Reinhard Mechler · Laurens M. Bouwer
Thomas Schinko · Swenja Surminski
JoAnne Linnerooth-Bayer
Editors

Loss and Damage from Climate Change

Concepts, Methods and Policy Options

Editors
Reinhard Mechler
International Institute for Applied Systems Analysis
Laxenburg, Austria

Laurens M. Bouwer
Deltares
Delft, The Netherlands

and

Climate Service Center Germany (GERICS)
Hamburg, Germany

Thomas Schinko
International Institute for Applied Systems Analysis
Laxenburg, Austria

Swenja Surminski
London School of Economics
London, UK

JoAnne Linnerooth-Bayer
International Institute for Applied Systems Analysis
Laxenburg, Austria

https://doi.org/10.1007/978-3-319-72026-5

Foreword I: Perspective from Saint Lucia

In his valedictory address, my son recently quoted a passage from a Dr. Seuss book that I often read to him and his brother at bedtime: "*You have brains in your head. You have feet in your shoes. You can steer yourself any direction you choose*". Words cannot describe how proud I am of both of my courageous young boys and their well-earned accomplishments and expectations of the bright future ahead. And yet, I am concerned that this future may not unfold on the small Caribbean island that my family calls home. I fear that the feet in those shoes will soon be submerged by rising seas and the direction in which they will be able to steer themselves will grow more and more limited, as our small island economy continues to be battered by the effects of climate change. For those of us from small island developing states climate change threatens our very survival, as sea levels rise, storm surges become ever more devastating, hurricanes become increasingly severe, the ocean acidifies, and rising temperatures lead to aridity and dwindling freshwater resources.

This is why representatives from Small Island Developing States (SIDS) fought so hard for the 1.5 °C global temperature limit in the Paris Agreement. For us, it is a matter of survival. While I remain optimistic that concerted global action will achieve the ambitious goal of reducing greenhouse gas emissions to limit temperature rise to 1.5 °C, in the interim, the particularly vulnerable, including our small island populations, will experience impacts from climate change to which it will be impossible to adapt. The recognition that climate change will cause loss and damage that is "beyond adaptation" has been acknowledged by the IPCC as "limits to adaptation" and has further led to the establishment of a dedicated mechanism under the UNFCCC—the Warsaw International Mechanism (WIM)—to address loss and damage associated with climate change impacts. It has further resulted in the treatment of loss and damage in a stand-alone article in the Paris Agreement (Article 8). But recognition must be followed by action. SIDS and other vulnerable countries must be supported, as they bear the brunt of coping with unavoidable loss and damage associated with changes to the climate that are attributable to others. This is no easy task and the world needs to maintain the Paris momentum of 2015 for this global fight.

The scientific community is called upon to support policy-makers to ensure that we handle the challenge in the most effective and well-informed manner. This book provides a valuable contribution to this effort. For the first time, the current scientific research and resulting knowledge on loss and damage has been collected in one comprehensive volume, allowing us to take stock of what we know and don't know, especially in areas of critical importance to SIDS, including implementing comprehensive climate risk management approaches; addressing slow onset events; financing efforts to address loss and damage; and understanding what institutional and legal arrangements are required to ensure the most effective responses. Of particular importance to the sustainable future of small islands are the impacts from slow onset events—including sea level rise, permanent rises in temperature and ocean acidification. Understanding the nature of these events and their impacts will require dedicated attention, because they are already beginning to affect countries and are certain to continue. Slow impact events severely limit the applicability of traditional risk management approaches and require novel solutions. It is my hope that this book will lay a foundation for further research in this area and foster enhanced understanding and closer cooperation between the scientific community and policy-makers on this and other critical matters. This is essential as we move forward in our work with the aim of addressing loss and damage. There is much to be gained in terms of facilitating effective decision-making that is grounded in science and far too much to be lost if we continue to tarry or get it wrong on this exigent issue of loss and damage.

Dawn Pierre-Nathoniel
Deputy Chief, Sustainable
Development and Environment Officer
Department of Sustainable Development
Saint Lucia

Foreword II: Perspective of Germany

Climate change can manifest itself in many ways, often with the most dramatic consequences for the poor and vulnerable. While our generation still has the means to avert catastrophic outcomes by drastically cutting carbon emissions, some consequences are already felt today, with a profound effect to already pressing social, environmental and economic issues. "Every year a thousand people die here from cholera that is spread by flooding, and during the rainy season, many people are forced from their homes", Daviz Simango, Mayor of Beira, Mozambique, explains. The global community increasingly acknowledges climate risks and puts ever more effort into finding innovative ways to cope with them on the ground. Equally, development efforts need to build resilience against climate-related shocks and stressors. The Paris Agreement provides a solid basis and reminds rich countries of their responsibility. This is why Germany via the German Federal Ministry for Economic Cooperation and Development (BMZ) promotes comprehensive climate risk management, including mitigation of and adaptation to climate change, risk reduction measures as well as risk finance instruments.

For example, the BMZ supported the expansion of a renewables firm to East Africa, starting to install solar-based off-grid systems in Uganda. In the meantime, the company also offers trainings for young people to become electrical engineers. In addition, we invest in storage facilities to help coffee planters in Rwanda who are struggling with harvests due to increasing weather extremes. Along with the quality of harvests, the efforts safeguard their livelihoods and progress to sustainable development. We offer vocational training to households in Bangladesh whose entire arable land was destroyed due to riverbank erosion, forcing them to seek shelter in the bigger city nearby. Along with enhancing water, sanitation and energy infrastructure in cooperation with local residents, the programme helps migrants, small businesses and the urban commerce alike. Finally, we fund the InsuResilience Investment Fund (IIF), which invests in partner countries' insurance providers, such as the microfinance institution Caja Sullana in Peru. Supported by the IIF, Caja Sullana offers insurance against flood and drought to small farmers and businesses, triggering payouts of over USD 630,000 to almost 500 farmers and businesses to rebuild their destroyed assets.

These are examples for the many ways to counter the damage inflicted by climate change. However, not all adverse effects of climate change can be dealt with by reducing vulnerability, increasing resilience or providing pre-agreed finance. Other impacts of climate change, such as sea level rise, can also lead to non-economic losses when e.g. cultural sites get inundated. In situations where community members face slow-onset events, they often have to consider making decisive changes regarding e.g. their residency and livelihoods. We want to improve the understanding around the role of climate risks on human mobility patterns: how can partner countries be best assisted in facilitating seasonal or temporary migration and, as a last resort, planned relocation processes; how to ensure implementation in a participative manner and in close coordination with the hosting communities? Because of the multi-faceted impacts of climate change on humankind, we acknowledge the importance of dealing with climate change and its impact on human lives and livelihoods and support our partner countries bilaterally and through our collaboration with international organizations. We have a long-standing engagement with the Warsaw International Mechanism (WIM) since its inception at the COP 19 in Warsaw and support its catalytic role to reach a common understanding of the most pressing issues and existing and emerging approaches to deal with them. The WIM is a good example of how solutions can be achieved together, through the cooperation of states, academia, civil society and the private sector.

We have already translated our willingness to act into many projects and programmes and continue to do so, also by supporting partner countries in tackling climate risks with tailor-made solutions (see box on a Climate Risk Management Framework in the chapter by Schinko et al. 2018, page 98). But it is of paramount importance to continuously study climate change, its known impacts and potential threats and interlinkages to improve the answers to these challenges. Current and future research can help us to understand the planetary boundaries and relevant tipping points. Such insights can facilitate an informed public debate driven by academia, civil society, private sector as well as governments. The BMZ is and will remain a strong partner in supporting all those actors on different levels. Only by fostering partnerships will we be able to address the challenges that lie ahead. This book is a valuable contribution to the dialogue and fosters a common understanding of key issues regarding Loss and Damage, thus further strengthening much-needed exchange.

Ingrid-Gabriela Hoven
Director-General Global Issues
Federal Ministry of Economic Cooperation
and Development (BMZ)
Germany

Preface

Climate change is rapidly proceeding, and climate-related risks are being exacerbated. The year 2018 brought about new temperature records in regions of Africa and Asia (with temperatures exceeding unprecedented 50 °C), the hottest European summer in recent history with heatwaves from Algeria to the Arctic, also bringing along forest fires and drought, severe flooding in southern India and Bangladesh, as well as massive cyclone damage in Fiji. While, largely involuntarily, people and their assets are increasingly located in harm's way, the IPCC has shown that the frequency and severity of climate-related hazards is being adversely shaped by anthropogenic climate change. Evidence is increasing that those risks have the potential to significantly affect lives and livelihoods across the globe, as well as push vulnerable people, communities and countries to their physical and socio-economic adaptation limits.

The Loss and Damage (L&D) discourse, initiated almost three decades ago by Small Island States worried about sea level rise, has given voice to concerns for climate change-related impacts that may be irreversible and beyond physical and social adaptation limits. The discourse has become institutionalised in international climate policy through the Warsaw Mechanism on Loss and Damages adopted in 2013 and was given firm consideration in the Paris Agreement in 2015. While expectations by policy advisors and civil society for the L&D discourse are looming large, the science has been trailing behind. This is impeding a step-change from debate to concrete policy deliberation and on-the-ground implementation.

This book provides science-based insight and inroads into the L&D discourse. The volume, made up of 22 chapters by experts and two forewords by L&D policymakers and negotiators, articulates the multiple concepts, principles and methods as well as place-based insight relevant for L&D. It additionally identifies a number of propositions that may serve as a foundation for improved policy formulation. The volume is the first comprehensive outcome of the "Loss and Damage Network", a partnership effort by scientists and practitioners bringing together members from more than twenty-five institutions around the globe.

In addition to providing information on critical climate risks and requisite responses to the public throughout, we are hopeful that the book may inform the L&D discourse at a critical time with the review of the Warsaw Mechanism underway and evidence of limits 'beyond adaptation' increasing. The network stands ready to further conduct relevant research, provide capacity building as well as support policy deliberation.

We dearly thank all authors for their valuable contributions. In particular, we thank Florentina Simlinger for editorial support and interaction with the L&D Network colleagues. Special thanks go to Fritz Schmuhl of Springer International for all the support and advice during this project.

Laxenburg, Austria — Reinhard Mechler
Hamburg, Germany — Laurens M. Bouwer
London, UK — Thomas Schinko
August 2018 — Swenja Surminski
JoAnne Linnerooth-Bayer

Contents

Part I Setting the Stage: Key Concepts, Challenges and Insights

1 **Science for Loss and Damage. Findings and Propositions** 3
Reinhard Mechler, Elisa Calliari, Laurens M. Bouwer, Thomas Schinko, Swenja Surminski, JoAnne Linnerooth-Bayer, Jeroen Aerts, Wouter Botzen, Emily Boyd, Natalie Delia Deckard, Jan S. Fuglestvedt, Mikel González-Eguino, Marjolijn Haasnoot, John Handmer, Masroora Haque, Alison Heslin, Stefan Hochrainer-Stigler, Christian Huggel, Saleemul Huq, Rachel James, Richard G. Jones, Sirkku Juhola, Adriana Keating, Stefan Kienberger, Sönke Kreft, Onno Kuik, Mia Landauer, Finn Laurien, Judy Lawrence, Ana Lopez, Wei Liu, Piotr Magnuszewski, Anil Markandya, Benoit Mayer, Ian McCallum, Colin McQuistan, Lukas Meyer, Kian Mintz-Woo, Arianna Montero-Colbert, Jaroslav Mysiak, Johanna Nalau, Ilan Noy, Robert Oakes, Friederike E. L. Otto, Mousumi Pervin, Erin Roberts, Laura Schäfer, Paolo Scussolini, Olivia Serdeczny, Alex de Sherbinin, Florentina Simlinger, Asha Sitati, Saibeen Sultana, Hannah R. Young, Kees van der Geest, Marc van den Homberg, Ivo Wallimann-Helmer, Koko Warner and Zinta Zommers

2 **The Ethical Challenges in the Context of Climate Loss and Damage** 39
Ivo Wallimann-Helmer, Lukas Meyer, Kian Mintz-Woo, Thomas Schinko and Olivia Serdeczny

3 **Observed and Projected Impacts from Extreme Weather Events: Implications for Loss and Damage** 63
Laurens M. Bouwer

4 **The Risk and Policy Space for Loss and Damage: Integrating Notions of Distributive and Compensatory Justice with Comprehensive Climate Risk Management** 83
Thomas Schinko, Reinhard Mechler and Stefan Hochrainer-Stigler

Part II Critical Issues Shaping the Discourse

5 **Attribution: How Is It Relevant for Loss and Damage Policy and Practice?** 113
Rachel A. James, Richard G. Jones, Emily Boyd, Hannah R. Young, Friederike E. L. Otto, Christian Huggel and Jan S. Fuglestvedt

6 **The Politics of (and Behind) the UNFCCC's Loss and Damage Mechanism** 155
Elisa Calliari, Swenja Surminski and Jaroslav Mysiak

7 **Legal Responses to Climate Change Induced Loss and Damage** 179
Florentina Simlinger and Benoit Mayer

8 **Non-economic Loss and Damage and the Warsaw International Mechanism** 205
Olivia Serdeczny

9 **The Impacts of Climate Change on Ecosystem Services and Resulting Losses and Damages to People and Society** 221
Kees van der Geest, Alex de Sherbinin, Stefan Kienberger, Zinta Zommers, Asha Sitati, Erin Roberts and Rachel James

10 **Displacement and Resettlement: Understanding the Role of Climate Change in Contemporary Migration** 237
Alison Heslin, Natalie Delia Deckard, Robert Oakes and Arianna Montero-Colbert

Part III Research and Practice: Reviewing Methods and Tools

11 **The Role of the Physical Sciences in Loss and Damage Decision-Making** 261
Ana Lopez, Swenja Surminski and Olivia Serdeczny

12 **Integrated Disaster Risk Management and Adaptation** 287
W. J. Wouter Botzen, Laurens M. Bouwer, Paolo Scussolini, Onno Kuik, Marjolijn Haasnoot, Judy Lawrence and Jeroen C. J. H. Aerts

13 **Exploring and Managing Adaptation Frontiers with Climate Risk Insurance** 317
Laura Schäfer, Koko Warner and Sönke Kreft

14 Integrated Assessment for Identifying Climate Finance Needs for Loss and Damage: A Critical Review 343
Anil Markandya and Mikel González-Eguino

Part IV Geographic Perspectives and Cases

15 Understanding Loss and Damage in Pacific Small Island Developing States 365
John Handmer and Johanna Nalau

16 Climate Migration and Cultural Preservation: The Case of the Marshallese Diaspora 383
Alison Heslin

17 Supporting Climate Risk Management at Scale. Insights from the Zurich Flood Resilience Alliance Partnership Model Applied in Peru & Nepal 393
Reinhard Mechler, Colin McQuistan, Ian McCallum, Wei Liu, Adriana Keating, Piotr Magnuszewski, Thomas Schinko, Finn Laurien and Stefan Hochrainer-Stigler

18 Loss and Damage in the Rapidly Changing Arctic 425
Mia Landauer and Sirkku Juhola

Part V Policy Options and Other Response Mechanisms for the L&D Discourse

19 Towards Establishing a National Mechanism to Address Losses and Damages: A Case Study from Bangladesh 451
Masroora Haque, Mousumi Pervin, Saibeen Sultana and Saleemul Huq

20 The Case of Huaraz: First Climate Lawsuit on Loss and Damage Against an Energy Company Before German Courts 475
Will Frank, Christoph Bals and Julia Grimm

21 Insurance as a Response to Loss and Damage? 483
JoAnne Linnerooth-Bayer, Swenja Surminski, Laurens M. Bouwer, Ilan Noy and Reinhard Mechler

22 Technology for Climate Justice: A Reporting Framework for Loss and Damage as Part of Key Global Agreements 513
Marc van den Homberg and Colin McQuistan

Index 547

List of Figures

Fig. 1.1	Evolution of the Loss and Damage discourse under the UNFCCC	6
Fig. 1.2	Co-evolution of climate change research reported by the IPCC and the UNFCCC process	8
Fig. 1.3	Risk as a function of hazard, exposure and vulnerability	12
Fig. 1.4	The risk concept as applied to sudden-onset and slow-onset processes	13
Fig. 3.1	Risk framework for the analysis of extreme event impacts	65
Fig. 3.2	Past, current and future risk from extreme weather events, and the relation to Loss and Damage	76
Fig. 4.1	Characterisation of climate-related risks relevant for Loss&Damage	86
Fig. 4.2	Selected key risks and potential for adaptation for small islands	89
Fig. 4.3	Degree of confidence in the detection of observed impacts of climate change versus degree of confidence in attribution to climate change drivers for tropical small islands	93
Fig. 4.4	Framing risk acceptance and (in)tolerance	94
Fig. 4.5	Elements of the dynamic principled approach to Loss and Damage	95
Fig. 4.6	Identifying the risk and policy options space for Loss and Damage	97
Fig. 4.7	Climate risk management (CRM) six step approach	98
Fig. 4.8	Defining acceptable and unacceptable risks for accident risks in Switzerland	101
Fig. 4.9	Conceptualising risk layering	102
Fig. 4.10	Understanding risk and risk layering for the case of flood risk in Bangladesh	103
Fig. 4.11	Global map identifying high-level risks	104

Fig. 5.1 A schematic diagram illustrating a spectrum of views on L&D identified by Boyd et al. (2017) 122
Fig. 5.2 A conceptual causal network illustrating multiple potential "causal chains" between anthropogenic changes in GHGs and aerosols, climate and weather, and L&D 128
Fig. 5.3 Example of a simplified detection and attribution study for global temperature 129
Fig. 5.4 A schematic illustration of the probability distribution of a climate variable (such as temperature or precipitation) with and without human influence on climate 130
Fig. 5.5 Schematic illustration of the assessment by the National Academy of Sciences of the state of attribution science for different types of extreme weather events 131
Fig. 5.6 Schematic diagram from the IPCC WGII Chap. 18 on detection and attribution of observed impacts 132
Fig. 5.7 An analysis by Hansen and Stone, revisiting impacts in the IPCC WGII report to assess whether they can be linked to anthropogenic forcing 134
Fig. 5.8 Sensitivity of estimated contributions to global mean surface temperature increase to the choice of forcing components included in attribution analysis. 136
Fig. 5.9 Map demonstrating the location of weather stations in the Global Historical Climatology Network, as well as the number of detected impacts reported in the IPCC AR5 for Annex I countries, Non-Annex I countries, and regions not party to the UNFCCC 141
Fig. 6.1 Timeline of L&D milestones 159
Fig. 6.2 The WIM in the UNFCCC architecture 160
Fig. 6.3 Evolution of Party groupings/coalitions 167
Fig. 8.1 Cases and categories of NELD as reported in the literature published by 2015 210
Fig. 9.1 Conceptual framework for understanding the role of ecosystem services 225
Fig. 9.2 Temperature change in degrees Celsius per decade from 1951 to 2013 228
Fig. 9.3 Coefficient of variation of rainfall from 1951 to 2013 228
Fig. 9.4 Difference in the number of years that received adequate rainfall for sorghum and millet (1990–2009 compared to 1950–1969) 228
Fig. 9.5 The drying of Lake Chad. 230
Fig. 9.6 Flooding in the peanut basin south of Kaolack, Senegal (September 2007). 231

Fig. 10.1 IOM migration-related terminology by motivation and destination . . . 239
Fig. 10.2 UN migration-related terminology by motivation and destination . . . 239
Fig. 10.3 Migration totals, measured as total foreign-born population . . . 241
Fig. 10.4 New internal displacements per year from conflict and natural disasters . . . 242
Fig. 10.5 Total number of new internally displaced by natural disasters 2008–2016 . . . 243
Fig. 10.6 The main reasons for moving in Kiribati 2005–2015 . . . 247
Fig. 11.1 The uncertainty cascade in the modelling chain from climate model forcings to the estimation of the climate hazard (the physical impact of climate change) . . . 269
Fig. 12.1 Layered disaster risk management . . . 290
Fig. 12.2 Flood risk in Jakarta measured as annual expected damage . . . 293
Fig. 12.3 Conceptual framework of the flood risk assessment of Ho Chi Minh City . . . 294
Fig. 12.4 Increase in flood risk (expected annual damage—EAD—and annual potential casualties) of floods in Ho Chi Minh City, from the present to year 2050 and 2100, for three combinations of climate and socio-economic scenarios . . . 295
Fig. 12.5 Performance of several adaptation measures and strategies in reducing the future impacts of sea level rise, compared to the situation without adaptation . . . 296
Fig. 12.6 Net Present Value and normalised Benefit/cost ratio of flood risk adaptation measures for Ho Chi Minh City for three combinations of climate change and socio-economic scenarios . . . 298
Fig. 12.7 Steps taken in Dynamic Adaptive Pathways Planning (DAPP) . . . 307
Fig. 12.8 Example of an adaptation pathways map and a scorecard presenting the costs and benefits of the nine alternative pathways presented in the map . . . 308
Fig. 13.1 Acceptable, tolerable and intolerable risk . . . 321
Fig. 13.2 The role of insurance in managing adaptation frontiers . . . 323
Fig. 13.3 Risk layering . . . 329
Fig. 14.1 Total damages, residual damages and adaptation expenditures . . . 346
Fig. 14.2 Temperature pathways for low and high damage scenarios . . . 348
Fig. 14.3 Residual damages estimates for the case of **a)** low damages-high discount rate; **b)** high damages-low discount rate (in billion 2005 US) . . . 349

Fig. 14.4 Residual costs as percentage of adaptation costs for the case of **a)** low damages-high discount rate; **b)** high damages-low discount rate (in billion 2005 US) 355
Fig. 14.5 Damage (% GDP) for different damage functions and ECS parameters 358
Fig. 15.1 Map of the South Pacific 367
Fig. 15.2 Visualisation of risk and options spaces for the SW Pacific 370
Fig. 15.3 Damage from tropical cyclone Pam in 2015 in north Efate island, Vanuatu 374
Fig. 16.1 The Republic of the Marshall Islands 385
Fig. 16.2 Outrigger Canoe traditionally used in ocean navigation, Majuro Atoll, Republic of the Marshall Islands 387
Fig. 16.3 Typical landscape, Arno Atoll, Republic of the Marshall Islands 388
Fig. 17.1 The practice imperative—connecting disaster preparedness and livelihood development 396
Fig. 17.2 Partners and roles in the Flood Resilience Alliance 399
Fig. 17.3 Flood risk context in the Karnali river basin in Nepal (left panel) and the Rimac river valley in Peru (right panel) 401
Fig. 17.4 Adaptive management cycle used in the ZFRA to foster Shared Resilience Learning 403
Fig. 17.5 Methodological approach for understanding and learning about risk and resilience 405
Fig. 17.6 Screenshot of Risk Geo-Wiki. Modelled global flood risk data overlaid on satellite imagery at the regional level for the Karnali, Nepal 407
Fig. 17.7 Community and NGO members mapping into OpenStreetMap with mobile devices in the Karnali basin, Nepal 408
Fig. 17.8 Conventional hand-drawn community risk map, capacity map, and social map versus digital community map produced via a participatory and collaborative mapping approach 409
Fig. 17.9 Zurich Flood Resilience Measurement Framework implementation process 411
Fig. 17.10 Measuring resilience in Nepal as compared to the global measurement 412
Fig. 17.11 Application of the Flood Resilience Game provoking discussion at an NGO workshop in Jakarta 415
Fig. 17.12 Flood Resilience Systems Framework (FLORES)—a simplified view 416
Fig. 17.13 Prospective forensics for projecting flood risk in Peru 419

Fig. 17.14 Tracing methods and tools developed in the Zurich Flood Resilience Alliance in time and space connecting risk and resilience research with practice. 420
Fig. 18.1 VOSviewer visualisation of Arctic literature sample 432
Fig. 18.2 Institutional and jurisdictional framework, as well as socio-economic, cultural and political settings affect adaptation threshold of Arctic communities, and can be drivers of Loss and Damage 437
Fig. 18.3 Risk and Indigenous Peoples in Alaska 440
Fig. 19.1 Multi-hazard map of Bangladesh 454
Fig. 19.2 Areas at risk of flooding in Bangladesh 455
Fig. 19.3 River embankment in Bangladesh 456
Fig. 19.4 Institutions, policy frameworks and organisations comprising the disaster management system in Bangladesh 458
Fig. 19.5 Disaster Management Regulatory Framework of Bangladesh 461
Fig. 19.6 Allocation of funding for projects by the Bangladesh Climate Change Trust Fund (BCCTF) 465
Fig. 19.7 Proposed functions of the national mechanism to address climate induced loss and damage. 470
Fig. 20.1 Location of Lake Palcacocha and the city of Huaraz 477
Fig. 20.2 Palcacocha Glacier Lake with the provisional pumping system in need of upgrading 478
Fig. 20.3 Detection and attribution for climate impacts in Central and South America 478
Fig. 21.1 Overview of 'risk management applications' of insurance, in the context of loss and damage 487
Fig. 21.2 Costs contributing to catastrophe insurance premium. 492
Fig. 21.3 The R4 Rural Resilience Initiative 496
Fig. 22.1 Community information board in the Banke and Bardia district in Nepal explaining appropriate flood mitigation measures and the community-based early warning system. . . . 515
Fig. 22.2 Overview of underlying climate justice principles and means of implementation 517
Fig. 22.3 Overview of the relationship of the risk of losses and damages to the three pillars of climate action and key global agreements (Sendai and SDG) 526
Fig. 22.4 Reporting framework for technology to address Loss and Damage and contribute to climate justice 534

List of Tables

Table 1.1 Classifying losses and damages 11
Table 2.1 Difference in policy priority depending on how adaptation and L&D are distinguished 43
Table 2.2 Overview of differences between analysing L&D within a framing of compensatory justice and distributive justice 45
Table 2.3 Indicative list of measures for different categories of losses and damages. Note that listed measures are not exhaustive and that these measures could apply under both compensatory or distributive justice framings 49
Table 2.4 Categorisation of the differentiated remedial responsibilities of countries to foster L&D measures without exclusively relying on outcome responsibility 57
Table 3.1 Observed changes in weather extremes and attribution to human greenhouse gas emissions 68
Table 3.2 Normalisation studies of weather-related disaster loss records 72
Table 3.3 Comparison of changes in extreme weather hazards (regardless of human contribution) and observed change in losses 75
Table 4.1 Classifying loss and damage 87
Table 6.1 Party/Grouping calling for compensation in the period 1991–2016 172
Table 7.1 Legal responses, their challenges and potential next steps 198
Table 8.1 NELD impacts reported in the literature 209
Table 14.1 Residual damages across three IAMs: high damages-low discount rate (USD billion 2005) 350
Table 14.2 Residual damages across three IAMs: low damages-high discount rate (USD billion 2005) 351
Table 14.3 Adaptation and residual costs for selected regions (high damages-low discount rate) 353

Table 14.4 Adaptation and residual costs for selected regions (low damages-high discount rate) 354
Table 15.1 Loss & Damage concepts applied to the SW Pacific. 369
Table 17.1 Characteristics and applicability of different decision-support tools for ex-ante and ex-post disaster risk management. 413
Table 18.1 Categories of Arctic studies focusing on risks and impacts of climate change (N=164) 430
Table 18.2 Examples limiting Arctic communities to adapt to climate change. 438
Table 19.1 Annual allocations to the trust fund are as follows (BCCT) 464
Table 21.1 Examples of risk financing arrangements at micro, intermediary and macro scales. 488
Table 21.2 Financing instruments for protecting government budgets. . . . 489
Table 21.3 An overview of preventative and curative functions of climate risk insurance 505
Table 22.1 Practical Action's framework for technology justice with five components 518
Table 22.2 Overview of public and private flood risk actions and their intended effect on losses and damages 524
Table 22.3 Transparency in the three key global agreements: reporting mechanisms, indicators related to impacts and risks, and means of implementation for technology, with some detail on Bangladesh, India and Nepal. 531
Table 22.4 Injustices identified in current flood early warning systems in South Asia. 536

Part I
Setting the Stage: Key Concepts, Challenges and Insights

Chapter 1
Science for Loss and Damage. Findings and Propositions

Reinhard Mechler, Elisa Calliari, Laurens M. Bouwer, Thomas Schinko, Swenja Surminski, JoAnne Linnerooth-Bayer, Jeroen Aerts, Wouter Botzen, Emily Boyd, Natalie Delia Deckard, Jan S. Fuglestvedt, Mikel González-Eguino, Marjolijn Haasnoot, John Handmer, Masroora Haque, Alison Heslin, Stefan Hochrainer-Stigler, Christian Huggel, Saleemul Huq, Rachel James, Richard G. Jones, Sirkku Juhola, Adriana Keating, Stefan Kienberger, Sönke Kreft, Onno Kuik, Mia Landauer, Finn Laurien, Judy Lawrence, Ana Lopez, Wei Liu, Piotr Magnuszewski, Anil Markandya, Benoit Mayer, Ian McCallum, Colin McQuistan, Lukas Meyer, Kian Mintz-Woo, Arianna Montero-Colbert, Jaroslav Mysiak, Johanna Nalau, Ilan Noy, Robert Oakes, Friederike E. L. Otto, Mousumi Pervin, Erin Roberts, Laura Schäfer, Paolo Scussolini, Olivia Serdeczny, Alex de Sherbinin, Florentina Simlinger, Asha Sitati, Saibeen Sultana, Hannah R. Young, Kees van der Geest, Marc van den Homberg, Ivo Wallimann-Helmer, Koko Warner and Zinta Zommers

Abstract The debate on "Loss and Damage" (L&D) has gained traction over the last few years. Supported by growing scientific evidence of anthropogenic climate change amplifying frequency, intensity and duration of climate-related hazards as well as observed increases in climate-related impacts and risks in many regions, the

---

E. Calliari · L. M. Bouwer · T. Schinko · S. Surminski · J. Linnerooth-Bayer · J. Aerts · W. Botzen · E. Boyd · N. D. Deckard · J. S. Fuglestvedt · M. González-Eguino · M. Haasnoot · J. Handmer · M. Haque · A. Heslin · S. Hochrainer-Stigler · C. Huggel · S. Huq · R. James · R. G. Jones · S. Juhola · A. Keating · S. Kienberger · S. Kreft · O. Kuik · M. Landauer · F. Laurien · J. Lawrence · A. Lopez · W. Liu · P. Magnuszewski · A. Markandya · B. Mayer · I. McCallum · C. McQuistan · L. Meyer · K. Mintz-Woo · A. Montero-Colbert · J. Mysiak · J. Nalau · I. Noy · R. Oakes · F. E. L. Otto · M. Pervin · E. Roberts · L. Schäfer · P. Scussolini · O. Serdeczny · A. de Sherbinin · F. Simlinger · A. Sitati · S. Sultana · H. R. Young · K. van der Geest · M. van den Homberg · I. Wallimann-Helmer · K. Warner · Z. Zommers
International Institute for Applied Systems Analysis (IIASA), Laxenburg, Austria

R. Mechler (✉)
International Institute for Applied Systems Analysis (IIASA), Laxenburg, Austria
e-mail: mechler@iiasa.ac.at

R. Mechler
Vienna University of Economics and Business, Vienna, Austria

R. Mechler et al. (eds.), *Loss and Damage from Climate Change*, Climate Risk Management, Policy and Governance, https://doi.org/10.1007/978-3-319-72026-5_1

"Warsaw International Mechanism for Loss and Damage" was established in 2013 and further supported through the Paris Agreement in 2015. Despite advances, the debate currently is broad, diffuse and somewhat confusing, while concepts, methods and tools, as well as directions for policy remain vague and often contested. This book, a joint effort of the Loss and Damage Network—a partnership effort by scientists and practitioners from around the globe—provides evidence-based insight into the L&D discourse by highlighting state-of-the-art research conducted across multiple disciplines, by showcasing applications in practice and by providing insight into policy contexts and salient policy options. This introductory chapter summarises key findings of the twenty-two book chapters in terms of five propositions. These propositions, each building on relevant findings linked to forward-looking suggestions for research, policy and practice, reflect the architecture of the book, whose sections proceed from setting the stage to critical issues, followed by a section on methods and tools, to chapters that provide geographic perspectives, and finally to a section that identifies potential policy options. The propositions comprise (1) Risk management can be an effective entry point for aligning perspectives and debates, if framed comprehensively, coupled with climate justice considerations and linked to established risk management and adaptation practice; (2) Attribution science is advancing rapidly and fundamental to informing actions to minimise, avert, and address losses and damages; (3) Climate change research, in addition to identifying physical/hard limits to adaptation, needs to more systematically examine soft limits to adaptation, for which we find some evidence across several geographies globally; (4) Climate risk insurance mechanisms can serve the prevention and cure aspects emphasised in the L&D debate but solidarity and accountability aspects need further attention, for which we find tentative indication in applications around the world; (5) Policy deliberations may need to overcome the perception that L&D constitutes a win-lose negotiation "game" by developing a more inclusive narrative that highlights collective ambition for tackling risks, mutual benefits and the role of transformation.

Keywords Science · Policy · Practice · Climate justice · Limits to adaptation Climate risk management · Transformation

1.1 Understanding and Reviewing the Evidence for Advancing Science and Policy

The debate on Loss and Damage (L&D)[1] has gained traction over the last few years. Although the discourse started already during the establishment of the United Nations Framework Convention on Climate Change (UNFCCC) in the early 1990s with a proposal by the Alliance of Small Island States (AOSIS) on compensation and

[1] In this chapter and in the book throughout, we will use the plural form and lowercase letters ('losses and damages') to refer broadly to (observed) impacts and (projected) risks, and the capitalized singular form ('Loss & Damage') where reference is made to the policy debate.

insurance for losses due to sea-level rise (INC 1991), it took about 20 years, alongside increasing evidence and public awareness of climate change impacts and risks as collated prominently in reports by the Intergovernmental Panel on Climate Change (IPCC), for it to be recognised at the institutional level. In 2007 UNFCCC's 13th Conference of the Parties (COP 13) in Bali first broadly considered means to address Loss and Damage, yet only in 2012 at COP 18 in Doha did Parties for the first time decide to consider institutional arrangements to address L&D, which in 2013 led negotiators at COP 19 to establish the "Warsaw International Mechanism for Loss and Damage associated with Climate Change Impacts" (WIM) (UNFCCC 2013). In 2015 at COP 21, the Paris Agreement established a separate article on L&D endorsing the Mechanism (UN 2015) (see Fig. 1.1). Since its establishment, the WIM, whose Executive Committee has devised work programmes to inform the deliberations, has been subject to intense debate. While some consider it a distinct building block of negotiations under the UNFCCC alongside mitigation and adaptation, others suggest that it is supposed to be an integral part of the negotiations under climate change adaptation. The implications and final directions for this Mechanism, which will undergo review in 2019, are, however, largely unclear.

The debate currently is broad, diffuse and somewhat confusing, while concepts, methods and tools, as well as directions for policy remain vague and contested. Over the last few years, research has been requested to provide actionable input and has increasingly become active. Scholarship has started to provide evidence on losses and damages in vulnerable countries (Warner and van der Geest 2013), coined and critically examined definitions, the rationale and plural perspectives on the discourse (Verheyen and Roderick 2008; James et al. 2015; Van der Geest and Warner 2015; Vanhala and Hestbaek 2016; Boyd et al. 2017), employed applicable methods and models (Gall 2015; Birkmann and Welle 2015; Schinko and Mechler 2017), reviewed roles for justice and equity considerations (Huggel et al. 2016a; Roser et al. 2015; Wallimann-Helmer 2015), spent due attention on non-economic losses (Serdeczny et al. 2017; Tschakert et al. 2017; Wewerinke-Singh 2018a), supported crafting of policy and governance options (Pinninti 2013; Page and Heyward 2017; Mechler and Schinko 2016; Crosland et al. 2016; Biermann and Boas 2017) and examined the role of legal responses to L&D (Mace and Verheyen 2016; Mayer 2016; Wewerinke-Singh 2018b).

Many gaps remain, not the least in terms of communication across the science-policy interface. Analysts and observers, including the authors of this book, have argued that these gaps have hampered understanding and progress towards effective policy formulation, as well as practical implementation. As we demonstrate in this book, a more strongly evidence-based dialogue is desirable and feasible, and we see a number of promising options for instilling more coherence into the debate and foster alignment with other policy agendas, particularly with regard to climate change adaptation (CCA), current international efforts on disaster risk reduction (DRR), as well as the United Nations Sustainable Development Goals (SDGs).

This book thus aims at providing insights into the L&D discourse by highlighting state-of-the-art research from multiple disciplines as well as policy contexts related to L&D. It articulates the multiple concepts, principles and methods relevant for L&D,

Fig. 1.1 Evolution of the Loss and Damage disco.urse under the UNFCCC. *Source* UNFCCC (2018)

including those that have only recently become available. As such, this volume is the first comprehensive outcome of the Loss and Damage Network, a partnership effort by scientists and practitioners, which includes members from more than 40 institutions around the globe. Aimed at informing research, policy, practice and the interested public, this book:

- discusses the political, legal, economic and institutional dimensions of L&D,
- introduces normative and ethical questions central to the discourse,
- highlights the role of climate risks and climate risk management,
- presents salient case studies from around the world,
- identifies practical and evidence-based policy and implementation options, and thus
- supports the science-policy dialogue and possible future directions of the L&D discourse, both under and outside the Paris Agreement.

The volume overall is organised into five sections: Sect. 1 **sets the stage with key concepts and insights** regarding trends in impacts and risks, while Sect. 2 presents **critical issues that increasingly are shaping the policy discourse**. In Sect. 3, **methods and tools for research and practice are reviewed** in terms of their applicability, Sect. 4 presents **place-based evidence** and insights on losses and damages as well as any soft and hard limits **across geographies**, and finally in Sect. 5, **policy options and other actions for the L&D discourse** are discussed. This introductory chapter further elaborates on the evolution of the discourse, presents key concepts of relevance and salience that arise from the book, shortly summarises the individual chapters, and concludes by outlining a number of propositions that link relevant findings to forward-looking suggestions for research, practice and policy.

1.2 Evolution of the Policy Discourse

Formal and informal deliberations regarding "dangerous" climate-related risks and sharing the burdens (including justice considerations) associated with responses to climate change have been fundamental for shaping the climate debate since the beginning (see also chapter by Calliari et al. 2018; see Fig. 1.1). Science, in particular as reported by the IPCC assessments, has had a major impact on policy formulation and decisions as part of the UNFCCC (see Fig. 1.2). Given the ultimate objective as stipulated by the UNFCCC in 1992 "to prevent dangerous anthropogenic interference with the climate system" (UN 1992, Art. 2), the focus of the UNFCCC was originally–and continues to predominantly be–on climate mitigation responses. The first discussions about L&D were initiated by the Alliance of Small Island States (AOSIS) in the early 1990s with due linkages to mitigation. During the negotiations that led to adoption of the UNFCCC in 1992, AOSIS proposed the establishment of, what they called, an international insurance scheme–also referred to by some as a compensation fund–to be supported by mandatory contributions from industrialised parties on the basis of their gross national product and relative greenhouse gas emissions (INC 1991).

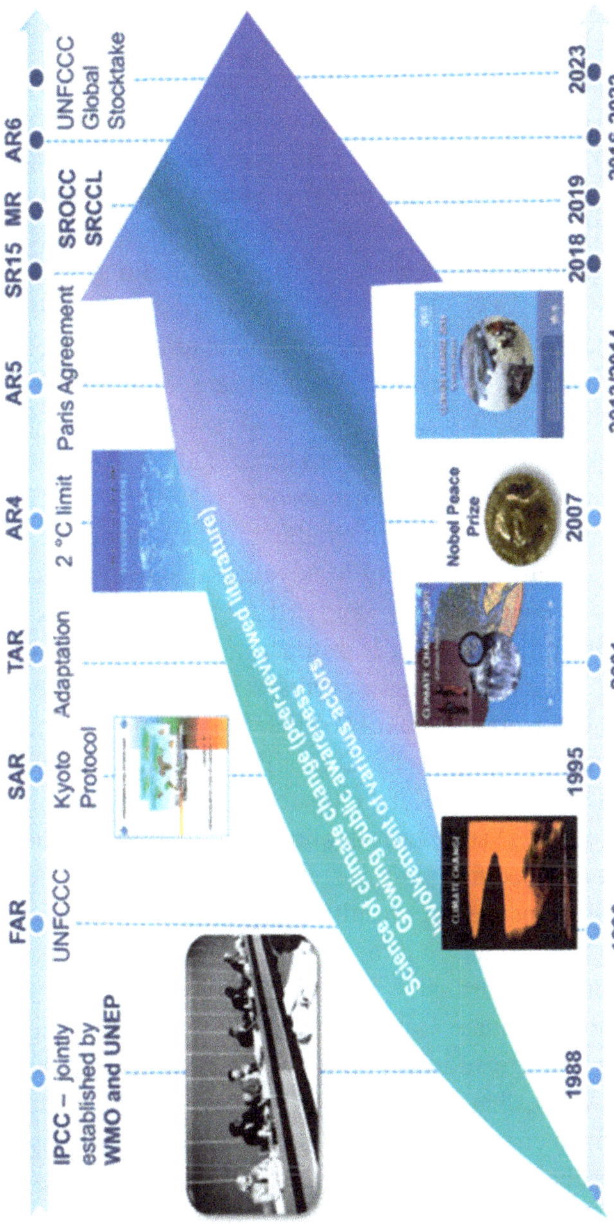

Fig. 1.2 Co-evolution of climate change research reported by the IPCC and the UNFCCC process. *Source* IPCC 2018

The scheme was intended to compensate small island- and low-lying developing nations for climate-related impacts from sea-level rise (Linnerooth-Bayer et al. 2003; AOSIS 2008; see the chapters by Schäfer et al. 2018 and Linnerooth-Bayer et al. 2018). While the proposal was eventually dropped, discussions on compensation and insurance as a means to address the adverse effects of climate change prevailed with expert workshops convened in 2003 and 2007 on the basis of COP decisions 5/CP 7 and 1/CP 10 and COP13 started to consider means to address Loss and Damage (Mace and Verheyen 2016).

In 2008, AOSIS submitted an expanded version of the 1991 proposal to the Ad Hoc *Working Group on Long-term Cooperative Action under the Convention* (AWG-LCA). This *Multi Window Mechanism to Address Loss and Damage from Climate Change Impacts* in Small Island Developing States (SIDS) and other developing countries particularly vulnerable to the impacts of climate change comprised three interdependent components: (1) insurance; (2) rehabilitation/compensation; and (3) risk management (AOSIS 2008). The idea of an "international mechanism addressing risk management and risk reduction strategies and insurance related risk sharing and risk transfer mechanisms" was reiterated a year later in the AOSIS proposal for a Copenhagen Protocol (UNFCCC 2009).

After losses and damages were mentioned in the 2007 *Bali Action Plan* (UNFCCC 2007), the 2010 *Cancun Adaptation Framework* (UNFCCC 2010) initiated formal UNFCCC activities on the issue with the establishment of an ad hoc work programme (UNFCCC 2011). The latter was meant to advance technical work on L&D in three thematic areas over the course of 2011 and 2012: (1) assessing the risk of L&D and the current knowledge on the same; (2) proposing a range of approaches to address L&D from both extreme and slow onset events, taking into consideration experience at all levels; and (3) determining the role of the Convention in enhancing the implementation of approaches to address L&D (UNFCCC 2012). Since its inception, the work programme has conducted several calls for submissions asking parties (national government representatives) and observers (other organisations attending UNFCCC meetings) for input on specific questions. These calls gave parties, observers and non-admitted organisations the opportunity to lay out their views on thematic issues, institutional questions, governance arrangements and suggestions on how to take the L&D work programme forward.

As part of the Doha Climate Gateway in 2012, the Parties decided to establish institutional arrangements to address L&D at COP 19. This laid the groundwork for the creation of the WIM, that is charged to "address loss and damage associated with impacts of climate change, including extreme events and slow onset events, in developing countries that are particularly vulnerable to the adverse effects of climate change" (UNFCCC 2013, para 1). COP19 also established an Executive Committee (ExCom) to guide the implementation of functions of the WIM through an initial 2-year work plan. A distinct L&D article in the Paris Agreement (UNFCCC 2015, Article 8) at COP 21 meant further recognition for L&D and the WIM, and arguably, institutional anchoring within the UNFCCC architecture.

The action areas for work under the WIM have been broad and diverse, ranging in scope and focus. Action areas include considering particularly vulnerable countries, populations and ecosystems, dealing with both slow- and sudden-onset events, and paying particular attention to non-economic losses. Policy areas include consideration for resilience, recovery and rehabilitation efforts, migration, displacement and mobility, as well as financial instruments including insurance. The work plan is intended to integrate also with other on-going work under the UNFCCC, such as on finance and technology.

Fundamental to this book, and the climate policy debate in general, has been the concept of comprehensive risk management including transformational approaches. The mandate of the WIM includes enhancing understanding of and promoting both short- and medium-term risk management, including risk analysis, risk reduction, risk transfer and risk retention. Furthermore, the WIM is to consider transformational approaches that help to build and strengthen the long-term resilience of countries and communities (UNFCCC 2016, Decision 3/CP.22). Since the establishment of the WIM, the ExCom has met several times and has transitioned from its initial 2-year work plan to a 5-year rolling work plan. Achievements and the WIM will officially be reviewed at COP 25 in 2019.

Recent non-climate policy developments, such as the compact on Sendai (UNISDR 2015), the SDGs (UN 2015), as well as the Nansen Initiative on Displacement (nanseninitiative.org) and its follow-up, the Platform on Disaster Displacement (Displacement Solutions 2015) provide potential opportunities to increase understanding of and respond to growing climate-related risks, including L&D. However, these approaches and preliminary actions are scattered across several sectors and actors, and their relevance to L&D has not yet been systematically evaluated with little exchange between research and policy. In addition, attention to L&D in research and policy has tended to focus heavily on only a few aspects, such as insurance. Broader reflection, particularly on the different dimensions of L&D decision-making has been largely lacking.

While it is difficult to summarise the different strands of the discourse(s), it may be argued that essentially three issues have been highlighted with varying levels of emphasis over time:

1. Burden sharing for the costs of managing climate impacts and risks (losses and damages) including compensation arrangements.
2. Awareness regarding the sensitivity and limitations of human and natural systems to climate change, and the need to respond with stringent climate mitigation policies for limiting warming to 1.5 °C or 2 °C.
3. Support for further risk reduction and risk management interventions for enhancing climate change adaptation and building climate resilience.

Some observers have suggested that there has been a shift in the debate away from "harmful wrongdoing" (1.) to mostly considering support for risk and climate insurance mechanisms (3.) (see Serdeczny and Zamarioli 2018). While indeed, insurance mechanisms have been given substantial attention, it seems that the debate overall has become more comprehensive and the three discursive lines rather exist in parallel offering potential to be further aligned as delineated in this book (see also Mechler 2017).

1.3 The Research Perspective: Definitions and Concepts

1.3.1 Defining Losses and Damages

Many of the issues associated with the L&D discourse are controversial, and given the various perspectives on what exactly L&D might refer to, it is unsurprising that there is no official UNFCCC definition for "Loss and Damage." There are, however, some aspects of L&D that have been relatively widely accepted. UNFCCC documentation consistently states that L&D refers to climate-related impacts and risks from both sudden-onset extreme events, such as flooding and cyclones, and slow-onset events, including sea level rise, glacial retreat, desertification, and others (UNFCCC 2013, 2015). Some analysts have also made a distinction between *losses* associated with irreversibility, for example, fatalities from heat-related disasters or the permanent destruction of coral reefs, while *damages* are referred to as impacts that can be alleviated or repaired, such as damages to buildings (Boyd et al. 2017). Another useful distinction, which has been adopted by many authors (including in this book), was made by Verheyen and Roderick (2008) between *avoided*, *unavoided* and *unavoidable* losses and damages (see Table 1.1).

Avoided losses and damages are those that have been and will be avoided by DRR and CCA. Unavoided impacts and risks are and will not be reduced due to socio-economic constraints and trade-offs (finance, governance, political economy). These unavoided losses and damages are also called residual impacts and risks in the literature (Warner and van der Geest 2013) and are characterised by limits impeding avoidance and reduction. Losses and damages can be material (i.e., physical) or immaterial, as well as economic (measurable in financial or economic terms) and non-economic, with some overlap between these categories (Schäfer and Balogun 2015; Serdeczny 2018). Many consider the L&D discourse to deal particularly with losses and damages "beyond adaptation" and limits to adaptation, that is, unavoided or unavoidable impacts that go beyond adaptation potentials (Verheyen and Roderick 2008; van der Geest and Warner 2015). While adaptation opportunities and barriers

Table 1.1 Classifying losses and damages

Avoided	Unavoided	Unavoidable
Avoidable losses and damages that *can* and *will be* avoided by climate change mitigation and/or adaptation measures	Avoidable losses and damages that are and *will not be* addressed by further mitigation and/or adaptation measures, even though avoidance would be possible. Financial, technical and political constraints, as well as case-specific risk preferences narrow down the adaptation space	Losses and damages that *cannot be* avoided and adapted to through further mitigation and/or adaptation measures, for instance impacts from slow onset processes that have kicked-off already, such as sea level rise and melting glaciers

Classification further developed based on Verheyen and Roderick (2008)

are enablers/disablers for adaptation planning and implementation, adaptation limits have been defined by Klein et al. (2014) as loci at which adaptation actions can no longer guarantee key actor objectives or system's needs can no longer be achieved in the presence of intolerable risks (Dow et al. 2013). These limits can be hard (meaning adaptive technologies and actions are not physically feasible), or soft (technology and/or important socio-economic trade-offs affect priorities today, yet there is potential for overcoming limits in the future) (see also chapter by van den Homberg and McQuistan 2018).

1.3.2 Loss and Damage in the Context of Climate and Disaster Risk Management

In L&D discussions, risk management approaches have received increasing attention. Climate risk management has become the widely accepted methodological framework for assessing potential impacts and devising strategies for adaptation. The IPCC (2014a, p 5.) defines risk as:

> The potential for consequences where something of value is at stake and where the outcome is uncertain, recognizing the diversity of values. Risk is often represented as probability of occurrence of hazardous events or trends multiplied by the impacts if these events or trends occur. Risk results from the interaction of vulnerability, exposure, and hazard.

IPCC's Special Report on Extreme Events (SREX 2012) and the IPCC 5th Assessment Report (IPCC 2014b) define climate risk management (CRM) as an integrative

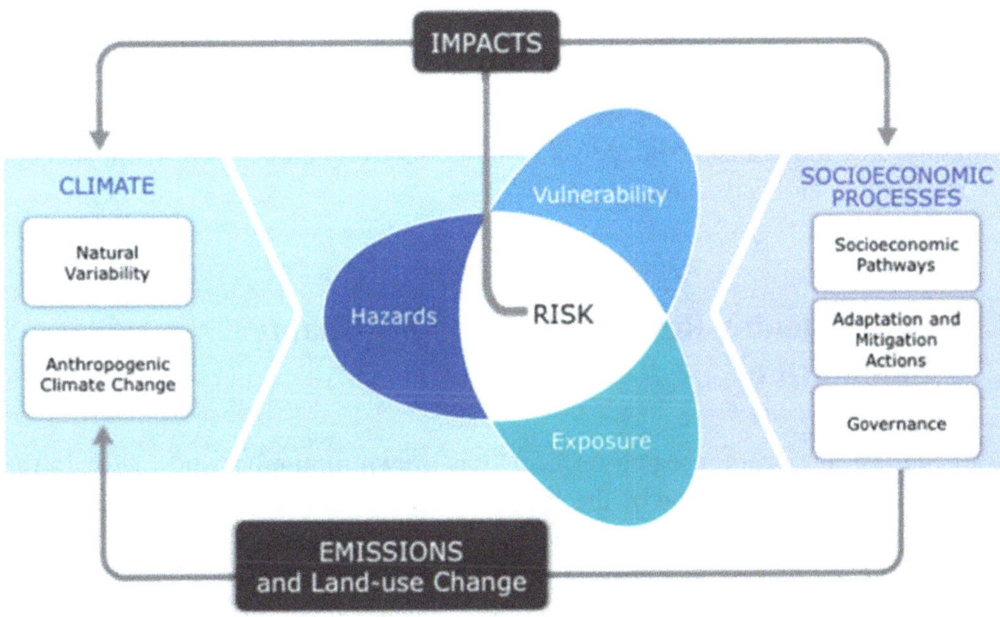

Fig. 1.3 Risk as a function of hazard, exposure and vulnerability. *Sources* IPCC (2012, 2014a)

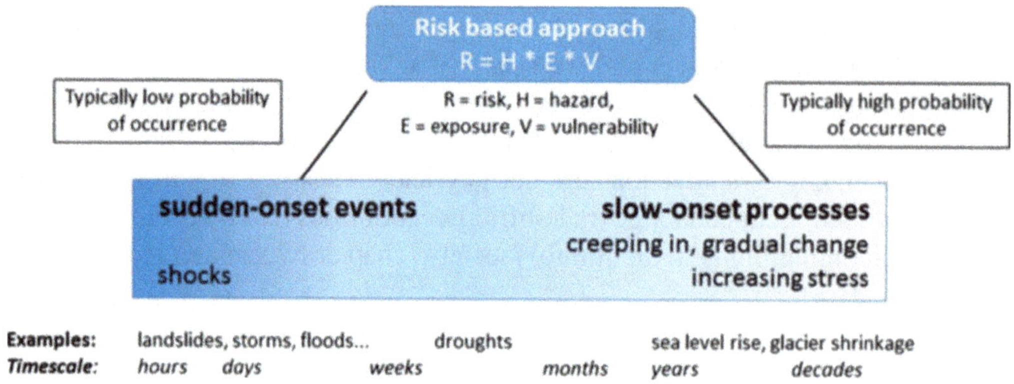

Fig. 1.4 The risk concept as applied to sudden-onset and slow-onset processes. *Source* Huggel et al. (2016a)

framework for understanding and addressing climate-related risks (see Fig. 1.3). CRM broadly may be defined as comprehensively reducing, preparing for, and financing climate-related risk, while tackling the underlying risk drivers, including climate-related and socio-economic factors (Schinko et al. 2016). Climate risk management can build on expertise developed in DRR and CCA research and practice. Firstly, it considers climate risk as a function of hazard (and any climate-related changes), exposure and vulnerability; secondly, it gives proper attention to variability and probability (low frequency vs. high frequency events), calling for probabilistic risk analytical approaches; and thirdly, it accounts for differences in risk perception and the various types of outcomes.

In principle, this climate risk concept can be applied to sudden-onset events and slow-onset climate-related processes unfolding over timescales from hours to days (landslides, storms, floods) to weeks and months (droughts, heat waves), to years (sea-level rise and impacts), and decades (glacial shrinkage) (see Fig. 1.4). In practice, risk analysis has so far usually been applied to phenomena lasting from hours to months. While risk analysis is a key policy tool for climate risk management, including dealing with unavoided losses and damages, it cannot effectively address those impacts that are irreversible and permanent.

1.4 A Broadening Research Landscape–Chapter Summaries

Over the last few years research on L&D has grown in number and focus. In this section, we summarise some of the most relevant findings from the various book chapters providing a review of key topics addressed in the book. Building on forewords by policy makers and negotiators from developing (Dawn Pierre-Nathoniel of the Small Island State of Saint Lucia) and developed countries (Ingrid-Gabriela

Hoven of Germany), the book is divided into five sections, for which we shortly summarise the respective chapters.

1.4.1 Setting the Stage: Key Concepts, Challenges and Insights

The chapter on the **Ethical Challenges in the Context of Climate Loss and Damage** by Ivo Wallimann-Helmer, Lukas Meyer, Kian Mintz-Woo, Thomas Schinko and Olivia Serdeczny sets out the main types of justice and ethical challenges relevant to the L&D debate. The authors argue that a clear differentiation between mitigation, adaptation policy domains and L&D policy is important to understand the normative implications of L&D. They show why *distributive* and *compensatory justice* perspectives are of key relevance to capture all ethical entitlements stemming from adaptation needs and the materialisation of L&D. Of particular importance, the chapter presents a distributive justice perspective for understanding ethical implications of L&D in the short- to medium-term, arguing that L&D can be understood as undeserved harm demanding redistribution to even out this unfairness.

Laurens M. Bouwer in his contribution on **Observed and Projected Impacts from Extreme Weather Events: Implications for Loss and Damage** presents the current knowledge on observed and projected impacts, and risks from extreme weather events in light of anthropogenic climate change. Research on the subject has focused on three key drivers: changes in extreme weather hazards due to natural climate variability and anthropogenic climate change, changes in exposure and vulnerability, and any implemented risk reduction efforts. Studies currently identify increasing exposure as the dominant driver, through growing populations and increases in assets at risk. The chapter further elaborates on how residual weather-related losses (i.e., impacts after implemented risk reduction and adaptation) have not yet been attributed to anthropogenic climate change. The author holds that globally increasing asset exposure will lead to increases in risk, yet presents evidence that vulnerability has declined; thus, it appears there is potential for reducing risks through DRR and adaptation. At country scale, and particularly for developing countries, the evidence points towards increasing risk, indicating the need to significantly upgrade climate risk management efforts and international support. This stage-setting chapter thus shows the challenges in understanding global trends in losses and damages, impacts, and risks from disasters in light of climate change.

Thomas Schinko, Reinhard Mechler and Stefan Hochrainer-Stigler build on the discussions on ethics and trends in impacts and risks. In their chapter on the **Risk and Policy Space for Loss and Damage: Integrating Notions of Distributive and Compensatory Justice with Comprehensive Climate Risk Management** they ask whether a policy framework can be developed around a broad notion of risk to identify a distinct L&D policy space. The authors see ample potential in aligning comprehensive climate risk analytics with distributive and compensatory justice considerations alongside principles of need and responsibility linked to risk-based actions. Building on the findings of the trends and ethics chapters, the authors develop a policy proposal arguing for international support for needs-based comprehensive climate risk management. At the same time, they also propose to include action on liabilities attributable to anthropogenic climate change and associated impacts. They identify a policy space composed of, what they call *curative* and *transformative* measures. Transformative measures are measures that go beyond the standard toolbox of risk management, also involving actions that change fundamental systems' attributes. Curative action would be triggered through the identification of unavoided and unavoidable losses and damages attributed with relatively *high confidence* to climate change (examples are impacts linked to sea-level rise and glacial retreat; see IPCC 2014a). Presenting and going beyond a public finance application, the authors maintain that the broad risk and justice approach developed may be applied to other highly contested L&D issues such as migration and the preservation of cultural heritage, as discussed elsewhere in the book.

1.4.2 Critical Issues Shaping the Discourse

A number of issues have been critical for shaping the discourse. Importantly, the role of attribution has been in the limelight. The chapter on **Attribution: How is it Relevant for Loss and Damage Policy and Practice?** by Rachel A. James, Richard G. Jones, Emily Boyd, Hannah R. Young, Friederike E. L. Otto, Christian Huggel and Jan S. Fuglestvedt provides an overview of the state of scientific evidence linking losses and damages to anthropogenic greenhouse gas emissions, and takes a critical look at the relevance of this science for L&D policy and practice. The authors' point of departure is a consideration of the existing understanding and perceptions of attribution among policy-makers and observers to L&D discussions. Following several years of research into stakeholder perspectives on attribution and L&D, they find that attribution is often associated with responsibility and blame, and therefore, some might prefer to avoid discussions of attribution. Yet, as the authors argue, attribution science itself is not about responsibility, but rather is a scientific investigation of causal links between elements of the earth system and society. The chapter therefore outlines available research into the causal connections between anthropogenic climate change and L&D from a climate science view focused on changes in hazard, but also from a risk research view that examines the drivers of exposure and vulnerability. The chapter closes with an examination of potential applications of attribution research, highlighting its importance to inform practical actions to avert, minimise and address L&D.

As mentioned, the L&D debate has been strongly shaped by political rationale. Elisa Calliari, Swenja Surminski and Jaroslav Mysiak's chapter on the **Politics of (and behind) the UNFCCC's Loss and Damage Mechanism** reviews political science research and takes an international relations view on the L&D discourse to enhance understanding of current negotiation processes. It also points out ways forward for research and policy. Adopting a multi-faceted notion of power drawing on neorealist, liberal and constructivist schools of thought, the authors examine the *structuralist paradox* in L&D negotiations in light of the fact that smaller parties to the convention have been able to successfully negotiate key milestones with stronger parties. The authors emphasise the relevance of discursive power for L&D decisions. Framing L&D in ethical and legal terms has been important to developing standards shared and agreed upon beyond the UNFCCC context, including basic moral norms linked to island states' narratives of survival and the reference to international customary law (see also the ethics chapter by Wallimann-Helmer et al. 2018). Looking forward, they however argue that a change in narrative may be conducive to truly achieve collective action on L&D as an issue of common concern countering the risk of the policy debate becoming a win-lose negotiation "game."

Legal actions on climate change have been proliferating in recent years. Florentina Simlinger and Benoit Mayer explore the current status of debate around **Legal Responses to Climate Change Induced Loss and Damage**. The discussion reviews the legal literature, scoping out the spectrum of potential legal actions on L&D including key challenges and possible directions for further research. The discussion broadly examines private and public climate change litigation with examples from around the world. It also lays out how human rights issues have been applied in international law with a view towards L&D. As one focus, the authors examine the applicability of the *no-harm principle* in climate change. This principle, which has long been applied in international law, requires states to refrain from activities that have potential to cause significant transboundary harm, and to prevent actors within its jurisdiction from carrying out such activities. The chapter, furthermore, presents legal actions with relevance for L&D negotiations. A synopsis of the various legal responses to L&D highlighting their premises, specific challenges and proposed remedies, provides a succinct summary of the discussion.

Non-economic Loss and Damage (NELD) is a distinct theme in the work plan of the Loss and Damage Executive Committee (WIM Excom). The chapter on **Non-economic Loss and Damage and the Warsaw International Mechanism** by Olivia Serdeczny starts by providing a definition of NELD as climate-related material- and non-material impacts, risks to well-being, and assets and goods not commonly traded in the market. Examples comprise loss of cultural identity, sacred places, as well as human health and lives. Initial analysis shows that the two main characteristics of non-economic values are their context-dependence and incommensurability. The author suggests that these attributes need to be preserved and respected when considering measures to avoid the risk of NELDs as part of comprehensive risk management approaches. Addressing NELDs in a central mechanism under the UNFCCC requires substantial understanding of the permanently lost values and their functions for those negatively affected.

Studies of L&D from climate change have focused strongly on human systems and tended to overlook the mediating role of ecosystems and the services ecosystems provide to society. This is a significant knowledge gap as losses and damages to human systems often result from permanent or temporary disturbances to ecosystems services caused by climatic stressors. The chapter on the **Impacts of Climate**

Change on Ecosystem Services and Resulting Losses and Damages to People and Society written by Kees van der Geest, Alex de Sherbinin, Stefan Kienberger, Zinta Zommers, Asha Sitati, Erin Roberts and Rachel James advances understanding of the impacts of climatic stressors on ecosystems in light of the implications for losses and damages to people and society. The chapter develops a conceptual framework for studying the complex relations, which is applied to a case study of multi-annual drought in the drylands of the West-African Sahel. This case study exhibits the complexity of causal links between climate change, climate variability and specific weather and climate events leading to losses and damages, including warming, multi-decadal drought, and flooding. The authors conclude the chapter by advising against the oversimplification of causality and suggest that governance and natural resource management should be given attention in future research and policy discussions.

How do we understand displacement and resettlement in the context of climate change? Alison Heslin, Natalie Delia Deckard, Robert Oakes and Arianna Montero-Colbert's contribution on **Displacement and Resettlement: Understanding the Role of Climate Change in Contemporary Migration** presents challenges and debates in the literature on climate change impacts and the growing global flow of people. The authors position their discussion within the literature on environmental migration, presenting associated definitions, forms of environmental migration and ways to measure the movement of people. The literature on the reception of migrants and migrant resettlement is also presented. The discussion is contextualised through a selection of cases where the environment plays a role in displacing populations, including sea level rise in Pacific Island States, cyclonic storms in Bangladesh, desertification in West Africa, and deforestation in South America's Southern Cone. The examples highlight the complex set of losses and damages incurred by population displacement in each case.

1.4.3 Research and Practice: Reviewing Methods and Tools

The chapter on the **Role of the Physical Sciences in Loss and Damage Decision-Making** by Ana Lopez, Swenja Surminski and Olivia Serdeczny elaborates on contributions that physical climate science can make to improve decision-makers' understanding of climate-related losses and damages. For climate science both the present and future are of relevance when estimating actual and potential losses and damages associated with climate change. For both timescales climate science seeks to understand those aspects that determine the climate-hazard, including the links between human induced changes in climate and climate variability, the probability of occurrence of extreme meteorological events (e.g., rainfall), and the resulting hazards leading to losses and damages (e.g., flood). The chapter reviews the approaches used to assess this component of risk. Particular attention is paid to the identification of sources of uncertainty and the potential for providing robust information to support decision-making. As the authors demonstrate, uncertainty does not imply policy inaction. To this end, they present tools and approaches developed in the context of CCA and DRR, which, as the authors show, are also of relevance for L&D.

Understanding all components of impacts and risks is crucial for considering further policy actions. Wouter Botzen, Laurens Bouwer, Paolo Scussolini, Onno Kuik, Marjolijn Haasnoot, Judy Lawrence and Jeroen Aerts present approaches for **Integrated Disaster Risk Management and Adaptation** aimed at informing L&D policymakers. Insights provided refer to how risk management and adaptation options interact with options discussed in the L&D debate (such as insurance), as well as how L&D-related activities may support risk reduction and adaptation in vulnerable communities and countries. The authors particularly focus on outlining how risk management can help people and societies to adapt to the increasing impacts of weather-related disasters in relation to anthropogenic climate change. The perspective established is one of holistic risk management comprising state-of-the-art risk assessment methods, socio-economic evaluations of risk management and adaptation options—including household-scale risk reduction strategies and insurance schemes for residual risk. The method of adaptation pathways is presented as an innovative contribution for coping with uncertainty in the timing and intensity of climate change impacts. Case studies on Jakarta, Ho Chi Minh City, Mexico, Bangladesh, Netherlands, New Zealand and Germany illustrate each of these topics with concrete insight.

Laura Schäfer, Koko Warner and Sönke Kreft's contribution on **Exploring and Managing Adaptation Frontiers with Climate Risk Insurance** follows a similar vein as the adaptation pathways proposition discussed above. The authors suggest that climate insurance, a key focus of policy discussion and implementation, may serve as an entry point and tool for exploring adaptation frontiers, which are closely linked to the concept of limits and defined in the literature as a "transitional space between safe and unsafe domains" (Preston et al. 2014). Introducing climate risk insurance (also covered in the chapter by Linnerooth-Bayer et al. 2018), the authors propose three routes through which an insurance focus may contribute to this exploration. The first route provides an action-focussed framework for signalling the magnitude, location, and exposure to climate-related risks, as well as on any actual and potential adaptation limits. The second route supports actors in moving away from adaptation limits by improving ex-ante decision making, incentivising risk reduction and reducing uncertainty around climate-resilient development, while the third route helps actors to stay within the tolerable risk space by facilitating financial buffering as part of risk financing approaches. The authors also highlight that insurance-based approaches are not a silver bullet, and suggest that these are effectively embedded in a comprehensive climate risk management framework integrating other risk-reduction and management strategies (for a similar point, see the chapter by Wallimann-Helmer et al. 2018).

Unsurprisingly, climate finance has been a hot topic for the L&D debate and has been receiving a lot of emphasis in current policy dialogue (in 2018 it is the focus of the so-called *Suva Dialogue* under the UNFCCC informing potential actions on finance leading up to the WIM review in 2019). The evidence base is, however, almost non-existent and there are very few empirical and model-based estimates of L&D finance needs. Anil Markandya and Mikel González-Eguino present what we can learn about possible L&D finance needed from an economic angle in the chapter on **Integrated Assessment for Identifying Climate Finance Needs for Loss and Damage: A Critical Review**. This economic perspective presents and critically reviews a methodological approach that builds on economic rationality for modelling market-based and monetised risks, and actual and perceived trade-offs between investment into income-generating actions, climate mitigation and adaptation. Specifically, the authors present estimates using Economic Integrated Assessment Modelling (EIAM), which calculates economically optimal responses to climate change mitigation and adaptation in terms of maximising welfare (GDP) a few decades into the future. Interpreting modelled residual damages as unavoided losses and damages, a number of implications emerge from the analysis. The authors emphasise that uncertainties are very large and any meaningful projections of residual damages in the medium to long term are currently not feasible. Furthermore, residual damages are found to strongly vary by region as well as by climate scenario. Overall, the chapter finds residual damages to appear significant under a variety of models, and for a range of climate scenarios for both developing and developed countries.

1.4.4 Geographic Perspectives and Cases

Many chapters in this volume contextualise their discussions and findings with examples of place-based insight. The section on geographic perspectives and cases focuses strongly on local experience in relation to L&D. Small Island Developing States (SIDS), being highly vulnerable to climate change due to, among others impacts, sea-level rise and associated consequences, started the discussion on L&D and are very vocal in the debate. John Handmer and Johanna Nalau localise the global debate by focusing on Pacific SIDS in their contribution on **Understanding Loss and Damage in Pacific Small Island Developing States**. Specifically, the authors provide commentary regarding the risk and options space (as discussed in Schinko et al. 2018 and Mechler and Schinko 2016) in the Western Pacific SIDS context, particularly in Vanuatu, where many of the livelihood activities are subsistence-based, reliant on the current climate and its variability, and already seriously disrupted by extreme weather events. As the authors show, for some low-lying island states climate change poses an existential threat, and the region is increasingly recognised as one that is most immediately vulnerable to potential mass migration and relocation due to climate change. The authors thus find the options-policy space for SIDS very constrained as demonstrated through evidence on soft (intolerable risk) and hard limits (irreversible high-level risk). The authors conclude with a proposal to mainstream L&D aspects into sectoral policies and strategies in Pacific SIDS in order to better manage the soft limits and understand any hard limits that could affect vulnerable communities.

Migration and displacement driven by climate-related impacts and risks is a reality in the Pacific and other regions. The chapter on **Climate Migration and Cultural**

Preservation: The Case of the Marshallese Diaspora by Alison Heslin expands that conversation by addressing the consequences of the relocation of Marshallese Islanders on their cultural heritage, an important component of NELD. The low-lying islands of the Republic of the Marshall Islands, with little capacity to withstand even minor increases in sea level and tides, are an important case in point, as its population is faced with relocation in the immediate future. Interestingly, nearly a third of the population already lives outside of the Marshall Islands, benefitting from visa free entry into the United States. This provides an evidence base for helping to anticipate future challenges faced by those who will be displaced by rising sea levels. The study draws on data from interviews with migrants from the Marshall Islands regarding accounts of life in the United States and identifies challenges (differences in livelihoods, family structures, food habits, etc.), as well as opportunities (better access to various forms of employment, improved healthcare and cultural preservation in the midst of the Marshallese diaspora). The study closes by laying out how understanding the means through which Marshallese migrants maintain cultural traditions and the challenges they face can help to address potentially irreversible, but in this case, avoidable losses of cultural traditions in the event of mass displacement from these small islands.

Suggestions have increasingly been brought forward regarding the potential for partnerships between public and private sectors and civil society for devising and implementing options that manage critical climate-related risks at scale. But how are such models and partnerships organised? What can be learned from existing activities and how can learning be upscaled? The chapter **Supporting Climate Risk Management at Scale: Insights from the Zurich Flood Resilience Alliance Partnership Model Applied in Peru and Nepal** by Reinhard Mechler, Colin McQuistan, Ian McCallum, Wei Liu, Adriana Keating, Piotr Magnuszewski, Thomas Schinko and Finn Laurien reports on the learnings from one such partnership, the Zurich Flood Resilience Alliance–a multi-actor partnership launched in 2013 to enhance communities' resilience to floods at local to global scales. The chapter presents learnings from two cases where flood risk, amplified by climate change, has been eroding livelihoods leading to some soft limits. In the Karnali and Koshi river basins in Nepal, communities are facing rapid on-set flash floods during the monsoon season that, in the absence of appropriate early warning technology, have led to severe loss of life and assets. In the Rimac and Piura river basins in Peru, the wellbeing of communities in the absence of effective preparedness has been severely affected by low probability, but high impact El Niño episodes. Options to overcome these impacts have included identifying novel evacuation routes and emergency plans, the development of flood brigades, and supporting communities to interact with local governments on DRR planning. This critical examination of the experience across geographies and scales leads the authors towards suggestions for identifying novel organisational, funding and support models involving NGOs, researchers and the private sector, side by side with public sector institutions.

The Arctic is a "laboratory" of physical transformation, where climate change is happening about two times faster than the global average; there is high evidence that meltwater from Arctic sources accounts for 35 percent of the current global sea level rise. Local impacts are of relevance as well, particularly those on social systems and responses. Arctic communities have had to seek ways to deal with rapidly changing environmental conditions that are leading to social impacts such as through outmigration, similar to the experience in the global South. Yet, the international debate on L&D has not sufficiently addressed the Arctic region so far. In their chapter on **Loss and Damage in the Rapidly Changing Arctic** Mia Landauer and Sirkku Juhola provide the first such research contribution reviewing the literature to show what impacts of climate change are already visible in the Arctic. The authors present a literature review with local cases to provide empirical evidence of climate losses and damages in the region. Particularly, they show that there is solid evidence and examples of outmigration and relocation. In addition to the implications of Arctic losses and damages for the international debate, the authors suggest a need for new governance mechanisms and institutional frameworks to tackle losses and damages in this quickly changing region.

1.4.5 Policy Options and Other Response Mechanisms for the L&D Discourse

The final section of the book deals with policy options and other response mechanisms relevant to L&D. The chapter by Masroora Haque, Mousumi Pervin, Saibeen Sultana and Saleemul Huq on **Towards Establishing a National Mechanism to Address Loss and Damage: A Case Study from Bangladesh** reports on innovative efforts that are underway to establish a national mechanism that addresses losses and damages in Bangladesh–a highly climate-vulnerable country which, at the same time, is one of the forerunners in comprehensive risk management. Bangladesh has a history of well-established DRR policies involving institutions at national and sub-national levels, as well as political and regulatory institutions. Furthermore, the country has been one of the first to establish a National Adaptation Programme of Action (NAPA), which has led to the Bangladesh Climate Change Strategy and Action Plan. Loss and Damage is currently not explicitly addressed, yet particularly the work area on comprehensive Disaster Management provides an entry point with activities underway or planned on insurance, as well as on tackling climate migration and displacement. Taking explicit account of L&D is the main gap in Bangladesh's adaptation and DRR policy framework, and thus the motivation behind the plans is to set up a legislative, institutional and policy-related mechanism to address climate-induced losses and damages.

As presented by Florentina Simlinger and Benoit Mayer, legal actions on climate change are proliferating. The contribution by William Frank, Christoph Bals and Julia Grimm on the **Case of Huaraz: First Climate Lawsuit on Loss and Damage against an Energy Company before German Courts** reports on the first climate litigation lawsuit in Germany and the first specifically on L&D. The case has been brought forward by the plaintiff, Saul Luciano Lliuya of the city of Huaraz in the

Andes nestled just below the Palcacocha glacial lake. Global warming has led to dangerous increases in the lake's volume, increasing the risk of a glacial ice avalanche. Such an avalanche would cause an outburst flood from the lake potentially leading to massive destruction and loss of life. As a precedent, in 1941 an outburst flood killed more than 5,000 people in Huaraz. Saúl Luciano Lliuya's climate lawsuit, brought forward with support from the German NGO Germanwatch in 2016 against the German energy company RWE, seeks support from the company to make a contribution to risk measures that avoid such a glacial lake flood, proportional to the company's share in historical CO_2 emissions (about 0.5% overall). The case, dismissed in the first instance, has since been accepted by a higher regional court in Germany after an appeal, and is now (mid 2018) in the midst of the evidentiary stage.

Much of the L&D debate has focused on climate risk insurance as a possible response mechanism. This policy response is explored by JoAnne Linnerooth-Bayer, Swenja Surminski, Laurens M. Bouwer, Ilan Noy and Reinhard Mechler in **Insurance as a Response to Loss and Damage?** The chapter reflects on recent evidence and questions whether insurance instruments can serve the *prevention* and *cure* intentions of the WIM and the Paris Agreement, in terms of reducing climate-related risk and providing an equitable response to L&D from weather extremes in developing countries. The chapter lays out the forms and functions of insurance for climate-related extremes and emphasises the substantial benefits as well as the substantial costs of both micro-insurance programs and regional insurance pools for providing post-disaster relief and reconstruction. Notwithstanding the actual and potential benefits, the authors find that absent significant intervention in their design and implementation, insurance mechanisms as currently implemented, will likely fall short of fully serving the *preventive* and *curative* aspirations of developing country parties to the WIM. The authors emphasise the importance of burden-sharing, as insurance is generally *loaded* with an expense and risk margin in addition to the profit margin for commercial insurance. The chapter, while advising caution about relying largely on market solutions to provide insurance for fulfilling the prevention and cure aspirations, thus emphasises the criticality of international and public intervention in climate risk insurance provision.

Technology plays a critical role in coping with climate impacts and risks so that adaptation limits are not further breached. Yet, vulnerable communities disproportionally impacted by climate change, often cannot benefit from existing technology. Those engaging in the L&D debate have only very recently sought dialogue with discussions on technology, such as under the UNFCCC. The chapter **Technology for Climate Justice: A Reporting Framework for Loss and Damage as part of Key Global Agreements** by Marc van den Homberg and Colin McQuistan examines how technology can shape limits to adaptation and how international reporting on technology (in)justice as part of key global agreements may help. The authors develop a technology-reporting framework with components of access, use and innovation, which is consequently applied via the example of transboundary early warning systems deployed in South Asia. They find that for vulnerable countries only a limited set of state-of-the-art technologies is available, and the reality of capacity and funding gaps means only the bare minimum, largely copycat types of technology, is utilised.

Similar to the ethics chapter, the authors thus argue that more attention to distributive, compensatory and procedural climate justice principles in terms of distributing technology, building capacity and providing finance is sorely needed to widen the access, use and innovation of the technology spectrum available to developing countries. The authors finally suggest to include technology for climate justice in the Adaptation Communications, and making reporting mandatory on actual and expected impacts of L&D measures.

1.5 From Findings to Propositions for the Loss and Damage Debate

The book chapters cover specific issues showing the wide variety of research on L&D, as well as the many interconnections, shared concepts, tools and methods. In this section, we align some of the key findings and suggestions for moving forward. We identify five key propositions that, as we assert, hold potential for providing a roadmap for further 'grounding' the so far highly political debate. The propositions are essentially cross-cutting and reflect the architecture of the book in terms of considering insights from the various sections (setting the stage, critical issues, methods and tools, cases, policy options). The propositions each build on relevant findings that then inform suggestions for an actionable element to be taken forward by research, policy and practice.

Proposition 1 *Risk management is an effective entry point for aligning perspectives and debates. Framed comprehensively, coupled with climate justice considerations and linked to established risk management practice, it may help to identify a distinct policy space for Loss and Damage.*

The L&D debate has been polarised between those advocating for compensation for actual losses and damages, and others suggesting support for tackling future risks by (further) employing disaster risk management and climate insurance solutions. While L&D remains a political concept developed during the UNFCCC negotiations, it has (some of) its technical roots in risk management, which can be built upon to identify a joint and distinct policy space (see chapters by Schinko et al. 2018; Botzen et al. 2018; van den Homberg and McQuistan 2018).

Risk management brings along established practices for dealing with extreme events and any trends therein, and thus may provide an operational framework with a tested set of methods and tools (see Bouwer 2018; Botzen et al. 2018). Yet, a broader perspective on climate risk research and policy appears sorely needed. In its 5th Assessment Report (IPCC 2014b), the IPCC laid the foundations for such a perspective by broadly defining climate-related risks and the potential (as well as limits) for adaptation to key risks faced by geographic regions both today and in the future, characterised by scenarios of aggressive or business-as-usual mitigation and adaptation. This perspective requires to take into account non-economic losses and damages (NELD) such as to human health and lives, but also losses of cultural identity and sacred places. The issue of NELD, which has garnered substantial attention in the discourse, but is generally not accounted for in standard DRR approaches, implies a need for well considering its two main characteristics, context-dependence and incommensurability (Serdeczny 2018).

Understanding and acting on climate risks is intricately linked to justice and ethical considerations. Justice and fairness issues have played a key role in the climate change policy and academic discourse since the beginning of the UNFCCC process–most prominently through the distributive justice principle of "common but differentiated responsibilities" (UNFCCC 1992). These considerations also come into play when contemplating issues of compensatory justice due to the unequal distribution of historical and current greenhouse gas emissions, the adverse distribution of impacts between the global North and South, and the understanding that climate change is projected to lead to unavoidable and potentially irrecoverable losses and damages (chapter by Wallimann-Helmer et al. 2018). Building on risk and justice principles, Schinko et al. 2018 propose a distinct L&D policy action space that can be identified by aligning a needs-based, distributive justice perspective, proposing support for transformative climate risk management beyond adaptation possibilities, with a compensatory justice perspective which upholds considerations for curative options for liabilities attributable to anthropogenic climate change (see also Mechler and Schinko 2016).

Interestingly, both types of principles and policy actions are already seeing some, if incipient, attention today. *Transformative risk management* is increasingly debated in the L&D discourse, and involves issues such as offering alternative livelihoods to those that are being affected (e.g., switching from smallholder farming to service sector employment) and assisting with voluntary migration where needed. Options under this rubric exhibit substantial overlap with interventions of disaster risk reduction and adaptation, yet may be focussed further on avoiding and managing intolerable risks that touch on hard and soft limits. Insurance applications, a mainstay of policy attention, e.g., through the G20/V20 InsuResilience initiative (InsuResilience 2017), can in principle be a useful entry point for tackling transformation; yet, caution must be exercised about commercial insurance products that place the full burden on the most vulnerable. Premium support in the form of subsidies and technical assistance can potentially transform insurance into a mechanism that meets the aspirations of the L&D discussions. Insurance options furthermore hold additional potential by serving as a concept and tool for exploring the magnitude and locations of adaptation frontiers, "socio-ecological system's transitional … operating spaces between safe and unsafe domains" (Preston et al. 2014) (see chapters by Schäfer et al. 2018 and Linnerooth-Bayer et al. 2018).

Complementing transformative risk management, largely appropriate for sudden-onset impacts and risks, with efforts for dealing with slow-onset events, the space for *curative* measures overlaps to some extent with demands for compensation, which have been ruled out by the Paris Agreement, but not from the debate in general (see chapters by Simlinger and Mayer 2018; Schinko et al. 2018). In addition to policy proposals in the domain of insurance, essentially a pre-arranged compensation mechanism for any losses and damages funded by premium payments of those at-risk, via a climate attribution-triggered capitalisation mechanism (see proposition 4), the most advanced ideas in the context of curative measures have been articulated with regard to support for involuntary climate-induced displacement and forced migration. A climate displacement facility is being discussed under the WIM and proposals for approaches to address climate-induced displacement have been made (e.g., through the Nansen Principles on Climate Change and Displacement (NRC & IDMC 2011) and the Peninsula Principles on Climate Displacement within States (Displacement Solutions 2015).

Identifying the financial costs associated with such a distinct risk and policy L&D space is currently extremely difficult–particularly as the remit of action has not been concretised. There are some limited studies extrapolating from estimates of climate impact and adaptation costs. If L&D is framed as dealing with residual impacts after adaptation, models using economic optimality reasoning calculate impact and option costs in the billions of US dollars; yet, as Markandya and González-Eguino (2018) find, there is currently *low confidence* regarding damage costs, cost of adaptation and residual impacts. Beyond finance considerations, the risk management approach to L&D—if framed comprehensively (with associated principles, methods and tools)—may indeed embrace some of the other salient perspectives of the discourse, such as those emphasising burden sharing and the limits to adaptation, and thus help to constitute a systematic platform for future work of the WIM and beyond (see chapter by Lopez et al. 2018).

Proposition 2 *Attribution science is advancing rapidly, leading to increased understanding of the causal connections between emissions, climate, human systems, and Loss and Damage. While the science has often been associated with responsibility and blame, its aim is to analyse drivers of change fundamental to informing actions to minimise, avert, and address loss and damage.*

Climate change attribution research originally focused on examining drivers of observed changes in global temperature. Attributing losses and damages is much more complex and requires investigating how anthropogenic greenhouse gases (GHGs) influence many other climatic variables apart from global temperature, as well as their influence on the oceans, cryosphere, biosphere, and human systems on a range of timescales. It also requires a comparison of the influence of anthropogenic emissions on hazards, with other potential drivers (for example land use change, and aerosols), as well as drivers of exposure and vulnerability. Therefore, this is not only a question for climate scientists, but requires integration of research from a number of scientific fields. Researchers are stepping up to this grand challenge and have made rapid advances, particularly in a new field of climate change attribution research focusing on single extreme weather events. This now allows statements to be made about how anthropogenic emissions have influenced the likelihood or magnitude of specific heatwaves, heavy rainfall events, wind storms, and droughts. Several recent event attribution studies have also demonstrated the influence of GHG emissions on the probability of monetary losses from flooding and loss of life from cold- and heat-related events (see chapter by James et al. 2018).

The evidence base on climate impacts is growing. As summarised in IPCC's AR5, impacts of climate change have been observed on all continents and across all oceans. There is *high confidence* that worldwide glacial retreat, permafrost thawing, and mass bleaching of coral reefs can be mainly attributed to climate change (IPCC 2014a). Yet, impacts to human systems and specific events are much harder to assess due to multifactorial causation, and in particular, since vulnerability reducing actions have been employed in many locations and for many weather-related hazards (see chapters by Bouwer 2018; Lopez et al. 2018). Therefore, despite the advances, it may never be possible to generate a complete inventory of L&D attributable to anthropogenic emissions. In addition to the uncertainties inherent in the attribution problem, a lack of robust time series data in many hot spot locations hinders progress in research and risk management (Huggel et al. 2016b). Thus, policy-advisors and negotiators should not expect the emergence of fully conclusive evidence regarding the influence of climate variability and change on specific incidences of losses and damages and, in particular, should not expect the strength of evidence to be equivalent between events and between countries.

Some of the most frequently discussed applications of attribution science for L&D have been made in relation to liability and legal responses. Attribution research is relevant to private and public administration litigation as well as to breaches of customary international law—the *no-harm principle* (see chapter by Simlinger and Mayer 2018). In the case of litigation before a national or international court or tribunal, legal cases are faced with a myriad of technical difficulties, particularly what concerns the issue of causality. Litigation requires diligence to prevent or minimise harm, as well as considering the indirect consequences of harmful wrongdoing in addition to direct impacts, which are normally considered in litigation. Thus, the case of Lliuya versus RWE, which is currently (mid 2018) in the evidentiary stages after having been admitted to a higher regional court in Germany, is exemplary in two regards. It is considered the first case on L&D in Germany and elsewhere, as several tort-based cases have been rejected by, for example, courts in the USA. It also innovatively seeks remuneration for risk management efforts to be undertaken to avoid future, irreversible risk (loss of life) associated with glacial lake outburst flooding affected by glacial retreat attributed with high confidence to anthropogenic climate change (see chapter by Frank et al. 2018). Given the many technical difficulties to be addressed, for legal actions overall, it may be interesting to consider working with a so-called *modified general causation test*—as has been done successfully for other risk classes, such as tobacco, nuclear risk etc. (see chapter by Simlinger and Mayer 2018). This would mean focusing on proving that GHG emissions are *generally* capable of causing damages and that a causal link between action and damage is *probable*. Such a rationale would render the requirement to attribute a specific climatic event to the emissions of a specific person or entity unnecessary. Therefore, a lack of attribution evidence may not necessarily be a limiting factor in some legal responses. Overall, attribution research has the potential for much broader applicability. It has an important role to play in helping to understand losses and damages, including through the quantification of risks; investigating the relative importance of different drivers of change; and identifying timescales on which significant impacts of climate change emerge in different regions of the world. All of these applications are fundamental to informing actions to address, avert and minimise losses and damages.

Proposition 3 *Climate change research has focused on understanding physical/hard limits to adaptation, but less so on the soft limits, which are strongly shaped by social processes. Applying a multiple lines of evidence framework, we find that soft limits to intolerable risk are already being breached in several geographies globally. Climate change is a key factor, yet exposure growth and vulnerability dynamics particularly need attention for a comprehensive understanding.*

While research on adaptation limits is still in its infancy, the L&D debate has had some focus on adaptation limits, which have been defined as points beyond which actors' objectives are compromised by intolerable risks. Adaptation research has focused on how climate-related hazards lead to hard adaptation limits, that is, where no adaptive technologies and actions are feasible anymore (see also chapter by van den Homberg and McQuistan 2018). Soft adaptation limits, characterised by a lack of options and concurrent socio-economic trade-offs, have received less attention. In addition, empirical research on losses and damages has only recently started to consider the mediating role of ecosystems and their services provided to society (van der Geest et al. 2018). Notably, a very recent volume co-edited by Johanna Nalau, an author in this book, provides a first comprehensive overview of research and experience on adaptation limits (see Filho and Nalau 2018). As one methodological contribution along a multiple lines of evidence approach, risk analysis shows a way forward for identifying hard and particularly soft limits. Starting with risk identification for assessing risks in monetary and/or non-monetary terms, the process of risk evaluation examines the ability of agents (households, private and public sectors) to respond to risk leading to qualifications and quantifications of risk (in)tolerance.

The cases presented in this volume provide a multiple lines of evidence approach for considering any actual or potential adaptation limits. The research documented in the book has generated evidence that poor and vulnerable people and communities already persist at the edges of these boundaries and limits. Overall, the case studies in this book report multiple instances where soft and hard adaptation limits are (at risk of) being breached. Climate change is generally a key factor, yet other drivers and constraints also need to be understood and addressed. In addition, observed vulnerability dynamics imply that adaptation and building resilience lead to reductions in vulnerability.

Pacific Island states are particularly vulnerable to sea level rise, high tides, and salinisation, but also to droughts. Some communities experience seasonal food shortages, and malnutrition is common, indicating that part of the Pacific (as discussed for the state of **Vanuatu**) is already at or near the tolerable/intolerable interface. As a result, relocations and some resettlement are already occurring or planned (Handmer and Nalau 2018). As people move, understanding the means through which SIDS migrants maintain cultural traditions and the challenges current migrants face can help address potentially irreversible, but avoidable, losses of cultural traditions in the event of mass displacement as analysed for the **Marshall Islands** (Heslin 2018).

Faced with the increasing impacts of climate change and recognising that gains in development and poverty alleviation are severely hampered by climate change, the government of **Bangladesh** is planning to set up a national L&D mechanism to support those that have already incurred significant losses and damages beyond adaptation (Haque et al. 2018). Flood climate risk management case studies on **Nepal, India, Bangladesh** and **Peru** show limits to adaptation due to inadequate transboundary governance, insufficient devolution of mandates and funding to lower administrative levels, as well as inadequate access to and use of technology (chapters by Mechler et al. 2018b; van den Homberg and McQuistan 2018).

A case study on the **Sahel** and the semi-arid drylands of **East Africa** discusses how climate variability and change have affected primary productivity and food production as supporting and provisioning ecosystem services. Losses and damages reported in this context are livestock losses, food insecurity, displacement, cultural losses (including traditional livelihood systems), and finally, conflict related to these. The case also shows that oversimplification must be avoided in a context of multiple risk factors, including the governance or management of natural resources. Examples for risk factors presented are a lack of investment in water-related infrastructure, gaps in access to agricultural technology, barriers to pastoralists' freedom of movement, or lack of health care services, which have also contributed to increasing losses and damages (van der Geest et al. 2018).

Migration, particularly if forced, is an example of "beyond the limits of adaptation." Contextualising migration as multifactorial, a selection of cases including sea level rise in **Pacific Island States**, cyclonic storms in **Bangladesh**, and desertification in **West Africa**, as well as deforestation in **South America**'s Southern Cone, presents instances of migration driven by climate change and variability, as well as other factors (Heslin et al. 2018). The **Arctic** case on relocation and outmigration provides examples of instances "beyond adaptation" due to institutional, political, organisational and jurisdictional factors hindering implementation of adaptation to climate impacts, thus leading to losses and damages (Landauer and Juhola 2018).

Proposition 4 *Insurance mechanisms can only serve the prevention and cure aspects emphasised in the L&D debate if they are made affordable with support from outside the insurance pool, and if they are purposefully designed to encourage or prescribe risk reduction. While their applications are limited to sudden onset events, insurance instruments can help to explore adaptation frontiers, in which many factors, including technology, play a role.*

Climate insurance has been one of the foci of debate on L&D and the WIM work plan. Recent experience, however, shows that insurance instruments can only serve as a risk-reducing and equitable response to losses and damages from weather extremes in developing countries if they are designed to explicitly reward risk-reducing behaviour and if they are supported by those outside the insurance pool. Commercial insurance is based on the principle of mutuality, according to which the insured participate in a disaster pool according to their risk class and pay a risk-based premium. Thus, the commercial insurance approach, unless subsidised or otherwise supported, does not share risk beyond the at-risk insured community.

This stands in contrast to most micro-insurance and regional insurance pools, which for the most part receive substantial support from the international community. Support appears to be increasingly based on the concept of *solidarity*, consistent with the humanitarian principles underlying development assistance, and not on attribution or responsibility for climate change impacts experienced by vulnerable countries. A common challenge with the solidarity principle, which features subsidies and other support to reduce premiums, is its failure to incentivise policyholders to reduce their risk. In meeting this challenge, international financial institutions, development agencies and other donors will need to reconcile the contending equity and preventive objectives in their support of climate insurance programs.

Two examples of insurance instruments serving the poor, the African R4 micro-insurance program and the African Risk Capacity (ARC) regional insurance pool, combine these goals. Neither is a commercial insurance enterprise; neither is fully characterised by risk-based premiums underlying the principle of mutuality; and both are highly subsidised. The R4 program's success has largely been attributed to its close connection with public safety net programs in the participating countries, while ARC requires member governments to develop disbursement plans to ensure that the most vulnerable parts of the population benefit from the macro scheme. Moreover, ARC's innovative Extreme Climate Facility (XCF) program may additionally bring in the concept of *accountability*, motivated by a perceived ethical or legal obligation for compensating those experiencing climate-attributed losses and damages, linked to changes in observed extreme weather in the region (Linnerooth-Bayer et al. 2018).

In general terms, insurance is a pre-arranged compensation mechanism for losses incurred and can be offered by both private and public actors. Public relief or catastrophe funds serve a similar function, while neither collecting premiums nor (typically) estimating risks. Many countries in the world have contingency funds to support victims of disasters. In Bangladesh, there is debate on whether to set up a national mechanism that would reimburse climate-related losses incurred by farmers and households that go beyond their adaptation possibilities (for example, if flooding pushes people to leave their homesteads or drought renders farming not profitable) (Haque et al. 2018).

In such a context, insurance in a wider sense (including national compensation pools) may innovatively be used as a navigational tool for exploring the adaptation frontiers (broad loci around adaptation limits). Such exploration may involve: (i) signalling the magnitude, location, and exposure to climate-related risks and cases where adaptation limits are approached or breached; (ii) supporting actors to move away from adaptation limits through improved ex-ante decision making and incentivising risk reduction and adaptation by creating a more certain environment for decisions on climate resilient development; and (iii) enabling actors with access to appropriate risk financing measures to remain in the tolerable risk space. One proposition is thus to embed climate insurance and other related instruments in a comprehensive climate risk management approach accompanied by other risk reduction and management strategies in international cooperation programs and projects (Schäfer et al. 2018).

Proposition 5 *Policy deliberations have exhibited characteristics of a win-lose negotiation "game." A more inclusive narrative highlighting collective ambition, mutual benefits and the role of transformation can point a way forward.*

The L&D discourse has exhibited strong ethical and legal undertones appealing to standards shared or agreed beyond the UNFCCC context, such as demanding redistribution for harm via international customary law. While it is useful to prove the need for action on L&D by appealing to moral standards recognised by both contending parties in international arenas, a change of narrative may be conducive to achieving collective action and to avoid turning the issue into a win-lose negotiation "game" (chapter by Calliari et al. 2018).

With evidence that climate impacts and risks are also strongly affecting industrialised countries directly (e.g., Arctic) and indirectly (e.g., through migration), it may be fruitful to frame the debate in terms of the benefits that acting on adaptation and its possible limits and failures could bring for developed countries. Considerations could range from working towards more resilient global supply chains to gaining support for climate displacement and refugees. Exploring mutual gains would contribute to bolstering collective action on an issue of common concern, as well as to elevate and better integrate L&D into other climate negotiation agenda items, such as capacity building, technology and the global stocktake.

A general and joint entry point is the SDG agenda, essentially supporting UN member states' transformation around a set of global developmental goals. The SDGs, passed in 2015, constitute a universal set of 17 goals and 169 targets defining development aspiration and ideally, collective transformation for all signatory countries (UN 2015). The SDG debate casts an integrated and unifying perspective on development. Integrated—as it requires a synergistic look across these broad development goals, and unifying—as it involves all signatories (Dodds and Donoghue 2016). Risk is fundamental in many regards. There are down-side risks (disasters and climate-related impacts as at the heat of the L&D discourse), which are explicitly and implicitly mentioned in many of the SDGs. The need for and benefits of up-side risk taking through increased investment into the socio-economic development objectives is another one of the cross-cutting issues.

Transformative risk management, which, as we argue, should be one of the pillars of the L&D policy space, thus may be one of those issues of common concern (Schinko et al. 2018). Innovative polycentric science-society partnership models are springing up to support the implementation of transformative risk management options that manage critical disaster risks "on the ground". Evidence from hotspots, not only has potential to inform better development policies, but may also support actions in industrialised countries facing similar issues (Mechler et al. 2018b). The role of technology is crucial in this context, as it shapes risks and limits to adaptation and risk management. Yet, access in developing countries is constrained. National hydrological and meteorological services in developing countries, for example, are limited in their possibilities to improve the spatial and temporal resolution of flood forecasts. This is because these countries lack the funding and capacity necessary to use state-of-the-art technology (i.e., computing power, advanced hydrological and meteorological models) and acquire or collect more granular data, such as digital-elevation-model data. In addition, the poor and the vulnerable can often not benefit from early warning/early action information due to the digital divide.

As an area of future work, progressive levels of innovation and technology are required to lead from incremental to transformative change, where the UNFCCC's Technology Mechanism can play a more prominent role (van den Homberg and McQuistan 2018). The WIM Executive Committee may innovatively consider an assessment of technologies from a climate justice perspective, which means rethinking access, use, innovation, finance, and (bottom-up) governance mechanisms from the perspective of the poor and vulnerable.

Enabling joint learning regarding technologies (and other means of implementation) for buffering against high-level risks is necessary for understanding how to overcome soft and avoid hard limits. This may be appealing for developed and developing countries sharing similar exposure and risk, where limits to adaptation need attention (e.g., in the Arctic, mountain areas with glacial retreat, etc.). A joint narrative will be needed to support and incentivise the requisite transformation of energy generation, consumption, but also adaptation efforts across the globe. An improved understanding of actual and potential "dangerous interference with the climate system" at risk management scales and across geographies may indeed be a decisive enabler.

1.6 Conclusions

The book has been a joint effort of the Loss and Damage Network that brings together scientists and practitioners from more than 40 institutions around the globe to inform the L&D debate. Offering a detailed overview of the multiple facets of knowledge emerging on the topic of L&D, the volume is a first comprehensive review of the state of play regarding the science, political debate, practice as well as any policy proposals seeing or looking for implementation. The WIM is now well into its 5-year work plan, and after COP23 in Bonn, the first climate summit chaired by a small island state (Fiji), the WIM stands to deliver on its various workstreams. In 2018, one focus is on the role of finance in supporting actions to address L&D, for which the so-called Suva expert dialogue was carried out in mid-2018 to project a way forward. This and other activities will inform the review of the WIM by the UNFCCC Parties during sessions of the subsidiary bodies in 2019, leading to proper review at COP25 in Rio. As we demonstrated, the science has matured, and interest in the issues is increasing. The IPCC has started to pick up on the discussion and considers L&D in its 1.5 °C report published in October 2018, in special reports on oceans and the cryosphere, and land, as well as in its 6th Assessment Report due in 2022.

Further work is to be done, ideally in close collaboration with policy advisors, negotiators, civil society, private- and public-sector representatives and, particularly, those vulnerable people and communities around the world that are actually and potentially affected by climate-related impacts and risks. The partners in the Loss and Damage Network stand ready to further contribute to the debate and help to identify actions to avert, address and minimise Loss&Damage.

References

Forewords

Pierre-Nathoniel D (2018) Perspective from St. Lucia. In: Mechler R, Bouwer L, Schinko T, Surminski S, Linnerooth-Bayer J (eds) Loss and damage from climate change. Concepts, methods and policy options. Springer, Cham, pp v–vi

Hoven I-G (2018) Perspective of Germany. In: Mechler R, Bouwer L, Schinko T, Surminski S, Linnerooth-Bayer J (eds) Loss and damage from climate change. Concepts, methods and policy options. Springer, Cham, pp vii–viii

Book Chapters (In Sequential Order)

Mechler R, et al (2018a) Science for loss and damage. findings and propositions. In: Mechler R, Bouwer L, Schinko T, Surminski S, Linnerooth-Bayer J (eds) Loss and damage from climate change. Concepts, methods and policy options. Springer, Cham, pp 3–37

Wallimann-Helmer I, Meyer L, Mintz-Woo K, Schinko T, Serdeczny O (2018) The ethical challenges in the context of climate loss and damage. In: Mechler R, Bouwer L, Schinko T, Surminski S, Linnerooth Bayer J (eds) Loss and damage from climate change. Concepts, methods and policy options. Springer, Cham, pp 39–62

Bouwer LM (2018) Observed and projected impacts from extreme weather events: implications for loss and damage. In: Mechler R, Bouwer L, Schinko T, Surminski S, Linnerooth-Bayer J (eds) Loss and damage from climate change. Concepts, methods and policy options. Springer, Cham, pp 63–82

Schinko T, Mechler R, Hochrainer-Stigler S (2018) The risk and policy space for loss and damage: integrating notions of distributive and compensatory justice with comprehensive climate risk management. In: Mechler R, Bouwer L, Schinko T, Surminski S, Linnerooth-Bayer J (eds) Loss and damage from climate change. Concepts, methods and policy options. Springer, Cham, pp 83–110

James RA, Jones RG, Boyd E, Young HR, Otto FEL, Huggel C, Fuglestvedt JS (2018) Attribution: how is it relevant for loss and damage policy and practice? In: Mechler R, Bouwer L, Schinko T, Surminski S, Linnerooth-Bayer J (eds) Loss and damage from climate change. Concepts, methods and policy options. Springer, Cham, pp 113–154

Calliari E, Surminski S, Mysiak J (2018) The Politics of (and behind) the UNFCCC's loss and damage mechanism. In: Mechler R, Bouwer L, Schinko T, Surminski S, Linnerooth-Bayer J (eds) Loss and damage from climate change. Concepts, methods and policy options. Springer, Cham, pp 155–178

Simlinger F, Mayer B (2018) Legal responses to climate change induced loss and damage. In: Mechler R, Bouwer L, Schinko T, Surminski S, Linnerooth-Bayer J (eds) Loss and damage from climate change. Concepts, methods and policy options. Springer, Cham, pp 179–203

Serdeczny O (2018) Non-economic Loss and damage and the Warsaw international mechanism. In: Mechler R, Bouwer L, Schinko T, Surminski S, Linnerooth-Bayer J (eds) Loss and damage from climate change. Concepts, methods and policy options. Springer, Cham, pp 205–220

van der Geest K, de Sherbinin A, Kienberger S, Zommers Z, Sitati A, Roberts E, James R (2018) The impacts of climate change on ecosystem services and resulting losses and damages to people and society. In: Mechler R, Bouwer L, Schinko T, Surminski S, Linnerooth-Bayer J (eds) Loss and damage from climate change. Concepts, methods and policy options. Springer, Cham, pp 221–236

Heslin A, Deckard D, Oakes R, Montero-Colbert A (2018) Displacement and resettlement: understanding the role of climate change in contemporary migration. In: Mechler R, Bouwer L, Schinko T, Surminski S, Linnerooth-Bayer J (eds) Loss and damage from climate change. Concepts, methods and policy options. Springer, Cham, pp 237–258

Lopez, A, Surminski S, Serdeczny O (2018) The role of the physical sciences in loss and damage decision-making. In: Mechler R, Bouwer L, Schinko T, Surminski S, Linnerooth-Bayer J (eds) Loss and damage from climate change. Concepts, methods and policy options. Springer, Cham, pp 261–285

Botzen W, Bouwer LM, Scussolini P, Kuik O, Haasnoot M, Lawrence J, Aerts JCJH (2018) Integrated disaster risk management and adaptation. In: Mechler R, Bouwer L, Schinko T, Surminski S, Linnerooth-Bayer J (eds) Loss and damage from climate change. Concepts, methods and policy options. Springer, Cham, pp 287–315

Schäfer L, Warner K, Kreft S (2018) Exploring and managing adaptation frontiers with climate risk insurance. In: Mechler R, Bouwer L, Schinko T, Surminski S, Linnerooth-Bayer J (eds) Loss and damage from climate change. Concepts, methods and policy options. Springer, Cham, pp 317–341

Markandya A, González-Eguino M (2018) Integrated assessment for identifying climate finance needs for loss and damage: a critical review. In: Mechler R, Bouwer L, Schinko T, Surminski S, Linnerooth-Bayer J (eds) Loss and damage from climate change. Concepts, methods and policy options. Springer, Cham, pp 343–362

Handmer J, Nalau J (2018) Understanding loss and damage in Pacific Small Island developing states. In: Mechler R, Bouwer L, Schinko T, Surminski S, Linnerooth-Bayer J (eds) Loss and damage from climate change. Concepts, methods and policy options. Springer, Cham, pp 365–381

Heslin A (2018) Climate migration and cultural preservation: the case of the Marshallese diaspora. In: Mechler R, Bouwer L, Schinko T, Surminski S, Linnerooth-Bayer J (eds) Loss and damage from climate change. Concepts, methods and policy options. Springer, Cham, pp 383–391

Mechler R, McQuistan C, McCallum I, Liu W, Keating A, Magnuszewski P, Schinko T, Szoenyi M, Laurien F (2018b) Supporting climate risk management at scale. Insights from the Zurich flood resilience alliance partnership model applied in Peru & Nepal. In: Mechler R, Bouwer L, Schinko T, Surminski S, Linnerooth-Bayer J (eds) Loss and damage from climate change. Concepts, methods and policy options. Springer, Cham, pp 393–424

Landauer M, Juhola S (2018) Loss and damage in the rapidly changing arctic. In: Mechler R, Bouwer L, Schinko T, Surminski S, Linnerooth-Bayer J (eds) Loss and damage from climate change. Concepts, methods and policy options. Springer, Cham, pp 425–447

Haque M, Pervin M, Sultana S, Huq S (2018) Towards establishing a national mechanism to address loss and damage: a case study from Bangladesh. In: Mechler R, Bouwer L, Schinko T, Surminski S, Linnerooth-Bayer J (eds) Loss and damage from climate change. Concepts, methods and policy options. Springer, Cham, pp 451–473

Frank W, Bals C, Grimm J (2018) The case of Huaraz: first climate lawsuit on loss and damage against an energy company before German courts. In: Mechler R, Bouwer L, Schinko T, Surminski S, Linnerooth-Bayer J (eds) Loss and damage from climate change. Concepts, methods and policy options. Springer, Cham, pp 475–482

Linnerooth-Bayer J, Surminski S, Bouwer LM, Noy I, Mechler R (2018) Insurance as a response to loss and damage? In: Mechler R, Bouwer L, Schinko T, Surminski S, Linnerooth-Bayer J (eds) Loss and damage from climate change. Concepts, methods and policy options. Springer, Cham, pp 483–512

van den Homberg M, McQuistan C (2018) Technology for climate justice: a reporting framework for loss and damage as part of key global agreements. In: Mechler R, Bouwer L, Schinko T, Surminski S, Linnerooth-Bayer J (eds) Loss and damage from climate change. Concepts, methods and policy options. Springer, Cham, pp 513–545

Other References

AOSIS (2008) Proposal to the AWG-LCA multi-window mechanism to address loss and damage from climate change impacts. 1–8

Biermann F, Boas I (2017) Towards a global governance system to protect climate migrants: taking stock. In: Mayer B, Crepeau F (eds) Research handbook on climate change, migration and the law. Edward Elgar Publishing, Cheltenham, UK, Northampton, MA, USA, pp 405–419

Birkmann J, Welle T (2015) Assessing the risk of loss and damage: exposure, vulnerability and risk to climate-related hazards for different country classification. Int J Global Warming 8(2):191–212

Boyd E, James RA, Jones RG, Young HR, Otto F (2017) A typology of loss and damage perspectives. Nat Clim Change 7:723–729

Crosland T, Meyer A, Wewerinke-Singh M (2016) The Paris agreement implementation blueprint: a practical guide to bridging the gap between actions and goal and closing the accountability deficit (Part 1). Environ Liability 25:114–125

Displacement Solutions (2015) Annual Report. http://displacementsolutions.org/ds-annual-report-2015. Accessed 23 May 2017

Dodds F, Donoghue D (2016) Negotiating the sustainable development goals: a transformational agenda for an insecure world. Routledge, Milton Park, UK

Dow K, Berkhout F, Preston BL, Klein RJT, Midgley G, Shaw MR (2013) Limits to adaptation. Nat Clim Change 3:305–307. https://doi.org/10.1038/nclimate1847

Filho LW, Nalau J (2018) Limits to climate change adaptation. Springer, Heidelberg, Germany

Gall M (2015) The suitability of disaster loss databases to measure loss and damage from climate change. Int J Global Warming 8(2):170–190

Huggel C, Bresch D, Hansen G, James R, Mechler R, Stone D, Wallimann-Helmer I (2016a) Attribution of irreversible loss to anthropogenic climate change. In: EGU General Assembly Conference Abstracts, p 8557

Huggel C, Stone D, Eicken H, Hansen G (2016b) Reconciling justice and attribution research to advance climate policy. Nat Clim Change 6:901–908

INC (1991) Vanuatu: Draft annex relating to Article 23 (Insurance) for inclusion in the revised single text on elements relating to mechanisms (A/AC.237/WG.II/Misc.13) submitted by the Co-Chairmen of Working Group II

InsuResilience (2017) Joint statement on the InsuResilience Global Partnership. 14 November 2017. Bonn

IPCC (2012) Managing the risks of extreme events and disasters to advance climate change adaptation. A special report of working groups i and ii of the intergovernmental panel on climate change. In: Field CB, Barros V, Stocker TF, Qin D, Dokken DJ, Ebi KL, Mastrandrea MD, Mach KJ, Plattner G-K, Allen SK, Tignor M, Midgley PM (eds). Cambridge University Press, Cambridge, UK, and New York, NY, USA

IPCC (2014a) Summary for policymakers. Climate change 2014: impacts, adaptation, and vulnerability. Part A: global and sectoral aspects. contribution of working group II to the fifth assessment report of the intergovernmental panel on climate change. In: Field CB, Barros VR, Dokken DJ,

Mach KJ, Mastrandrea MD, Bilir TE, Chatterjee M, Ebi KL, Estrada YO, Genova RC, Girma B, Kissel ES, Levy AN, MacCracken S, Mastrandrea PR, White LL (eds) Cambridge University Press. Cambridge, United Kingdom and New York, NY, USA, pp 1–32

IPCC (2014b) Climate change 2014: impacts, adaptation, and vulnerability. Part A: global and sectoral aspects. contribution of working group ii to the fifth assessment report of the intergovernmental panel on climate change. In: Field CB, Barros VR, Dokken DJ, Mach KJ, Mastrandrea MD, Bilir TE, Chatterjee M, Ebi KL, Estrada YO, Genova RC, Girma B, Kissel ES, Levy AN, MacCracken S, Mastrandrea PR, White LL (eds) Cambridge University Press. United Kingdom and New York, NY, USA, Cambridge, p 1132

IPCC (2018) The IPCC and the Sixth Assessment cycle. IPCC: Geneva, Switzerland. http://ipcc.ch/pdf/ar6_material/AC6_brochure_en.pdf

James R, Otto F, Parker H, Boyd E, Cornforth R, Mitchell D, Allen M (2015) Characterizing loss and damage from climate change. Nat Clim Change 4:938–939

Klein R, Midgley GF, Preston BL, Alam M, Berkhout F, Dow K, Shaw MR (2014) Adaptation opportunities, constraints, and limits. In: Climate change 2014: impacts, adaptation, and vulnerability. part a: global and sectoral aspects. Contribution of working group II to the fifth assessment report of the intergovernmental panel of climate change. In: Field CB, Barros VR, Dokken DJ, Mach KJ, Mastrandrea MD, Bilir TE, Chatterjee M, Ebi KL, Estrada YO, Genova RC, Girma B, Kissel ES, Levy AN, MacCracken S, Mastrandrea PR, White LL (eds). Cambridge University Press, Cambridge, United Kingdom and New York, NY, USA, pp 899–943

Linnerooth-Bayer J, Mace MJ, Verheyen R (2003) Insurance-related actions and risk assessment in the context of the UNFCCC. Background paper for UNFCCC workshop on insurance-related actions and risk assessment in the framework of the UNFCCC, 11–15 May 2003, Bonn, Germany

Mace MJ, Verheyen R (2016) Loss, damage and responsibility after COP21: All options open for the Paris Agreement. Rev European Commun Int Environ Law 25:197–214. https://doi.org/10.1111/reel.12172

Mayer B (2016) The relevance of the no-harm principle to climate change law and politics. Asia Pacific J Environ Law 19:79–104. https://doi.org/10.4337/apjel.2016.01.04

Mechler R (2017) Climate policy: transparency for loss and damage. Nat Clim Change 7:687–688

Mechler R, Schinko T (2016) Identifying the policy space for climate loss and damage. Science 354(6310):290–292

Mechler R, Bouwer LM, Linnerooth-Bayer J, Hochrainer-Stigler S, Aerts JCJH, Surminski S, Williges K (2014) Managing unnatural disaster risk from climate extremes. Nat Clim Change 4:235–237. https://doi.org/10.1038/nclimate2137

Norwegian Refugee Council/Internal Displacement Monitoring Centre (NRC/IDMC) (2011) The Nansen conference: climate change and displacement in the 21st Century, 7 June 2011. http://www.refworld.org/docid/521485ef4.html. Accessed 23 May 2018

Page EA, Heyward C (2017) Compensating for climate change loss and damage. Polit Stud 65(2):356–372

Pinninti KR (2013) Climate Change Loss and Damage. Econ Leg Found. Springer, Berlin

Preston B, Dow K, Berhout F (2014) The climate adaptation frontier. Sustainability 5(3):1011–1035

Roser D, Huggel C, Ohndorf M, Wallimann-Helmer I (2015) Advancing the interdisciplinary dialogue on climate justice. Clim Change 133:349–359

Schäfer L, Balogun K (2015) Stocktaking of climate risk assessment approaches related to loss and damage. UNUEHS Working Paper, No. 20. United Nations University Institute of Environment and Human Security: Bonn, Germany

Schinko T, Mechler R (2017) Applying recent insights from climate risk management to operationalize the loss and damage mechanism. Ecol Econ 136:296–298. https://doi.org/10.1016/j.ecolecon.2017.02.008

Schinko T, Mechler R, Hochrainer-Stigler S (2016) A methodological framework to operationalize climate risk management: managing sovereign climate-related extreme event risk in Austria. Mitig Adapt Strat Glob Change. https://doi.org/10.1007/s11027-016-9713-0

Serdeczny O, Zamarioli L (2018) Loss and damage financing must push beyond market-based measures. Climate Analytics January 29, 2018. http://theenergymix.com/2018/01/29/loss-and-damage-financing-must-push-beyond-market-based-measures/

Serdeczny O, Waters E E, Chan S (2017) Non-economic loss and damage in the context of climate change (Discussion Paper 3/2016). Bonn, Germany, German Development Institute (DIE)

Tschakert P, Coauthors (2017) Climate change and loss, as if people mattered: values, places, and experiences. Wiley Interdiscip. Rev Clim Chang 8:e476. https://doi.org/10.1002/wcc.476

UN (1992) United Nations Framework Convention on Climate Change. United Nations, New York

UN (2015) Transforming our world: the 2030 agenda for sustainable development, A/RES/70/1

UNFCCC (2007) Decision 1/CP.13, Bali Action Plan, UN Doc FCCC/CP/2007/6/Add.1

UNFCCC (2009) Ideas and proposals on the elements contained in paragraph 1 of the Bali Action Plan

UNFCCC (2010) Decision 1/CP.16, The Cancun agreements: outcome of the work of the ad hoc working group on Long-term Cooperative Action under the Convention, UN Doc FCCC/CP/2010/7/Add.1

UNFCCC (2012) Decision 3/CP.18, Approaches to address loss and damage associated with climate change impacts in developing countries that are particularly vulnerable to the adverse effects of climate change to enhance adaptive capacity, UN Doc FCCC/CP/2012/8/Add.1

UNFCCC (2013) Decision 2/CP.19, Warsaw International Mechanism for loss and damage associated with climate change impacts, UN Doc FCCC/CP/2013/10/Add.1

UNFCCC (2015) Decision 1/CP.21, Adoption of the Paris Agreement, UN Doc FCCC/CP/2015/10/Add.1

UNFCCC (2016) Decision 3/CP.22, Warsaw international mechanism for loss and damage associated with climate change impacts, UN Doc FCCC/CP/2016/10/Add.1

UNFCCC (2018) Loss and damage: Online guide. Available at: https://unfccc.int/sites/default/files/resource/Online_guide_on_loss_and_damage-May_2018.pdf

UNISDR (2015) Sendai framework for disaster risk reduction 2015–2030, A/CONF.224/CRP.1. http://www.unisdr.org/files/43291_sendaiframeworkfordrren.pdf. Accessed 31 Mar 2015

Van der Geest K, Warner K (2015) Editorial: loss and damage from climate change: emerging perspectives. Int J Global Warming 8(2):133–140

Vanhala L, Hestbaek C (2016) Framing climate change loss and damage in UNFCCC negotiations. Global Environ Politics 16:111–129. https://doi.org/10.1162/GLEP_a_00379

Verheyen R, Roderick P (2008) Beyond adaptation—the legal duty to pay compensation for climate change damage. WWF-UK, Climate Change Programme discussion paper, p 2008

Wallimann-Helmer I (2015) Justice for climate loss and damage. Clim Change 133:469–480

Warner K, Van der Geest K (2013) Loss and damage from climate change: local-level evidence from nine vulnerable countries. Int J Global Warming 5:367. https://doi.org/10.1504/IJGW.2013.057289

Wewerinke-Singh M (2018a) Climate migrants' right to enjoy their culture. In: Behrman S, Kent A (eds) Climate refugees: beyond the legal impasse? Earthscan/Routledge: Abingdon. UK and New York, NY, USA

Wewerinke-Singh M (2018b) State responsibility for human rights violations associated with climate change. In: Sébastien D, Sébastien J, Alyssa J (eds) Routledge handbook of human rights and climate governance, Routledge, Abingdon, UK and New York, NY, USA

Chapter 2
The Ethical Challenges in the Context of Climate Loss and Damage

Ivo Wallimann-Helmer, Lukas Meyer, Kian Mintz-Woo, Thomas Schinko and Olivia Serdeczny

Abstract This chapter lays out what we take to be the main types of justice and ethical challenges concerning those adverse effects of climate change leading to climate-related Loss and Damage (L&D). We argue that it is essential to clearly differentiate between the challenges concerning mitigation and adaptation and those ethical issues exclusively relevant for L&D in order to address the ethical aspects pertaining to L&D in international climate policy. First, we show that depending on how mitigation and adaptation are distinguished from L&D, the primary focus of policy measures and their ethical implications will vary. Second, we distinguish between a *distributive* justice framework and a *compensatory* justice scheme for delivering L&D measures. Third, in order to understand the differentiated remedial responsibilities concerning L&D, we categorise the measures and policy approaches available. Fourth, depending on the kind of L&D and which remedies are possible, we explain the difference between *remedial* and *outcome* responsibilities of different actors.

Keywords Loss and Damage · Justice · Responsibility · Compensation Liability · Distributive justice · Compensatory justice · Ethics

I. Wallimann-Helmer (✉)
Center for Ethics, University of Zurich, Zurich, Switzerland
e-mail: wallimann@philos.uzh.ch

L. Meyer · K. Mintz-Woo
Department of Philosophy, Section Moral and Political Philosophy, University of Graz, Graz, Austria

T. Schinko
International Institute for Applied Systems Analysis (IIASA), Laxenburg, Austria

O. Serdeczny
Climate Analytics GmbH, Berlin, Germany

R. Mechler et al. (eds.), *Loss and Damage from Climate Change*, Climate Risk Management, Policy and Governance, https://doi.org/10.1007/978-3-319-72026-5_2

2.1 Introduction

Debate in ethics concerning climate change has mainly investigated questions of how to deal with mitigation and adaptation. Much of the debate has been on climate justice asking how to distribute the benefits and burdens of mitigation and adaptation fairly; dealing with the rights of those facing the impacts of climate change; or discussing the individual moral duty to change lifestyles in order to contribute to climate protection. An important detail of this debate is that mitigation and adaptation are often discussed under one and the same heading. Potential differences between duties related to climate change mitigation and those of adaptation are rarely analysed. Research dealing with this distinction, however, shows that there are crucial differences between the ethical challenges of mitigation and those of adaptation (Jagers and Duus-Otterström 2008; Wallimann-Helmer 2015, 2016). We build on this distinction to discuss a further distinctive area of climate change research and policy: the adverse effects of climate change leading to climate related Loss and Damage (for short: L&D). As we argue and demonstrate throughout, in order to address the ethical aspects pertaining to L&D in international climate policy it is essential to clearly differentiate between the challenges concerning mitigation and adaptation and those ethical issues exclusively relevant for L&D.

This chapter lays out what we take to be the main ethical challenges concerning climate L&D. Building on this diagnosis, we develop criteria to categorise measures as being appropriate for dealing with L&D and analyse how the responsibilities coming with these measures must be distributed to be just. First, we show that depending on how mitigation and adaptation are distinguished from L&D, the primary focus of policy measures and their ethical implications will vary (2.2). Second, we distinguish between a *distributive* justice framework and a *compensatory* justice scheme for delivering L&D measures. We discuss some theoretical advantages of distributive justice frameworks, but do not decide the issue. One key advantage for a distributive justice approach is that it covers all L&D rather than only the fraction that is anthropogenically induced (2.3). Third, in order to understand the types of measures that these justice approaches could apply to, we analyse the appropriateness of different measures and policy approaches available (2.4). Fourth, depending on the kind of L&D and which remedies are possible, responsibilities of different actors are found to vary (2.5). In particular, we discuss the distinction between *remedial* responsibility and *outcome* responsibility. Overall, while our primary aim here is to map out the most important arguments and principles in climate ethics dealing with L&D, we also argue that the capacity to most efficiently and effectively contribute to even out undeserved harm from L&D is crucial. One of our suggestions is that it is the differentiated capacities of those able to support the ones in need of assistance that should matter the most when differentiating remedial responsibilities to tackle L&D.

2.2 Two Approaches to Distinguish Between Adaptation and L&D

Some argue that the three pillars of climate policy at the UNFCCC level are mitigation, adaptation, and L&D (see introduction by Mechler et al. 2018; chapter by Calliari et al. 2018). While mitigation can be distinguished from adaptation quite easily (mitigation involves reducing GHG emissions and enhancing sinks and reservoirs whereas adaptation involves the processes, practices, and structures to moderate potential negative impacts), L&D is more challenging to differentiate from adaptation. Nevertheless, we can adopt a standard definition which helps to separate the two: in a climate change context, L&D may refer to actions dealing with the residual, adverse impacts of climate change which remain after mitigation and adaptation measures have been adopted (Mace and Verheyen 2016). We call this the "beyond adaptation" approach. This is similar to what the parties to the UNFCCC acknowledge in Decision 2/CP.19 when they state that L&D "involves more than, that which can be reduced by adaptation" (UNFCCC 2014).

In the literature, an alternative approach to the distinction is that adaptation involves responses to keep risks within the range of tolerable risk whereas L&D involves responses to risks that cannot be kept within the range of tolerable risks and so become intolerable. This means that despite adaptation measures these risks exceed socially negotiated norms or values defining tolerability (Dow et al. 2013a, b; Wallimann-Helmer 2015; see chapter by Schinko et al. 2018). We call this the "risk tolerance" approach. Depending on which of these approaches is chosen, different kinds of responsibilities and measures will become the primary focus of policy. In the following, we first show why this is the case and then argue why in setting these priorities both approaches complement each other.

The question of which responsibilities and measures the "beyond adaptation" approach encompasses can be elaborated by considering whether the climate-related impacts *cannot* be avoided or *will not* be avoided in the future by mitigation or adaptation (Mace and Verheyen 2016). In the literature, this same distinction has also been discussed in terms of *unavoidable* and *unavoided* impacts (Roderick and Verheyen 2008). According to this approach, a key reason why some adaptation measures that could have been taken will not be taken is that actors may be subject to socio-economic constraints. Typically, L&D measures are not taken due to a lack of international financing, implementation restrictions, or political constraints leading to soft and hard limits (Chambwera and Mohammed 2014). The Intergovernmental Panel on Climate Change (IPCC) sees soft limits if adaptation constraints can in principle be overcome in contrast to hard adaptation limits, where constraints lead to limits that cannot be overcome (Klein et al. 2014).

To illustrate this, imagine a scenario in which members of the Alliance of Small Island States (AOSIS), without international financing, may be unable to afford large-scale beach renourishment needed to guard against the impacts of high sea level rise. In turn, such adaptation would be taken were there sufficient financial (or other) resources available. The impacts associated with the inability to conduct such large-scale beach renourishment can be considered losses and damages that *will not* be avoided. But it does not fall within the category of hard adaptation limits: impacts that *cannot* be avoided. Impacts that *cannot* be avoided are losses and damages that will materialize whatever measures are taken to adapt. For instance, AOSIS groups relocating due to sea-level rise that leads to loss of their homelands and damages to many of their valued assets (see chapters by Handmer and Nalau 2018; Heslin 2018). These losses and damages, which comprise market and non-market values, cannot be avoided by adapting to the new conditions regardless of the level of financial and other assistance.

This first "beyond adaptation" approach distinguishes L&D from adaptation by focusing on whether the different impacts can be avoided or will be avoided by appropriate measures without any assessment by those facing potential L&D. This is different from the "risk tolerance" approach. This second approach to distinguishing between adaptation and L&D focuses on how those facing the risks of L&D evaluate these risks. Risks of climate impacts that are judged to be intolerable are considered L&D and are contrasted with tolerable risks that are understood to be avoidable through adaptation (Dow et al. 2013a, b; Mechler and Schinko 2016; Wallimann-Helmer 2015). Such an evaluation of risks as intolerable, and thus relevant for L&D, presupposes value judgments that can only be taken by those facing those risks. Thus, according to the "risk tolerance" approach, it is crucial that those potentially facing climate impacts can assess the risks they are facing. Since different communities might assess similar risks differently, they will demand different measures that might fall within either the category of adaptation or L&D (see chapter by Schinko et al. 2018).

The "risk tolerance" approach primarily relies on the value judgments of those facing potential climate impacts. This not only shows why, according to this approach, the distinction between adaptation and L&D tends to be blurred. It also shows why it is most probably associated with a primary concern to foster appropriate structures and institutions for collective decision-making and capacity building within and among potentially impacted communities. The decisions regarding what measures should be taken, by whom and how they should be implemented are relegated to secondary importance. Thus, priorities regarding climate L&D tend to differ depending on the way of distinguishing adaptation from L&D (see Table 2.1). For the "beyond adaptation" approach, priority lies with fostering implementation of efficient and effective L&D measures, i.e. measures not being prone to soft and hard adaptation limits. For the "risk tolerance" approach, in contrast, priority lies with supporting capacity building in order for communities facing climate impacts to be better able to collectively assess the risks they face.

Thus, while the first approach to distinguishing adaptation and L&D mainly focuses on the impacts and the measures they demand to differentiate responsibilities, the second approach primarily derives the responsibilities to be differentiated from whether and to what extent capacity building is necessary. On the "risk tolerance" approach, although support for implementing L&D measures is of secondary concern, it may in fact be more effective for support to be provided if needed. As suggested by adaptation research, implementation of L&D measures is likely to be

Table 2.1 Difference in policy priority depending on how adaptation and L&D are distinguished

	Beyond adaptation	Risk tolerance
1st policy priority	Implementing the most efficient and effective measures to deal with unavoided and unavoidable L&D	Fostering collective decision-making and capacity building to assess climate risks as acceptable, tolerable or intolerable
2nd policy priority	Involving local communities to secure efficient and effective implementation of measures to be taken	Implementing those measures understood to be most efficient and effective to deal with the threats as evaluated

more effective and efficient if accompanied by capacity building and involvement of local communities in decisions and management (cf. Kaswan 2016). Responsibilities for capacity building and fostering involvement thus also follow as important concerns when distributing responsibilities from the "beyond adaptation" perspective to distinguish adaptation and L&D. Even though the two approaches to distinguish adaptation and L&D tend to set different priorities, the foci they suggest regarding the measures to be taken complement each other.

This is so, because, regardless of the approach used to distinguish L&D from adaptation, in the end L&D concerns impacts that are in fact expected to materialise. Thus, L&D measures are expected to *respond to* or *minimise the* socio-*economic or human effects* of these impacts, but these measures are not expected to *prevent* these impacts altogether. In practical terms, they are expected to e.g. enhance transformative capacities to comprehensively deal with climate-related risks beyond traditional adaptation or to enhance trust and respect between countries facing L&D and those contributing to it.[1] Consequently, preventing climate impacts from materialising is a goal only to be ascribed to mitigation and adaptation—but not to L&D measures. There are a variety of measures which can be used to address L&D demanding different kinds of responsibilities, which we classify below (Sects. 2.3 and 2.4). Before it is possible to come to this classification, however, we must first be clearer about the nature of measures that can fall within the category of L&D. In this regard and as discussed below, paragraph 52 of decision 1/CP.21 accompanying the Paris agreement becomes highly relevant.

2.3 Neither Compensation Nor Liability Under the UNFCCC

When a damage or a loss occurs, it seems natural to ask who is liable for that harm and to demand repair or compensation of the damage or loss (Shue 1999, 2017). This is why the most natural way to investigate the ethical implications of

[1] For discussion of this latter point see Cohen (2016), O'Neill (2017), Thompson and Otto (2015).

L&D would be by considering *compensatory* or *rectificatory* justice. These kinds of justice considerations define the appropriate remedy for a damage or a loss. A classical compensatory principle, for example, demands that the victim is made whole again. The victims should find themselves in the same condition as they had been before infliction; to wit, as they would have been had the harm never occurred (Wallimann-Helmer 2015; Page and Heyward 2016). According to considerations of compensatory justice it is key to identify the inflictors contributing to the occurrence of harm, because, according to the most common understanding of compensation, those causing harm are seen as liable to make those they inflicted whole again. In terms of climate L&D, such a principle requires that those facing L&D should be made whole again by those liable for these harms. This is first and foremost the major greenhouse gas emitters who contribute or have contributed the most to climate change and in so doing to climate-related L&D.

Although such considerations of compensatory justice are plausible and important, in the following we argue that a different justice framing of how to consider the ethical implications of climate L&D must be considered alternatively or in conjunction with the intuitive compensatory view. This alternative framing is based on considerations of *distributive* justice. There are at least two reasons for considering this alternative framework. First, on pragmatic grounds in light of paragraph 52 of decision 1/CP.21 such an alternative framing may make acceptance of L&D measures among potential donor countries more feasible, at least under current political conditions. This is so, because decision 1/CP.21 makes explicit that "Article 8 of the [Paris] Agreement does not involve or provide a basis for any liability or compensation" (UNFCCC 2015).[2] Second, this alternative framing allows to fully capture the exigence of those actually facing L&D since it allows not only assignment of remedial responsibilities for anthropogenic climate L&D as is the case with compensatory claims but also responsibilities for L&D caused by natural climate variability (remedial responsibilities are discussed at greater length in 2.5). Compensatory justice is only owed for anthropogenic L&D because, conceptually speaking, those inflicting harm on others are only under a duty to compensate for the harms they cause while natural climate variation is not addressed. For the remainder of this section we elaborate on the differences between compensatory and distributive justice framings (see Table 2.2).

Compensatory Justice

To better understand the differences in framing ethical implications of L&D in terms of distributive justice, it is helpful to clarify some issues in analysing these implications from the perspective of compensatory justice. We can distinguish several prominent and intuitively plausible principles to justify duties of compensation (cf. Gardiner et al. 2010). As already mentioned, in the case of L&D the most plausible responsibility bearer for compensatory duties is the emitter. The corresponding principle of justice is usually called the *Polluter Pays Principle* (PPP). A second prominent principle of justice to warrant compensatory duties identifies the benefi-

---

[2]For other readings on the legal perspective see for example Lees (2016), Mayer (2017) and the chapter by Simlinger and Mayer (2018).

Table 2.2 Overview of differences between analysing L&D within a framing of compensatory justice and distributive justice

	Compensatory justice	Distributive justice
Scope	Differentiating responsibilities in light of compensatory reasons and liability	L&D understood as undeserved harm demanding redistribution to even out this unfairness
Redistribution based on	Wrongful emitting	Undeserved harms
Temporal context	Backward-looking	Forward-looking
Implementation horizon	Long-term, once attribution challenges can be tackled	Short- to medium-term, while attribution challenges still exist and are a main barrier

ciary of emissions as responsible for providing compensation. This is the *Beneficiary Pays Principle* (BPP). In the literature, both principles most often identify individuals as responsibility bearers. But they can also refer to corporations or countries. This is why sometimes a third principle in some sense combining the first two is invoked. The Community *Pays Principle* (CoPP) ascribes the responsibility for compensation to the polluting and benefitting community. All three principles assign liability for compensation either to the polluters (PPP), the beneficiaries (BPP) or communities (CoPP).[3] They hold that by emitting, these differing agents acquire responsibility to make whole again those harmed by the consequences of their emissions. Thus, decision 1/CP.21 seems to suggest, these agents become liable to compensate for the L&D they are contributing to causing.

It is important to note that on ethical grounds compensatory duties for climate L&D are more difficult to justify than it at first appears. There are at least three basic problems for justifying compensation for L&D (Meyer and Roser 2010; Meyer 2013; Kolstad et al. 2015): a. Potential duty bearers might not have *wrongfully emitted* by exceeding their fair shares of emissions and thus have not acquired any legitimate compensatory duties; b. Potential duty bearers might have been *(blamelessly) ignorant* about the harmfulness of their emissions and can therefore not be said to be (fully) responsible to compensate; and c. Potential recipients might be said not to be *wrongfully harmed* since they are only wrongfully harmed if they are worse off due to (wrongful) emissions than they would otherwise be or if they fall below a specified threshold of harm due to (wrongful) emissions (or both).[4]

---

[3]Although we discuss these three principles as principles identifying the bearers of compensatory duties, these principles, and especially the beneficiary pays principle have also be shown to be important in identifying the bearers of duties of distributive justice (see Meyer and Sanklecha 2017).

[4]By such a threshold of harm, we mean that there is some sufficient (not necessarily minimal) level of well-being and any individual who falls below that is thereby harmed, regardless of the counterfactual arrangements (cf. Meyer 2003). In other words, individuals could be harmed by being below the threshold even if they had never had their interests thwarted by any other particular individual.

The challenges associated with identifying the legitimate agents to pay compensation and the legitimate claimants of compensation narrow down the number of potential recipients of compensatory payments. This number decreases even more when considering the conceptual challenge that strictly speaking compensation can only be demanded for anthropogenically induced L&D but not for natural climate variability (Huggel et al. 2016; Wallimann-Helmer 2015). Natural disasters without any human cause are tragic and individuals being threatened need to be assisted. However, this requirement of assistance can only be justified on humanitarian grounds and for reasons of distributive justice. They cannot be addressed by appeal to compensatory justice. This is why, in practice, compensatory claims for some specific (risk of) L&D demand the detection of anthropogenic cascades demonstrating why this L&D can be attributed to anthropogenic climate change (Huggel et al. 2013). Hence, the worry for the advocate of compensatory justice is that some victims of climate L&D might not be harmed in a normatively relevant sense, whereby considerations of compensation become unsuitable. Elaborating on these difficulties by considering individuals as duty bearers and claimants, it becomes possible that many emitters and legitimate claimants are not identified either as duty bearers or victims. Emitters only emitting within the limits of their fair shares cannot be identified as liable for compensation. Similarly, those individuals not wrongfully harmed, are not entitled to any compensatory payments. These reasons can be taken to be decisive against addressing L&D in terms of compensatory justice. However, considering the CoPP both these challenges must be qualified.

According to the assessments of the IPCC and the agreements under the UNFCCC countries, to wit communities, can definitively be identified as wrongful emitters not being legitimately excused by ignorance (Meyer and Sanklecha 2017). At least some agents of industrialised country parties (its citizens, companies or the countries as a whole) definitively exceed their fair shares of emissions (Shue 2017). Furthermore, with the publication of the first IPCC report it becomes difficult to argue for excusable ignorance from 1990 onwards. This suggests ways of how some of the challenges above can be met. However, even though industrialised countries and at least some of their companies can potentially be identified as duty bearers, the CoPP still only succeeds in justifying *some* compensation for L&D. As shown above, it can only justify them for *some* L&D from climate change but not for all since it only warrants payments for *anthropogenic* climate L&D but not for L&D caused by *natural* climate variability. To be clear, this is not necessarily a bad thing. Many developing countries facing climate L&D would already be much helped if they received some in contrast to no assistance. In addition, a compensatory approach can be said to be simple and more strongly in line with international law whereas distributive approaches are relatively untested in international fora. For instance, considering environmental issues in terms of reparations for injury has been dominant in legal history (the influential *Trail Smelter* case is based on "no harm" considerations, see Simlinger and Mayer 2018 for complexities in applying international environmental law to this issue).

Despite these pragmatic advantages, however, from an ethical point of view it seems highly problematic to only support those facing L&D in coping with part of the harm they face. This is so for three reasons. First, the fact that the main L&D occurs in regions which historically have contributed far less to anthropogenic climate change seems to unfairly burden those least responsible for these adverse effects. Second, those regions and countries most burdened with L&D are often (economically) less well equipped to manage climate impacts once they materialise. Third and most importantly, since many adverse effects of climate change are not immediate but linked to slow onset events, it seems appropriate to say that in many regions of the world we find a situation of more or less acute emergency due to climate change already.[5] In our view, it seems clear that in a case of emergency, *someone* is under duty to assist irrespective of whether that agent has caused the threat ("remedial responsibility"). Such assistance usually is due up to the point where those under threat are safe again. Thus, it seems inappropriate to only help countries in need of assistance with L&D up to the point it can be attributed to anthropogenic climate change and then leave them on their own. That would be like helping someone drowning to as far to the shore as one has thrown him in, but then swim away. Rescuing someone drowning means to try one's best to bring him safely to the shore irrespective of how much one contributed to the threat. Because of this, we believe that even in cases in which no one can be ascribed compensatory responsibility, all of those afflicted by climate L&D are entitled to assistance if they do not have the capacity to make themselves whole again. This especially applies to those who, due to climate L&D, fall below a specified threshold of harm.

Distributive Justice

Especially to meet this last challenge, we suggest to also considering an alternative framing of the ethical implications of L&D, namely the framing of distributive justice. According to this alternative framing, rather than regarding L&D as reasons for compensation only, L&D also provides reasons for redistribution due to *undeserved harms*. That is, *wrongful emitting* would be relinquished as a relevant criterion to identify the duty bearers for payments in case of L&D. Instead, the focus would be on the *wrongfulness of harms* as defined from the perspective of distributive justice. In other words, the alternative framing to be considered demands redistribution in case of unfair disadvantage but not compensation due to wrongful emitting.

One way to distinguish between redistribution and compensation starts with the premise that there is some *baseline distribution* of goods or bads that is just. This baseline distribution is on the one hand determined by certain criteria or principles of justice (such as the priority view, the strict egalitarian view or any other) and on the other hand by legitimate changes to the distribution (as determined by criteria or principles of justice) which someone experiences as a result of her own *responsible (and non-wrongful) choices*. Deviations from this baseline then call for two different kinds of reactions. In case the reaction the deviation calls for is *based on the wrongfulness* of what occurred, we are operating in the realm of *compensatory justice*. In case the reaction the deviation calls for is based on the idea of *evening out undeserved* benefits or harms (which are due to bad luck, for example, or harmful

[5] Notably we here understand climate change to encompass both anthropogenic climate change and natural climate variability.

but non-wrongful actions), we are operating in the realm of *distributive justice* since these undeserved benefits or harms demand redistribution (Meyer 2004; Meyer and Roser 2010). On the distributional justice approach in the case of L&D, the situation of communities, who just happen to have "bad luck" to be living in regions more heavily exposed to climate change, calls for an evening out of these undeserved harms.

Hence, if necessary to avoid political deadlock in light of decision 1/CP.21 and to secure assistance not only for the part of L&D that is anthropogenic, but for all L&D threatening countries and communities, one may speak in terms of *undeserved harms* rather than focusing on impacts brought about by wrongful emitters demanding compensation from those liable. Any responsibilities concerning L&D would then be understood as responsibilities that fall into the category of redistribution. In this manner, L&D-related responsibilities would be regarded as grounded in the objective of levelling undeserved harms. So, on the one hand, what could be looked for are ways of differentiating responsibilities without relying on the wrongfulness of emissions, liability and compensation. However, on the other hand, as attribution research matures and international climate policy develops, it may become more feasible to rely on causal explanations to help determine the differentiation of responsibilities in line with a compensatory approach (Boran and Heath 2016; Thompson and Otto 2015; see chapter by James et al. 2018), although doing so may be ambitious at this point (Huggel et al. 2013; James et al. 2014; Huggel et al. 2016).[6]

2.4 Categorising L&D Measures to Differentiate Responsibilities

The previous section leads to an important ethical consideration. Irrespective of the justice framework applied, the fact that developing countries carry such a large share of L&D cries out for *some* kind of response. Such a response makes it necessary to clarify two issues. On the one hand, it is necessary to be clear about what kinds of L&D can become relevant since these determine what approaches and policy measures are most appropriate for either compensation or redistribution. On the other hand, it is necessary to discuss how responsibilities to provide assistance should be differentiated. Before analysing the differentiation of responsibilities in the next section, here we discuss the first of these two issues. We argue that it makes a significant difference which kinds of climate L&D are at stake since different kinds of L&D demand different measures requiring varying forms of competence and

[6]To be sure, one implication of the distributive justice framing is that it brings legitimate claims for assistance in case of climate L&D on a par with any other claims for assistance in case of undeserved harm or even more generally any undeserved socio-economic disadvantage. This can be considered a strength of this alternative framing, because it shows that climate L&D cannot be appropriately dealt with in isolation (Caney 2012; Wallimann-Helmer 2015). However, it also points to the weakness of this framing, namely that it expands concerns about L&D beyond what is currently dealt with under the umbrella of the UNFCCC.

Table 2.3 Indicative list of measures for different categories of losses and damages. Note that listed measures are not exhaustive and that these measures could apply under both compensatory or distributive justice framings

	Replaceable L&D (economic and some non-economic L&D)	Non-replaceable L&D (non-economic L&D)
Sudden-onset extremes (insurable L&D)	Measures (A) • Risk transfer - Insurance (e.g. with subsidised premiums) - Micro insurance - Insurance/Risk pools - Catastrophe bonds • National and international disaster funds • Risk reduction - Early warning systems - Preventive building measures - Planned relocation • Technology transfer	Measures (B) • Recognition of loss (accompanied by financial payments or not) • Active remembrance (e.g. through museum exhibitions, school curricula) • Counselling • Official apologies
Slow-onset processes (non-insurable L&D)	Measures (C) • Risk reduction - Preventive building measures - Physical risk reduction measures (sea walls) - Planned relocation • Technology transfer • Risk transfer via catastrophe bonds • Redress • Rehabilitation	Measures (D) • Alternative livelihoods provision • Recognition of loss (accompanied by financial payments or not) • Active remembrance (e.g. through museum exhibitions, school curricula) • Counselling • Official apologies

involvement of those responsible to contribute to the measures to be taken (for an overview of categories and measures see Table 2.3).[7]

L&D needs to be rectified in order to ensure justice. Within the distributive justice framework, this means redistribution aiming at a baseline distribution where no undeserved harm had ever occurred. In case of climate impacts, this means aiming at overcoming undeserved burdens on some regions, communities, and individuals due to climate variability and extremes. In contrast to compensatory claims for redistribution to even out undeserved harms it is only necessary that the harm in fact can be neutralised by human action. This makes the distributive framing more comprehensive. It not only captures L&D caused by anthropogenic climate change

[7]By thus arguing we implicitly assume the ability-to-pay principle as the appropriate principle for differentiating responsibilities. In the next section we explain more thoroughly how we think this principle must be understood in case of L&D.

but also climate impacts brought about by natural climate variability and extremes. However, a large amount of the responsibilities involved by these considerations does not concern natural climate variability but anthropogenic climate change. Most responsibilities captured in a distributive framework would also directly apply in a compensatory framework as well.

The categorisation of appropriate measures to respond to different kinds of L&D significantly depends on whether the distinction between adaptation and L&D is drawn using a "beyond adaptation" or a "risk tolerance" approach. While according to the "risk tolerance" approach, the appropriateness of measures does depend on how those potentially affected assess different kinds of risk for L&D, the "beyond adaptation" approach can do so without involving them. Focusing on the "beyond adaptation" approach for now, the relevant climate impacts concern L&D that *cannot* and also in some cases *will not* be avoided. L&D that cannot be avoided must be considered undeserved harm to the extent that those facing climate impacts did not contribute to their occurrence. L&D that will not be avoided is undeserved harm to the degree that it can be traced back to adaptation constraints that are not self-inflicted. In both cases, redistributive responses will have to differ depending on whether they are designed to deal with replaceable or non-replaceable values, values which can be non-economic/non market-based or economic/market-based L&D.

In the case of economic/market-based L&D, measures will have to either manage/transfer financial risks or to provide adequate monetary/financial redress for L&D. However, in the non-economic case, novel approaches for ends-displacing have to be identified (Wallimann-Helmer 2015). Many such assets (encompassing material goods and non-material services) fall into the category of non-economic values, which have entered the L&D discourse as the concept of *non-economic loss and damage* or, after COP21 in Paris, *non-economic losses* (NELD; see also chapter by Serdeczny 2018). Commonly cited examples of NELD include loss of life, human health, cultural heritage, ecosystem services and indigenous knowledge (e.g. Fankhauser et al. 2014; Morrissey and Oliver-Smith 2013). NELD can occur as direct and indirect consequences of climate change, including negative side effects of adaptation (Serdeczny et al. 2016). They share the criterion that they are not commonly traded in the market.[8]

Non-economic L&D can be replaceable or non-replaceable. Non-replaceable, non-economic L&D or simply "losses" might be perceived as losses of irreplaceable ends by those affected. In other words, the assets lost in case of this kind of L&D might be perceived as ends in themselves. Following Goodin (1983), characteristics for regarding assets as irreplaceable are typically tied to (1) personal integrity, both bodily and mentally; (2) history; and (3) variety. Many assets typically listed as NELD correspond to these characteristics. Loss of cultural identity, sense of place or indigenous knowledge, for example, are inextricably tied to a community´s integrity (Bell 2004; Heyward 2014; Zellentin 2010, 2015). A fishing community having lost its traditional fishing grounds will never be the same again because it lacks a central

[8]For this reason, "non-market losses" might be a more adequate description of such losses, but the term was not adopted in the policy process.

part of its own integrity. Loss of cultural heritage relates to historical characteristics, where no replica of the lost object will be regarded as equivalent to the original. Finally, biodiversity, another often quoted NELD distinct from ecosystem services, is valued as an asset of variety.

Offsetting losses of irreplaceable ends necessarily relies on providing alternative ends that are perceived by those affected as being able to provide a similar level of wellbeing compared to before the loss. The fishermen's community might receive funding enabling them to become farmers with comparable income levels, food security and social status as before. However, according to Goodin (1989), a shift in preferences will have been forced upon them, infringing upon their integrity and personal autonomy and ultimately leaving them in a state of undeserved harm. What follows is that actions that inflict the loss of irreplaceable assets on others can never be fully addressed by any amount of remedy. This is especially important considering financial payments. Whatever amount of money is paid to a harmed community, if the ends are irreplaceable, by definition such payments cannot make the community whole again. But financial payments and other actions recognising the fact of undeserved L&D are certainly important steps for regaining a just baseline distribution (cf. Thompson and Otto 2015; Huggel et al. 2016).

Non-economic but replaceable values can either fulfil different ends or constitute ends in themselves, with the distinction being culturally- or even individually-contingent. Ecosystem services, for example, are often valued as a means because they provide important resources for human health and nourishment. The value of cultural heritage in turn might be understood by some as a means to the end of community identity or social stability or by others as an end in itself. In case the losses are means towards some end, an appropriate response would ideally replace those lost means, i.e. to provide those affected with new means to achieve the same ends (cf. Goodin 1989). Following such an understanding, loss of ecosystem services (e.g. health and nourishment) could sensibly be responded to by providing medication to maintain human health and supporting agricultural production to maintain previous (if adequate) levels of nourishment. In other words, in order to even out undeserved harms due to climate change, non-economic values which fulfil ends require measures for their replacement by other non-economic values or by financial payments. In contrast to irreplaceable assets, if non-economic values are perceived as replaceable, the undeserved harm can be fully addressed and the just baseline can be maintained despite infliction of harm. This is more clearly the case when economic assets are at issue. In many cases, economic goods can be replaced by simply reimbursing their economic costs or by providing a substitute of the same (market) value.

It is far from clear, however, what mechanisms will lead to progress in making the most vulnerable more resilient to climate change. In line with policy proposals and current literature on mechanisms to tackle L&D (e.g. AOSIS 2008; Burkett 2014; Mace and Verheyen 2016; Mechler and Schinko 2016), we identify L&D measures comprising the following three components (see chapter by Schinko et al. 2018): (1) *Comprehensive risk management* to support and promote risk management tools to reduce the risk of future losses and damages in addition to mitigation and adaptation, (2) *risk financing* comprising *risk-transfer, sharing and pooling* to support particularly vulnerable countries to manage their increasing financial risks due to increasingly frequent and severe extreme weather events, and (3) *curative measures* such as *redress and rehabilitation* mechanisms to tackle irreversible impacts due to progressive slow-onset processes (e.g. sea level rise, ocean acidification, increasing land and sea surface temperatures) and sudden-onset extreme events that cannot or will not be avoided.

Factoring in the distinction between economic and non-economic L&D, it seems clear that risk management and risk-financing mechanisms—the intuitively most plausible tools to deal with L&D—will not be sufficient in all cases (Surminski et al. 2016). This is why, in addition to comprehensive risk management, including risk-financing tools such as insurance, we may require curative action for redress and rehabilitation (Mechler and Schinko 2016). Such action may address a further important pillar of L&D measures, namely climate-related impacts that are deemed uninsurable. This is either because insurance is not the right instrument for tackling certain climate-related impacts, particularly those linked to slow-onset processes, such as loss of territory with attendant human displacement (Burkett 2014), or because commercial insurance is just not economically feasible.

Furthermore, it not only makes a difference whether risks of climate impacts are insurable or not. It also makes a difference whether L&D measures are designed to tackle sudden-onset extreme events or slow-onset processes. While risk financing instruments such as insurance are a theoretically feasible strategy to tackle extreme event risks, insurance is not applicable to deal with potential L&D caused by slow-onset processes. Indeed, insurance mechanisms also have been found to encounter limitations even in the case of sudden-onset risks (Mechler et al. 2014; chapters on insurance in this book by Schäfer et al. 2018 and Linnerooth-Bayer et al. 2018). Insurance may only be available for certain risks within a certain probability range or for what would be considered "acceptable" by those underwriting to the "risks based" distinction between adaptation and L&D and, hence, may not apply to L&D. Risk transfer and sharing schemes do not directly reduce the probability of occurrence or the severity of negative impacts from climate risks, although they can provide incentives to that end (Linnerooth-Bayer and Mechler 2009). Moreover, inappropriately constructed insurance schemes can have unwanted consequences and may neither benefit the poor nor foster climate resilience (Vivid Economics 2015).

What seems to be needed to appropriately address L&D is something like the "Multi-Window Mechanism to address loss and damage" suggested by AOSIS (AOSIS 2008) or what Roderick and Verheyen (2008) as well as Burkett (2014) call a "Compensation Protocol" and a "Small Island Compensation and Rehabilitation Commission to deal with impacts of slow-onset processes" (also cf. Boran and Heath 2016).[9] However, in our suggested framing the focus of such institutions would not only be on compensation and identifying the wrong-doers but rather on distributive justice. This would amount to redistributive mechanisms aiming at evening out

[9]The mechanism suggested by AOSIS consists of three inter-dependent components: (1) an insurance component, (2) a rehabilitation/compensatory component, and (3) a risk management component, which taken together aim at enhancing overall adaptive capacities in SIDS.

undeserved L&D due to climate variability and extremes. What would be needed is a coordinated redistributive scheme, which could be operationalised under the UNFCCC as the body with the largest expertise and a clear focus on climate change and relevant approaches to cope with it.

Notably, such a scheme neutralising undeserved L&D incorporating and combining all of the components of L&D measures mentioned in this section will require substantial amounts of funding. Even though L&D is addressed in its own dedicated Article 8 of the Paris Agreement, no new funding stream for addressing L&D has been created. Nevertheless, as Mace and Verheyen (2016) point out, Article 8.3's reference to 'action and support', which should come through the WIM and the parties' action, demands financial mechanisms. With the exception of early voluntary commitments by developed countries to support the insurance component of L&D measures, it remains an open question what kind of existing funding schemes could be accessed or which additional funding windows should be established to address further components of L&D measures. Based on the two framings of compensatory and distributive justice, in the next section we set out to answer the question of who bears what responsibility for providing adequate levels of assistance in financial and non-financial terms to establish a comprehensive portfolio of L&D measures.

2.5 Differentiating Responsibilities for L&D Measures

Responsibilities will vary depending on whether we are adopting a compensatory or a distributive approach. Regarding the former approach, it is necessary to determine who or which groups have contributed to the harm. This is challenging from the point of view of attribution science as well as the applicability of national and international law (cf. chapter on attribution by James et al. 2018 and chapter on legal issues by Simlinger and Mayer 2018). Regarding the latter approach, redistribution to secure differentiated support for those facing L&D for undeserved harms is required. This is challenging from the point of view of being considerably more ambitious and counter to the agreements contained under the umbrella of the UNFCCC. However, since we are addressing the demands of justice here, it may be that justice requires radical restructuring. In this section we argue that in order to be effective and efficient a scheme to tackle L&D must take into account differences in capacity to provide specific support but also communal ties. Under a distributive framing, this leads to an extended ability to pay principle, incorporating considerations concerning how to most efficiently and effectively remedy undeserved harm due to L&D. According to this scheme, depending on the kinds of L&D at issue, different countries and regions have different duties in light of their abilities to pay. If adopting a compensatory approach, ability to pay might be a mitigating factor, but the compensation would primarily stem from the responsibility a group had for the occurrence of the harms in question.

To clarify the distinction between responsibility for the occurrence of undeserved harm and responsibility for remedy of harm we suggest to consider the distinction between outcome responsibility and remedial responsibility: *outcome responsibility* denotes responsibility for bringing about a certain state of affairs and *remedial responsibility* denotes responsibility to even out harm (Hart and Honoré 2002; Honoré 2010; Miller 2007). Whilst the first kind of responsibility is backward-looking the second looks forward. In principle, both these conceptions of responsibility are independent. Irrespective of whether or not someone brought about a certain harm, she can be responsible to (help) remedy that harm. We believe that seeing somebody drowning puts us under duty to help, irrespective of whether we are responsible for that person drowning. By contrast, being outcome responsible for a certain harm does not always imply responsibility to (help) remedy this harm. Somebody who trips and falls thereby pushing another person in front of him might be responsible in terms of outcome but not necessarily in terms of remedy. If the one pushing could not avoid tripping and tripping is not due to a fault of her own then this is bad luck for both persons involved but no one is usually seen under duty for remedy.

In order to legitimately claim a connection between outcome responsibility and remedial responsibility, some kind of normatively relevant tie between the two must be established. Miller (2007) suggests moral failure, responsibility for the outcome and mere causal contribution as legitimate reasons for assigning remedial responsibilities based on outcome responsibility. If this kind of connection is or can be established, then we are in the realm of compensatory justice, because in this case it is the assignment of responsibility for a certain state of affairs that justifies remedial responsibility. Generally speaking, the most obvious way to differentiate responsibilities in case of harm like climate L&D would be to assign responsibilities for remedy in proportion to the contribution to the harm, like levels of greenhouse gas emissions. In case of L&D, the reasons linking outcome responsibility to remedial responsibility would amount to wrongful emitting, non-wrongful but significant contribution to the harm, or causal contribution. Whichever of these three reasons is operative in justifying a connection between outcome responsibility and remedial responsibility, it operates within the framing of compensatory justice. Those bringing about a harm are assigned responsibilities to make whole again those whom were impacted by their behaviour.

The potential reasons for linking outcome responsibility with remedial responsibility mentioned above are backward-looking, as is compensatory justice. When a harm has materialised, considerations of compensatory justice aim at identifying those responsible for the harm in order to assign remedial responsibilities. However, in light of our discussion such a (purely) backward-looking assignment of remedial responsibilities may not be fully appropriate for two reasons. First, in light of paragraph 52 of decision 1/CP.21 it may become politically unfeasible since it would amount to compensation and liability. This means that a "responsibility vacuum" might emerge when, for political reasons, duty-bearers do not step up to their remedial responsibilities. Furthermore, only a portion of experienced L&D would be covered were remedial responsibility to be based on outcome responsibility only. As shown before, natural climate variability as well as socio-economic factors on the ground contribute to much of the L&D as well.

Relying on Miller (2007) once again, there are at least three additional reasons allowing the differentiated assignment of remedial responsibilities without relying on backward looking considerations of outcome responsibility. That is, reasons applicable within a distributive justice framing. First, and in modification of the already mentioned BPP, those currently benefitting the most from emissions contributing to climate change are most often those also financially and technologically best able to foster L&D measures. Second, those with the best know-how to support one or several of the three components (comprehensive risk management, risk financing and curative measures) of a comprehensive scheme of L&D measures mentioned before can most efficiently and effectively provide assistance. Third, indigenous and other cultural knowledge shared by communities affected not only leads to special duties among them but also might help to provide more appropriate and effective support in practice. In the case of many communities and countries, the assignment of remedial responsibilities according to the first two reasons will most probably overlap because both determine the developed country parties to the UNFCCC to be under remedial duty. The third reason, by contrast, probably identifies developing country parties; e.g. members of AOSIS, to be under specified remedial duties.

Following on from Sect. 2.3 and independent of the reasons employed to assign remedial responsibilities, support must be differentiated at least along the following two lines: (a) whether L&D is replaceable or not, and (b) whether L&D measures shall tackle slow-onset processes or sudden-onset extreme events (see Table 2.3). The discussion in the previous section reveals that the first type of differentiation roughly corresponds but is not identical with the distinction between economic and non-economic L&D. The second type of differentiation largely correlates with whether L&D is insurable or not. These differentiations/categories need to be taken into account because a comprehensive scheme to appropriately tackle climate L&D must ultimately differentiate responsibilities in an efficient and effective way in order to be considered just. Notably, in terms of support for L&D, pledging finance is likely not enough and probably not the most efficient and effective form of support for communities and countries in need of assistance. What is further needed is assistance in capacity building and technology transfer in order for these communities to be able to take action allowing them efficiently and effectively to mediate the social and economic costs of climate L&D.

Transfer of technology without know-how available tends to be less effective. In order to be effective, we claim that a fair differentiation of responsibilities must not only befall those able to foster L&D measures but also those potentially harmed. As already mentioned, the effectiveness of measures is substantially increased if those profiting from them are also involved in their implementation and maintenance. Similarly, shared indigenous or cultural knowledge especially in countries and regions facing similar risks of L&D can become relevant as well. We believe that such ties as well as geographic proximity can significantly increase the efficiency and effectiveness of implementation and maintenance of measures (Wallimann-Helmer 2016). Furthermore, without transfer of know-how, pledging finance might contribute to unfairness when it comes to applying for financial support to implement L&D measures. For instance, there is far less detected and attributed climate events in countries probably facing the most severe climate impacts (Huggel et al. 2016). This is not only the case because in these regions of the world measurement stations are lacking but also because there is missing capacity to establish and analyse the necessary data for effective risk management.

According to these considerations for assigning remedial responsibilities in relation to the four categories of L&D measures, we believe that replaceable L&D can most probably be moderated by appropriate schemes of risk management and detection in combination with mechanisms of risk financing like insurance (see Table 2.4). This is especially the case if that L&D is of an economic nature and occurs due to expected sudden-onset extreme events. Countries under the greatest duties in this case are those able to financially contribute to these schemes and/or possessing the know-how to assist in implementing them. However, responsibilities might befall other countries when slow-onset processes are at issue since these processes might contribute to non-replaceable and non-insurable L&D. Although in such cases financial payments might have great importance in the sense of providing recognition for undeserved harms, transfer of know-how between communities with similar cultural experiences and under similar threats of L&D seems to be central to efficiently and effectively helping even out the undeserved harms due to climate change. In case of non-replaceable L&D, ends-displacing becomes necessary, a competence most probably possessed by those communities already having gone through similar processes of transformation.

Deciding whether or not non-economic L&D can be deemed replaceable is an issue that is not easily determined without involving those facing these impacts (Wallimann-Helmer 2015). This is so, because by definition non-economic L&D is not traded in the market and cannot be weight up with any established market price. This also makes it difficult to decide whether or not non-economic but replaceable L&D can be insured since for insurance assessment of the financial value in economic terms becomes key. And even if non-economic L&D can be deemed insurable, its value to be insured cannot objectively be decided without involving those whose assets are potentially damaged or lost due to sudden-onset extreme events or slow-onset processes. For these reasons, for differentiating remedial responsibilities we believe it to be crucial to also consider the differentiated competences to foster appropriate decision-structures and capacity building within potentially threatened communities. Indeed, this may apply either relying on outcome responsibilities or reasons independent of responsibilities for the occurrence of L&D.

Once appropriate decision-making structures and capacity are established within communities and countries potentially threatened by climate L&D and in need of assistance, they acquire remedial responsibilities to other threatened countries as well (Wallimann-Helmer 2016). Appropriate finance and technology provided, developing countries not only acquire responsibilities for implementing and maintaining L&D measures in their own regions. Since they also gain specific know-how on how to most efficiently and effectively respond to the specific L&D they face, they also become more responsible to assist those facing the same or similar L&D. Consequently, the more developed the decision-structures and capacities in communities initially in need of assistance become, the more they acquire responsibilities to assist

Table 2.4 Categorisation of the differentiated remedial responsibilities of countries to foster L&D measures without exclusively relying on outcome responsibility

	Replaceable L&D (economic and some non-economic L&D)	Non-replaceable L&D (non-economic L&D)
Sudden-onset extremes (insurable L&D)	For measures (A) mainly countries are remedially responsible that are best able to: • financially support risk transfer (e.g. insurance or catastrophe bonds) schemes • financially support risk reduction (e.g. preventive building measures) and relocation schemes and/or • provide technology and know-how in setting up and maintaining such schemes	For measures (B) mainly countries are remedially responsible that are best able to: • financially support securing recognition, remembrance of loss and counselling and/or • provide experience and know-how how to overcome loss
Slow-onset processes (non-insurable L&D)	For measures (C) mainly countries are remedially responsible that are best able to: • financially support risk reduction and relocation schemes • financially support catastrophe bonds schemes for countries at risk and/or • provide technology and know-how in setting up and maintaining such schemes	For measures (D) mainly countries are remedially responsible that are best able to: • financially support securing recognition, remembrance of loss and counselling and/or • provide experience and know-how how to achieve alternative livelihoods

other communities and countries still in need of assistance. To increase efficiency and effectiveness, it seems plausible that those countries are also under a duty to assist those in need of assistance who are facing similar (risks of) L&D as they were or are threatened with themselves.

2.6 Conclusions

In this chapter we aimed at mapping out the most important ethical considerations relevant in case of climate L&D. Especially in light of the Paris Agreement and the multi-causality of factors beyond anthropogenic climate change contributing to L&D, we elaborated on the ethical implications of L&D—in the short to medium term—within a distributive framework. In addition to differentiating responsibilities in light of compensatory considerations and liability, we argued that L&D could also be understood as undeserved harms demanding redistribution to even out unfairness. As we have shown, evening out such unfairness demands being able to specify the measures exclusively relevant for L&D either defined as being beyond adaptation and/or as intolerable levels of risks, where coping capacities of communities are breached. However, regardless of the appropriate framing, it becomes essential to foster appropriate decision-making structures and capacity building for those facing the risks of L&D. These capacities significantly contribute to the efficiency and effectiveness of L&D measures, measures which comprise a complex net of approaches including comprehensive risk management, risk finance schemes and curative mechanisms.

The advantage of the alternative framing of distributive justice is to help overcome political deadlock and potential conceptual confusion. Notably, we do not claim compensatory justice to be irrelevant for differentiating responsibilities for L&D. Much of our deliberations were motivated by paragraph 52 of decision 1/CP.21 which posits that Article 8 of the Paris Agreement does not provide any basis for compensation or liability. From this we read that implementing support for L&D based on compensatory justice may be currently politically unfeasible. However, political infeasibility is not to be mistaken with moral appropriateness. We have argued that the conditions for compensatory justice to apply, i.e. no excusable ignorance and exceeding fair shares of emissions, potentially limit the application of compensatory claims at the individual level. Here, the difficulty in attributing L&D to anthropogenic climate change poses a further practical challenge.

However, we also argued that these considerations must be qualified at the community level of whole countries: No country can be excused anymore for ignorance after publication of the IPCC reports, and the emissions of a large number of countries have been deemed to exceed fair shares on multiple accounts. According to these considerations, compensatory justice thus clearly becomes relevant and should drive action of countries under the UNFCCC from a moral point of view. Notably, it should drive increased mitigation ambition as it is clear that some of the losses due to climate change are irreplaceable and those affected cannot be made whole again. But as long as compensation for L&D creates political deadlock and in order to secure that those under threat get full and not only partial assistance, a framework based on distributive justice to even out undeserved harm should be considered relevant in implementing practical approaches to L&D and identifying responsibilities for doing so as well.

Acknowledgements Ivo Wallimann-Helmer would like to acknowledge generous support from the Swiss National Science foundation, which made possible to extensively work on this chapter during a very fruitful research visit at the School of Politics and International Relations of the University College Dublin. He also wants to thank Alexa Zellentin for her kind invitation. Kian Mintz-Woo would like to acknowledge support from the Austrian Science Fund (FWF) under research grant W 1256-G15 (Doctoral Program on Climate Change—Uncertainties, Thresholds and Coping Strategies). We are grateful for very helpful comments on an earlier drafts of this paper by Benoit Mayer, Laura García-Portela, Sadhbh O Neill, and the editors of this volume.

References

AOSIS (2008) Submission of alliance of Small Island States. In: Ideas and proposals on the elements contained in paragraph 1 of the Bali Action Plan, Submissions from Parties, Addendum, Part I (UN Doc. FCCC/AWGLCA/2008/Misc.5/Add.2 (Part I), pp 9–32

Bell DR (2004) Environmental refugees: what rights? which duties? Res Publica 10:135–152

Boran I, Heath J (2016) Attributing weather extremes to climate change and the future of adaptation policy. Ethics Policy Environ 19(3):239–255

Burkett M (2014) Loss and damage. Clim Law 4(1–2):119–130

Calliari E, Surminski S, Mysiak J (2018) The politics of (and behind) the UNFCCC's loss and damage mechanism. In: Mechler R, Bouwer L, Schinko T, Surminski S, Linnerooth-Bayer J (eds) Loss and damage from climate change. Concepts, methods and policy options. Springer, Cham, pp 155–178

Caney S (2012) Just emissions. Philos Public Aff 40(4):255–300

Chambwera M, Mohammed K (2014) 7. Economic analysis of a community-based adaptation project in Sudan. In: Ensor J, Berger R, Huq S (eds) Community-based adaptation to climate change. Practical Action Publishing, Rugby: Warwickshire, United Kingdom, pp 111–128

Cohen AI (2016) Corrective vs. distributive justice: the case of apologies. Ethic Theor Moral Practice 19(3):663–677

Dow K, Berkhout F, Preston BL, Klein RJ (2013a) Limits to adaptation. Nat Clim Change 3(4):305–307

Dow K, Berkhout F, Preston BL (2013b) Limits to adaptation to climate change: a risk approach. Current Opin Environ Sustain 5(3–4):384–391

Fankhauser S, Dietz S, Gradwell P (2014) Non-economic losses in the context of the UNFCCC work programme on loss and damage (policy paper). London School of Economics – Centre for Climate Change Economics and Policy, Grantham Research Institute on Climate Change and the Environment

Gardiner SM, Caney S, Jamieson D, Shue H (eds) (2010) Climate ethics: essential readings. Oxford University Press, Oxford, New York

Goodin RD (1983) The ethics of destroying irreplaceable assets. Int J Environ Stud 21(1):55–66

Goodin RE (1989) Theories of compensation. Oxford J Legal Stud 9(1):56–75

Handmer J, Nalau J (2018) Understanding loss and damage in Pacific Small Island developing states. In: Mechler R, Bouwer L, Schinko T, Surminski S, Linnerooth-Bayer J (eds) Loss and damage from climate change. Concepts, methods and policy options. Springer, Cham, pp 365–381

Hart HLA, Honoré T (2002) Causation in the law (2nd edn) reprinted by Clarendon Press, Oxford

Heslin A (2018) Climate migration and cultural preservation: the case of the marshallese diaspora. In: Mechler R, Bouwer L, Schinko T, Surminski S, Linnerooth-Bayer J (eds) Loss and damage from climate change. Concepts, methods and policy options. Springer, Cham, pp 383–391

Heyward C (2014) Climate change as cultural injustice. In: Brooks T (ed) New waves in global justice. New waves in global justice. Palgrave Macmillan: Basingstoke, Hampshire, UK, pp 149–169

Honoré A (2010) Causation in the law. In: Zalta EN (ed) Stanford encyclopedia of philosophy. Stanford University (online), Stanford, pp 1–22

Huggel C, Stone D, Auffhammer M, Hansen G (2013) Loss and damage attribution. Nat Clim Change 5:694–696

Huggel C, Wallimann-Helmer I, Stone DA, Cramer W (2016) Reconciling justice and attribution research to advance climate policy. Nat Clim Change 6(10):901–908

Jagers SC, Duus-Otterström G (2008) Dual climate change responsibility: on moral divergences between mitigation and adaptation. Environ Politics 17(4):576–591

James R, Otto F, Parker H, Boyd E, Cornforth R, Mitchell D, Allen M (2014) Characterizing loss and damage from climate change. Nat Clim Change 4(11):938–939

James RA, Jones RG, Boyd E, Young HR, Otto FEL, Huggel C, Fuglestvedt JS (2018) Attribution: how is it relevant for loss and damage policy and practice? In: Mechler R, Bouwer L, Schinko T,

Surminski S, Linnerooth-Bayer J (eds) Loss and damage from climate change. Concepts, methods and policy options. Springer, Cham, pp 113–154

Kaswan A (2016) Climate change adaptation and theories of justice. Archiv für Rechts- und Sozialphilosophie 149 (Beihefte):97–118

Klein R, Midgley GF, Preston BL, Alam M, Berkhout F, Dow K, Shaw MR (2014) Adaptation opportunities, constraints, and limits. In: Climate change 2014: impacts, adaptation, and vulnerability. Part A: global and sectoral aspects. Contribution of working group II to the fifth assessment report of the intergovernmental panel of climate change. In: Field CB, Barros VR, Dokken DJ, Mach KJ, Mastrandrea MD, Bilir TE, Chatterjee M, Ebi KL, Estrada YO, Genova RC, Girma B, Kissel ES, Levy AN, MacCracken S, Mastrandrea PR, White LL (eds). Cambridge University Press, Cambridge, United Kingdom and New York, NY, USA, pp 899–943

Kolstad C, Urama K, Broome J, Bruvoll A, Fullerton D, Gollier C, Hahnemann WM, Hassan R, Jotzo F, Khan MR, Meyer L, Mundaca L, Olvera C (2015) Social, economic, and ethical concepts and methods. In: Ottmar E et al (eds) Climate change 2014. mitigation of climate change. Working group III contribution to the fifth assessment report of the intergovernmental panel on climate change. Cambridge University Press, New York, pp 207–282

Lees E (2016) Responsibility and liability for climate loss and damage after Paris. Clim Policy 17(1):59–70

Linnerooth-Bayer J, Mechler R (2009) Insurance Against Losses from Natural Disasters in Developing Countries. DESA Working Paper No. 85 ST/ESA/2009/DWP/85

Linnerooth-Bayer J, Surminski S, Bouwer LM, Noy I, Mechler R (2018) Insurance as a response to loss and damage? In: Mechler R, Bouwer L, Schinko T, Surminski S, Linnerooth-Bayer J (eds) Loss and damage from climate change. Concepts, methods and policy options. Springer, Cham, pp 483–512

Mace MJ, Verheyen R (2016) Loss, damage and responsibility after COP21: all options open for the Paris agreement. RECIEL 25(2):197–214

Mayer B (2017) Climate change reparations and the law and practice of state responsibility. AsianJIL 7(01):185–216

Mechler R, Schinko T (2016) Identifying the policy space for climate loss and damage. Science 354(6310):290–292

Mechler R, Bouwer LM, Linnerooth-Bayer J, Hochrainer-Stigler S, Aerts JCJH, Surminski S, Williges K (2014) Managing unnatural disaster risk from climate extremes. Nat Clim change 4(4):235–237

Mechler R et al (2018) Science for loss and damage. Findings and propositions. In: Mechler R, Bouwer L, Schinko T, Surminski S, Linnerooth-Bayer J (eds) Loss and damage from climate change. Concepts, methods and policy options. Springer, Cham, pp 3–37

Meyer LH (2003) Past and future: the case for an identity-independent notion of harm. In: Meyer LH, Paulson SL, Pogge T (eds) Rights, culture, and the law: themes from the legal and political philosophy of Joseph Raz. Oxford University Press, Oxford, pp 143–159

Meyer LH (2004) Compensating wrongless historical emissions of grennhouse gases. Ethical Perspect 11(1):20–35

Meyer LH (2013) Why historical emissions should count. Chicago J Int Law 13(2):598–614

Meyer LH, Roser D (2010) Climate justice and historical emissions. Critical Rev Int Soc Polit Philos 13(1):229–253

Meyer LH, Sanklecha P (2017) On the significance of historical emissions for climate ethics. In: Meyer L, Sanklecha P (ed) Climate justice and historical emissions. Cambridge University Press: Cambridge

Miller D (2007) National responsibility and global justice. Oxford University Press, Oxford

Morrissey J, Oliver-Smith A (2013) Perspectives on non-economic loss and damage. Understanding values at risk from climate change. In: Warner K, Kreft S (eds) Perspectives on non-economic loss and damage

O'Neill J (2017) The price of an apology: justice, compensation and rectification. Camb J Econ 41:1043–1059

Page EA, Heyward C (2016) Compensating for climate change loss and damage. Polit Stud 65(2):356–372

Roderick P, Verheyen R (2008) Beyond adaptation—the legal duty to pay compensation for climate change damage. WWF-UK, Climate Change Programme discussion paper 2008

Schäfer L, Warner K, Kreft S (2018) Exploring and managing adaptation frontiers with climate risk insurance. In: Mechler R, Bouwer L, Schinko T, Surminski S, Linnerooth-Bayer J (eds) Loss and damage from climate change. Concepts, methods and policy options. Springer, Cham, pp 317–341

Schinko T, Mechler R, Hochrainer-Stigler S (2018) The risk and policy space for loss and damage: integrating notions of distributive and compensatory justice with comprehensive climate risk management. In: Mechler R, Bouwer L, Schinko T, Surminski S, Linnerooth-Bayer J (eds) Loss and damage from climate change. Concepts, methods and policy options. Springer, Cham, pp 83–110

Serdeczny O (2018) Non-economic loss and damage and the Warsaw international mechanism. In: Mechler R, Bouwer L, Schinko T, Surminski S, Linnerooth-Bayer J (eds) Loss and damage from climate change. Concepts, methods and policy options. Springer, Cham, pp 205–220

Serdeczny O, Waters E, Chan S (2016) Non-economic loss and damage: addressing the forgotten side of climate change impacts. German Development Institute Briefing Paper 2016/3

Shue H (1999) Global environment and international inequality. Int Affairs 75(3):531–545

Shue H (2017) Responsible for what? Carbon producer CO_2 contributions and the energy transition. Clim Change 144(4):591–596

Simlinger F, Mayer B (2018) Legal responses to climate change induced loss and damage. In: Mechler R, Bouwer L, Schinko T, Surminski S, Linnerooth-Bayer J (eds) Loss and damage from climate change. Concepts, methods and policy options. Springer, Cham, pp 179–203

Surminski S, Bouwer LM, Linnerooth-Bayer J (2016) How insurance can support climate resilience. Nat Clim Change 6(4):333–334

Thompson A, Otto FEL (2015) Ethical and normative implications of weather event attribution for policy discussions concerning loss and damage. Clim Change 133(3):439–451

UNFCCC (2014) Report of the Conference of the Parties on its nineteenth session, held in Warsaw from 11 to 23 November 2013: Part two: Action taken by the Conference of the Parties at its nineteenth session

UNFCCC (2015) COP 21 Adoption of the Paris agreement

Vivid Economics (2015) Building an evidence base on the role of insurance-based mechanisms in promoting climate resilience. http://www-cif.climateinvestmentfunds.org/events/ppcr-sub-committee-meeting-thursday-november-12-2015-130-pm 500-p

Wallimann-Helmer I (2015) Justice for climate loss and damage. Clim Change 133(3):469–480

Wallimann-Helmer I (2016) Differentiating responsibilities for climate change adaptation. Archiv für Rechts- und Sozialphilosophie 149 (Beihefte):119–132

Zellentin A (2010) Climate migration: cultural aspects of climate change. Analyse & Kritik 1:63–86

Zellentin A (2015) Climate justice, small island developing states & cultural loss. Clim Change 133(3):491–498

Chapter 3
Observed and Projected Impacts from Extreme Weather Events: Implications for Loss and Damage

Laurens M. Bouwer

Abstract This chapter presents current knowledge of observed and projected impacts from extreme weather events, based on recorded events and their losses, as well as studies that project future impacts from anthropogenic climate change. The attribution of past changes in such impacts focuses on the three key drivers: changes in extreme weather hazards that can be due to natural climate variability and anthropogenic climate change, changes in exposure and vulnerability, and risk reduction efforts. The chapter builds on previous assessments of attribution of extreme weather events, to drivers of changes in weather hazard, exposure and vulnerability. Most records of losses from extreme weather consist of information on monetary losses, while several other types of impacts are underrepresented, complicating the assessment of losses and damages. Studies into drivers of losses from extreme weather show that increasing exposure is the most important driver through increasing population and capital assets. Residual losses (after risk reduction and adaptation) from extreme weather have not yet been attributed to anthropogenic climate change. For the Loss and Damage debate, this implies that overall it will remain difficult to attribute this type of losses to greenhouse gas emissions. For the future, anthropogenic climate change is projected to become more important for driving future weather losses upward. However, drivers of exposure and especially changes in vulnerability will interplay. Exposure will continue to lead to risk increases. Vulnerability on the other hand may be further reduced through disaster risk reduction and adaptation. This would reduce additional losses and damages from extreme weather. Yet, at the country scale and particularly in developing countries, there is ample evidence of increasing risk, which calls for significant improvement in climate risk management efforts.

Keywords Extreme weather · Flood · Storm · Losses · Risk · Normalisation Attribution

L. M. Bouwer (✉)
Climate Service Center Germany (GERICS), Hamburg, Germany
e-mail: laurens.bouwer@hzg.de

L. M. Bouwer
Deltares, Delft, The Netherlands

R. Mechler et al. (eds.), *Loss and Damage from Climate Change*, Climate Risk Management, Policy and Governance, https://doi.org/10.1007/978-3-319-72026-5_3

3.1 Introduction

3.1.1 Impacts from Extreme Weather

Impacts from anthropogenic climate change are often equated with impacts from weather-related natural hazards, such as floods, droughts and windstorms. Extreme weather events can lead to substantial impacts, including loss of life, damages to buildings, agricultural production and natural capital, as well as longer term economic effects. The discussion on Loss and Damage from climate change therefore warrants a discussion on the extent to which increases in impacts from extreme weather have already occurred, what impacts can be expected in the future, and which losses cannot be prevented or reduced through risk reduction and adaptation.

In this chapter "climate change" is defined according to the definition by the Intergovernmental Panel (IPCC 2012), which includes both natural variability, as well as human induced climate change from anthropogenic forcing such as greenhouse gas emissions. Losses and damages have varying definitions, and we discuss these in the light of current understanding of impacts from weather extremes. As explained in the introductory chapter (Mechler et al. 2018), "losses" refer to monetary losses, while "damages" are meant to cover non-monetary impacts as well as irreversible effects. Losses from extreme weather can include both types; monetary losses (damages to buildings and other property that can be repaired or replaced), as well non-monetary impacts such as loss of life, health impacts, and irreversible damages such as coastal erosion, ecosystem impacts and societal impacts (for instance retreat after severe flooding).

Current understanding shows that the changes in impacts from extreme weather hazards are largely moderated by the extent to which humans and assets are exposed to these hazards, and to what extent they are vulnerable or sensitive to these hazards. This implies that apart from the actual occurrence of the hazards, the level of impacts—relevant to the Loss and Damage debate—is influenced by non-climatic factors. Quantitative risk assessment methods and approaches practiced since many decades in natural hazard research can help to assess risk from weather and geophysical extremes using the combination of these processes. The framework that combines these elements of hazard, exposure, and vulnerability as developed by the IPCC (2012) has now become widely accepted by the climate change research community to understand and study the occurrence as well as temporal changes in the impacts from extremes (e.g. Huggel et al. 2013; see framework depicted in Fig. 3.1).

The hazard driver is influenced by changes in climate; both from anthropogenic climate change, resulting from greenhouse gas emissions, as well as natural climate variability. Exposure is influenced by changes in development, including population growth and economic development that lead to increased accumulation of people and capital assets in locations that are at risk from natural hazards. Vulnerability and exposure may change because of adaptation and risk reduction actions that increase the protection from weather hazards and reduce sensitivity to these extremes that would otherwise results in negative impacts. Governance can influence land-use

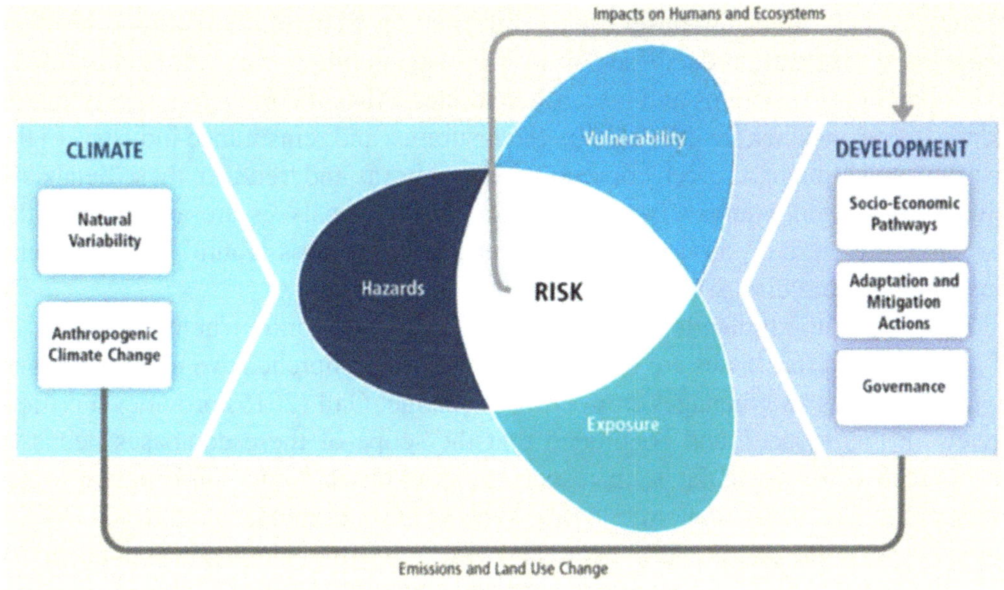

Fig. 3.1 Risk framework for the analysis of extreme event impacts. *Source* IPCC (2012)

planning that helps to reduce exposure, as well as the absorption of losses through risk transfer such as insurance, thereby changing vulnerability.

3.1.2 Extreme Weather Impacts and Loss and Damage

Impacts from anthropogenic climate change are manifold, and there are mostly negative consequences, especially with higher rates of warming, as well as a few positive effects. Here we focus on the impacts from extreme weather events. This provides only a partial picture of Loss and Damage, as there may be negative consequences from climate change that are not related to extreme weather events. Such impacts occur because of more gradual shifts, often called slow-onset processes, in climate variables such as average (seasonal) land-surface temperatures, average rainfall, as well as other variables, such as sea-level rise, loss of ice and snow-cover, and increasing temperatures of water bodies such as rivers, lakes and oceans. These impacts include shifts or loss of ecosystems and biodiversity, coastal erosion and loss of land, submergence of low-lying islands and atolls, changes in agricultural yield, and loss of indigenous and cultural practices and traditions. Many of such impacts are treated in this book in the chapters by Serdeczny (2018) and van der Geest et al. (2018).

Still, a considerable share of impacts on natural and human systems is associated with changes in weather extremes as a result of natural climate variability, and possibly also anthropogenic climate change. An advantage for research is that impacts from extreme weather events are relatively well-documented across the globe, compared to impacts such from slow-onset events. Information on extreme weather impacts is available in observation databases on past disasters collected by humanitarian and development organisations and research institutes. Also, records of monetary losses from extreme weather are collected by the insurance and reinsurance industry. In the disasters and climate research community, the patterns and trends in these databases have been studied extensively, and therefore several analyses are available in the academic literature on observed impacts for many locations around the world, and these analyses are discussed in this chapter.

With regard to climate losses and damages, the question is whether the records of observed disaster losses are fit for the purpose of comprehensive monitoring and analysing losses and damages from climate change. Gall (2015) provides a critical review in this respect, and concluded that the scope of these databases needs to be broadened, in particular with respect to slow-onset events, and include other impacts besides direct economic losses, such as indirect impacts and losses. While not exhaustive, the disaster loss records provide at this moment the best opportunity to assess and monitor changes in socioeconomic impacts, at least for extreme weather and climate change.

In addition, many studies have projected future changes in risk from extreme weather events, for the purpose of disaster risk reduction planning and climate adaptation. These studies also take into account future changes in hazard, exposure and vulnerability, on the basis of physical modelling and scenarios (Bouwer 2013), and therefore serve to indicate what impacts are expected for the near and more distant future, that could inform Loss and Damage discussions.

As shown in other chapters such as the contribution by James et al. (2018), wider definitions and viewpoints on Loss and Damage can include the impacts from present-day climate, so without much influence of climate change. This implies that losses and damages could also include impacts from extreme weather that are not attributable to anthropogenic climate change, but simply to (baseline) risk that occurs because of occurrence of extreme weather. This risk has occurred always, regardless of climate change, or occurs because of natural variability or increased exposure of people and capital. In this context, understanding present-day risks from extreme weather, and understanding the role of drivers of changes in that risk, is important for discussions on Loss and Damage. These drivers and the way they are understood to determine risk, ultimately also determine the scope of losses and damages from these extreme events.

There seems to be some agreement that the Loss and Damage debate refers to residual impacts, i.e. after adaptation ("losses beyond adaptation") (see James et al. 2018). Also, losses and damages can refer to actual impacts that have already occurred, as well as potential future risks of further impacts and damages (see introduction by Mechler et al. 2018).

In this context, all drivers of weather related risks should be considered. This is because non-climatic drivers of risk (influencing exposure, and vulnerability) may consciously (through adaptation) or unconsciously be influenced, as for instance with increasing development and wealthy societies become better protected from extreme weather hazards.

This chapter builds on previous major reviews of changes in past extreme weather events and their impacts, including the relevant summaries contained in IPCC reports, such as the Special Report on Managing the Risks of Extreme Events and Disasters to Advance Climate Change Adaptation (IPCC SREX; IPCC 2012), as well as the Fifth Assessment Report (IPCC 2013, 2014), and extends these with recent published studies. In addition, it provides a discussion of expectations of future losses under projected climate change. The discussion is complementary to other chapters that focus on the attribution of anthropogenic climate change (chapter by James et al. 2018), and decision making in the context of Loss and Damage (chapter by Lopez et al. 2018) as well as on risk management in the chapter by Botzen et al. (2018). The following topics are covered

- Observed changes in weather extremes and their relation with anthropogenic climate change;
- Observed changes in impacts from extreme weather, and their relation to changing weather extremes;
- Observed changes in exposure and vulnerability, leading to altered impacts from extreme weather;
- Possible changes in the future in terms of extreme weather impacts and losses and damages, based on projections from quantitative impact studies.

3.2 Observed Changes in Weather Extremes

The occurrence of weather extremes has been studied extensively, both in natural hazard research for the purpose of hazard probability estimation and design of protection, as well as in climate change research. At the same time, uncertainties in the attribution of extremes (such as windstorms) to anthropogenic climate change are larger than for slow-onset processes (such as annual average temperature change and sea-level rise) (IPCC 2013). This is partly because of the rare nature of extremes, which are often analysed at return periods of 100 years or more, and also because they often occur at spatial scales that are smaller than slow-onset events. For instance, tropical cyclones occur over smaller areas than major heat-wave or drought events. However, over recent years the attention to extreme weather events has increased, and possibilities to analyse and model the occurrence and intensity of these events have improved. For a number of extreme weather events, there is considerable evidence that these have increased in frequency and for some that anthropogenic emissions of greenhouse gases are a major cause of this increase.

Table 3.1 provides an overview of past changes in weather extremes and the role of anthropogenic forcing, as assessed by the IPCC in the SREX (IPCC 2012) and the Working Group I volume of the Fifth Assessment Report (IPCC 2013). From this table it can be concluded that the detection of changes and attribution to anthropogenic emissions has been established for extremes related to temperature and sea-level rise.

Table 3.1 Observed changes in weather extremes and attribution to human greenhouse gas emissions

Weather extreme	Observed past changes	Human contribution
Warmer (and/or fewer cold) days and nights[a]	• Very likely increase (decrease) in frequency over most land areas	• Very likely
Heat waves[a]	• Medium confidence in increase on global scale • Likely increase in large parts of Europe, Asia and Australia	• Likely
Heavy precipitation[a]	• Likely increases over more land areas than decreases	• Medium confidence
River floods[b]	• Limited to medium evidence for changes in frequency of river floods at the regional level • Low confidence for sign of change of river floods at the global level	—
Drought[a]	• Low confidence in change on a global level • Likely changes in some regions (increase in Mediterranean and West Africa; decreases in central North America and north-west Australia)	• Low confidence
Tropical cyclones[a]	• Low confidence in increase in activity (intensity and frequency) on timescales of 100 years • Virtually certain in North Atlantic since 1970	• Low confidence
Extra-tropical cyclones[b]	• Likely pole-ward shift of storm tracks on the northern and southern hemispheres	—
Extreme sea-levels[a]	• Likely increase since 1970	• Likely

Note Based on SREX and Fifth Assessment Report WGI reports from the IPCC (2012, 2013). For definition of confidence levels see IPCC (2013)
[a]IPCC (2013) (Summary for Policymakers). [b]IPCC (2012) (Summary for Policymakers)

For rainfall related extremes, including droughts and river flooding, findings regarding the detection of changes is more mixed, as is the attribution of these changes to human greenhouse gas emissions. For windstorms, in the tropical and extra-tropical regions, both the changes and the precise human contribution to these changes are even more uncertain. In addition, there is an extensive literature that has looked at how the likelihood of individual extreme weather events has possibly changed due to anthropogenic forcing (see James et al. 2018). In addition to monotonic changes from anthropogenic forcing, the role of natural variability in shaping the impacts from natural disasters can be very large. This is an important reason why even when trends in extremes are found, related to large decadal variability in the occurrence of extremes related to natural variability, the attribution of smaller changes over time to anthropogenic emissions. This is for instance the case for tropical cyclones, where large natural variability complicates the detection of any remaining trend (Knutson et al. 2010).

3.3 Observed Impacts Based on Disaster Loss Records

3.3.1 Loss Data and Normalisation

Several records are available of disaster losses. The most notable global databases consist of those managed by CRED (EM-DAT database,[1] Munich Reinsurance Company (NatCatSERVICE database),[2] and Swiss Reinsurance Company (SIGMA database).[3] Besides these global databases, several combined are available under Desinventar.[4] While these databases provide a good overall understanding of loss frequency and trends, several other records of natural hazard impacts exist that are more detailed, including national accounts of disaster losses and national and local insurance records. Some of these are also assessed in the studies reported here.

Several researchers have analysed disaster loss records, to assess the frequency and size of impacts from these hazards. In addition, many have analysed which drivers (hazard, exposure, or vulnerability) may have led to changes in these impacts over time. An often-used approach is so-called normalisation, which tries to account for changes in exposure over time, by applying correction factors to the observed loss record. These factors are based on the total size of the exposed assets and their value (see Pielke and Landsea 1998). This is also common practise in the insurance industry in order to arrive at a common reference baseline of historical loss events that can be compared to catastrophe models that simulate risks for today's exposure and vulnerabilities or for a specific baseline year (Pielke et al. 1999). Many

[1] http://www.emdat.be.

[2] https://www.munichre.com/en/reinsurance/business/non-life/natcatservice/index.html.

[3] http://institute.swissre.com/research/overview/sigma_data/.

[4] https://www.desinventar.org/ and http://www.desinventar.net/.

of the studies that applied loss normalisation also refer to "attribution of changes in impacts." This is however different from the formal detection and attribution as approached by the climate research community, which usually refers to the detection[5] of statistically significant changes in climate variables, and attribution[6] of these changes to natural forcing and anthropogenic greenhouse gas emissions. In the case of studies on disaster losses, attribution takes two steps: first attribution of the observed change in disaster losses to socioeconomic drivers (exposure, vulnerability), and next establish whether there is a remaining trend, that could be attributed to changing weather hazard conditions, usually regardless of human causes (e.g. Huggel et al. 2013). Other lines of research, include so-called event attribution studies put a direct link between the occurrence of individual extreme events and increased likelihood of these events that is due to anthropogenic forcing. In a few cases, also the impacts or losses from these events are included in the models (e.g. Pall et al. 2011), but not changes in other variables beside climate, such as changes in catchment hydrology or flood defences that would also influence flood risk (Schaller et al. 2016). These event attribution studies are further discussed in the chapter by James et al. (2018).

3.3.2 Analysis of Loss Trends

A number of assessments is available of the current understanding of disaster loss records on the basis of individual studies, most notably the IPCC SREX report (IPCC 2012), including the chapter on human and ecosystem impacts by Handmer et al. (2012), and in the contribution from Working Group II to the Fifth Assessment report, including the chapters on attribution by Cramer et al. (2014), and on the insurance sector in the chapter by Arent et al. (2014). Throughout these chapters, it is acknowledged that losses from natural hazards have increased, regardless of causation of the increase. In addition, it is noted that losses from weather-related hazards have increased more rapidly than from geophysical events such as earthquakes (e.g. Handmer et al. 2012). The assessments of IPCC have concluded the following on the causes of the upward trends in losses from extreme weather events:

> Long-term trends in economic disaster losses adjusted for wealth and population increases have not been attributed to climate change, but a role for climate change has not been excluded (SREX SPM, IPCC 2012).
>
> Economic losses due to extreme weather events have increased globally, mostly due to increase in wealth and exposure, with a possible influence of climate change (Cramer et al. 2014).

---

[5]Detection: "Detection of change is defined as the process of demonstrating that climate or a system affected by climate has changed in some defined statistical sense, without providing a reason for that change" (IPCC 2013: Annex III Glossary).

[6]Attribution: "Attribution is defined as the process of evaluating the relative contributions of multiple causal factors to a change or event with an assignment of statistical confidence" (IPCC 2013: Annex III Glossary).

In sum, while increasing trends are found for losses from past extreme weather events, increasing exposure has been the main driver, and climate change (both anthropogenic climate change as well as natural climate variability) could have an additional role, but this role was not substantiated. The confidence of the role of anthropogenic climate change as driver in the upward trend in disaster loses is however *low*. Results from these previous reviews, as well as more recent studies on disaster loss databases, are displayed in Table 3.2. In total 34 studies are included. Most of these studies have analysed monetised losses from extreme weather events, although in some cases the losses concern quantified impacts, such as volume of damaged timber wood. And most studies account for increasing exposure, using either data on exposed capital assets, population, wealth indicators, and an inflation correction.

While this overview is perhaps neither exhaustive nor complete, it provides a comprehensive overview of scientific studies on impacts from major extreme weather types, such as tropical and extra-tropical cyclones, rainfall flooding, hailstorms, wildfires and convective weather types. While coastal flooding is often included in tropical cyclone losses, drought events are underrepresented in these studies. A few studies detect trends at the regional or national level, the overall conclusion is that very few upward trends are found, after normalising for changes in exposure.

There are several issues related to the normalisation approach, as well as the interpretation of normalised losses. First of all, the general assumption is that the change in the major driver of losses, that is increasing exposure of assets, has a proportional (linear) relation with the losses (e.g. Pielke and Landsea 1998; Bouwer 2011a; Handmer et al. 2012). But alternative approaches such as from Estrada et al. (2015) show that alternative formulations of statistical models with explanatory variables may lead to different trends in losses, such as for US hurricanes. Such approaches are however not yet conclusive, and need further confirmation in consecutive studies (Hallegatte 2015).

In addition, the interpretation of the normalised record is also not straightforward. As Visser et al. (2014) and Visser and Petersen (2012) show, different statistical methods for trend detection may lead to different interpretation of upward, downward or no trends found in the normalised loss records of extreme weather events. And how fluctuations in the normalised loss-record are interpreted, possibly related to natural climate variability, is another matter of discussion.

What is clear from the normalisation studies listed here (Table 3.2) is that most do not find an increasing trend in losses, after the records have been normalised for increasing exposure. This implies that the main driver of the observed losses likely has been an increasing number of population and assets, and not a change in the hazard frequency or severity. A few studies however do find increases in losses, also after normalisation. These include most notably convective weather events, including thunderstorms and hailstorms, where three studies find increasing trends for over several decades. With increasing temperatures, there is a possibility that extremes related to convective weather could become more frequent. However, IPCC (2012)

Table 3.2 Normalisation studies of weather-related disaster loss records

Hazard	Location	Period	Normalised loss	References
Tropical cyclones (9 studies)				
Tropical storm	Latin America	1944–1999	No trend	Pielke et al. (2003)
Tropical storm	India	1977–1998	No trend	Raghavan and Rajesh (2003)
Tropical storm	USA	1900–2005	No trend	Pielke et al. (2008)
Tropical storm	USA	1950–2005	Increase since 1970; no trend since 1950	Schmidt et al. (2009)
Tropical storm	China	1983–2006	No trend	Zhang et al. (2009)
Tropical storm	USA	1900–2008	Increase since 1900	Nordhaus (2010)
Tropical storm	USA	1900–2005	No trend	Bouwer and Botzen (2010)
Tropical storm	USA	1900–2005	Increase since 1900	Estrada et al. (2015)
Tropical storm	China	1984–2013	No trend	Fischer et al. (2015)
Extra-tropical cyclones (3 studies)				
Windstorm	USA	1952–2006	Increase since 1952	Changnon (2009b)
Windstorm	Europe	1970–2008	No trend	Barredo (2010)
Windstorm	Switzerland	1859–2011	No trend	Stucki et al. (2014)
Snow storms (1 study)				
Ice, blizzard and snow storms	USA	1949–2003	Increase since 1949	Changnon (2007)
Convective weather (7 studies)				
Thunderstorm	USA	1949–1998	Increase since 1974	Changnon (2001)
Tornado	USA	1890–1999	No trend	Brooks and Doswell (2001)
Tornado	USA	1900–2000	No trend	Boruff et al. (2003)
Hailstorm	USA	1951–2006	Increase since 1992	Changnon (2009a)
Hailstorm	Southwest Germany	1974–2003	Increase over last 20 years	Kunz et al. (2009)
Tornado	USA	1950–2011	No trend	Simmons et al. (2013)
Thunderstorm	USA	1970–2009	Increasing trend since 1990	Sander et al. (2013)
Flooding (7 studies)				
River flood	USA	1926–2000	No trend	Downton and Pielke (2005)
River flood	China	1950–2001	Increase since 1987	Fengqing et al. (2005)

(continued)

Table 3.2 (continued)

Hazard	Location	Period	Normalised loss	References
River flood	Europe	1970–2006	No trend	Barredo (2009)
River flood	Korea	1971–2005	Increase since 1971	Chang et al. (2009)
River flood and landslides	Switzerland	1972–2007	No trend	Hilker et al. (2009)
River flood	Spain	1971–2008	No trend	Barredo et al. (2012)
River flooding	Spain	1975–2013	No trend	Pérez-Morales et al. (2018)
Wildfire (1 study)				
Bushfire	Australia	1925–2009	No trend	Crompton et al. (2010)
Various weather (9 studies)				
Weather (hurricanes, floods)	USA	1951–1997	No trend	Choi and Fisher (2003)
Weather (flood, thunderstorm, hail, bushfires)	Australia	1967–2006	No trend	Crompton and McAneney (2008)
Weather (hail, storm, flood, wildfire)	World	1950–2005	Increase since 1970; no increase since 1950	Miller et al. (2008)
Weather (floods, convective events, winter storms, tropical cyclones, heatwaves)	World	1980–2008	No trend	Neumayer and Barthel (2011)
Weather (winter storms, heatwaves)	Germany	1980–2008	Increase since 1980	Neumayer and Barthel (2011)
Weather (floods, convective events	Germany	1980–2008	No trend	Neumayer and Barthel (2011)
Weather (floods, convective events, winter storms, tropical cyclones, heatwaves)	USA	1980–2008	Increase since 1980	Neumayer and Barthel (2011)
Natural disasters (including extreme temperatures, floods, mass movement, storms, wildfire)	China	1990–2011	No trend	Zhou et al. (2013)
Weather (tropical cyclones, flooding, drought)	India (Odisha)	1972–2009	No trend	Bahinipati and Venkatachalam (2016)

Updated from Bouwer (2011a), including Handmer et al. (2012), Cramer et al. (2014), Arent et al. (2014) and other recent publications noted that there is insufficient evidence[7] to conclude that severe convective weather has already become more frequent.

Other weather hazards for which positive loss trends are found include studies on tropical storms. While Nordhaus (2010) found a positive trend for US hurricane losses after normalisation, Bouwer and Botzen (2011) found no trend using other loss records and alternative normalisation of the same events. The study by Estrada et al. (2015) used an alternative formulation, assuming a non-linear relation between changes in exposure and losses, which has not yet been confirmed by other studies, nor has there been a sufficient explanation for the cause of the remaining increase in losses (Hallegatte 2015). Schmidt et al. (2009) found an increasing trend in US hurricane losses after normalisation since 1970, but this is likely due to natural variability (Bouwer 2011a); in this case the low frequency of landfalling hurricanes in the North Atlantic and Caribbean in the 1970s, and the subsequent increase in the 1990s and early 2000s. For river flooding some studies find increases after normalisation (Fengqing et al. 2005; Chang et al. 2009), but these are relatively short-lived, and it is unclear whether these increases are related to changes in flood hazard driven by natural variability or anthropogenic climate change.

Finally, there are some studies that indicate increasing losses after normalisation at the global level, for several types of weather extremes (Miller et al. 2008; Neumayer and Barthel 2011), but these trends are also over recent times (over 30 years or less), and here it is also unclear whether any related changes in hazard are driven by natural variability or anthropogenic climate change.

3.3.3 Interpretation of Drivers of Losses

As shown above, few studies find signals in losses beyond the driver of increasing exposure. Less is known about the role of vulnerability changes that potentially may play an important role. As societies become wealthier, they are likely to start to invest more in risk reduction and adaptation, thereby reducing impacts from weather related hazards. This may result in reduced losses over time. For normalisation studies, this may imply that accounting for increases in exposure only, would downplay the role of any other contributing factors, including anthropogenic climate change (Nicholls 2011). Indeed, there are studies that show that especially loss of life and also monetary losses have decreased, despite increasing exposure (Mechler and Bouwer 2015; Bahinipati and Patnaik 2015; Kreibich et al. 2017; Bouwer and Jonkman 2018). Jongman et al. (2015) for instance stress that despite the fact that total losses from river flooding have increased, fatalities and monetised losses as a share of population and GDP, have fallen over past decades. However, the question is how significant these changes in vulnerability are, compared to the very rapid increase in exposure (Bouwer 2011b). While loss of life clearly has benefitted from improved early

[7]"There is low confidence in observed trends in small spatial-scale phenomena such as tornadoes and hail because of data inhomogeneities and inadequacies in monitoring systems" (IPCC 2012:8).

warning and evacuation, and vulnerability has substantially declined (Mechler and Bouwer 2015; Bouwer and Jonkman 2018), monetary losses can only be substantially prevented from improved protection, such as through flood prevention, improved building construction, and alternative agricultural practices. There are however very few longitudinal studies that have assessed these effects over sufficiently long periods over time, to establish the long-terms effects, compared to increasing exposure. The studies indicating substantial reductions in monetary losses have considered the most recent decades (Jongman et al. 2015; Kreibich et al. 2017), and while efforts may have been successful at improving the current situation, they can hardly make up for substantial development in vulnerable areas that has been taken place over the last 100 years.

Finally, for attributing changes in extreme weather impacts, in the context of Loss and Damage, any remaining trend after normalisation and after accounting for vulnerability reduction would need to be demonstrated to have a relation with changes in extreme weather hazards. And this change in extreme weather hazard in turn should be attributed to anthropogenic climate change. Table 3.3 summarises the results from the review of loss normalisation studies (Table 3.2), as well as the observed changes in weather extremes (Table 3.1). While for several weather extremes, increasing occurrence has been observed, and often also attributed to anthropogenic greenhouse gas forcing (Table 3.1), these changes are not reflected in loss records, or at least cannot be recognised. No substantial evidence is present for long-term increases in normalised losses from these types of extreme weather, based on quantified loss records. And while a few studies show that losses from convective weather may have increased, in particular losses from hail and thunderstorm events (Changnon 2001; Changnon 2009a; Kunz et al. 2009; Sander et al. 2013), these are yet to be linked to structural changes in the occurrence of convective weather events, related to greenhouse gas forcing (IPCC 2012, 2013).

Table 3.3 Comparison of changes in extreme weather hazards (regardless of human contribution) and observed change in losses

Type	Increase in extreme weather hazard?	Increase in observed losses?
Heat wave	Very likely	Unknown
Heavy precipitation	Likely	Unknown
River floods	Limited/medium evidence	No increase
Drought	Low confidence	Unknown
Tropical cyclones	Low confidence	No increase
Extra-tropical cyclones	Likely poleward shift	No increase
Extreme sea-levels	Likely	Unknown
Wildfires	Unknown	No increase
Convective weather	Unknown	Possible increase?

3.4 Projections of Future Extreme Weather Losses

As a stylised case, Fig. 3.2 provides an illustration of how past risk from extreme weather has increased, and how this risk can be reduced or avoided through disaster risk reduction (protection and prevention). There will always remain a residual risk (see also chapter by Schinko et al. 2018), which cannot be reduced in a cost-efficient way, i.e. the costs of eliminating the risk are considered higher than incurring the costs. However, current risk has increased by increasing exposure, and possibly by anthropogenic climate change. Part or all of this risk is related to the Loss and Damage debate, depending on whether or not residual impacts are considered to be included. Future risk will increase further due to anthropogenic climate change, leading to an increasing amount of losses and damages, not addressed by disaster risk reduction and adaptation. However, as vulnerability is likely to be further reduced (see also evidence discussed in Sect. 3.3), the share avoided by disaster risk reduction and adaptation will also increase. The losses and damages after adaptation include unavoidable losses and damages, potentially including the residual risks that will remain.

Various studies also project quantified future losses from extreme weather, mostly for risk assessment purposes in the context of vulnerability and adaptation studies at national or international level, and also for planning and design purposes at local level. These studies are assessed by several authors, including IPCC (e.g. Handmer et al. 2012; Arent et al. 2014). Overall, these studies recognise that changing weather hazards have a role, driven by anthropogenic climate change as major driver of

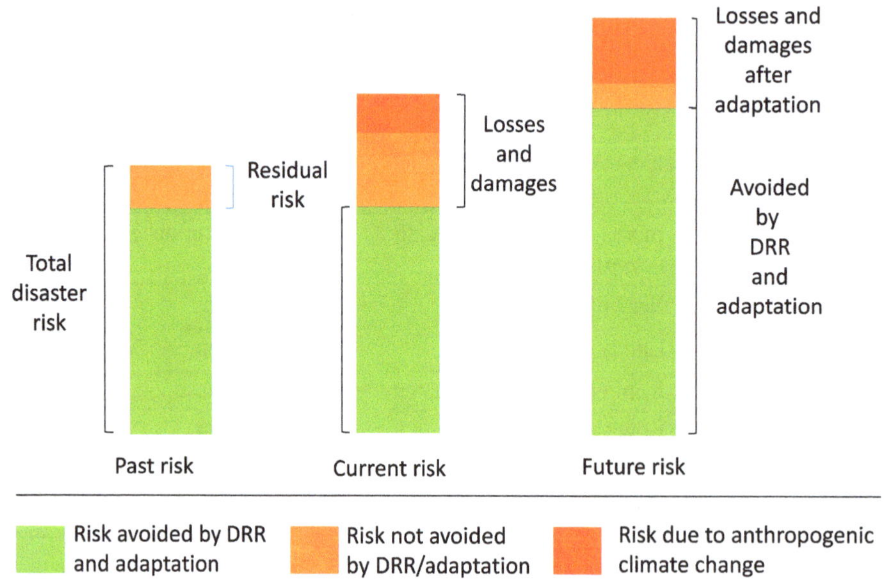

Fig. 3.2 Past, current and future risk from extreme weather events, and the relation to Loss and Damage

risk. The hazards that are studied include tropical and extra-tropical cyclones, river flooding, coastal flooding, as well as small scale phenomena such as hailstorms.

Exposure and vulnerability are also considered as important drivers of future risks. Many but not all of these studies also integrate projections of increasing population and wealth or capital at risk in the quantitative estimates of future risk. A comparison of these estimates shows that for tropical cyclones and extra-tropical cyclones, the effects of future increases in exposure are much larger than from increasing hazard frequency as a consequence of anthropogenic climate change (Bouwer 2013). Some recent studies have analysed these signals together in a single analysis, such as Crompton et al. (2011). They show that for tropical cyclones in the USA, it will take at least until the end of this century before the effects from anthropogenic climate change can be disentangled from the loss record. Muis et al. (2016) show for Indonesia that coastal and river flood risk in the future will be largely driven by increasing exposure. Preston (2013) shows for various weather hazards in the USA that exposure potentially will have a major impact on losses until the year 2050. Strader et al. (2017) show for tornado risk, that increasing expansion of urban areas in the US outweighs the effects of increasing severe weather occurrence.

Only very few studies have analysed the effects of a further decline in vulnerability, as a result of increasing risk reduction and adaption efforts, in comparison to projected future climate change. Jongman et al. (2015) shows that when considering vulnerability reduction (e.g., through adaptation and disaster risk reduction), future absolute losses from river flooding in terms of loss of life and monetary impacts could be substantially reduced, at the global scale than without adaptation, and under an optimistic scenario even declining, compared to today's risks. Also, Mechler and Bouwer (2015) show for Bangladesh that increases in risks are potentially lower when dynamic vulnerability is considered.

These projection studies imply that for Loss and Damage, it will remain difficult which elements of the actual losses from extreme weather are attributed to greenhouse gas emissions; first of all, increasing exposure could still play a dominant role. But in addition, successful vulnerability reduction could increasingly lead to a lowered pace of risk increases, compared to the past. Changes are observed in the frequency of several weather extremes, and anthropogenic climate change is an important driver for several of these. Also, losses, including monetary losses, from extreme weather events have increased, as can be seen from several observational records. The records of losses discussed above are focused on monetary losses, while several other types of impacts, including non-monetised damages and irreversible impacts from extreme weather, are underrepresented, complicating the assessment of losses and damages. Studies into drivers of losses from extreme weather show that increasing exposure has been the most important driver, through increasing population and capital assets. Anthropogenic climate change is currently not an important driver for changes in losses from events related to extreme wind, rainfall, and flooding, except perhaps for convective weather events (thunderstorms and hail). Other extreme weather types (such as extreme heat) have not been addressed in this chapter, and monetary losses are rarely assessed for extreme temperatures. It is known that anthropogenic climate change is increasing heatwave frequency, and mortality and morbidity have been high in recent events. Residual losses (after risk reduction and adaptation) from extreme weather have not yet been attributed to anthropogenic climate change. For the Loss and Damage debate, this implies that overall it is currently difficult to attribute losses to greenhouse gas emissions.

Anthropogenic climate change is projected to become more important for driving future weather losses upward. However, drivers of exposure and especially vulnerability reduction will interplay. Exposure will continue to lead to risk increases. Vulnerability on the other hand may to be further reduced if disaster risk reductionand adaptation is taken forward. As modelling studies show this would reduce losses and damages from extreme weather at the global scale. In the most optimistic scenario with high adaptation assumed, it could even reduce the burden from extreme weather. Yet, at national scales and particularly for developing countries there is ample evidence of increasing risk, which calls for a significant upgrade of climate risk management efforts.

References

Arent DJ, Tol RSJ, Faust E, Hella JP, Kumar S, Strzepek K, Tóth FL, Yan D (2014) Key economic sectors and services. In: Field CB, Barros VR, Dokken DJ, Mach KJ, Mastrandrea MD, Bilir TE, Chatterjee M, Ebi KL, Estrada YO, Genova RC, Girma B, Kissel ES, Levy AN, MacCracken S, Mastrandrea PR, White LL (eds) Climate change 2014: impacts, adaptation, and vulnerability. Part A: global and sectoral aspects. Contribution of working group II to the fifth assessment report of the intergovernmental panel of climate change. Cambridge University Press, Cambridge, United Kingdom and New York, NY, USA, pp 659–708

Bahinipati CS, Patnaik U (2015) The damages from climatic extremes in India: do disaster-specific and generic adaptation measures matter? Environ Econ Policy Stud 17:157–177

Bahinipati CS, Venkatachalam L (2016) Role of climate risks and socio-economic factors in influencing the impact of climatic extremes: a normalisation study in the context of Odisha, India. Reg Environ Change 16(1):177–188

Barredo JI (2009) Normalised flood losses in Europe: 1970–2006. Nat Hazards Earth Syst Sci 9:97–104

Barredo JI (2010) No upward trend in normalised windstorm losses in Europe: 1970–2008. Nat Hazards Earth Syst Sci 10:97–104

Barredo JI, Sauri D, Carmen-Llasat MC (2012) Assessing trends in insured losses from floods in Spain 1971–2008. Nat Hazards Earth Syst Sci 12:1723–1729

Boruff BJ, Easoz JA, Jones SD, Landry HR, Mitchem JD, Cutter SL (2003) Tornado hazards in the United States. Climate Res 24:103–117

Botzen W, Bouwer LM, Scussolini P, Kuik O, Haasnoot M, Lawrence J, Aerts JCJH (2018) Integrated disaster risk management and adaptation. In: Mechler R, Bouwer L, Schinko T, Surminski S, Linnerooth-Bayer J (eds) Loss and damage from climate change. Concepts, methods and policy options. Springer, Cham, pp 287–315

Bouwer LM (2011a) Have disaster losses increased due to anthropogenic climate change? Bull Am Meteor Soc 92(1):39–46

Bouwer LM (2011b) Reply to comments on "Have disaster losses increased due to anthropogenic climate change?" Bull Am Meteorol Soc 92(6):792–793

Bouwer LM (2013) Projections of future extreme weather losses under changes in climate and exposure. Risk Anal 33(5):915–930

Bouwer LM, Botzen WJW (2011) How sensitive are US hurricane damages to climate? Comment on a paper by W.D. Nordhaus. Clim Change Econ 1(2):1–7

Bouwer LM, Jonkman SN (2018) Global mortality from storm surges is decreasing. Environ Res Lett 13(1):014008

Brooks HE, Doswell CA (2001) Normalized damage from major tornadoes in the United States: 1890–1999. Weather Forecast 16:168–176

Chang H, Franczyk J, Kim C (2009) What is responsible for increasing flood risks? The case of Gangwon Province, Korea. Nat Hazards 48:339–354

Changnon SA (2001) Damaging thunderstorm activity in the United States. Bull Am Meteor Soc 82:597–608

Changnon SA (2007) Catastrophic winter storms: an escalating problem. Clim Change 84:131–139

Changnon SA (2009a) Increasing major hail losses in the U.S. Clim Change 96:161–166

Changnon SA (2009b) Temporal and spatial distributions of windstorm damages in the United States. Clim Change 94:473–483

Choi O, Fisher A (2003) The impacts of socioeconomic development and climate change on severe weather catastrophe losses: Mid-Atlantic region (MAR) and the U.S. Clim Change 58:149–170

Cramer W, Yohe G, Auffhammer M, Huggel C, Molau U, Da Silva Dias MAF, Solow A, Stone D, Tibig L (2014) Detection and attribution of observed impacts. In: Field CB, Barros VR, Dokken DJ, Mach KJ, Mastrandrea MD, Bilir TE, Chatterjee M, Ebi KL, Estrada YO, Genova RC, Girma B, Kissel ES, Levy AN, MacCracken S, Mastrandrea PR, White LL (eds) Climate change 2014: impacts, adaptation, and vulnerability. Part A: global and sectoral aspects, Chap 18. Contribution of working group II to the fifth assessment report of the intergovernmental panel of climate change. Cambridge University Press, Cambridge, United Kingdom and New York, NY, USA, pp 979–1037

Crompton RP, Pielke RA Jr, McAneney KJ (2011) Emergence time scales for detection of anthropogenic climate change in US tropical cyclone loss data. Environ Res Lett 6:014003

Crompton RP, McAneney KJ (2008) Normalised Australian insured losses from meteorological hazards: 1967–2006. Environ Sci Policy 11:371–378

Crompton RP, McAneney KJ, Chen K, Pielke RA Jr, Haynes K (2010) Influence of location, population, and climate on building damage and fatalities due to Australian bushfire: 1925-2009. Weather Clim Soc 2(10):300–310

Downton M, Pielke RA Jr (2005) How accurate are disaster loss data? The case of U.S. flood damage. Nat Hazards 35:211–228

Estrada F, Botzen WJW, Tol RSJ (2015) Economic losses from US hurricanes consistent with an influence from climate change. Nat Geosci 8:880–884

Fengqing J, Cheng Z, Guijin M, Ruji H, Qingxia M (2005) Magnification of flood disasters and its relation to regional precipitation and local human activities since the 1980s in Xinxiang, northwestern China. Nat Hazards 36:307–330

Fischer T, Su B, Wen S (2015) Spatio-temporal analysis of economic losses from tropical cyclones in affected provinces of China for the last 30 years (1984–2013). Nat Hazards Rev 16(4). https://doi.org/10.1061/(ASCE)NH.1527-6996.0000186

Gall M (2015) The suitability of disaster loss data bases to measure loss and damage from climate change. Int J Global Warming 8(2):170–190

Hallegatte S (2015) Unattributed hurricane damage. Nat Geosci 8:819–820

Handmer J, Honda Y, Kundzewicz ZW, Arnell N, Benito Z, Hatfield J, Mohamed IF, Peduzzi P, Wu S, Sherstyukov B, Takahashi K, Yan Z (2012) Changes in impacts of climate extremes: human systems and ecosystems. In: Field CB, Barros V, Stocker TF, Qin D, Dokken DJ, Ebi KL, Mastrandrea MD, Mach KJ, Plattner G-K, Allen SK, Tignor M, Midgley PM (eds) Chapter 4. Cambridge University Press, USA, Cambridge, UK, and New York, NY, USpp 231–290

Hilker N, Badoux A, Hegg C (2009) The Swiss flood and landslide damage database 1972–2007. Nat Hazards Earth Sys Sci 9:913–925

Huggel C, Stone D, Auffhammer M, Hansen G (2013) Loss and damage attribution. Nat Clim Change 3(8):694–696

IPCC (2012) Managing the risks of extreme events and disasters to advance climate change adaptation. A special report of working groups I and II of the intergovernmental panel on climate change. In: Field CB, Barros V, Stocker TF, Qin D, Dokken DJ, Ebi KL, Mastrandrea MD, Mach KJ, Plattner G-K, Allen SK, Tignor M, Midgley PM (eds). Cambridge University Press, USA, Cambridge, UK, and New York, NY, US, 582 pp

IPCC (2013) Climate change 2013: the physical science basis. Contribution of working group I to the fifth assessment report of the intergovernmental panel on climate change. In: Stocker TF, Qin D, Plattner G-K, Tignor M, Allen SK, Boschung J, Nauels A, Xia Y, Bex V, Midgley PM (eds). Cambridge University Press, Cambridge, United Kingdom and New York, NY, USA, 1535 pp

IPCC (2014) Climate change 2014: impacts, adaptation, and vulnerability. Part A: global and sectoral aspects. In: Field CB, Barros VR, Dokken DJ, Mach KJ, Mastrandrea MD, Bilir TE, Chatterjee M, Ebi KL, Estrada YO, Genova RC, Girma B, Kissel ES, Levy AN, MacCracken S, Mastrandrea PR, White LL (eds) Contribution of working group II to the fifth assessment report of the intergovernmental panel on climate change. Cambridge University Press, Cambridge, United Kingdom and New York, NY, USA, 1132 pp

James RA, Jones RG, Boyd E, Young HR, Otto FEL, Huggel C, Fuglestvedt JS (2018) Attribution: how is it relevant for loss and damage policy and practice? In: Mechler R, Bouwer L, Schinko T, Surminski S, Linnerooth-Bayer J (eds) Loss and damage from climate change. Concepts, methods and policy options. Springer, Cham, pp 113–154

Jongman B, Winsemius HC, Aerts JCJH, Coughlan de Perez E, Van Aalst MK, Kron W, Ward PJ (2015) Declining vulnerability to river floods and the global benefits of adaptation. Proc Natl Acad Sci USA 112(18):E2271–E2280

Knutson TR, McBride JL Chan J, Emanuel K, Holland G, Landsea C, Held I, Kossin JP, Srivastava AK, Sugi M (2010) Tropical cyclones and climate change. Nat Geosci 3:157–163

Kreibich H, Aerts JCJH, Apel H, Arnbjerg-Nielsen K, Di Baldassarre G, Bouwer LM, Bubeck P, Caloiero T, Cortés M, Do C, Gain AK, Giampá V, Kuhlicke C, Kundzewicz ZW, Llasat MC, Mård J, Matczak P, Mazzoleni M, Molinari D, Nguyen VD, Petrucci O, Schröter K, Slager K, Thieken AH, Vorogushyn S, Merz B (2017) Reducing flood risk by learning from past events. Earth's Future 5(10):953–965

Kunz K, Sander J, Kottmeier C (2009) Recent trends of thunderstorm and hailstorm frequency and their relation to atmospheric characteristics in southwest Germany. Int J Climatol 29:2283–2297

Lopez, A, Surminski S, Serdeczny O (2018) The role of the physical sciences in loss and damage decision-making. In: Mechler R, Bouwer L, Schinko T, Surminski S, Linnerooth-Bayer J (eds) Loss and damage from climate change. Concepts, methods and policy options. Springer, Cham, pp 261–285

Mechler R, Bouwer LM (2015) Understanding trends and projections of disaster losses and climate change: is vulnerability the missing link? Clim Change 133(1):23–35

Mechler R et al (2018) Science for loss and damage. Findings and propositions. In: Mechler R, Bouwer L, Schinko T, Surminski S, Linnerooth-Bayer J (eds) Loss and damage from climate change. Concepts, methods and policy options. Springer, Cham, pp 3–37

Miller S, Muir-Wood R, Boissonnade A (2008) An exploration of trends in normalized weather-related catastrophe losses. In: Diaz HF, Murnane RJ (eds) Climate extremes and society. Cambridge University Press, Cambridge, pp 225–347

Muis S, Verlaan M, Winsemius HC, Aerts JCJH, Ward PJ (2016) A global reanalysis of storm surges and extreme sea levels. Nat Commun 7:11969

Neumayer E, Barthel F (2011) Normalizing economic loss from natural disasters: a global analysis. Glob Environ Change 21(1):13–24

Nicholls N (2011) Comments on "Have disaster losses increased due to anthropogenic climate change?". Bull Am Meteor Soc 92(6):791

Nordhaus WD (2010) The economics of hurricanes and implications of global warming. Clim Change Econ 1:1–20

Pall P, Aina T, Stone DA, Stott PA, Nozawa T, Hilberts AGJ, Lohmann D, Allen MR (2011) Anthropogenic greenhouse gas contribution to flood risk in England and Wales in autumn 2000. Nature 470:382–385

Pérez-Morales A, Gil-Guirado S, Olcina-Cantos J (2018) Housing bubbles and the increase of flood exposure. Failures in flood risk management on the Spanish south-eastern coast (1975–2013). J Flood Risk Manag 11(S1):S302–S313

Pielke RA Jr, Landsea CW, Musulin RT, Downton M (1999) Evaluation of catastrophe models using a normalized historical record: why it is needed and how to do it. J Insur Regul 18(2):177–194

Pielke RA Jr, Rubiera J, Landsea C, Fernandez ML, Klein R (2003) Hurricane vulnerability in Latin America and the Caribbean: normalized damage and loss potentials. Nat Hazards Rev 4:101–114

Pielke AR Jr, Gratz J, Landsea CW, Collins D, Saunders M, Musulin R (2008) Normalized hurricane damages in the United States: 1900–2005. Nat Hazards Rev 9:29–42

Pielke RA Jr, Landsea CW (1998) Normalized hurricane damage in the United States: 1925–95. Weather Forecast 13:621–631

Preston BL (2013) Local path dependence of U.S. socioeconomic exposure to climate extremes and the vulnerability commitment. Glob Environ Change 23(4):719–732

Raghavan S, Rajesh S (2003) Trends in tropical cyclone impact: a study in Andhra Pradesh, India. Bull Am Meteor Soc 84:635–644

Sander J, Eichner JF, Faust E, Steuer M (2013) Rising variability in thunderstorm related U.S. losses as a reflection of changes in large-scale thunderstorm forcing. Weather Clim Soc 5:317–331

Schaller N, Kay AL, Lamb R, Massey NR, Van Oldenborgh GJ, Otto FL, Sparrow SN, Vautard R, Yiou P, Ashpole I, Bowery A, Crooks SM, Haustein K, Huntingford C, Ingram WJ, Jones RG, Legg T, Miller J, Skeggs J, Wallom D, Weisheimer A, Wilson S, Stott PA, Allen MA (2016) Human influence on climate in the 2014 southern England winter floods and their impacts. Nat Clim Change 6:627–634

Schinko T, Mechler R, Hochrainer-Stigler S (2018) The risk and policy space for loss and damage: integrating notions of distributive and compensatory justice with comprehensive climate risk management. In: Mechler R, Bouwer L, Schinko T, Surminski S, Linnerooth-Bayer J (eds) Loss and damage from climate change. Concepts, methods and policy options. Springer, Cham, pp 83–110

Schmidt S, Kemfert C, Höppe P (2009) Tropical cyclone losses in the USA and the impact of climate change: a trend analysis based on data from a new approach to adjusting storm losses. Environ Impact Assess Rev 29:359–369

Serdeczny O (2018) Non-economic loss and damage and the Warsaw international mechanism. In: Mechler R, Bouwer L, Schinko T, Surminski S, Linnerooth-Bayer J (eds) Loss and damage from climate change. Concepts, methods and policy options. Springer, Cham, pp 205–220

Simmons KM, Sutter D, Pielke R (2013) Normalized tornado damage in the United States: 1950-2011. Environ Hazards 12(2):132–147

Strader SM, Ashley WS, Pingel TJ, Krmenec AJ (2017) Projected 21st Century changes in tornado exposure, risk and disaster potential. Climatic Change 141:301–313

Stucki P, Brönnimann S, Martius O, Welker C, Imhof M, Von Wattenwyl N, Philipp N (2014) A catalog of high-impact windstorms in Switzerland since 1859. Nat Hazards Earth Sys Sci 14:2867–2882

van der Geest K, de Sherbinin A, Kienberger S, Zommers Z, Sitati A, Roberts E, James R (2018) The impacts of climate change on ecosystem services and resulting losses and damages to people and society. In: Mechler R, Bouwer L, Schinko T, Surminski S, Linnerooth-Bayer J (eds) Loss and damage from climate change. Concepts, methods and policy options. Springer, Cham, pp 221–236

Visser H, Petersen AC, Ligtvoet W (2014) On the relation between weather-related disaster impacts, vulnerability and climate change. Clim Change 125(3–4):461–477

Visser H, Petersen A (2012) Inferences on weather extremes and weather-related disasters: a review of statistical methods. Clim Past 8(1):265–286

Zhang Q, Wu L, Liu Q (2009) Tropical cyclone damages in China: 1983–2006. Bull Am Meteor Soc 90:489–495

Zhou Y, Li N, Wu W, Wu J, Gu X, Ji Z (2013) Exploring the characteristics of major natural disasters in China and their impacts during the past decades. Nat Hazards 69(1):829–843

Chapter 4
The Risk and Policy Space for Loss and Damage: Integrating Notions of Distributive and Compensatory Justice with Comprehensive Climate Risk Management

Thomas Schinko, Reinhard Mechler and Stefan Hochrainer-Stigler

Abstract The Warsaw Loss and Damage Mechanism holds high appeal for complementing actions on climate change adaptation and mitigation, and for delivering needed support for tackling intolerable climate related-risks that will neither be addressed by mitigation nor by adaptation. Yet, negotiations under the UNFCCC are caught between demands for climate justice, understood as compensation, for increases in extreme and slow-onset event risk, and the reluctance of other parties to consider Loss and Damage outside of an adaptation framework. Working towards a jointly acceptable position we suggest an actionable way forward for the deliberations may be based on aligning comprehensive climate risk analytics with distributive and compensatory justice considerations. Our proposed framework involves in a short-medium term, needs-based perspective support for climate risk management beyond countries ability to absorb risk. In a medium-longer term, liability-based perspective we particularly suggest to consider liabilities attributable to anthropogenic climate change and associated impacts. We develop the framework based on principles of need and liability, and identify the policy space for Loss and Damage as composed of curative and transformative measures. Transformative measures, such as managed retreat, have already received attention in discussions on comprehensive climate risk management. Curative action is less clearly defined, and more contested. Among others, support for a climate displacement facility could qualify here. For both sets of measures, risk financing (such as 'climate insurance') emerges as an entry point for further policy action, as it holds potential for both risk management as well as

T. Schinko (✉) · R. Mechler · S. Hochrainer-Stigler
International Institute for Applied Systems Analysis (IIASA), Laxenburg, Austria
e-mail: schinko@iiasa.ac.at

R. Mechler
Vienna University of Economics and Business, Vienna, Austria

R. Mechler et al. (eds.), *Loss and Damage from Climate Change*, Climate Risk Management, Policy and Governance, https://doi.org/10.1007/978-3-319-72026-5_4

compensation functions. To quantify the Loss and Damage space for specific countries, we suggest as one option to build on a risk layering approach that segments risk and risk interventions according to risk tolerance. An application to fiscal risks in Bangladesh and at the global scale provides an estimate of countries' financial support needs for dealing with intolerable layers of flood risk. With many aspects of Loss and Damage being of immaterial nature, we finally suggest that our broad risk and justice approach in principle can also see application to issues such as migration and preservation of cultural heritage.

Keywords Climate justice · Loss and Damage space · Transformative measures Curative measures · Climate risk management

4.1 Tackling Climate-Related Risk in a Contested Policy Context

The 19th conference of the Parties (COP 19) in Warsaw in 2013 saw the establishment of the "Warsaw International Mechanism for Loss and Damage" (UNFCCC 2014). With Article 8 of the Paris Agreement (UNFCCC 2015a) Loss and Damage (L&D) can now be regarded as a sort of "3rd pillar of the work under the UNFCCC in addition to mitigation and adaptation" (Verheyen 2012). The terrain is extremely contested with highly-at risk countries of the global South (such as those of the Alliance of Small Island States, AOSIS) demanding compensation payments for *actual* past, present and future incurred losses and damages due to climate change, while Annex I countries are unwilling to consider such framing and any related actions (see introduction by Mechler et al. 2018; chapters by Calliari et al. 2018; chapter by Wallimann-Helmer et al. 2018). Yet, these parties have shown willingness to support climate change adaptation (CCA) and have supported 'good' risk management over the years to tackle *potential* loss and damage, as evidenced by intense debates on moral responsibility that preceded the approval of the Sendai Framework of Action (SFA) in March 2015. Interestingly, this discussion also saw heated debate as developing countries started to frame their interventions around the common, but differentiated responsibility logic, which has been fundamental for the UNFCCC discussion (Mysiak et al. 2015).

Liability and compensation on the one hand, and support for disaster risk management plus insurance on the other hand remain key negotiation positions for the parties. The divergence in perspectives (see also chapter by James et al. 2018) has led to difficult negotiations for the Executive Committee, which was established in 2015 to support the implementation of an informational work programme. Currently, the work programme somewhat balances the two perspectives without explicitly referring to justice and equity principles (more on the politics behind L&D can be found in the chapter by Calliari et al. 2018).

The science behind climate-related risks relevant for the L&D debate is equally complex. It has made great leaps forward with IPCC's SREX and IPCC's Working Group II reports as well as the UNGAR publications, which discuss climate and non-climate drivers of climate-related risk, the role of uncertainty, the role of attribution and the relevance of climate risk management (CRM) (IPCC 2012, 2013, 2014; UNISDR 2015). Overall, the science shows that, while anthropogenic climate change indeed amplifies intensity, frequency and duration of many hazards, a clear causal link from anthropogenic CO_2 emissions as a driver of risk to quantified socioeconomic risks cannot be established, and that therefore a principle of strict liability cannot (yet) be applied to climate risk (for more details on the frontiers in science regarding L&D see the chapters Bouwer 2018; James et al. 2018 and Lopez et al. 2018). In this context, Mechler and Schinko (2016) proposed a policy framework that builds on recent IPCC framing and evidence on climate-related risk, and Schinko and Mechler (2017) suggested to apply recent insights from CRM, an approach that strives for linking disaster risk reduction (DRR) and CCA agendas under one umbrella (see Schinko et al. 2016) to L&D. The authors argued that a better understanding of climate-related disaster risk and risk management can inform effective action on CCA and point a way forward for L&D policy as well as practice.

This chapter takes this proposition forward to the L&D debate and suggests to find a balance between notions of compensatory and distributive justice. While the compensatory justice notion's scope is distributing responsibilities in light of compensatory reasons and liability, the notion of distributive justice understands L&D as undeserved harm demanding redistribution to even out this unfairness (see also chapter by Wallimann-Helmer et al. 2018; Dellink et al. 2009 on the fair distribution of CCA costs). As a principle of strict liability cannot yet be applied to climate-related risk, we suggest an actionable way forward for the deliberations under the WIM based on the concept of CRM, which allows for an alignment of distributive and compensatory justice over time. The approach involves in a short-medium, needs-based perspective, international support for risk management beyond individual countries' ability to cope with climate-related risk; in a medium-longer term, rights-based perspective, we particularly argue for a strong consideration for liabilities attributable to human induced climate change. The discussion can be integrated towards a principled framework for identifying the space for Loss and Damage composed of curative and transformative measures.

As another key element to operationalise CRM in the context of L&D in practice, we put forward 'risk layering' as an actionable concept of risk and risk management (Mechler et al. 2014). This concept involves identifying efficient and acceptable interventions based on recurrence as well as severity of climate-related risks. For example, for flood risk, this would mean identifying physical flood protection to deal with more frequent events, considering risk financing for infrequent disasters as well as relying on public and international compensation for extreme catastrophes. Risk layering overall points towards considering risk comprehensively as determined by climatic and non-climatic factors as well as considering portfolios of options that manage risks today and in the future.

The further discussion in this chapter is organised as follows: Sect. 4.2 provides a short definition of L&D and aims at identifying major building blocks of a framework for L&D. Section 4.3 takes this discussion forward, and based on our three building blocks identifies the risk and policy space for Loss and Damage. The concept of risk layering based on risk-based modelling is put forward as a method for quantifying the Loss and Damage space in Sect. 4.4, which is followed by some short conclusions.

4.2 Building Blocks of a Principled Framework for Loss and Damage

Many analysts and parties have argued that the WIM is to deal with climate-related risks 'beyond adaptation' when coping capacities of communities and countries are exceededv (see e.g. Verheyen 2012). This is also reflected in what the parties to the UNFCC acknowledge in decision 2/CP.19 when they state that L&D "includes, and in some cases involves more than, that which can be reduced by adaptation" (UNFCC 2014). Beyond this consensus, little common ground exists and particularly ethical aspects have been the elephant in the room ever since the early stages of the debate on L&D. The following discussion aims at overcoming the ethical challenges involved in the discourse by referring to the debate via notions of climate justice and a CRM perspective (see also the chapter by Wallimann-Helmer et al. 2018 for more detailed exploration of the ethical challenges in the debate).

Defining Losses and Damages

Climate-related risks considered in the Loss and Damage discussion are associated with sudden-onset extreme events, such as flooding and cyclones, and slow-onset impacts including sea level rise and melting glaciers (see Fig. 4.1).

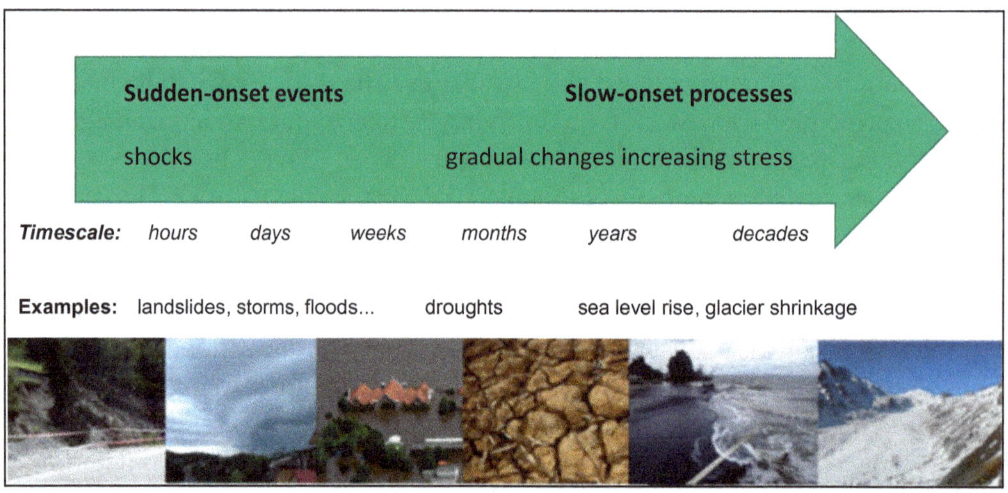

Fig. 4.1 Characterisation of climate-related risks relevant for Loss&Damage. Based on Huggel et al. (2016). *Pictures Source* Wikimedia Commons

Table 4.1 Classifying loss and damage

Avoided	Unavoided	Unavoidable
Avoidable loss and damage that can and will be avoided by climate change mitigation and/or adaptation measures	Avoidable loss and damage that will not be addressed by further mitigation and/or adaption measures, even though the avoidance would be possible. Financial, technical and political constraints as well as case-specific risk preferences narrow down the adaptation space	Loss and damage that cannot be avoided through further mitigation and/or adaptation measures, e.g. loss and damage due to slow onset processes that have kicked-off already, such as sea level rise, and extreme event risk where no adaptation efforts would help preventing the physical impacts

Source Table based on Verheyen and Roderick (2008)

While there is no official definition, losses in this context have been associated with irreversibility, e.g. fatalities from disasters or households stuck in poverty traps post-event, while damages have been referred to as impacts that can be rectified in principle. A useful distinction made that we build on has been between avoided, unavoided and unavoidable loss and damage (Verheyen and Roderick 2008) (see Table 4.1). In the literature, this same distinction has also been discussed with regard to whether climate-related impacts *cannot* or *will not* be addressed by mitigation or adaptation (cf. Mace and Verheyen 2016).

An example for *unavoidable* impacts or loss and damage that *cannot* be addressed either by mitigation or adaptation are extreme event risks where no adaptation efforts would help preventing the physical damage (Verheyen and Roderick 2008). A reason that some adaptation measures *will not be taken* or losses and damages remain *unavoided* is that actors may be subject to socio-economic constraints, especially international financing, and/or implementation constraints, although at least in theory these measures could have been taken (Chambwera and Mohammed 2014). Further constraints to adaptation planning and implementation comprise a lack of technological or knowledge resources and institutional characteristics that impede action.

4.2.1 *Risk Identification: Analytics for Defining Avoidable and Unavoidable Losses and Damages*

Over the last few years, with consequences of climate change becoming visible on all continents and in all oceans (IPCC 2014), assessments of climate change impacts have changed in focus from an initial analysis of the problem to the assessment of actual observed and potential future impacts, and finally, to the consideration of specific risk analytical methods to assess and manage future increases in risks. Originally focussed on incremental risk induced by anthropogenic climate change to identify dangerous levels of global risk (IPCC's five reasons for concerns), a risk perspective has prominently gained traction in recent IPCC reports where climate risk at different scales has been considered to be both shaped by natural climate variability and climate change, as well as by socioeconomic exposure and vulnerability. This evolved framing has opened doors for considering DRR as an important part of climate adaptation and lead to novel considerations organised around CRM, involving the management of total climate-related risk including any current adaptation deficits (Jones et al. 2014).

To inform thinking and action on CRM, a sort of 'climate risk language' has been developed by IPCC's working group II in its 5th assessment report (IPCC 2014). In doing so, working group II has built on IPCC's multiple lines of evidence philosophy, including collating empirical evidence on impacts and risks with information on adaptation options, and the modelling of future risks, as well as using expert judgment. The IPCC report succinctly summarises climate risks and the potential (as well as the limits) for adaptation for key risks and three time steps (present, near- and long-term 2 and 4 °C).

While adaptation constraints or barriers are defined as "factors that make it harder to plan and implement adaptation actions," an adaptation limit is "the point at which an actor's objectives or system's needs cannot be secured from intolerable risks through adaptive actions." (Klein et al. 2014) Furthermore, soft and hard limits to adaptation can be distinguished. The latter concept describes limits where no adaptive actions are possible to avoid intolerable risks, while in the former concept adaptive action might be possible in the future but no measures are currently available (IPCC 2014). The distinction between barriers and limits to adaptation as well as between soft and hard limits is coherent in theory, yet many difficulties might arise in operationalising it in practice. What determines when a limit is breached and who decides what the limits are? For example, Fig. 4.2 visualizes risks from sea level rise and high-water events as well as the corresponding adaptation potential in Small Island States. Building on the identification of key hazard drivers, sea level rise and cyclones interacting with high tide events, it finds the level of risk, essentially for coastal flooding, to currently be at medium levels and increasing with future warming to very high levels, particularly for the 4 °C warming scenario. While the risk bar, which is the product of the IPCCC's meta-analysis of available literature on climate-related risks in SIDS, shows overall risk (given adaptation actions taken), this visualization also teases out the potential for additional adaptation efforts in terms of further reducing risk.

IPCC's analysis applied to key world regions shows that the potential for adaptation is large for many regions and suggests that many risks are avoidable (although actions are not yet fully implemented thus defining a soft adaptation limit). Yet, for some regions and risks (particularly in natural systems) and at higher levels of warming, limits to adaptation are found to be reached, and these climate-related risks may become unavoidable (see chapters by Handmer and Nalau 2018; Haque et al. 2018; van der Geest et al. 2018; Landauer and Juhola 2018). An example is the bleaching of tropical coral reefs beyond 1.5/2 and 4 °C, where no options for adaptation exist (hence defining a hard limit to adaptation) (Magrin et al. 2014).

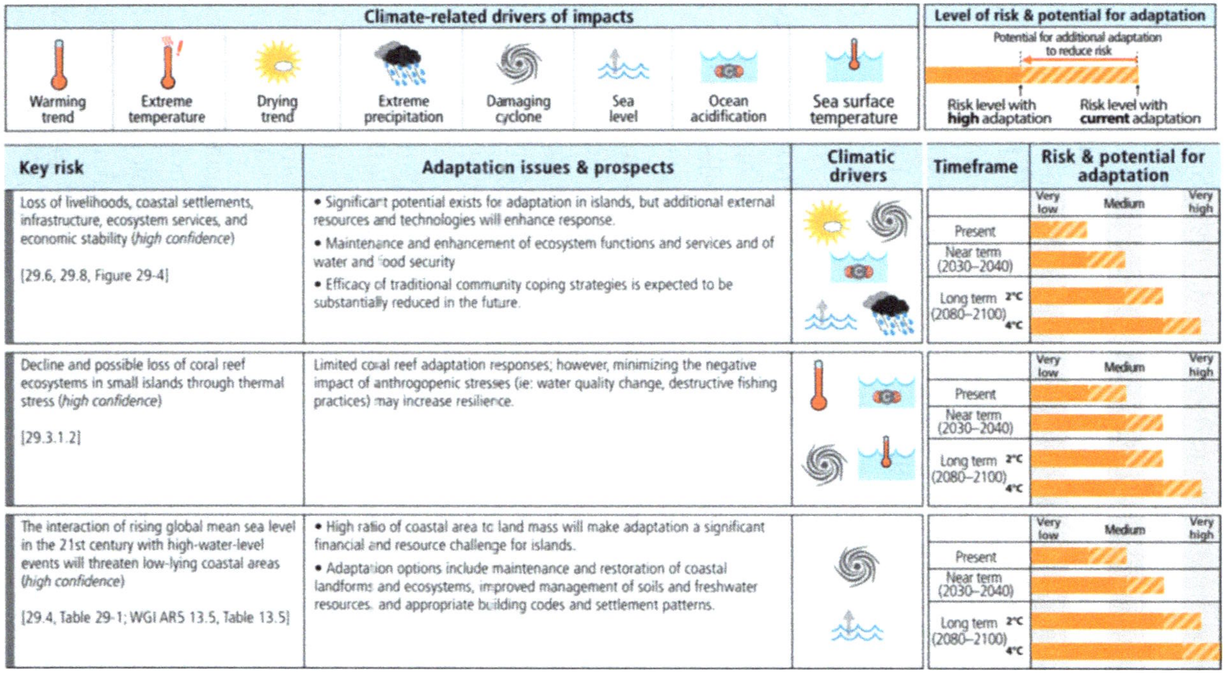

Fig. 4.2 Selected key risks and potential for adaptation for small islands. *Source* Nurse et al. (2014), p. 1635

4.2.2 *Climate Attribution of Unavoidable Losses and Damages: Establishing a Role for Climate Justice*

Ethical considerations in the form of questions regarding justice and fairness have played a key role in the policy and academic discourse on climate change (see e.g. Brown et al. 2006; Gardiner 2004a, b, 2006; Jamieson 1992, 2001, 2005; Ott 2004; Posner and Weisbach 2010; Shue 1992, 1993, 1999; Singer 2002, 2006; Vanderheiden 2008; chapter by Wallimann-Helmer 2018) ever since the beginning of the UNFCCC process, prominently exemplified by the principle of common but differentiated responsibilities in the Rio Declaration (United Nations 1992, Article 3.1).

For climate change mitigation and adaptation the discourse has largely circled around distributive justice (Grasso 2007; Posner and Weisbach 2010). In the mitigation domain different principles of distributive justice, applicable to the sharing of mitigation burdens have been discussed (Klinsky and Dowlatabadi 2009; Vanderheiden 2008). Due to inertia in the climatic system, no matter how effective global GHG mitigation efforts turn out to be, humanity will be faced with risks due to climate change that have direct and indirect (e.g. through ecosystem services) impacts on human welfare and which will require substantial adaptation efforts (IPCC 2012, 2014). The justice debate in the adaptation domain has thus centred on the question of how the costs (and benefits) of adaption should be distributed across countries (Adger et al. 2006; Dellink et al. 2009; Paavola and Adger 2006).

With the L&D debate, another notion of climate justice has now formally entered the international climate policy scene: compensatory justice. Basically two kinds of justice are especially applicable in the context of L&D (see chapter by Wallimann-Helmer et al. 2018). Forward-looking contexts are concerned with distributive justice, especially when distributing the risks of damages that cannot be adapted to. Backward-looking contexts are concerned with compensatory justice, especially in legal or procedural attributions of responsibility and liability. Compensatory justice suggests that it is those agents who primarily caused climate change who should compensate the agents which are experiencing losses and damages due to climate change without having substantially contributed to the problem themselves. This in turn implies that the agents who are not responsible for climate change are given a right for compensation by the agents who are found responsible and hence liable for particular risks that climate change increases the likelihood for (i.e. the outcome). Distributive justice (based on the ability to pay principle) suggests that it is those agents who are able or have the capacity to pay for managing residual risks should bear the lion's share of the costs, and those agents in greatest need for financial assistance should be allocated the bulk of the benefits, i.e. the resources globally available.

The IPCC has attributed trends in slow onset climate change processes and many climate extremes to anthropogenic greenhouse gas emissions (IPCC 2012). Moreover, climate model results evaluated in the latest IPCC report show peak windstorm velocity of tropical storms is set to increase, rainfall to become more volatile and sea levels to rise as ice caps melt, altogether leading to even more severe adverse impacts of climate change in the future (IPCC 2013). These findings imply an explicit and moral obligation for enhanced action on managing climate-related risks. Different principles of distributive justice, such as capacity to pay or greatest needs, may be applied to share the associated costs among agents, a principle which indeed the international community has built on as it supports the most vulnerable countries[1] (Posner and Weisbach 2010). In addition, climate change also brings along a need for considering issues of compensatory justice due to the unequal distribution of historical and current emissions as the root cause of global warming, the adverse distribution of impacts of climate change between the global North and the global South, and the fact that climate change is projected to lead to unavoidable and potentially irrecoverable losses and damages, such as of low-lying islands in the wake of strong sea-level rise (Roser et al. 2015).

Climate science has been making great progress in climate attribution research even with regard to specific events (see chapter by James et al. 2018). Recent research has shown a significant human element in mega events (Trenberth et al. 2015) such as superstorms Sandy in 2013 in the US, the Australian heatwave in 2013 (Herring et al. 2014), the 2016 drought in Kenia (WWA 2017). Mann et al. (2017) found that amplified arctic warming, influenced by climate change, makes temperature patterns (so called "planetary waves") that cause heatwaves, droughts and floods across Europe, North America and Asia more likely. Yet, causally linking anthropogenic emissions to extreme weather events and eventually to risks on people and property has not conclusively been achieved and will remain complex, as risks from climate-related events are shaped by many factors, including climate variability, rising exposure of people and assets as well as socio-economic vulnerability dynamics (Stone et al. 2013). While basic evidence to link anthropogenic GHG emissions to climate impacts is there (Schaller et al. 2016), making the concrete, enforceable case will remain much harder (Huggel et al. 2015; chapter by Bouwer 2018). Hence, and as argued above, the causal attribution and strict liability principle cannot be invoked currently (e.g. for legal action). Nevertheless, we suggest it is kept in the background, when decisions are made in the meanwhile based on principles of distributive justice. In the medium to longer-term, as evidence from climate change attribution studies potentially increases, we argue for a gradual integration of the compensatory justice dimension.

[1]Current international support for the most vulnerable countries is primarily based on implied responsibility and moral duty, as well as humanitarian reasons. Donor countries are currently not acting on explicit responsibilities.

To this effect, again, IPCC is the scientific authority with its methodological framework for detection and attribution. This systematic approach first focusses on detecting any trend in changes of key variables, then seeks to attribute those to climate change (e.g. change in local temperature and other system variables) (Cramer et al. 2014). As one example, Fig. 4.3 shows a summary application of the framework in terms of specifying the degree of confidence in the detection of observed impacts of climate change versus the degree of confidence in attribution to climate change drivers for tropical small islands. While, for example, it finds for "greater rates of sea level rise relative to global means" (a coastal system impact) both very high confidence levels of detection and attribution, it detects trends at very high confidence levels for tightly associated impacts in human systems (environmental degradation and casualties), albeit only at low levels of confidence, as risks in human systems are importantly shaped by socio-economic vulnerability and exposure.

4.2.3 Risk Evaluation: Considering Risk Preference and Risk Tolerance for Identifying Soft and Hard Adaptation Limits

Establishing risk as the overarching concept and metric naturally leads to addressing the question of risk coping or risk preference. While risk identification assesses risks in monetary and/or non-monetary terms, risk evaluation, involving socioeconomic analysis, leads to the notion of risk preference and risk tolerance. The process of risk evaluation examines agents' (households, private and public sectors) ability to respond to risk, also termed risk tolerance. Economics has distinguished risk preference around risk aversion, neutrality and risk loving (Eeckhoudt et al. 2005). Risk analysis, e.g. Dow et al. (2013), building on Klinke and Renn (2002), conceptually break risk tolerance down into acceptable—no formal risk reduction interventions necessary; tolerable—risk reduction measures are necessary and implemented depending on resources available; and intolerable risks-risk cannot be taken on, i.e. action is required irrespective of costs but often no further action is possible, thus essentially defining risks that exceed the limits of adaptation (see Fig. 4.4).

Following such framing, one could argue that, backed up by considerable evidence (UNFCCC 2015b) as well as heuristics, the intolerable risk space (globally) with regard to 'dangerous interference with the climate system,' as put down in Article 2 of the UNFCCC, has been determined by the Paris agreement as starting beyond 1.5 °C of average global warming. The 1.5 °C line is a political compromise based on intense negotiations and normative discourse, which was informed by science. It is not a 'hard' system boundary and already today, with good levels of confidence, the IPCC has identified many communities and countries as facing substantial stress from climate change-exacerbated impacts on agriculture in Africa (high confidence), sea surge in small islands states (high confidence) and riverine flooding in Bangladesh (medium confidence) (IPCC 2014).

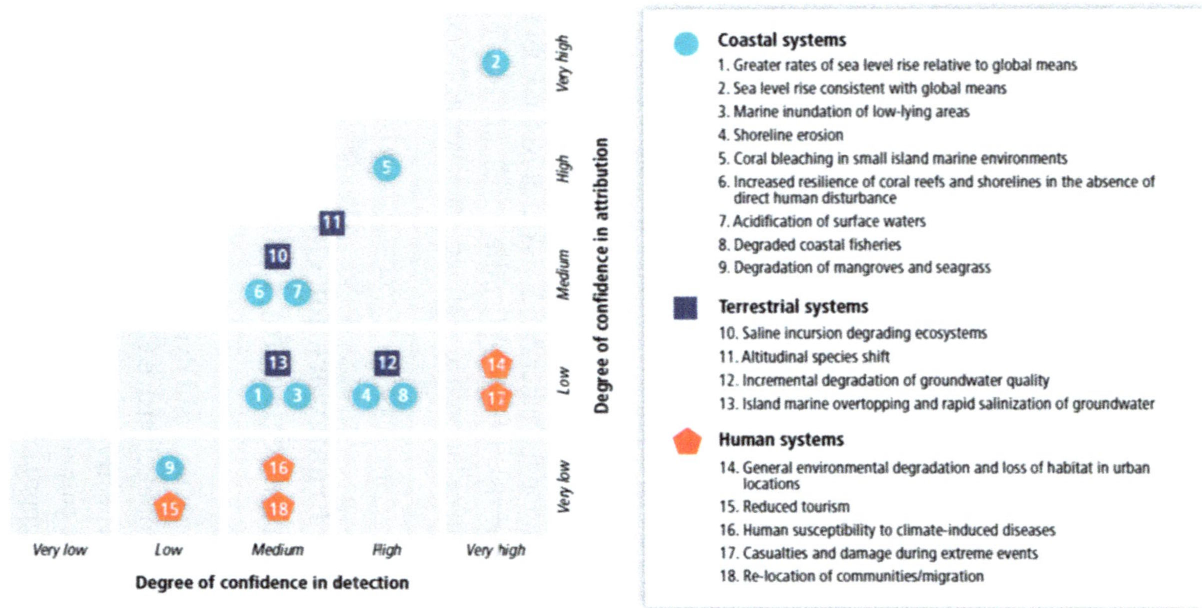

Fig. 4.3 Degree of confidence in the detection of observed impacts of climate change versus degree of confidence in attribution to climate change drivers for tropical small islands. *Source* Nurse et al. (2014, p. 1627)

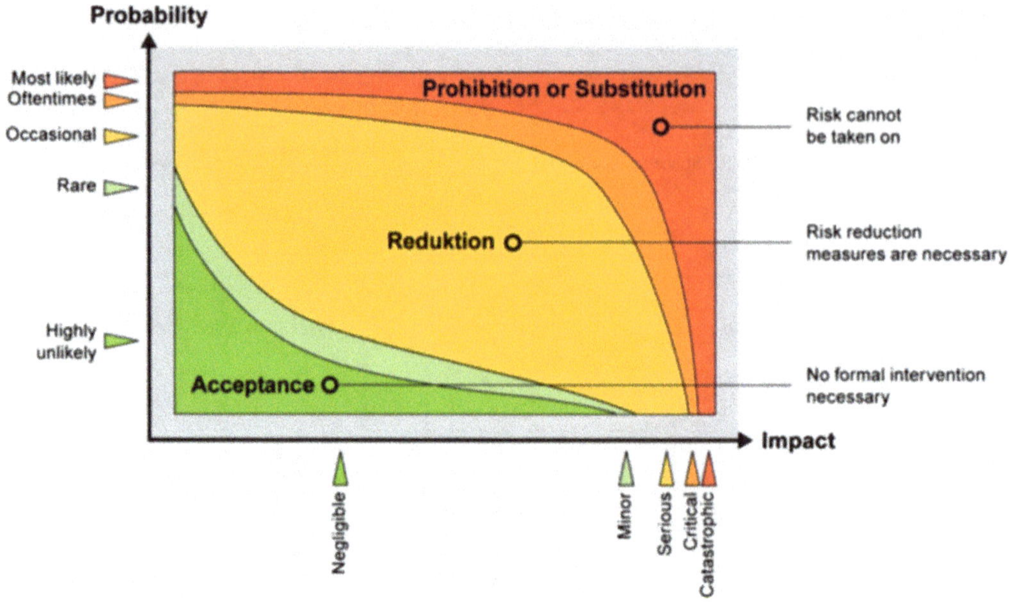

Fig. 4.4 Framing risk acceptance and (in)tolerance. *Source* Klinke and Renn (2002)

Eventually, what constitutes acceptable, tolerable, and intolerable risk can be defined in a subjective/normative or technical/science-based way. Risk tolerance is strongly determined by social, cultural, and economic factors and often requires subjective judgment (Dow et al. 2013). The IPCC Working Group II in 2014, for example, used expert judgement for determining levels of low, medium and high risk in its regional risk assessments. On the other hand, risk analysis has developed analytical procedures for segregating risk according to differential ability to bear risk to which risk policy instruments can be tailored to - termed risk layering (Mechler et al. 2014).

4.3 An Actionable Framework for Outlining the Risk and Policy Options Space for Loss and Damage

Overall, we argue for a practical and dynamic policy approach to the L&D debate based on the concept of comprehensive CRM and balancing the ethical principles of compensatory justice and distributive justice (see also Dellink et al. 2009, discussing a similar approach for the case of CCA). Figure 4.5 conceptualizes a dynamic needs and liability-based CRM approach to the L&D debate. It summarizes the two different notions of justice (compensatory and distributive) as linked to the different political principles (capacity and needs, liability and rights) on which policies tackling residual

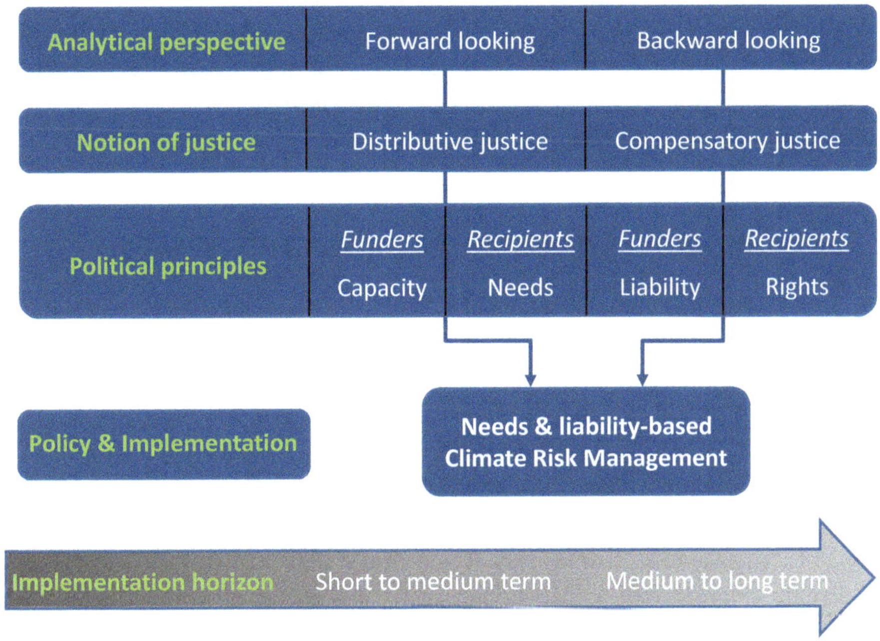

Fig. 4.5 Elements of the dynamic principled approach to Loss and Damage. *Source* Own Figure

risks in the domain of L&D are based. Given the present difficulties of attributing climate related losses and damages to (1) anthropogenic climate change and further (2) to certain agents, we propose taking on a distributive justice perspective for the short to medium-term. We argue for supporting comprehensive CRM based on the capacity to pay principle in those countries with the greatest need, identified, e.g. by a country level risk assessment based on risk layering (such as presented in Sect. 4.4), and focusing on both national and local levels.

Particularly in the medium to longer-term, as evidence from climate change attribution studies is bound to increase, we see a strong consideration of a compensatory justice dimension into the practical policy approach, by taking on (in addition) a liability-based perspective. This is important given the evidence on climate impacts and the fact that compensation will remain a central normative aspect in the climate negotiations and has to be dealt with in order to establish healthy long-term international relations, which themselves are a precondition for implementing just and effective responses to global climate change (Thompson and Otto 2015).

Naturally, the question emerges whether and how the three building blocks—risk identification, risk evaluation, and climate attribution and justice–which have been discussed in the previous section, can now be brought together and how to fill the principled approach outlined here with life to identify and visualise the Loss and Damage space? Our discussion builds on the policy proposal made by Mechler and

Schinko (2016) that considers key contributions from these fields of research and synthesizes respective insights into a visual representation of, what we consider, constitutes the risk and policy space for Loss and Damage.

4.3.1 The Loss and Damage Risk and Options Space

Synthesising existing literature, in particular building on IPCC assessments and the UNFCCC stocktake that led to defining the Paris ambition of 1.5 °C respectively 2 °C of change as the upper global warming limit (UNFCCC 2015b), the summary chart (Fig. 4.6) shows stylised past, present, and future climate-related risk levels and corresponding CRM portfolios for a given community or country (here again shown via the example of the Small Island States, whose risk profile has been presented in Fig. 4.2) facing severe climate risk today and expecting further increases in risk due to climate change (the socio-economic component is kept constant for ease of presentation, which does not affect our argumentation). In line with the three cornerstones presented above, the key foci are to (i) consider total climate-related risk incl. the adaptation deficit, (ii) include risk preference in terms of acceptable, tolerable and intolerable risk, (iii) consider risk of irreversible loss.

The options portfolio comprises actual and potential cumulative action in terms of CRM, implemented as part of separate or synergistic efforts related to DRR and climate adaptation. It is important to note here that while IPCC (2012) highlights the need to look at all drivers of risk and to synergistically manage those, in the context of climate anthropogenic climate change is at the centre of interest. The IPCC (2012) has suggested that "Effective climate risk management portfolios integrate sound risk analysis, risk reduction, risk financing, response and opportunities for learning." (see also chapter by Lopez et al. 2018; chapter by Botzen et al. 2018). How can those concepts be further operationalised at scale? As one example, Box 4.1 presents a comprehensive CRM framework developed for the case of informing Indian state and national-level policymakers, which may act as a blueprint for taking action on climate-related losses and damages.

Comprehensive risk management and policy can be broken down to comprise incremental (e.g., raising dikes), fundamental (e.g., floodplains instead of dikes) and transformative (e.g., voluntary migration from floodplains) interventions (see also Mechler and Schinko 2016). Accepting this stylised visualisation (Fig. 4.6), the options space for Loss and Damage may be determined as follows: (i) with climate change amplifying risk, there is a legitimate case for international action in the *Loss and Damage transformative risk space* to push risk down from intolerable to tolerable levels complementing the DRR and adaptation policy domains; (ii) the *Loss and*

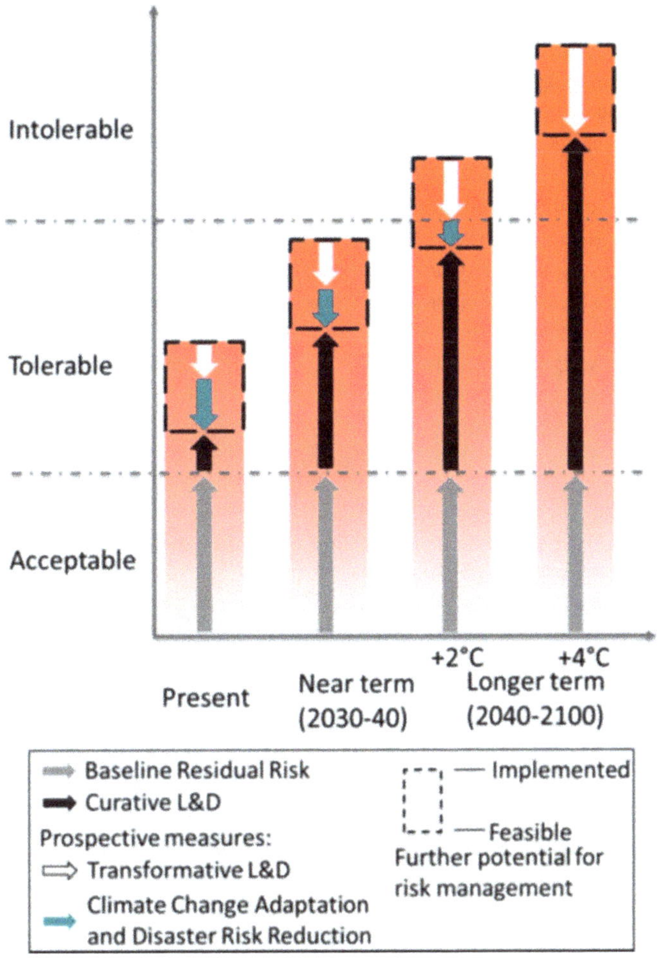

Fig. 4.6 Identifying the risk and policy options space for Loss and Damage. *Source* Own Figure based on Mechler and Schinko (2016)

Damage curative space opens up when technical and feasible risk reduction becomes limited over time with risk increasing, e.g. sea level rise leading to irreversible and unavoidable loss of land and induced migration, limiting the societally negotiated pathway, and foreclosing development opportunities (people being pushed to migrate from their homelands).

Box 4.1 A Climate Risk Management (CRM) framework for India

On behalf of the German Federal Ministry for Economic Cooperation and Development (BMZ), the German development assistance agency GIZ with partners developed a CRM framework that can be utilised to assess climate-related risks and identify management measures at various scales. In close cooperation with IIASA, KPMG and IIT Delhi, a six step process operationalising the CRM process at scale was developed (Fig. 4.7). The CRM process is embedded in a learning framework, which allows for updating decisions over time with mounting evidence and insights. Traditional DRR and CCA policy typically operates via incremental adjustments to existing management approaches. While such incremental learning is important in the short term, climate-related (residual) risks require a particular focus on locally-applicable bottom-up techniques for understanding risks and risk management interventions. Such techniques are, for example, Vulnerability Capacity Assessments (VCAs) and community-led focus groups. In the face of financial, technical and institutional constraints, fundamental and transformative learning is needed. These advanced learning loops aim at achieving the required adjustments of management processes at national and subnational levels in order to be able to deal with increasing risk over time.

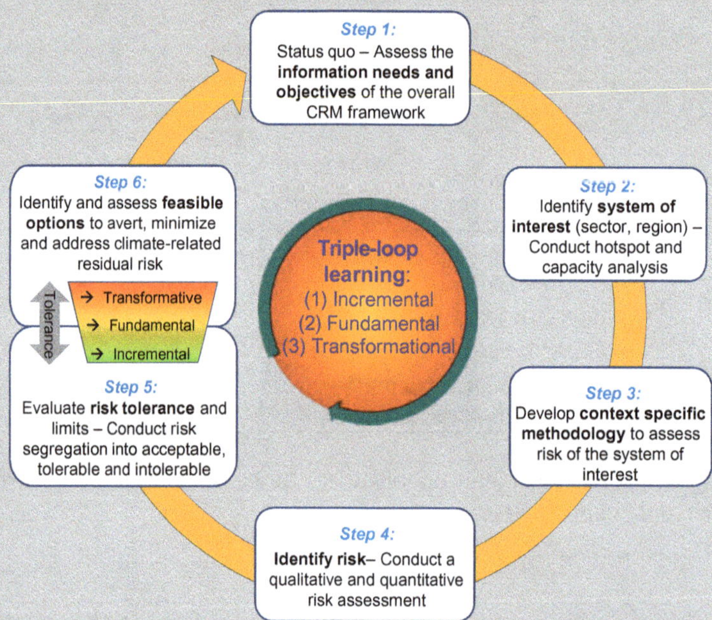

Fig. 4.7 Climate risk management (CRM) six step approach. *Source* GIZ et al. (2018 unpublished)

An exemplary application of the comprehensive framework to Tamil Nadu in India (cyclone and flood risk) served to test the methodological approach and glean its usefulness at state and local levels. The application showed that risks are on the rise due to climate and socio-economic drivers, and that risks are significantly affecting key objectives of households and the public sector. Furthermore, risk responses by farmers and households are largely of incremental, yet increasingly also of fundamental and importantly transformative nature. Governmental DRR and CCA institutions work well within their remit to provide incremental assistance, yet are usually not charged to deal with fundamental and transformative interventions. The assessment revealed that the risk management policy options space needs more attention and further deliberation with those at risk and in charge to deploy interventions with public support from state, national to international levels.

Transformative Measures

With sea level rise alone threatening to displace 72–187 million people by 2100 (Nicholls et al. 2011), transformative measures are increasingly needed, such as offering alternative livelihoods (e.g., switching from smallholder farming in coastal areas to services in cities) and assisting with voluntary migration, as compared with curative support for forced migration, which we discuss below (se also Mechler and Schinko 2016). Hino et al. (2017) find that managed retreat—"the strategic relocation of structures or abandonment of land"—is a potentially important transformational option when limits to structural protection or other adaptation measures to manage climate-related risks are reached. It is important to note that even though considered transformational, managed retreat is confronted by its own set of case-specific complexities and challenges, whether political, social, or legal (Hino et al. 2017).

Curative Measures

The space for curative measures is much less clear, and has not seen a lot of attention owing to the fact that it overlaps largely with demands for compensation, which have been ruled out from the Paris agreement, and because of existing limitations in the causal attribution of losses and damages from slow-onset processes and sudden-onset extreme events to anthropogenic climate change. The most advanced ideas in the context of curative measures have been articulated with regard to support for involuntary climate-induced displacement and forced migration. A climate displacement facility is being discussed under the WIM and proposals for approaches to deal with climate-induced displacement have been made, such as the Nansen Principles on Climate Change and Displacement (Nansen Conference 2011), and the Peninsula Principles on Climate Displacement Within States (Displacement Solutions 2015). Yet, concrete ideas for operationalisation are largely lacking.

For the contested discourse around international compensation for climate-related impacts exacerbated by climate change, only few concrete options have been put on the table so far. Sprinz and Bünau (2013), for example, find that no convincing mechanism has yet been found to compensate for climate-related impacts. The authors present a conceptual outline for a voluntary, internationally organized compensation fund and highlight the need for specialized, independent climate courts. At the national level, however, the establishment of national mechanisms to address climate induced losses and damages is being discussed, e.g. for Bangladesh. The chapter by Haque et al. (2018) suggests to make use of a reserve fund of approximately USD

140 million accumulated by unspent finance from the Bangladesh Climate Change Trust Fund in order to deal with those climate-related impacts not tackled by conventional DRR or CCA measures. This would also include ex-post compensation for losses and damages triggered by climate change induced slow onset events, salinity intrusion and increased intensity of cyclones.

4.4 Identifying the Space for Loss and Damage: An Application

Science can provide insights into defining the Loss and Damage risk space and associated policy response options. As indicated by the list of building blocks for a framework outlined above and also demonstrated by other chapters in this volume (see particularly chapters by Lopez et al. 2018; Botzen et al. 2018; Serdeczny 2018), science for L&D has to essentially be transdisciplinary and multifaceted. This requires input by, among others, climatology, meteorology, ethics and philosophy, geography, risk science and social sciences including economics. We proceed with an application building on transdisciplinary analysis and focused on one aspect, identifying fiscal risk tolerance with respect to managing climate-related extreme events.

4.4.1 From Risk Identification to Risk Evaluation: Risk Layering and Risk Tolerance

Climate risk assessments generally go through a structured process, starting with the identification of risks based on qualitative and quantitative methodologies. Risk identification is then followed by risk evaluation for determining risk tolerance, as the next step in the structured process, which, again, can build on various methods, such as eliciting stated risk preferences via focus groups, studying behaviour in markets to reveal preference, or use risk and economic modelling. Box 4.2 reports on the political decision-making process for defining acceptable and unacceptable risks for accident risks in Switzerland. Risk analytics has provided the scientific basis for the political decision in that case, but has tended to only matter up to a certain point. After all, the delimiters of acceptable to not acceptable risk areas have mostly been determined by the political process.

Box 4.2 Defining acceptable and unacceptable risks for accident risks in Switzerland

This example distinguishes different levels of accident risk acceptance as specified in the Swiss Industrial Accident Regulation, building on various inputs and procedures. The acceptable risk area demarcated in green and aggregating small risks (low extent of damage) is defined and regulated by specifications made in the Swiss Labour Act. Beyond the transition zone (marked in yellow), risks are considered not acceptable (catastrophic, large-scale accidents) and identified in red. Here it is the (national-level) political decision-making process, building on analytics, but also other inputs, that determine risk areas as (non) acceptable, thus putting emphasis on rolling out a proper democratically-legitimated process for managing risks and appropriate risk management actions.

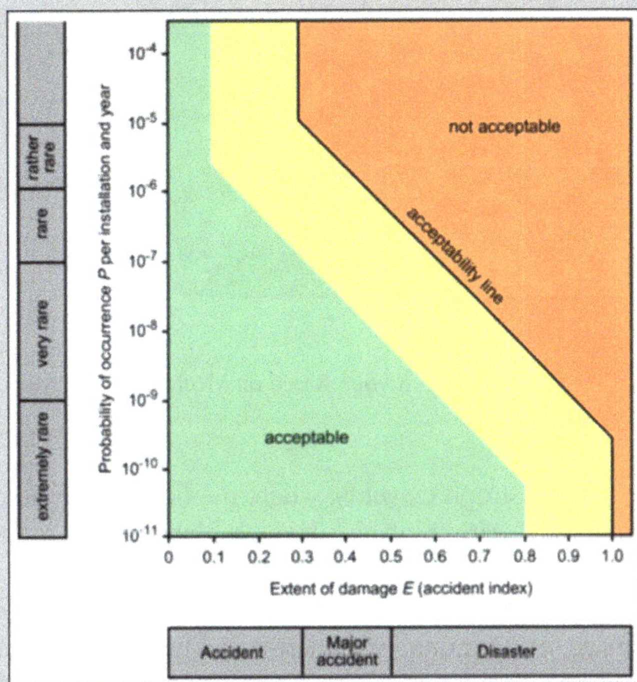

Fig. 4.8 Defining acceptable and unacceptable risks for accident risks in Switzerland. *Source* WBGU (1998)

As one promising analytical component of a CRM approach, the concept and practice of *risk layering* has seen increasing attention (Mechler et al. 2014; Mechler and Schinko 2016; Schinko and Mechler 2016). Risk layering involves segmenting risk into acceptable, tolerable and intolerable layers and allocating roles and responsibilities to reduce, finance or accept risks. We suggest to build on risk analytics in terms of a risk portfolio approach that breaks down total risk (as determined by probability and impacts/losses) into 4 distinct layers: (i) a layer for frequent risks for action on risk reduction, (ii) a medium layer of risks, where risk reduction will be combined with insurance and other risk-financing instruments that transfer residual risk; (iii)

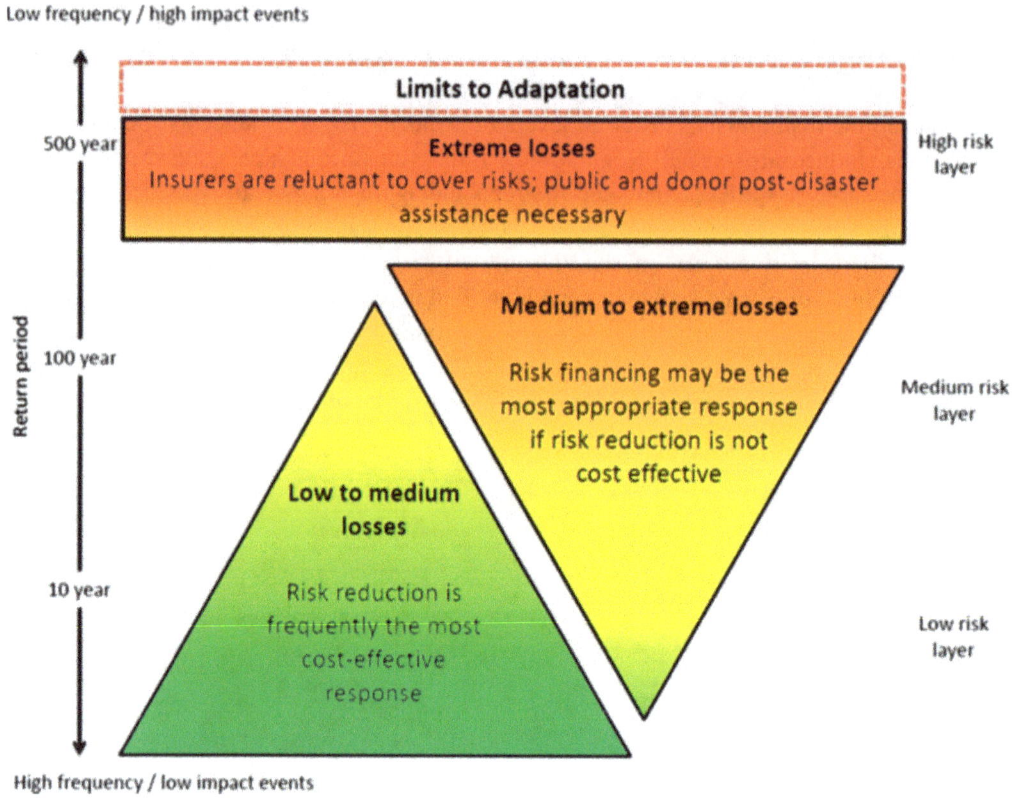

Fig. 4.9 Conceptualising risk layering. *Source* Based on Mechler et al. (2014)

a layer for infrequent catastrophic events, where public and international assistance is decisive, and (iv) a very rare, high risk layer, which will require assistance from international climate funding sources (see Fig. 4.9).

We argue that risk layering can be a valuable tool to define the Loss and Damage risk and options space for economic or market-based losses and damages, which can be quantified and costed. Employing a climate risk lens, a focus on loss distributions is appropriate as it provides information on the whole risk spectrum and not only on expected or average losses. Average annual (or expected) losses may differ greatly compared to potential losses of low probability events, e.g. for Bangladesh average losses associated with cyclone hazard are estimated to be around 0.5 billion USD, while a 500 year event is gauged to cause losses 40 times higher (UNISDR 2015). In addition, the risk layering approach can help determine the increase or decrease of climate-related risks, and disentangle the increase according to the underlying drivers of risk—hazard, exposure and vulnerability. This has important implications for the prioritisation of instruments within the options space.

As one example, Fig. 4.10 provides results from an application of the risk layering approach to the fiscal implications of flood risk in Bangladesh, the dominant climate-related risk in the country (based on Mechler et al. 2014; Mechler and Bouwer 2015; Hochrainer-Stigler et al. 2016) (for a more detailed discussion of the case of Bangladesh see the chapter by Haque et al. 2018). The quantitative risk assessment

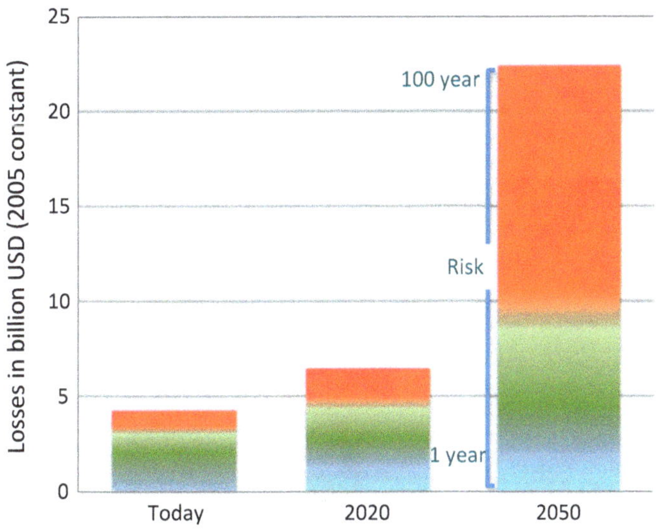

Fig. 4.10 Understanding risk and risk layering for the case of flood risk in Bangladesh. *Note* The different colours represent acceptable, tolerable and intolerable risk layers ranging from high probability, low impact events (1 year) to low probability, high impact events (100 years). *Source* Adapted from Mechler et al. (2014)

carried out with the IIASA CATSIM model (see Hochrainer-Stigler et al. 2014) builds on hydrological and socio-economic modelling and estimates increasing flood risk for 1 to 100 year events for present, 2020 to 2050 periods. A 100 year event today would cost about USD 4.7 billion, and increase in 2050 to more than USD 20 billion absent additional risk management measures. Much of the burden (infrastructure losses and support for households and business) generally may end up with the public sector and we find fiscal risk tolerance, determined by the country's capacity to absorb risk by national means and international assistance, is already today exceeded at events with a return period of less than 25 years (the area shaded in red). This fiscal risk threshold is expected to move down to even lower return periods over time and the costs are estimated to strongly increase, for which national (the planned compensation fund) and international funding will be required to pick up the burden. Risk layering thus not only helps to identify appropriate measures for tackling different layers of climate-related risk, but also provides an opportunity to investigate how risk layers will change in the future and what portions of risk may eventually become intolerable.

The logic of risk layering can be expanded to global analysis, which may be used to identify countries that are in need of international support for transformative and curative CRM measures. Figure 4.11 shows results from such an exercise identifying fiscal risk tolerance as the gap return period in financial resources available. Countries shaded in red face such instances of fiscal intolerance at particularly low return period events.

The fiscal risk evaluation methodology, while only covering certain aspects of the problem, enables analysts to determine global funding arrangements to support countries that face risks beyond their financial tolerance and may assist the international community in prioritising investment decisions with regard to transformative and curative CRM measures. Such a fund may build on available sovereign risk pooling arrangements in the Caribbean, Pacific, Africa and the Indian oceans (see chapters by Linnerooth-Bayer et al. 2018 and Schaefer et al. 2018).

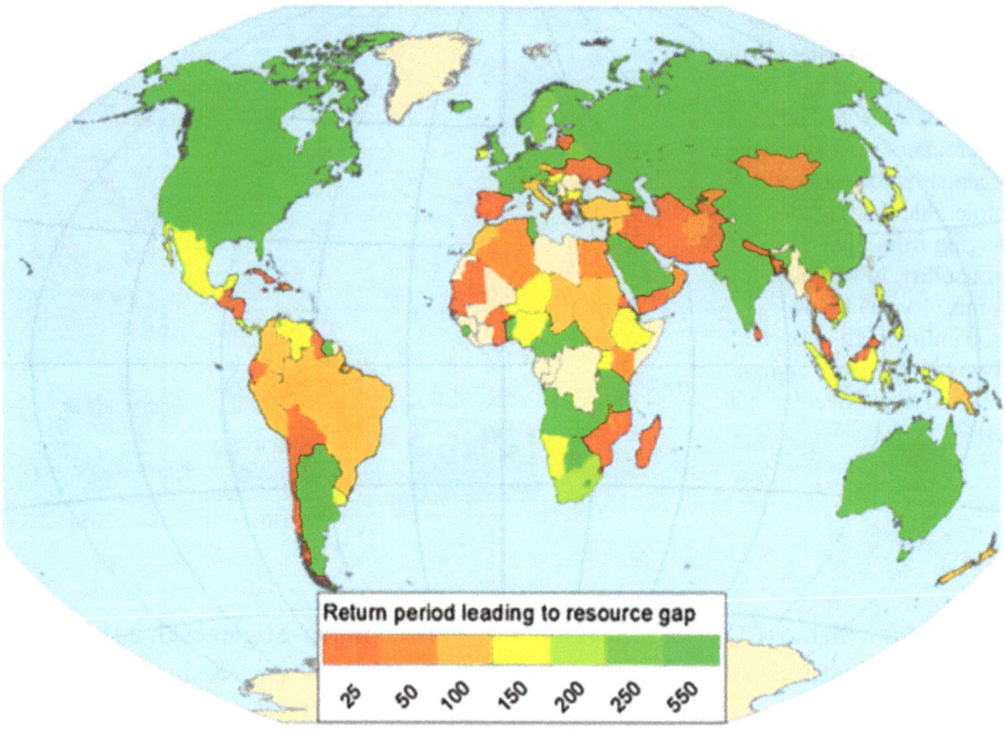

Fig. 4.11 Global map identifying high-level risks. *Note* The lower the return period the higher are the chances of a gap event. *Source* Based on Hochrainer-Stigler et al. (2014)

Overall, a risk-layering plus risk tolerance-based approach supports the integrated assessment of risk portfolios across global to country, down to local levels—a feature that is beneficial especially in the context of identifying the Loss and Damage risk space and corresponding implementation measures. As mentioned throughout, decision makers, communities or societies will differ in their understanding of what constitutes acceptable, tolerable and intolerable risk. Thus, risk layers will differ according to decisions at stake, context, and stakeholders involved.

4.5 Implications for Research and Policy

The L&D debate has been contested among those advocating compensation for *actual* losses and damages, versus those that have been suggesting support should be extended for tackling *potential* losses and damages, most prominently as part of further employing disaster risk management and climate insurance applications. Our discussion proposed an actionable way forward for the deliberations based on a broad interpretation and conceptualisation of comprehensive CRM, importantly aligning and balancing notions of distributive and compensatory justice. The suggested approach involves in a short-medium term, needs-based perspective, support for risk management actions, which fall beyond countries' ability to prevent and absorb risk; these actions to be supported internationally would largely comprise of fundamental and transformative risk management interventions. Particularly in a medium-longer term liability-based perspective, we emphasise consideration for liabilities attributable to climate change. As we suggest, these considerations can be integrated into a policy-oriented framework, which identifies the policy space for Loss and Damage as composed of curative and transformative measures.

Transformative measures exhibit substantial overlap with DRR and adaptation agendas, yet focus on high-level risks. This set of measures is seeing attention, mostly focussed on climate insurance (e.g. the G7 Initiative; GIZ 2015; Schäfer et al. 2018). Many analysts and advocates, however, see a need for broadening this debate towards comprehensive CRM, so that risk prevention and preparedness are better integrated and linked with risk financing. The curative action space is less clearly defined, while heavily contested. Beyond the calls for compensation for actual losses and damages, which are currently ruled out in the Paris agreement, the set-up of and support for a climate displacement facility has been in the spotlight and may qualify as an action item in this space.

Common to both sets of measures, and discussed as a working element of the agenda, is a need for committing finance for the genuine implementation of the WIM. Such commitments to finance may have a prospective and transformative function in terms of financial support for CRM, encompassing financing for climate insurance premium subsidies, reserve capital and technical assistance. The curative function involves finance for dealing ex-post with unavoided and unavoidable loss and damage, on top of mechanisms that deal with avoidable risk. An important aspect to emphasise is that our proposed principled approach, ideally to be linked to international commitments to support, can serve as a sort of "canary in the coal mine" where risks, costs and implications detected now and modelled for later time horizons at local to regional risk management scales can help to inform the ultimate remit of the UNFCCC, which is to harness collective global action for "avoiding dangerous interference with the climate system" (United Nations 1992).

There is analytical and modelling expertise that can be employed to identify risks 'beyond adaptation' and to define the Loss and Damage risk and options space. We argued that risk layering can be a valuable tool—at least for market-based losses and damages. Non-economic or non-market based impacts may require alternative assessment tools. When taking a climate risk lens, probabilistic loss distributions are useful to provide information about the whole risk spectrum beyond expected or average losses only. The risk layering approach can also provide support for determining any increase (or decrease) of climate-related risks, and disentangle the contributing drivers of risk—hazard, exposure and vulnerability, which has important consequences for the prioritisation of instruments within the options space. It is important to note, however, that disentangling anthropogenic and natural drivers of risk is still not conclusively possible.

Our application of a risk analytical approach, comprising risk layering and risk-based probabilistic modelling to the case of flood risk in Bangladesh and at the global level represents a methodological approach for determining countries' financial needs for dealing with intolerable risk layers. Notwithstanding the fact that our example dealt with monetary losses, we hold that, with many aspects of being of immaterial nature, our broad risk and justice approach, with a different set of methods and tools, is also applicable to issues such as migration and preservation of cultural heritage. Such and other assessments at national as well as at regional and global scales may provide the basis for tackling the salient follow-up question towards the genuine implementation of the WIM around justice aspects: who will provide (receive) which share of the required levels of financial support, and based on which burden-sharing principle? After all, if any of the options discussed here and as part of the WIM process are to see acceptance and implementation, they need strong embedding in a framework based on principles of justice.

References

Adger WN, Huq S, Paavola J, Mace MJ (2006) Fairness in adaptation to climate change. MIT Press, Cambridge, MA

Botzen W, Bouwer LM, Scussolini P, Kuik O, Haasnoot M, Lawrence J, Aerts JCJH (2018) Integrated disaster risk management and adaptation. In: Mechler R, Bouwer L, Schinko T, Surminski S, Linnerooth-Bayer J (eds) Loss and damage from climate change. Concepts, methods and policy options. Springer, Cham, pp 287–315

Bouwer LM (2018) Observed and projected impacts from extreme weather events: implications for loss and damage. In: Mechler R, Bouwer L, Schinko T, Surminski S, Linnerooth-Bayer J (eds) Loss and damage from climate change. Concepts, methods and policy options. Springer, Cham, place, pp 63–82

Brown D, Lemons J, Tuana N (2006) The importance of expressly integrating ethical analysis into climate change policy formation. Clim Policy 5(5):549–552

Calliari E, Surminski S, Mysiak J (2018) The politics of (and behind) the UNFCCC's loss and damage mechanism. In: Mechler R, Bouwer L, Schinko T, Surminski S, Linnerooth-Bayer J (eds) Loss and damage from climate change. Concepts, methods and policy options. Springer, Cham, pp 155–178

Chambwera M, Mohammed K (2014) 7. Economic analysis of a community-based adaptation project in Sudan. In: Ensor J, Berger R, Huq S (eds) Community-based adaptation to climate change. Practical Action Publishing, Rugby, Warwickshire, United Kingdom, pp 111–128

Cramer W, Yohe GW, Auffhammer M, Huggel C, Molau U, Silva Dias MAF, Solow A, Stone DA, Tibig L (2014) Detection and attribution of observed impacts. In: Field CB, Barros VR, Dokken DJ, Mach KJ, Mastrandrea MD, Bilir TE, Chatterjee M, Ebi KL, Estrada YO, Genova RC, Girma B, Kissel ES, Levy AN, MacCracken S, Mastrandrea PR, White LL (eds) Climate change 2014: impacts, adaptation, and vulnerability. Part A: global and sectoral aspects. contribution of working group II to the fifth assessment report of the intergovernmental panel of climate change. Cambridge University Press, Cambridge, United Kingdom and New York, NY, USA, pp 979–1037

Dellink R, den Elzen M, Aiking H, Bergsma E, Berkhout F, Dekker T, Gupta J (2009) Sharing the burden of financing adaptation to climate change. Glob Environ Change 19(4):411–421

Displacement Solutions (2015) Peninsula Principles on Climate Displacement within States (Aug. 19, 2015). http://displacementsolutions.org/peninsula-principles/. Accessed 11 Oct 2017

Dow K, Berkhout F, Preston B, Klein R, Midgley G, Shaw M (2013) Limits to adaptation. Nat Clim Change 3:305–307

Eeckhoudt L, Gollier C, Schlesinger H (2005) Economic and financial decisions under risk. Princeton University Press

Gardiner S (2004a) Ethics and global climate change. Ethics 114:555–600

Gardiner S (2004b) The global warming tragedy and the dangerous illusion of the Kyoto Protocol. Ethics Int Aff 18(1):23–39

Gardiner S (2006) A perfect moral storm. Environ Values 15(3):397–413

GIZ (2015) Climate risk insurance for strengthening climate resilience of poor people in vulnerable countries. GIZ, Eschborn

GIZ, IIASA, KPMG India (2018) Climate Risk Management (CRM) Framework for India. GIZ

Grasso M (2007) A normative ethical framework in climate change. Clim Change 81(3):223–246

Handmer J, Nalau J (2018) Understanding loss and damage in Pacific Small Island developing states. In: Mechler R, Bouwer L, Schinko T, Surminski S, Linnerooth-Bayer J (eds) Loss and damage from climate change. Concepts, methods and policy options. Springer, Cham, pp 365–381

Haque M, Pervin M, Sultana S, Huq S (2018) Towards establishing a national mechanism to address loss and damage: a case study from Bangladesh. In: Mechler R, Bouwer L, Schinko T, Surminski S, Linnerooth-Bayer J (eds) Loss and damage from climate change. Concepts, methods and policy options. Springer, Cham, pp 451–473

Herring S et al (eds) (2014) Special supplement to the bulletin of the American Meteorological Society 95

Hino M, Field CB, Mach KJ (2017) Managed retreat as a response to natural hazard risk. Nat Clim Change 7:828–832. https://doi.org/10.1038/NCLIMATE3252

Hochrainer-Stigler S, Mechler R, Pflug GC, Williges K (2014) Funding public adaptation to climate-related disasters. Estimates for a global fund. Glob Environ Change 25:87–96. https://doi.org/10.1016/j.gloenvcha.2014.01.011

Hochrainer-Stigler S, Mochizuki J, Pflug G (2016) Impacts of global and climate change uncertainties for disaster risk projections: a case study on rainfall-induced flood risk in Bangladesh. J Extreme Events 3(1). https://doi.org/10.1142/s2345737616500044

Huggel C, Mechler R, Bouwer L, Schinko T, Surminski S, Wallimann-Helmer I (2016) Science for loss and damage. Four research contributions to science for loss and damage. Four research contributions to the debate. Working paper by the loss and damage network, prepared for COP22 in Marrakech. http://www.lse.ac.uk/GranthamInstitute/wp-content/uploads/2016/11/LD-Forum-paper-COP-22-final.pdf. Accessed 11 Oct 2017

Huggel C, Stone D, Eicken H, Hansen G (2015) Potential and limitations of the attribution of climate change impacts for informing loss and damage discussions and policies. Clim Change 133:453–467

IPCC (2012) Managing the risks of extreme events and disasters to advance climate change adaptation. In: Field CB, Barros V, Stocker TF, Qin D, Dokken DJ, Ebi KL, Mastrandrea MD, Mach KJ, Plattner G-K, Allen SK, Tignor M, Midgley PM (eds) A special report of working groups I and II of the intergovernmental panel on climate change. Cambridge University Press, Cambridge, UK, and New York, NY, USA, 582 pp

IPCC (2013) Climate change 2013: the physical science basis. In: Stocker TF, Qin D, Plattner G-K, Tignor M, Allen SK, Boschung J, Nauels A, Xia Y, Bex V, Midgley PM (eds) Contribution of working group I to the fifth assessment report of the intergovernmental panel on climate change. Cambridge University Press, Cambridge, United Kingdom and New York, NY, USA, 1535 pp

IPCC (2014) Climate change 2014: impacts, adaptation, and vulnerability. Part A: global and sectoral aspects. In: Field CB, Barros VR, Dokken DJ, Mach KJ, Mastrandrea MD, Bilir TE, Chatterjee M, Ebi KL, Estrada YO, Genova RC, Girma B, Kissel ES, Levy AN, MacCracken S, Mastrandrea PR, White LL (eds) Contribution of working group II to the fifth assessment report of the intergovernmental panel on climate change. Cambridge University Press, Cambridge, United Kingdom and New York, NY, USA, 1132 pp

James RA, Jones RG, Boyd E, Young HR, Otto FEL, Huggel C, Fuglestvedt JS (2018) Attribution: how is it relevant for loss and damage policy and practice? In: Mechler R, Bouwer L, Schinko T, Surminski S, Linnerooth-Bayer J (eds) Loss and damage from climate change. Concepts, methods and policy options. Springer, Cham, pp 113–154

Jamieson D (1992) Ethics, public policy and global warming. Sci Technol Human Values 17(2):139–153

Jamieson D (2001) Climate change and global environmental justice. In: Miller C, Edwards P (eds) Changing the atmosphere: expert knowledge and environmental governance. MIT Press, Cambridge, MA, pp 287–307

Jamieson D (2005) Adaptation, mitigation and justice. In: Sinnott-Armstrong W, Howarth R (eds) Perspectives on climate change: science, economics, politics, ethics, vol 5. Elsevier, Amsterdam, pp 217–248

Jones R, Patwardhan A, Cohen S, Dessai S, Lammel A, Lempert R, Mirza M, von Storch H (2014) Foundations for decision making. In: Field CB, Barros VR, Dokken DJ, Mach KJ, Mastrandrea MD, Bilir TE, Chatterjee M, Ebi KL, Estrada YO, Genova RC, Girma B, Kissel ES, Levy AN, MacCracken S, Mastrandrea PR, White LL (eds) Climate change 2014: impacts, adaptation, and vulnerability. Part A: global and sectoral aspects. Contribution of working group II to the fifth assessment report of the intergovernmental panel of climate change. Cambridge University Press, Cambridge, United Kingdom and New York, NY, USA, pp 195–228

Klein RJT, Midgley GF, Preston BL, Alam M, Berkhout FGH, Dow K, Shaw MR (2014) Adaptation opportunities, constraints, and limits. In: Field CB, Barros VR, Dokken DJ, Mach KJ, Mastrandrea MD, Bilir TE, Chatterjee M, Ebi KL, Estrada YO, Genova RC, Girma B, Kissel ES, Levy AN, MacCracken S, Mastrandrea PR, White LL (eds). Climate change 2014: impacts, adaptation, and vulnerability. Part A: global and sectoral aspects. Contribution of working group II to the fifth assessment report of the intergovernmental panel of climate change. Cambridge University Press, Cambridge, United Kingdom and New York, NY, USA, pp. 899–943.

Klinke A, Renn O (2002) A new approach to risk evaluation and management: risk-based, precaution-based, and discourse-based strategies. Risk Anal 22:1071–1094

Klinsky S, Dowlatabadi H (2009) Conceptualizations of justice in climate policy. Clim Policy 9:88–108

Landauer M, Juhola S (2018) Loss and damage in the rapidly changing arctic. In: Mechler R, Bouwer L, Schinko T, Surminski S, Linnerooth-Bayer J (eds) Loss and damage from climate change. Concepts, methods and policy options. Springer, Cham, pp 425–447

Linnerooth-Bayer J, Surminski S, Bouwer LM, Noy I, Mechler R (2018) Insurance as a response to loss and damage? In: Mechler R, Bouwer L, Schinko T, Surminski S, Linnerooth-Bayer J (eds) Loss and damage from climate change. Concepts, methods and policy options. Springer, Cham, pp 483–512

Lopez A, Surminski S, Serdeczny O (2018) The role of the physical sciences in loss and damage decision-making. In: Mechler R, Bouwer L, Schinko T, Surminski S, Linnerooth-Bayer J (eds) Loss and damage from climate change. Concepts, methods and policy options. Springer, Cham, pp 261–285

Mace MJ, Verheyen R (2016) Loss, damage and responsibility after COP21: all options open for the Paris agreement. Rev Eur Commun Int Environ Law 25:197–214

Magrin GO, Marengo JA, Boulanger J-P, Buckeridge MS, Castellanos E, Poveda G, Scarano FR, Vicuña S (2014) Central and South America. In: Field CB, Barros VR, Dokken DJ, Mach KJ, Mastrandrea MD, Bilir TE, Chatterjee M, Ebi KL, Estrada YO, Genova RC, Girma B, Kissel ES, Levy AN, MacCracken S, Mastrandrea PR, White LL (eds) Climate change 2014: Impacts, adaptation, and vulnerability. Part A: global and sectoral aspects. Contribution of working group II to the fifth assessment report of the intergovernmental panel of climate change. Cambridge University Press, Cambridge, United Kingdom and New York, NY, USA, pp 1499–1566

Mann ME, Rahmstorf S, Kornhuber K, Steinman BA, Miller SK, Coumou D (2017) Influence of anthropogenic climate change on planetary wave resonance and extreme weather events. Nat Sci Rep 7:45242. https://doi.org/10.1038/srep45242

Mechler R, Bouwer L (2015) Reviewing trends and projections of global disaster losses and climate change: is vulnerability the missing link? Clim Change 133(1):23–35

Mechler R, Bouwer L, Linnerooth-Bayer J, Hochrainer-Stigler S, Aerts J, Surminski S (2014) Managing unnatural disaster risk from climate extremes. Nat Clim Change 4:235–237

Mechler R et al (2018) Science for loss and damage. Findings and propositions. In: Mechler R, Bouwer L, Schinko T, Surminski S, Linnerooth-Bayer J (eds) Loss and damage from climate change. Concepts, methods and policy options. Springer, Cham, pp 3–37

Mechler R, Schinko T (2016) Identifying the policy space for climate loss and damage. Science 354(6310):290–292. https://doi.org/10.1126/science.aag2514

Mysiak J, Surminski S, Thieken A, Mechler R, Aerts J (2015) Brief communication: Sendai framework for disaster risk reduction—success or warning sign for Paris? Nat Hazards Earth Sys Sci - Discuss 3:3955–3966. https://doi.org/10.5194/nhessd-3-3955-2015

Nansen Conference (2011) Climate change and displacement in the 21 Century, Oslo, Norway, June 5–7, 2011. www.unhcr.org/4ea969729.pdf. Accessed 11 Oct 2017

Nicholls RJ, Marinova N, Lowe JA, Brown S, Vellinga P, De Gusmão D, Hinkel J, Tol RSJ (2011) Sea-level rise and its possible impacts given a 'beyond4 ∘C world' in the twenty-first century. Philos Trans Royal Soc A 369:161–181

Nurse LA, McLean R, Agard J, Briguglio L, Duvat-Magnan V, Pelesikoti N, Webb A (2014) Small islands. In: Barros VR, Field CB, Dokken DJ, Mastrandrea MD, Mach KJ, Bilir TE, Chatterjee M, Ebi KL, Estrada YO, Genova RC, Girma B, Kissel ES, Levy AN, MacCracken S, Mastrandrea PR, White LL (eds). Cambridge University Press, Cambridge, United Kingdom and New York, NY, USA, pp 1613–1654

Ott K (2004) Ethical claims about the basic foundations on climate change policies. Workshop on Climate Policies, Greifswald, Germany

Paavola J, Adger WN (2006) Fair adaptation to climate change. Ecol Econ 56(4):594–609

Posner EA, Weisbach D (2010) Climate change justice. Princeton University Press

Roser D, Huggel C, Ohndorf M, Wallimann-Helmer I (2015) Advancing the interdisciplinary dialogue on climate justice. Clim Change 133:349–359

Schäfer L, Warner K, Kreft S (2018) Exploring and managing adaptation frontiers with climate risk insurance. In: Mechler R, Bouwer L, Schinko T, Surminski S, Linnerooth-Bayer J (eds) Loss and damage from climate change. Concepts, methods and policy options. Springer, Cham, pp 317–341

Schaller et al (2016) Human influence on climate in the 2014 southern England winter floods and their impacts. Nat Clim Change 6:627–634. https://doi.org/10.1038/NCLIMATE2927

Schinko T, Mechler R (2017) Applying recent insights from climate risk management to operationalize the loss and damage mechanism. Ecol Econ 136:296–298. https://doi.org/10.1016/j.ecolecon.2017.02.008

Schinko T, Mechler R, Hochrainer-Stigler S (2016) Developing a methodological framework for operationalizing iterative climate risk management based on insights from the case of Austria. Mitig Adapt Strat Glob Change 22(7):1063–1086. https://doi.org/10.1007/s11027-016-9713-0

Serdeczny O (2018) Non-economic loss and damage and the Warsaw international mechanism. In: Mechler R, Bouwer L, Schinko T, Surminski S, Linnerooth-Bayer J (eds) Loss and damage from climate change. Concepts, methods and policy options. Springer, Cham, pp 205–220

Shue H (1992) The unavoidability of justice. In: Hurrell A, Kingsbury B (eds), The international politics of the environment: actors, interests and institutions. Clarendon Press, Oxford, pp 373–397

Shue H (1993) Subsistence emissions and luxury emissions. Law and Policy 15(1):39–59

Shue H (1999) Global environment and international inequality. Int Aff 75(3):531–545

Singer P (2002) One world: the ethics of globalization. Yale University Press, New Haven, CT

Singer P (2006) Ethics and climate change. Environ Values 15(3):415–422

Sprinz D, von Bünau S (2013) The compensation fund for climate impacts. Weather Clim Soc 5:210–220. https://doi.org/10.1175/WCAS-D-12-00010.1

Stone D et al (2013) The challenge to detect and attribute effects of climate change on human and natural systems. Clim Change 121:381–395. https://doi.org/10.1007/s10584-013-0873-6

Thompson A, Otto FEL (2015) Ethical and normative implications of weather event attribution for policy discussions concerning loss and damage. Clim Change 133:439–451

Trenberth K, Fasullo JT, Shepherd TG (2015) Attribution of climate extreme events. Nat Clim Change 5:725–730. https://doi.org/10.1038/nclimate2657

UNFCCC (2014) Decision 2/CP.19. Warsaw international mechanism for loss and damage associated with climate change. http://unfccc.int/resource/docs/2013/cop19/eng/10a01.pdf#page=6. Accessed 11 Oct 2017

UNFCCC (2015a) Adoption of the Paris agreement FCCC/CP/2015/L.9/Rev1. United Nations Framework Convention on Climate Change

UNFCCC (2015b) Report on the structured expert dialogue on the 2013 2015 review. Decision FCCC/SB/2015/INF.1

UNISDR (2015) Making development sustainable: the future of disaster risk management. Global assessment report on disaster risk reduction. United Nations Office for Disaster Risk Reduction (UNISDR), Geneva, Switzerland

United Nations (1992) UN Framework Convention on Climate Change (UNFCCC). United Nations, New York

van der Geest K, de Sherbinin A, Kienberger S, Zommers Z, Sitati A, Roberts E, James R (2018) The impacts of climate change on ecosystem services and resulting losses and damages to people and society. In: Mechler R, Bouwer L, Schinko T, Surminski S, Linnerooth-Bayer J (eds) Loss and damage from climate change. Concepts, methods and policy options. Springer, Cham, pp 221–236

Vanderheiden S (2008) Atmospheric justice: a political theory of climate change. Oxford University Press, Oxford

Verheyen R, Roderick P (2008) Beyond adaptation—the legal duty to pay compensation for climate change damage. WWF-UK, Climate Change Programme discussion paper

Verheyen R (2012) Tackling loss & damage–a new role for the climate regime? Climate and Development Knowledge Network

Wallimann-Helmer I, Meyer L, Mintz-Woo K, Schinko T, Serdeczny O (2018) Ethical challenges in the context of climate loss and damage. In: Mechler R, Bouwer L, Schinko T, Surminski S, Linnerooth-Bayer J (eds) Loss and damage from climate change. Concepts, methods and policy options. Springer, Cham, pp 39–62

WBGU-German Advisory Council on Global Change (1998) World in transition: strategies for managing global environmental risks. Springer, Berlin

WWA (2017) Kenya Drought, 2016. World Weather Attribution. https://wwa.climatecentral.org/analyses/kenya-drought-2016/. Accessed 11 Oct 2017

Part II
Critical Issues Shaping the Discourse

Chapter 5
Attribution: How Is It Relevant for Loss and Damage Policy and Practice?

Rachel A. James, Richard G. Jones, Emily Boyd, Hannah R. Young, Friederike E. L. Otto, Christian Huggel and Jan S. Fuglestvedt

Abstract Attribution has become a recurring issue in discussions about Loss and Damage (L&D). In this highly-politicised context, attribution is often associated with responsibility and blame; and linked to debates about liability and compensation. The aim of attribution *science*, however, is not to establish responsibility, but to further scientific understanding of causal links between elements of the Earth System and society. This research into causality could inform the management of climate-related risks through improved understanding of drivers of relevant hazards, or, more widely, vulnerability and exposure; with potential benefits regardless of political positions on L&D. Experience shows that it is nevertheless difficult to have open discussions about the science in the policy sphere. This is not only a missed opportunity, but also problematic in that it could inhibit understanding of scientific results and uncertainties, potentially leading to policy planning which does not have sufficient scientific

---

R. A. James (✉) · F. E. L. Otto
Environmental Change Institute, University of Oxford, Oxford, UK
e-mail: rachel.james@eci.ox.ac.uk

E. Boyd
LUCSUS, Lund University, Lund, Sweden

C. Huggel
Department of Geography, University of Zurich, Zurich, Switzerland

J. S. Fuglestvedt
CICERO, Oslo, Norway

R. A. James
Department of Oceanography, University of Cape Town, Cape Town, South Africa

R. G. Jones
School of Geography and the Environment, University of Oxford, Oxford, UK

R. G. Jones
Met Office Hadley Centre, Exeter, UK

E. Boyd
Department of Geography, University of Reading, Reading, UK

H. R. Young
Department of Meteorology, University of Reading, Reading, UK

R. Mechler et al. (eds.), *Loss and Damage from Climate Change*, Climate Risk Management, Policy and Governance, https://doi.org/10.1007/978-3-319-72026-5_5

evidence to support it. In this chapter, we first explore this dilemma for science-policy dialogue, summarising several years of research into stakeholder perspectives of attribution in the context of L&D. We then aim to provide clarity about the scientific research available, through an overview of research which might contribute evidence about the causal connections between anthropogenic climate change and losses and damages, including climate science, but also other fields which examine other drivers of hazard, exposure, and vulnerability. Finally, we explore potential applications of attribution research, suggesting that an integrated and nuanced approach has potential to inform planning to avert, minimise and address losses and damages. The key messages are

- In the political context of climate negotiations, questions about whether losses and damages can be attributed to anthropogenic climate change are often linked to issues of responsibility, blame, and liability.
- Attribution science does not aim to establish responsibility or blame, but rather to investigate drivers of change.
- Attribution science is advancing rapidly, and has potential to increase understanding of how climate variability and change is influencing slow onset and extreme weather events, and how this interacts with other drivers of risk, including socio-economic drivers, to influence losses and damages.
- Over time, some uncertainties in the science will be reduced, as the anthropogenic climate change signal becomes stronger, and understanding of climate variability and change develops.
- However, some uncertainties will not be eliminated. Uncertainty is common in science, and does not prevent useful applications in policy, but might determine which applications are appropriate. It is important to highlight that in attribution studies, the strength of evidence varies substantially between different kinds of slow onset and extreme weather events, and between regions. Policy-makers should not expect the later emergence of conclusive evidence about the influence of climate variability and change on specific incidences of losses and damages; and, in particular, should not expect the strength of evidence to be equal between events, and between countries.
- Rather than waiting for further confidence in attribution studies, there is potential to start working now to integrate science into policy and practice, to help understand and tackle drivers of losses and damages, informing prevention, recovery, rehabilitation, and transformation.

Keywords Loss and Damage · Attribution · Climate change · Science-policy interface

5.1 Introduction

The science of attributing observed phenomena to human-induced and natural climate drivers has seen remarkable progress since its emergence in the 1990s. The first studies demonstrated that the late 20th century increase in global mean surface temperature would not have occurred without human influence on concentrations of greenhouse gases (GHGs) and aerosols (Tett et al. 1999; Stott et al. 2000). In subsequent years, many more studies of global temperature supported this finding, leading to greater and greater confidence in anthropogenic influence on global warming (Santer et al. 1995; Mitchell et al. 2001; Hegerl et al. 2007; Bindoff et al. 2013), and, the most recent report of the Intergovernmental Panel on Climate Change (IPCC) states that anthropogenic drivers are "extremely likely [or>95% probability] to have been the dominant cause of the observed warming since the mid-20th century" (IPCC 2014). These scientific attribution statements provide a fundamental underpinning for the United Nations Framework Convention on Climate Change (UNFCCC; UN 1992), demonstrating that recent warming was predominantly caused by human emissions of carbon dioxide, methane, and short-lived climate forcings (SLCFs), and modifications to GHG concentrations associated with land use change (LUC); and thus establishing the imperative for mitigation.

As the UNFCCC's mandate has extended beyond mitigation, to include adaptation, and now Loss and Damage (L&D) from climate change impacts (UNFCCC 2013, 2015; see introductory chapter by Mechler et al. 2018), new challenges and questions are emerging about the science of attribution, and its role in policy. Whilst there is strong evidence from attribution studies that human activity is influencing global and regional temperatures (Bindoff et al. 2013), and also other global and regional scale changes (including sea level rise, e.g. Church et al. 2013; and atmospheric moisture content, e.g. Santer et al. 2007), understanding how anthropogenic drivers influence losses and damages in particular ecosystems, economies, and communities is a very different endeavour, which raises questions extending far beyond physical climate science. When referring to the loss of coastline from a storm surge, fatalities during a heat wave, or famine during a drought, the issue of causality becomes more challenging scientifically. As we will explore in this chapter, at this scale and complexity, multiple factors contribute to a specific loss or damage, and the signal from climate change is more difficult to detect relative to the many other potential influences on hazard occurrence, exposure, and vulnerability (Huggel et al. 2013).

Questions about attribution of specific losses and damages also make the implications of the scientific research more political than the implications of studies into global or regional climate. Now questions are being asked about the influence of human actions (through anthropogenic GHGs) on specific people, and often not the same people who were responsible for the majority of GHG emissions. It is therefore not difficult to understand why, in the context of L&D policy discussions, attribution has often been associated with responsibility, blame, and liability. For scientists, research into causality is a fundamental route towards understanding how the Earth System works, and attribution research is not necessarily intended to identify responsible parties. In the context of political negotiations, however, even mentioning attribution science can be seen as, and arguably often is, a political move.

If attribution science is to be helpful in this controversial policy space, scientists must not only push the boundaries of their physical scientific analyses, but also improve their understanding of policy mechanisms, and the motivations, perceptions, and knowledge of policy-makers and practitioners. Interdisciplinary research in collaboration with social scientists, and transdisciplinary studies with stakeholders in policy and practice, are fundamental to identify whether there are entry points for physical attribution science. In response to this need, the authors have been investigating the potential relevance of attribution science for L&D by attending UNFCCC meetings (James et al. 2014a; Parker et al. 2015; Otto et al. 2015a), interviewing stakeholders about attribution (Parker et al. 2017a), playing participatory games about attribution science and its role in L&D (Parker et al. 2016), and more broadly analysing perspectives of what L&D signifies (Boyd et al. 2017). This research has highlighted the challenge of applying attribution science in a context where it is difficult to even discuss climate change science (James et al. 2014a). There are many vested interests in the outcomes of attribution research, and, for negotiators of climate policy, clarity on exactly what can and cannot be attributed might not be considered helpful.

Unsurprisingly, then, our research also suggests that stakeholders to the L&D debate have quite different understandings of what can and cannot be attributed to anthropogenic climate change (Parker et al. 2017a). Yet, we find that attribution is an issue which recurs in negotiations: and there is a risk that, without improved understanding, policy planning could proceed based on assumptions about the science, and then later find that the evidence available is either stronger or weaker than expected. In this chapter, we revisit the question of whether and how attribution science might be useful for L&D policy and practice, first examining existing understandings of attribution in L&D policy discussions, then outlining the science itself and what it can offer, and finally turning to potential applications. We hope to open up opportunities for more informed dialogue between researchers, policy-makers, and practitioners: helping scientists to understand the L&D policy context, the perceptions and implications of attribution, helping policy-makers and practitioners to understand what the science can offer, and identifying areas which might require further integration for progress (see Box 5.1 for key messages).

Box 5.1 Key Messages

- In the political context of climate negotiations, questions about whether losses and damages can be attributed to anthropogenic climate change are often linked to issues of responsibility, blame, and liability.
- Attribution science does not aim to establish responsibility or blame, but rather to investigate drivers of change.
- Attribution science is advancing rapidly, and has potential to increase understanding of how climate variability and change is influencing slow onset and extreme weather events, and how this interacts with other drivers of risk, including socio-economic drivers, to influence losses and damages.
- Over time, some uncertainties in the science will be reduced, as the anthropogenic climate change signal becomes stronger, and understanding of climate variability and change develops.
- However, some uncertainties will not be eliminated. Uncertainty is common in science, and does not prevent useful applications in policy, but might determine which applications are appropriate. It is important to highlight that in attribution studies, the strength of evidence varies substantially between different kinds of slow onset and extreme weather events, and between regions. Policy-makers should not expect the later emergence of conclusive evidence about the influence of climate variability and change on specific incidences of losses and damages; and, in particular, should not expect the strength of evidence to be equal between events, and between countries.
- Rather than waiting for further confidence in attribution studies, there is potential to start working now to integrate science into policy and practice, to help understand and tackle drivers of losses and damages, informing prevention, recovery, rehabilitation, and transformation.

Section 5.2 summarises findings from our transdisciplinary research of perspectives on attribution in L&D policy discussions, drawing directly on qualitative evidence from stakeholder interviews (see Box 5.2). Section 5.3 then provides an overview of sources of evidence about attribution of L&D to climate variability and anthropogenic climate change. This is not restricted to physical climate science, but also includes other fields of enquiry which investigate causative links between L&D, climate and weather, and human activity. Section 5.4 will discuss if and how such attribution science might be applied to support L&D policy and practice, taking into account previous ideas from the L&D literature, and stakeholder interviews (see 5.2), but also drawing on our own conclusions and ideas about potentially fruitful applications.

Box 5.2 Evidence from stakeholder interviews

The discussion of perspectives of attribution in the context of L&D policy in this chapter draws on qualitative evidence from two research projects which included interviews with stakeholders to L&D discussions. The first project aimed to explore stakeholders' understandings of probabilistic event attribution in relation to L&D (Parker et al. 2017a), and the second project was designed to more broadly investigate stakeholder perspectives on L&D (Boyd et al. 2017). In both projects we asked stakeholders what kind of scientific evidence might be relevant for L&D policy, and how; and both projects led to insights into stakeholder perspectives on attribution science, including some consistent findings. The methodologies are described more thoroughly in the key academic papers, but here we provide a brief overview of the interview design and participants to provide context for the quotations that are included in this chapter. All interview data were anonymised and analysed for the respective papers, and here we draw on key quotations which emerged from these analyses.

The focus of the Parker et al. (2017a) study was on just one area of attribution research: probabilistic event attribution (PEA), a rapidly emerging field which aims to explore the extent to which anthropogenic emissions influence the likelihood and magnitude of specific extreme weather events such as heatwaves, floods and droughts in a specific location (see Sect. 5.3). Qualitative, semi-structured interviews were conducted between November 2013 and July 2014 with 31 stakeholders including UNFCCC delegates, representatives from non-governmental organisations, climate scientists, and social scientists. Interview questions focusing on the extent to which the interviewees understood PEA, and their views about its relevance to L&D policy.

The broader study of stakeholder perspectives on L&D, described in Boyd et al. (2017), was prompted by the authors' work on the relevance of attribution science for L&D policy (including Parker et al. 2017a). One of the emerging insights from the initial engagement with L&D discussions was the difficulty of initiating detailed discussions about science and practice to understand and address L&D, given the controversy of the topic, but also the lack of clarity on the concept of L&D (James et al. 2014a). This prompted an in-depth investigation of stakeholder perspectives of L&D, in which interviewees were asked how they would define L&D, the relationship between L&D and adaptation, and what actions might be needed to address L&D. On the basis of these interviews a diverse spectrum of ideas about L&D was identified, characterised as a typology of four perspectives (see Fig. 5.1). The interviews included questions about the relevance of anthropogenic climate change in the context of L&D and what kind of science might be needed for L&D policy, and it is these aspects which we discuss in this chapter. 36 qualitative, semi-structured interviews were conducted between April and November 2015 with stakeholders from science, policy, and practice, including negotiators, adaptation and disaster risk practitioners, and researchers with expertise in climate science, social science, law, philosophy, and economics.

5.2 Attribution in the Context of L&D: Why Is Attribution a Critical Issue?

5.2.1 Recurring Questions: Is This Really About Anthropogenic Climate Change?

The UNFCCC has a mandate to address anthropogenic climate change (UN 1992). Its ultimate objective is to "achieve stabilization of greenhouse gas concentrations in the atmosphere at a level that would prevent dangerous anthropogenic interference with the climate system" (UN 1992:4), and therefore the original focus of UNFCCC discussions was on mitigation, or reducing GHGs. However, there has long been a recognition that some climate change impacts cannot be avoided (e.g. Meehl 2005; Wigley 2005); and the UNFCCC now has frameworks and mechanisms to address climate change impacts in terms of adaptation (UNFCCC 2011) and more recently L&D (UNFCCC 2013, 2015; see also introductory chapter by Mechler et al. 2018).

In seeking to address the *impacts* of anthropogenic climate change, the boundaries of the UNFCCC's mandate become less clear. Efforts to help people cope with climate change include risk reduction, e.g. by reducing vulnerability or more generally by enhancing adaptive capacity, and improving disaster response and recovery. These activities are already important ambitions for institutions which focus on development, disaster risk management, and humanitarian aid. An obvious question is therefore: what is distinct about adaptation and/or L&D? How should the UNFCCC interact with UNDP (the UN Development Programme), UNISDR (the UN Office for Disaster Risk Reduction), and a whole host of other UN agencies and international organisations? Which activities are specific to *climate change*?[1] In the case of L&D, the term—"losses and damages"—has been used in disaster risk reduction for many years.[2] Losses and damages from natural disasters have occurred and would continue to occur without climate change. So, which losses and damages are relevant for the UNFCCC? What further effort is needed to address the new and/or additional losses and damages which will result from climate change?

These questions about institutional mandates and responsibilities lead to questions about attribution: about which losses and damages can be attributed to anthropogenic climate change. It is not easy to find conclusive scientific answers, partly because these attribution questions are motivated and posed differently to research questions in scientific studies (Otto et al. 2016), and partly due to the complexity of isolat-

---

[1]Similar questions were raised by many of the stakeholders we interviewed (see Box 5.2), for example one said: "That's a fundamental question—am I fighting climate change or poverty?", and one interviewee described the challenge in UNFCCC L&D discussions to "draw the distinction about what's considered adaptation and L&D, and some of the humanitarian and DRR issues", explaining "we had a very long discussion in the committee meeting just to discuss whether the humanitarian assistance can be counted for climate finance".

[2]As one interviewee highlighted (see Box 5.2), the "use of this phrase in this very policy context is very different from use of the phrase in the disaster risk management community, where they're looking at L&D from all events".

ing the influence of anthropogenic climate change on specific losses and damages. Scientific attribution studies usually take anthropogenic emissions as their starting point, and ask what influence those emissions have had on climate and weather. In policy discussions, attribution questions emerge from questions of how to address specific cases of losses and damages, and what proportion of the losses or damages can be related to anthropogenic climate change. As we will outline in Sect. 5.3, at a local scale it becomes more challenging to understand how the influence of anthropogenic climate change interacts with natural variability in weather and climate. Furthermore, the influence of hazards resulting from local climate changes and extreme weather events on people (through impacts on health, water resources, food systems, infrastructure and beyond) interacts with a whole range of other drivers. These include the vulnerability and exposure components of coupled human-natural systems (see chapters by Bouwer 2018; Lopez et al. 2018 and Botzen et al. 2018). These complexities and uncertainties perhaps start to explain why questions about attribution recur in UNFCCC negotiations[3]: there are obvious and practical reasons to ask which L&D is related to climate change, but no straightforward answers.

5.2.2 *Questions with Political Implications: Controversy and Ambiguity in the Negotiations*

The answers to attribution questions also have important political implications. Attributing specific losses and damages to GHG emissions might imply responsibility for emitters (potentially including countries, regions, sectors, companies, and individuals). Some of the stakeholders we interviewed (see Box 5.2) highlighted that mentions of attribution in the negotiation context were likely to be politically motivated, associated with attempts to push for compensation for climate change impacts.[4] They also suggested that the political motivations might influence how attribution science would be represented, i.e. negotiators might "*choose what they know*" (Parker et al. 2017a).[5] When developed countries mention attribution in UNFCCC negotiations they might highlight the uncertainty and imply inability to attribute losses and

[3]Recurring questions about whether L&D is related to climate change, and specifically about attribution, were witnessed in our own participant observation of UNFCCC discussions (see Boyd et al. 2017), notably including one quote from a member of the Executive Committee to the WIM "it's a question of attribution which we always get back to". Interviewees (see Box 5.2) also commented on the recurring nature of the topic in UNFCCC discussions, for example "there's a lot of unproductive exchanges that say 'how can we be sure this is related to anthropogenic changes," explaining "it's not an explicit agenda item, but it always pops up."

[4]For example, one interviewee said "When you talk about attribution, there's an important sense of who's paying for it and who's to blame… people look at attribution as a way to get compensation."

[5]Another interviewee said, referring to attribution science: "I think there will be different ways in which people interpret this and use this to get what they want, and to avoid having to do/pay for things."

damages to anthropogenic forcing.[6] Conversely, vulnerable countries might want to highlight the strength of attribution evidence to try to prompt action from emitters[7] (see also chapter by Calliari et al. 2018).

Therefore, whilst on an institutional level it seems important to distinguish losses and damages which are attributable to climate change, and losses and damages which might not be relevant to the UNFCCC, doing so is not only scientifically challenging, but also politically contentious. Perhaps in order to make progress in the presence of this controversy, and to achieve agreement across different Parties, deliberately ambiguous language has been used in the official L&D text under the UNFCCC, including in the Warsaw International Mechanism (WIM) (UNFCCC 2013) and Article 8 of the Paris Agreement (UNFCCC 2015).[8] The WIM refers to L&D from climate change impacts, but it is unclear how those losses and damages might be distinguished from L&D from natural disasters (James et al. 2014a).

5.2.3 Perspectives from Practitioners: Is It More Pragmatic to Avoid Isolating Anthropogenic Climate Change Impacts from Other Losses and Damages?

The ambiguity in international policy leaves room for multiple perspectives on the relevance of anthropogenic climate change to L&D, and the potential role for attribution science. Boyd et al. (2017) asked stakeholders whether they thought actions to address losses and damages should refer only to the impacts of anthropogenic climate change, or to any adverse effects from climate variability and change (see Fig. 5.1). This revealed a divide in opinion. In 9 of the 36 interviews, stakeholders were clear that, since the WIM was part of the UNFCCC, it should focus on anthropogenic climate change. Nine others, predominantly practitioners, argued that it would be more pragmatic to address all weather and climate-related losses and damages together (in keeping with several working definitions of L&D, Warner and van der Geest 2013; UNEP 2016).[9]

Many of the remaining interviewees also expressed caution about limiting L&D actions too strictly to those impacts that could be attributed to anthropogenic climate change. This was partly due to awareness of the political connotations of attribution

---

[6]For example, Vanhala and Hastbaek (2016) refer to the response of New Zealand to an AOSIS proposal, in which they rejected the proposal on the basis that it is not possible to attribute any specific extreme event to climate change.

[7]One interviewee discussed the challenge of attribution science for vulnerable countries: "the risk is that L&D may well go unattributed to climate change and once the opportunity to compensate is lost, in the scheme of things it's lost…It's difficult, obviously you want to attribute everything."

[8]According to Vanhala and Hastbaek (2016), the ambiguous nature of the WIM was central to its establishment; or as one interviewee in Boyd et al.'s (2017) study stated "they've made it fuzzy to get people to sign on".

[9]In the remaining 18 interviews, a conclusive opinion about this question was not expressed.

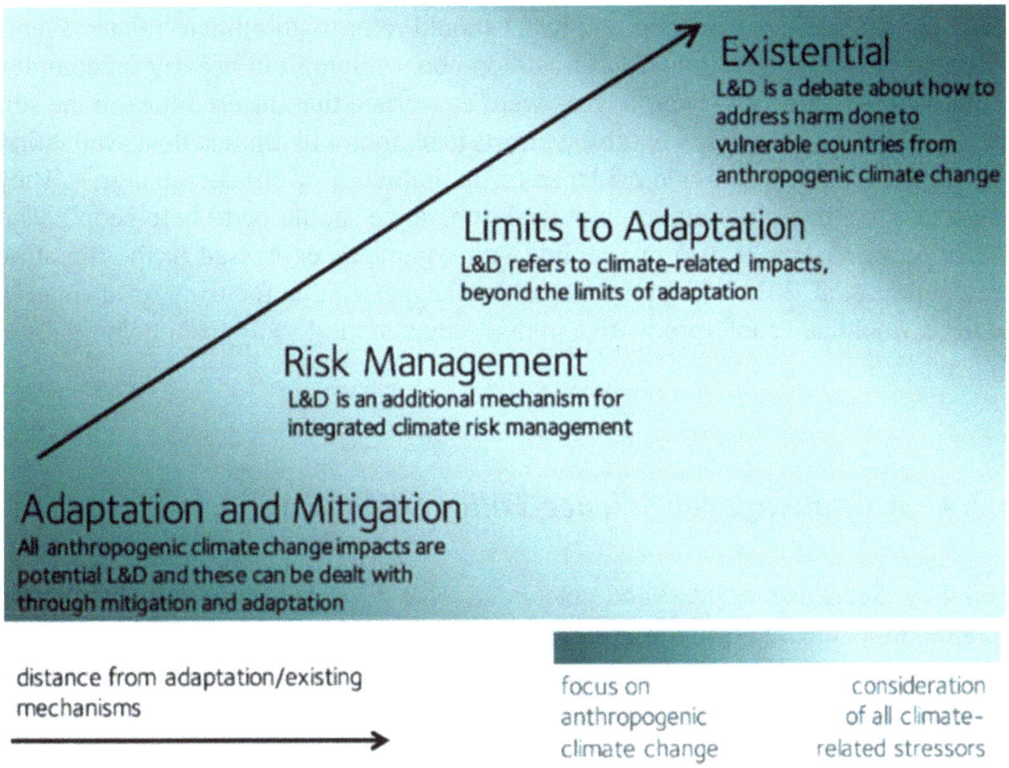

Fig. 5.1 A schematic diagram illustrating a spectrum of views on L&D identified by Boyd et al. (2017). Each of the four perspectives are arranged along an axis in terms of how far suggested approaches to address losses and damages are distinct from, or go beyond, existing adaptation mechanisms. The shading illustrates how the perspectives differ in terms of the relevance of anthropogenic climate change: for two of the perspectives identified, L&D refers to anthropogenic climate change impacts only, for the other two perspectives, there is an emphasis on addressing all climate-related risk. Adapted from Boyd et al. (2016, 2017)

in the negotiations,[10] and the suggestion that more progress might be possible if the mandate of L&D mechanisms remained vague and inclusive.[11] It was also partly due to frustration at the inefficiencies of multiple institutions in disaster risk, humanitarian aid, development, adaptation, and now potentially L&D, working on separate but related issues without effective coordination[12]; and an appeal for more integrated risk

[10]This was expressed several times when this question was linked to issues of compensation and attribution by the interviewee, e.g. "to get political consensus around attribution, and therefore compensation, is just never going to happen."

[11]For example: "If you push too hard the discussion on defining, other than the quagmire semantics and politics it takes you into, it actually works against the idea that you have to address the problem comprehensively."

[12]For example: "There are too many forms of funding coming out of development, the problem with that is that you need a broad resilience approach to short term risk and long term stresses which can create conflict related to climate change."

management.[13] The suggestion that L&D should refer to all climate-related events was also related to an expression of caution about relying too heavily on complex scientific assessments.[14] Interviewees were concerned that uncertainties in the science could delay progress,[15] or inhibit efforts in regions with limited data availability and limited ability to provide evidence of the influence of climate change.[16] They suggested that the more important ethical imperative should be to help people who are suffering.[17] This is also in keeping with comments expressed in the literature (e.g. Hulme et al. 2011). Several stakeholders suggested that focusing on attributing hazards would be counterproductive in diverting attention away from helping those in need.[18]

5.2.4 A Challenge for Science-Policy Dialogue

In policy (Sects. 5.2.1, 5.2.2) and practice (Sect. 5.2.3), questions about attribution may therefore emerge from questions about which institutions and countries should take responsibility for dealing with L&D; about who should pay for L&D. Many see that assigning responsibility is politically challenging, and addressing climate change impacts in isolation is impractical. Attribution, by association, is sometimes seen as unhelpful or irrelevant.[19]

For scientists, questions about attribution have different motivations, objectives, and implications. Analysis of causality is an important way to further understanding of the Earth System. There are many important reasons to ask attribution questions besides establishing responsibility. And, it is worth highlighting that the results of scientific attribution studies are not sufficient to indicate responsibility. Attribution studies can estimate the extent to which certain drivers (such as GHGs) contributed to certain outcomes (such as flooding), but this "contribution" is very different from

---

[13]For example: "disaster risk management thinking and also climate change thinking has to be integrated with this big development perspective."

[14]For example: "that places too great a weight upon scientific evidence in ethical and political negotiations, which cannot be borne by climatic science."

[15]For example: "We cannot wait for them [climatologists] to determine to what extent this is about climate change or not" (Parker et al. 2017a).

[16]For example: "Science can establish maybe for some impacts earlier than others, there's some differences", and "there's a big issue with that in that the data for developing countries, we have less certainty on what is climate enhanced disaster in the south, simply because we don't have the data sets. We don't have the information to say with certainty that that was caused by climate change."

[17]For example: "the more urgent issue is… actually… responding to or adapting to extreme weather events, whether it's caused by people or not".

[18]In the words of one interviewee: "trying to disentangle the climate change portion of that risk might be useful from a political point but it's actually counterproductive in terms of having an impact on reducing risk". Similar points were expressed by stakeholders interviewed specifically about attribution science (Parker et al 2017a).

[19]For example: "I know there's this question around attribution, if you think it is key, then the science is very important. In my mind it isn't and I don't think that is the way forward."

"responsibility", which is a moral or ethical issue (Gardiner 2004; Muller et al. 2009; Skeie et al. 2017). Even where a scientific study might demonstrate that a country's, or company's, emissions contributed to a particular loss, that would not necessarily equate to responsibility to act or compensate, for example, if the emitter were unaware of the influence of their emissions. Ethical questions about responsibility extend far beyond the domain of climate science (ethical issues and perspectives are treated in the chapter by Wallimann-Helmer et al. 2018 of this book).

Yet many of the stakeholders interviewed appear to see a direct association between attribution and blame, liability, or compensation.[20] Several also suggested that the motivation for attribution research is blame or compensation.[21] This might explain why mentioning attribution science can receive a hostile, or wary, reception in many L&D discussions.[22] As one interviewee said: "the minute you talk about anthropogenic climate change, the purpose in talking about that is to figure out who is to blame and who to pay for the effects of it."

The assumption of political motives behind scientific inquiry or discussion poses a dilemma for science-policy dialogue: it is difficult to talk about attribution and climate change signals in connection with L&D, but it seems important that policy-makers are aware of what the science can offer, and what it cannot. And, if policy is to address losses and damages from climate change, it is important to understand changing risks. A central aim of attribution research, to investigate how rising GHGs are influencing climate and the occurrence of extreme weather events, would appear to be quite fundamental in order to prepare for climate change and address losses and damages.

Initial evidence suggests that the current understanding of attribution science amongst stakeholders involved in the L&D discussions is quite limited (Parker et al. 2017a). There are several opinions about the science which were found amongst the interviewees which might be problematic. First, several implied that scientific evidence would later become stronger which would provide more evidence for policy, particularly for compensation.[23] Whilst the science is advancing rapidly, some

[20]In many of the interviews, attribution was mentioned in the same sentence or fragment as blame, compensation, and liability, for example: "attribution and culpability of climate damage," "attribution of blame and taking compensation," "attribution, and therefore compensation," "the compensation or liability issues, as well as attribution," "how do you attribute and get compensation." This was often with the implication that the main purpose of attribution is to establish responsibility, or that the only reason why attribution would be needed is to establish responsibility e.g. "Is this about making an argument that there is an ethical responsibility on polluters to compensate for damage caused by pollution. In which case, attribution of weather events to particular cases in the atmosphere becomes important".

[21]For example: "There will at some point be a growing need for a politically motivated answer that looks at attribution, but the reason for that is not practical it is political", and: "climate attributions are trying to understand what's climate change doing to extremes and slow onset events and suggesting that this can create a call for compensation"

[22]Based on research team's experience of attending >20 meetings with a focus on L&D (Boyd et al. 2017).

[23]For example: "the science … that's kind of the one thing that's lagging" and "that issue of attribution around which political consensus will not occur in the next 5 years or 10." One interviewee

uncertainty will always remain, and it is important to help these stakeholders understand what the science might be able to offer, and where it might be insufficient. On the other hand, many other stakeholders highlighted the challenges and difficulties of attribution,[24] some even saying that it is impossible,[25] which perhaps misses an opportunity, as there may be useful research available which they are unaware of. In the next section, we review sources of attribution evidence to examine the extent to which they might provide useful information about the changing risk of losses and damages.

5.3 The Science of Attribution: What Kind of Evidence Is Available About the Influence of Anthropogenic Climate Change on L&D?

Climate change attribution research initially focused on investigating drivers of observed global warming (e.g. Tett et al. 1999; Stott et al. 2000). However global mean surface temperature does not have direct influence on people or infrastructure. Attribution of losses and damages is a much more challenging and more interdisciplinary scientific problem.

Attributing losses and damages involves investigating how anthropogenic GHGs influence many other climatic variables besides global temperature, as well as their influence on the oceans, cryosphere and biosphere, on a range of timescales. UNFCCC documents (e.g. UNFCCC 2013, 2015) consistently state that losses and damages refers to impacts from both extreme events (including heatwaves, flooding, tropical cyclones, and drought), and "slow onset" events or climatic processes (including glacier retreat, sea level rise, ocean acidification and desertification).[26] Understanding this wide range of environmental processes requires input from many different scientific disciplines (from physical climate science, to hydrology, to ecology, to economics), and collaboration between them. It is worth highlighting that the

---

described attribution science as the key to unlocking liability, implying that it would later emerge: "we don't have to enter the rooms on liability and compensation, those doors are locked behind a door called attribution. The key to that door lies with the scientific community, it is still being forged."

[24]For example: "Attribution is just really difficult," "as we know attribution is very difficult," and "the whole attribution thing is tricky."

[25]On being asked whether L&D should refer to L&D which can be attributed to anthropogenic climate change, or all climate-related L&D, one interviewee said "there's no science that can distinguish between the two," and another said "I think in many cases, it's just simply impossible to differentiate between the two. And I cannot think about one methodology that would allow a small island state to argue whether a storm surge is part of a natural variability or climate change."

[26]In decision 1/CP.16 (UNFCCC 2011), it was noted that approaches to address losses and damages should consider climatic impacts "including sea level rise, increasing temperatures, ocean acidification, glacial retreat and related impacts, salinization, land and forest degradation, loss of biodiversity and desertification"

distinction in policy, between extreme events and slow onset events, is not consistent with the way the events are studied by scientists; and losses and damages in many cases result from the interplay between incremental change (including "slow onset processes") and rare (extreme) events. For instance, sea level rise is often experienced through an increase in the height of storm surges. Gradually increasing temperatures may have their largest impact during a drought.

Attribution to anthropogenic climate change requires a comparison between the influence of human GHGs and the influence of other potential drivers. The first climate change attribution studies compared the "forcing" on global temperature from anthropogenic GHGs and aerosols, with natural drivers including solar variations and volcanic aerosols (Tett et al. 1999; Stott et al. 2000). Attribution of global temperature also, importantly, considers the role of natural modes of variability, such as the El Nino Southern Oscillation or Atlantic Multi-Decadal Oscillation (e.g. Fyfe et al. 2010; Foster and Rahmstorf 2011; Folland et al. 2013), which can modify the global temperature from year to year or even decade to decade (Parker et al. 2007). At a regional or local scale, the role of natural variability on weather and climate is even more pronounced, and it is therefore a very important factor to consider in attribution of losses and damages. In addition, the climatic and environmental hazards which lead to losses and damages have many other drivers besides anthropogenic emissions and natural variability, for example changes in land use (such as deforestation, urbanisation, agricultural development) which have important influences, for example via the hydrological cycle, meaning more confounding variables need to be taken into account in an attribution analysis.

To understand losses and damages, it is essential to not only study drivers of environmental hazards, but also to investigate other components of risk: influences on exposure and vulnerability (Huggel et al. 2013; chapters by Bouwer 2018; Schinko et al. 2018; Lopez et al. 2018; Botzen et al. 2018). The extent of losses and damages during a flood, for example, will be determined by the scale of the meteorological and hydrological hazard, but also the exposure of populations (are there people living in the floodplain?), and their vulnerability (are houses flood-resilient? are there early warning systems and procedures for emergency response? do people have insurance?). Furthermore, losses and damages might include monetary losses, loss of life, damage to infrastructure, detrimental effects on ecosystems, and a diverse array of non-monetary or non-economic losses and damages (NELs/NELD), such as loss of identity, or psychological distress (Serdeczny et al. 2016; Clayton et al. 2017; chapter by Serdeczny 2018). Attribution of such a range of quantifiable and non-quantifiable variables poses further uncertainties and challenges.

Attributing losses and damages may start to sound like an impossible challenge. As we will explore, it is not currently possible, and it may never be possible, to generate a complete inventory of losses and damages from anthropogenic emissions. Yet that should not prevent scientists from seeking to develop a fuller understanding of the drivers of losses and damages, and it does not mean that the science that is already available is not useful for policy-makers, who are accustomed to dealing with incomplete information and uncertainties. There are several important fields of enquiry which can already contribute evidence to help us understand how anthropogenic climate change is influencing losses and damages, and steps are already being made to integrate these disciplines. For example, recent work has estimated the monetary losses attributable to anthropogenic emissions from damage to housing following the 2013/2014 winter flooding in the UK (Schaller et al. 2016), and the number of heat-related deaths attributable to anthropogenic emissions during the 2003 European heatwave (Mitchell et al. 2016).

Here we review fields of study that might contribute to more such analyses in the future, for each giving a brief overview of how the science works, examples of the kind of attribution findings it can deliver, an evaluation of the strength of evidence which is currently available, and future directions in the field. Given the scale of the challenge, we cannot not hope to be comprehensive, but rather to give an introduction alongside references which could provide more detailed insights. Figure 5.2 summarises some of the causal connections between anthropogenic activity and losses and damages, and illustrates contributions from the different scientific fields described in Sects. 5.3.1–5.3.4. Several authors have described a "causal chain" between anthropogenic emissions, climate and weather, and local impacts (Stone and Allen 2005; Hansen et al. 2016). Here we show there are many interacting causal chains, which might be conceived of as a web or network of natural and anthropogenic interactions.

5.3.1 *Attribution of Climate Change and Extreme Weather Events to Anthropogenic Forcing*

The science of attributing observed climate and weather to external drivers, including attribution of climate change trends, and attribution of extreme weather events, is the type of research which physical climate scientists are usually referring to when they use the term "attribution," and this is also how "attribution" is used in the IPCC Working Group I (WGI) reports (Bindoff et al. 2013). Here, attribution is defined as "the process of evaluating the relative contributions of multiple causal factors to a change or event with an assignment of statistical confidence" (Hegerl et al. 2010: 2; Bindoff et al. 2013: 872). The aim is to investigate the influence of human-induced changes in GHGs and other short-lived climate forcers (SLCFs) on climate or extreme weather events, relative to the influence of other drivers, including modes of natural climate variability, solar variability, and volcanic eruptions. The studies usually focus on climate and weather, and therefore do not necessarily provide information about impacts or losses and damages, therefore the results are most relevant for the links shown in the top left of Fig. 5.2. What follows is a brief overview of the relevance of attribution research to L&D. For more detailed information, several reviews are available (Hegerl and Zwiers 2011; Bindoff et al. 2013; Stott et al. 2016; National Academies of Sciences, Engineering, and Medicine 2016).

Until very recently climate change attribution studies analysed trends, most notably the increase in global mean surface temperature. In these attribution studies,

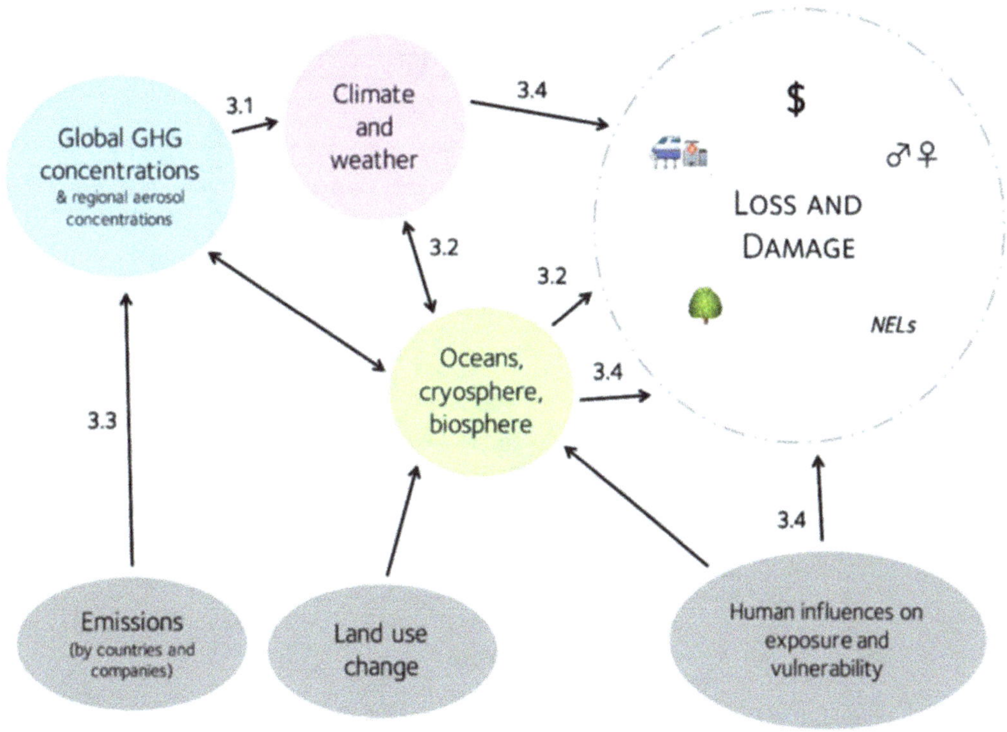

Fig. 5.2 A conceptual causal network illustrating multiple potential "causal chains" between anthropogenic changes in GHGs and aerosols, climate and weather, and L&D. The figure is designed to be illustrative rather than comprehensive, showing the influence of human factors (shown in grey at the bottom of the figure) on L&D, including monetary losses, fatalities, damage to infrastructure and ecosystems, and non-economic losses (NELs). The arrows are labelled with the section of the chapter which deals with scientific research relevant to that link in the network: importantly not all of the links are labelled, highlighting again that this chapter is not comprehensive, and there may be other fields of research which could be integrated into L&D research and practice to better understand L&D

observed trends are compared to model simulations with and without certain drivers (including GHGs, anthropogenic aerosols, solar variability, and volcanic aerosols) to test the relative importance of each forcing factor (see Fig. 5.3). These studies have demonstrated that anthropogenic activity has influenced global warming, and also regional warming on six continents, as well as global changes in related variables, such as atmospheric water vapour. The global increase in sea level rise has also been attributed to anthropogenic GHGs (Bindoff et al. 2013). Trend attribution can therefore provide relevant information about the influence of climate change on some "slow onset" events including sea level rise, and increasing temperatures. It is also possible to conduct trend attribution studies on long term trends in extreme weather events, for example the global increase in heavy precipitation events has been attributed to anthropogenic emissions (Zhang et al. 2013).

In the last 10 years, a new field of climate change attribution research has rapidly emerged, which focuses on single extreme weather events (Stott et al. 2016). It is now possible to make statements about how anthropogenic emissions have influenced specific heatwaves, heavy rainfall events, wind storms, and droughts. Since

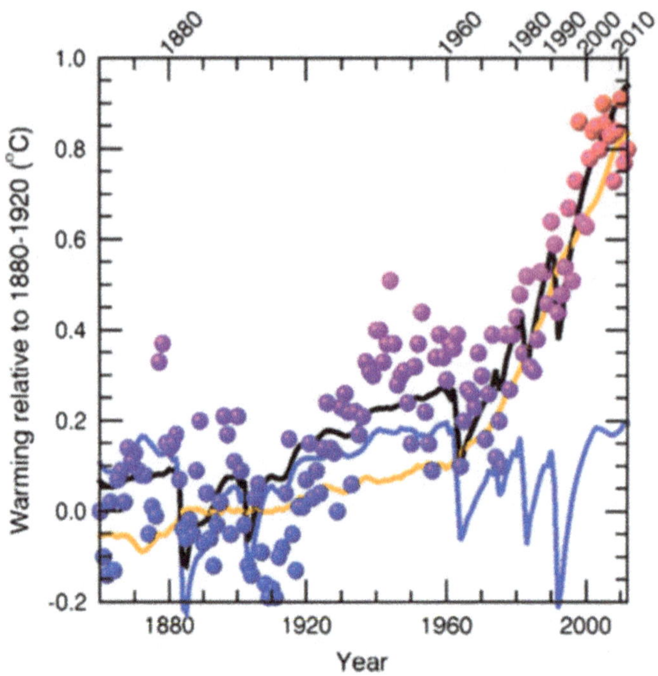

Fig. 5.3 Example of a simplified detection and attribution study for global temperature. Points show observed global temperature anomalies relative to 1880–1920 (shaded blue to pink to represent cooler to warmer temperatures). These are compared to model simulated temperatures with natural forcings only (blue), anthropogenic forcing only (orange), and a combination of natural and anthropogenic forcings (black). As shown, the observations can only be reproduced with both natural and anthropogenic forcing. *Source* Bindoff et al. (2013) IPCC AR5 WGI, Box 10.1 Fig. 1, p. 876

extreme weather events are rare, and their occurrence is strongly influenced by natural variability, it is not possible to say that a specific event would not have occurred without anthropogenic interference. However, it is possible to investigate whether and how anthropogenic emissions influenced the probability and magnitude. There are several different methods for examining the influence of anthropogenic climate change on extreme weather events, including observational and model-based studies (Stott et al. 2016). All methods use either large ensembles of climate models or statistical models to estimate the likelihood of an event occurring in the current climate as well as with the anthropogenic climate drivers removed. The resulting frequency distributions can be used to estimate the change in the probability due to anthropogenic interference (as in Fig. 5.4).

Extreme event attribution studies are increasingly being applied to understand contemporary extreme events, and for the past 6 years the *Bulletin of the American Meteorological Society* has published a summary of attribution studies referring to the previous year (Peterson et al. 2012, 2013; Herring et al. 2014, 2015, 2016, 2018). The science is advancing rapidly, evidenced in the large growth in the number of studies published, and the ability to make attribution statements more quickly: scientists are investigating the possibility of operational event attribution which could deliver statements in the weeks and months following an event

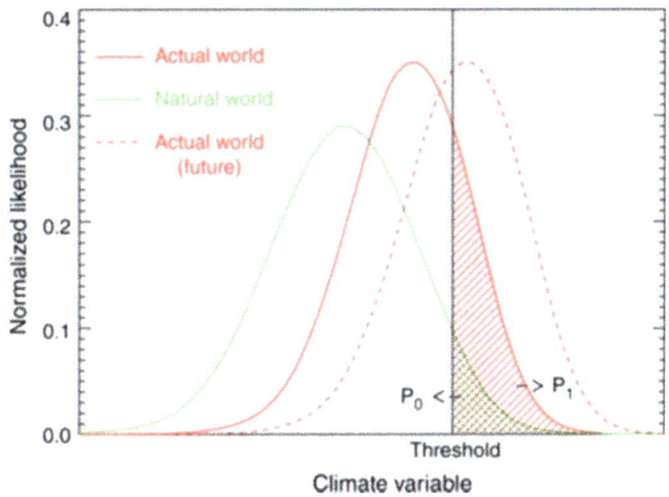

Fig. 5.4 A schematic illustration of the probability distribution of a climate variable (such as temperature or precipitation) with (solid red line) and without (green line) human influence on climate. Extreme event attribution studies use statistics or climate models to estimate these distributions and then calculate the change in probability associated with anthropogenic forcing (i.e. the difference between the green hatched area—P_0—and the red hatched area—P_1). The red dashed line illustrates how the probability distribution of the variable might change in future. *Source* Stott et al. (2016)

(see www.climatecentral.org). For example, the flooding in Louisiana in August 2016 was attributed to have been made twice as likely due to anthropogenic climate change, two weeks after the event occurred (van der Wiel et al. 2017). A large signal from anthropogenic climate change on the early 2017 drought in Kenya could be excluded while the event was still unfolding (Uhe et al. 2017).

It is currently not possible to conduct scientifically viable attribution studies for all types of extreme weather events leading to losses and damages (see Fig. 5.5), and some specific cases can be particularly difficult to model due to rare and complex weather patterns, as was found for flooding in Pakistan in 2010 (e.g. Christidis et al. 2013). There are also important variations in the availability and quality of attribution evidence between regions. Currently, many more studies have been conducted for developed than developing countries (Otto et al. 2015a). There are efforts to change this (e.g. wwa.climatecentral.org), but limited availability of data in developing countries is a barrier (Huggel et al. 2015a). This is highly relevant for L&D, because it means it is challenging to make attribution statements about losses and damages from some disasters. It is also important to highlight that in some cases anthropogenic climate change is found to decrease the probability of extreme events, such as spring flooding from snowmelt in the UK (Kay et al. 2011) or not to alter the likelihood of the event occurring, as for the 2014–15 droughts in the Sao Paolo area (Otto et al. 2015b).

Uncertainties associated with event attribution studies can make the results challenging to communicate and apply in policy (Otto et al. 2015a), as with projections of climate change (Weaver et al. 2013). The results of attribution studies also depend on

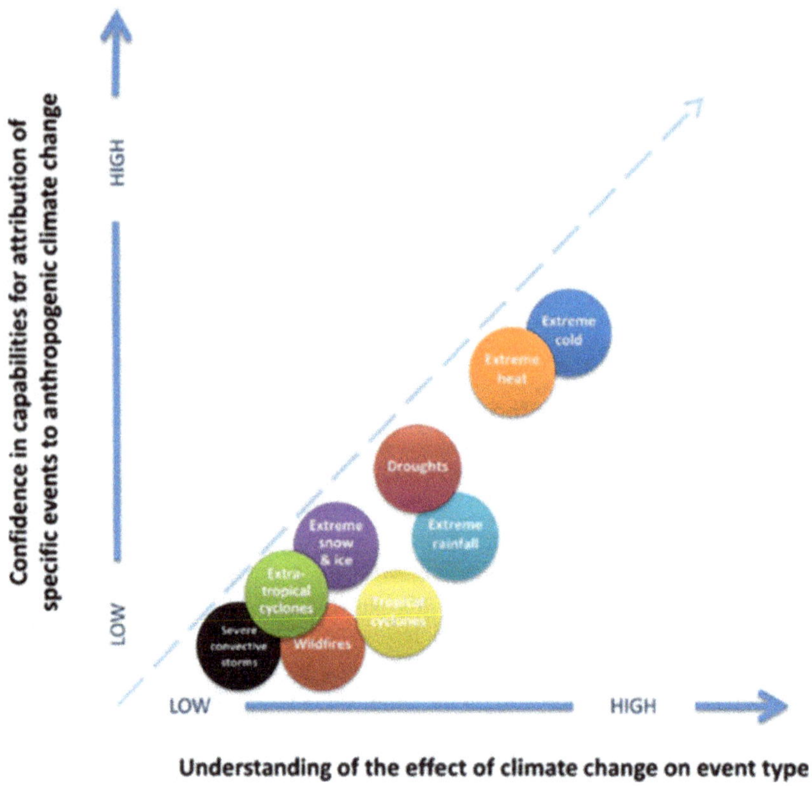

Fig. 5.5 Schematic illustration of the assessment by the National Academy of Sciences of the state of attribution science for different types of extreme weather events, both in terms of the general understanding of the impact of climate change on this kind of events, and in terms of the attribution of specific extreme events to anthropogenic forcing. *Source* National Academies of Sciences, Engineering and Medicine (2016)

how events are defined, how attribution questions are asked, and the methodologies used (Dole et al. 2011; Rahmstorf and Coumou 2011; Otto et al. 2012), which has led to some disagreements between scientists about the strength of evidence which they provide (Trenberth et al. 2015; Otto et al. 2016). This does not preclude the use of evidence about changing risks from attribution studies, but highlights a need for research to explore how the science might contribute to decision analyses (see chapter by Lopez et al. 2018; chapter by Botzen et al. 2018), potentially building on existing efforts to combine and translate sources of uncertainty into a common confidence language (Stone and Hansen 2016).

As GHG concentrations increase, and the Earth System adjusts to this perturbation to the energy balance, the signal from climate change will be strengthened, and therefore it is likely that the Earth will experience more regional changes, and more extreme events which show a detectable influence from anthropogenic emissions (e.g. Lee et al. 2016; Frame et al. 2017). The rapid developments in the science also suggest that there will be a continued growth in available literature, and now there are also increasing efforts to extend extreme event attribution studies beyond climatic variables to also consider ecological and hydrological impacts (e.g. Marthews et al.

2015; see Sect. 5.3.2), loss of life (Mitchell et al. 2016), and monetary losses (Schaller et al. 2016), as well as linking with research into the sources of anthropogenic forcing (see Sect. 5.3.3). However, it is worth highlighting that some uncertainties in the science will not be eliminated, and the research is unlikely to provide an even evidence base for all countries and events: some events will always be easier to study due to differences between events in the strength of the climate signal, availability of data, and ability of models to simulate them.

5.3.2 *Attribution of Climate Change Impacts*

There is a growing body of evidence about how recent changes in climate have influenced natural and human systems. As part of the IPCC AR5 Working Group II (WGII) report this evidence is drawn together to assess the detection and attribution of climate change impacts on the cryosphere, water resources, coastal systems, terrestrial and oceanic ecosystems, and on human systems, including analysis of food systems and the livelihoods of indigenous people (Cramer et al. 2014). In this context, attribution "addresses the question of the magnitude of the contribution of climate change to change in a system" (Cramer et al. 2014, 985), and that contribution is evaluated as being "major" or "minor". This is a slightly different approach to the attribution of climate changes and weather events in WGI (Sect. 5.3.1; see Fig. 5.6), and in particular, does not necessarily imply that the change in question

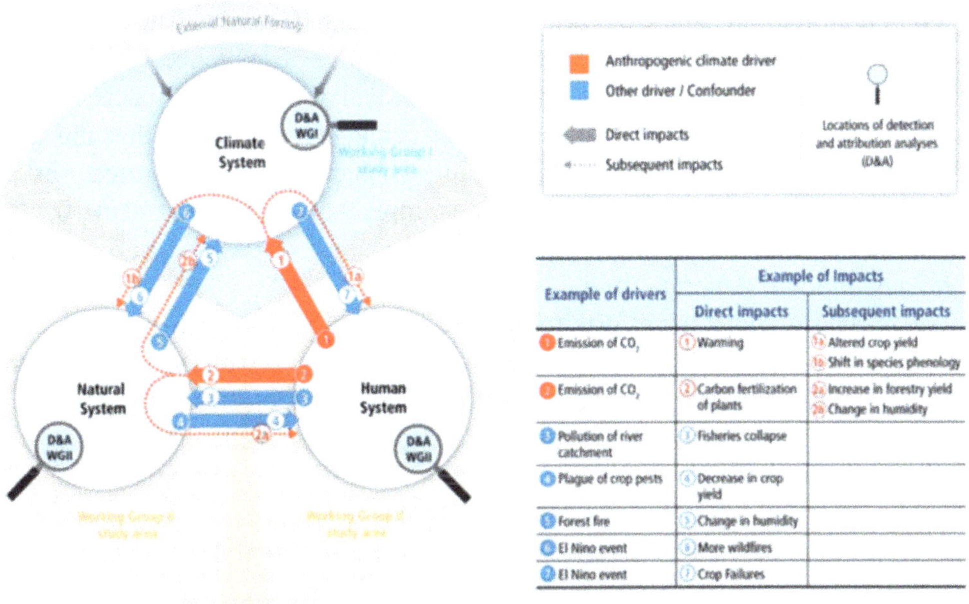

Example of drivers	Example of impacts	
	Direct impacts	Subsequent impacts
1 Emission of CO_2	1 Warming	1a Altered crop yield 1b Shift in species phenology
2 Emission of CO_2	2 Carbon fertilization of plants	2a Increase in forestry yield 2b Change in humidity
3 Pollution of river catchment	3 Fisheries collapse	
4 Plague of crop pests	4 Decrease in crop yield	
5 Forest fire	5 Change in humidity	
6 El Nino event	6 More wildfires	
7 El Nino event	7 Crop Failures	

Fig. 5.6 Schematic diagram from the IPCC WGII Chap. 18 on detection and attribution of observed impacts, which illustrates how WGII work on impacts attribution (here Sect. 5.3.2) relates to WGI work on attribution of climate and weather (here Sect. 5.3.1) and wider research into changes in climate, natural, and human systems. *Source* Cramer et al. (2014) IPCC AR5 WGII, Fig. 18-1, 985

can be traced back to anthropogenic emissions. Given the challenges of attribution to anthropogenic emissions for certain variables, notably precipitation changes, this flexible approach allows for evidence to be gathered even where the signal-to-noise ratio from anthropogenic activity is so far small.

The basic premise of impacts attribution research is consistent with the atmospheric research (Sect. 5.3.1). Once a change in a certain variable has been detected, potential drivers of that change are compared: the influence of regional or local climate change is compared with other confounding variables such as pollution and land use change, and sometimes technological innovation, or social and demographic changes. The precise methodologies vary between disciplines (Stone et al. 2013), but for a causal relationship to be established it is essential to understand the processes by which climate change contributed to the observed impact, which is often explored using ecological, hydrological, agricultural, or epidemiological models.

Over the past couple of decades, evidence about the observed impacts of climate change has grown substantially (Hansen 2015). In the IPCC report of 2001, strong evidence was restricted to the cryosphere and terrestrial ecosystems in northern latitudes or mountainous regions (Gitay et al. 2001; Arnell et al. 2001). In the AR5, impacts of recent climate change were observed on all continents and across all oceans. There is high confidence that worldwide glacial retreat, permafrost warming and thawing, and mass bleaching of coral reefs can be mainly attributed to climate change. There is evidence that the livelihoods of indigenous people in the Arctic have been altered by climate change, and emerging evidence for indigenous people in other regions (Cramer et al. 2014).

As might be expected, understanding causal relationships is very challenging for human systems, and there is often a strong role for social and economic factors, making it difficult to isolate the role of climate change (Cramer et al. 2014). Hansen and Cramer (2015) also highlight that the availability of evidence varies markedly between regions. Often there is less evidence available about impacts in regions considered to be most vulnerable to climate change: suggesting that the lack of evidence does not indicate that climate change impacts have not occurred, but rather than there are fewer studies available. For example, between 2000 and 2010, 10,544 scientific studies were published about climate change impacts in Europe, and just 1987 about South America (ibid).

Increasingly, there are efforts to analyse whether impacts attributed to climate change can also be attributed to anthropogenic emissions, as well as to extend extreme event attribution studies of weather to also investigate impacts (i.e. linking Sects. 5.3.1 and 5.3.2). Attribution to anthropogenic emissions has been demonstrated for global scale studies of shrinking glaciers (Marzeion et al. 2014), ecological studies at a global aggregate level of a meta-analysis (Rosenzweig et al. 2008), changing water runoff, for example in the western United States (Barnett et al. 2008), and changes in ecosystem productivity (Sippel et al. 2018). Hansen and Stone (2016) analysed the role of anthropogenic emissions across all of the impacts assessed in the IPCC WGII report (Cramer et al. 2014), and found that approximately 65% of the impacts related to changes in atmospheric or ocean temperature could be confidently attributed to anthropogenic forcing (Fig. 5.7). The strongest evidence exists for shrinking glaciers,

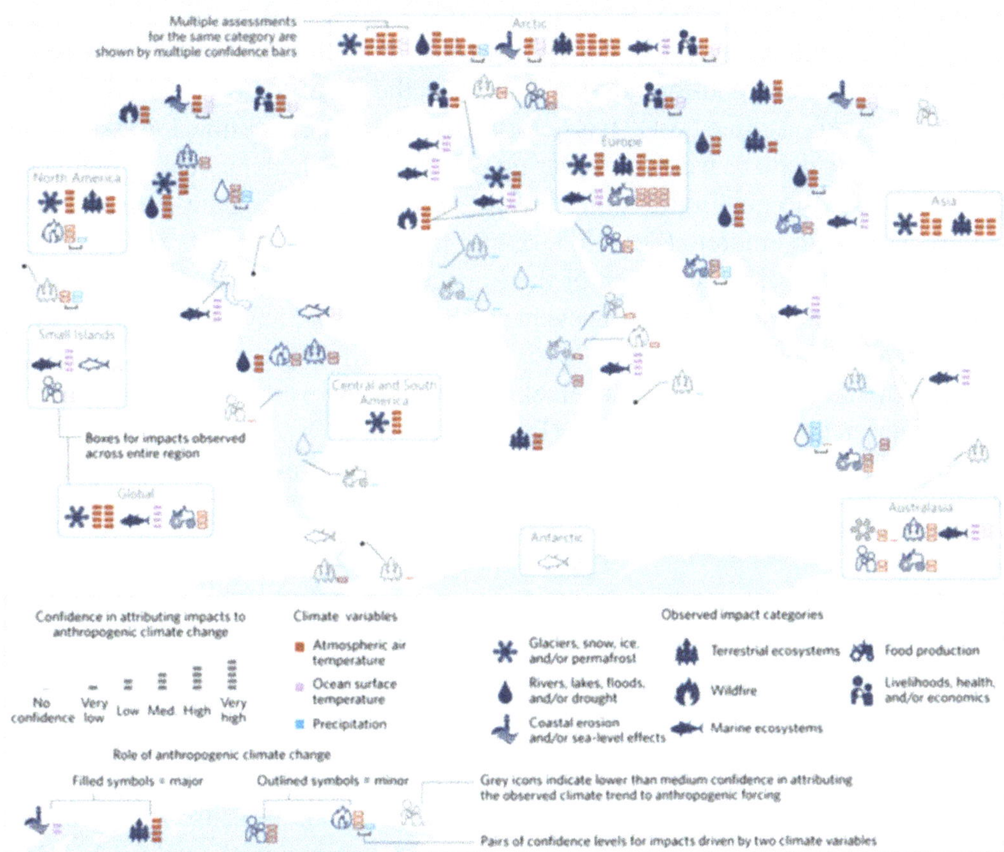

Fig. 5.7 An analysis by Hansen and Stone, revisiting impacts in the IPCC WGII report to assess whether they can be linked to anthropogenic forcing. *Note* Blue symbols show impacts which have been attributed to anthropogenic forcing with at least medium confidence, and confidence bars indicate the confidence level, with the colour of the confidence bars indicating whether the observed impact is related to changes in air temperature (red), ocean surface temperature (violet) or precipitation (blue). Impacts that are linked to regional climate trends, but with little evidence for anthropogenic forcing are shown in grey. *Source* Hansen and Stone (2016)

permafrost degradation, bleaching and decline of coral reefs, increasing forest fires, and the increase in shrub cover in Arctic regions. For impacts-related to precipitation, the evidence of anthropogenic forcing is still weak, and for many impacts, the evaluation of the relative contribution of anthropogenic climate change is still qualitative. It is currently difficult to make quantitative statements due to the limited availability of long-term, high quality data on the potential (non-climatic) drivers of change required to perform a comprehensive analysis.

However, despite the remaining gaps and challenges, there is already substantial evidence available about the attribution of climate change impacts (see Fig. 5.7), which can contribute to an understanding of how anthropogenic climate change is influencing losses and damages. The steps taken to integrate impacts research (Sect. 5.3.2) with climate research (Sect. 5.3.1), are promising, and several authors have proposed frameworks, and provided examples to illustrate, "end-to-end" attribution (Stone and Allen 2005; Stone et al. 2013; Huggel et al. 2015a; Hansen et al. 2016), which might be useful for further research. There is a question about whether this constitutes true "end-to-end" attribution in the case of L&D. Do all climate change impacts constitute L&D? It is notoriously unclear exactly how L&D should be defined, but it is perhaps worth considering various other elements which might contribute to an "end-to-end" attribution of L&D, including extending the "causal chains" from emissions to emitters (Sect. 5.3.3), and towards disaster losses (Sect. 5.3.4). It is also worth considering which of the impacts attributed (in e.g. Fig. 5.7) might already be considered L&D. Recent event attribution studies have analysed monetary losses from flooding (Schaller et al. 2016); and loss of life from cold- and heat-related events (Christidis et al. 2010; Mitchell et al. 2016). Huggel et al. (2016a) also examine the Hansen and Stone (2016) data (Fig. 5.7) to consider which impacts constitute irreversible losses, finding evidence for the attribution of irreversible loss of glaciers, coral reefs, or livelihoods of Arctic communities.

5.3.3 Attributing Anthropogenic Forcing to Regions, Countries, and Sectors

IPCC (2013) stated "Human influence on the climate system is clear." This overarching statement can be decomposed on the *response side* of the cause-effect chain in terms of various types of impacts and their regional distribution (Sects. 5.3.1, 5.3.2). But it is also possible to do so on the *driver side*—along several dimensions. Firstly, there are different emissions and surface changes that perturb the radiative balance of the earth-atmosphere system and cause radiative forcing; greenhouse gases such as CO_2, CH_4 and N_2O, aerosols such as sulphate and black carbon, and albedo changes from land surface changes. Secondly, these factors also have a regional resolution; i.e., the emissions and changes in albedo from land use changes can be distributed to regions and nations, and economic sectors. Thirdly, these changes have occurred at different points in time; e.g. early deforestation and coal burning versus late emissions from more modern sectors (e.g. aviation) and technologies (e.g. halogenated gases). Several studies have quantified contributions to climate change by regions (den Elzen et al. 2005), nations (e.g. Matthews 2016; Skeie et al. 2017), sectors (e.g. Fuglestvedt et al. 2008) and even companies (Heede 2014).

To investigate the contributions to climate change, simple climate models are used to test the influence of specified quantities of emissions, or types of radiative forcing, on climatic changes, primarily global temperature. Contributions to climate change are often defined in counterfactual terms; i.e., how would the change in the chosen climate indicator (usually global mean surface temperature) be different if a particular subset of emissions were removed? A large number of simulations are used to test many different subsets of emissions. Due to non-linearities the individual contributions do not necessarily add up to 100% and there are various methods to adjust for this. Availability of emissions data is also a key issue. Various emission

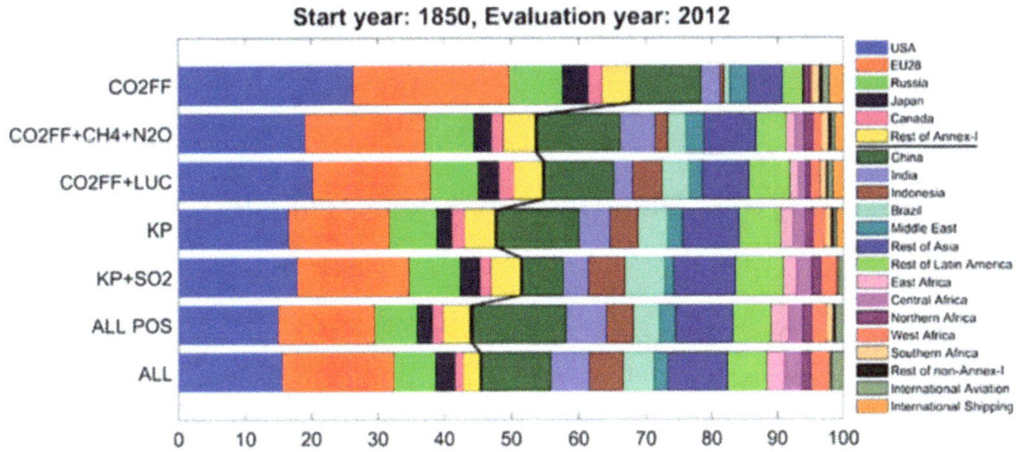

Fig. 5.8 Sensitivity of estimated contributions to global mean surface temperature increase to the choice of forcing components included in attribution analysis. CO_2FF: CO_2 from fossil-fuel combustion and cement production. LUC: Land use change. KP: Kyoto Protocol gases (CO_2, CH_4, N_2O, HFC, SF_6, PFC). ALL POS: All warming components. *Source* Skeie et al. (2017)

databases and inventories are used and often assumptions and inter/extrapolations are needed (see Skeie et al. 2017).

The results of these studies depend strongly on various choices taken during the analysis. Among the choices that have to be made are start and end dates for emissions that are considered, *when* to measure the effect of the emissions, what indicator of climate change is chosen (temperature, precipitation, extremes, sea level rise, etc.), which drivers (GHGs, aerosols, land use changes) are included, how to frame the emissions by the selected entities (extraction/territorial/consumption based emissions), and whether the contributions should be normalised by population size. An alternative could also be to normalise the contributions by the Gross Domestic Product (GDP) of the countries. Figure 5.8 shows how the choice of emission components included can impact the resulting calculations of how much each region or country has contributed to change in global mean surface temperature up to 2012 (Skeie et al. 2017).

As discussed by Skeie et al. (2017), and Fuglestvedt and Kallbekken (2015) there is no simple and single answer to the contribution question. Thus, it is not straightforward to ask how much a particular country, company, or sector contributed to observed global warming. The answer varies depending on many choices in the methodology, and these choices are associated with many open value-related and ethical questions. Scientists might therefore best support policy-makers by presenting a spectrum of results showing how the calculated contributions vary according to various choices.

A natural research question to ask is whether it will be possible to go further and attribute other implications of climate change to nations' emissions. Otto et al. (2017) for the first time explore the link between emissions from countries to radiative forcing and temperature contributions, and changes in the probability of extreme weather events, demonstrating how this area of work might be integrated with attribution of climate and weather events (Sect. 5.3.1) and impacts (Sect. 5.3.2).

5.3.4 Assessing and Analysing Losses and Damages from Disasters

To understand L&D from anthropogenic climate change, it is also important to consider disaster assessments and disaster research. Before the establishment of L&D as an area within the UNFCCC, there was already a great deal of work seeking to quantify and analyse losses and damages from natural hazards. Not all of this work examines causality, and therefore might not be considered attribution research, but integrating knowledge, expertise, and analysis tools from disaster research with climate change and climate impacts attribution research (Sects. 5.3.1, 5.3.2, 5.3.3) could be a fruitful way to obtain a fuller understanding of L&D, and in particular to compare the influence of anthropogenic climate change with drivers of exposure and vulnerability.

Loss and damage assessments are routinely conducted after major disasters, and the results are widely available in disaster databases including at global (EM-DAT: Guha-Sapir et al. 2009; DesInventar 2015), and national levels. Reinsurance companies also hold disaster databases,[27] but these are generally not publically available. Disaster databases represent an impressive resource, however the quality, consistency and completeness varies between regions and between events. The results also vary between datasets: there is no consensus about how to collect data following disasters (Huggel et al. 2015b), and different methodologies can have quite different results (Kron et al. 2012). Collecting data about losses and damages from slow onset events such as drought is very challenging, due to the timescales of data collection, and the many other drivers which might play a role over this longer time period. Developing countries are poorly represented (Gall et al. 2009), and in particular there is a lack of information at the subnational scale in vulnerable countries (Huggel et al. 2015b).

Disaster risk research uses these databases to examine trends in losses from disasters, including extreme weather events, and including analysis of causal relationships with climatic variability (Bouwer 2011; chapter by Bouwer 2018). It is generally accepted that the observed global increase in disaster losses is largely attributable to increases in exposure to hazard, with more wealth situated in locations that are at risk (Bouwer 2011; IPCC 2012). Research on the role of changes in vulnerability on observed losses and damages is still very scarce and needs to be investigated in more detail, although there is evidence that vulnerability to flood hazard is decreasing in some places (Mechler and Bouwer 2015; Jongman et al. 2015; Kreibich et al. 2017). Disaster databases often focus on a few key variables such as monetary losses and fatalities. The range of losses and damages considered under the UNFCCC extends far beyond these quantities (Serdeczny et al. 2016) and therefore it is also important

---

[27] E.g. www.munichre.com/natcatservice; www.swissre.com/sigma.

to consider social science research to understand losses from disasters at a local level (e.g. Warner and van der Geest 2013).

Perhaps the greatest opportunity for integration with attribution research lies with "disaster forensics" and related fields which seek to examine past disasters, and draw lessons for future disaster risk management (e.g. Keating et al. 2016). Techniques include root-cause analysis (Blaikie et al. 2014), meta-analytical reviews (Mitchell 1999), longitudinal analysis of multiple disasters in a specific location (Erikson 1976; Oliver-Smith and Hoffman 1999; Kreibich et al. 2017), and retrospective scenarios (Jones et al. 2008).

5.4 Policy Implications: How Might Attribution Science Be Applied to Support Actions to Address Losses and Damages?

To date, it has been challenging to initiate detailed conversations in the policy arena about the potential relevance of attribution science to L&D: in part due to the controversy surrounding L&D, and the association which is often made between attribution and responsibility, blame, and liability (see Sect. 5.2). In this chapter we seek to highlight that attribution science itself does not aim to establish responsibility; and to outline some of the motivations, methods, and findings of different forms of attribution research, also considering how the integration of these fields could lead to a fuller understanding of the influence of anthropogenic climate change on losses and damages (Sect. 5.3). Now, having reviewed the available attribution evidence, we consider whether this science might have any useful applications to support L&D mechanisms, policies, and practice.

Many attribution scientists have suggested that their research could be useful for adaptation and/or L&D (e.g. Pall et al. 2011; Mitchell et al. 2016; Parker et al. 2017b). Parker et al. (2017a)'s literature review highlighted that climate scientists frequently refer to the potential applications of PEA. However, they found that in the L&D literature itself, including, for example, publications from non-governmental organisations, there was little mention of attribution science. This suggests that there is a need for science-policy dialogue to explore potential applications (in agreement with e.g. Stott and Walton 2013); and to this end, there have already been a number of studies involving interviews with decision-makers about the potential uses of attribution science (e.g. Sippel et al. 2015).

One potential barrier in identifying applications for L&D is that it is not yet clear exactly what actions to address losses and damages would entail, with different stakeholders holding different perspectives and priorities (Boyd et al. 2017; Fig. 5.1). Previous literature has already highlighted that the potential role for science in relation to L&D might be different depending on what is meant by L&D, and what L&D mechanisms aim to do (Surminski and Lopez 2015; Huggel et al. 2015a; chapters by Lopez et al. 2018 and Schinko et al. 2018). Here we explore potential applications for attribution science in a L&D context with a very broad view of what L&D might signify, including a large range of actions to address losses and damages, as identified by different stakeholders (Boyd et al. 2017), for example adaptation, risk reduction, risk transfer, insurance, risk pooling, risk management, recovery, rehabilitation, and compensation.

5.4.1 *Catalysing Action*

Many papers, and stakeholder interviews, have highlighted an important role for attribution in catalysing action (Bouwer 2011; Surminski and Lopez 2015; Parker et al. 2017a). This refers to action in terms of greater mitigation ambition, as well as actions to better prepare for disasters. Stott and Walton (2013) highlight that attribution of extreme weather events could help aid agencies to encourage preparation for disasters, and research projects are now underway to develop attribution studies with DRR agencies to pilot such an approach (www.climatecentral.org). Promoting mitigation could also be seen as an important element in relation to L&D. Several interviewees in the Boyd et al. (2017) study highlighted that one of the important goals of L&D negotiations is to heighten ambition to mitigate, in order to avoid impacts and risks. If the interviewees and commentators are correct, that attribution evidence could motivate mitigation (see Parker et al. 2017a), presumably by demonstrating quantitative evidence and examples of how GHGs and aerosols are affecting people; this motivates further attribution research, and also further efforts to communicate the results in an understandable form for policy-makers and the public (following existing work e.g. wwa.climatecentral.org).

5.4.2 *Providing Evidence for Liability and Compensation*

The most frequently discussed applications of attribution science for L&D arguably relate to liability and compensation (Allen 2003; Allen et al. 2007; Stone et al. 2009; Thompson and Otto 2015; Parker et al. 2016, 2017a; Thornton and Covington 2016). L&D has its origins in calls from small islands states for some form of compensation for climate change impacts, particularly sea level rise (Mace and Verheyen 2016), and L&D is sometimes still discussed with reference to some notion of a global compensation mechanism. In this context, attribution is often raised in terms of whether it could provide sufficient evidence for such a mechanism (e.g. Craeynest 2010). For example, one interviewee from Boyd et al. (2017)'s study explained: "In order to have a reliable L&D compensation mechanism, you'll need to have a very high confidence about the causes of L&D, if the science is not 100% or close, there'll always be room to contest" (see similar discussions in Parker et al. 2017a). For one stakeholder, attribution science was even described as the key to unlocking liability: "we don't have to enter the rooms on liability and compensation, those doors are locked behind a door called attribution. The key to that door lies with the scientific community, it is still being forged."

These interviews took place before the Paris Climate Conference, when the following text was included in Decision 1/CP. 21, referring to the article of the Paris Agreement about L&D: "Article 8 of the Agreement does not involve or provide a basis for any liability or compensation;" (UNFCCC 2015, paragraph 51). Subsequent analysis suggests that this does not prevent liability or compensation per se, but rather only in connection with Article 8 (Mace and Verheyen 2016; Calliari 2016). It does not, for example, prevent actions outside the framework of the UNFCCC, such as legal action against individual countries or companies.

The potential for attribution evidence to support ad hoc litigation, outside of the UNFCCC, has also received considerable attention in the literature, with mixed views about whether the science would be strong enough to stand up in court (e.g. Farris 2009; Adam 2011; Wrathall et al. 2015; Hannart et al. 2016; Thornton and Covington 2016; see also the chapter by Simlinger and Mayer 2018).

Drawing on the review of available evidence in Sect. 5.3, it would seem that any form of liability and compensation which relies on a complete "causative chain" from monetary losses—to weather and climate—to anthropogenic climate change—to emitters, might currently struggle to find many examples with sufficient evidence. Given the progress of the science, such examples will however emerge, albeit with uncertainties (Otto et al. 2017). It will then become a legal question of whether and how these might support individual lawsuits. Existing analysis suggests that the requirements of quantitative evidence would be rather different, for example if the case is examined in tort law or in the context of human rights (Marjanac and Patton 2018).

Beyond ad hoc litigation, the idea of a global compensation mechanism based on fully attributable losses and damages is currently far from reality. This is not to say that some kind of global insurance and/or compensation mechanism is not possible, but rather that trying to base payments on quantitative attribution evidence at a local level is unlikely to lead to fair outcomes, as the strength of available evidence will vary between places and events. In fact, the evidence at the disposal of poor countries, typically highly vulnerable to climate change, is very limited as compared to richer countries with long-term and high-quality data series and information (Huggel et al. 2016b; Fig. 5.9). Several proposals for global insurance mechanisms in the context of L&D have been developed (e.g. Linnerooth-Bayer et al. 2009; chapter by Linnerooth-Bayer et al. 2018),[28] and these have not necessarily required a full causative chain of attribution evidence (see also introduction by Mechler et al. 2018).

[28]The original proposal from the Alliance of Small Islands States for to establish a 'collective loss-sharing scheme' to 'compensate the most vulnerable small island and low-lying coastal developing countries for losses and damages' is described in Mace and Verheyen (2016), and can be found in an annex at http://unfccc.int/resource/docs/a/15_2.pdf.

5.4.3 *Informing the Distribution of Adaptation or L&D Funding*

Another frequent, and related, discussion about the potential use of attribution science concerns whether it might be applied to help inform distribution of adaptation or (potential) L&D funding. Currently projects which seek support from the Green Climate Fund are judged against a list of criteria, for example expected reduction in vulnerability and ability to strengthen institutional capacity (the investment framework is documented in e.g. GCF 2015). It is conceivable that some kind of attribution evidence might be required as part such a checklist. In the context of L&D, some have suggested a separate fund could be established for projects which seek to address losses and damages (e.g. Richards and Boom 2015). Such a fund would presumably also have a list of necessary criteria which could include attribution evidence. The concept of a L&D fund is related to the idea of a global compensation mechanism, but here we discuss it separately, since it could, for example, be based on voluntary contributions, and it is perhaps useful to think about how evidence might be applied to *distribute available funds* rather than to extract new funding from emitters.

Several authors (Hoegh-Guldberg et al. 2011) and stakeholders interviewed (in Parker et al. 2017a; Sippel et al. 2015) have suggested that attribution science could be used to help allocate resources. However, others argue that, given disparities in the strength of evidence, it would be counterproductive or unfair to give priority only to projects which address impacts that can be confidently attributed to anthropogenic

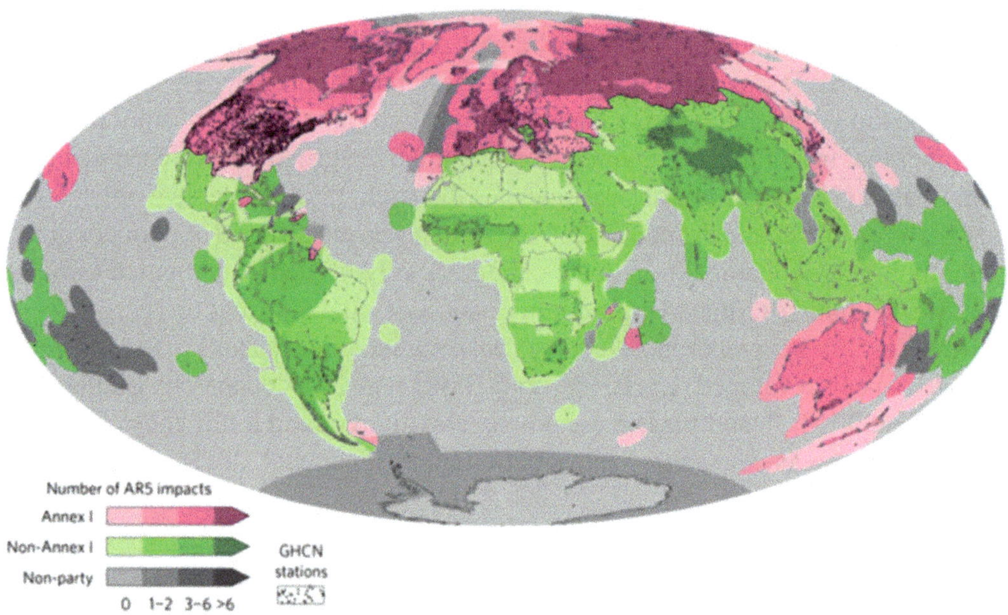

Fig. 5.9 Map demonstrating the location of weather stations in the Global Historical Climatology Network (black points), as well as the number of detected impacts reported in the IPCC AR5 for Annex I countries (in purple), Non-Annex I countries (in green), and regions not party to the UNFCCC (in grey). *Source* Huggel et al. (2016b)

climate change (Hulme et al. 2011). Referring again to Fig. 5.9, it is clear that some countries and regions have more data available than others, and whilst this is not the only factor that determines confidence in attribution studies (Otto et al. 2013), the strength of evidence will continue to vary between regions, and between climate change impacts. The discussion about who is most deserving of funding raises ethical questions which cannot be answered by scientists, and highlights that incorporating attribution science into a system for distributing funding would not be straightforward. In the final section we explore a potentially less controversial, and perhaps more fundamental way in which the science can be used in helping to decide which actions might address losses and damages.

5.4.4 Analysing Drivers of L&D to Inform Practical Actions to Avert, Minimise, and Address Losses and Damages

Rather than being used to help answer *political* and *ethical* questions about *who* should pay, and *who* should receive support (see chapter by Wallimann-Helmer et al. 2018), attribution science could instead help to answer *practical* questions about *how* to spend the money: *How* should risks be managed? *What* can be done to minimise and address losses and damages? *Which* actions can be taken to help people to recover from L&D? In order to prepare for changing risks, it is fundamental to understand their causes, including drivers of changes in hazard, as well as vulnerability and exposure. Anthropogenic climate change is just one driver of changing hazard, but a fundamental driver which must be incorporated into risk analyses in order to identify risk management options which will be most effective in a changing climate (see Mechler and Schinko 2016; chapter by Schinko et al. 2018). As demonstrated in Sect. 5.3, attribution science is focused on establishing causality and, alongside other climate change research, is an important element in a toolkit for climate risk management.

From a climate risk management perspective, the key is to be able to quantify current risks and how these may evolve in the future in a changing climate (and, more broadly, a changing world). The importance of future climate model projections is frequently highlighted with reference to adaptation planning (e.g. Giorgi et al. 2009) and, more recently, with reference to planning to address losses and damages (Surminski and Lopez 2015). It is also increasingly recognised that, to understand risk, climate projections should be combined with projections of future changes in exposure and vulnerability (Mechler and Bouwer 2015). Attribution science can be a complementary source of evidence, which (a) provides important additional information about changing risk in the presence of uncertainty, (b) offers an assessment of how risks are changing now (whilst future projections might not be relevant for 30 years or more), and (c) helps to diagnose the causes of losses and damages, which could be useful in prioritising actions to reduce risk. The need to assess science investigating the role of climate and non-climate drivers in recent high-impact events, and how those drivers are changing across time and spatial scales, in order to inform adaptation and risk management, has been recognised as a key priority for the next IPCC report (RC/RCCC 2017). Here we give a few examples to illustrate the importance of this approach.

In East Africa, many climate models suggest that the region will become wetter in future (Shongwe et al. 2011; James et al. 2014b), which might imply the need to adapt to wetter conditions, and potential for losses and damages from extreme precipitation or flooding (Shongwe et al. 2011; Taylor et al. 2013). However, observations suggest that there has been a recent increase in drought (Rowell et al. 2015), and analysis of the climate processes associated with precipitation decline suggest it could be caused by warming of the Indian Ocean, which is expected under anthropogenic climate change (Copsey et al. 2006; Williams and Funk 2011; Williams et al. 2012). An attribution study of the drivers of the climate hazards that resulted in the extreme drought in 2010–11 (Lott et al. 2013) showed that it was influenced by both climate change and natural variability (with an important role for the El Nino Southern Oscillation). By combining evidence from attribution research with observational evidence, physical understanding, and future projections, it seems clear that adaptation and L&D planning for East Africa should not assume wetter futures (Funk 2011), and should strengthen measures to respond to drought, which could continue to occur due to natural variability, and may be amplified by climate change.

Another reason that attribution research can provide important evidence to help address losses and damages, is that it offers an assessment of how risk is changing now. For many decision-makers, information about how climate might change in 30 years is not relevant because their planning horizons are much shorter (Jones et al. 2017). This is true for several of the approaches which have been suggested to address losses and damages. For example, there has been a great deal of emphasis on risk pooling schemes and (re)insurance. These systems rely on estimates of the probability of extreme weather events based on historical data, which may no longer be relevant in a changing climate. Attribution studies can provide an estimate of the current probability of extreme weather events. Finally, the above has focused on the hazard component of climate risk management but attribution science can also be extended to provide relevant information on the vulnerability and exposure components. This principle is demonstrated by considering the impact of different responses to two category 4 tropical cyclones in Mozambique (Benessene 2007; UNISDR 2010). This showed significantly less loss of life in a more recent event in 2007 compared to 2000, as a result of better early warning systems reducing human exposure to a hazard of similar magnitude. Another example by Otto et al. (2015b) showed that climate change had not altered the likelihood of the precipitation deficit associated with the 2014–15 droughts in the Sao Paolo area. Thus higher losses in this case compared to earlier events could not be attributed to a change in the hazard and so were attributable to higher vulnerability and exposure resulting from socio-economic changes. These examples demonstrate that attribution science can be useful to guide the design of improved future responses to climate-related risks.

5.5 Conclusions

In this chapter we have discussed how attribution science might be useful for L&D policy and practice. As has been widely recognised, the concept of L&D from climate change is still vague and contested with a diverse range of perspectives held amongst stakeholders. This makes it challenging to say exactly what kind of scientific input is needed. Here we take a broad approach to consider how attribution science might be relevant to L&D discussions, and a range of possible options for L&D policy and practice. The first step was to examine the discourse surrounding L&D and existing mentions of, and debates about, attribution in the L&D policy space (Sect. 5.2). If scientists, practitioners, and policy-makers are to jointly integrate science into actions to address losses and damages, it is important to understand the baseline understandings and associations held by different stakeholders. We have followed policy discussions for a number of years, and directly asked many participants in L&D discussions about their views on attribution, including through stakeholder interviews (Box 5.2). This research has demonstrated that attribution is a controversial but also recurring issue in L&D discussions. In our interviews with stakeholders and observations of meetings about L&D, attribution was often mentioned. Few stakeholders demonstrated in-depth knowledge of attribution science, but they often raised questions about whether losses and damages could be attributed to climate change. These questions relate to practical issues about the mandate of the UNFCCC, but also have important political implications. Attribution is often mentioned alongside responsibility, blame and liability.

It therefore appears that attribution is a key issue of relevance to L&D discussions, but it is so far very difficult to discuss in detail how the science might be used, because it is considered to be a controversial topic. If scientists are to effectively engage in dialogue with policy-makers, it would be helpful for them to be aware of these associations and controversies; and also aware that policy-makers work in an environment where science is often used for political motives, and clarity is not always helpful or asked for. In fact, climate negotiators may be mandated to avoid certain topics or terminology. Communicating scientific results is therefore not sufficient to support policy: it must be communicated in a language that policy-makers can work with. At the same time, it would be helpful if policy-makers and practitioners were made more aware of the findings and methodologies of attribution studies and the fact that attribution science itself is not primarily designed to establish responsibility. The political and ethical implications are far beyond the realm of physical scientists, and many scientists are keen to remain impartial purveyors of information, without becoming involved in politics: a potentially useful resource for policy-makers in a landscape where most actors do have political motives.

A more in-depth discussion between scientists, practitioners, and policy-makers about attribution science would likely reveal much that is relevant to averting and addressing losses and damages, regardless of political positions. As outlined in Sect. 5.3, there are a number of fields of inquiry that are advancing rapidly which could be integrated to better understand the influence of anthropogenic climate change on losses and damages, and how this compares with other drivers of risk. There are uncertainties, and the level of evidence available is not even between countries, regions, or between different climate change impacts. It may therefore be challenging to use attribution science for the kind of applications which are most frequently suggested. Notably it might be challenging to use attribution science for some kind of global compensation mechanism, or to allocate funding to address climate change impacts. Such systems might benefit from being informed by global estimates of attributable changes and evidence for the emergence of climate change impacts in different regions, rather than being informed by attribution studies for specific events or specific losses. However, as well as the difficult political and ethical questions about *who* should pay for losses and damages, and *who* deserves support to address losses and damages, there are also fundamental practical questions about *how* to help people prepare for, and recover from, climate change impacts and losses and damages. To address these questions most effectively, and manage risks in a changing climate, understanding drivers of risk is fundamental, and attribution science has a key role to play.

To end, *how is attribution science relevant for L&D policy and practice? And could it be useful?* While in a political context attribution is often associated with compensation for climate change impacts, we show that the science of attribution has the potential for much broader applications. Attribution has an important role to play in helping understanding L&D, including through quantification of risks, investigating of the relative importance of different drivers of change, and identifying timescales on which significant impacts of climate change emerge in different regions of the world. Regardless of the policy mechanisms for addressing losses and damages, it is important to foster a better understanding of how climate change is influencing losses and damages. With further scientific integration, including integrating attribution studies with future projections, and through informed science-policy-practice dialogue, attribution could contribute towards the development of useful practical actions to avert and address losses and damages.

References

Adam D (2011) Climate change in court. Nat Clim Change 1(3):127. https://doi.org/10.1038/nclimate1131

Allen M (2003) Liability for climate change. Nature 421:891–892. https://doi.org/10.1038/421891a

Allen M, Pall P, Stone D, Stott P, Frame D, Min S-K, Nozawa T, Yukimoto S (2007) Scientific challenges in the attribution of harm to human influence on climate. University of Pennsylvania Law Rev 1353–1400

Arnell N, Compagnucci L, Cunha R, da L, Hanaki K, Howe C, Shiklomanov GM SEI (2001) Hydrology and water resources. In: McCarthy J, Canziani O, Leary N, Dokken DWK (eds) Climate change 2001: impacts, adaptation and vulnerability. Contribution of working group II to the third assessment report of the intergovernmental panel on climate change. Cambridge University Press, Cambridge, United Kingdom and New York, NY, USA, pp 192–233

Barnett TP, Pierce DW, Hidalgo HG, Bonfils C, Santer BD, Das T, Bala G, Wood AW, Nozawa T, Mirin AA, Cayan DR, Dettinger MD (2008) Human-Induced changes in the hydrology of the Western United States. Science 319:1080–1083

Benessene MV (2007) Experience in coping with floods in Central Mozambique. http://www.iisd.org/pdf/2007/climate_early_moises_benessene.pdf. Accessed 12 Jun 2010

Bindoff NL, Stott PA, AchutaRao KM, Allen MR, Gillett N, Gutzler D, Hansingo K, Hegerl G, Hu Y, Jain S et al (2013) Detection and attribution of climate change: from global to regional. In: Stocker TF, Qin D, Plattner G-K et al (eds) Climate change 2013: the physical science basis. contribution of working group I to the fifth assessment report of the intergovernmental panel on climate change. Cambridge University Press, Cambridge, United Kingdom and New York, NY, USA, pp 867–952

Blaikie P, Cannon T, Davis I, Wisner B (2014) From event analysis to global lessons: disaster forensics for building resilience. Routledge, New York

Bouwer LM (2011) Have disaster losses increased due to anthropogenic climate change? Bull Am Meteor Soc 92:39–46. https://doi.org/10.1175/2010BAMS3092.1

Botzen W, Bouwer LM, Scussolini P, Kuik O, Haasnoot M, Lawrence J, Aerts JCJH (2018) Integrated disaster risk management and adaptation. In: Mechler R, Bouwer L, Schinko T, Surminski S, Linnerooth-Bayer J (eds) Loss and damage from climate change. Concepts, methods and policy options. Springer, Cham, pp 287–315

Boyd E, James R, Jones R (2016) Policy brief: a spectrum of views on loss and damage. http://www.eci.ox.ac.uk/publications/161101.pdf

Boyd E, James RA, Jones RG, Young HR, Otto FE (2017) A typology of loss and damage perspectives. Nat Clim Change 7:723. https://doi.org/10.1038/nclimate3389

Bouwer LM (2018) Observed and projected impacts from extreme weather events: implications for loss and damage. In: Mechler R, Bouwer L, Schinko T, Surminski S, Linnerooth-Bayer J (eds) Loss and damage from climate change. Concepts, methods and policy options. Springer, Cham, pp 63–82

Calliari E (2016) Loss and damage: a critical discourse analysis of Parties' positions in climate change negotiations. J Risk Res 9877:1–23. https://doi.org/10.1080/13669877.2016.1240706

Calliari E, Surminski S, Mysiak J (2018) Politics of (and behind) the UNFCCC's loss and damage mechanism. In: Mechler R, Bouwer L, Schinko T, Surminski S, Linnerooth-Bayer J (eds) Loss and damage from climate change. Concepts, methods and policy options. Springer, Cham, pp 155–178

Christidis N, Stott PA, Zwiers FW, Shiogama H, Nozawa T (2010) Probabilistic estimates of recent changes in temperature: a multi-scale attribution analysis. Clim Dyn 34:1139–1156. https://doi.org/10.1007/s00382-009-0615-7

Christidis N, Stott PA, Scaife AA et al (2013) A new HADGEM3-a-based system for attribution of weather- and climate-related extreme events. J Clim 26:2756–2783. https://doi.org/10.1175/JCLI-D-12-00169.1

Church JA, Monselesan D, Gregory JM, Marzeion B (2013) Evaluating the ability of process based models to project sea-level change. Environ Res Lett 8:14051. https://doi.org/10.1088/1748-9326/8/1/014051

Clayton S, Manning CM, Krygsman K, Speiser M (2017) Mental health and our changing climate: impacts, implications, and guidance. American Psychological Association, and ecoAmerica: Washington, DC

Copsey D, Sutton R, Knight JR (2006) Recent trends in sea level pressure in the Indian Ocean region. Geophys Res Lett 33:L19712. https://doi.org/10.1029/2006GL027175

Craeynest L (2010) Loss and damage from climate change: the cost for poor people in developing countries. Action Aid International Discussion Paper

Cramer W, Yohe GW, Auffhammer M, Huggel C, Molau U, Dias MAF, Leemans R (2014) Detection and attribution of observed impacts. In: Field CB, Barros VR, Dokken DJ, Mach KJ, Mastrandrea MD, Bilir TE, Chatterjee M, Ebi KL, Estrada YO, Genova RC, Girma B, Kissel ES, Levy AN, MacCracken S, Mastrandrea PR, White LL (eds) Climate change 2014: impacts, adaptation, and vulnerability. Part A: global and sectoral aspects. Contribution of working group

II to the fifth assessment report of the intergovernmental panel of climate change. Cambridge University Press, Cambridge, United Kingdom and New York, NY, USA, pp 979–1037

den Elzen M, Fuglestvedt J, Höhne N, Trudinger C, Lowe J, Matthews B, Romstad B, de Campos CP, Andronova N (2005) Analysing countries' contribution to climate change: scientific and policy-related choices. Environ Sci Policy 8:614–636. https://doi.org/10.1016/j.envsci.2005.06.007

DesInventar (2015) DesInventar Online Edition 2013. In: Inventar. Desastr. Dispon. https://www.desinventar.net/

Dole R, Hoerling M, Perlwitz J, Eischeid J, Pegion P, Zhang T, Quan X-W, Xu T, Murray D (2011) Was there a basis for anticipating the 2010 Russian heat wave? Geophys Res Lett 38:1–5. https://doi.org/10.1029/2010GL046582

Erikson KT (1976) Everything in its path. Simon and Schuster, New York

Farris M (2009) Compensating climate change victims: the climate compensation fund as an alternative to tort litigation. Sea Grant Law Policy 2:49–62

Folland CK, Colman AW, Smith DM, Boucher O, Parker DE, Vernier J-P (2013) High predictive skill of global surface temperature a year ahead. Geophys Res Lett 40:761–767. https://doi.org/10.1002/grl.50169

Foster G, Rahmstorf S (2011) Global temperature evolution 1979–2010. Environ Res Lett 6:44022. https://doi.org/10.1088/1748-9326/6/4/044022

Frame D, Joshi M, Hawkins E, Harrington LJ, de Roiste M (2017) Population-based emergence of unfamiliar climates. Nat Clim Change. https://doi.org/10.1038/NCLIMATE3297

Fuglestvedt J, Berntsen T, Myhre G, Rypdal K, Skeie RB (2008) Climate forcing from the transport sectors. Proc Natl Acad Sci 105:454–458. https://doi.org/10.1073/pnas.0702958104

Fuglestvedt JS, Kallbekken S (2015) Climate responsibility: fair shares? Nat Clim Change. https://doi.org/10.1038/nclimate2791

Funk C (2011) We thought trouble was coming. Nature 476:7

Fyfe JC, Gillett NP, Thompson DWJ (2010) Comparing variability and trends in observed and modelled global-mean surface temperature. Geophys Res Lett 37. https://doi.org/10.1029/2010gl044255

Gall M, Borden KA, Cutter SL (2009) When do losses count? Bull Am Meteor Soc 90:799–809. https://doi.org/10.1175/2008BAMS2721.1

Gardiner SM (2004) Ethics and global climate change. Ethics 114:555–600. https://doi.org/10.1086/382247

GCF (2015) Decisions of the board—ninth meeting of the board, 24–26 March 2015, GCF/B.09/23

Giorgi F, Jones C, Asrar GR (2009) Addressing climate information needs at the regional level: the CORDEX framework. World Meteorological Organization (WMO) Bulletin 58:175–183

Gitay H, Brown S, Easterling W, Jallow B, Antle J, Apps M, Beamish R, Chapin T, Cramer W, Frangi JLJ (2001) Ecosystems and their goods and services. In: McCarthy J, Canziani O, Leary N, Dokken DWK (eds) Climate change 2001: impacts, adaptation and vulnerability. Contribution of working group II to the third assessment report of the intergovernmental panel on climate change. Cambridge University Press, Cambridge, United Kingdom and New York, NY, USA, pp 235–342

Guha-Sapir D, Below R, Hoyois P (2009) EM-DAT: The CRED/OFDA international disaster database. In: Cent. Res. Epidemiol. Disasters (CRED), Univ. Cathol. Louvain

Hannart A, Pearl J, Otto FEL, Naveau P, Ghil M (2016) Causal counterfactual theory for the attribution of weather and climate-related events. Bull Am Meteor Soc 97:99–110. https://doi.org/10.1175/BAMS-D-14-00034.1

Hansen G (2015) The evolution of the evidence base for observed impacts of climate change. Curr Opin Environ Sustain 14:187–197. https://doi.org/10.1016/j.cosust.2015.05.005

Hansen G, Cramer W (2015) Global distribution of observed climate change impacts. Nat Clim Change 5:182–185. https://doi.org/10.1038/nclimate2529

Hansen G, Stone D (2016) Assessing the observed impact of anthropogenic climate change. Nat Clim Change 6:532–537. https://doi.org/10.1038/nclimate2896

Hansen G, Stone D, Auffhammer M, Huggel C, Cramer W (2016) Linking local impacts to changes in climate: a guide to attribution. Reg Environ Change 16:527–541. https://doi.org/10.1007/s10113-015-0760-y

Heede R (2014) Tracing anthropogenic carbon dioxide and methane emissions to fossil fuel and cement producers, 1854–2010. Clim Change 122:229–241. https://doi.org/10.1007/s10584-013-0986-y

Hegerl GC, Zwiers FW, Braconnot P, Gillett NP, Luo Y, Marengo Orsini JA, Nicholls N, Penner JE, Stott PA (2007) Understanding and attributing climate change. In: Solomon SD, Qin M, Manning Z, Chen M, Marquis KB, Averyt MT, Miller HL (eds) Climate change 2007: the physical science basis. Contribution of working group I to the fourth assessment report of the intergovernmental panel on climate change. Cambridge University Press, Cambridge, United Kingdom and New York, NY, USA

Hegerl G, Hoegh-Guldberg O, Casassa G, Hoerling MP, Kovats RS, Parmesan C, Pierce DW, Stott PA (2010) Good practice guidance paper on detection and attribution related to anthropogenic climate change. In: Stocker T, Field C, Dahe Q et al (eds) Meeting report: IPCC expert meeting on detection and attribution related to anthropogenic climate change

Hegerl G, Zwiers F (2011) Use of models in detection and attribution of climate change. Wiley Interdisc Rev: Clim Change 2:570–591. https://doi.org/10.1002/wcc.121

Herring S, Hoerling M, Peterson T, Stott P (2014) Explaining extreme events of 2013 from a climate perspective. Bull Am Meteor Soc 95(9):S1–S96

Herring SC, Hoerling MP, Kossin JP, Peterson TC, Stott PA (2015) Explaining extreme events of 2014 from a climate perspective. Bull Am Meteor Soc 96:S1–S172. https://doi.org/10.1175/BAMS-D-15-00157.1

Herring SC, Christidis N, Hoell A, Kossin JP, Schreck CJ, Stott PA (eds) (2018) Explaining extreme events of 2016 from a climate perspective. Bull Amer Meteor Soc 99(1):S1–S157

Herring SC, Hoell A, Hoerling MP, Kossin JP, Schreck CJ III, Stott PA (2016) Explaining extreme events of 2015 from a climate perspective. Bull Am Meteor Soc 97:1–145

Hoegh-Guldberg O, Hegerl G, Root T, Zwiers F, Statt P, Pierce D, Allen M (2011) Difficult but not impossible. Nat Clim Change 1:72–72. https://doi.org/10.1038/nclimate1107

Huggel C, Stone D, Auffhammer M, Hansen G (2013) Loss and damage attribution. Nat Clim Change 3:694–696. https://doi.org/10.1038/nclimate1961

Huggel C, Stone D, Eicken H, Hansen G (2015a) Potential and limitations of the attribution of climate change impacts for informing loss and damage discussions and policies. Clim Change 133:453–467. https://doi.org/10.1007/s10584-015-1441-z

Huggel C, Raissig A, Rohrer M, Romero G, Diaz A, Salzmann N (2015b) How useful and reliable are disaster databases in the context of climate and global change? A comparative case study analysis in Peru. Nat Hazards Earth Sys Sci 15:475–485. https://doi.org/10.5194/nhess-15-475-2015

Huggel C, Bresch D, Hansen G, James R, Mechler R, Stone D, Wallimann-Helmer I (2016a) Attribution of irreversible loss to anthropogenic climate change. EGU General Assembly Conference 2016, held 17–22 April 2016 Vienna Austria, p 8557 18:8557

Huggel C, Wallimann-Helmer I, Stone D, Cramer W (2016b) Reconciling justice and attribution research to advance climate policy. Nat Clim Change 6:901–908. https://doi.org/10.1038/nclimate3104

Hulme M, O'Neill SJ, Dessai S (2011) Is weather event attribution necessary for adaptation funding? Science 334:764–765. https://doi.org/10.1126/science.1211740

IPCC (2012) Managing the risks of extreme events and disasters to advance climate change adaptation. A special report of working groups I and II of the intergovernmental panel on climate change. In: Field CB, Barros V, Stocker TF, Qin D, Dokken DJ, Ebi KL, Mastrandrea MD, Mach KJ, Plattner G-K, Allen SK, Tignor M, Midgley PM (eds). Cambridge University Press, Cambridge, UK, and New York, NY, USA

IPCC (2013) Climate change 2013: the physical science basis. contribution of working group I to the fifth assessment report of the intergovernmental panel on climate change. In: Stocker TF, Qin

D, Plattner G-K, Tignor M, Allen SK, Boschung J, Nauels A, Xia Y, Bex V, Midgley PM (eds). Cambridge University Press, Cambridge, United Kingdom and New York, NY, USA, 1535 pp

IPCC (2014) Climate change 2014: synthesis report. Contribution of Working Groups I, II and III to the fifth assessment report of the intergovernmental panel on climate change. In: Core Writing Team RK, Pachauri, Meyer LA (eds). IPCC, Geneva, Switzerland, 151 pp

James R, Otto F, Parker H, Boyd E, Cornforth R, Mitchell D, Allen M (2014a) Characterizing loss and damage from climate change. Nat Clim Change 4:938–939. https://doi.org/10.1038/nclimate2411

James R, Washington R, Rowell DP (2014b) African climate change uncertainty in perturbed physics ensembles: implications of global warming to 4 °C and beyond. J Clim 27:4677–4692. https://doi.org/10.1175/JCLI-D-13-00612.1

Jones LM, Bernknopf R, Cox D et al (2008) The shakeout scenario. US Geol Survey Open-File Report 1150:308

Jones L, Champalle C, Chesterman S, Cramer L, Crane TA (2017) Constraining and enabling factors to using long-term climate information in decision-making. Clim Policy 17:551–572. https://doi.org/10.1080/14693062.2016.1191008

Jongman B, Winsemius HC, Aerts JCJH, Coughlan de Perez E, Van Aalst MK, Kron W, Ward PJ (2015) Declining vulnerability to river floods and the global benefits of adaptation. Proc Natl Acad Sci USA 112(18):E2271–E2280

Kay AL, Crooks SM, Pall P, Stone DA (2011) Attribution of Autumn/Winter 2000 flood risk in England to anthropogenic climate change: a catchment-based study. J Hydrol 406:97–112. https://doi.org/10.1016/j.jhydrol.2011.06.006

Keating A, Venkateswaran K, Szoenyi M, MacClune K, Mechler R (2016) From event analysis to global lessons: disaster forensics for building resilience. Nat Hazards Earth Sys Sci 16:1603–1616. https://doi.org/10.5194/nhess-16-1603-2016

Kreibich H, Di Baldassarre G, Vorogushyn S, Aerts JCJH, Apel H, Aronica GT, Arnbjerg-Nielsen K, Bouwer LM, Bubeck P, Caloiero T (2017) Adaptation to flood risk: results of international paired flood event studies. Earth's Future. https://doi.org/10.1002/2017EF000606

Kron W, Steuer M, Löw P, Wirtz A (2012) How to deal properly with a natural catastrophe database—analysis of flood losses. Nat Hazards Earth Sys Sci 12:535–550. https://doi.org/10.5194/nhess-12-535-2012

Lee D, Min S-K, Park C, Suh M-S, Ahn J-B, Cha D-H, Lee D-K, Hong S-Y, Park S-C, Kang H-S (2016) Time of emergence of anthropogenic warming signals in the Northeast Asia assessed from multi-regional climate models. Asia-Pacific J Atmos Sci 52:129–137. https://doi.org/10.1007/s13143-016-0014-z

Linnerooth-Bayer J, Warner K, Bals C, Hoppe P, Burton I, Loster T, Haas A (2009) Insurance, developing countries and climate change. Geneva Papers in Risk Insurance-Issues and Practice 34:381–400. https://doi.org/10.2307/41953037

Linnerooth-Bayer J, Surminski S, Bouwer LM, Noy I and R Mechler (2018) Insurance as a response to loss and damage? In: Mechler R, Bouwer L, Schinko T, Surminski S, Linnerooth-Bayer J (eds) Loss and damage from climate change. Concepts, methods and policy options. Springer, Cham, pp 483–512

Lopez A, Surminski S, Serdeczny O (2018) The role of the physical sciences in loss and damage decision-making. In: Mechler R, Bouwer L, Schinko T, Surminski S, Linnerooth-Bayer J (eds) Loss and damage from climate change. Concepts, Methods and policy options. Springer, Cham, pp 261–285

Lott FC, Christidis N, Stott PA (2013) Can the 2011 East African drought be attributed to human-induced climate change? Geophys Res Lett 40:1177–1181. https://doi.org/10.1002/grl.50235

Mace MJ, Verheyen R (2016) Loss, damage and responsibility after COP21: all options open for the Paris agreement. Rev Eur Compar Int Environ Law 25:197–214. https://doi.org/10.1111/reel.12172

Marjanac S, Patton L (2018) Extreme weather event attribution science and climate change litigation: an essential step in the causal chain? J Energy Nat Res Law. https://doi.org/10.1080/02646811.2018.1451020

Marthews TR, Otto FEL, Mitchell D, Dadson SJ, Jones RG (2015) The 2014 drought in the horn of Africa: attribution of meteorological drivers. In: Herring SC, Hoerling MP, Kossin JP et al (eds) Explaining extreme events of 2014 from a climate perspective. Bulletin of the American Meteorological Society

Marzeion B, Cogley JG, Richter K, Parkes D (2014) Attribution of global glacier mass loss to anthropogenic and natural causes. Science 345:919–921. https://doi.org/10.1126/science.1254702

Matthews HD (2016) Quantifying historical carbon and climate debts among nations. Nat Clim Change 6:60–64. https://doi.org/10.1038/NCLIMATE2774

Mechler R, Bouwer LM (2015) Understanding trends and projections of disaster losses and climate change: is vulnerability the missing link? Clim Change 133:23–35. https://doi.org/10.1007/s10584-014-1141-0

Mechler R, Schinko T (2016) Identifying the policy space for climate loss and damage. Science (80-)354:290–292

Mechler R et al (2018) Science for loss and damage. Findings and propositions. In: Mechler R, Bouwer L, Schinko T, Surminski S, Linnerooth-Bayer J (eds) Loss and damage from climate change. Concepts, methods and policy options. Springer, Cham, pp 3–37

Meehl GA (2005) How much more global warming and sea level rise? Science 307:1769–1772. https://doi.org/10.1126/science.1106663

Mitchell D, Heaviside C, Vardoulakis S, Huntingford C, Masato G, Guillod BP, Frumhoff P, Bowery A, Wallom D, Allen M (2016) Attributing human mortality during extreme heat waves to anthropogenic climate change. Environ Res Lett 11:74006. https://doi.org/10.1088/1748-9326/11/7/074006

Mitchell JFB, Karoly DJ Hegerl GC, Zwiers FW, Allen MR, Marengo J (2001) Detection of climate change and attribution of causes. Climate change 2001: The scientific basis. Cambridge University Press, Cambridge, United Kingdom and New York, NY, USA, pp 697–738

Mitchell JK (1999) Megacities and natural disasters: a comparative analysis. GeoJournal 49:137–142. https://doi.org/10.1023/A:1007024703844

Muller B, Hohne N, Ellerman C (2009) Differentiating (historic) responsibilities for climate change. Clim Policy 9:593–611. https://doi.org/10.3763/cpol.2008.0570

National Academics of Sciences, Engineering and Medicine (2016) Attribution of extreme weather events in the context of climate change. National Academies Press: Washington, D.C. https://doi.org/10.17226/21852

Oliver-Smith A, Hoffman SM (1999) The angry earth: disaster in anthropological perspective. Routledge, New York

Otto FEL, Massey N, Van Oldenborgh GJ, Jones RG, Allen MR (2012) Reconciling two approaches to attribution of the 2010 Russian heat wave. Geophys Res Lett 39:1–5. https://doi.org/10.1029/2011GL050422

Otto FEL, Jones RG, Halladay K, Allen MR (2013) Attribution of changes in precipitation patterns in African rainforests. Philos Trans Royal Soc Londin B: Biol Sci 368:20120299–20120299. https://doi.org/10.1098/rstb.2012.0299

Otto FEL, Boyd E, Jones RG, Cornforth RJ, James R, Parker HR, Allen MR (2015a) Attribution of extreme weather events in Africa: a preliminary exploration of the science and policy implications. Clim Change 132:531–543. https://doi.org/10.1007/s10584-015-1432-0

Otto FEL, Coelho C a. S, King A, et al (2015b) Factors other than climate change, main drivers of 2014/5 water shortage in southeast Brazil. In: Herring SC, Hoerling MP, Kossin JP et al (eds) Explaining extreme events of 2014 from a climate perspective. Bull Am Meteorol Soc 96:35–40

Otto FEL, van Oldenborgh GJ, Eden J, Stott PA, Karoly DJ, Allen MR (2016) The attribution question. Nature. Clim Change 6:813–816. https://doi.org/10.1038/nclimate3089

Otto FEL, Skeie RB, Fuglestvedt JS, Bernsten T, Allen MR (2017) Assigning historical responsibilities for extreme weather events. Nat Clim Change 7:757–759. https://doi.org/10.1038/nclimate3419

Pall P, Aina T, Stone DA, Stott PA, Nozawa T, Hilberts AGJ, Lohman D, Allen MR (2011) Anthropogenic greenhouse gas contribution to flood risk in England and Wales in autumn 2000. Nature 470:382–385. https://doi.org/10.1038/nature09762

Parker D, Folland C, Scaife A, Knight J, Colman A, Baines P, Dong B (2007) Decadal to multidecadal variability and the climate change background. J Geophys Res Atmos 112:1–18. https://doi.org/10.1029/2007JD008411

Parker HR, Cornforth RJ, Boyd E, James R, Otto FE, Allen MR (2015) Implications of event attribution for loss and damage policy. Weather 70:268–272. https://doi.org/10.1002/wea.2540

Parker HR, Cornforth RJ, Suarez P et al (2016) Using a game to engage stakeholders in extreme event attribution science. Int J Disaster Risk Sci 7:353–365. https://doi.org/10.1007/s13753-016-0105-6

Parker HR, Boyd E, Cornforth RJ, James R, Otto FE, Allen MR (2017a) Stakeholder perceptions of event attribution in the loss and damage debate. Clim Policy 17:533–550. https://doi.org/10.1080/14693062.2015.1124750

Parker HR, Lott FC, Cornforth RJ, Mitchell DM, Sparrow S, Wallom D (2017b) A comparison of model ensembles for attributing 2012 West African rainfall. Environ Res Lett 12:14019. https://doi.org/10.1088/1748-9326/aa5386

Peterson TC, Stott PA, Herring S (2012) Explaining extreme events of 2011 from a climate perspective. Bull Am Meteorol Soc 93:1041–1067. https://doi.org/10.1175/BAMS-D-12-00021.1

Peterson T, Stott P, Herring S (2013) Explaining extreme events of 2012 from a climate perspective. Bull Am Meteorol Soc 94:1–74

Rahmstorf S, Coumou D (2011) Increase of extreme events in a warming world. Proc Natl Acad Sci 108:17905–17909. https://doi.org/10.1073/pnas.1101766108

RC/RCCC (2017) Bridging science, policy and practice; report of the international conference on climate risk management—pre-scoping meeting for the IPCC sixth assessment report (5–7 April 2017, Nairobi)

Richards J-A, Boom K (2015) Big oil, coal and gas producers paying for their climate damage

Rosenzweig C, Karoly D, Vicarelli M, Neofotis P, Qigang Wu, Casassa G, Menzel A, Root TL, Estrella N, Seguin B (2008) Attributing physical and biological impacts to anthropogenic climate change. Nature 453:353–357. https://doi.org/10.1038/nature06937

Rowell DP, Booth BBB, Nicholson SE, Good P (2015) Reconciling past and future rainfall trends over East Africa. J Clim 28:9768–9788. https://doi.org/10.1175/JCLI-D-15-0140.1

Santer BD, Mears C, Wentz FJ, Taylor KE, Gleckler PJ, Wigley TML, Barnett TP, Boyle JS, Brugge-mann W, Gillet NP (2007) Identification of human-induced changes in atmospheric moisture content. Proc Natl Acad Sci 104:15248–15253. https://doi.org/10.1073/pnas.0702872104

Santer BD, Wigley TML, Barnett TP, Anyamba E (1995) Detection of climate change and attribution of causes. In: Houghton JT, Meira Filho LG, Callander BA et al (eds) Climate change 1995: the science of climate change. Contribution of working group I to the second assessment report of the intergovernmental panel on climate change. Cambridge University Press, Cambridge, United Kingdom and New York, NY, USA

Schaller N, Kay AL, Lamb R, Massey NR, van Oldenborgh GJ, Otto FEL, Sparrow SN, Vautard R, Yiou P, Ashpole I, Bowery A, Crooks SM, Haustein K, Huntingford C, Ingram WJ, Jones RG, Legg T, Miller J, Skeggs J, Wallom D, Weisheimer A, Wilson S, Stott PA, Allen MR (2016) Human influence on climate in the 2014 southern England winter floods and their impacts. Nat Clim Change 6:627–634. https://doi.org/10.1038/nclimate2927

Schinko T, Mechler R, Hochrainer-Stigler S (2018) The risk and policy space for loss and damage: integrating notions of distributive and compensatory justice with comprehensive climate risk management. In: Mechler R, Bouwer L, Schinko T, Surminski S, Linnerooth-Bayer J (eds) Loss and damage from climate change. Concepts, methods and policy options. Springer, Cham, pp 83–110

Serdeczny O, Waters E, Chan S (2016) Non-economic loss and damage in the context of climate change: understanding the challenges. German Development Institute No. 03/16: Berlin

Serdeczny O (2018) Non-economic loss and damage and the warsaw international mechanism. In: Mechler R, Bouwer L, Schinko T, Surminski S, Linnerooth-Bayer J (eds) Loss and damage from climate change. Concepts, methods and policy options. Springer, Cham, pp 205–220

Shongwe ME, van Oldenborgh GJ, van den Hurk B, van Aalst M (2011) Projected changes in mean and extreme precipitation in Africa under global warming. Part II: East Africa. J Clim 24:3718–3733. https://doi.org/10.1175/2010JCLI2883.1

Simlinger F, Mayer B (2018) Legal responses to climate change induced loss and damage. In: Mechler R, Bouwer L, Schinko T, Surminski S, Linnerooth-Bayer J (eds) Loss and damage from climate change. Concepts, methods and policy options. Springer, Cham, pp 179–203

Sippel S, Walton P, Otto FEL (2015) Stakeholder perspectives on the attribution of extreme weather events: an explorative enquiry. Weather Clim Soc 7:224–237. https://doi.org/10.1175/WCAS-D-14-00045.1

Sippel S, El-Madany TS, Migliavacca M, Mehecha MD, Carrara A, Flach M, Kaminski T, Otto FEL, Tonicke K, Reichstein M (2018) Response in ecosystem functioning on the Iberian Peninsula. Bull Am Meteorol Soc 99:S80–S85. https://doi.org/10.1175/BAMS-D-17-0135.1

Skeie RB, Fuglestvedt J, Berntsen T, Peters GP, Andrew R, Allen M, Kallbekken S (2017) Perspective has a strong effect on the calculation of historical contributions to global warming. Environ Res Lett 12:24022. https://doi.org/10.1088/1748-9326/aa5b0a

Stone DA, Allen MR, Stott PA, Pall P, Min SK, Nozawa T, Yukimoto S (2009) The detection and attribution of human influence on climate. Ann Rev Environ Res 34:1–16. https://doi.org/10.1146/annurev.environ.040308.101032

Stone D, Auffhammer M, Carey M, Hansen G, Huggel C, Cramer W, Lobell D, Molau U, Solow A, Tibig L (2013) The challenge to detect and attribute effects of climate change on human and natural systems. Clim Change 121:381–395. https://doi.org/10.1007/s10584-013-0873-6

Stone DA, Allen MR (2005) The end-to-end attribution problem: from emissions to impacts. Clim Change 71:303–318. https://doi.org/10.1007/s10584-005-6778-2

Stone DA, Hansen G (2016) Rapid systematic assessment of the detection and attribution of regional anthropogenic climate change. Clim Dyn 47:1399–1415. https://doi.org/10.1007/s00382-015-2909-2

Stott PA, Tett SFB, Jones GS, Allen MR, Mitchell JFB, Jenkins GJ (2000) External control of 20th century temperature by natural and anthropogenic forcings. Science 290:2133–2137. https://doi.org/10.1126/science.290.5499.2133

Stott P, Walton P (2013) Attribution of climate-related events: understanding stakeholder needs. Weather. https://doi.org/10.1002/wea.2152

Stott PA, Christidis N, Otto FEL, Sun Y, Vanderlinden J-P, van Oldenborgh GJ, Vautard R, von Storch H, Walton P, Yiou P (2016) Attribution of extreme weather and climate-related events. Wiley Interdisc Rev: Clim Change 7:23–41. https://doi.org/10.1002/wcc.380

Surminski S, Lopez A (2015) Concept of loss and damage of climate change—a new challenge for climate decision-making? A climate science perspective. Clim Develop 7:267–277. https://doi.org/10.1080/17565529.2014.934770

Taylor RG, Todd MC, Kongola L, Maurice L, Nahozya E, Hosea Sanga, MachDonald AM (2013) Evidence of the dependence of groundwater resources on extreme rainfall in East Africa. Nat Clim Change 3:374–378. https://doi.org/10.1038/nclimate1731

Tett SF, Stott PA, Allen MR, Ingram WJ, Mitchell JF (1999) Causes of twentieth-century temperature change near the Earth's surface. Nature 399:569–572. https://doi.org/10.1038/21164

Thompson A, Otto FEL (2015) Ethical and normative implications of weather event attribution for policy discussions concerning loss and damage. Clim Change 133:439–451. https://doi.org/10.1007/s10584-015-1433-z

Thornton J, Covington H (2016) Climate change before the court. Nat Geosci 9:3–5. https://doi.org/10.1038/ngeo2612

Trenberth KE, Fasullo JT, Shepherd TG (2015) Attribution of climate extreme events. Nat Clim Change 5:725–730. https://doi.org/10.1038/nclimate2657

Uhe P, Sjoukje P, Kew S, Shah K, Otto F, van Oldenborgh GJ, Singh R, Arrighi J, Cullen H (2017) Kenya Drought, 2016—World Weather Attribution. https://wwa.climatecentral.org/analyses/kenya-drought-2016/ Accessed 13 Jun 2017

UN (1992) The United Nations framework convention on climate change. United Nations, Rio de Janeiro. https://unfccc.int/resource/docs/convkp/conveng.pdf

UNEP (2016) Loss and Damage: The Role of Ecosystem Services. Nairobi, Kenya. https://uneplive.unep.org/media/docs/assessments/loss_and_damage.pdf

UNFCCC (2011) Decision 1/CP.16 The Cancun agreements: outcome of the work of the ad hoc working group on long-term cooperative action under the convention

UNFCCC (2013) Decision 2/CP.19: Warsaw international mechanism for loss and damage associated with climate change impacts

UNFCCC (2015) Adoption of the Paris agreement. FCCC/CP/2015/10/Add.1. Paris, France

UNISDR (2010) Guidance note on recovery: governance, International Recovery Platform & United Nations Development Programme India. https://www.unisdr.org/we/inform/publications/16774 Accessed 13 Jun 2017

van der Wiel K, Kapnick SB, van Oldenborgh GJ, Whan K, Philip S, Vecchi GA, Singh RK, Arrighi J, Cullen H (2017) Rapid attribution of the August 2016 flood-inducing extreme precipitation in south Louisiana to climate change. Hydrol Earth Syst Sci 21:897–921. https://doi.org/10.5194/hess-21-897-2017

Vanhala L, Hestbaek C (2016) Framing loss and damage in the UNFCCC negotiations: the struggle over meaning and the Warsaw international mechanism. Global Environ Politics 16:111–129. https://doi.org/10.1162/GLEP_a_00379

Wallimann-Helmer I, Meyer L, Mintz-Woo K, Schinko T, Serdeczny O (2018) Ethical challenges in the context of climate loss and damage. In: Mechler R, Bouwer L, Schinko T, Surminski S, Linnerooth-Bayer J (eds) Loss and damage from climate change. Concepts, methods and policy options. Springer, Cham, pp 39–62

Warner K, Van der Geest K (2013) Loss and damage from climate change: local-level evidence from nine vulnerable countries. Int J Global Warming 5:367. https://doi.org/10.1504/IJGW.2013.057289

Weaver CP, Lempert RJ, Brown C, Brown C, Hall JA, Revell D, Sarewitz D (2013) Improving the contribution of climate model information to decision making: the value and demands of robust decision frameworks. Wiley Interdisc Rev: Clim Change 4:39–60. https://doi.org/10.1002/wcc.202

Wigley TML (2005) The climate change commitment. Science 307:1766–1769. https://doi.org/10.1126/science.1103934

Williams AP, Funk C (2011) A westward extension of the warm pool leads to a westward extension of the Walker circulation, drying eastern Africa. Clim Dyn 37:2417–2435. https://doi.org/10.1007/s00382-010-0984-y

Williams AP, Funk C, Michaelsen J, Rauscher SA, Robertson I, Wils THG, Koprowski M, Eshetu Z, Loader NJ (2012) Recent summer precipitation trends in the Greater Horn of Africa and the emerging role of Indian Ocean sea surface temperature. Clim Dyn 39:2307–2328. https://doi.org/10.1007/s00382-011-1222-y

Wrathall DJ, Oliver-Smith A, Fekete A, Gencer E, Reyes ML, Sakdapolrak P (2015) Problematising loss and damage. Int J Global Warming 8:274–294

Zhang X, Wan H, Zwiers FW, Hegerl GC, Min SK (2013) Attributing intensification of precipitation extremes to human influence. Geophys Res Lett 40:5252–5257. https://doi.org/10.1002/grl.5101

Chapter 6
The Politics of (and Behind) the UNFCCC's Loss and Damage Mechanism

Elisa Calliari, Swenja Surminski and Jaroslav Mysiak

Abstract Despite being one of the most controversial issues to be recently treated within climate negotiations, Loss and Damage (L&D) has attracted little attention among scholars of International Relations (IR). In this chapter we take the "structuralist paradox" in L&D negotiations as our starting point, considering how IR theories can help to explain the somewhat surprising capacity of weak parties to achieve results while negotiating with stronger parties. We adopt a multi-faceted notion of power, drawing from the neorealist, liberal and constructivist schools of thought, in order to explain how L&D milestones were reached. Our analysis shows that the IR discipline can greatly contribute to the debate, not only by enhancing understanding of the negotiation process and related outcomes but also by offering insights on how the issue could be fruitfully moved forward. In particular, we note the key importance that discursive power had in the attainment of L&D milestones: Framing L&D in ethical and legal terms appealed to standards relevant beyond the UNFCCC context, including basic moral norms linked to island states' narratives of survival and the reference to international customary law. These broader standards are in principle recognised by both contending parties and this broader framing of L&D has helped to prove the need for action on L&D. However, we find that a change of narrative may be needed to avoid turning the issue into a win-lose negotiation game. Instead, a stronger emphasis on mutual gains through adaptation and action on L&D for both developed and developing countries is needed as well as clarity on the limits of these strategies. Examples of such mutual gains are more resilient global supply chains, reduction of climate-induced migration and enhanced security. As a result, acting on

E. Calliari (✉) · J. Mysiak
Euro-Mediterranean Center on Climate Change (CMCC) and Ca' Foscari, University of Venice, Venice, Italy
e-mail: elisa.calliari@cmcc.it

S. Surminski
Grantham Research Institute on Climate Change and the Environment, London School of Economics and Political Science (LSE), London, UK

R. Mechler et al. (eds.), *Loss and Damage from Climate Change*, Climate Risk Management, Policy and Governance, https://doi.org/10.1007/978-3-319-72026-5_6

L&D would not feel as a unilateral concession developed countries make to vulnerable ones: it would rather be about elaborating patterns of collective action on an issue of common concern.

Keywords Loss and Damage · AOSIS · UNFCCC · International relations Neorealism · Liberalism · Constructivism

6.1 Foundations for an International Relations' Contribution to the Debate

In recent years, the academic community has made important contributions to the Loss & Damage (L&D) debate, especially by (i) framing it through a disaster and climate risk management perspective (Mechler et al. 2014; Fekete and Sakdapolrak 2014; Birkmann and Welle 2015; Mechler and Schinko 2016); (ii) looking at the connection between L&D and the limits to adaptation (Warner and van der Geest 2013, 2015); (iii) outlining how attribution studies could support the assessment of L&D (Huggel et al. 2013; James et al. 2014); and (iv) discussing L&D's connection with the concept of state responsibility in international law (Tol and Verheyen 2004; Verheyen 2012, 2015; Mayer 2014; Mace and Verheyen 2016). Some authors have also provided historical overviews on the emergence of L&D in the international debate, analysed the role of the UNFCCC in addressing it, and discussed the possible implications of the Warsaw International Mechanism (WIM) (Huq et al. 2013; McNamara 2014; Mathew and Akter 2015; Roberts and Huq 2015; Stabinsky and Hoffmaister 2015). Against this background, contributions by political science and International Relations (IR) scholars have been almost absent (recent exceptions are Johnson (2017), Vanhala and Hestbaek (2016) and Calliari (2016a)).

This is only partly surprising. Overall, limited attention has been devoted to climate change within the discipline, especially when considering adaptation-related issues (Crump and Downie 2015). While contributions on mitigation are somewhat more common, where the need for international cooperation is more evident, this is not the case for adaptation and its (possible) failures and limits (i.e., L&D). Yet, there are a number of reasons why the current discourse on adaptation and its limits/constraints should be of interest to those exploring global policy and international power relations (Khan 2016): These include the self-interest of states and how in a globalised and interconnected world they are exposed to the effects of social, economic, political, environmental, and technological events, even when those occur in a different corner of the world. In addition, norms, values and justice imperatives also feature as a base for collective action on adaptation (Brown and Weiskel 2002) and play an even more important role when considering L&D.

Moreover L&D provides a very interesting case to be studied by IR scholars given the relevance of power dynamics in the climate change negotiations setting and its complex, asymmetrical and multilateral characteristics. Decision-making under the

UNFCCC relies on consensus: disagreement around the voting majority required for certain decisions has until now prevented the adoption of the rules of procedure (draft art. 42). This implies that, differently from other multilateral fora where each Party is bestowed a single vote and thus given equal weight, final outcomes in the UNFCCC will likely mirror Parties' capacity to shape and influence the decision-making process. In this context, it is important to point out that, on their initiative, developing countries managed to establish the WIM in 2013 and obtain a dedicated article on L&D in the Paris Agreement in 2015. A leading role in the process was assumed by the Alliance of Small Island States (AOSIS), a coalition of small island and low-lying coastal countries sharing similar development challenges and vulnerabilities to climate change impacts, and regarded among the most vocal groups in climate talks. Generally considered as the parties with less negotiation power, at least in terms of sheer delegation sizes, these achievements appear particularly remarkable.

The case of AOSIS has been characterised as an example of the so-called "structuralist paradox" in negotiations (Betzold 2010), i.e., the case that weaker parties are often able to effectively negotiate with stronger parties and get something out of the process (Zartman and Rubin 2002). More specifically, AOSIS' capacity to influence the UNFCCC has been explained in terms of moral leadership (de Águeda Corneloup and Mol 2014), capacity to "borrow power" (Betzold 2010), promotion of collaborative approaches to knowledge building and cooperative institutional mechanisms (Larson 2003). While importantly shedding light on a relatively overlooked topic, these contributions only explore limited timeframes[1] and, by design, are not able to capture evolutions and diversifications in the use of power sources. Moreover, none of them specifically addresses L&D negotiations, instead applying a broader adaptation lense.

In this chapter we specifically focus on the L&D process over time in order to consider its emergence and evolution from the negotiation of the UNFCCC (1991) to the entry into force of the Paris Agreement (2016). Taking the "structuralist paradox" in L&D negotiations as our starting point, we look beyond aggregate measures of power (like GDP, population size or military forces) and consider different sources of influence that AOSIS might have activated to shape L&D outcomes. We analyse L&D negotiations through the lenses of the main schools of thought in IR—the neorealist, liberal and constructivist (Snyder 2004)—to better understand the complexities of finding international agreement on L&D issues. This approach might look unorthodox, given that these schools of thought are based on hardly reconcilable premises. Nevertheless, conceptual pluralism around the notion of power is much needed to understand how global outcomes are produced (Barnett and Duvall 2005), as different forms of power might capture different and interrelated ways through which actors are enabled or constrained in pursuing their objectives.

[1]Betzold (2010) focuses on AOSIS's negotiating strategies in the climate change regime from 1990 to 1997; de Águeda Corneloup and Mol (2014) consider the period 2007–2009; while Larson (2003) analyses AOSIS' 1994 position paper: "Draft Protocol to the United Nations Framework Convention on Climate Change on Greenhouse Gas Emissions Reduction".

The chapter is organised as follows. We first provide an overview of the L&D process within the UNFCCC from AOSIS's first proposals to the PA, looking at the historic developments and actions by different actors that led to the emergence of L&D as a pillar of the UNFCCC architecture. We then consider the negotiating process through the lenses of IR theories to understand how L&D outcomes have been produced. By analysing the actors involved, their positions, the negotiation process and related outcomes, we finally identify opportunities, both for research and policy, to move this contested discourse forward.

6.2 Positioning of L&D in the UNFCCC Negotiations

As discussed in the introductory chapter (Mechler et al. 2018), the debate on L&D has been spearheaded by AOSIS since the early 1990s, by calling for an insurance pool to compensate vulnerable small island and low-lying developing countries for the impacts of sea level rise (INC 1991) (Fig. 6.1).

It took more than 20 years to institutionalise the debate within the UNFCCC architecture through the creation of the WIM in 2013 and eventually the stipulation of the stand-alone article 8 in the Paris Agreement. Figure 6.2 shows the positioning of the Executive Committee of the WIM (ExCom), which the COP established to guide the implementation of functions of the WIM through an initial 2-year work plan, in the UNFCCC architecture. ExCom is a body constituted under the Convention, and is guided by and accountable to the COP.

COP 20 finalised the governance of the ExCom by bestowing 10 members each to Annex I and non-Annex I Parties.[2] However, disagreement around regional representation within Annex I parties caused substantial delays in nominating ExCom members, convening of the ExCom first meeting (September 2015), and implementing the activities of the WIM. The balanced representation among Parties is also reflected in the Chairmanship, with the two Co-chairs being elected from Annex I and non-Annex I respectively to serve for 1 year.[3] The ExCom may establish expert groups, subcommittees, panels, thematic advisory groups or task-focused ad hoc working groups to help execute its advisory role.

The initial 2-year work plan of the WIM comprises 9 action areas focusing on: (1) Particularly vulnerable developing countries, population, ecosystems; (2) Comprehensive risk management approaches; (3) Slow onset events; (4) Non-economic losses; (5) Resilience, recovery and rehabilitation; (6) Migration, displacement and human mobility; (7) Financial instruments and tools; (8) complementing and drawing upon the work of and involvement other bodies; and (9) development of a 5-

[2]Members from non-Annex I Parties include 2 members from each of the African, the Asia-Pacific, and the Latin American and Caribbean States, 1 member from SIDS, 1 member from the LDC Parties, and 2 additional members from non-Annex I Parties.

[3]During the first meeting of the ExCom in 2017, co-chairmanship went from Tuvalu and USA to Jamaica and European Union.

Fig. 6.1 Timeline of L&D milestones. *Source* UNFCCC (2018)

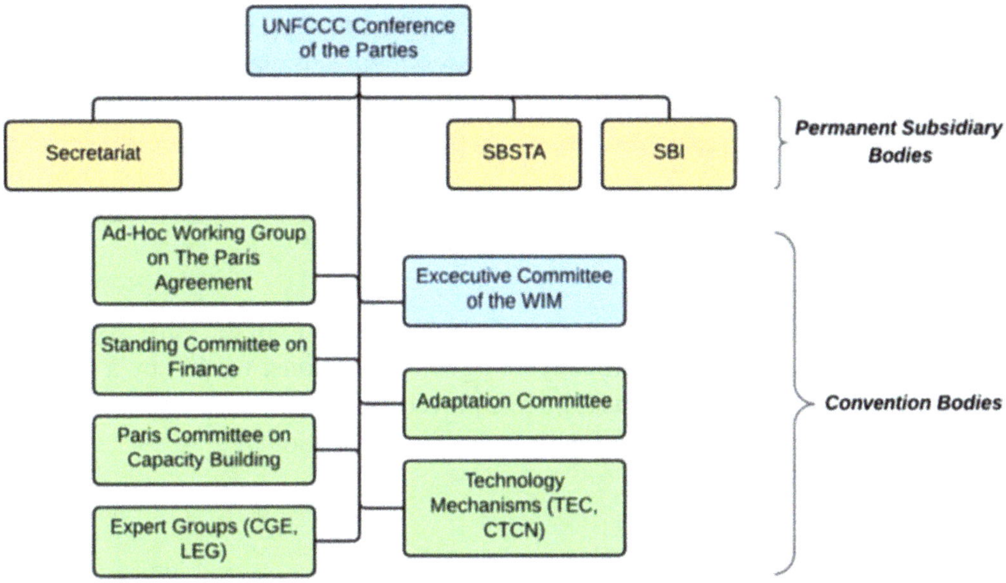

Fig. 6.2 The WIM in the UNFCCC architecture. According to Decision 2/CP. 19, the WIM reports annually to the COP. *Source* Adapted from own elaboration

year rolling work plan. As for the latter, its strategic workstreams were approved at COP23 and call for enhanced cooperation on: (1) Slow onset events; (2) Non-economic losses; (3) Comprehensive risk management approaches; (4) Migration, displacement and human mobility; and (5) action and support, including finance, technology and capacity-building.

The "structure, mandate and effectiveness" of the WIM is to be periodically reviewed, with the first review to be held in 2019 and subsequent ones to take place no more than 5 years apart (UNFCCC 2017). Reviews should consider progress on the implementation of the ExCom's work plan but also adopt a long-term vision to reflect on how the WIM may be enhanced and strengthened. As an input to the 2019 review, decision 4/CP.22 called for a "technical paper (to) be prepared by the secretariat elaborating the sources of financial support". At COP 23 it was agreed that the latter should be informed by an expert dialogue (baptised as "Suva Expert Dialogue") that took place in May 2018, in order "to explore a wide range of information, inputs and views on ways for facilitating the mobilisation and securing of expertise, and enhancement of support, including finance, technology and capacity-building, for averting, minimising and addressing loss and damage" (SBI and SBSTA 2017).

Besides the WIM, a major institutional milestone on L&D was reached with the adoption of the Paris Agreement. A stand-alone article 8 recognises L&D as distinct from adaptation, elevating it almost as a third pillar of climate action. Through the article "Parties recognize the importance of averting, minimizing and addressing loss and damage associated with the adverse effects of climate change, including extreme weather events and slow onset events" (UNFCCC 2015). The article sanctions the permanence of the WIM, whilst leaving the door open for it to be "enhanced and strengthened" through future COP decisions. It also calls Parties to work "on a cooperative and facilitative basis" to "enhance understanding, action and support" in areas including early warning systems, comprehensive risk assessment and management, risk insurance facilities, climate risk pooling, and non-economic losses (UNFCCC 2015).

6.3 Actors and Positions in the L&D Debate

The inclusion of L&D as a distinct concept from adaptation in the Paris Agreement was the result of a series of politically charged negotiations, fuelled by a range of actors with a variety of viewpoints. The role played by each of these actors, including their negotiation positions, is briefly discussed in this section.

6.3.1 Developing Countries and Their Representative Groups

As recognised above, developing countries and their representative groups have provided much of the impetus for the recognition of L&D within the UNFCCC. AOSIS has been particularly important, having first campaigned for the inclusion of L&D in climate change negotiations in the early 1990s and continuing to do so in conjunction with other representative groups. Other key events have included:

- In 2005 at COP11, Bangladesh on behalf of the LDC Group called for the compensation of climate change damages (Vanhala and Hestbaek 2016);
- In 2013, G77 with support from AOSIS and LDCs pushed for (and achieved) the adoption of the WIM (Calliari 2016a); and
- Prior to the commencement of COP21, members of the G77, China bloc, the Climate Vulnerable Forum, LDCs, AOSIS and the Africa Group all emphasised the importance of L&D to the Paris negotiations (Hoffmeister and Huq 2015).

The negotiating position of developing countries in general has been to (i) consider L&D as distinct from adaptation; (ii) treat climate change negotiations as an appropriate forum to discuss L&D; (iii) hold developed countries liable for L&D; and (iv) call for compensation (Huq and De Souza 2016). At the same time, they have raised concerns that the emphasis of L&D discourse on financial compensation could have a trivialising effect on addressing the underlying needs of developing countries (Hoffmaister et al. 2014).

6.3.2 Developed Countries

Developed countries have generally been critical and provided the opposite stance to developing countries on negotiations around L&D. Particular resistance was made in recognising L&D as distinct from adaptation. This is reflected, for instance, in developed countries' attempts to have L&D treated outside the Paris Agreement through a COP decision, or inside the text of the agreement but under the same article as adaptation. As for compensation, any references to such a concept have mostly been avoided, with developed countries shifting instead the attention to non-economic L&D, such as "losses of lives and negative impacts for health", and "loss of biodiversity and ecosystem services necessary to sustain livelihoods" (Norway 2013). The US also raised ethical concerns, by claiming that considering compensation would have meant "put[ting] a monetary value on the lives, livelihoods and assets of the most vulnerable countries and populations" (UNFCCC 2012a).

Not surprisingly, in Paris they rejected compensatory language (e.g. "rehabilitation", "compensation" and "liability") for fear of creating a legal liability for L&D suffered by developing countries (Huq and De Souza 2016). Former U.S. Secretary of State John Kerry explained the US' reluctance in relation to this as follows: "We're not against [loss and damage]. We're in favour of framing it in a way that doesn't create a legal remedy because Congress will never buy into an agreement that has something like that…the impact of it would be to kill the deal" (Goodell 2015).

Ultimately, Article 8 can be viewed as a compromise for developed countries; although they conceded the treatment of L&D as a separate pillar for climate action, they made it clear that they continue rejecting any liability for L&D, and emphasised a strong role for climate risk management. This attempt to move the L&D discourse under the less contested and binding disaster risk reduction framework or under the wider humanitarian arena is not new and has characterised developed countries' position since the inception of the L&D work programme. A central argument for it has been the extreme difficulty in attributing "the incidence of loss and damage to climate change, as opposed to natural climate variability and/or vulnerabilities stemming from non-climatic stresses and trends like deforestation and development patterns", as put by the US (UNFCCC 2012a).

6.3.3 NGOs

Generally speaking, NGOs have been highly supportive of the efforts of developing countries to create a liability and compensation mechanism for L&D. Such support has its roots in climate justice considerations; for example, ECO noted at the time of COP19 that L&D is a matter of "climate justice…It is time for those who are mainly responsible for climate change to act here in Warsaw" (Vanhala and Hestbaek 2016). In particular, NGOs:

- *Have advocated for the development of an L&D mechanism*. For example, Germanwatch, supported by the Munich Climate Insurance Initiative (MCII) (together with other partner institutions), launched the Loss and Damage in Vulnerable Countries Initiative in 2012 (CDKN et al. 2012). Similarly, the ACT Alliance, a network consisting of 140 humanitarian and development organisations, advocated for L&D during COP19: "Governments should recognise that we cannot choose between mitigation, adaptation and loss and damage. … The lower the mitigation ambition, the higher the adaptation need. The lower the adaptation support available to help poor communities and countries, the more serious the limits to adaptation become from climatic changes, the more loss and damage ensues" (Vulturius and Davis 2016)

- *Have helped to stimulate interest in L&D in developing countries*. For example, LDCs participating in a MCII workshop developed much greater interest in the development of an L&D mechanism than they held prior to participation (Vanhala and Hestbaek 2016);
- *Have acted as enablers for change*. For example, the pro bono Legal Response Initiative (LRI)[4] operated by WWF-UK and Oxfam-GB has provided legal support to LDCs during climate change negotiations. A similar role was played by the Foundation for International Environmental Law and Development (FIELD), a non-governmental research institute based at the Law Department at SOAS, University of London (see for instance Hyvarinen (2012)). A recent advisory group employed by the Republic of Marshall Islands and AOSIS is the New York based Independent Diplomat (Carter 2015);
- *Have sought public support on L&D*. For example, through reports produced by ActionAid, Care, and WWF (ActionAid 2010; ActionAid et al. 2012, 2013);
- *Have continued to pursue options for compensation outside of climate change negotiations*. For example, Greenpeace has used the Philippines Human Rights Commission to accuse a number of major companies of human rights abuses for carbon emissions. The Commission on Human Rights of the Philippines contacted those companies in 2016 to give them an opportunity to respond to Greenpeace's allegations (Vidal 2016).

6.3.4 The Private Sector and the Insurance Industry

There is limited evidence of private sector actors playing a role in the development of L&D as a concept and mechanism, with the exception of some insurance companies. Indeed, from a private sector point of view, the conceptual separation of L&D, adaptation, and disaster risk reduction might appear a highly theoretical and academic exercise, with limited relevance (Surminski and Eldridge 2015). However, back in 2011, when the UNFCCC consulted on an L&D mechanism, a number of responses to the UNFCCC called for greater engagement with the private sector in climate risk management. For example:

- Norway noted that 'broad participation from stakeholders [including the private sector] would be crucial to a good outcome of the work programme' (Norway 2011);
- Gambia asked 'to seek (private sector) contribution for a successful mechanism to address L&D in LDCs' (Gambia 2011)—but explicit detail of what this 'con-

[4] http://legalresponseinitiative.org/.

tribution' means remains lacking. Gambia also referenced the need to provide the private sector in LDCs with tools and information to help them respond to the risk of L&D. The submission specifically mentions 'climate services for users in both the public and private sector in LDCs and other vulnerable countries, (… including the) strengthening of meteorological services in developing countries to facilitate free sharing of data and information' (Gambia 2011).

The World Health Organization, International Labour Organization, and UNISDR have all made similar calls. However, while these submissions point to a clear deficit in integrating the private sector, they do not provide much detail on the expectations that come with it. The US has been more specific in explaining the aim of this private sector engagement: 'increase collaboration with the private sector (…) to achieve effective and comprehensive risk management. (…) We should also prioritise the development of strategies that leverage private sector resources and create market-based mechanisms that are not overly reliant on public sector budgets, and that are sustainable in the long term' (USA 2011).

ExCom's 2016 report makes several references to the private sector. In particular the ExCom (SBSTA and SBI 2016):

- has recommended to the COP that the private sector be invited to cooperate and collaborate on issues relating to L&D where relevant.
- has initiated engagement with the private sector to identify how to enhance the implementation of comprehensive risk management approaches relating to L&D.
- has reached out to private investors to encourage them to incorporate climate risk and resilience into development projects.

The only sector that has been engaged in the L&D discussions under the UNFCCC is the insurance industry. In fact, the dominant focus on insurance-related instruments within the WIM is likely to have been influenced by the presence and engagement of these insurance companies.

A particularly prominent role has been played by MCII. MCII was initiated as a charitable organisation by representatives of insurers, research institutes and NGOs in 2005 in response to the rising interest in insurance-related solutions for climate adaptation. It brings together a broad range of insurers, policy researchers, NGOs and other climate change experts in a single forum. The UNFCCC is recognised as an 'observer' and 'friend' of MCII. Between 2008 and 2011, MCII's submissions to the UNFCCC focused on the role of insurance for weather-related risks in the context of adaptation (MCII 2012). Notably, some elements of a 2008 MCII proposal for a climate risk management module, comprising prevention and insurance pillars to facilitate adaptation (MCII 2008), were eventually included in the Cancun Adaptation Framework and the SBI Work Program on L&D.

Other parts of the insurance industry are also showing an emerging interest in L&D. This has been highlighted by the Philippines, which hosted a UNFCCC Standing Committee on Finance forum in early September 2016. The forum was designed to support the work of the WIM and ExCom. The programme for the forum was designed by the UNEP FI Principles for Sustainable Insurance (PSI) Initiative, and members of the Philippines insurance industry participated in the forum by providing technical expertise. A separate event was also hosted by the PSI together with the Philippines Insurers and Reinsurers Association the day following the forum (UNEPFI 2016). This event involved discussion of the L&D, and involved members of ExCom. Chapters 13 (Schäfer et al.) and 21 (Linnerooth-Bayer et al.) of this book look at the role of insurance for L&D in greater detail.

6.4 The L&D Negotiation Process Through the Lenses of IR Theories

In the previous section attention was drawn to the different actors involved in L&D negotiations, describing their positions and contributions. In particular, we emphasised that developing countries' negotiators, including AOSIS, after long negotiations managed to reach at least a partial victory in terms of the WIM and Art. 8 of the Paris Agreement. We now investigate this somewhat surprising victory from different IR perspectives to better understand the complexities of finding international agreement on L&D solutions. More specifically, we look at L&D negotiations through the lenses of the main school of thoughts in IR, namely neorealism, liberalism and constructivism (Snyder 2004). We believe that a pluralistic approach is necessary to understand how global outcomes are produced (Barnett and Duvall 2005).

In general terms, a neorealist viewpoint is useful to highlight resource-endowment asymmetries and highlight strategies to overcome them. Neorealism is a very influential strand in IR and sees states as pursuing their self-interest (which is ultimately security or wealth) in an international system defined by anarchy. States possess varying capabilities, or power, that they use to turn deals in their favour. The power States possess depends on their resource endowment, including the economy, population, and military forces. Nevertheless, aggregate measures of power might explain little about power positions when considering a specific bargaining circumstance (climate talks, in this case). What becomes relevant, instead, is "issue-specific power"; that is, the amount of relevant resources a Party can use for a specific conflict or concern (Habeeb 1988). In a multilateral setting such as the UNFCCC, two main resources acquire particular relevance and are considered for our analysis: delegation size and capacity.

Liberalism shares some assumptions with realism (anarchy of the international system and rationality of actors), but rejects power as the sole explaining factor and stresses the role of international cooperation and mutual benefits in shaping international outcomes. In particular, liberalism postulates that (i) it is the interdependence among state preferences to influence world politics [that promotes international cooperation,] and that (ii) states' preferences mirror the views of some subset of (domestic) social groups (Moravcsik 2008). The first assumption derives from the special emphasis liberals place on globalisation as a characteristic of the international political-economic system. In an interconnected world, characterised by high degrees of complexity and feed-back effects, state interactions are daily occurrences in a number of realms, including society, economy, politics and technology. These interactions are fuelled by specific state preferences (as determined by domestic actors), without which a state would not have any incentive to engage in the international context. Liberalist lenses are thus useful to investigate how asymmetry between states' preferences affect L&D outcomes.

Finally, constructivism is a relatively recent theoretical paradigm, challenging in many aspects both realist and liberal theories in explaining international negotiations and power relations. What fundamentally distinguishes constructivism from the former schools of thought is its ontological assumption of the world as being socially constructed. This means, as Hurd (2008) puts it, that "*how people and states think and behave in world politics is premised on their understanding of the world around them, which includes their own beliefs about the world, the identities they hold about themselves and others, and the shared understandings and practices in which they participate*". One of the most important contributions of constructivism is showing that norms matter (Price 2008) and thus ethical and legal standards are important in guiding world politics (Snyder 2004).

We suggest all these viewpoints are necessary to understand L&D negotiations. In the following sections we apply such competing theories to the L&D case by assuming the particular perspective of small island states, AOSIS being their most proactive proponent on the L&D issue.

6.4.1 Neorealism

In terms of aggregate power, AOSIS—a coalition of socially, economically and environmentally vulnerable small island nations—would be defined as a low-power actor in international negotiations. Its members are home to less than 1% of the world population; the sum of their 39 GDPs equals the annual economy of the city of London[5]; and almost half of the states have no or limited armed forces (Barbey 2015). Yet, such traditional indicators of power might explain little in a specific bargaining situation like climate negotiations. In this setting, two "issue-specific power" resources acquire particular relevance: delegation size and capacity. Both are reflections of a country's GDP. The size of national budgets influences the number of personnel and experts in the government and the ministries back home that can develop national negotiation positions, as well as the size of the delegations (Panke 2012). Developing countries often cannot afford to send big negotiating teams to COPs, and some initiatives have been put in place in response to that. One of them is the *Trust Fund for Participation in the UNFCCC* established under the Convention, which is nevertheless based on limited and decreasing voluntary contributions and can only support around two additional delegates per eligible developing Party (UNFCCC 2016). These circumstances inevitably hamper developing countries' full participation in the negotiation process.

[5]Own calculations based on the World Development Indicators by the World Bank (2015).

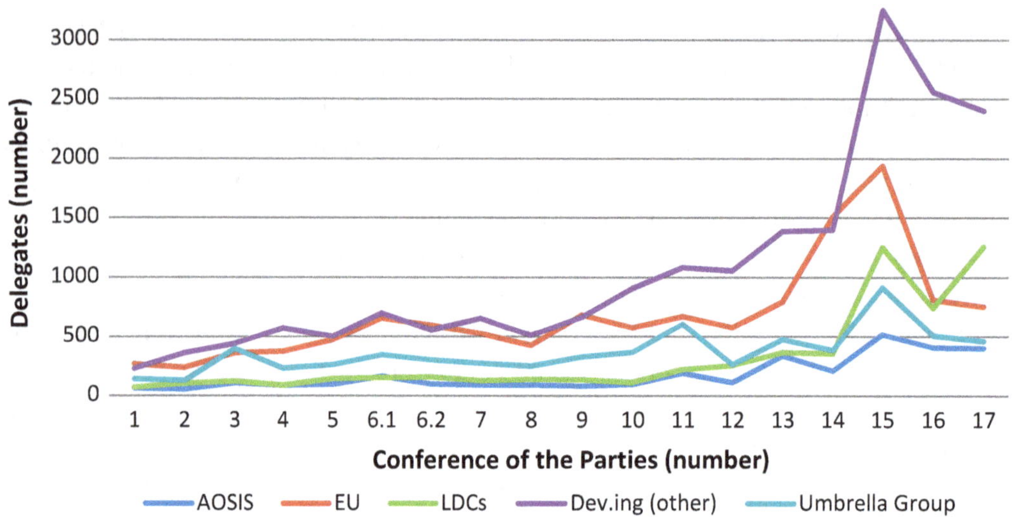

Fig. 6.3 Evolution of Party groupings/coalitions. *Note* Dev.ing (other) refers to G77 & China minus AOSIS. *Source* Own elaboration based on Böhmelt (2013)

Delegations composed of a small number of people only are unlikely to possess the range of technical expertise needed to follow different negotiation streams and are physically unable to cover simultaneous or exhaustingly long sessions (Chasek 2005; Michaelowa and Michaelowa 2012). The smaller the delegation, the less it will also be able to participate in the informal side of UNFCCC negotiations (where the most contentious issues are likely to be solved) and to exploit the networking opportunities offered by COPs.

AOSIS' "issue-specific power" is evident when considering the evolution of the group's delegations at COPs. A comparison among the sizes of UNFCCC Party-groupings between 1995 and 2011 (own elaboration based on Böhmelt (2013)[6] confirms AOSIS as the smallest one, with its size increasing at a slower pace compared to other non-Annex 1 Parties (Fig. 6.3).[7]

Although some authors consider size as an indicator of bargaining skills (Weiler 2012), other non-material resources like knowledge and expertise influence Parties' capacity at the negotiating table. Developing countries are typically ascribed a "capacity gap", only partially alleviated by the support offered by non-state actors (Schroeder et al. 2012). The case of AOSIS is somewhat different as the personal leadership of its negotiators and the early engagement of NGOs as knowledge brokers turned the group into one of the most vocal and proactive in climate talks. This is at least true when considering some key issues like the 1.5 °C target, adaptation and L&D, on which the group has been more cohesive. On topics of specific concern, members have started to increasingly negotiate out of the group, for instance on

[6] Latest available data.

[7] We are aware that a more accurate consideration of AOSIS' resource-endowment in L&D negotiations would require disaggregated data on the number of delegates effectively working on the issue, to be compared with their counterparts in other groups. Unfortunately this information does not yet exist.

the issue of reducing emissions from deforestation and forest degradation (REDD) (Betzold et al. 2012).

Yet, it is not just about resources. "Issue-specific power" can be increased using "behavioural power", i.e. tactics to alter perceived or real power structures (Habeeb 1988). Teaming up with NGOs was one of the strategies employed by AOSIS to rectify power asymmetries on L&D. The other was to pull resources and gain influence through coalition-building with other non-Annex I groupings. The alignment with LDCs, the African Group and the G77+China was arguably a result of a conceptual "reshaping" of the L&D concept in the 2000s. While originally AOSIS' claims only focused on losses resulting from sea level rise (as in its 1991 proposal), consideration for the residual impacts from slow onset events as a whole and the financial risk associated with extremes (e.g. AOSIS 2008) made a stronger case for other developing countries to support the cause. This is not to say that all these groupings had the same position on L&D and, even less, the same idea about what L&D is. If AOSIS stressed the life-threatening dimension of L&D, the LDCs focused more on the connection with development and how L&D could affect the quality of life, livelihoods, food security, and social fabric at the community/household level. At the same time, Bolivia defined L&D as lost development opportunities and pointed at the deferral of payments to international institutions, debt relief and similar measures as a way to address them (UNFCCC 2012a). However, common denominators laid in the request for L&D to be a stand-alone pillar in UNFCCC architecture and in the need for supporting developing countries' limited capacity to address climate change impacts. The G77+China is worthy of separate consideration. While its position was decisive for the establishment of the WIM and the creation of a separate article on L&D in the Paris Agreement (see, for instance, the work done within the Ad Hoc Working Group on the Durban Platform for Enhanced Action—ADP), future alignment with AOSIS' positions cannot be taken for granted. This is mainly because of the heterogeneity of the group which makes synthesis among its members' positions challenging to reach. Recent examples of difficulties in finding common ground include the review of the WIM at COP22 (Calliari 2016b) and the quarrels between China and AOSIS on the need (supported by the former) to erase the reference to "particularly" vulnerable developing countries in defining beneficiaries of L&D support.[8]

While AOSIS has surely benefitted from liaising with other developing countries in bringing L&D high on the UNFCCC Agenda, this cannot deterministically explain why outcomes on L&D were obtained. Coalition-building in itself is not a sure means for any grouping to impact substantively on negotiations (Cooper and Shaw 2009) and even less in a consensus-based setting such as the UNFCCC (Deitelhoff and Wallbott 2012). As the institutional context does not level power asymmetries—for instance through a one state-one vote system—weaker Parties will be unable to succeed by relying on their resource-endowment only. Thus, trying to explain L&D negotiations through "realist eyes" does not allow for going beyond the "structuralist paradox". It is therefore worth investigating other sources of power beyond the neorealist perspective to get more insight on how AOSIS' outcomes on L&D were obtained.

[8]Personal observations at COP 22.

6.4.2 Liberalism

By stressing the role played by preferences, *liberals* point to their interdependence as a determinant of bargaining outcomes. Some liberals ascribe particular importance to economic preferences in determining state behaviour. In the L&D case, developed countries would be incentivised to support their vulnerable developing counterparts so as to guarantee their viability as commercial partners or to safeguard their delocalised supply-chains. Global trade systems can indeed transmit a variety of negative impacts, as exemplified by the billion dollar losses incurred by the American corporation Intel that resulted from the collapse of the Thai electronic industry following flooding in 2011 (Struck 2011). Actually, this liberal argument was also employed by AOSIS when it called on the international community to consider the "increased interdependence of global economy and society" and to address "the cascading effects that climate change impacts in poor and vulnerable regions can globally have" as it would be "cost-effective" (AOSIS 2008). It is worth noting, however, that this argument was incidentally used by developing countries and that they largely approached the debate in ethical and legal terms.

While making the case for increased international cooperation on L&D, liberal theory also allows for highlighting some of the "hampering factors" that have affected developing countries in L&D negotiations. These are related to the liberal conceptualisation of power, which differs significantly from realist theory. According to Kehoane and Nye (1977), one form of international influence derives from the "asymmetric interdependence" of preferences among states. The more interdependent a state is and the more intense its preference for a given outcome, the more power others potentially have over it (Moravcsik 2008). In other words, the salience an actor attaches to an issue is inversely linked to its success at the negotiating table as the actor will be more willing to make concessions to get the result (Schneider 2005). Moreover, salience is linked to the existence of an outside option: if a state has alternatives to the negotiated agreement it will exploit the circumstance to ask for a higher "price" to take part in it. Translating this reasoning to L&D negotiations, it easy to see how AOSIS has negotiated since the beginning from a disadvantageous position. By virtue of their extreme vulnerability and the existential threat posed by climate change, small islands states can only rely on ambitious mitigation efforts and support for adaptation and rehabilitation by developed countries to address L&D. This has two intertwined implications: (i) as they do not have control over the issue at stake (mostly in terms of mitigation), small island states can do nothing but wait for developed countries to act; and (ii) not having bargaining power, small island states are forced to accept a sub-optimal solution compared to what they would prefer.

Beyond salience, liberals stress the importance that domestic actors have in shaping negotiating outcomes. Governments facing a strong opposition back home—and thus looking less powerful—can convince counterparts that only a minimum commitment is possible (Schneider 2005). While not really applying to AOSIS' member states (as domestic actors should agree with the survival of their country), this can be observed in a relevant counterpart of the L&D debate: the US. One of the leitmotifs of the US delegation at COP21 was that any reference to legal remedies in the Paris Agreement would have encountered the opposition of the Congress and had the effect "to kill the deal". The US ratification constraint (Putnam 1988) forced AOSIS to put aside their responsibility claims and go for a compromise solution. Talks between the US and small island states, labelled a "meeting of the minds" by Secretary Kerry (Friedman 2015), were held at the onset of the second negotiation week, with Saint Lucia minister Fletcher describing their objective as "ensur[ing] that everybody was comfortable with the agreement" (CarbonBrief 2015). Yet, the compromise solution (paragraph 52 of the accompanying decision to the Agreement excluding basis for any liability or compensation claims) did not make everybody comfortable. The Philippines expressed deep concern and Bolivia stated that "no clause can deny people and countries' rights to ask for compensation" and that "all the necessary institutional means will be used so that [climate] justice can be made" (Bolivia 2015).

As made evident by this discussion, a liberalist view of L&D negotiations does not really help to explain the structuralist-paradox. In fact, it reinforces it. This is the result of considering, as in realism, negotiation outcomes a function of the (static) characteristics—being Parties' features or capabilities—of a particular negotiation. In other words, for liberals and neorealists it is material power (military hardware, strategic resources, and money) that ultimately matters (Hurd 2008). On the contrary, constructivists argue that both material and discursive power are necessary for understanding world politics (Hopf 1998). We therefore turn our attention to the constructivist approach and the role that ethical and legal discourses have had in shaping L&D negotiations.

6.4.3 *Constructivism*

Along the constructivism line, L&D negotiations would have been shaped not only by material power or state interest but also by a competition between states around different understandings and framings (i.e. discourses) of L&D. Developing countries have largely framed L&D in ethical and legal terms and made a case for this conceptualisation since the beginning of climate talks. They have pointed to the unfairness of climate change (affecting first those least responsible for the problem) and to the threats for survival it poses for the most exposed societies. By analysing developing countries' submissions to the SBI and ADP (2011–2015) and High Level Segment statements from COP 16 to COP 21 (see Calliari (2016a) for the material employed), it is possible to find references to the concepts of fairness, international solidarity; equity and intergenerational equity. The legal counterpart of these ethical arguments is the concept of state responsibility–compensation (see Chap. 7 on legal issues: Simlinger and Mayer 2018), which seeks reparation for wrongful acts attributable to states. In terms of citation frequency, this is the most-cited principle in the (wide) sample of submissions we analysed, and it is often accompanied by the Polluter Pays Principle; Common but differentiated responsibility and respective capabilities (CBDR-RC) and references to precautionary measures. On the contrary, as explained above, developed countries have mostly avoided any references to compensation, and have tried instead to shift the attention to non-economic L&D. This is interesting if we consider that, up to the establishment of the WIM, developing countries tended to associate L&D to (in principle) the quantifiable and monetisable effects of climate change, like physical impacts—e.g. loss of land because of sea level rise—and economic impacts, such as the loss of development opportunities advanced by Bolivia (UNFCCC 2012a). As a whole, developed countries have tried to shift L&D to the less contested DRR and humanitarian frameworks; used scientific knowledge (issues of attribution) to neutralise the developing Parties' compensation claims; and employed ethical claims to avoid the 'monetisation' of the discourse, by hinting at the inappropriateness of placing price tags on the lives, livelihoods and assets of the most vulnerable societies (Calliari 2016a).

If power, in a simplified constructivist view, is about "convince[ing] others to adopt [ones] ideas" (Snyder 2004), can AOSIS be deemed successful on the L&D issue? Can the WIM and Article 8 be seen as a result of AOSIS' discursive power? Undoubtedly, the developing countries managed to institutionalise the idea of L&D as something beyond adaptation both in the text of Decision 2/CP.19 establishing the WIM and with a stand-alone article for L&D in the Paris Agreement. Thus, they were able to "convince" developed countries on this point. The result was obtained by framing the L&D debate in such a way that Parties' resources and interests became irrelevant as the playground was moved into the legal and moral fields. While narratives of survival (and thus moral issues) have also been employed by AOSIS in other UNFCCC negotiation streams (for instance, in asking for ambitious mitigation actions), the massive recourse to state Responsibility-compensation claims was the main factor in determining AOSIS' outcomes. It can be argued that, rather than being an objective per se, calls for compensation were used strategically to get concessions from Annex 1 Parties. This idea is somehow reinforced when looking at the timing of compensation claims (Table 6.1).

Most of them concentrated before 2013, at the time of the discussion for an institutional mechanism to address L&D (what was going to be the WIM). After that, reference was made episodically by AOSIS and the G77+China in the proposal for a Climate Change Displacement Coordination Facility. Among the performed functions, the facility was to provide "compensation measures for people displaced by climate change"—a provision that was dropped without excessive clamour on the road to Paris. And while at COP 21 requests for compensation were "traded" for a dedicated L&D article, they reappeared in a number of interpretative declarations to the instruments of ratification of the Paris Agreement (see Bolivia, the Philippines, Nauru, Marshall Islands, Cook Islands, Solomon Islands and Tuvalu). This is not to imply that such calls for retributive justice were not genuine: they are consistent with the unfairness that developing countries ascribe to the climate change problem. However, some tactical considerations are discernible behind their use in climate talks.

In terms of the "status" that L&D has in the UNFCCC architecture, AOSIS and other developing countries were less successful in "convincing" their counterparts

Table 6.1 Party/Grouping calling for compensation in the period 1991–2016

Year	Party/grouping
1991	AOSIS
2008	AOSIS; Sri Lanka
2009	Brazil; Colombia; India; Nicaragua on behalf of Guatemala, Dominican Republic, Honduras, Panama and Nicaragua; Turkey; Tuvalu; Cook Island; Algeria on behalf of the African group; AOSIS; Bolivia;
2010	Bolivia; Ghana; AOSIS; Maldives; The Bolivarian Republic of Venezuela on behalf of Cuba, Bolivia, Ecuador and Nicaragua; Alba;
2011	Mexico[a], Sri Lanka
2012	AOSIS; Gambia for the LDCs; Swaziland for the African Group; Ghana; Bolivia with Ecuador, China, El Salvador, Guatemala, Thailand, Philippines, Nicaragua;
2013	AOSIS
2014	Central American Integration System (SICA, in Spanish)
2015 (pre-PA)	AOSIS, G 77
2015–2016 (post-PA)	Bolivia, Nicaragua, Cook Islands; Micronesia (Federated States of); Nauru; Niue; Solomon Islands; Tuvalu

[a]Mexico does not properly call for compensation, but rather highlights it among the mechanisms that could be "identified, prioritised and developed"

in placing L&D as a truly third pillar of climate action. In particular, L&D does not seem to be placed on an equal footing with mitigation and adaptation in the climate regime designed by the Paris Agreement as no reference is made to Article 8 by other treaty provisions. It is not mentioned in the purpose of the Agreement (Article 2), in the context of the "ambitious efforts" required to achieve it (Article 3), in the related transparency framework (Article 13), or in the global stocktake process (Article 14). This signals not only the "last minute" nature of the agreement reached at COP 21, but also—and most importantly—the contested status that L&D continues to have under the UNFCCC. Besides the symbolic meaning of keeping L&D separate from adaptation, Article 8 contains nothing more than tentative and cautious language.

6.5 From Theory to Practice: Next Steps and Key Questions for Moving the L&D Discourse Forward

Despite being one of the most controversial issues to be recently treated within climate negotiations, L&D has attracted little attention among IR scholars. Yet, the discipline can greatly contribute to the debate, not only by enhancing understanding of the negotiation process and related outcomes but also by offering insights on how the issue could be fruitfully moved forward. This chapter specifically adopted a multi-faceted notion of power, drawing from the neorealist, liberal and constructivist schools of thought, in order to explain how L&D milestones were reached. This allowed for overcoming the "structuralist paradox" in negotiations, i.e. the apparently surprising capacity of weak parties to take home results while negotiating with stronger parties.

Developing countries' achievements on L&D (WIM and Article 8) are only surprising when considering power in its purely materialistic form. If discursive power is added to the picture, then achievements can be ascribed to developing countries' capacity to shape their fate rather than to fortunate circumstances. This is not to say that material power does not play any role. Developing countries are faced with resource and capacity constraints which make it harder for their needs to be fully addressed within the UNFCCC. Consistently, NGO support will continue to play a crucial role in levelling current asymmetries in terms of capabilities, together with other initiatives to fund developing countries' participation in the process.

Yet, other sources of power besides the realist and liberal ones can be decisive for obtaining desired international outcomes. Our analysis has shown the key importance that discursive power, by framing L&D in ethical and legal terms, had in the attainment of L&D milestones. First, it moved the debate to a playground where resources and interests became irrelevant, therefore putting developed and developing countries on an equal foot. Second, it appealed to standards somehow shared or agreed beyond the UNFCCC context, including the basic moral norms linked to island states' narratives of survival and the reference to international customary law (state responsibility-compensation principles). This was useful to prove the need for action on L&D recurring to standards in principle recognised by both contending parties in other international arenas. Although this was not enough to impose developing countries' view on what L&D is and how it should be addressed, it at least moved developed countries' position towards the direction paved by the former.

At the same time, however, this strategy prevented Parties from starting a process towards the creation of shared meaning and understanding around L&D. Indeed, definitional issues have been carefully avoided in order not to stumble into the taboo reference of 'compensation'. As a result, no official definition of L&D has been agreed at the UNFCCC level yet and Parties rely on a working one formulated under the SBI (UNFCCC 2012b). This is not just a matter of form, but a more important matter of substance. Without clarity around L&D conceptual boundaries, it will ultimately be difficult to go beyond the explorative mandate the WIM was given. In particular, concrete guidance is needed in order to implement the WIM's third function on enhancing "action and support to address loss and damage", which also includes finance. For example, there is a need for establishing relevant criteria to identify L&D projects on the ground, as well as defining the level of adaptation beyond which L&D materialises. Does L&D arise when social, technical and physical limits are surpassed, or should also economic and institutional constraints be considered? The answers cannot but be political.

Yet, we are not claiming that agreeing on a definition is the only way to have meaningful action on L&D. We are aware that the discussion still causes discomfort and may lead to political deadlock. We thus believe that a more fruitful way forward entails adopting a different perspective and agreeing on shared principles against which action could be tested (see chapter on justice by Wallimann-Helmer et al. 2018). Such shared principles would support an L&D working space where solutions can be developed (see chapter by Schinko et al. 2018), including tools to address irreversible losses, which are mostly associated with slow-onset events. While there is general accord around the use of comprehensive risk management approaches (including risk assessment, reduction, transfer, retention), how to deal with impacts from slow onset events remains an open question. Discourse about those impacts and efforts to develop creative or transformative instruments in response has been somewhat limited, often hampered by the taboo of compensation. A change of narrative is therefore needed. Framing L&D exclusively in terms of justice might have turned the issue into a win-lose negotiation game. Instead, a bigger emphasis on mutual gains through adaptation and action on L&D for both developed and developing countries is needed, as well as more clarity on the limits of those strategies. Examples of such mutual gains are more resilient global supply chains, reduction of climate refugees and enhanced security. As a result, acting on L&D would not feel as a unilateral concession developed countries make to vulnerable ones: it would rather be about elaborating patterns of collective action on an issue of common concern.

References

ActionAid (2010) Loss and damage from climate change: the cost for poor people in developing countries. Johannesburg

ActionAid, Care, WWF (2012) Tackling the limits to adaptation: an international framework to address "Loss and Damage" from climate change impacts. Johannesburg

ActionAid, Care, WWF (2013) Tackling the climate reality: a framework for establishing an international mechanism to address loss and damage at COP19. Johannesburg

AOSIS (2008) Proposal to the AWG-LCA multi-window mechanism to address loss and damage from climate change impacts. 1–8

Barbey C (2015) Non-militarisation: countries without armies. Identification criteria and first findings. Mariehamn, Åland, Finland

Barnett M, Duvall R (2005) Power in international politics. Int Org 59:39–75

Betzold C (2010) "Borrowing" power to influence international negotiations: AOSIS in the climate change regime, 1990–1997. Politics 30:131–148. https://doi.org/10.1111/j.1467-9256.2010.01377.x

Betzold C, Castro P, Weiler F (2012) AOSIS in the UNFCCC negotiations: from unity to fragmentation? Clim Policy 12:591–613. https://doi.org/10.1080/14693062.2012.692205

Birkmann J, Welle T (2015) Assessing the risk of loss and damage: exposure, vulnerability and risk to climate-related hazards for different country classifications. Int J Global Warming 8:191–212

Böhmelt T (2013) A closer look at the information provision rationale: civil society participation in states' delegations at the UNFCCC. Rev Int Organ 8:55–80. https://doi.org/10.1007/s11558-012-9149-6

Bolivia (2015) Intervención Bolivia COP21 - Ministro René Orellana. https://www.youtube.com/watch?v=kQOEdNZBqFs. Accessed 22 Jan 2016

Brown DA, Weiskel T (2002) American heat: ethical problems with the United States' Response to global warming. Rowman & Littlefield Publishers

Calliari E (2016a) Loss and damage: a critical discourse analysis of Parties' positions in climate change negotiations. J Risk Res 1–23. https://doi.org/10.1080/13669877.2016.1240706

Calliari E (2016b) Review of the L&D mechanism agreed in Marrakech. Int Clim Policy 43:12–13

CarbonBrief (2015) COP21 video: St Lucia's James Fletcher on loss and damage

Carter G (2015) Establishing a Pacific voice in the climate change negotiations. ANU Press, Acton

CDKN, GERMANWATCH, ICCCAD et al (2012) Loss and damage in vulnerable countries initiative

Chasek PS (2005) Margins of power: coalition building and coalition maintenance of the South Pacific island states and the alliance of small island states. Rev Eur Commun Int Environ Law 14:125–137. https://doi.org/10.1111/j.1467-9388.2005.00433.x

Cooper AF, Shaw T (2009) The diplomacies of small states. Palgrave Macmillan UK, London

Crump L, Downie C (2015) Understanding climate change negotiations: contributions from international negotiation and conflict management. Int Negot 20:146–174. https://doi.org/10.1163/15718069-12341302

de Águeda Corneloup I, Mol APJ (2014) Small island developing states and international climate change negotiations: the power of moral leadership'. Int Environ Agreements: Politics, Law Econ 14:281–297. https://doi.org/10.1007/s10784-013-9227-0

Deitelhoff N, Wallbott L (2012) Beyond soft balancing: small states and coalition-building in the ICC and climate negotiations. Cambridge Rev Int Aff 25:345–366. https://doi.org/10.1080/09557571.2012.710580

Fekete A, Sakdapolrak P (2014) Loss and damage as an alternative to resilience and vulnerability? Preliminary reflections on an emerging climate change adaptation discourse. Int J Disaster Risk Sci 5:88–93. https://doi.org/10.1007/s13753-014-0012-7

Friedman L (2015) Kerry sees progress on key issues. In: E&E news. https://www.eenews.net/stories/1060029174

Gambia (2011) Submission by the Gambia on behalf of the least developed countries group on loss and damage overview. https://unfccc.int/files/adaptation/application/pdf/submission_by_the_gambia_on_behalf_of_the_least_developed_countries_on_loss_and_damage.pdf. Accessed 12 Aug 2017

Goodell J (2015) John Kerry on climate change: the fight of our time. In: Rolling-Stone. http://www.rollingstone.com/politics/news/john-kerry-on-climate-change-the-fight-of-our-time-20151201. Accessed 12 Aug 2017

Habeeb WM (1988) Power and tactics in international negotiation: how weak nations bargain with strong nations. Johns Hopkins University Press, Baltimore, Maryland

Hoffmaister PJ, Talakai M, Damptey P, Barbosa AS (2014) Warsaw international mechanism for loss and damage: moving from polarizing discussions towards addressing the emerging challenges faced by developing countries. Bonn, Germany

Hoffmeister V, Huq S (2015) Loss and damage in INDCs. An investigation of Parties' statements on L&D and prospects for its inclusion in a Paris Agreement. Dacca, Bangladesh

Hopf T (1998) The promise of constructivism in international relations theory. Int Secur 23:171. https://doi.org/10.2307/2539267

Huggel C, Stone D, Auffhammer M, Hansen G (2013) Loss and damage attribution. Nat Clim Change 3:694–696. https://doi.org/10.1038/nclimate1961

Huq S, Roberts E, Fenton A (2013) Loss and damage. Nat Clim Change 3:947–949. https://doi.org/10.1038/nclimate2026

Huq S, De Souza R-M (2016) Climate compensation: how loss and damage fared in the Paris agreement. In: New Security Beat. https://www.newsecuritybeat.org/2016/01/loss-damage-fared-paris-agreement/. Accessed 1 Aug 2017

Hurd I (2008) Constructivism. In: Snidal Christian Reus-Smit Duncan (ed) The oxford handbook of international relations. Oxford University Press, Oxford, pp 298–316

Hyvarinen J (2012) Loss and damage caused by climate change : legal strategies for vulnerable countries. http://re.indiaenvironmentportal.org.in/files/file/field_loss__damage_legal_strategies_oct_12.pdf. Accessed 24 Apr 2018

INC (1991) Vanuatu: Draft annex relating to Article 23 (Insurance) for inclusion in the revised single text on elements relating to mechanisms (A/AC.237/WG.II/Misc.13) submitted by the Co-Chairmen of Working Group II. Intergovernmental Negotiating Committee for a Framework Convention on Climate Change, Working Group II

James R, Otto F, Parker H et al (2014) Characterizing loss and damage from climate change. Nat Clim Change 4:938–939

Johnson CA (2017) Holding polluting countries to account for climate change: Is? Loss and damage? Up to the task? Rev Policy Res 34:50–67. https://doi.org/10.1111/ropr.12216

Keohane RO, Nye JS (1977) Power and interdependence: world politics in transition. Little Brown and Company

Khan MR (2016) Climate change, adaptation and international relations theory. In: Sosa-Nunez G, Atkins E (eds) Environment, climate-change, and international relations. E-International Relations, Bristol, England, pp 14–28

Larson MJ (2003) Low-power contributions in multilateral negotiations: a framework analysis. Negot J 19:133–149. https://doi.org/10.1023/A:1023645817323

Mace MJ, Verheyen R (2016) Loss, damage and responsibility after COP21: all options open for the Paris agreement. Rev Eur Commun Int Environ Law 25:197–214. https://doi.org/10.1111/reel.12172

Mathew LM, Akter S (2015) Loss and damage associated with climate change impacts. In: Chen W-Y, Seiner J, Suzuki T, Lackner M (eds) Handbook of climate change mitigation and adaptation, 1st edn. Springer, New York, pp 1–23

Mayer B (2014) Whose " loss and damage"? Promoting the agency of beneficiary states. Clim Law 4:267–300

MCII (2008) Insurance instruments for adapting to climate risks a proposal for the Bali Action Plan

MCII (2012) Insurance solutions in the context of climate change-related loss and damage: needs, gaps, and roles of the Convention in addressing loss and damage

McNamara KE (2014) exploring loss and damage at the international climate change talks. Int J Disaster Risk Sci 5:242–246. https://doi.org/10.1007/s13753-014-0023-4

Mechler R, Bouwer LM, Linnerooth-bayer J et al (2014) Managing unnatural disaster risk from climate extremes. Nat Clim Change 4:235–237. https://doi.org/10.1038/nclimate2137

Mechler R, Schinko T (2016) Identifying the policy space for climate loss and damage. Science 354:290–292. https://doi.org/10.1126/science.aag2514

Mechler R et al (2018) Science for loss and damage. Findings and propositions. In: Mechler R, Bouwer L, Schinko T, Surminski S, Linnerooth-Bayer J (eds) Loss and damage from climate change. Concepts, methods and policy options. Springer, Cham, pp 3–37

Michaelowa K, Michaelowa A (2012) Negotiating climate change. Clim Policy 12:37–41. https://doi.org/10.1080/14693062.2012.693393

Moravcsik A (2008) The New Liberalism. In: Reus-Smit C, Snidal D (eds) The oxford handbook of international relations. Oxford University Press, Oxford, UK

Norway (2011) Submission on approaches to enhance adaptive capacity in developing countries that are particularly vulnerable to the adverse effects of climate change when addressing loss and damage associated with climate change impacts. http://unfccc.int/files/documentation/submissions_from_parties/application/pdf/norway_loss_and_damage.pdf. Accessed 12 Aug 2017

Norway (2013) Institutional arrangements under the UNFCCC for approaches to address loss and damage associated with climate change impacts in developing countries that are particularly vulnerable to the adverse effects of climate change to enhance adaptive capacity. 1–5

Panke D (2012) Dwarfs in international negotiations: how small states make their voices heard. Cambridge Rev Int Aff 25:313–328. https://doi.org/10.1080/09557571.2012.710590

Price R (2008) The ethics of constructivism. In: Reus-Smit C, Snidal D (eds) The oxford handbook of international relations. Oxford University Press, Oxford, pp 317–326

Putnam RD (1988) Diplomacy and domestic politics: the logic of two-level games. Int Org 42:427. https://doi.org/10.1017/S0020818300027697

Roberts E, Huq S (2015) Coming full circle: the history of loss and damage under the UNFCCC. Int J Global Warming 8:141–157

SBI, SBSTA (2017) Report of the executive committee of the warsaw international mechanism for loss and damage associated with climate change impacts. UNFCCC, Bonn, Germany

SBSTA, SBI (2016) Report of the executive committee of the Warsaw international mechanism for loss and damage associated with climate change impacts report of the executive committee of the Warsaw international mechanism for loss and damage associated with climate change impacts*

Schinko T, Mechler R, Hochrainer-Stigler S (2018) The risk and policy space for loss and damage: Integrating notions of distributive and compensatory justice with comprehensive climate risk management. In: Mechler R, Bouwer L, Schinko T, Surminski S, Linnerooth-Bayer J (eds) Loss and damage from climate change. Concepts, methods and policy options. Springer, Cham, pp 83–110

Schneider G (2005) Capacity and concessions: bargaining power in multilateral negotiations. Millennium—J Int Stud 33:665–689. https://doi.org/10.1177/03058298050330031901

Schroeder H, Boykoff MT, Spiers L (2012) Equity and state representations in climate negotiations. Nat Clim Change 2:834–836. https://doi.org/10.1038/nclimate1742

Simlinger F, Mayer B (2018) Legal responses to climate change induced loss and damage. In: Mechler R, Bouwer L, Schinko T, Surminski S, Linnerooth-Bayer J (eds) Loss and damage from climate change. Concepts, methods and policy options. Springer, Cham, pp 179–203

Snyder J (2004) One world, rival theories. Foreign Policy 53–62. https://doi.org/10.2307/4152944

Stabinsky D, Hoffmaister JP (2015) Establishing institutional arrangements on loss and damage under the UNFCCC : the Warsaw international mechanism for loss and damage. Int J Global Warming 8

Struck H (2011) After thai floods, companies reconsider risk. Forbes

Surminski S, Eldridge J (2015) Observations on the role of the private sector in the UNFCCC' s loss and damage of climate change work program. Int J Global Warming 8:213–230

Tol RS, Verheyen R (2004) State responsibility and compensation for climate change damages—a legal and economic assessment. Energy Policy 32:1109–1130. https://doi.org/10.1016/S0301-4215(03)00075-2

UNEPFI (2016) UNFCCC, UNEP and Philippine insurance industry collaborate for climate and disaster risk solutions through international events in Manila « UNEP FI Principles for Sustainable Insurance. http://www.unepfi.org/psi/unfccc-unep-and-philippine-insurance-industry-collaborate-for-climate-and-disaster-risk-solutions-through-international-events-in-manila/. Accessed 7 Sep 2017

UNFCCC (2012a) (FCCC/SBI/2012/MISC.14/Add.1) Views and information from Parties and relevant organizations on the possible elements to be included in the recommendations on loss and damage in accordance with decision 1/CP.16. 1–7

UNFCCC (2012b) A literature review on the topics in the context of thematic area 2 of the work programme on loss and damage: a range of approaches to address loss and damage associated with the adverse effects of climate change Note by the secretariat. Bonn, Germany

UNFCCC (2015) Adoption of the Paris Agreement

UNFCCC (2016) Budget performance for the biennium 2016–2017 as at 30 June 2016. 1–57

UNFCCC (2018) Loss and damage: Online guide. Available at: https://unfccc.int/sites/default/files/resource/Online_guide_on_loss_and_damage-May_2018.pdf

USA (2011) Submission by the United States of America Work program on loss and damage associated with the adverse effects of climate change. https://unfccc.int/files/adaptation/cancun_adaptation_framework/application/pdf/usa_25_february_2011.pdf. Accessed 12 Aug 2017

Vanhala L, Hestbaek C (2016) Framing climate change loss and damage in UNFCCC negotiations. Global Environ Polit 16:111–129. https://doi.org/10.1162/GLEP_a_00379

Verheyen R (2012) Loss & damage: tackling loss & damage. Bonn, Germany

Verheyen R (2015) Loss and damage due to climate change: attribution and causation—where climate science and law meet. Int J Global Warming 8:158–169

Vidal J (2016) World's largest carbon producers face landmark human rights case. In: The Guardian. https://www.theguardian.com/environment/2016/jul/27/worlds-largest-carbon-producers-face-landmark-human-rights-case. Accessed 12 Aug 2017

Vulturius G, Davis M (2016) Defining loss and damage: the science and politics around one of the most contested issues within the UNFCCC. Stockholm

Wallimann-Helmer I, Meyer L, Mintz-Woo K, Schinko T, Serdeczny O (2018) The ethical challenges in the context of climate loss and damage. In: Mechler R, Bouwer L, Schinko T, Surminski S, Linnerooth-Bayer J (eds) Loss and damage from climate change. concepts, methods and policy options. Springer, Cham, pp 39–62

Warner K, van der Geest K (2013) Loss and damage from climate change : local-level evidence from nine vulnerable countries. Int J Global Warming 5

Warner K, van der Geest K (2015) Editorial: loss and damage from climate change: emerging perspectives. Int J Global Warming 8:133–140

Weiler F (2012) Determinants of bargaining success in the climate change negotiations. Clim Policy 12:552–574. https://doi.org/10.1080/14693062.2012.691225

Zartman IW, Rubin JZ (2002) Power and negotiation. University of Michigan Press

Chapter 7
Legal Responses to Climate Change Induced Loss and Damage

Florentina Simlinger and Benoit Mayer

Abstract Legal issues are central to ongoing debates on Loss and Damage associated with climate change impacts and risks (L&D). These debates shed light, in particular, on the remedial obligations of actors most responsible for causing climate change towards those most affected by its adverse impacts. The aim of this chapter is to take stock of the legal literature on the topic, to identify potential legal approaches to L&D, identify challenges and to explore possible directions for further research. It looks at the feasibility of private and administrative climate change litigation while providing examples from around the world. Subsequently, we explore how human rights issues have been applied in international law to address L&D. The discussion particularly addresses the question whether the no-harm rule can be applied to climate change and would in fact trigger legal responsibility for greenhouse gas emissions. In addition, we examine relevant legal actions with relevance for L&D taken under the UNFCCC and the Warsaw International Mechanism on Loss and Damage. The chapter concludes with a synopsis of the various legal responses to L&D highlighting their premises, specific challenges and proposed remedies.

Keywords Climate change litigation · Climate regime · No-harm rule
Loss and Damage

7.1 Introduction and Preliminary Notes

Legal issues are central to the ongoing debate on Loss and Damage associated with climate change impacts (L&D). These debates on L&D shed light, in particular, on the remedial obligations of the actors most responsible for causing climate change

F. Simlinger (✉)
Department of European, International and Comparative Law,
University of Vienna, Vienna, Austria
e-mail: f.simlinger@outlook.com

B. Mayer
Faculty of Law, The Chinese University of Hong Kong, Hong Kong, China
e-mail: bmayer@cuhk.edu.hk

R. Mechler et al. (eds.), *Loss and Damage from Climate Change*, Climate Risk Management, Policy and Governance, https://doi.org/10.1007/978-3-319-72026-5_7

towards those most affected by its adverse impacts. Ethical perspectives are explored in the chapter by Wallimann-Helmer et al. (2018) in this book, and the aim of the present chapter is to take stock of the legal literature on the topic, to identify potential legal approaches to L&D, and to explore possible directions for further research. While the Warsaw International Mechanism is an important institutional development, it does not appear as the unique entry point for providing redress for the adverse impacts of climate change. In outlining how diverse domestic or international legal frameworks could approach L&D, this chapter engages with the relation between legal arguments and necessary political or scientific developments at different scales of the regime complex for climate change.

The chapter is organised as follows. Section 7.2 presents different approaches to climate law litigation before domestic courts and highlights the most prominent cases relevant to L&D. Section 7.3 briefly discusses whether regional and international human rights law is of avail to those affected most by the impacts of climate change. Section 7.4 highlights the potential of international litigation based on principles of customary international law. Section 7.5 turns to the developments taking place under the UN Framework Convention on Climate Change, including the Warsaw International Mechanism on Loss and Damage (WIM). Section 7.6 finally discusses the different legal responses analysed and concludes with possible ways forward.

7.2 National Laws

Recent years have seen a rapid development of national laws related to climate change. From only a few climate laws in the pre-Kyoto Protocol era, there are now more than 1,200 laws and policies world-wide (Nachmany et al. 2017). Beyond a general focus on climate change mitigation, some of these laws have sought to address the damages caused by climate change.

Developments have also taken place before national courts, often driven by individuals or groups interested in bypassing the inertia of political institutions. Generally speaking, litigation is more likely in “common law” jurisdictions, as largely based on the doctrine of precedent—the application of the rule identified by a court in a given case to any similar subsequent cases. Most English-speaking countries apply a system of “common law,” while other countries apply a form of “civil law,” based on extensive codes covering fundamental areas of law.

Litigation can be based on private or public law. Through private law litigation, a person (individual or group) may seek a court’s finding regarding the responsibility of another person or private entity for harms suffered. Through public law litigation, a person may seek a court’s finding regarding the obligation of the government or another public administration to take a particular course of action, for instance to mitigate climate change, to adapt to the impacts of climate change, or to compensate for losses and damages. Whether litigation leads to a favourable court decision or not, it contributes to raising awareness and creating political momentum for further developments.

7.2.1 Public Law Litigation

Public law litigation puts the action or inaction of national authorities under scrutiny. In common law jurisdictions, such "judicial review" often takes place before an ordinary court, whereas civil law jurisdictions often have specific courts in charge of administrative and, mostly, constitutional oversight. Normally, public law litigation is based on the inconsistency of an act or omission of a national authority with a rule of higher hierarchical standing. For instance, a regulation could be struck by a court because it is incompatible with a statute, or the application of a statute could be suspended when it is incompatible with the constitution.

Public law litigation related to climate change has often focused on the obligation of a state to mitigate climate change rather than directly on ways to address losses and damages. The decision of the US Supreme Court in *Massachusetts v. Environmental Protection Agency*, for instance, forced the Environmental Protection Agency to regulate GHGs as air pollutants. As another example, in 2015, a decision of the District Court of The Hague in the case of *Urgenda Foundation v. The State of the Netherlands* found the government of the Netherlands in breach of its obligation to mitigate climate change under international law and ordered it to take measures to reduce national greenhouse gas emissions by at least 25% until the end of 2020 based on the 1990 levels. This judgment is currently under appeal and the final decision is still pending at the time of publication.

The Netherlands is one of very few jurisdictions where international law obligations are recognised a legal value similar to that of the constitution, thus providing a strong basis for public law litigation on the implementation of international commitments. Nevertheless, the success of the *Urgenda* case in a first instance judgment inspired many similar cases such as *Juliana v. United States of America* on the constitutional protection of future generations against climate change and decision W109 2000179-1/291E [2007] on the adverse ruling to a third runway on the Vienna Airport due to climate change concerns (which has however been reversed by the constitutional Court in June 2017).

Likewise, public law litigation can be used to push a government to promote climate change adaptation or otherwise address L&D. The case of *Ashgar Leghari v. Federation of Pakistan* regarded an alleged inconsistency of the limited efforts by the government of Pakistan to promote climate change adaptation with constitutional provisions on the protection of fundamental rights. In 2015, the High Court of Lahore recognised that "the delay and lethargy of the State in implementing the Framework offend[ed] the fundamental rights of the citizens which need to be safeguarded" (W.P. No. 25501/2015, at para. 8). Accordingly, the court ordered the government of Pakistan to take action to promote climate change adaptation under the supervision of an *ad hoc* panel of experts reporting to the court. As this case illustrates, redress can extend far beyond compensation.

The effect of public law litigation is limited by the rules on the basis of which the action or omission of national authorities can be contested. Domestic constitutional provisions on the protection of fundamental rights, invoked in the case of *Ashgar*

Leghari, are often limited to the territory of the state: they do not usually provide ground for a Court to recognise the obligation of a state to address L&D beyond its own jurisdiction. International law, on the other hand, can sometimes be invoked before domestic courts in support of public litigation, as illustrated in the case of *Urgenda*, although national courts are often reluctant to implement international law obligations.

7.2.2 *Private Law Litigation*

Private law litigation sheds light on the obligations of any person (individual or group granted legal personality within a particular legal system) towards another. Courts in common law jurisdictions apply various concepts of "tort" such as nuisance, trespass, or a risk-based regime of strict liability. By contrast, courts in civil law jurisdictions refer to particular provisions of their respective Civil Code on "extra-contractual responsibility." Absent more specific statutory developments, Courts in civil law jurisdictions could theoretically play an extensive role in interpreting such principle of responsibility to the context of climate change.

Private law litigation on L&D face a myriad of hurdles and, to date, most have been unsuccessful. A first hurdle is the issue of attribution. It is generally impossible to attribute a certain climatic event to human induced climate change, and certainly not to the emissions of a specific person or entity. While it is beyond doubt that GHG emissions, as a general proposition, cause harm, it is currently impossible to trace specific damages to certain emitters. Most legal systems require a direct causal relation for damages to be granted, but climate science only offers probabilistic attribution (see e.g. Pall et al. 2016). Some authors have suggested that courts should apply a modified general causation test as have sometimes been developed on "toxic tort cases" (Grossman 2003: 23). It would accordingly be sufficient to prove that GHG emissions are generally capable of causing damages and that a causal link between action and damage is *probable* thus render the requirement to attribute a specific climatic event to the emissions of a specific person or entity unnecessary (Grossman 2003).

A second hurdle is the deference of the courts to other branches of government. Courts have usually been reluctant to touch matters which require a fine-tuned balance between different interests, especially when the executive and the legislature have already seized themselves of the matter. These concerns may be phrased in the terms of the "political question doctrine" in the United States or in more or less implicit considerations of the "justiciability" of disputes brought before domestic courts in other jurisdictions. This is an even greater obstacle in civil law countries, where courts are posited to simply apply the law created by the legislative branch.

In *American Electric Power Co. v. Connecticut* the US Supreme Court regarded the alleged nuisance constituted by the greenhouse gas emissions of five US power utilities. It unanimously rejected the claim in 2011 on the ground that the regulation of greenhouse gas emissions by the Environmental Protection Agency precluded the application of tort law of nuisance. In this view, compliance with domestic provisions on greenhouse gas emissions protects the power utilities from private law litigation. This doctrine was also one of the obstacles that precluded the inhabitants of the Alaskan village of Kivalina from obtaining damages from major hydrocarbons and power companies. In 2012, the Ninth Circuit Court of Appeals found that the Clean Air Act had displaced tort-based claims for damages and efforts to appeal before the US Supreme Court have been unsuccessful (*Native Village of Kivalina v. ExxonMobil Corp.*, 696 F.3d 849 (9th Cir. 2012)) (see also chapter by Landauer and Juhola 2018).

A similar case was initiated by a Peruvian farmer against RWE, a German utility company. A German district court dismissed the lawsuit as it held that the plaintiff had not established that RWE was legally responsible for protecting the city of Huaraz from flooding and because of lack of direct chain of causation. In January 2017, the plaintiff filed an appeal, which was rejected on grounds of unclear causality and inadequacy. The case has since been taken to the higher regional court in Hamm, where it was finally admitted in November 2017 and has now proceeded to the evidentiary stage (see also chapter by Frank et al. 2018).

7.3 Regional and International Human Rights Law

Multiple regional and international human rights instruments recognise the obligation of states to respect, protect and fulfill the human rights of individuals within their jurisdiction. International institutions have been established to promote compliance with these obligations. These include regional human rights courts such as the European Court of Human Rights, the Inter-American Court of Human Rights and the African Court of Human and Peoples' Rights, as well as regional commissions. The Human Rights Council and its special procedures as well as international human rights treaty bodies have also contributed to naming and shaming governments failing to comply with their obligations.

The impact of climate change on the enjoyment of human rights are well recognised (e.g., Preamble of the Paris Agreement). The UN Human Rights Council, for instance, emphasised that "the adverse effects of climate change have a range of implications … for the effective enjoyment of human rights" (2015, recital 8). Various regional and international human rights that are affected by L&D include the right to life (e.g., International Covenant on Civil and Political Rights, art. 6; see also Human Rights Committee 2017, para. 65), the right to property (Protocol 1 ECHR, art. 1), the right to a clean environment (African Charter on Human and Peoples' Rights, art. 24) and the right to enjoy one's own culture (International Covenant on Economic, Social and Cultural Rights, art. 27). Yet, human rights law has generally been of little help in addressing L&D. While states have an obligation to take positive steps to protect and fulfill the rights of individuals within their jurisdiction, this obligation is limited to their available means. More importantly, it is generally understood that the obligation to protect human rights is limited to individuals within the states' own jurisdiction or, at most, to individuals under their effective control (see e.g. *Al-Skeini v. UK*). Thus, from a legal perspective, states have no obligation to take into account the effects of their policies on the enjoyment of human rights outside their jurisdiction or effective control.

To comply with their obligation to protect and fulfill human rights, states must also take measures necessary to prevent human rights violations by private actors under their jurisdiction. However, this is again limited to human rights violations within the jurisdiction of the state. Efforts to promote responsibility of states for companies that commit human rights violations extra-territorially have seen increased support. For instance, the Commission on Human Rights of the Philippines, which has the power to investigate alleged barriers to the enjoyment of human rights, investigates whether carbon majors in causing climate change and ocean acidification violate human rights. The petition filed by Greenpeace Southeast Asia and Philippine Rural Reconstruction Movement is based partly on the expert drafted, legally non-binding Maastricht Principles on Extraterritorial Obligations of States in the Area of Economic, Social and Cultural Rights (ETO Consortium 2013). The investigation was still ongoing as of the time of writing.

However, also cases invoking the failure of a state to address L&D within its own jurisdiction appear extraordinarily unlikely to succeed before human rights institutions. The petitioner would first need to establish that greenhouse gas emissions of a particular state caused him or her to lose the enjoyment of a right within that jurisdiction. Then, further evidence would need to be provided that the cause of such loss in the enjoyment of a right was the failure of the state to take appropriate measures to prevent such greenhouse gas emissions. Lastly, the petitioner would have to rebut likely arguments by the state according to which the protection of human rights can be limited in the pursuance of objectives of general interest such as economic growth or development. Before an international human rights body, the petitioner would need to make the latter argument in a manner sufficiently compelling to persuade judges or commissioners that the state's balance of human rights protection with such objectives of general interest was not within the national "margin of appreciation," so-called by the European Court of Human Rights, in the protection of human rights.

For instance, in 2005, the Inuit Circumpolar Conference submitted a petition to the Inter-American Commission on Human Rights against the United States for their failure to prevent greenhouse gas emissions resulting in a violation of the human rights of Inuit communities. Following a public hearing, the Commission dismissed the petition (Chapman 2010).

However, cases are more likely to succeed when invoking the obligation of a state to protect the human rights of its population in isolation from its responsibility for climate change. An example of such successful proceedings before domestic courts was mentioned in Sect. 7.2 in the case of *Ashgar Leghari v. Federation of Pakistan*. Similar cases could be brought in in every circumstance where a state fails to take appropriate measures to protect its population against the adverse circumstances which may relate to impacts of climate change. Yet, this approach does not properly provide for redress for the impacts of climate change as it relies on the state on whose territory a person is present for the protection of the human rights of this person. Thus, the burden of addressing L&D falls disproportionately on developing states rather than on those states responsible for most greenhouse gas emissions.

A particular question related to human rights law surrounds the protection of individuals displaced in circumstances related to climate change impacts. Some arguments have been made for an international protection of "climate refugees" either in application of existing international law or through the development of new international legal frameworks. In existing international law, however, a "refugee" is narrowly defined as a person fleeing out of a well-founded fear of being persecuted on the ground of his race, religion, nationality, membership of a particular social group or political opinion (Convention relating to the Status of Refugees, art. 1(A)(2)). Even when states have extended this definition to people living in a situation of generalised violence, environmental factors have not generally been recognised as a ground for international protection. For instance, claims for asylum based on the environmental conditions in Tuvalu were rejected by the New Zealand Immigration and Protection Tribunal in 2009 (*In Re: AD (Tuvalu)*). Arguably, the lives of people migrating from a state seriously impacted by climate change are threatened if they are returned to that state. However, national courts have previously considered that provisions of international human rights treaties dealing with the right to life, such as art. 6 of the International Covenant on Civil and Political Rights, did not prevent the expulsion of an individual whose country of origin is seriously affected by impacts of climate change (see e.g. for instance *Teitiota v Chief Executive of the Ministry of Business Innovation and Employment*) or was in violation of the principle of *non-refoulement* (see e.g. *AC (Tuvalu)*).

Further developments could, however, occur. Ongoing developments include for instance the Platform on Disaster Displacement which continues the work of the Nansen Initiative on Disaster-Induced Cross-Border Displacement and the work by the ILC on the protection of persons in the event of disasters (ILC 2016), as further discussed in the chapter by Heslin et al. (2018).

7.4 Customary International Law

National and international human rights laws are too limited in scope to fully address L&D. This is because climate change responsibilities and harms are geographically split. Most greenhouse gas emissions take place in industrialised nations, whereas most L&D affects individuals in the least developed or developing states. Human rights protection may reduce the harm caused to particular communities, including through adaptation measures, but its effectivity largely depends on the resources available to national authorities. Without enhanced support from the international community, the most vulnerable states may have little capacity to effectively protect their populations. This suggests that approaches to address L&D are more likely to take place at an international level.

There are two main sources of international law: customs and treaties (Statute of the International Court of Justice, art. 38(1)). Norms of customary international law are constituted by the general practice of states accepted as law (Statute of the International Court of Justice, art. 38(1)(b)). A treaty is instead an agreement through which two or several states voluntarily commit to comply with certain obligations. When a state fails to respect its international obligations, including obligations stemming from customary international law and treaty law, this state has a secondary obligation to cease the wrongful act and perform its international obligation and to make adequate reparation to any state injured (ILC Articles on Responsibility of States for Internationally Wrongful Acts, arts. 29–31).

Section 7.4.1 examines whether excessive greenhouse gas emissions could constitute a breach of a norm of customary international law—the no-harm principle—and consequently entails an obligation to make reparation for the injury caused to the territory of other states. Section 7.4.2 turns to the treaty-based international climate law regime. Thus, we elude, for the sake of brevity, any discussion of other treaty-based regimes, such as the provisions on pollution of the marine environment contained in the UN Convention on the Law of the Seas or the work of the International Law Commission on the protection of the atmosphere.

7.4.1 The Obligation of States Not to Cause Serious Environmental Harm

The contemporary international legal system is based on the principle that states are equal sovereigns. States could not be equal sovereigns if it was permitted for one state to interfere with the internal affairs of another state in any manner that would seriously affect the latter. Likewise, states would not be genuinely equal sovereigns if one state was permitted to render the territory of another state uninhabitable or otherwise to significantly affect the conditions under which that territory can be used, for instance through causing serious environmental harms across international borders (see Order of 13 December 2013 in the joined proceedings *Construction of a Road in Costa Rica along the San Juan River (Nicaragua v. Costa Rica); Certain Activities Carried Out by Nicaragua in the Border Area (Costa Rica v. Nicaragua)*, Provisional Measures ICJ Rep 2013, 398).

The no-harm principle, as a corollary of the principle of equal sovereignty, was first recognised in the 1941 arbitral award in the *Trail Smelter* case. This case concerned a dispute between Canada and the United States over air pollution arising from a smelter in Canada, which was brought by dominant winds towards the US State of Washington, causing serious environmental damages. In an oft-cited passage, the tribunal declared that:

> under the principles of international law [...] no state has the right to use or permit the use of its territory in such a manner as to cause injury by fumes in or to the territory of another or the properties of persons therein, when the case is of serious consequences and the injury is established by clear and convincing evidence (*Trail Smelter Arbitration*: 1905).

This principle was confirmed in further decisions of international courts and tribunals (e.g. *Corfu Channel*, 22; *Case concerning the Gabcikovo-Nagymaros Project*, para. 53; *Case Concerning Pulp Mills on the River Uruguay*, paras. 101, 193 [hereinafter: Pulp Mills]). It was also recognised in international declarations (e.g. United Nations Rio Declaration on Environment and Development, principle 2; Declaration of the United Nations Conference on the Human Environment, principle 21; UNGA Res. 2996 (XXVII)) and, although less systematically, in treaties, including a mention in the preamble to the UN Framework Convention on Climate Change. In the *Advisory Opinion on the Legality of the Threat or Use of Nuclear Weapons*, the International Court of Justice recognised

> the general obligation of States to ensure that activities within their jurisdiction and control respect the environment of other States or of areas beyond national control is now part of the corpus of international law relating to the environment (para 29).

The no-harm principle requires states to refrain from engaging in activities which would cause significant transboundary harm and to prevent persons or entities within its jurisdiction to carry out such activities. Beyond this general understanding, the modalities of the no-harm principle are debated. As with any customary norm, it is difficult to establish the exact scope of this duty to prevent significant transboundary harm. In its previous cases, the ICJ has clarified little the content of the duty to prevent significant transboundary harm. Generally, it has been understood as one of due diligence (*Pulp Mills*, para 101; ILC 2001:154, para. 7). This means that a state is required to act in a way that can be expected from a "good government" (ILC 2001: 155, para. 17) and to exert its best efforts to minimise the risk of significant transboundary harm (ILC 2001: 154, para. 7). As such, the no-harm principle is an obligation of conduct, not of result. Thus, a state is not responsible for harm that occurs despite its reasonable efforts to prevent it or—in case that it is not possible—to minimise the risk. The International Law Commission has acknowledged in its work on the Articles on the Prevention of Transboundary Harm from Hazardous Activities that a different degree of care is expected from states with fewer capacities and economic difficulties (ILC 2001:155, para. 17). When applying this criterion to climate change, it must also be kept in mind that treaties may contribute in different ways to the development of customary international law. Despite the continuing work of the ILC on the role of treaties in identifying customary international law (see e.g. Wood 2015: 14 ff), there remain fundamental uncertainties on how the multilateral environmental agreements shape, crystallise and form the content of customary international law.

State practice and cases where the no-harm rule was invoked generally dealt with activities at or around a shared border. These activities included for instance emitting toxic fumes that caused damages in the woods of the neighbouring state, dredging in a shared river and altering its waters (e.g. *Lac Lanoux Arbitration*) or else polluting it through mills (e.g. *Pulp Mills*) or construction activities close to it. This raises the question whether the no-harm principle is applicable to climate change.

Climate change differs from most aforementioned cases in at least three pivotal points. Firstly, damages from climate change result not from a single activity of a state but of its reliance on fossil fuels as an economic motor, i.e. from many activities. Secondly, damages from climate change results not from the conduct of a single state but from the concomitant conduct of multiple states, with the resulting harm not confined to a single state but affecting virtually all states. Thirdly and relatedly, the harm results not from any particular activity, but from an accumulation of activities over decades.

For these reasons, in the 1990s, the International Law Commission excluded phenomena such as creeping pollution and pollution deriving from ordinary economic activities from its work on the Articles on the Prevention of Transboundary Harm from Hazardous Activities (Rao 2000:9). The International Law Commission considered these situations too complex, and possibly too politically sensitive, to make statements about their legal nature. Although the Articles are not binding as such and do not reflect existing customary international law in their entirety, this is indicative of the difficulty of applying the no-harm principle to new situations.

The multiplicity of states contributing to climate change and impacted by its consequences at least complicates the application of the no-harm rule. Scholars have questioned the applicability of the no-harm principle to circumstances where harm is caused not directly by a single source, but by multiple diffuse sources over a long period of time, which accumulate and result in harm (Zahar 2014; Okawa 2010:307; Scovazzi 2001:61). Most cases before the international courts and tribunals are decided over situations where a single activity caused harm to another state. Environmental harm accruing because of the conduct of multiple states was discussed in the pleadings before the ICJ in one case. In their submissions on the *Legality of the Threat or Use of Nuclear Weapons*, some states raised concerns with the possibility that the repeated use of nuclear weapons over a relatively short span of time would create a "nuclear winter"—a cataclysmic upheaval of the climate system which could wipe out most of life on our planet (Mexico 1995, para 65; Egypt 1995, para 32; Ecuador, para D). When mentioning that the damages caused by nuclear weapons could not "be contained in either space or time" and had "the potential to destroy all civilization and the entire ecosystem of the planet," (*Legality of the Threat or Use of Nuclear Weapons*, para. 35) the International Court of Justice made no distinction between mediated damages and damages caused by cumulative causation but implied that the no-harm principle applied equally to both (see also Dissenting Opinion of Judge Weeramantry: 456–458; Mayer 2015:8).

If there is indeed an obligation for states not to cause transboundary environmental harms through greenhouse gas emissions, its modalities remain ill-defined (see also Mayer 2016b, 2018a). In particular, the scope of the no-harm principle is ill-determined. In general, the duty to prevent significant harm exists whenever a state has or should have been able to foresee the risk of harm. Unfortunately, there is no interpretation of these modalities of the no-harm principle by the International Court of Justice or sufficient clarification through the work of the International Law Commission. However, it appears possible to assume that a state must have had at least some scientific hints of the impacts of greenhouse gas emissions. Thus, the historical failure of a state to prevent activities generating excessive greenhouse gas emissions does not constitute a breach of the no-harm rule until at least some scientific evidence suggested that they may have a serious impact on the climate system. It is also unclear to what extent a state must have been able to foresee the specific damage that might occur. Very few cases involving indeterminate damage have been decided by international courts and tribunals. In the *Naulilaa* case, an Arbitral Panel held that Germany should have anticipated that its attack on some Portuguese colonies would likely expose Portugal to further turmoil in an unstable colonial context, although Germany could not have foreseen the nature and extent of the turmoil that unfolded. On this basis, the Panel condemned Germany to the payment of an "equitable additional compensation" established *ex aequo et bono* (*Responsabilité de l' Allemagne à raison des dommages causés dans les colonies portugaises du sud de l'Afrique*: 1032-3).

Another area of uncertainty exists with regards to the stringency of the due diligence obligation of states under the no-harm principle. The International Court of Justice held that in order to fulfil its obligation to exercise due diligence in preventing significant transboundary environmental harm, a state must carry out an environmental impact assessment when there is a risk of such harm and, if the risk of significant transboundary harm is confirmed, notify and consult with any states potentially affected (see e.g. *Certain Activities and Construction of a Road*, paras. 104, 168). Where a state has acted in due diligence to prevent significant transboundary harm, it cannot be made responsible for harm that occurs nonetheless, in which case a state has to prevent further damages. This, however, does not result in a right for a state to veto an activity conducted in another state. Notably, in relation to environmental matters, the ICJ has often put emphasis on procedure, including the obligation to conduct an environmental impact assessment, rather than substantive obligations to refrain from a certain conduct. However, it is reasonable to assume that a state must ultimately refrain from certain activities if that is the only way to prevent significant harm. Nevertheless, the question of the actual content of the no-harm rule, especially in the context of climate change where procedural processes such as consulting with all potentially affected states is often unhelpful, will remain difficult to be answered.

States certainly are not under an obligation to stop all greenhouse gas emissions at once (see e.g. Voigt 2015:162). The scope of their due diligence obligation depends on their capacity. The obligation of all states under the no-harm principle is one of employing all their best efforts to limit and reduce greenhouse gas emissions from activities within their jurisdiction in order to prevent and minimise injurious effects on other states. In any event, the question whether a state has fulfilled its obligations of due diligence must be assessed in the light of the specific circumstances and the norms of customary international law emerging from the general practice of states accepted as law (see e.g. *Certain Activities carried out by Nicaragua in the Border Area*, Separate Opinion of Judge Donoghue, para. 10). Especially, the extent to which efforts of economic growth shape the understanding of due diligence remains unclear and should be further researched within the concept of sustainable development.

Thus, there remain many difficulties in defining the modalities of application of the no-harm principle in relation to climate change. Some authors such as Verheyen (2005: 146) conclude that the vagueness of the customary no-harm rule provides for space for interpretation. Certainly, only an authoritative interpretation by an international court or tribunal, or possibly by the International Law Commission, could help disentangling the debates. In 2013, the International Law Commission has initiated a project on the protection of the atmosphere, which could possibly address the issue of climate change.

7.4.2 *State Responsibility Following a Breach of the No-Harm Principle*

The breach of an obligation is to be sanctioned for a legal system to be meaningful. Accordingly, it is a well-established principle of customary international law that a state whose conduct breaches its international obligation commits an internationally wrongful act entailing its international responsibility (ILC Articles on the Responsibility of States for Internationally Wrongful Acts, art. 1 and 2). Whereas the above section discusses whether and under which assumptions greenhouse gas emissions could amount to a breach of the no-harm rule, this section will look at the legal consequences resulting from these emissions, based on the hypothetical premise that they constitute an internationally wrongful act. It is important to bear in mind that certain questions, such as foreseeability and multiplicity of actors, are problematic not only concerning the characterisation of a state conduct as an internationally wrongful act, but also to assess whether any particular state is responsible for it.

State responsibility involves two main legal consequences: the continued duty of performance—which involves the obligation to cease a continuing internationally wrongful act—and the obligation to make reparation for any injury (ibid, art. 28–39). The obligations following a breach of the no-harm rule depends on the content of this obligation in the context of climate change, which is difficult to determine. As a consequence of the continued duty of performance, states would have to cease these emissions that are considered an internationally wrongful act. Of greater importance to the present discussion is the other consequence involved by the international responsibility of a state, namely, the obligation to make good for any injury caused by the internationally wrongful act. This obligation is generally analysed by reference to the judgment of the Permanent Court of International Justice in the case of the *Factory at Chorzów*, according to which "reparation must, as far as possible, wipe out all the consequences of the illegal act and re-establish the situation which would, in all probability, have existed if that act had not been committed" (at 47). Accordingly, the International Law Commission concluded that "[f]ull reparation for the injury caused by the internationally wrongful act shall take the form of restitution, compensation and satisfaction, either singly or in combination" (ILC Articles on the Responsibility of States for Internationally Wrongful Acts, art. 34). "Full reparation" is understood as reparation for the full value of the injury. Restitution consists often in returning something wrongfully taken, whereas compensation—in practice the most common form of reparation—is the payment of the financial value of something that cannot be returned or other damage done. Satisfaction relates to measures such as apologies, usually limited to reparation for symbolic harms.

For a claim for reparation to be successful, it is, presumably, necessary to establish that an activity has caused harm in a way that the harm would not have occurred without the activity. The causal link between greenhouse gas emissions and its adverse impacts is a long and complex one, which will make this argument difficult to establish. Yet, the law of state responsibility appears slightly more flexible in this regard than many national legal systems. Rather than a strict limitation to the "direct" consequence, injury in international law is extended to any consequence *unless* it is "too indirect, remote, and uncertain to be appraised" (*Trail Smelter Arbitration*: 1931; ILC 2001: 92, para. 10). Assessing the value of the injury on the basis of which compensation should be paid would however face many difficulties. Particular damages would have to be attributed to climate change in abstraction from the multitude of natural or social processes in which they unfold. Things that have no inherent economic value (e.g. human lives, health, culture, ecosystems) would have to be given one (see chapter by Serdeczny 2018). The value of future harms would need to be discounted at an arbitrary rate. Responsibility would then need to be allocated among states on the basis of their respective share of the wrongdoing, despite the indeterminacy of the threshold beyond which greenhouse gas emissions become excessive and wrongful and the contribution of the injured state to its damages (see e.g. Reis 2011:183). This would lead to never-ending controversies, nullifying the role of international law in settling international disputes through pacific means.

However, such a perilous analysis may not be necessary. When concluding that responsibility for an internationally wrongful act involves an obligation to make "full reparation," the International Law Commission referred to the usual practice of international courts and tribunals dealing with relatively small quantum of damages (ILC 2000: 2). Like in the *Naulilaa* case (*Responsabilité de l' Allemagne à raison des dommages causés dans les colonies portugaises du sud de l'Afrique*), larger injuries—such as reparations for wars and other mass atrocities, for unlawful trade measures, for nation-wide expropriation programs or for hazardous activities—have never led to full reparation, but rather to an agreement on lump-sum compensation. Relevant judicial decisions or international negotiations considered the capacity of the responsible state to pay, the need of the injured parties for reparation, the possible disproportion of the injury to the "culpability" of the responsible state, and the limits of the fundaments for a collective responsibility (Mayer 2017; Eritrea-Ethiopia Claims Commission:522, para. 22; Mayer 2016a). The International Law Commission has promoted in its work on the allocation of loss in the case of transboundary harm arising out of hazardous activities an approach to balance the interests of the responsible and the injured party (ILC 2006: 58ff).

7.4.3 Relationship Between the Climate Regime and the No-Harm Principle

A possible objection to the reasoning presented in this section relates to the existence of a treaty-based international climate law regime. Some scholars argued that the UN Framework Convention on Climate Change and following treaties as well as decisions adopted by the Conference of the Parties precluded the application of norms of international law such as the no-harm principle and the law of state responsibility for L&D (see Zahar 2015).

Such an argument would have to be based on the doctrine of *lex specialis* ("special law"). This notion prescribes that a more specific rule prevails over a general one. However, this is only the case when there is an actual norm conflict between the two rules. In this context, the International Law Commission stated that for the *lex specialis* doctrine to apply, "it is not enough that the same subject matter is dealt with by two provisions; there must be some actual inconsistency between them, or else a discernible intention that one provision is to exclude the other" (ILC 2001:140; see also *Mavrommatis Palestine Concessions*: 31). Absent such actual inconsistency or discernible intention to exclude the more general rule, both rules should be "be interpreted so as to give rise to a single set of compatible obligations" (ILC 2006:178).

There is certainly no ground to believe that states, as a whole, intended to exclude the application of the no-harm rule when establishing the international climate law regime. Similarly, inconsistencies between the climate regime and the customary no-harm rule do not necessarily arise (Mayer 2014; Verheyen 2005). The ultimate objective of the UNFCCC, to "prevent dangerous anthropogenic interference with the climate system" (UNFCCC, art. 2), is certainly not inconsistent with the no-harm principle, and the specific commitments made by states under successive international climate agreements do not exclude the existence of more demanding obligations under customary international law. The obligation to prevent significant transboundary harm, insofar as it may apply to emissions of greenhouse gases, should thus be interpreted consistently with the climate regime "so as to give rise to a single set of compatible obligations" (ILC 2006a, para. 4). Hence, the commitments entered into through the climate regime do not replace the no-harm rule—and *vice versa* –but both simultaneously work towards bringing states closer to compliance with their obligations arising under international law (see Mayer 2018b). In this regard a number of vulnerable states have made several statements emphasising that successive international climate change agreements do not in principle derogate the application of principles of general international law (see e.g. Declarations of Kiribati, Fiji, and Nauru upon signature of the UNFCCC and other declarations upon signature of the Paris Agreement. Arguably, the customary rule, should it apply and be triggered in the context of climate change, requires efforts that go beyond that of the climate regime in so far as those are not sufficient to actually prevent harm.

7.5 The International Climate Law Regime

After this overview of customary international law, the present section turns to international obligations based on climate treaties. Several treaties have been negotiated to address climate change, in particular the UN Framework Convention on Climate Change (UNFCCC 1992), the Kyoto Protocol (1997), and the Paris Agreement (2015). These treaties establish an institutional framework composed in particular by a Secretariat and a Conference of the Parties. The Conference of the Parties adopts decisions at its annual meetings. The treaties and decisions adopted under them form what is often referred to as the international climate law regime.

In contrast with customary international law, the international climate law regime is negotiated by states. More powerful states have naturally a greater say in the negotiations. Diplomatic and financial pressure is often exercised on weaker states. This political determination of the international climate law regime has significantly hindered efforts of vulnerable nations to bring up the question of L&D because, often, the most powerful states, responsible for the largest share of greenhouse gas emissions, are also the most influential in international negotiations on climate change.

In the following, a first subsection recounts the progressive *mezzo voce* recognition of something possibly akin to "responsibility" in the international climate law regime. A second subsection then discusses the initiation of a workstream dedicated to negotiations on L&D over the last decade (see also introduction by Mechler et al. 2018 and chapter by Calliari et al. 2018).

7.5.1 An Ambivalent Recognition of Responsibilities

In a declaration adopted in the Caracas Summit of the G77 in 1989, most developing states took a common position on climate change. They declared that, "[s]ince developed countries account for the bulk of the production and consumption of environmentally damaging substances, they should bear the main responsibility in the search for long-term remedies for global environmental protection" (*Caracas Declaration*, paras. II-34). Two years later, Small Island Developing States submitted a proposal for an instrument to address "loss and damage" associated with climate change by "compensat[ing] the most vulnerable small island and low-lying coastal developing countries for loss and damage resulting from sea level rise" (Vanuatu 1991:2).

Yet, no provision recognising the "main responsibility" of developed states or their obligation to "compensate" the most vulnerable nations was inserted in the final draft of the UNFCCC, adopted at the Earth Summit, in Rio de Janeiro, in June 1992. Rather, this treaty focused on forward-looking efforts to mitigate climate change in order to "achieve … stabilization of greenhouse gas concentrations in the atmosphere at a level that would prevent dangerous anthropogenic interference with the climate system" (UNFCCC, art. 2). Nevertheless, since negotiations had been pursued on the basis of consensus, the position of developing states had been taken into consideration, if only marginally. Developed states agreed to the insertion of elements of language containing constructive ambiguities which, without entirely rejecting the demands of developing states, did not fulfil them either.

One such provision is the principle of "common but differentiated responsibilities," which was inserted in the UNFCCC and in the Rio Declaration on Environment and Development adopted at the same time (UNFCCC, art. 3; Rio Declaration, principle 7). Including the word "responsibility" gave some satisfaction to developing states, but the word could be understood alternatively as a ground for reparation based on culpability or simply an obligation to cooperate based on each state's capacities. Thus, the position of the United States, reflected on their written statement on the Rio Declaration, was that this concept highlighted "the special leadership role of the developed countries, based on [their] industrial development, [their] experience with environmental protection policies and actions, and [their] wealth, technical expertise and capabilities." To avoid any doubt, the United States stated on record that they did not accept any interpretation of this concept "that would imply a recognition or acceptance … of any international obligations or liabilities, or any diminution in the responsibilities of developing countries" (United States 1992, para. 16).

Likewise, small island developing states secured the insertion in the UNFCCC of a provision recognising the duty of developed states to "assist the developing country Parties that are particularly vulnerable to the adverse effects of climate change in meeting costs of adaptation to those adverse effects" (UNFCCC, art. 4(4)). This, again, was of a limited avail. "Meeting costs of adaptation" does not mean "meeting [all] *the* costs of adaptation" (Bodansky 1993). The obligation accepted by developed states was simply one of contributing *something* to the costs of adaptation in developing states.

A stream of negotiations on climate change adaptation appeared, for long, as a potential entry point for claims for compensation for losses and damages. Since the adoption of the UNFCCC and despite the creation of an adaptation fund under the Kyoto Protocol, international financial assistance to adaptation in developing states has remained limited, especially when compared to financial assistant to climate change mitigation (Buchner et al. 2015). A growing frustration of some advocates led them to push for a distinct conceptual framework within international negotiations on climate change, where claims for compensation could emerge. Yet, any mention of compensation or reparation was a non-starter.

7.5.2 The Workstream and Mechanism on Loss and Damage

A workstream on L&D was initiated in 2007 through the Bali Action Plan adopted by a decision of the 13th Session of the Conference of the Parties to the UNFCCC (COP13). The Kyoto Protocol had just entered into force and, although measures to mitigate climate change were being designed or implemented, there was a clear sense that much more had to be done through future agreements. Accordingly, the Bali Action Plan aimed "to launch a comprehensive process to enable the full, effective and sustained implementation of the Convention" (UNFCCC 2007, Decision 1/CP.13, Bali Action Plan, para. 1). Much attention was starting to be put on emerging economies and other developing states, whose greenhouse gas emissions were increasing much faster than the greenhouse gas emissions of developed states could possibly be reduced. In this context, "enhanced action on adaptation" was one of the concessions that developed states agreed in exchange of an increase commitment of developing states to "enhanced … action on mitigation" (UNFCCC 2007, Decision 1/CP.13, Bali Action Plan, 1(b) and 1(c)).

One of the items listed under "enhanced action on adaption" in the Bali Action Plan was "disaster reduction strategies and means to address losses and damages associated with climate change impacts in developing countries that are particularly vulnerable to the adverse effects of climate change" (UNFCCC 2007, Decision 1/CP.13, Bali Action Plan, para. 1(c)(iii)). The length of the concept reflected the difficulty of its insertion in a COP decision. There was no clear understanding on whether the two branches of this provision—"disaster reduction" and "loss and damage"—were necessarily related, that is, whether losses and damages would necessarily stem from (sudden-onset) disasters. Nor were there any clear understanding of the differences between "loss," "damage," "impacts," and the "adverse effects of climate change." Yet, a great achievement of the Bali Action Plan was the insertion of a provision hinting to the obligation of developed states to pay reparation for the injury caused by excessive greenhouse gas emissions.

The Bali Action Plan initiated a new stream of negotiations. However, this was largely side-lined, in the following years, by intense negotiations on climate change mitigation and the reluctance of developed states to virtually anything (Warner and Zakieldeen 2012:4). Not much had been achieved when, 3 years later, the Cancún Agreements recognised "the need to strengthen international cooperation and expertise in order to understand and reduce loss and damage associated with the adverse effects of climate change, including impacts related to extreme weather events and slow onset events" (UNFCCC 2010, Decision 1/CP.16, para. 25).

The Cancún Agreements created a "work programme" were negotiations could be pursued. Thematic areas were defined in 2011 and further explored in 2012 (UNFCCC 2011, Decision 7/CP.17, paras. 6–15; UNFCCC 2012, Decision 3/CP.18). More specifically, COP18 expressed a common desire "to enhance action on addressing loss and damage" (UNFCCC 2012, Decision 3/CP.18, para. 6). The following year, COP19 established the Warsaw International Mechanism on Loss and Damage (WIM), a subsidiary body of the UNFCCC (UNFCCC 2013, Decision 2/CP.19). The objective of the WIM was to "fulfil the role under the Convention of promoting the implementation of approaches to address loss and damage … in a comprehensive, integrated and coherent manner," including through "enhancing knowledge and understanding," "strengthening dialogue, coordination, coherence and synergies among relevant stakeholders," and "enhancing action and support, including finance, technology and capacity-building, to address loss and damage" (UNFCCC 2013, Decision 2/CP.19, para. 5). More specific arrangements were made at COP20, including the composition of the Executive Committee of the WIM, basic rules on procedure, and a 2-year workplan (UNFCCC 2014, Decision 2/CP.20, para. 5). This

2-year workplan was followed by a "five-year rolling workplan" adopted at COP22 (UNFCCC 2016, Decision 3/CP.22).

The inclusion of an article on L&D in the Paris Agreement was another ambiguous concession to developing states. Through Article 8, the Parties of the Paris Agreement "recognize the importance of averting, minimizing and addressing loss and damage … and the role of sustainable development in reducing the risk of loss and damage" (Paris Agreement, art. 8(1)). It places the WIM under the "authority and guidance" of the Conference of the Parties serving as the meeting of the Parties to the Paris Agreement (Paris Agreement, art. 8(2)). It also highlights some areas of cooperation and facilitation such as on "early warning systems," "emergency preparedness," "slow onset events" and "events that may involve irreversible and permanent loss and damage" (Paris Agreement, art. 8(4)). Yet, Article 8 does not imply any substantive international legal obligation beyond a vague statement that the Parties "*should* enhance understanding, action and support … as appropriate, on a cooperative and facilitate basis with respect to loss and damage associated with the adverse effects of climate change" (Paris Agreement, art. 8(3)). In that sense, Article 8 of the Paris Agreement does not really go further than Article 4(4) of the UN Framework Convention on Climate Change.

Even such provision, however, was only inserted in the treaty after hard-fought negotiations and was accompanied by a caveat. COP21, in its decision on the adoption of the Paris Agreement, asserted that "Article 8 of the Agreement does not involve or provide a basis for any liability or compensation" (UNFCCC 2015, Decision 1/CP.21, para. 51). The legal nature of COP decisions has been discussed extensively by scholars (see e.g. Mace and Verheyen 2016; Verheyen 2005:67ff; Brunnée 2002; Gehring 2007; Churchill and Ulfstein 2000:639). However, it only states the obvious: nothing in Article 8 could be taken to imply any liability or compensation, as the language is weak and the concepts are undefined. Moreover, it goes without saying that this does not exclude the possible applicability of customary international law and possible arguments for state liability that stem from an alleged breach of the no-harm principle.

Ten years after the initiation of a workstream on L&D, few concrete steps have been taken. Instead, a work programme led to a 2-year workplan which led to a 5-year rolling workplan. The concept of L&D became more prominent in international negotiations on climate change but no agreement was reached on how to implement it. COP21 decision on the adoption of the Paris Agreement requested that the WIM establish a "clearing house for risk transfer" and a "task force … to develop recommendations for integrated approaches to avert, minimize and address displacement related to the adverse impacts of climate change" (UNFCCC 2015, decision 1/CP.21, paras. 48 and 49). These developments suggest a growing role of the WIM in sharing good practices and issuing recommendations, rather than providing compensation. It may thus replicate the evolution of the concept of adaptation in international negotiations on climate change, from claims for remedies for the wrongs caused by excessive greenhouse gas emissions in industrialised states, to a regime of international oversight on national measures supported only very partially by insufficient international financial support.

7.6 Discussion and Conclusions

This chapter has given an overview over the potential remedies in law to L&D. National laws have started to address this issue, including public law litigation forcing governments to address L&D in mitigation and adaptation efforts and private law litigation trying to hold private actors responsible for excessive greenhouse gas emissions. While most legal systems could theoretically be applied to excessive greenhouse gas emissions, their potential has not yet been fully recognised by national courts. The main caveat is the reluctance of courts to decide on something they perceive as a political decision: whether these emissions are falling within the competence of the court to decide. Human rights on the other hand do recognise their importance to the discourse relating to L&D. However, conceptual weaknesses regarding their application and enforcement make them an unlikely forum to address L&D. The enforcement of even these vague obligations is often reliant on their implementation in national laws and, on the international level, of the political will to exercise pressure on high emitting states.

We have also reviewed the applicability of the customary obligation not to cause serious environmental harm to other states and the viability of the climate change treaties to address L&D. While the no-harm rule is generally accepted as binding in international law, it remains unclear whether and, even more, how it applies to climate change. In the case of litigation before an international court or tribunal, it would be faced with a myriad of technical difficulties, not least the issue of causality and the required diligence to prevent or minimise harm. Certainly, the obligations under the UNFCCC, the Kyoto Protocol and the Paris Agreement do not replace the obligations under customary international law, but they may shape the understanding of what is to be considered as "best possible efforts" required under customary international law. Even where an international wrongful act is considered, difficulties remain to determine the quantum of remedies. The breach of an obligation entails the obligation to cease the wrongful act, if it is continuing, and to make good for damages it caused. However, how to disentangle the injury caused through climate change and the harm caused due to other socio-economic factors in the state concerned will remain difficult. In any event, it is unlikely that such a case would go before an international court or tribunal, as states would be reluctant to agree to their jurisdiction. Treaties, on the other hand, mostly provide for the jurisdiction of an international court or tribunal. However, it has become clear in their negotiation history that states are reluctant to accept legal responsibility. They thus fail to establish clear rules can be breached by parties.

Table 7.1 summarises the common legal approaches to climate change induced losses and damages and shortly highlights the main challenges to their efficacy and potential remedies to those challenges. The table is only supposed to serve as a potential starting point for further research and in no way intends to be complete or perfect in any way.

While the previous analysis of the available means to address L&D through the legal framework does not seem promising for real change, it is important to notice that

Table 7.1 Legal responses, their challenges and potential next steps

National laws			
	Public law litigation		Private law litigation
Rationale	States have obligations to protect their citizens from the adverse effects of climate change		Companies are responsible for damages from climate change and the costs of remedial action
Challenges	Dismissal based on lack of legal causality	Dismissal based on political nature of claim, international treaties not directly applicable to national courts	Dismissal based on lack of legal causality, complexity and multiplicity of causation
Potential remedy	Broader interpretation of causality; progress in attribution science	New or amendment of existing laws	Broader interpretation of causality; progress in attribution science. New or amendment of existing laws
Regional and international human rights law			
	Various human rights to life and safety		Refugee law
Rationale	States have an obligation to ensure health and safety of people within their jurisdiction		States have an obligation to grant asylum to climate refugees
Challenges	Cases are likely to be dismissed based on lack of legal causality	States have a "margin of appreciation" of human rights	No sufficient legal basis
Potential remedy	Courts apply a broader interpretation of causality requirements	Amending regional and international human rights treaties	Enhanced negotiation and work on international levels such as via the Platform on Disaster Displacement
Customary international law			
Rationale	States have a customary obligation not to harm other states and therefore must refrain from emitting greenhouse gases that cause harm to other states		
Challenges	States are unlikely to agree to the jurisdiction of the ICJ or an international tribunal		Content of the no-harm rule relating to climate change is unclear and not specific enough
Potential remedy	Addressing fears of escalating responsibility; limiting jurisdiction to specific problems		ICJ or international tribunal issues judgment or advisory opinion on that matter; further research on the relationship between climate regime and the customary no-harm rule; further research on required due diligence, especially relating to sustainable development
Climate change regime			
Rationale	States that excessively emit greenhouse gases are in breach of international treaties relating to the UN climate convention		
Challenges	Obligations are not clear and specific enough		
Potential remedy	Addressing fears of escalating responsibility; amending convention treaty text		Enhanced negotiations and work on the international level, such as through the WIM

the behaviour of states is not only motivated by binding, enforceable law. So-called soft law, i.e. law that is not legally binding, has often proved to be more effective than binding, enforceable international law. Although the pace of the progress of the WIM workstream can be frustrating, it shows that the issue of L&D is being picked up by the political bodies.

Previous treaties and institutions have developed from political bodies and strenuous negotiations—this evolution might also come true for the issue of L&D. Moreover, it seems that efforts at the national levels are increasing. While the overwhelming amount of the cases have been dismissed, it shows that public awareness is increasing. Mostly, it is not the science that is failing, it is the political will of the states. Understandably, what they fear is escalating responsibility for historic and present emissions. However, Gsottbauer et al. (2017) argue that a liability regime can under certain circumstances indeed promote precaution to prevent L&D. Moreover, law is flexible and can be adapted to the specific concerns of the states—provided there is political will to negotiation (see also Lees 2016). Thus, while legal responses to climate change induced L&D might not be as clear now, they probably will be at a later point in time.

References

Articles, Books and Reports

Bodansky D (1993) The united nations framework convention on climate change: a commentary. Yale J Int Law 18(2):451–558

Brunnée J (2002) COPing with consent: law-making under multilateral environmental agreements. Leiden J Int Law 15(1):1–52

Buchner B, Herve-Mignucci M, Trabacchi C, Wilkinson J, Stadelmann M, Boyd R, Mazza F, Falconer A, Micale V (2015) Global landscape of climate finance 2015. Climate Policy Institute

Calliari E, Surminski S, Mysiak J (2018) The Politics of (and behind) the UNFCCC's loss and damage mechanism. In: Mechler R, Bouwer L, Schinko T, Surminski S, Linnerooth-Bayer J (eds) Loss and damage from climate change. Concepts, methods and policy options. Springer, Cham, pp 155–178

Caracas Declaration (1989) Special ministerial meeting of the group of Seventy-seven, paras. II-34

Chapman M (2010) Climate change and the regional human rights systems. Sustain Develop Law Policy 10(2):37–38

Churchill RR, Ulfstein G (2000) Autonomous institutional arrangements in multilateral agreements. Am J Int Law 94(4):623–659

ETO Consortium (2013) Maastricht principles on extraterritorial obligations of states in the area of economic, social and cultural rights

Frank W, Bals C, Grimm J (2018) The case of Huaraz: first climate lawsuit on loss and damage against an energy company before German courts. In: Mechler R, Bouwer L, Schinko T, Surminski S, Linnerooth-Bayer J (eds) Loss and damage from climate change. Concepts, methods and policy options. Springer, Cham, pp 475–482

Gehring T (2007) Treaty-making and treaty evolution. In: Brunnee J, Hey E, Bodansky D (eds) The oxford handbook of international environmental law. Oxford University Press, Oxford, pp 467–497

Grossman D (2003) Warming up to a not-so-radical idea: Tort-based climate change litigation. Columbia J Environ Law 28(1):1–61
Gsottbauer E, Gampfer R, Bernold E, Delas AM (2017) Broadening the scope of loss and damage to legal liability: an experiment. Clim Policy. https://doi.org/10.1080/14693062.2017.1317628
Heslin A, Deckard D, Oakes R, Montero-Colbert A (2018) Displacement and resettlement: understanding the role of climate change in contemporary migration. In: Mechler R, Bouwer L, Schinko T, Surminski S, Linnerooth-Bayer J (eds) Loss and damage from climate change. Concepts, methods and policy options. Springer, Cham, pp 237–258
Human Rights Committee (2017) General comment No. 36 on article 6 of the international covenant on civil and political rights, on the right to life. Revised draft prepared by the Rapporteur, Advance Unedited Version
ILC (2016) Protection of persons in the event of disasters, UN Doc A/CN.4/L.871
ILC Articles on the Prevention of Transboundary Harm from Hazardous Activities, UN Doc UNGA A/RES/62/68
ILC Articles on the Responsibility of States for Internationally Wrongful Acts, UN Doc UNGA A/RES/56/83
Landauer, M, Juhola S (2018) Loss and damage in the rapidly changing arctic. In: Mechler R, Bouwer L, Schinko T, Surminski S, Linnerooth-Bayer J (eds) Loss and damage from climate change. Concepts, methods and policy options. Springer, Cham, pp 425–447
Lees E (2016) Responsibility and liability for climate loss and damage after Paris. Clim Policy 17(1):59–70
Mace MJ, Verheyen R (2016) Loss, damage and responsibility after COP21: all options open for the Paris agreement. Rev Eur Commun Int Environ Law 25(2):197–214
Mayer B (2014) State responsibility and climate change governance: a light through the storm. Chin J Int Law 13(3):539–575
Mayer B (2015) The applicability of the principle of prevention to climate change: a response to Zahar. Clim Law 5(1):1–24
Mayer B (2016a) Less-than-full reparations in international law. Indian J Int Law 56(3–4):463–502
Mayer B (2016b) The relevance of the no-harm principle to climate change law and politics. Asia-Pacific J Environ Law 19:79–104
Mayer B (2017) Climate change reparations and the law and practice of state responsibility. Asian J International Law 7(1):185–216
Mayer B (2018a) The international law on climate change. Cambridge University Press, Cambridge, UK
Mayer B (2018b) Construing international climate change law as a compliance regime. Transn Environ Law 7(1):115–137
Mechler R et al (2018) Science for loss and damage. findings and propositions. In: Mechler R, Bouwer L, Schinko T, Surminski S, Linnerooth-Bayer J (eds) Loss and damage from climate change. Concepts, methods and policy options. Springer, Cham, pp 3–37
Nachmany M, Fankhauser S, Setzer J, Averchenkova A (2017) Global trends in climate change legislation and litigation, 2017 Update
Okawa P (2010) Responsibility for environmental damage. In: Fitzmaurice M, Ong DM, Merkouris P (eds) Research handbook on international environmental law. Edward Elgar Publishing, Cheltenham/Northampton, pp 303–319
Pall P, Wehner M, Stone D (2016) Probabilistic extreme event attribution. In: Li J, Swinbank R, Grotjahn R, Volkert H (eds) Dynamics and predictability of large-scale, high-impact weather and climate events. Cambridge University Press: Cambridge, pp 37–46
Reis T (2011) Compensation for environmental damages under international law: the role of the international judge. Kluwer Law International, Alphen aan den Rijn
Scovazzi T (2001) State responsibility for environmental harm. In Ulfstein G, Werksman J et al (eds) Yearbook Int Environ Law 12:43–67
UN (1972) Declaration of the united nations conference on the human environment (1972) 11 ILM 1416 (16 Jun 1972)

UN Human Rights Council (2015) Human rights and climate change, UN Doc A/HRC/29/L. 21, Res 29/15 (2 Jul 2015)
UNFCCC (2007) Decision 1/CP.13, Bali Action Plan, UN Doc FCCC/CP/2007/6/Add.1
UNFCCC (2010) Decision 1/CP.16, The Cancun agreements: Outcome of the work of the ad hoc working group on long-term cooperative action under the convention, UN Doc FCCC/CP/2010/7/Add.1
UNFCCC (2011) Decision 7/CP.17, Work programme on loss and damage, UN Doc FCCC/CP/2011/9/Add.2
UNFCCC (2012) Decision 3/CP.18, Approaches to address loss and damage associated with climate change impacts in developing countries that are particularly vulnerable to the adverse effects of climate change to enhance adaptive capacity, UN Doc FCCC/CP/2012/8/Add.1
UNFCCC (2013) Decision 2/CP.19, Warsaw international mechanism for loss and damage associated with climate change impacts, UN Doc FCCC/CP/2013/10/Add.1
UNFCCC (2014) Decision 2/CP.20, Warsaw international mechanism for loss and damage associated with climate change impacts, UN Doc FCCC/CP/2014/10/Add.2
UNFCCC (2015) Decision 1/CP.21, Adoption of the Paris Agreement, UN Doc FCCC/CP/2015/10/Add.1
UNFCCC (2016) Decision 3/CP.22, Warsaw international mechanism for loss and damage associated with climate change impacts, UN Doc FCCC/CP/2016/10/Add.1
UNGA Res. 2996 (XXVII), International responsibility of States in regard to the environment, UN Doc A/RES/2996(XXVII)
United Nations Rio Declaration on Environment and Development (1992), 31 ILM 874 (13 June 1992)
Universal Declaration of Human Rights (1948), UN Doc UNGA Res 217 A (III)(10 Dec 1948)
Verheyen R (2005) Climate change damage and international law: prevention duties and state responsibility. Martinus Nijhoff Publishers, Leiden/Boston
Voigt C (2015) The potential roles of the ICJ in climate-change related claims. In: Faure M (ed) Elgar encyclopedia of environmental law, Elgar online: 152–166
Warner K, Zakieldeen S (2012) Loss and damage due to climate change: an overview of the UNFCCC negotiations, European capacity building initiative
Wallimann-Helmer I, Meyer L, Mintz-Woo K, Schinko T, Serdeczny O (2018) The ethical challenges in the context of climate loss and damage. In: Mechler R, Bouwer L, Schinko T, Surminski S, Linnerooth-Bayer J (eds) Loss and damage from climate change. Concepts, methods and policy options. Springer, Cham, pp 39–62
Zahar A (2014) Mediated versus cumulative environmental damage and the international law association's legal principles on climate change. Clim Law 4(3–4):217–233
Zahar A (2015) Methodological issues in climate law. Clim Law 5(1):25–34

ILC Yearbooks and Reports by UN Special Rapporteurs

ILC (2000) Yearbook of the International Law Commission 2000, Vol. I., UN Doc A/CN.4/SER.A/2001
ILC (2001) Yearbook of the International Law Commission 2001, Vol. II, Part Two, UN Doc A/CN.4/SER.A/2001/Add.1 (Part 2)
ILC (2006) Yearbook of the International Law Commission 2006, Vol. II, Part Two, UN Doc A/CN.4/SER.A/2006/Add.l (Part 2)
Rao PS (2000) Third report on international liability for injurious consequences arising out of acts not prohibited by international law (prevention of transboundary damage from hazardous activities), UN Doc A/CN.4/510
Wood M (2015) Third report on identification of customary international law, UN Doc A/CN.4/682

International Treaties

African Charter on Human and Peoples' Rights (signed 27 June 1981, entered into force 21 October 1986) 1520 UNTS 217

Convention relating to the Status of Refugees (signed 28 July 1951, entered into force 22 April 1954) 189 UNTS 137

International Covenant on Civil and Political Rights (adopted 16 December 1966, entered into force 23 March 196) 999 UNTS 171

International Covenant on Economic, Social and Cultural Rights (adopted 16 Dec 1966, entered into force 3 January 1976) 993 UNTS 3

Paris Agreement (adopted 12 December 2015, entered into force November 2016), UNTS Registration No. 54113

Protocol 1 to the European Convention for the Protection of Human Rights and Fundamental Freedoms (signed 20 March 1952, entered into force 18 May 1954) ETS 9

Statute of the International Court of Justice (signed 26 June 1945, entered into force 24 October 1945) Annex to the Charter of the UN

United Nations Framework Convention on Climate Change (signed 9 May 1992, entered into force 21 March 1994) 1771 UNTS 107

Decisions by International Courts and Tribunals

Al-Skeini v. UK, ECtHR 55721/07 (7 Jul 2011)

Case Concerning Pulp Mills on the River Uruguay (Argentina v. Uruguay) [2010] Judgment, ICJ Rep 14

Case concerning the Gabcikovo-Nagymaros Project (Hungary v. Slovakia) [1997] Judgment, ICJ Rep 7

Certain Activities carried out by Nicaragua in the Border Area Separate Opinion of Judge Donoghue

Corfu Channel (United Kingdom v. Albania) [1949] Merits, Judgment, ICJ Rep 4

Eritrea-Ethiopia Claims Commission, decision of 17 August 2009, Final Award: Eritrea's Damages Claims, decision of 17, XXVI Reports of International Arbitral Awards 505

Factory at Chorzów (Merits), PCIJ, Judgment of 13 September 1928, Series A.17

Lac Lanoux Arbitration (France v Spain) (1957) RIAA, Vol XII, pp 281– 317

Legality of the Threat or Use of Nuclear Weapons, Advisory Opinion, [1996] ICJ Rep 226

Legality of the Threat or Use of Nuclear Weapons, Advisory Opinion, [1996] ICJ Rep 226, Dissenting Opinion of Judge Weeramantry, pp 456–458

Mavrommatis Palestine Concessions, 1924, PCIJ, Series A, No. 2

Order of 13 December 2013 in the joined proceedings Construction of a Road in Costa Rica along the San Juan River (Nicaragua v. Costa Rica); Certain Activities Carried Out by Nicaragua in the Border Area (Costa Rica v. Nicaragua), Provisional Measures ICJ Rep 2013, 398

Responsabilité de l' Allemagne à raison des dommages causés dans les colonies portugaises du sud de l'Afrique (Portuval v. Germany), PCIJ, [1928] UNRIAA, Vol. II, p 1011

Trail Smelter Arbitration (United States v. Canada) [1938, 1941] UNRIAA, vol. III, p 1905

Decisions by Domestic Courts

AC (Tuvalu) (2014) Immigration and Protection Tribunal New Zealand, NZIPT 800517-520
American Electric Power Company v. Connecticut (2011) 564 US 410
Ashgar Leghari v. Federation of Pakistan (2015) W.P. No. 25501/2015, Lahore High Court Green Bench
Decision W109 2000179-1/291E (2007) BVwG Österreich
In Re: AD (Tuvalu) Immigration and Protection Tribunal of New Zealand (2014) 501370-371
Juliana v. United States of America (2016) 6:15-cv-01517-TC (D. Or. Nov. 10, 2016)
Massachusetts v. Environmental Protection Agency (2007) 549 US 497
Native Village of Kivalina v. ExxonMobil Corp. (2012) 696 F.3d 849 (9th Cir. 2012)
Teitiota v Chief Executive of the Ministry of Business Innovation and Employment (2015) New Zealand Supreme Court, NZSC 107
Urgenda Foundation v. The State of the Netherlands (2015) C/09/456689/HA ZA 13-1396

Statements by States

Egypt (1995) Written Statement of the Government of Egypt (transmitted on 20 June 1995)
Ecuador (1995) Letter dated 20 June 1995 from the General Director for Multilateral Organizations at the Ministry of Foreign Affairs of Ecuador
Kiribati, Fiji, and Nauru (1992) Declarations upon signature of the UNFCCC, 1771 UNTS 317–318
Mexico (1995) Written Statement by the Government of Mexico
Vanuatu (1991) Draft annex relating to insurance: Submission by Vanuatu. In: INCFCC, Negotiation of a Framework Convention on Climate Change: Elements relating to mechanisms, A/AC.237/WG.II/CRP.8
United States (1992) Written statement of the United States on Principle 7 of the Rio Declaration, in Report of the United Nations Conference on Environment and Development, A/CONF.151/26 (Vol. IV) (28 September 1992)

Chapter 8
Non-economic Loss and Damage and the Warsaw International Mechanism

Olivia Serdeczny

Abstract Non-economic Loss and Damage (NELD) forms a distinct theme in the documents outlining both the initial 2-year workplan that concluded in 2017 and the future work areas as outlined in the next 5-year rolling workplan of the Executive Committee of the Warsaw International Mechanism on Loss and Damage (WIM Excom). NELD refers to the climate-related losses of items both material and non-material that are not commonly traded in the market, but whose loss is still experienced as such by those affected. Examples of NELD include loss of cultural identity, sacred places, human health and lives. Within the context of the WIM the goal is to raise awareness of the kinds of NELD that occur and, for an expert group, to "develop inputs and recommendations to enhance data on and knowledge of reducing the risk of and addressing non-economic losses" (UNFCCC Secretariat 2014). Initial analysis shows that the two main characteristics of non-economic values are their context-dependence and their incommensurability. These attributes need to be preserved and respected when integrating measures to (i) avoid the risk and (ii) address NELD by a central mechanism under the UNFCCC. While (i) will rely on integrating NELD into existing comprehensive risk management approaches, (ii) requires thorough understanding of lost values and the functions they fulfilled for those affected.

Keywords Loss and Damage · Values · Assessment · Justice

8.1 Introduction

Climate change affects people and their environments in multiple adverse ways. Extreme heat waves like the Central Asian one in 2010 damage agricultural crops and undermine food security (Barriopedro et al. 2011); sea-level rise endangers coastal infrastructure and related economic activities such as tourism and transport (Wong

O. Serdeczny (✉)
Climate Analytics, Berlin, Germany
e-mail: olivia.serdeczny@climateanalytics.org

R. Mechler et al. (eds.), *Loss and Damage from Climate Change*, Climate Risk Management, Policy and Governance, https://doi.org/10.1007/978-3-319-72026-5_8

et al. 2014); diseases like malaria spread into previously unaffected regions posing novel health risks (Siraj et al. 2014). Many of these impacts of climate change can and have been quantified and monetised. A common example of monetised and aggregate impact assessments is the social cost of carbon. It measures the economic effects of climate change as an aggregate of changes in net agricultural productivity, human health, property damages and wider economic effects from, e.g., increased flood risk, and changes in energy system costs per unit of emitted carbon (United States Environmental Protection Agency 2015). The social cost of carbon thus derived is used to calculate the benefits of mitigation and adaptation policies and to weigh those against the costs of climate policies to arrive at an optimal level of mitigation and adaptation.

However—as has long been recognised (e.g. IPCC 1996:9; Tol 2005)—not all the negative consequences of climate change have been captured in the assessments of the social cost of carbon, as well as other assessments that rely either on qualitative or quantified data. For example, mental distress has been observed at the individual level following forced relocation due to deteriorating rural livelihoods. The distress has been linked to such losses as loss of social networks or physical surroundings that provided for a feeling of familiarity and belonging (Tschakert et al. 2013). At the collective level, the disruption of informal networks as a consequence of migration can cause losses in the form of a population´s diminished capacity to cope with continued climate impacts, further increasing the toll of climate change (Olsson et al. 2014). The effects of such often intangible losses on human wellbeing are often hard to measure and are rarely included in estimates of observed and projected climate impacts, particularly where aggregates are sought. This can be considered a serious limitation. The fact that values other than economic are of substantive importance for people is evidenced in livelihood decisions that involve trade-offs to the benefit of retaining social or cultural capital at the cost of potential economic gains. An example of such decisions are cases where migration is desisted despite its expected positive effects on income (Bebbington 1999). There is thus good reason to pay attention to non-economic values and to integrate them into policies that may lead to or prevent their losses if the overall goal is to safeguard and protect human well-being. Notably, adjustments have been made to earlier economic assessments of climate impacts in order to account for non-market losses. Nordhaus (2014), for example, reports an adjustment of 25% of the monetised damages to reflect non-monetised impacts.[1]

The concept of NELD takes into focus the dimensions of climate change impacts that are hard to quantify and whose value cannot easily be determined through the market. The term non-economic losses, which is often used interchangeably with non-economic losses and damages, originates from medical malpractice law. Methods for the assessment and expression of non-economic values in monetary units have been developed but remain controversial (see Box 8.1). Non-market losses might be a more adequate description, which, however, has not been adopted in the policy-

[1] It should be noted, however, that his list of non-monetised impacts includes extreme events, catastrophic events that are inherently difficult to model, and some other which are not considered NELD under the UNFCCC, as explained below.

process. In the following, the term of non-economic losses is used synonymously with non-market losses. Non-economic values are understood to be the object of non-economic losses.

In recognition of the importance that non-economic values hold particularly for vulnerable developing countries, NELD has been included in the workplan of the Warsaw International Mechanism as a specific work area (UNFCCC Secretariat 2014). While not spelled out as such, the two central tasks that work under the WIM will be faced with concerning NELD are the development of instruments (i) to avoid the risk of non-economic losses occurring ex ante and (ii) to respond to unavoided losses ex post. A rich body of knowledge can be drawn upon when developing approaches to both these tasks. Avoiding or reducing the risk of non-economic losses will most likely rely on the integration of the value of potential non-economic losses into comprehensive risk management. Literature on adequate assessment methods and participatory approaches to adaptation planning is available in this regard, including on the integration of NELD into wider economic assessments and the drawbacks of such integration. Addressing unavoided losses, in turn, raises questions of justice and questions of fair remedy (Wallimann-Helmer 2015) that require further critical academic debate but whose solutions ultimately need to be politically negotiated.

8.2 NELD—Causal Pathways and Examples

Impacts related to NELD as reported in the literature are direct or indirect effects of climate-related changes that were experienced as adverse by those affected. While they are triggered by climate-related environmental changes, they are always mediated by social factors that drive the vulnerability of a human system to environmental stressors, and by cultural factors that provide the context in which losses are experienced as such. The social and cultural factors notwithstanding, direct and indirect causal pathways can be identified which show how NELD impacts are caused by climate change.

NELD can be a direct consequence of climate change, for example, when losses are incurred due to physical damage of natural environments or cultural sites. High coral reef mortality due to rising sea-surface temperatures, as observed at a large scale during the 2015/2016 El Nino event (Eakin et al. 2016) is one such example of how climate change may directly cause non-economic loss of biodiversity in the future, adding to the sizeable toll of economic losses associated with the loss of biodiversity and other ecological functions (e.g. TEEB 2010). Loss of territory due to sea-level rise presents another way in which climate change may lead to NELD (Albert et al. 2016). Indeed, projections over two millennia show that under 3 °C global mean warming 3–12 countries will have lost more than half of their territory due to sea-level rise (Marzeion and Levermann 2014). Non-economic losses and damages directly related to climate change are often compounded by human activity such as marine pollution and unsustainable groundwater extraction.

Examples of indirectly induced NELD change include adverse impacts on human health following the contamination of freshwater due to sea level rise or heavy flooding (Nunn 2009). Loss of sense of place, traditional knowledge or cultural identity are often indirect consequences of climate change if migration is necessary for populations or individuals to safeguard their survival (see chapter by Heslin et al. 2018). Migration is frequently framed as a form of adaptation deliberately chosen by migrants (Tacoli 2009). However, indirect non-economic losses are often incurred involuntarily as negative side-effects of adaptation. For example, following heavy flooding and submersion of informal housing in Douala, Cameroon a government official was quoted saying: "*We think the only way to put an end to such catastrophe in the future is to demolish and force people out of these risky and vulnerable zones*" (Ngalame 2015). While such decisions are certain to avoid some non-economic losses, most notably loss of human lives, it may also lead to loss of social cohesion and agency. This shows how preserving non-economic values is complicated in situations of necessary trade-offs, which often occur in the context of climate change and resource scarcity.

The first three reports that have been published on NELD yield a catalogue of diverse recorded types of NELD that are summarised and categorised in Table 8.1/Fig. 8.1. (UNFCCC 2013a—same as Fankhauser and Dietz 2014; Morrissey and Oliver-Smith 2013; Andrei et al. 2015). The studies rely either on literature review (UNFCCC 2013) expert knowledge (Morrissey and Oliver-Smith 2013) or interviews (Andrei et al. 2015).

All authors referenced in Table 8.1/Fig. 8.1 stress that presented types and related cases are often inter-related with economic losses. Further, it is stressed that the lists provided are non-exhaustive: Climate impacts in other regional settings and cultural value systems can in principle result in different and additional types of NELD than those listed here, depending on respective cultural values. Reporting bias in the literature may mean that NELD—both types and instances—go unnoticed either because they are not comprehensively investigated or because losses in regions where they occur are not assessed. This has led to calls for a stronger involvement of qualitative climate impact research (Tschakert 2015).

8.3 Conceptualising NELD

In order to better understand why such highly diverse NELD as displayed in Table 8.1 is grouped under one activity area under the WIM it is helpful to direct attention at the shared attributes of non-economic values: (i) context-dependence and (ii) incommensurability, i.e. the lack of a common unit of measurement (see below). These attributes also shed light on some of the challenges that NELD pose to decision- and policy-making, particularly in the centralised setting of the UNFCCC.

Table 8.1 NELD impacts reported in the literature

UNFCCC (2013)/Fankhauser and Dietz 2014 (Table 2)	Morrissey and Oliver-Smith (2013) (Fig. 1)	Andrei et al. (2015)
Loss of life	Loss of life	
Health	Adverse health impacts	Physical and psychological well-being
Human mobility (Dignity; Security; Agency)		
Territory (Sovereignty; Sense of place)	Territory abandonment	
Cultural heritage (Social cohesion, Identity)		
Indigenous knowledge (Social cohesion, Identity)	Decline of indigenous knowledge	
Biodiversity	Biodiversity loss	Biodiversity/species
Ecosystem services		Ecosystem services
	Destruction of cultural sites	
	Loss of culturally important landscapes	
	Habitat destruction	
	Loss of identity and ability to solve problems collectively	
	Loss of knowledge/ways of thinking that are part of lost livelihood systems	
	Social cohesion, peacefully functioning society	
		Education
		Traditions/religion/customs
		Social bonds/relations

Note Terms in parentheses refer to terms listed as descriptions in UNFCCC 2013 rather than as losses themselves. *Source* Adapted from Serdeczny et al. (2016b)

8.3.1 Context-Dependence

Most non-economic values are the result of specific human-environment interactions. This renders them highly context-dependent. For example, the loss of biodiversity will be experienced differently by a community whose culture is built around a particular natural ecosystem than by a community that does not relate to this ecosystem. Kirsch (2001) in his analysis of the legal struggle for compensation for "culture loss" suffered by Marshall Islanders following nuclear weapons testing by the United States, reports the specific value that land holds in different contexts. Quoting

Fig. 8.1 Cases and categories of NELD as reported in the literature published by 2015. *Source* Serdeczny et al. (2016b)

the anthropologist and Enewetak ethnographer Carucci in his testimony before the Nuclear Claims Tribunal Kirsch writes:

> He [Carucci] noted that Americans move on average six times during their lifetimes and treat land as a commodity, 'something that is used, purchased and sold.' Relationships to place are temporary, and land is 'something that one can buy, utilize for a short period of time, and pass on.' Our attachment to place, in Carucci's estimation, is 'quite modest.' In contrast, the Marshallese regard land as a 'different kind of entity,' an element 'of one's very person' and an 'integral part of who people are and how they situate themselves in the world.' Their 'sense of self, both personal and cultural, is deeply embedded in a piece of land,' their weto or land parcel (Kirsch 2001:173).

Similarly, Morrissey and Oliver Smith (2013) relate the high value of glaciers to Andean villagers whose culture is composed of a system of traditional knowledge and cultural narratives around these glaciers. Such context-dependence makes communication of the relevance of non-economic values for those affected by their potential loss particularly challenging. Instruments aimed at avoiding or responding to non-economic losses within a centralised setting like the UNFCCC need to be able to accommodate such context-dependence of non-economic values. Rather than relying on a finite set of indicators, standardised assessment rules could determine what would be officially recognized as loss of non-economic values that merits international attention and action (Serdeczny et al. 2016a).

8.3.2 *Incommensurability*

Most non-economic values are considered to be incommensurable. According to (Chang 2013) "[p]*erhaps the most frequently recurring idea that falls under the label 'the incommensurability of values' is that values lack a common unit of measurement*" (p. 5). This means that while individual items might be comparable in terms of priority or importance ranking or according to an imprecise unit, they cannot be measured on one unitary scale. In contrast, if all values could be expressed by one unitary unit, then the difference between them would be merely one of quantity. Chang illustrates such a case:

> For example, if the value of one's child can be measured by the same unit that measures the value of a beach vacation, then our attitudes toward the loss of value of each should be a matter of degree. Insofar as our practical attitudes are driven by the value of their objects, our attitudes toward our children should differ from our attitudes toward beach vacations only in quantity, not in quality. (Chang 2013: 6)

A standard unitary unit of value is a monetary numéraire. Monetisation, as the process of assigning monetary values, effectively puts all values on one scale and expresses their difference as one in quantity. Which values are considered incommensurable is culturally contingent and may change over time. For example, while the value of ecosystems is frequently expressed in monetary terms (Sukhdev et al. 2014), some raise objections to such valuation and question the benefits of monetisation for biodiversity conservation (e.g. Gomez-Baggethun and Ruiz-Perez 2011).

Conceptually speaking monetisation as a valuation technique is thus not compatible with the incommensurability of value. Consequently, if incommensurability of non-economic values is respected then alternative means of valuation, as well as communication and weighting of values are needed. This presents a challenge to decision-making particularly in systems where cost-benefit analyses are drawn upon as the primary method for decision-making (see Box 8.1).

Box 8.1 Incommensurability and economic valuation

One way of integrating non-economic values with decision-making that is based on cost-benefit analyses is through the economic valuation or monetisation of non-economic values. Methods to do so exist, primarily through revealed preference, which trace consumer behaviour that indirectly relates to a non-economic good (e.g. health expenditures), or stated preference, where respondents are asked how much they would be willing to pay to preserve a certain good or how much they would be willing to accept in compensation for the loss of a good. The application of such methods is not without controversy and has been subject to much debate and scrutiny (UNFCCC 2013a).

Methodological issues—and moral concerns regarding cost-benefit analyses in general—aside, it is worth noting that assigning monetary value to incommensurable goods rests on a number of assumptions which themselves may be in conflict with values or interests in different cultural and political contexts. Assuming that a price can be assigned to certain goods or services may bereave them of what constitutes their value, namely the very fact that they cannot be bought or sold. The value of friendship is an example of such constitutive incommensurability (O´Neill 2001). Climate change affects livelihoods across cultures, who may have differing understandings of which values are undermined by the idea of assigning them market value; the application of economic valuation effectively imposes one interpretation, namely that there is no constitutive incommensurability, over any others. Further, the application of economic valuation masks questions of power and rights to ownership, which are often at the basis of conflicting values and are of high relevance for decision-making. While it is not the purpose of economic valuation to solve these issues, the problem is that "its application assumes that an answer has already been given" (O´Neill 2001:1868). Thus, while economic valuation may present a useful way of integrating non-economic values into cost-benefit analyses, this should be done critically and without diverting attention away from questions that require political and public deliberation.

Alternative approaches to integrating NELs into cost-benefit analyses could be further explored. For example, in analogy to attempts of incorporating a rights-based approach into cost-benefit analyses (Lowry and Peterson 2012), non-economic values could be integrated into cost-benefit analyses through the establishment of safeguards or output filters. In the case of output filters, any decisions that are based on cost-benefit analyses are excluded if they violate certain rights (or losses), e.g. the right to bodily integrity (or loss of life). However, it should be noted that this might be challenging to apply for all non-economic values in the context of climate change, resource scarcity and the virtually unavoidable risks that come with any course of action.

8.4 Developing Solutions

The role of the WIM in promoting instruments to address NELD is still evolving. In order to get some orientation regarding the scope and level of implementation of instruments under the WIM it is helpful to review the three function of the WIM as outlined in Decision 3/CP.18: (a) Enhancing knowledge and understanding of comprehensive risk management approaches to address Loss and Damage; (b) Strengthening dialogue, coordination, coherence and synergies among relevant stakeholders; (c) Enhancing action and support, including finance, technology and capacity building (UNFCCC 2012). With regards to NELD, function (a) is being addressed through the establishment of an expert group,[2] which will likely also positively affect fulfilment of function (b). Function (c) has not yet been addressed. Further elaboration on this function, agreed upon according to Decision 2/CP.19 (UNFCCC 2013b), (c) can offer some insights on what might be expected in the future and is worth quoting in full length:

i. Providing technical support and guidance on approaches to address loss and damage associated with climate change impacts, including extreme events and slow onset events;
ii. Providing information and recommendations for consideration by the Conference of the Parties when providing guidance relevant to reducing the risks of loss and damage and, where necessary, addressing loss and damage, including to the operating entities of the financial mechanism of the Convention, as appropriate;
iii. Facilitating the mobilization and securing of expertise, and enhancement of support, including finance, technology and capacity-building, to strengthen existing approaches and, where necessary, facilitate the development and implementation of additional approaches to address loss and damage associated with climate change impacts, including extreme weather events and slow onset events; (Decision 2/CP.19)

As is evidenced in the reference to the financial mechanism of the Convention, guidance and potential standards developed under the WIM can be expected to have consequences for countries affected by losses and damages, and by extensions NELD. Any financial mechanism is likely to rely on standardised assessment criteria for deciding which projects to fund. This is for example the case for the Green Climate Fund, where a set of criteria and sub-criteria has been developed to guide the rating of project proposals (Green Climate Fund 2014). It is open to question whether consideration of NELD will ever precipitate into concrete rules under which conditions pre-determined levels of support will be granted explicitly for addressing NELD. In either case, it is clear that recommendations developed under the WIM in the coming years are likely to be of lasting effect for the treatment of NELD under the UNFCCC.

Placed under the UNFCCC, NELD is an area of concern for the international community and responses will be guided by the principle of common but differentiated responsibility. This means that considerations of fair burden sharing need to accompany the development and implementation of both measures to avoid risks linked to NELD and measures to respond to unavoided NELD impacts. In the context of

[2]See http://unfccc.int/adaptation/groups_committees/loss_and_damage_executive_committee/items/9694.php.

such considerations, questions of adequate scales and conditions for support and fair remedy will be particularly relevant. Insights into the application of comprehensive risk management and the integration of non-economic values into decision-making can guide the development of practical guidelines for implementation of preventive measures. The questions of fair responses to unavoided NELD impacts as well as fair burden sharing and appropriate scales of support for preventive measures can be further clarified academically but their response is of ultimately political nature.

8.4.1 Avoiding and Reducing NELD

The literature on comprehensive risk management and decision making offers valuable insights into means of integrating non-economic values into decision-making processes (see also Box 8.1). The technical paper on NELD commissioned by the UNFCCC lists a number of methods to valuation of non-economic values and their integration into decision-making. Proposed methods are economic valuation, multi-criteria decision analysis, composite risk indices and qualitative and semi-quantitative methods (UNFCCC 2013a). The choice of method will ultimately depend on scale and availability of resources. While the active involvement and empowerment of local communities has been suggested as the preferable mode of work with non-economic values (NELD 2015), the qualitative methods that go with such approaches often hinder large coverage and comparability between cases.

On a country-basis, some countries have started to implement policy measures safeguarding non-economic values. Faced with the prospect of losing large parts of inhabitable land, the State of Kiribati has embarked on a programme of "migration with dignity", which entails vocational training and support for early migrants (Office of the President Republic of Kiribati 2016). In a situation of future necessity, this programme introduces an element of choice through the long-term planning horizon provided to individuals or communities, as well as institutional support. While no explicit reference is made to the preservation of agency, community ties and social cohesion, it is clear that such a programme is well suited to preserve such values that might otherwise be lost in the process of forced and unplanned migration. The example of Kiribati illustrates how knowledge and understanding of non-economic values can shape policies aimed at avoiding the risks of climate change at large: If relocation will have to be an option, then a better understanding of the values that people care for can guide policies in support of preserving these values. Notably neither quantification nor monetisation are necessary for the approach chosen by Kiribati.

Related to the question of support for the implementation of comprehensive risk management measures, it is not clear whether standards will be developed to account for the protection of NELD. While Loss and Damage is not treated under the Green Climate Fund, criteria developed to guide funding decisions show that environmental and social co-benefits, which in many cases include non-economic values, are considered alongside criteria of economic efficiency (Green Climate Fund 2014). It is, however, not clear how they are weighted with other criteria or what an appropriate weighting would be. More research is also needed on the costs that come with the integration of NELD into preventive planning. Where integration is cost-neutral, protection of NELD would be a no-regret strategy and could be implemented by default.

8.4.2 Responding to Unavoided NELD

It needs to be expected that not all NELD can and will be avoided. This is so particularly because adaptation to climate change brings with it negative side-effects which can be considered as losses and damages (Warner and Geest 2013; see introduction by Mechler et al. 2018). Many of the negative side-effects from adaptation are non-economic in kind. The example of Kiribati is a case in point, where despite careful measures, sense of place and territory are likely to be lost: With reference to census according to which most I-Kiribati want to remain on their islands (Uan 2016), officials explicitly frame migration as a last resort (Office of the President Republic of Kiribati 2016).

Having said this, not all non-economic values will necessarily continue to be perceived as important or mourned by those affected. As people adapt to gradually or abruptly changing environments it can be expected that their value preferences may shift as well (Tschakert 2016). Fishermen, for example, losing their traditional livelihoods may find new identities in alternative means of income and social exchange: new goals and preferences in their lives will likely emerge. However, it is open to question which of the lost values will continue to be mourned by those affected in the future and which will prove to be temporary. Nor is it clear whether temporarily mourned losses, which could have been avoided had climate change been avoided, can simply be ignored or whether they too merit some form of fair remedy. After all, those affected are forced to shift to new goals rather than freely choosing to do so.

Questions of what constitutes a fair remedy to unavoided non-economic losses touch on the means and instruments that are available as responses as well as on questions of who bears the duty to remedy. Bracketing the question of identifying the duty bearer it is helpful to approach non-economic values with Goodin´s theories of compensation (Goodin 1989). Goodin distinguishes between means replacing compensation, where people are provided with the means to pursue the same ends that have been lost and ends-displacing compensation, where people are enabled "to pursue some other ends in a way that leaves them subjectively as well off overall as they would have been had they not suffered the loss at all" (Goodin 1989:60). In the case of irreplaceable losses where no substitute can be found, means replacing compensation is not possible, leaving ends-displacing compensation as the only option. Goodin argues for the moral superiority of means replacing compensation as it does not forcibly interfere with the "unity and coherence in a person´s life" (Goodin 1989:68) and does not undermine a person´s autonomy. In contrast, in ends-displacing compensation, people are forced to shift their goals and pursue new ends, as if their preferences and goals were "one undifferentiated mass" (Goodin 1989:67).

For responses to NELD this means that ways should be sought that allow those affected to pursue the same goals as prior to the loss. Whether and how exactly this can be achieved will depend on the loss in question as some but not all incommensurable values are irreplaceable. Designing responses to unavoided NELD impacts will consequently require a thorough understanding of the function that a lost value had for those affected by its loss. For example, if a community is forced to relocate and is faced with loss of traditional knowledge then locations for relocation could be sought which allow as much of the knowledge to still be applied as possible. Granting migrants the rights needed to re-establish their livelihoods according to their own preferences would be another way of effective means-replacement in order to enable the pursuit of lost ends.

In cases where no substitute for what has been lost is conceivable, as might for example be the case with loss of lives or sacred places, it is important to acknowledge that ends-displacing compensation does not legitimise the policy that led to this loss (Goodin 1989:73). This does not imply that ends-displacing compensation, as for example monetary compensation for irreplaceable goods, should be avoided. Indeed, claims for compensation for culture loss as quoted by (Kirsch 2001) show that communities affected by such losses seek justice through the form of monetary recompense despite the perceived incommensurability of culture which conceptually prohibits its economic valuation. This might appear as conceptual inconsistency or dishonesty by those affected. However, as O´Neill (2001) argues, forward-looking economic valuations are distinct from backward-looking ones in that the latter are associated with notions of rectificatory justice whereas the former are not. Along these lines, monetary compensation for irreplaceable or incommensurable goods does not imply that those goods are replaced or that their value can be expressed on a single scale. Rather, ends-displacing compensation is an aspect of rectificatory justice and "surely better than nothing" (Goodin 1989:73), but it does not right a wrong. In the context of climate policy this translates into the clear preference that needs to be given to measures that prevent the risk of losses and damages, even if the difference between avoiding and compensating were cost-neutral. Finally, where losses are irreplaceble and require that those affected are forced to shift their goals, as will be the case with many of the non-economic values already observed and projected, it needs to be acknowledged that a residue of moral wrong will remain.

8.5 Conclusions

The concept of NELD spans a wide range of adverse effects of climate change that affect both human wellbeing and natural systems. Some of these effects are standardly considered in public policies on climate change (e.g. adverse effects on human health or human life) while others (e.g. loss of cultural heritage or social networks) remain less well reflected. With the particular focus now placed on NELD under the UNFCCC, the opportunity arises to widen the scope of current approaches and design comprehensive policies that accommodate the dimension of incommensurable values at risk from climate change and that are sensitive to context.

Debates on the most adequate and effective valuation methods, in particular controversies around economic valuation, are likely to continue in the context of NELD. Here, it will be important to not "jump the gun" and consider to which ends data and information on non-economic values will be needed. In cases of preventive measures, a deep understanding of the values and their functions for well-being that should be preserved despite choices that threaten these values and that are limited by resource availability, such as the choice to relocate despite high sense of place, is needed for an effective design of policies. The economic value of community ties, sense of place or traditional cultures would add little information to the design of such policies. Similarly, the identification of possibilities for means-replacing compensation will not rely on the monetary value of what has been lost but of the goals and ends that were pursued by those affected by NELD. What is, however, needed and currently lacking are economic estimates of the costs of preventing NELD impacts and risks. These will also inform the debate on adequate scales of international support and burden sharing that have not been addressed in this chapter (see chapter by Wallimann-Helmer et al. 2018).

Raising awareness on NELD and giving it appropriate weight in decision-making processes will continue to be a challenge. This is particularly the case in the international setting of the UNFCCC where different cultures are represented and where decisions on funding and support will likely rely on standardised criteria and centralised decision-making. The development of dedicated efforts to integrate NELD in the design and implementation of both preventive and reactive approaches at the national and regional level can be expected in the coming years. For these instruments to be effective it will be important to put them on a strong evidence base. Comprehensive geographical coverage of climate impact observations, including contributions from social disciplines such as human geography and environmental psychology can provide important insights in this regard. Similarly, academic discussions of the normative dimensions of NELD and adequate responses can clarify much of the debate. However, which values will count and how they will be weighed in decision-making both at the national and international level will in the end always be one of judgment and as such require political debate and deliberation.

References

Albert S, Leon JX, Grinham AR, Church JA, Gibbes BR, Woodroffe CD (2016) Interactions between sea-level rise and wave exposure on reef island dynamics in the Solomon Islands. Environ Res Lett 11:054011. https://doi.org/10.1088/1748-9326/11/5/054011

Andrei S, Rabbani G, Khan HI (2015) Non-economic loss and damage caused by climatic stressors in selected coastal districts of Bangladesh. Bangladesh: Bangladesh Centre for Advanced Studies. Supported by the Asian Development Bank. http://www.icccad.net/wp-content/uploads/2016/02/ADB-Study-on-Non-Economic-Losses-and-Damages-Report_Final-Version-Reduced-File-Size.compressed1.pdf. Accessed 22 Jan 2017

Barriopedro D, Fischer EM, Luterbacher J, Trigo RM, Garcia-Herrera R (2011) The hot summer of 2010: redrawing the temperature record map of Europe. Science 332:220–224

Bebbington A (1999) Capitals and capabilities: a framework for analyzing peasant viability, rural livelihoods and poverty. World Dev 27:2021–2044

Chang R (2013) Incommensurability (and Incomparability). Int Encycl Ethics 2591–2604. https://doi.org/10.1002/9781444367072.wbiee030

Eakin MC, Liu G, Gomez AM, De La Cour JL, Heron S, Skirving, Strong AE (2016) Global coral bleaching 2014–2017. Status and appeal for observations. Reef Encounter 31:20–26

Fankhauser S, Dietz S (2014) Non-economic losses in the context of the UNFCCC work programme on loss and damage (policy paper). London School of Economics—Centre for Climate Change Economics and Policy, Grantham Research Institute on Climate Change and the Environment

Gomez-Baggethun E, Ruiz-Perez M (2011) Economic valuation and the commodification of ecosystem services. Prog Phys Geogr 35:613–628. https://doi.org/10.1177/0309133311421708

Goodin RE (1989) Theories of compensation. Oxford J Legal Stud 9:56–75. https://doi.org/10.1093/ojls/9.1.56

Green Climate Fund (2014) Investment Framework GCF/B.07/06. https://www.greenclimate.fund/documents/20182/24943/GCF_B.07_06_-_Investment_Framework.pdf/. Accessed 22 Jan 2017

Heslin A, Deckard D, Oakes R, Montero-Colbert A (2018) Displacement and resettlement: understanding the role of climate change in contemporary migration. In: Mechler R, Bouwer L, Schinko T, Surminski S, Linnerooth-Bayer J (eds) Loss and damage from climate change. Concepts, methods and policy options. Springer, Cham, pp 237–258

IPCC (1996) Climate change 1996. Economic and social dimensions of climate change. contribution of working group III to the second assessment report of the intergovernmental panel on climate change. Cambridge University Press, New York, USA and Melbourne Australia

Kirsch S (2001) Lost worlds: environmental disaster, “culture loss”, and the law. Curr Anthropol 42:167–198. https://doi.org/10.1086/320006

Lowry R, Peterson M (2012) Cost-benefit analysis and non-utilitarian ethics. Politics Philos Econ 11:258–279. https://doi.org/10.1177/1470594X11416767

Marzeion B, Levermann A (2014) Loss of cultural world heritage and currently inhabited places to sea-level rise. Environ Res Lett 9:34001. https://doi.org/10.1088/1748-9326/9/3/034001

Mechler R et al (2018) Science for loss and damage. Findings and propositions. In: Mechler R, Bouwer L, Schinko T, Surminski S, Linnerooth-Bayer J (eds) Loss and damage from climate change. Concepts, methods and policy options. Springer, Cham, pp 3–37

Morrissey J, Oliver-Smith A (2013) Perspectives on non-economic loss and damage: understanding values at risk from climate change. Loss and damage series, United Nations University Institute for Environment and Human Security, Bonn. http://loss-and-damage.net/download/7308.pdf Accessed 22 Jan 2017

NELD (2015) Non-economic loss and damage—what is it and why does it matter? Key outcomes of the 2015 NELD Expert Workshop. http://climate-neld.com/wp-content/uploads/2015/09/NELD.WS_Key.Outcomes_final1.pdf. Accessed 22 Jan 2017

Ngalame EN (2015) Flood-hit Cameroon to demolish low-lying urban homes. Retrieved from http://www.preventionweb.net/news/view/44976. Accessed 22 Jan 2017

Nordhaus W (2014) Estimates of the social cost of carbon: concepts and results from the DICE-2013R model and alternative approaches. J Assoc Environ Res Econ 1:273–312. https://doi.org/10.1086/676035

Nunn PD (2009) Responding to the challenges of climate change in the Pacific Islands: management and technological imperatives. Clim Res 40:211–231. https://doi.org/10.3354/cr00806

Office of the President Republic of Kiribati (2016) Relocation. http://www.climate.gov.ki/category/action/relocation/. Accessed 13 Aug 2016

Olsson LM, Opondo M, Tschakert P et al (2014) Livelihoods and poverty. In: Climate change 2014: Impacts, adaptation, and vulnerability. Part A: global and sectoral aspects. In: Field CB, Barros VR (eds) Contribution of working group II to the fifth assessment report of the intergovernmental panel on climate change. Cambridge University Press, Cambridge, United Kingdom and New York, NY, USA, pp 793–832

O´Neill J (2001) Markets and the environment: the solution is the problem. Econ Political Weekly 36:1865–1873

Serdeczny O, Waters E, Chan S (2016a) Non-economic loss and damage. Addressing the forgotten side of climate change impacts. German Development Institute briefing paper 2016, 3. https://www.die-gdi.de/uploads/media/BP_3.2016_neu.pdf. Accessed 22 Jan 2017

Serdeczny O, Waters E, Chan S (2016b) Non-economic loss and damage. Understanding the challenges. German Development Institute discussion paper 2016, 3. https://www.die-gdi.de/uploads/media/DP_3.2016.pdf. Accessed 22 Jan 2017

Siraj AS, Santos-Vega M, Bouma MJ, Yadeta D, Carrascal DR, Pascual M (2014) Altitudinal changes in malaria incidence in highlands of Ethiopia and Colombia. Science 343:1154–1158. https://doi.org/10.1126/science.1244325

Sukhdev P, Wittmer H, Miller D (2014) The economics of ecosystems and biodiversity (TEEB): challenges and responses. In: Nature in the balance: the economics of biodiversity. Oxford University Press, Oxford, UK

Tacoli C (2009) Crisis or adaptation? Migration and climate change in a context of high mobility. Environ Urbanization 21:513–525

TEEB (2010) The economics of ecosystems and biodiversity: mainstreaming the economics of nature: A synthesis of the approach, conclusions and recommendations of TEEB. http://doc.teebweb.org/wp-content/uploads/Study%20and%20Reports/Reports/Synthesis%20report/TEEB%20Synthesis%20Report%202010.pdf. Accessed 13 May 2017

Tol RSJ (2005) The marginal damage costs of carbon dioxide emissions: an assessment of the uncertainties. Energy Policy 33:2064–2074. https://doi.org/10.1016/j.enpol.2004.04.002

Tschakert P (2015) 1.5 °C or 2 °C: a conduit's view from the science-policy interface at COP20 in Lima. Peru. Climate Change Responses 2:1–11. https://doi.org/10.1186/s40665-015-0010-z

Tschakert P (2016) Non-economic losses (NELs): human mobility, territory, and indigenous knowledge—Presentation at 3rd meeting of the executive committee of the warsaw international mechanism on loss and damage associated with climate change

Tschakert P, Tutu R, Alcaro A (2013) Embodied experiences of environmental and climatic changes in landscapes of everyday life in Ghana. Emotion, Space Soc 7:13–25. https://doi.org/10.1016/j.emospa.2011.11.001

Uan L (2016) I-Kiribati want to migrate with dignity. http://www.climate.gov.ki/2013/02/12/i-kiribati-want-to-migrate-with-dignity/. Accessed 13 Aug 2016

UNFCCC (2012) Report of the conference of the parties on its eighteenth session, held in Doha from 26 November to 8 December 2012. Addendum. Part two: Action taken by the Conference of the Parties at its eighteenth session

UNFCCC (2013a) Technical Paper: Non-economic losses in the context of the work programme on loss and damage. http://unfccc.int/resource/docs/2013/tp/02.pdf. Accessed 13 Aug 2016

UNFCCC (2013b) Report of the Conference of the Parties on its nineteenth session, held in Warsaw from 11 to 23 November 2013. Addendum. Part two: action taken by the conference of the parties at its nineteenth session. https://cop23.unfccc.int/node/8387. Accessed 22 Jan 2017

UNFCCC Secretariat (2014) Subsidiary body for scientific and technological advice. Forty-first session, Lima 1–6 December 2014. Report of the executive committee of the Warsaw international mechanism for loss and damage associated with climate change impacts. Held in Lima from 1 to 6 Decemer 2014. http://unfccc.int/resource/docs/2014/sb/eng/04.pdf. Accessed 22 Jan 2018

United States Environmental Protection Agency (2015) Social cost of carbon. EPA Fact Sheet. https://www.epa.gov/sites/production/files/2016-12/documents/social_cost_of_carbon_fact_sheet.pdf. Accessed 13 May 2017

Wallimann-Helmer I (2015) Justice for climate loss and damage. Clim Change 133:469–480. https://doi.org/10.1007/s10584-015-1483-2

Wallimann-Helmer I, Meyer L, Mintz-Woo K, Schinko T, Serdeczny O (2018) The ethical challenges in the context of climate loss and damage. In: Mechler R, Bouwer L, Schinko T, Surminski S, Linnerooth-Bayer J (eds) Loss and damage from climate change. Concepts, methods and policy options. Springer, Cham, pp 39–62

Warner K, van der Geest K (2013) Loss and damage from climate change: local-level evidence from nine vulnerable countries. Int J Global Warming 5:367–386. https://doi.org/10.1504/IJGW.2013.057289

Wong PP, Losada IJ, Gattuso J-P, Hinkel J, Khattabi A, McInnes KL, Saito Y, Sallenger A (2014) Coastal systems and low-lying areas. In: Climate change 2014: impacts, adaptation, and vulnerability. Part A: global and sectoral aspects. In: Field CB, Barros VR, Dokken DJ, Mach KJ, Mastrandrea MD, Bilir TE, Chatterjee M, Ebi KL, Estrada YO, Genova RC, Girma B, Kissel ES, Levy AN, MacCracken S, Mastrandrea PR, White LL (eds) Contribution of working group II to the fifth assessment report of the intergovernmental panel on climate change. Cambridge University Press, Cambridge, United Kingdom and New York, NY, USA, pp 361–409

Chapter 9
The Impacts of Climate Change on Ecosystem Services and Resulting Losses and Damages to People and Society

Kees van der Geest, Alex de Sherbinin, Stefan Kienberger, Zinta Zommers, Asha Sitati, Erin Roberts and Rachel James

Abstract So far, studies of Loss and Damage from climate change have focused primarily on human systems and tended to overlook the mediating role of ecosystems and the services ecosystems provide to society. This is a significant knowledge gap because losses and damages to human systems often result from permanent or temporary disturbances to ecosystems services caused by climatic stressors. This chapter tries to advance understanding of the impacts of climatic stressors on ecosystems and

K. van der Geest (✉)
United Nations University Institute for Environment and Human Security (UNU-EHS), Bonn, Germany
e-mail: geest@ehs.unu.edu

A. de Sherbinin
Center for International Earth Science Information Network (CIESIN), The Earth Institute at Columbia University, New York, USA

S. Kienberger
Department of Geoinformatics – Z-GIS, University of Salzburg, Salzburg, Austria

Z. Zommers
Mercy Corps, London, UK

A. Sitati
University College London, London, UK

E. Roberts
King's College, London, UK

R. James
Department of Oceanography, Environmental Change Institute, University of Oxford, Oxford, UK

R. James
University of Cape Town, Cape Town, South Africa

R. Mechler et al. (eds.), *Loss and Damage from Climate Change*, Climate Risk Management, Policy and Governance, https://doi.org/10.1007/978-3-319-72026-5_9

implications for losses and damages to people and society. It introduces a conceptual framework for studying these complex relations and applies this framework to a case study of multi-annual drought in the West-African Sahel. The case study shows that causal links between climate change and a specific event, with subsequent losses and damages, are often complicated. Oversimplification must be avoided and the role of various factors, such as governance or management of natural resources, should be at the centre of future research.

Keywords Loss and Damage · Climate change · Ecosystem services Livelihoods · Adaptation limits and constraints · Sahel · Africa

9.1 Introduction

Climate change amplifies extreme weather events such as heatwaves and extreme rainfall, with implications for losses and damages affecting vulnerable populations around the world. Global surface temperature has increased already on average by 0.85 °C relative to pre-industrial temperature (IPCC 2014), and there is evidence that even with very ambitious mitigation measures, the Earth's atmospheric system may already be committed to warming of approximately 1.5 °C above pre-industrial levels by 2050 (World Bank 2014). While mitigation continues to be of paramount importance to limit losses and damages, the extent and magnitude of climate change impacts will almost certainly increase in the future. Decision makers will need to be prepared to implement both adaptation and risk reduction measures to avoid losses and damages and a suite of other approaches within comprehensive risk management frameworks to address losses and damages that are not averted (see introduction by Mechler et al. 2018).

Defining Losses and Damages

No universally agreed-upon definition of losses and damages as part of the Loss and Damage debate exists, and a fit-for-purpose working definition varies by scale and purpose. This chapter refers to losses and damages as the adverse effects of climate-related stressors that cannot be or have not been avoided through mitigation or managed through adaptation efforts (adapted from Van der Geest and Warner 2015). Losses and damages occur when adaptation measures are unsuccessful, insufficient, not implemented, or impossible to implement; when adaptation measures have unrecoverable costs; or when measures are maladaptive, making ecosystems and societies more vulnerable (Warner and van der Geest 2013).

Verheyen (2012) makes an important and policy-relevant distinction between avoided, unavoided and unavoidable losses and damages (see also Mechler et al. 2018). Avoided losses and damages refer to impacts and risks that have been prevented through mitigation and adaptation measures. For example, if an African rain-fed farmer has planted drought-resistant crop varieties that yielded well in a season of extremely low rainfall, he or she has avoided adverse effects of drought. Unavoided losses and damages refer to impacts of climate change that could in theory have been avoided but that have not been avoided because of inadequate efforts to reduce risks or adapt. For example, unavoided losses and damages may result if a coastal storm and high tide inundate properties because available measures to adapt to sea level rise were not adopted. By contrast, impacts and risks that are impossible to avoid through mitigation and adaptation efforts are characterised as "unavoidable losses and damages" (Verheyen 2012). In reality there is ambiguity around what can and what cannot be avoided. It depends on technological, social, economic or political limits to mitigation and adaptation, which are context-specific and subjective. Strong disaster mitigation, for example, might be technically possible but not politically feasible or economically viable. Similarly, if a small, low-lying atoll would be confronted with 6 m of sea level rise, it could be technically possible to build a dyke around the island, but the costs of such an effort would probably be prohibitive. This chapter does not attempt to resolve these ambiguities. However, it is important to acknowledge that they exist because there are important policy implications. In some cases, resources would be invested most efficiently in trying to avoid losses and damages, and in other cases it will be better to accept losses and find sustainable and dignified solutions for the people who are affected.

A useful concept in the discussion about avoidable and unavoidable losses and damages are 'adaptation limits' (Dow et al. 2013; Preston et al. 2013; Warner et al. 2013). According to the IPCC, adaptation limits are reached when adaptation is no longer able to "provide an acceptable level of security from risks to the existing objectives and values and prevent the loss of the key attributes, components or services of ecosystems" (Klein et al. 2014). An adaptation limits is considered 'hard' when no adaptive actions are possible to avoid intolerable risk, while soft adaptation limits occur when options are currently not available to avoid intolerable risk through adaptive action (Agard et al. 2014). In practice, it is not always clear whether an adaptation limit is hard or soft. Similarly, what renders risk acceptable, tolerable or intolerable is subjective, context-specific and socially constructed (Mechler and Schinko 2016).

A common way of analysing losses and damages is by differentiating economic and non-economic losses and damages (NELD). Economic losses are understood to be the loss of resources, goods and services that are commonly traded in markets, such as livestock and cash crops. Non-economic losses and damages involve things that are not commonly traded in markets (UNFCCC 2013). Examples of NELD in natural systems include loss of habitat and biodiversity and damage to ecosystem services. While such items are not traded in markets, there is a strong research community dedicated to valuing the services ecosystems provide, and hence also to quantifying losses when they occur (Costanza et al. 2014). Examples of NELD in human systems include cultural and social losses associated with the loss of ancestral land and forced relocation. Such climate change impacts are difficult to quantify but important to address (Morrissey and Oliver-Smith 2014; chapter by Serdeczny 2018).

Losses and damages can also be categorised as direct and indirect. Examples of direct losses and damages include loss of life, land, crops, or livestock–as well as damage to houses, properties, and infrastructure. Such losses and damages are generally quite well covered in disaster loss assessments (Gall 2015; chapter by Bouwer 2018). By contrast, indirect losses and damages are harder to quantify or estimate, so they are often underreported (UNFCCC 2012). Indirect losses and damages are associated with the measures actors implement to adapt to or cope with direct impacts. For example, if a community is displaced by flooding and has to live in a school building for six months, there will be indirect effects of the flood on the students' education level (Opondo 2013). When coping measures are beneficial in the short term but have adverse effects on livelihood sustainability in the longer-term, we speak of 'erosive coping' (van der Geest and Dietz 2004).

Research Gaps and Outline of Chapter

There is a long tradition of scholarly work on assessing disaster losses, and a small, but emerging body of literature on losses and damages from climate change. More research has been done about losses and damages from sudden onset disasters—such as cyclones and floods—than from slow onset processes—such as sea level rise, ocean acidification and drought. While scientific conceptualisations and empirical work on Loss and Damage has focused primarily on human impacts (Warner and van der Geest 2013; Wrathall et al. 2015), little attention has been given to the loss of ecosystem services and the cascading impacts on human societies resulting from this (Zommers et al. 2014). Yet, according to the IPCC's Fifth Assessment Report, "evidence of climate-change impacts is strongest and most comprehensive for natural systems" (IPCC 2014). Moreover, adaptation options for ecosystems are limited (IPCC 2014) and in the case of progressive and permanent change, current measures are unlikely to prevent loss and damage to ecosystems and their services.

This chapter[1] tries to enhance understanding of how impacts of climate change on ecosystem services result in losses and damages to people and society. This helps in determining what kind of interventions could reduce such losses and damages now and in the future. We first present a conceptual framework for studying how impacts of climate change on ecosystem services can result in losses and damages to human systems. The next section discusses current knowledge of climate change impacts on four types of ecosystem services—provisioning, regulating, supporting, and cultural. A case study follows where we present how losses and damages to ecosystem services affects human well-being in the drylands of the West African Sahel. The conclusion section of this chapter summarises key findings and discusses policy options. As well, we identify two important areas for future research and evidence gathering.

[1]This chapter builds on a report published by the United Nations Environment Program, entitled "Loss and Damage: The role of Ecosystem Services" (UNEP 2016).

9.2 Conceptual Framework for Understanding the Role of Ecosystem Services

The working definition we use in this chapter refers to losses and damages as the adverse effects of climate-related stressors that cannot be or have not been avoided through mitigation or managed through adaptation efforts (adapted from Van der Geest and Warner 2015). Following from this definition is the notion that there is a conceptual difference between climate impacts and losses and damages. Despite its negative connotation, the concept of losses and damages gives central stage to the role of mitigation and adaptation and the opportunities that exist for avoiding harm, as illustrated in Fig. 9.1. However, too many opportunities to mitigate or adapt are missed because of adaptation constraints, such as due to a lack in understanding, deficits in long-term commitment and motivation, and inadequate financial resources (Ayeb-Karlsson et al. 2016). Losses and damages result from these failures.

The purpose of this framework is to illustrate the central focus and storyline in this chapter. It does not elaborate on all elements and relations of the complex reality of climate change, impacts, and adaptation. Starting at the top of the diagram, climatic stressors affect human systems and natural systems. Impacts on human systems can be direct, or indirect through damage to natural systems and the ecosystem services they provide to society. When human systems are affected—be it directly or indirectly—adaptation options may exist. If adaptation measures are adopted and successful, there are no losses and damages. If there are no adaptation options at all, when adaptation limits have been surpassed, then losses and damages to human systems is inevitable. If there are possibilities to adapt, but adaptation action does not materialise or is not efficient because of adaptation constraints, then actors will also incur losses and damages. Often, successful adaptation is possible in theory, but doesn't happen in practice because of adaptation constraints, such as lack of knowledge, skills, and resources (chapter by Schinko et al. this 2018).

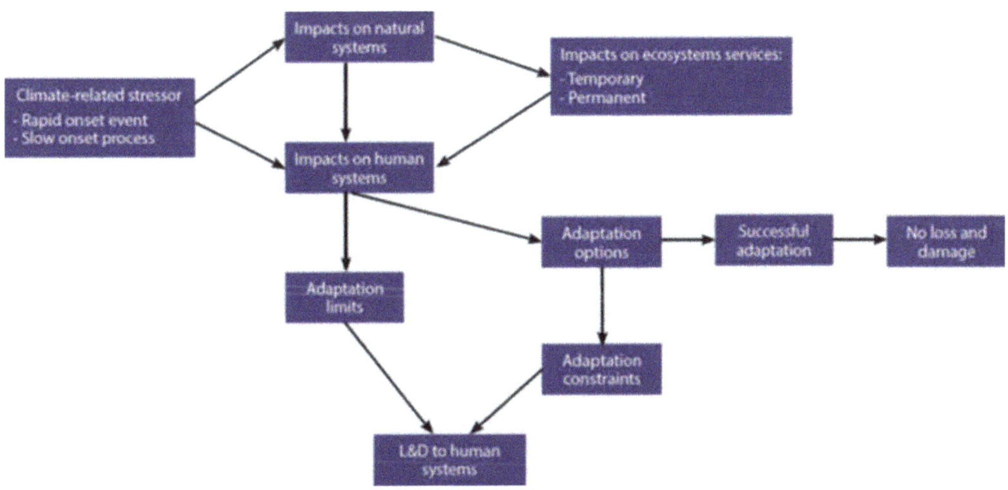

Fig. 9.1 Conceptual framework for understanding the role of ecosystem services

9.3 Impacts of Climate Change on Ecosystem Services-Current Knowledge

Ecosystems are collections of macro and microscopic biota that form critical life support systems. Degradation of ecosystems is occurring worldwide due to over-exploitation and because of insufficient recognition of the vital importance of the services that ecosystems provide to human well-being (WWAP 2015; MA 2005). Climate change has the potential to exacerbate ecosystem degradation and reduce the efficiency of ecosystem services (Staudinger et al. 2012; Bangash et al. 2013; Lorencová et al. 2013).

The Millennium Ecosystem Assessment defines ecosystem services as the benefits that people obtain from ecosystems (MA 2005) and distinguishes four types of ecosystem services :

- provisioning services (food, water, fuel and wood or fiber),
- regulating services (climate, flood and disease regulation and water purification),
- supporting services (soil formation, nutrient cycling and primary production),
- cultural services (educational, recreational, aesthetic and spiritual).

The quality of ecosystem services increases with the level of intactness, complexity, and/or species richness of ecosystems (Díaz et al. 2006). Many of the negative consequences human societies experience from climate change are related to the adaptation limits of individual species that provide us with food, fiber, fuel and shelter, as well as the services provided by whole ecosystems. Dow and others (2013) provide two telling examples of such adaptation limits. First, there is a limit to the temperature that rice in South Asia can cope with in the pollination and flowering phase: After a threshold temperature of 26 °C, every 1 °C increase in night-time temperature results in a 10% decline in yield. Beyond a night temperature of 35 °C it is impossible to grow current rice varieties there, which constitutes a hard adaptation limit beyond which different types actors (farmers, traders, the economy at large) incur losses and damages due to changes in the ecosystem service (Dow et al. 2013).

The second example demonstrates how a society itself can choose its adaptation limits: After settling in Greenland around 1000AD, the complex and advanced Norse society there ended around 1450. The settlements' collapse can be attributed to their adaptation limits. When harsh conditions began, Norse Greenlanders adopted new ways of exploiting marine mammals as declines in agriculture and domestic livestock production persisted. But faced with growing competition from Inuit hunters, declining trade in ivory and fur with Norway as pack ice blocked their access, and a generally chilling climate, these adaptations were insufficient to maintain risks to community continuity at tolerable levels. At the same time, the Norse settlers refused to adopt techniques that proved useful to the Inuit (Dow et al. 2013). Impacts of climate change on ecosystem services are characterised by high levels of complexity arising from interactions of biophysical, economic, political, and social factors at various scales (Ewert et al. 2015). These impacts are often specific to a given context or place, making generalisations difficult.

9.4 Case Study: Multi-annual Drought in the Drylands of the Sahel

While climate change impacts on ecosystem services are already highly localised, this applies even more to the resulting losses and damages to people and society. Differences between places in terms of culture, social organization, governance, development and adaptive capacity cause the local specificity of climate change impacts in human systems. This section uses a West African case study to further explore conceptual links between climate change and losses and damages to ecosystem services, and consequently to human well-being. The following questions are explored:

- What is the weather-related stressor and does climate change play a role?
- How does the stressor affect ecosystems and the services they provide?
- How does the change in ecosystem services affect human systems?
- What are adaptation options, and how effective are these at avoiding losses and damages?
- What is the evidence on losses and damages?
- What can be done in terms of better preparedness or adaptation to avoid future losses and damages?

The Sahel and the semi-arid drylands of East Africa are emblematic of climate change vulnerability. The regions have faced challenges such as crop and livestock losses, food insecurity, displacement, cultural losses including traditional livelihood systems, and conflict. A major factor in these challenges is climate variability exacerbated by climate change. In contrast with other parts of the world, most agriculture in Africa is rainfed and therefore crops yields are extremely sensitive to climatic conditions (Zaal et al. 2004). In early 2015 an estimated 20.4 million people were food insecure as a result of ongoing drought—mostly in Niger, Nigeria, Mali, and Chad where conflict and poverty compound food insecurity (ReliefWeb 2015). A number of climatic changes are occurring in the region. For one, it is becoming hotter, and this is clearly consistent with climate change. Temperature increases vary widely within the region, up to as much as 0.5 °C per decade from 1951 to the present (or 3.5 °C total) in a large part of Sudan and South Sudan; and are also high, 0.2–0.4 °C per decade, in large parts of Mauritania, Mali, Niger, Chad and Uganda (Fig. 9.2). Recent studies suggest that in some African regions the pace of warming is more than double the global and tropical average (Cook and Vizy 2015; Engelbrecht et al. 2015). Higher temperatures increase evaporation from soil and water surfaces and transpiration from vegetation—a process known collectively as evapotranspiration. Therefore, even in places where rainfall increases, it may not be sufficient to offset overall soil moisture loss, affecting primary productivity and food production, which are supporting and provisioning ecosystem services respectively.

In the drylands of Africa, there is high rainfall variability from year to year, and even from decade to decade. Figure 9.3 shows the rainfall variation for the Sahel

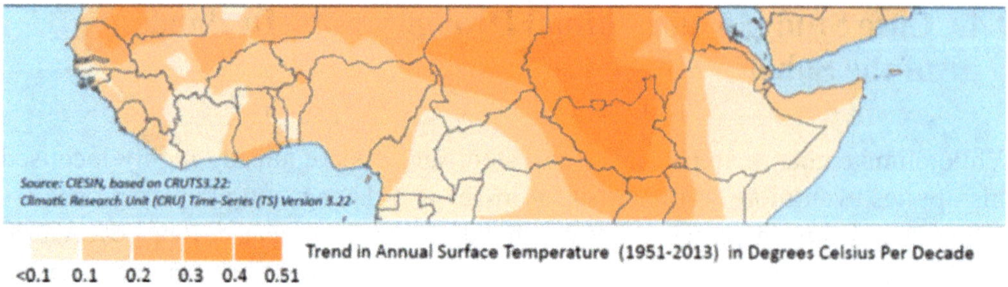

Fig. 9.2 Temperature change in degrees Celsius per decade from 1951 to 2013. *Source* UNEP (2016). *Notes* Trends are obtained by adjusting a linear trend to inter-annual anomalies (anomalies with respect to the average over the 63 year observation record), with no other filtering (not removing any other scales of variability). It is expressed in degrees C/decade

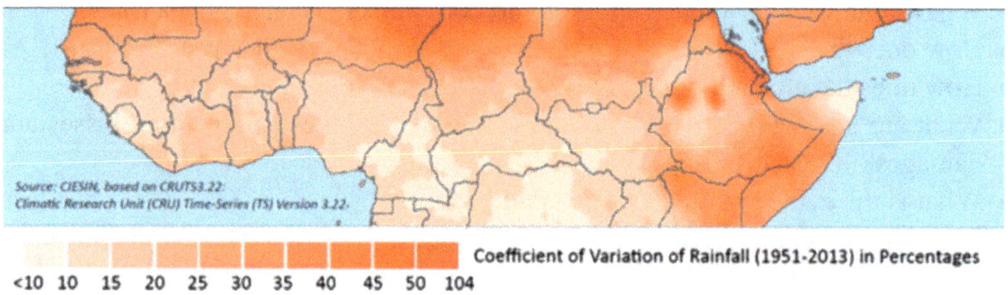

Fig. 9.3 Coefficient of variation of rainfall from 1951 to 2013 (in percent of the long-term average). *Source* UNEP (2016)

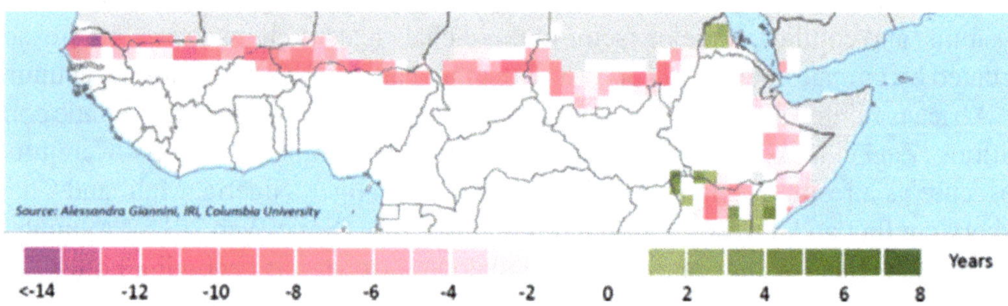

Fig. 9.4 Difference in the number of years that received adequate rainfall for sorghum and millet (1990–2009 compared to 1950–1969). *Source* UNEP (2016)

from 1951 to 2013. Large areas of the drylands have inter-annual rainfall variability that is ±30% of the mean.

During the 1970s and early 1980s the Sahel experienced a long and widespread drought that was associated with a devastating famine (Held et al. 2005; Conway et al. 2009). Trends for the late 20th and early 21st century suggest an increase in the intensity and length of droughts in West Africa (IPCC 2012), and a decline in rainfall of between 10 and 20%, with rainfall becoming less dependable (Turco et al. 2015). The region also has strong decadal variability, related to swings in ocean temperatures in the North Atlantic. Even controlling for the effect of decadal variability, pronounced shifts in rainfall are evident. For example, in the drylands of Mali and Burkina Faso, the number of years that exceed the minimum required to grow sorghum and millet has changed over time (Fig. 9.4). During the period 1950–69, generally recognised as a wet period for the Sahel, there was reliable rainfall for sorghum and millet in many regions, but in the last two decades the number of years that met the threshold was 60–80% lower. This demonstrates how climatic variability and change can threaten food production, an important ecosystem service.

Intra-annual variability is another issue. Within any growing season, large gaps in rainfall or extreme rainfall events can have important impacts on crop production—withering crops after they've sprouted or washing them away. The combined effects of decadal, inter-annual (between years), and intra-annual (within years) variability have important repercussions for food provisioning, which is an important ecosystem service.

Research on losses and damages from the 2004 and 2010 droughts in northern Burkina Faso showed that villagers have become less able to cope with droughts because of a decline in pastoralism and an increase in cropping (Traore and Owiyo 2013). Pastoralism has long been an important and well adapted livelihood strategy in the region; herders could move their cattle to areas where pasture was more abundant to accommodate localised water deficits. This was a way of life that brought resilience to droughts. With recent land use change policies and conflict, severe barriers to pastoralists' freedom of movement make them more vulnerable to droughts. Surveys found 96 and 87% of respondents felt the negative effects of droughts on crops and livestock, respectively, and that extreme droughts tend to have cascading effects. First, the water deficits affect seedling growth and crop yields, which then affects the availability of food for people and feed for livestock (Traore and Owiyo 2013).

At the geographic center of this large dryland region, for centuries Lake Chad—centred in Western Chad and straddling the Niger, Nigeria and Cameroon borders—was home to abundant fisheries and livestock herds. Temperature increase, rainfall unpredictability, and land use changes have negatively affected the Lake Chad basin. Once among Africa's largest lakes, the lake has shrunk from 25,000 sq. km in 1963 to around 1,000 sq. km (Fig. 9.5) (UNEP 2008).

A ridge that emerged during the drought in the 1970s and 1980s now divides Lake Chad in two. Despite the recovery of rainfall in the 1990s, the lake never fully recovered because irrigation withdrawals increased from the primary tributaries to the south, where rainfall is higher (Gao et al. 2011). The lake once supported a vital traditional culture of fishing and herding. As the lake receded, farmers and pastoralists shifted to the greener areas, where they compete for land resources with host communities (Salkida 2012). This has been compounded by violent conflict associated with the Boko Haram insurgency, which has spilled across the border from Nigeria (Taub 2017). Others have migrated to Kano, Abuja, Lagos, and other big cities. The decline of Lake Chad illustrates how changing climate patterns interacting with other anthropogenic modifications, conflict and poor governance result in losses and damages to ecosystems and societies.

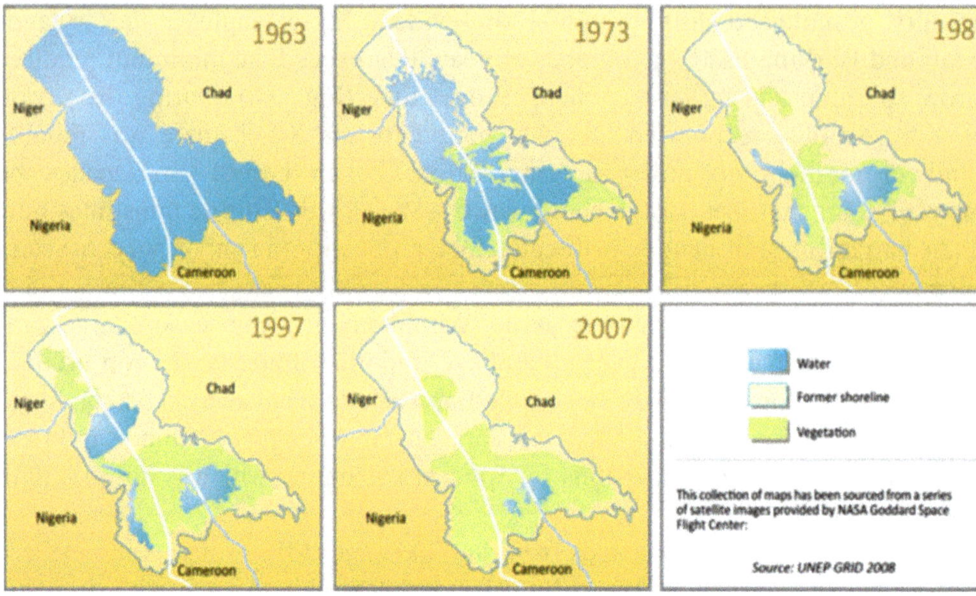

Fig. 9.5 The drying of Lake Chad. *Source* UNEP (2016)

In other parts of the Sahel, rainfall recovery in recent decades has brought flooding because the rainfall arrives in more intense cloudbursts rather than in a more evenly distributed manner (Giannini et al. 2013). In 2007, for example, rainfall extremes and consequent flooding in Senegal's peanut basin led to loss of property and crop loss because farmers often cultivate in and around natural depressions (Fig. 9.6).

Research in eastern Senegal on household perceptions of flood and drought indicate that climate variability brings crop, livestock and other economic losses (Miller et al. 2014). Over the decade preceding the survey, on average households reported experiencing 2.5–3 years of drought and 0.2–0.5 years with flooding, with higher incidence in the north than the south. It is unclear how climate change might influence the Sahel in future, with some climate change projections suggesting there might be a shift to wetter conditions while other projections suggest that conditions will become much drier (Druyan 2011). Despite the uncertainty about the potential influence of human-induced climate change in the region, there is ample evidence to demonstrate the vulnerability to climate shocks, as well as potential shifts in climate.

Adaptation measures implemented in the Sahel include crop-livestock integration, soil fertility management, planting of drought-resistant crops, water harvesting, dug ponds for watering animals, livelihood diversification, and seasonal or permanent migration. A number of these methods have been practiced for generations and are the norm for semi-arid regions. However, in a changing climate such practices will have to be scaled up and new methods developed, as adaption has not been sufficient to prevent losses. New methods may include breeding of more drought-resistant crops, or innovations such as index-based insurance. For the latter, payouts to participating farmers and herders are not made on the basis of actual losses but on the basis of changes in rainfall or drought indices, thereby reducing the overhead of

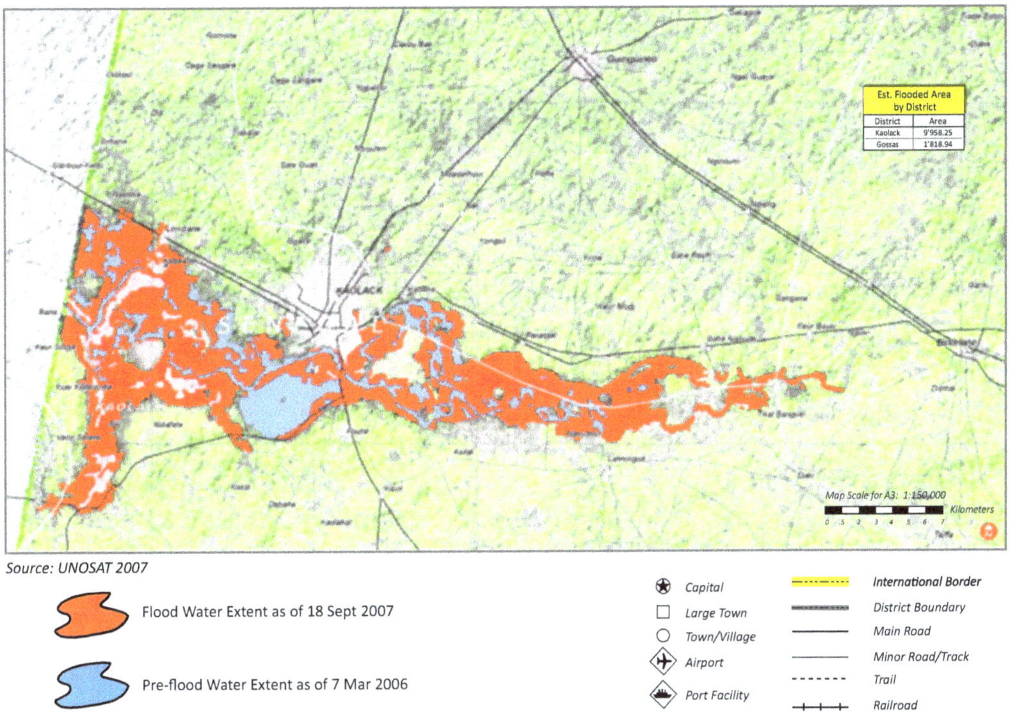

Fig. 9.6 Flooding in the peanut basin south of Kaolack, Senegal (September 2007). *Source* UNEP (2016)

claims inspections (chapter by Schafer et al. 2018). This has been tested successfully in Senegal, Ethiopia, and Northern Kenya (Greatrex et al. 2015).

In the future, temperature changes may create genuine hard limits to adaptation, for example, where temperature increases are beyond the limit of crops during critical points in their life cycle (Ericksen et al. 2011). According to the IPCC, in Africa

Climate change combined with other external changes (environmental, social, political, technological) may overwhelm the ability of people to cope and adapt, especially if the root causes of poverty and vulnerability are not addressed (Niang et al. 2014).

This may lead to migration as an adaptive response (Mortimore 2010; World Bank 2018), as it has in the past (de Sherbinin et al. 2012; UNEP 2011).

9.5 Conclusions

This chapter tried to enhance understanding of how and when climate change threats to ecosystems and the services they provide result in losses and damages to people and society. In doing so it addressed serious gaps in the emerging research and debate on Loss and Damage from climate change. The first generation of empirical work on losses and damages has focused primarily on human systems and tended to overlook the mediating role of ecosystems and the services ecosystems provide to society. The chapter introduced a conceptual framework for studying the complex relations between climatic stressors, impacts on ecosystems, ecosystem services, adaptation opportunities, limits and constraints and residual losses and damages. A case study from West Africa illustrated how this works out in a real-world setting.

The case study showed that causal links between climate change and a specific event, with subsequent losses and damages, are often complicated. Oversimplification must be avoided and the role of different factors, such as governance or management of natural resources, should be explored further. For example, lack of investment in water related infrastructure, agricultural technology, or health care services also increase the risk of losses and damages. In the Sahel, variability in rainfall patterns influences primary productivity, but barriers to pastoralists' freedom of movement have also increased their vulnerability to droughts.

The case also shows that while some adaptation measures have been implemented, losses and damages have nevertheless occurred. For instance, adaptation measures in Dryland West Africa include crop-livestock integration, soil fertility management, planting of drought-resistant crops, water harvesting, dug ponds for watering animals, livelihood diversification, and seasonal or permanent migration. A number of these methods have been practiced for generations. However, as climate change intensifies, promising practices will have to be scaled up and new methods will have to be devised. A win-win solution will be to invest in ambitious mitigation action to avoid the unmanageable, and comprehensive and holistic adaptation action to manage the unavoidable–including better management of ecosystems and their services, improved governance, and economic policies that support sustainable development.

Ultimately, a range of approaches is needed to address climate change impacts and to ensure that resilience building efforts and sustainable development can continue. This includes policy options to avert losses and damages, and to address losses and damages that have not been or cannot be averted through enhanced mitigation and adaptation. These options include risk transfer, which can be used to both avoid and address losses and damages; risk retention, such as social protection policies; migration, recovery, rehabilitation and rebuilding in the wake of extreme events; and tools to address non-economic losses and damages. Approaches to avert and limit losses and damages as well as to address the residual impacts of climate change will be more successful if they incorporate inclusive decision-making, account for the needs of a wide range of actors, and target the poor and vulnerable.

As Loss and Damage is a new and emerging topic in science and policy, there are more unanswered questions than answers at present. We identify two important areas for future research and evidence gathering. First, there is a need to increase understanding of how losses and damages to human well-being is mediated through losses and damages to ecosystem services and of the specific policy entry points. This includes more study of the adverse impacts of climate change, including climate extremes, on ecosystem functioning. Examples may include the effects of extreme heat and drought on forest ecosystems, the consequences of sea level rise and storm surge for coastal ecosystems ranging from sea grasses and marshes to mangroves, and the implications of glacier loss on downstream hydrology and riparian ecosystem functions.

Second, it is important to document and evaluate the effectiveness of efforts to avert losses and damages and identify how the efficacy of tools and measures can be improved, including how non-economic losses and damages associated with the loss of ecosystem services can be better addressed. This includes gathering evidence on the potential for, and the limits to, ecosystem-based adaptation in a number of areas. Examples may include the ability of intact mangrove ecosystems to limit coastal erosion from sea level rise and storm surge, the potential for wetlands to reduce flood damage by absorbing runoff from heavy rainfall and releasing water gradually, or the potential and the limits for greening urban areas to reduce heat stress and consequent remediation of health risks. In such evaluations of adaptation and risk management efforts, it is of paramount importance to include the views of beneficiaries, particularly when the intended project beneficiaries are vulnerable people with limited political capital (see also Pouw et al. 2017).

Acknowledgements The authors would like to acknowledge the contributions of Tricia Chai-Onn, Alphonse Pinto, and Sylwia Trzaska at CIESIN, and Alessandra Giannini at the International Research Institute for Climate and Society (IRI), Columbia University. The Division of Early Warning and Assessment (DEWA), sub-program SP-7, of the United Nations Environment Programme (UNEP) generously provided the funding for the report (UNEP 2016) on which this chapter is based. The report benefited from inputs and reviews by Ryan Alaniz, Stephanie Andrei, Barney Dickson, Adrian Fenton, Ebinezer Florano, Kashmala Kakakhel, Andrew Kruczkiewicz, Peter McDonald, Catherine McMullen, Sebastian d'Oleire-Oltmanns, Janak Pathak, Marco Poetsch, Hannah Reid, Alexandra Rüth, Pinya Sarasas, Olivia Serdeczny, Sylwia Trzaska, Koko Warner and David Wrathall.

References

Agard J, Schipper L, Birkmann J, Campos M, Dubeux C, Nojiri Y, Olsson L, Osman-Elasha B, Pelling M, Prather M, Rivera-Ferre M, Ruppel OC, Sallenger A, Smith K, St. Clair A (2014) WGII AR5 glossary. In: Field et al (eds) Climate change 2014: impacts, adaptation, and vulnerability. Part A: global and sectoral aspects. Contribution of working group II to the fifth assessment report of the intergovernmental panel on climate change. Cambridge University Press, Cambridge and New York

Ayeb-Karlsson S, van der Geest K, Ahmed I, Huq S, Warner K (2016) A people-centred perspective on climate change, environmental stress, and livelihood resilience in Bangladesh. Sustain Sci 11(4):679–694

Bangash RF, Passuello A, Sanchez-Canales M, Terrado M, López A, Elorza FJ, Ziv G, Acuna V, Schuhmacher M (2013) Ecosystem services in Mediterranean river basin: climate change impact on water provisioning and erosion control. Sci Total Environ 458:246–255

Bouwer LM (2018) Observed and projected impacts from extreme weather events: implications for loss and damage. In: Mechler R, Bouwer L, Schinko T, Surminski S, Linnerooth-Bayer J (eds) Loss and damage from climate change. Concepts, methods and policy options. Springer, Cham, pp 63–82

Cook KH, Vizy EK (2015) Detection and analysis of an amplified warming of the Sahara Desert. J Clim 28(16):6560–6580

Conway D, Persechino A, Ardoin-Bardin S (2009) Rainfall and water resources variability in Sub-Saharan Africa during the twentieth century. J Hydrometeorol 10(1):41–59. https://doi.org/10.1175/2008JHM1004.1

Costanza R, de Groot R, Sutton P, van der Ploeg S, Anderson SJ, Kubiszewski I, Farber S, Turner RK (2014) Changes in the global value of ecosystem services. Glob Environ Change 26:152–158 de Sherbinin A, Levy M, Adamo SB, MacManus K, Yetman G, Mara V, Razafindrazay L, Goodrich B, Srebotnjak T, Aichele C, Pistolesi L (2012) Migration and risk: net migration in marginal ecosystems and hazardous areas. Environ Res Lett 7:045602. https://doi.org/10.1088/1748-9326/7/4/045602

Díaz S, Fargione J, Chapin FS, Tilman D (2006) Biodiversity loss threatens human well-being. PLoS Biol 4(8):1300–1305

Dow K, Berkhout F, Preston B, Klein RJT, Midley G, Shaw R (2013) Limits to adaptation. Nat Clim Change 3:305–307

Druyan LM (2011) Studies of 21st-century precipitation trends over West Africa. Int J Climatol 31(10):1415–1424. https://doi.org/10.1002/joc.2180

Ericksen P, Thornton P, Notenbaert A, Cramer L, Jones P, Herrero M (2011) Mapping hotspots of climate change and food insecurity in the global tropics. CCAFS Report no. 5. CGIAR Research Program on Climate Change, Agriculture and Food Security (CCAFS). Copenhagen, Denmark

Engelbrecht F, Adegoke J, Bopape M-J, Naidoo M, Garland R, Thatcher M, McGregor J, Katzfey J, Werner M, Ichoku C, Gatebe C (2015) Projections of rapidly rising surface temperatures over Africa under low mitigation. Environ Res Lett 10(8):085004. https://doi.org/10.1088/1748-9326/10/8/085004

Ewert F, Rötter RP, Bindi M, Webber H, Trnka M, Kersebaum KC, Olesen JE, van Ittersum MK, Janssen S, Rivington M, Semenov MA (2015) Crop modelling for integrated assessment of risk to food production from climate change. Environ Model Softw 72:287–303

Gall M (2015) The suitability of disaster loss databases to measure loss and damage from climate change. Int J Global Warming 8(2):170–190

Gao H, Bohn TJ, Podest E, McDonald KC, Lettenmaier DP (2011) Environ Res Lett 6(3). Retrieved from: http://iopscience.iop.org/article/10.1088/1748-9326/6/3/034021/meta

Giannini A, Salack S, Lodoun T, Ali A, Gaye AT, Ndiaye O (2013) A unifying view of climate change in the Sahel linking intra-seasonal, interannual and longer time scales. Environ Res Lett 8(2):024010

Greatrex H, Hansen JW, Garvin S, Diro R, Blakeley S, Le Guen M, Rao KN, Osgood DE (2015) Scaling up index insurance for smallholder farmers: recent evidence and insights. CCAFS Report No. 14 Copenhagen: CGIAR Research Program on Climate Change, Agriculture and Food Security (CCAFS). www.ccafs.cgiar.org

Held IM, Delworth TL, Lu J, Findell KU, Knutson TR (2005) Simulation of Sahel drought in the 20th and 21st centuries. Proc Natl Acad Sci USA 102(50):17891–17896

IPCC (2012) Summary for policymakers. Managing the risks of extreme events and disasters to advance climate change adaptation. In: Barros V et al (eds) A special report of working groups I and II of the intergovernmental panel on climate change. Cambridge University Press, Cambridge

IPCC (2014) Climate change 2014: synthesis report. In: Core Writing Team, Pachauri RK, Meyer LA (eds) Contribution of working groups I, II and III to the fifth assessment report of the intergovernmental panel on climate change. IPCC, Geneva, Switzerland, 151 pp

IPCC (2014) Climate change 2014: impacts, adaptation, and vulnerability. Part A: global and sectoral aspects. In: Field CB et al (eds) Contribution of working group II to the fifth assessment report of the intergovernmental panel on climate change, vol 1. Cambridge, United Kingdom and New York, NY, USA: Cambridge University Press

Klein RJT, Midgley GF, Preston BL, Alam, M, Berkhout, FGH, Dow K, Shaw MR (2014) 2014: Adaptation opportunities, constraints, and limits. In: Climate change 2014: impacts, adaptation, and vulnerability. Part A: global and sectoral aspects. In: Field C et al (eds) Contribution of working group II to the fifth assessment report of the intergovernmental panel on climate change. Cambridge University Press, Cambridge, United Kingdom and New York, NY, USA, pp 899–943

Lorencová E, Frélichová J, Nelson E, Vačkář D (2013) Past and future impacts of land use and climate change on agricultural ecosystem services in the Czech Republic. Land Use Policy 33:183–194

MEA (Millennium Ecosystem Assessment) (2005) Ecosystems and human well-being: current state and trends. Island Press, Washington DC

Mechler R, Schinko T (2016) Identifying the policy space for climate loss and damage. Science 354(6310):290–292

Mechler R et al (2018) Introduction. Science for loss and damage. Findings and propositions. In: Mechler R, Bouwer L, Schinko T, Surminski S, Linnerooth-Bayer J (eds) Loss and damage from climate change. Concepts, methods and policy options. Springer, Cham, pp 3–37

Miller D, Wasson M, Trzaska S (2014) Senegal climate change vulnerability assessment and options analysis. Report of the African and Latin American resilience to climate change project. Washington DC: USAID

Morrissey J, Oliver-Smith A (2014) Perspectives on non-economic loss and damage: understanding value at risk from climate change. Germanwatch, Bonn

Mortimore M (2010) Adapting to drought in the Sahel: lessons for climate change. Wiley Interdisc Rev: Clim Change 1:134–143

Niang I, Ruppel OC, Abdrabo MA, Essel A, Lennard C, Padgham J, Urquhart P (2014) Chapter 22: Africa. IPCC A45, climate change 2014: impacts, adaptation and vulnerability. Cambridge University Press, Cambridge, UK

Opondo D (2013) Erosive coping after the 2011 floods in Kenya. Int J Global Warming 5(4):452–466

Pouw N, Dietz T, Belemvire A, De Groot D, Millar D, Obeng F, Rijneveld W, Van der Geest K, Vlaminck Z, Zaal F (2017) Participatory assessment of development; lessons learned from an experimental approach in Ghana and Burkina Faso. Am J Eval 38(1):47–59

Preston BL, Dow K, Berkhout F (2013) The climate adaptation frontier. Sustainability 5:1011–1035

ReliefWeb (2015) Sahel crisis: 2011–2015. http://reliefweb.int/disaster/ot-2011-000205-ner

Salkida A (2012) Africa's vanishing Lake Chad. Africa Renewal, April 2012, p 24. http://www.un.org/africarenewal/magazine/april-2012/africa%E2%80%99svanishing-lake-chad. Accessed 21 Nov 2015

Schäfer L, Warner K, Kreft S (2018) Exploring and managing adaptation frontiers with climate risk insurance. In: Mechler R, Bouwer L, Schinko T, Surminski S, Linnerooth-Bayer J (eds) Loss and damage from climate change. Concepts, methods and policy options. Springer, Cham, pp 317–341

Schinko T, Mechler R, Hochrainer-Stigler S (2018) The risk and policy space for loss and damage: integrating notions of distributive and compensatory justice with comprehensive climate risk management. In: Mechler R, Bouwer L, Schinko T, Surminski S, Linnerooth-Bayer J (eds) Loss and damage from climate change. Concepts, methods and policy options. Springer, Cham, pp 83–110

Serdeczny O (2018) Non-economic loss and damage and the Warsaw international mechanism. In: Mechler R, Bouwer L, Schinko T, Surminski S, Linnerooth-Bayer J (eds) Loss and damage from climate change. Concepts, methods and policy options. Springer, Cham, pp 205–220

Staudinger M, Grimm NB, Staudt A, Carter SL, Stuart III FS, Kareiva P, Stein BA (2012) Impacts of climate change on biodiversity, ecosystems, and ecosystem services: technical input to the 2013 National Climate Assessment (pp i–A). United States Global Change Research Program

Taub B (2017) Lake Chad: the world's most complex Humanitarian disaster. The New Yorker, December 4, 2017

Turco M, Palazzi E, von Hardenberg J, Provenzale A (2015) Observed climate change hotspots, geophysical research letters, 42. U.S. Census, Quick Facts, State of California. http://www.census.gov/quickfacts/table/PST045214/12,06,48,00

Traore S, Owiyo T (2013) Dirty droughts causing loss and damage in Northern Burkina Faso. Int J Global Warming 5(4):498–513

UNEP (2008) Lake Chad: almost gone. An Overview of the State of the World's Fresh and Marine Waters - 2nd Edition - 2008. http://www.unep.org/dewa/vitalwater/article116.html

UNEP (2011) Livelihood security: climate change, migration and conflict. UNEP, Nairobi

UNEP (2016) Loss and damage: the role of ecosystem services. United Nations Environment Programme, Nairobi, Kenya

UNFCCC (2012) A literature review on the topics in the context of thematic area 2 of the work programme on loss and damage: a range of approaches to address loss and damage associated with the adverse effects of climate change FCCC/SBI/2012/INF.14

UNFCCC (2013) Report of the conference of the parties on its eighteenth session, held in Doha from 26 November to 8 December 2012. FCCC/CP/2012/8. Add.1

Van der Geest K, Dietz T (2004) A literature survey about risk and vulnerability in drylands, with a focus on the Sahel. In: Dietz T, Rueben R, Verhagen J (eds) The impact of climate change on drylands. Kluwer, Cham, pp 117–146

Van der Geest K, Warner K (2015) What the IPCC fifth assessment report has to say about loss and damage. UNU-EHS Working Paper 21. Bonn: United Nations University Institute for Environment and Human Security

Verheyen R (2012) Tackling loss and damage. Germanwatch, Bonn

Warner K, van der Geest K (2013) Loss and damage from climate change: local-level evidence from nine vulnerable countries. Int J Global Warming 5(4):1–20

Warner K, van der Geest K, Kreft S (2013) Pushed to the limits: evidence of climate change-related loss and damage when people face constraints and limits to adaptation. Report No.11. Bonn, United Nations University Institute for Environment and Human Security (UNU-EHS)

World Bank (2014) Turn down the heat: confronting the new climate normal. World Bank, Washington, DC

World Bank (2018) Groundswell: preparing the way for internal climate migration Washington. World Bank, DC

Wrathall DJ, Oliver-Smith A, Fekete A, Gencer E, Reyes ML, Sakdapolrak P (2015) Problematising loss and damage. Int J Global Warming 8(2):274–294

WWAP (United Nations World Water Assessment Programme) (2015) The united nations world water development report 2015: water for a sustainable world. UNESCO, Paris

Zaal F, Dietz, T, Brons J, van der Geest K, Ofori Sarpong E (2004) Sahelian livelihoods on the rebound: a critical analysis of rainfall, drought index and yields in Sahelian agriculture. In: Dietz T, Rueben R, Verhagen J (eds) The impact of climate change on drylands. Kluwer, Cham, pp 61–78

Zommers Z, Wrathall D, van der Geest K (2014) Loss and damage to ecosystem services UNU-EHS Working Paper Series, No. 12. Bonn, United Nations Institute for Environment and Human Security

Chapter 10
Displacement and Resettlement: Understanding the Role of Climate Change in Contemporary Migration

Alison Heslin, Natalie Delia Deckard, Robert Oakes and Arianna Montero-Colbert

Abstract How do we understand displacement and resettlement in the context of climate change? This chapter outlines challenges and debates in the literature connecting climate change to the growing global flow of people. We begin with an outline of the literature on environmental migration, specifically the definitions, measurements, and forms of environmental migration. The discussion then moves to challenges in the reception of migrants, treating the current scholarship on migrant resettlement. We detail a selection of cases in which the environment plays a role in the displacement of a population, including sea level rise in Pacific Island States, cyclonic storms in Bangladesh, and desertification in West Africa, as well as the role of deforestation in South America's Southern Cone as a driver of both climate change and migration. We outline examples of each, highlighting the complex set of losses and damages incurred by populations in each case.

Keywords Migration · Internal displacement · Resettlement · Climate change Natural disasters · Environmental degradation · Loss and Damage · Refugee

10.1 Introduction

How do we understand displacement and resettlement in the era of climate change? Scholars, practitioners, and policy-makers have been grappling with ways to improve life outcomes for large numbers of refugees and migrants. In particular, the 21st conference of the Parties to the United Nations Climate Convention (UNFCCC) in Paris created a taskforce to work out recommendations to "avert, minimize, and address

A. Heslin (✉)
International Institute of Applied Systems Analysis, Laxenburg, Austria
e-mail: heslin@iiasa.ac.at

N. Delia Deckard · A. Montero-Colbert
Davidson College, Davidson, USA

R. Oakes
United Nations University, Bonn, Germany

R. Mechler et al. (eds.), *Loss and Damage from Climate Change*, Climate Risk Management, Policy and Governance, https://doi.org/10.1007/978-3-319-72026-5_10

displacement related to the adverse impacts of climate change" (UNFCCC 2017). In addressing the role of climate change in displacement, one must identify the ways that factors pertaining to environmental change generally drive migration, as this relationship will become all the more important and complex with climate change (IOM 2017b). This chapter addresses the ways that the natural environment relates to the global flow of people (Bettini and Andersson 2014; Bates 2002; Dun and Gemenne 2008). In addressing this relationship between the environment and displacement, we first outline the primary debates within the environmental displacement and migration literature, as well as challenges in the reception of migrants in host communities and nations. Using cases of climate-related displacement, we then highlight the complexity of the social effects of environmental factors and the process of migration.

10.2 Defining and Measuring Migration

The complexity of environmental migration begins with the process of setting concrete, agreed upon definitions, however, defining and subsequently measuring the process of environmental migration is not uniform throughout the literature (Dun and Gemenne 2008).

10.2.1 Definitions

To understand the various means by which one can define environmental migration, we may start by understanding the broader categories used to describe populations outside their habitual place of residence, including migrant, refugee, asylum seeker, and internally displaced person. In general, one may classify a person in these different categories based on the circumstances of their leaving their place of residence and the destination of their movement (outlined in Fig. 10.1). According to the International Organization for Migration, migrant is the most general term, encompassing any person who "has moved across an international border or within a State away from his/her habitual place of residence" (IOM 2018). By this definition, anyone who falls within our matrix outlined in Fig. 10.1 is a migrant, but depending on the circumstances of their movement, more precise labels and terminology can be used to describe them. For instance, if one flees across an international border due to a "well-founded fear of being persecuted for reasons of race, religion, nationality, membership of a particular social group or political opinion," they can be further classified as a refugee or asylum-seeker (UN 1951). In addition, one who is forced to flee their home, but has not crossed an international border is considered an internally displaced person (IDP) (IOM 2017c; UN 1998).

While the IOM definitions of refugees and IDPs are consistent with UN conventions, the definition of migrant used by the IOM differs from that of the UN, which uses a more narrow definition of migrant. According to the UN, a migrant is one

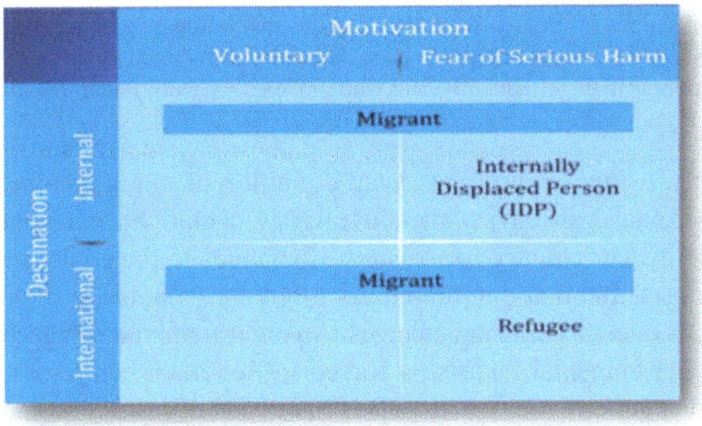

Fig. 10.1 IOM migration-related terminology by motivation and destination. *Source* IOM (2017c)

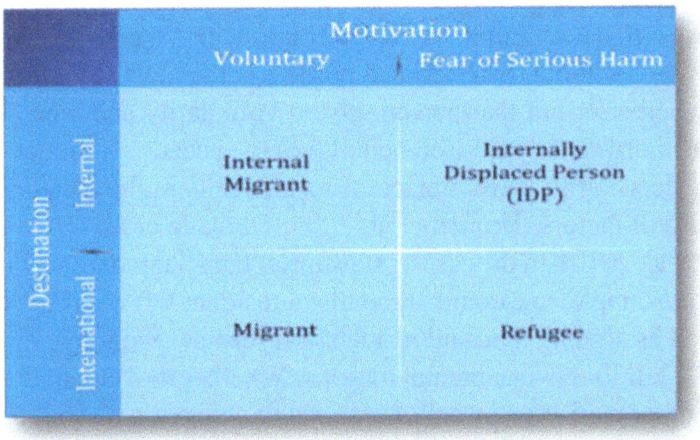

Fig. 10.2 UN migration-related terminology by motivation and destination. *Sources* UN (1951), UN (1990), UN (1998)

residing outside the country of which he/she is a national, not including those categorised as refugees or asylum seekers (UN 1990). By the UN definition, migrant would occupy only the bottom-left quadrant, shown in Fig. 10.2. This UN distinction is useful to differentiate the four categories into four separate, non-overlapping labels—internal migrant, internally displaced person, migrant, and refugee/asylum seeker—to be determined by two questions: Was the movement domestic or international? and was the movement voluntary or forced?

At its most simple, moving from migration broadly to environmental migration specifically entails maintaining the same categories, but restricting to cases in which the motivating factor for movement was environmentally-related, including those caused by climate change. The IOM does just this, maintaining the encompassing definition for migration, defining an environmental migrant as a person who

> for reasons of sudden or progressive changes in the environment that adversely affect their lives or living conditions, are obliged to have to leave their habitual homes, or choose to do so, either temporarily or permanently, and who move either within their territory or abroad (IOM 2017c).

Alternatively, using the more restricted definition of migrant from the UN (voluntary, international), an environmental migrant would be one who voluntarily resides outside his/her country for reasons of changes to the environment, sudden- or gradually-onset. Internal environmental migrants voluntarily relocate domestically for reasons of environmental changes. An environmental refugee would be one who, due to environmental factors, is forced to flee home and cross international borders, whereas an environmental IDP is also forced to leave home but remains within the state of which he/she is a national. While these terms may seem well defined, the process of identifying populations that fall into each category is rife with complications, leading to scientific and policy debates on the specific criteria of the definitions. In determining the category into which a person falls, locating the person as within or without their national borders is the most straightforward, while determining whether or not that person moved voluntarily and whether or not that movement was motivated by environmental factors, is cause for much debate in the literature. The decision to leave a place of residence is multifaceted, comprised of both push and pull factors (Bronen et al. 2009; Obokata et al. 2014; Renaud et al. 2007; Warner et al. 2010). In the case of slow onset land degradation, with decreasing crop yields, for example, one could argue that a resident left willingly or was forced to leave, as well as arguing that said resident left for new economic opportunities in a nearby city or left for environmental reasons. Whether movement is forced or voluntary and whether motivated by environmental or economic reasons encompasses a primary debate in the scientific literature on environmental migration (Bates 2002).

Additionally, because these definitions constitute legal classifications, identifying which category a population falls into can carry with it particular sets of entitlements or binding policy responses. For example, the UN High Commission on Refugees provides aid and resources to refugees according to their definition of refugees (Gill 2010). Accordingly, environmentally displaced populations may not be eligible for aid as refugees as they lack a "well founded fear of being persecuted" as outlined in the UN Convention Relating to the Status of Refugees. Without the inclusion of natural disasters or climate-related environmental degradation as forms of persecution, those displaced from these causes do not constitute refugees per this definition (Bronen et al. 2009; Warner et al. 2010). Despite this understanding from the UN, many studies have used the term environmental refugees to describe those displaced by environmental factors (Bates 2002; Myers 2002).

10.2.2 Measurement

A particular scientific implication of the definitional issues relating to environmental migration is the capacity to measure and predict flows of environmental migrants (per IOM definition). Data and empirical studies on environmental migration differ based

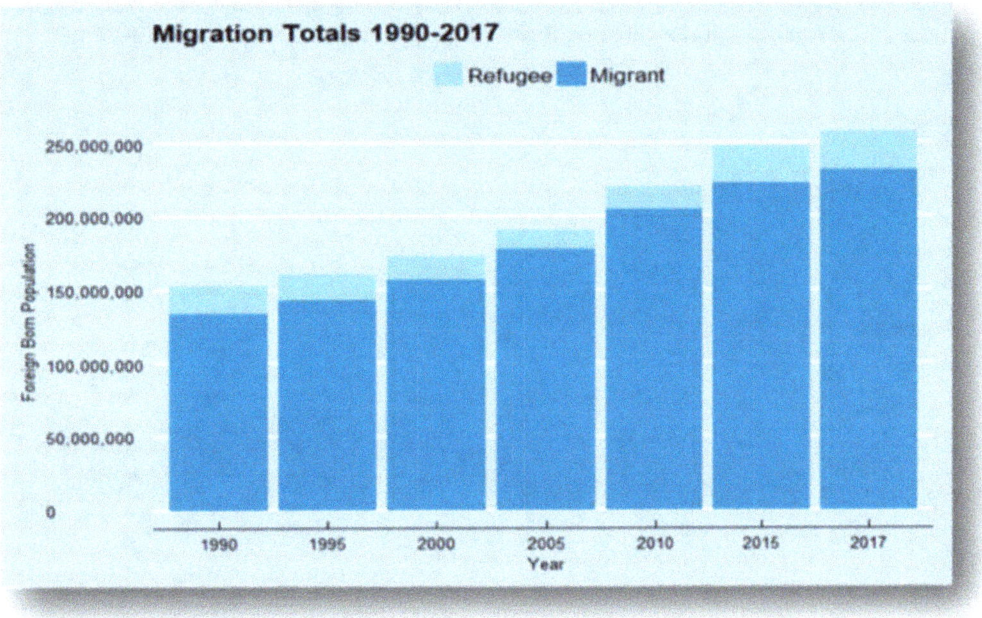

Fig. 10.3 Migration totals, measured as total foreign-born population. *Data Source* United Nations Population Division (2017)

on the criteria used to identify population movements as voluntary versus forced and environmentally or otherwise motivated.

Looking at international migration generally, data indicate increasing volumes of migration, but differ depending on the means of measurement. The United Nations, measuring migration as the total foreign-born population throughout the world, identifies the number of foreign-born residents of countries to be over 250 million in 2017, with over 25 million of those categorised as refugees and asylum-seekers (United Nations Population Division 2017). Figure 10.3 presents the United Nations data measuring the number of people living outside their country of birth, showing significant increases over the past 25 years.

While for foreign-born populations, there is readily available data, studies challenge this operationalisation of migration, as it fails to capture when people moved and from where. Abel and Sander (2014), for instance, estimate the volume of migration flows and direction since 1990, finding that while the stock of foreign-born populations globally has increased, there has not been a drastic increase in the flow of migrants in recent years, relative to the global population size or in absolute quantities. These differences in measurement paint very different pictures regarding contemporary global migration, with popular narratives often following UN data, shown in Fig. 10.3, indicating massive increases in migrants.

The process of measurement and analysis is further complicated when attempting to determine the cause of the movement.

Determining the proportion of international migrants who relocate due to environmental changes faces the same challenges as estimating migrant flows, with the

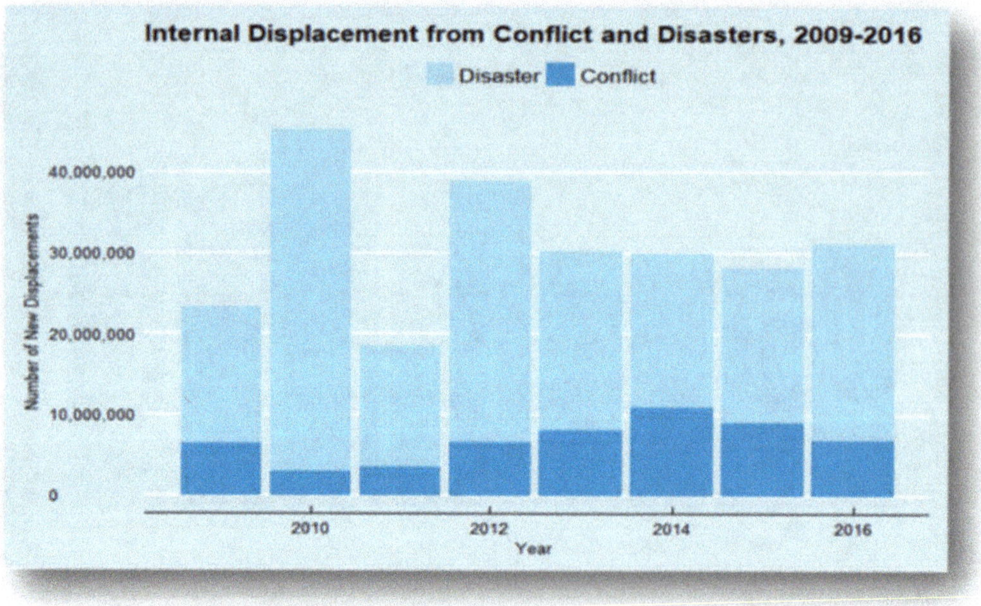

Fig. 10.4 New internal displacements per year from conflict and natural disasters. *Data Source* Internal Displacement Monitoring Centre 2016

additional challenges of parsing environmental motivators from economic, social, and political factors, which influence migration decisions in tandem (Black et al. 2011). Due to this complexity, as well as uncertainty in predicting future adaptive capacity, predictions of future movements of people from climate change and environmental causes vary from 25 million to 1 billion in 2050 (IOM 2017b).

In addition to international movement, populations move internally in massive numbers in the face of environmental factors, including those affected by climate change, such as natural disasters, environmental degradation, droughts, and floods. The Internal Displacement Monitoring Centre estimates the number of new internal displacements per year at values far above those estimates of international migration flows calculated by Abel and Sander (2014). As shown in Fig. 10.4, the number of internal displacements in 2016 was over 30 million. Of those displaced in 2016, nearly 25 million were displaced by natural disasters, with large volumes of displacements occurring in Asia, particularly China, India, and Pakistan, illustrated in Fig. 10.5 (IDMC 2017).

The current volume of displacements, internal and international, due to environmental stressors is striking. With climate change increasing extreme weather events as well as long-term climate variability, the IPCC finds evidence that current migration is partly driven by climate change and projects an increased displacement of people over the 21st century, yet assigns *low confidence* to quantitative projections (IPCC 2014).

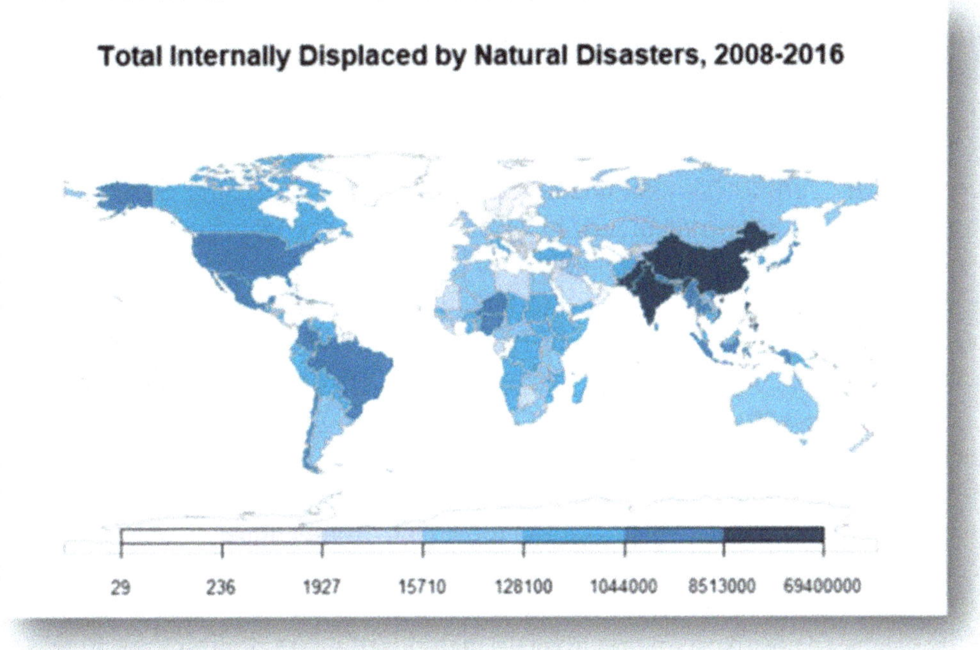

Fig. 10.5 Total number of new internally displaced by natural disasters 2008–2016. *Data Source* Internal Displacement Monitoring Centre 2016

10.3 Understanding Resettlement

Whether internal or international, the effects of displacement continue much beyond the moment of departure, and as such we briefly address the literature on the process of resettlement. This section provides an overview of the spaces and challenges faced by the displaced in the process of resettling, including those for the voluntary migrant as well as the refugee.

The figure of the voluntary migrant is often cast as one motivated by rational choices and systematic decisions. While conversations regarding refugees are framed largely through questions of the right to asylum and the politics of conflict, the migration question is consumed by questions regarding their capacity to contribute to the health and success of the local economy without detracting from local employment or host community culture (Deckard and Heslin 2016). The framing of migration in terms of economic contribution categorises the desirability and, subsequently, legality of migrants in a space (Golash-Boza 2015). Thus, anticipating the ways in which environmental migrants are received by a host country is a matter of understanding the economic desirability of that specific group in the country, which is subject to change with variations in the economic situation of the receiving area or country.

In the United States, for example, immigrants of Hispanic and Latino origin—often crossing the nation's Southern border escaping a difficult-to-disentangle combination of degraded natural resources, corruption, gang violence and economic disarray (Bender and Arrocha 2017)—represent a significant source of migrant labor to the nation and are associated with cheap, unskilled labor in the national discourse (Romero 2006). The inclusion of these migrants is metered by the degree to which they are seen as contributing to the national economy (Deckard and Browne 2015). This reality has become so anchored in the hegemonic common sense that a criminality has been constructed around migrant bodies, which are physically present while economically surplus (Gunkel and González Wahl 2012). To the degree to which migrants are seen as costing money in terms of social benefits or use of public goods, they are viewed as members of an out-group. Conversely, to the extent that they are perceived to work effectively and contribute to the general economic well-being, they are seen as meritorious of inclusion in national communities (Armenta 2017; Golash-Boza and Parker 2007).

The discourse around migrant labor is similar in other wealthy nations—most notably the construction of the African in Western Europe. Similar to the push factors propelling Latino immigrants to the United States, the home country realities of the French sans papiers vary in their combination of environmental degradation, conflict, economic hardship and corruption. Also, similarly undocumented migrants to France exist in the interstices of surplus labor and criminal (Schaap 2011). In sharp contrast to the extensive positive attention given to methods of incorporation for refugees and legal migrants—those who have been given permission to reside in the nation only so long as they perform work explicitly required in order to meet national economic goals—any need to integrate the economically surplus generated by global challenges has, apparently, been addressed with their widespread criminalisation.

In addition to the flows of voluntary migrants internally and internationally, mass events, such as natural disasters, can abruptly displace those living in a space, often en masse. When such large and sudden displacements occur, governments face logistical and political challenges in managing the flow of people internally and across international borders. In this process, the displaced can seek asylum, often settling temporarily in refugee camps, beginning a prolonged, indefinite state of transience.

Understanding the role and structure of the refugee camp is an important component of environmental migration, as refugee camps represent the political response to mass displacement, as possible through large scale natural disasters. Through such events, as well as large scale conflicts, displaced populations can flow into neighbouring countries at rates, which exceed the economic, political, or social capacity or willingness of the receiving country to accommodate. The structure of the camp itself speaks to its roots in political expediency for the host country. Following the established provisions in the 1951 Convention Relating to the Status of Refugees and 1967 Protocol, to maintain credibility globally, countries face international pressure to respond to mass displacement (Black 2001). The refugee camp thus arises out of the juxtaposition of the international pressure to act charitably towards those in need and a state's inclination to keep "space and distance" from the refugees themselves (Hyndman 2000).

In addressing the losses and damages of environmental displacement, one must engage with the realities of the refugee camp. Rather than initiating a process of assimilation, the camp inherently exists as a space of prolonged temporality, which serves to exclude refugees' participation in the economic and social activities of the host country, as well as from political representation and participation (Kibreab 2003; Ramadan 2013). Further, refugee initiatives are often conducted with limited input from the supposed beneficiaries of the aid (Silverman 2008; Hanafi and Long 2010), thereby inhibiting the development of refugee communities into societal structures of the host country and of the global economy at large (Hanafi and Long 2010). In contrast to refugee camps, asylum policies aim to initiate the process of resettlement for displaced persons. An asylum-seeker is one who has applied for refuge outside their own country and is awaiting official refugee status in their new country of residence. The refugee camp dweller is often not distinct from the asylum seeker, as applications for asylum start once an individual has arrived in a refugee camp, but also can begin following arrival to a host country legally by obtaining a work or student visa.

Asylum-seekers, however, face many barriers in the process of resettlement. First, because of bureaucratic process and the sheer number of applicants, central to the experience of the twenty first century asylee is the experience of years of waiting (Rotter 2016). The asylum-seeking process also requires costs associated with travel and paperwork fees, often making resettlement inaccessible to many whose livelihoods depend on it (Settlage 2009). Additionally, due to host citizens' belief that asylum-seekers take more than they give socially, destination countries may be less than welcoming in their public policy affecting accepted asylees in an effort to deter refugees from arriving. A study of the European Union indicates that countries compete in a race to the bottom for provision of services through five areas of asylum policy: 'safe third country' provisions, determination procedures, compulsory dispersal policy, welfare vouchers, and obstacles from employment (Thielemann 2004).

Critically, because the nation-state holds exclusive control over the bodies in its territory, the right of asylum following from international law is generally understood as a right for the state to grant or deny, rather than the right of an individual to claim (Boed 1994). To be granted asylum as a refugee, according to the UN 1951 Refugee Convention, one must have a "well-founded fear of being persecuted for reasons of race, religion, nationality, membership of a particular social group or political opinion" (United National 1951). As outlined above, the construction of climate-induced calamities as "natural" disasters, therefore, influences the perceived legitimacy of resulting claims to refugeehood and asylum (Shacknove 1985). That is, insofar as events such as hurricanes and droughts are interpreted as apolitical tragedies, the presumed contract between citizen and state that grounds refugee policy is never broken, thus lacking a sufficient claim of persecution.

10.4 Case Studies of Environmental Migration

The risks associated with climate change vary greatly between different geographic locations and different social structures (IPCC 2014). Correspondingly, the mechanisms by which climate change can influence the flow of people also vary widely from place to place, with corresponding sets of losses and damages faced by the affected populations at the time of departure as well as in the process of resettlement. In this section, we detail a selection of cases in which the environment plays a role in the displacement of a population, including sea-level rise, cyclonic storms, and desertification, as well as the role of deforestation as a driver of both climate change and migration. We outline examples of each, highlighting the complex set of losses and damages incurred by populations in each case.

10.4.1 Sea-Level Rise in Pacific Island States

The dominant media representation of Pacific Small Island Developing States (SIDS) is of drowning islands, with rising sea levels compelling residents to move (Barnett and Campbell 2010). However, this narrative is simplistic for two reasons. Firstly, while sea-level rise does cause erosion and more frequent, and intense flooding events (Nurse et al. 2014), and floods can damage property, destroy crops, contaminate water supplies and spread disease through penetrating septic tanks (ADB 2014), it is not the only climate hazard driving mobility. Changes in rainfall can combine with lack of aquifers to produce a shortage of water for bathing, drinking, cooking and agriculture (IPCC 2014) and the increase in CO_2 in the atmosphere is contributing to ocean acidification, impacting on fisheries (Manzello et al. 2017). Secondly, islanders are not automatons which respond to climate change in fixed way by moving away from the sea. Instead, they have a degree of individual and collective agency to respond, and adapt to climate change (Gemenne 2011). It is also true that both climate change risk perceptions and attitudes towards mobility are nuanced and differentiated within Pacific SIDS. Recent qualitative research on Kiribati found three distinct shared viewpoints on the themes. One group seemed to exempt itself from agency in the matter, claiming that God would decide the fate of Kiribati. Another group believed that climate change would likely result in some people leaving their islands, while a final group stressed the existential threats of climate change to islands, populations and culture (Oakes et al. 2016).

Nonetheless, when the impacts of climate change interact with the physical geography and developmental status of the SIDS, human mobility can and does occur and such movements have implications for Loss and Damage, with a general trend of the more agential the movement, the less severe losses and damages. Displacement can occur when an intensive natural hazard such as a storm or flood compels people to leave their place of residence. Forcibly displaced persons have little control over when, where and how they move and as a result are more likely to be subject to losses and damages. In Kiribati, a survey revealed that almost every household (94%) reported that they had been impacted by a natural hazard over the period 2005–2015, with sea-level rise affecting 80% of households (Oakes et al. 2016). The same study found that one in seven of all movements from 2005 to 2015 were attributed to environmental change (14%), and the vast majority of such movements were internal (Fig. 10.6). This is despite the fact that international movement is often

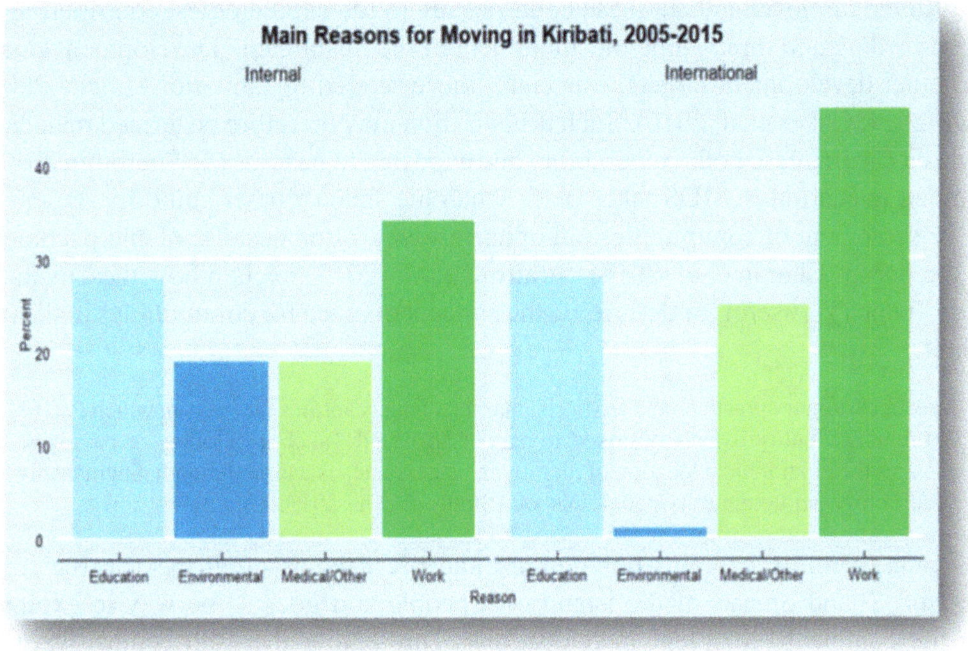

Fig. 10.6 The main reasons for moving in Kiribati 2005–2015. *Source* Oakes et al. (2016)

seen as desirable, suggesting a lack of choice in destination for people impacted by a climate-impacted environment.

Losses and damages suffered in the context of such climate change related displacement can be in the form of health, access to services and education, protection and culture (Unicef UK 2017). In Pacific SIDS, king tides cause frequent floods and are intensified by sea level rise and La Niña years (Lin et al. 2014). There can be very short intervals between king tides (Lin et al. 2014) meaning that households have little time to recover and can be locked into a vicious cycle of recovery. Vulnerable groups are particularly at risk. Climate change related environmental degradation has meant that children in Pacific SIDS have been forced to move to islands with more resilient infrastructure for schooling. Often this involves staying with extended families, which can place them at risk of all forms of abuse (PRRRT 2014).

Voluntary migration typically makes place as people seek more secure livelihoods less impacted by environmental hazards such as changes in rainfall, agricultural yields and fisheries. In such instances, losses and damages can be less severe. The I-Kiribati idea of "migration with dignity" has not been defined in a policy document, but revolves around facilitating voluntary migration through improving education and developing international networks (Voigt-Graf and Kagan 2017). In this manner, it is hoped that people can migrate, generating remittances to enable adaptation (IOM 2017a) improve their livelihoods (Gemenne and Blocher 2017) and in so doing reduce future losses and damages inducing displacement. However, in both Kiribati (Oakes et al. 2016) and Tuvalu (Milan et al. 2016) international migration is limited by finances and permits. In the absence of options to move internationally, the majority of internal movements in these countries are to the capital cities, contributing to overcrowding and threatening the attainment of the Sustainable Development Goals and other development targets, especially those related to sanitation (Locke 2009; ADB 2014; Oakes et al. 2016). Such urbanisation may therefore be termed maladaptive as it can increase both vulnerability and exposure to hazards (de Sherbinin 2013). Planned relocation in SIDS takes place when the state or other authority organises the re-settlement of communities out of harm's way, often because of encroachment by the ocean (Charan et al. 2017). Stratford et al. (2013) explain how the Tuvaluan word "Fenua" is useful for describing the concept of place for communities in Pacific SIDS:

> A set of customary practices and territorial markers, fenua captures the ways in which Pacific community identity is usually linked to part of an island—such as a valley or bay—and explains the biographical location of identity in place. Fenua is a term that indistinguishably bundles together community/people/places. (Stratford et al. 2013:69)

Fenua therefore explains how culture and life itself is often inextricable from the land, island or part of the island of a people and goes some way to explaining the complexity inherent in relocations. Throughout the 20th century various relocations took place within the Pacific region, many of which were unsuccessful for not considering livelihoods or cultural differences (Connell 2012) and even possibly contributing to deaths as people were exposed to new environmental risks (Donner 2015). Unsurprisingly, proposed relocations have been rejected by the moving community (Tabucanon and Opeskin 2011). Some people are reticent to move as potential migrants feel that they will lose a link to their past and their very cultural identity (Mortreaux and Barnett 2009). As a result, moving from home can bring feelings of grief and anxiety (Doherty and Clayton 2011) and people may stay in objectively risky areas (Oakes et al. 2016). Some recent relocations have been more successful where processes are participatory and consideration is given to culture and livelihoods (Tabucanon 2012). Guidelines of good practice have been produced to improve the experiences of those who relocate which may contribute to better results for both relocating and host communities (Brookings and UNHCR 2015), thereby minimising losses and damages.

10.4.2 Cyclonic Storms

Cyclonic storms affect tropical and subtropical regions, in the Atlantic, Caribbean and North-East Pacific as hurricanes and in North-West Pacific as typhoons and the South Pacific and Indian Ocean as cyclones. It is impossible to link a particular storm to climate change, and globally with increased temperatures, less storms could form due to changes in wind shear (Vecchi and Soden 2007). Nonetheless climate change will likely result in higher risk from cyclones through increased average sea temperatures causing more intense and wetter storms and sea-level rise magnifying the impact of storm surges—the main killer in cyclones (IPCC 2012). These climatic changes are occurring at the same time as economic and demographic changes, which result in larger, more vulnerable populations living in more exposed areas (Hugo 2011). As a result, globally millions of people are affected each year, with 12.9 million people displaced by storms in 2016 (IDMC 2017). Whether human mobility related to a cyclone is before or after the event, the losses and damages can be extensive.

Poorer countries are typically more exposed to cyclonic storms due to their locations in tropical regions and more vulnerable to their impacts due to poverty, livelihoods dependent on natural resources and low levels of education and healthcare (Blaikie et al. 2014). Bangladesh is low-lying and deltaic meaning that each year millions of vulnerable people are living in areas exposed to cyclones and floods. As such, according to the World Risk Index, in 2016 Bangladesh was the 5th most at risk country in the world (Garschagen et al. 2016). Although Bangladesh has early warning systems, these do not always grant sufficient time for people to leave in a manner to minimise losses and damages. Moreover, some people may stay to protect their livelihoods (Ayeb-Karlsson et al. 2016). There are also cultural barriers which may contribute to non-evacuation. Some people may be fatalistic about cyclones and conceptualise evacuation as against Allah's will (Haque 1995). Unaccompanied women might not go to the cyclone shelter, as it can be culturally taboo (Paul 2014). In cyclone shelters, and on the journey to them, women and children are at risk of disease through insanitary conditions and may even cause themselves harm through reluctance to go to the toilet in public (Unicef UK 2017).

After repeated displacements Bangladeshis may move either seasonally or permanently (Unicef UK 2017), making Dhaka one of fastest growing city in the world with residents subject to losses and damages. Almost half the population of Dhaka lives in slums where approximately a third have no access to sanitation (World Bank 2015) and are exposed to communicable disease (Banu et al. 2013). Children in Dhaka presented a significantly higher number of disability-adjusted life years (DALYs) than children who had not been displaced (Molla et al. 2014). Seasonal or permanent migration to a city can bring new or increased risks related to working conditions (Ayeb-Karlsson et al. 2016) and children can miss out on school if they are obliged to find work (Unicef UK 2017).

Rich countries are not immune to losses and damages associated with mobility related to cyclonic storms. The USA is frequently impacted by hurricanes, with 875,000 people displaced by Hurricane Matthew in 2016 (IDMC 2017). By mid-October, the 2017 Atlantic hurricane season had produced 15 storms, 10 hurricanes and 5 major hurricanes, while the month of September 2017 was the single most active month for Atlantic storms on record (The Weather Channel 2017). Projections for the North Atlantic show a 45% increase in the number of major hurricanes (category 3 or above) in the period 2016–2035 relative to 1986-2005 and an 11% increase in related rainfall (Knutson et al. 2010). Hurricanes Irene and Sandy in 2011 and 2012 respectively may provide evidence of a shift in the hurricane belt (IPCC 2012), which could have implications for a population lacking the experience and infrastructure to cope with hurricanes (Cutter et al. 2007).

The poorest and ethnic minority communities are typically those which suffer the most severe losses and damages through hurricane displacement. The natural and man-made processes which combined for Hurricane Katrina, meant that some termed the disaster "death by political economy" for the African America residents of Louisiana (Price 2008). Children are also more likely to be affected by hurricane displacement. Children displaced by Hurricane Katrina were five times more likely to suffer from emotional distress (Abramson et al. 2010) and those in a state of prolonged displacement and unable to return to the city were more likely to suffer from post-traumatic stress disorder and depression than those who moved within the city (Hansel et al. 2013). Over a third of children displaced by Hurricane Katrina were a year or more behind in school (Abramson et al. 2010). There were also ramifications on school behaviour, attendance, suspension, expulsion and drop-out rates (Pane et al. 2006; Ward et al. 2008).

In the USA, typically 20–30% of the affected populations fail to respond to evacuation orders and remain in the disaster area during storms (Redlener 2006). This can be attributed to differentiated risk perception, others fail to evacuate prior to the landfall of the hurricane to avoid perceived losses and damages that leaving entails. Reasons for not evacuating include the discomfort for elderly or infirm (Van Willigen et al. 2002) protecting one's home from looters (Riad et al. 1999), previous problems with evacuation traffic (Morss and Hayden 2010), anxiety about being arrested for undocumented workers (Tiefenbacher and Wilson 2012), reluctance to leave pets (Heath et al. 2001) and the need to be able to clean up after the storm as soon as possible (Dash and Morrow 2000).

10.4.3 The Desertification of West Africa and the Ascendance of Boko Haram

Natural disasters—however unnatural—are not the only movers of people across nations and regions. The changing terrain that accompanies widespread climate change also shifts geo-political realities, and with them the landscape of conflict. Here, we consider the ways in which slowly-worsening environmental conditions change people's locations and lives, specifically desertification and deforestation.

Desertification has made previously fertile agricultural land functionally uninhabitable in regions throughout the world (Bettini and Andersson 2014; Owusu 2013; Vieira et al. 2015). Existing research has linked this phenomenon to man-made climate change for nearly 25 years (Hulme and Kelly 1993; Calabrò and Magazù 2016). In the case of the Sahara, it has made already tenuous post-colonial regimes even more vulnerable, as fragile states struggle to maintain basic services while grappling with the arrival of citizens and migrants in transit (Ferris 2012). Traditional ways of life have been rendered obsolete as villages are overtaken by the sand of the Sahel and, in the case of Nigeria, the trend has worked to further impoverish the Northern provinces of the nation (Mantzikos 2010). In the Maiduguri province of Northern Nigeria, school teachers were unable to cultivate land or fish during school breaks. This newly found desperation contributed to their organising of students into the radical Islamist organisation referred to as Boko Haram (Deckard et al. 2015; Walker 2012).

With the rise of Boko Haram has come relentless attacks against Nigerian secular institutions—especially in the North (Mohammed 2014; Agbiboa 2013). Actual deaths since 2009 number approximately 100,000 (Tukur 2017), and churches (Michael Kpughe 2017), schools (Aghedo and Osumah 2012) and public spaces (Maiangwa et al. 2012) have all been targeted. The relentless violence has been met by similar attacks by the Nigerian military—resulting in thousands more civilian casualties. As of 2017, Boko Haram has displaced an estimated two million Northern Nigerians, sending families fleeing throughout Nigeria and into the neighbouring countries of Chad and Cameroon (Tukur 2017). Certainly, the actions of individual Boko Haram and Nigeria military members are to blame for this displacement, but also worth understanding is the way in which slow-moving environmental degradation has contributed to the conflict between the two parties, and subsequent displacement of millions. In the stories of the displaced, there is much discussion of deteriorating conditions and a wish to return to not only the geographical home—but the traditional one (Jacob et al. 2016). Given the realities of climate change, however, this traditional home may be considered a fictive one, as livelihoods are no longer sustainable.

10.4.4 The Deforestation of the Southern Cone and the Urbanisation of the Campesino

In the consideration of climate change as a driver of migration, we can see the ways in which natural disasters and sea-level rise displace populations, as well as consequences of damages to traditional livelihoods in the case of Nigeria. In addition to examples of displacement and conflict relating to climate change, there are development-related phenomena that are causal agents of climate change, while also working to drive migration. In such cases, as people are systematically moved, the land is cleared for further development, spurring both climate change at the local and global level and a continued feedback loop of migration and further development. Here, we treat the specific issue of monoculture-propelled deforestation in South America's Southern Cone—a documented cause of the type of slow-moving climate change that pushes intergenerational movement (Bonan 2008).

Soybean monoculture increasingly defines the landscape of the Southern Cone and the lives of the people in it (Oliveira and Hecht 2016). The link between soy, deforestation and changing climate is well-documented in both the scholarly literature and the collective memory of communities torn apart by soy (Fehlenberg, et al. 2017; Hetherington 2011). As deforestation continues apace, realities for peasant campesinos in Paraguay, Argentina, and Brazil are being upended (Fair 2011).

In response to their wholesale dispossession at the hands of agribusiness and with the collusion of the various national governments, campesinos have been migrating—both to urban areas within their own countries and abroad Parrado and Cerrutti (2003). The Paraguayan case is particularly instructive, given the nation's status as a paradigm of neoliberal governance in its post-dictatorship (Nickson and Lambert 2002; Ezquerro-Cañete 2016). As the state's "hands off" approach to both export-oriented agribusiness and migration has allowed the results of deforestation to affect the nation's social dynamics in a way that is largely uninfluenced by regulation or legislation.

Paraguayan campesinos overwhelmingly relocate to informal settlements in the nation's three largest urban centres (Hetherington 2011; Reed 2015). These slum areas, known as *bañados*, are completely without the presence of the state—with dwellings having no reliable access to power, no mailing addresses and complying with no legal building codes (Reed 2015; Cunningham et al. 2012). Despite the presence of privately built streets of various quality, the communities do not appear on maps. As indicated by the nomenclature, *bañados* are located in flood plains—leaving the residents to evacuate to public parks and street corners on higher ground in times of flood (Hetherington 2011). Although *bañados* have no permanent infrastructure, residences are inhabited multi-generationally, with adults in 2017 living with their children in the most desirably located *bañado* homes constructed by the grandparents as early as the 1930s. Although the families may be understood as displaced, their current homes are permanently in temporary spaces, and their government has no demonstrated intention of changing this reality.

10.5 Conclusions

As climate change continues to put at risk the livelihoods and personal security of populations throughout the world, the movement of people internally and across international borders will continue. Due to the numerous consequences of climate change and the ways climate change interacts with other environmental stressors and existing social structures, the pathways by which changes in climate displace populations differ greatly between places, overlapping in ways specific to a particular locale. In this chapter, we outlined examples of these overlapping climate risks in locations including Pacific Small Island Developing States, West Africa and the Southern Cone, highlighting the complex interactions between the environment, natural resources, extreme weather, and society. With the push of populations away from their homes through sea-level rise, cyclones, desertification, or other environmental change, we draw attention to the ways in which displaced populations are received and the challenges they face in resettlement. This piece is critical for understanding the losses and damages associated with dislocation, as risks to displaced populations do not end once they have left their homeland. Studies of climate-related displacement must address where people move to and how the political economy of the sending and receiving nations affects the capacity of migrants to resettle and succeed in their new country. Additionally, in considering future climate change and its effects on populations, we must also acknowledge that in the face of losses and damages to livelihoods and safety, not all are able to relocate. Studies of climate-induced migration will also need to take into account those left behind and whether they have sufficient resources to address future damages from climate change. In this way, future studies of climate and displacement must include both the process of leaving and resettling, as covered here, as well as an investigation into the standard of living for those who remained.

References

Abel GJ, Sander N (2014) Quantifying global international migration flows. Science 343:1520–1522

Abramson DM, Park YS, Stehling-Ariza T Redlener I (2010) Children as bellwethers of recovery: dysfunctional systems and the effects of parents, households, and neighborhoods on serious emotional disturbance in children after Hurricane Katrina. Disaster Med Public Health Preparedness 4(Suppl 1):S17–27

Agbiboa D (2013) The ongoing campaign of terror in Nigeria: Boko Haram versus the state. Stability: Int J Security Develop 2(3):1–18

Aghedo I, Osumah O (2012) The Boko Haram uprising: how should nigeria respond? Third World Q 33(5):853–869

Armenta A (2017) Racializing crimmigration: structural racism, colorblindness, and the institutional production of immigrant criminality. Sociol Race Ethnic 3(1):82–95

Asian Development Bank (ADB) (2014) Economic costs of inadequate water and sanitation: South Tarawa. Kiribati, Asian Development Bank

Ayeb-Karlsson S, Geest K, Ahmed I, Huq S, Warner K (2016) A people-centred perspective on climate change, environmental stress, and livelihood resilience in Bangladesh. Sustain Sci 11(4):679–694

Banu S, Rahman MT, Uddin MKM, Khatun R, Ahmed T, Rahman MM, Husain MA, van Leth F (2013) Epidemiology of tuberculosis in an urban slum of Dhaka City, Bangladesh. PloS one 8(10):e77721. https://doi.org/10.1371/journal.pone.0077721

Barnett J, Campbell J (2010) Climate change and small island states: power, knowledge, and the South Pacific. Earthscan, London

Bates DC (2002) Environmental refugees? Classifying human migrations caused by environmental change. Popul Environ 23(5):465–477

Bender SW, Arrocha WF (2017) Introduction. In: Bender SW, Arrocha WF (eds) Compassionate migration and regional policy in the Americas. Palgrave Macmillan UK, London, pp 1–15

Bettini G, Andersson E (2014) Sand waves and human tides: exploring environmental myths on desertification and climate-induced migration. J Environ Develop 23(1):160–185

Black R (2001) Fifty years of refugee studies: from theory to policy. Int Migr Rev 35(1):57–78

Black R, Bennett SRG, Thomas SM, Beddington JR (2011) Climate change: migration as adaptation. Nature 478:447–449. https://doi.org/10.1038/478477a

Blaikie P, Cannon T, Davis I, Wisner B (2014) At risk: natural hazards, people's vulnerability and disasters. Routledge, Oxon

Boed R (1994) The state of the right of asylum in international law. Duke J Compar Int Law 5(1):1–34

Bonan GB (2008) Forests and climate change: forcings, feedbacks, and the climate benefits of forests. Science 320(5882):1444–1449

Bronen R, Chandrasekhar D, Conde D, Kavanova K, Caro Morinière L, Schmidt K, Witter R (2009) Stay in place or migrate: a research perspective on understanding adaptation to a changing environment. In: Oliver-Smith A, Shen X (eds) Linking environmental change, migration and social vulnerability, studies of the university: research. Edication—Publication Series of the UNU-ERS, Counsel, pp 12–21

Brookings & UNHCR (2015) Guidance on Planned Relocation. http://www.unhcr.org/uk/protection/environment/562f798d9/planned-relocation-guidance-october-2015.html

Calabrò E, Magazù S (2016) Correlation between increases of the annual global solar radiation and the ground albedo solar radiation due to desertification—a possible factor contributing to climatic change. Climate 4(4):64

Charan D, Kaur M, Singh P (2017) Customary land and climate change induced relocation—a case study of Vunidogoloa Village, Vanua Levu, Fiji. In Climate Change Adaptation in Pacific Countries. Springer International Publishing, pp 19–33

Connell J (2012) Population resettlement in the Pacific: lessons from a hazardous history? Aust Geogr 43(2):127–142

Cunningham R, Simpson C, Keifer M (2012) Hazards faced by informal recyclers in the squatter communities of Asunción, Paraguay. Int J Occup Environ Health 18(3):181–187

Cutter SL, Johnson LA, Finch C, Berry M (2007) The U.S. Hurricane coasts: increasingly vulnerable? Environ: Sci Policy Sustain Develop 49(7):8–21

Dash N, Morrow B (2000) Return delays and evacuation order compliance: the case of Hurricane Georges and the Florida Keys. Global Environ Change Part B: Environ Hazards 2(3):119–128

de Sherbinin A (2013) Climate change hotspots mapping: what have we learned? Clim Change 123(1):23–37

Deckard ND, Barkindo A, Jacobson D (2015) Religiosity and Rebellion in Nigeria: considering Boko Haram in the radical tradition. Stud Conflict Terrorism 37(7):510–528

Deckard ND, Browne I (2015) Constructing citizenship: framing unauthorized immigrants in market terms. Citizsh Stud 19(6–7):664–681

Deckard N, Heslin A (2016) After postnational citizenship: constructing the boundaries of inclusion in neoliberal contexts. Sociol Compass 10(4):294–305

Doherty TJ, Clayton S (2011) The psychological impacts of global climate change. Am Psychol 66(4):265

Donner SD (2015) The legacy of migration in response to climate stress: learning from the Gilbertese resettlement in the Solomon Islands. Nat Res Forum 39(3–4):191–201

Dun O, Gemenne F (2008) Defining environmental migration. Forced Migr Rev 31(October):10–11

Ezquerro-Cañete A (2016) Poisoned, dispossessed and excluded: a critique of the neoliberal soy regime in Paraguay. J Agrarian Change 16(4):702–710

Fair EM (2011) The peasantary with modern capitalism: power, position, and class. The Global Labour University, London

Fehlenberg V, Baumann M, Ignacio N, Piquer-Rodrigueza M, Gavier-Pizarrod G, Kuemmerle T (2017) The role of soybean production as an underlying driver of deforestation in the South American Chaco. Glob Environ Change 45:24–34

Ferris E (2012) Internal displacement in Africa: an overview of trends and opportunities. Brookings-LSE Project on Internal Displacement, New York, pp 1–12

Garschagen M, Hagenlocher M, Comes M, Dubbert M, Sabelfeld R, Lee YJ, Grunewald L, Lanzendörfer M, Mucke P, Neuschäfer O, Pott S (2016) World Risk Report 2016

Gemenne F (2011) Why the numbers don't add up: a review of estimates and predictions of people displaced by environmental changes. Glob Environ Change 21(S1):41–S49

Gemenne F, Blocher J (2017) How can migration serve adaptation to climate change? Challenges to fleshing out a policy ideal. Geogr Journal 183(4):336–347

Gill N (2010) 'environmental refugees': Key debates and the contributions of geographers. Geography Compass 4:861–871

Golash-Boza T (2015) Deported: immigrant policing. NYU Press, Disposable Labor and Global Capitalism

Golash-Boza T, Parker D (2007) Human Rights in a globalizing world: who pays the human cost of migration? J Latino/Latin American Stud 2(4):34–46

Gunkel SE, González Wahl A-M (2012) Unauthorized migrants and the (Il)Logic of "Crime Control": a human rights perspective on us federal and local state immigration policies. Sociol Compass 6(1):26–45

Hanafi S, Long T (2010) Governance, governmentalities, and the state of exception in the Palestinian refugee camps of Lebanon. J Refugee Stud 23(2):135–159

Hansel TC, Osofsky JD, Osofsky HJ, Friedrich P (2013) The effect of long-term relocation on child and adolescent survivors of Hurricane Katrina. J Trauma Stress 26(5):613–620

Haque CE (1995) Climatic hazards warning process in Bangladesh: experience of, and lessons from, the 1991 April cyclone. Environ Manage 19(5):719–734

Heath SE, Kass PH, Beck AM, Glickman LT (2001) Human and pet-related risk factors for household evacuation failure during a natural disaster. Am J Epidemiol 153(7):659–665

Hetherington K (2011) Guerrilla auditors: the politics of transparency in neoliberal Paraguay. Duke University Press, Durham, NC

Hulme M, Kelly M (1993) Exploring the links between desertification and climate change. Environ: Sci Policy Sustain Develop 35(6):4–45

Hugo G (2011) Future demographic change and its interactions with migration and climate change. Glob Environ Change 21(S1):S21–S33

Hyndman J (2000) Managing displacement: refugees and the politics of humanitarianism. University of Minnesota Press, Minneapolis, MN

IDMC (2016) Global Internal Displacement Database. Internal Displacement Monitoring Centre

IDMC (2017) Global Report on Internal Displacement. Internal Displacement Monitoring Centre

IPCC (2012) Managing the risks of extreme events and disasters to advance climate change adaptation: special report of the intergovernmental panel on climate change. Cambridge University Press, Cambridge and New York

IPCC (2014) Climate change 2014: impacts, adaptation, and vulnerability—Part A: global and sectoral aspects. In: Field CB and others (eds) Contribution of working group II to the fifth assessment report of the intergovernmental panel on climate change. Cambridge University Press, Cambridge and New York

IOM (2017a) Making mobility work for adaptation to environmental changes: results from the MECLEP global research. International Organization for Migration, Geneva

IOM (2017b) Migration, climate change and the environment: a complex nexus. International Organization for Migration, Geneva

IOM (2017c) Migration, climate change and the environment: definitional issues. International Organization for Migration, Geneva

IOM (2018) Key migration terms. International Organization for Migration, Geneva

Jacob JU-U, Abia-Bassey M, Nkanga E, Aliyu A (2016) Narratives of displacement: conversations with boko haram displaced persons in Northeast Nigeria. Contemporary French and Francophone Studies 20(2):176–190

Kibreab G (2003) Displacement, host governments' policies, and constraints on the construction of sustainable livelihoods. Int Soc Sci J 55(175):57–67

Knutson TR, McBride JL, Chan J, Emanuel K, Holland G, Landsea C, Held I, Kossin JP, Srivastava AK, Sugi M (2010) Tropical cyclones and climate change. Nat Geosci 3:157–163

Lin CC, Ho CR, Cheng YH (2014) Interpreting and analyzing King Tide in Tuvalu. Nat Hazards Earth Sys Sci 14(2):209–217

Locke JT (2009) Climate change-induced migration in the Pacific region: sudden crisis and long-term developments. Geogr J 175(3):171–180

Maiangwa B, Uzodike UO, Whetho A, Onapajo H (2012) "Baptism by Fire": Boko Haram and the Reign of Terror in Nigeria. Africa Today 59(2):40–57

Mantzikos I (2010) The absence of the state in Northern Nigeria: the case of Boko Haram. Afr Renaissance 7(1):57–62

Manzello DP, Eakin CM, Glynn PW (2017) Effects of global warming and ocean acidification on carbonate budgets of eastern pacific coral reefs. In: Glynn PW, Manzello DP, Enouchs IC (eds) Coral reefs of the eastern tropical Pacific: persistence and loss in a dynamic environment. Springer, Netherlands, pp 517–533

Michael Kpughe L (2017) Christian churches and the Boko Haram insurgency in cameroon: dilemmas and responses. Religions 8(8):143

Milan A, Oakes R, Campbell J (2016) Tuvalu: climate change and migration—relationships between household vulnerability, human mobility and climate change Report No.18. Bonn: United Nations University Institute for Environment and Human Security (UNU-EHS). http://collections.unu.edu/view/UNU:5856

Mohammed K (2014) The message and methods of Boko Haram. In: de Montclos MP (ed) Boko Haram: Islamism, politics, security and the State in Nigeria. African Studies Centre - Institut Français de Recherche en Afrique (IFRA), Leiden, Netherlands, pp 9–32

Molla NA, Mollah KA, Fungladda W, Ramasoota P (2014) Multidisciplinary household environmental factors: influence on DALYs lost in climate refugees community. Environ Develop 9:1–11

Morss RE, Hayden MH (2010) Storm Surge and 'Certain Death': interviews with texas coastal residents following Hurricane Ike. Weather Clim Soc 2:174–189

Mortreux C, Barnett J (2009) Climate change, migration and adaptation in Funafuti, Tuvalu. Global Environ Change 19(1):105–112

Myers N (2002) Environmental refugees: a growing phenomenon of the 21st century. Phil Trans R Soc Lond B 357:609–613

Nickson A, Lambert P (2002) State reform and the 'Privatized State' in Paraguay. Public Admin Develop 22(2):163–174

Nurse LA, McLean RF, Agard J, Briguglio LP, Duvat-Magnan V, Pelesikoti N, Tompkins E, Webb A (2014) Small islands. In: Climate change 2014: impacts, adaptation, and vulnerability. Part B: regional aspects. Contribution of working group II to the fifth assessment report of the Intergovernmental Panel on Climate Change. Barros VR, Field CB, Dokken DJ, Mastrandrea MD, Mach KJ, Bilir TE, Chatterjee M, Ebi KL, Estrada YO, Genova RC, Girma B, Kissel ES, Levy AN, MacCracken S, Mastrandrea PR, White LL (eds.). Cambridge University Press, Cambridge, United Kingdom and New York, NY, USA, pp. 1613–1654

Oakes R, Milan A, Campbell J (2016) Kiribati: climate change and migration—relationships between household vulnerability, human mobility and climate change. Report No. 20. Bonn: United Nations University Institute for Environment and Human Security (UNU-EHS). http://collections.unu.edu/view/UNU:5903

Obokata R, Veronis L, McLeman R (2014) Empirical research on international environmental migration: a systematic review. Popul Environ 36:111–135

Oliveira G, Hecht S (2016) Sacred Groves, Sacrifice Zones and soy production: globalization, intensification and neo-nature in South America. J Peasant Stud 46(2):251–285

Owusu AB (2013) Measuring desertification in continuum: normalized difference vegetation index-based study in the upper east region, Ghana. Civil Environ Res 3(12):157–170

Pacific Regional Rights Resource Team (PRRRT) (2004) Commercial sexual exploitation of children and child sexual abuse in the Republic of Kiribati: a situation analysis. Tarawa, Kiribati: United Nations Children's Fund (UNICEF)

Pane JF, McCaffrey DF, Tharp-Taylor S, Asmus GJ, Stokes BR (2006) Student displacement in Louisiana after the hurricanes of 2005: experiences of public schools and their students. RAND Corporation, Santa Monica, CA

Parrado EA, Cerrutti M (2003) Labor migration between developing countries: the case of Paraguay and Argentina. Int Migrat Rev 37(1):101–132

Paul SK (2014) Determinants of evacuation response to cyclone warning in coastal areas of Bangladesh: a comparative study. Oriental Geographer 55(1–2):57–84

Price GN (2008) Hurricane Katrina: was there a political economy of death? Rev Black Political Econ 35(4):163–180

Ramadan A (2013) Spatialising the refugee camp. Trans Inst Br Geogr 38(1):65–77

Redlener IM (2006) Americans at Risk: why we are not prepared for Megadisasters and what we can do now. Knopf, New York, NY

Reed RK (2015) Environmental destruction, guaraní refugees, and indigenous identity in Urban Paraguay. In: Wood DC (ed) Climate change, culture, and economics: anthropological investigations. Emerald Group Publishing Limited, Bingley, UK, pp 263–292
Renaud F, Bogardi J, Dun O, Warner K (2007) Control, adapt or flee how to face environmental migration? Interdisciplinary Security Connections Publication Series of UNU-EHS 5
Riad JK, Norris FH, Ruback RB (1999) Predicting evacuation in two major disasters: risk perception, social influence, and access to resources. J Appl Soc Psychol 29(5):918–934
Romero M (2006) Racial profiling and immigration law enforcement: rounding up of usual suspects in the Latino community. Critical Sociol 32(2–3):447–473
Rotter R (2016) Waiting in the Asylum determination process: just an empty interlude? Time Soc 25(1):80–101
Schaap A (2011) Enacting the right to have rights: JacquesRanciére's critique of Hannah Arendt. Eur J Polit Theor 10(1):22–45
Settlage RD (2009) Affirmatively denied: the detrimental effects of a reduced grant rate for affirmative asylum seekers. Boston Univ Int Law J 27(61):61–113
Shacknove AE (1985) Who is a refugee? Ethics 95(2):274–284
Silverman SJ (2008) Redrawing the lines of control: political interventions by refugees and the sovereign state system. Dead/Lines: Contemporary Issues in Legal and Politics Theory 1–27
Stratford E, Farbotko C, Lazrus H (2013) Tuvalu, sovereignty and climate change: considering Fenua, the archipelago and emigration. Island Stud J 8(1):67–83
Tabucanon G (2012) The Banaban resettlement: implications for Pacific environmental migration. Pacific Stud 35(3):343–370
Tabucanon G, Opeskin B (2011) The resettlement of Nauruans in Australia: an early case of failed environmental migration. J Pacific History 46(3):337–356
Thielemann ER (2004) Why Asylum policy harmonisation undermines refugee Burden-sharing. Eur J Migr Law 6:47–65
The Weather Channel (2017) September 2017 Was the Most Active Month on Record for Atlantic Hurricanes. https://weather.com/storms/hurricane/news/september-2017-most-active-month-on-record for-atlantic-hurricanes
Tiefenbacher JP, Wilson SN (2012) The barriers impeding precautionary behaviours by undocumented immigrants in emergencies: the hurricane Ike experience in Houston, Texas, USA. Environ Hazards 11(3):194–212
Tukur S (2017) 100,000 Killed, two million displaced by Boko Haram insurgency, Borno Governor Says. Premium Times, 13 February
Unicef UK (2017) No place to call home: protecting children's rights when the changing climate forces them to flee. London: Unicef. https://downloads.unicef.org.uk/wp-content/uploads/2017/04/No-Place-To-Call-Home.pdf?_ga=2.73316244.623674493.1494945170-1964912592.1483624860
United Nations (UN) (1951) 1951 Convention Relating to the Status of Refugees. Geneva
United Nations (UN) (1990) International Convention on the Protection of the Rights of All Migrant Workers and Members of their Families
United Nations (UN) (1998) OCHA Guiding Principles on Internal Displacement. New York and Geneva
United Nations Framework Convention on Climate Change (UNFCCC) (2017) Task force on displacement at a glance. The Warsaw International Mechanism for Loss and Damage, United Nations
United Nations Population Division (2017) Trends in International migrant stock: The 2017 revision. Department of Economic and Social Affairs. (United Nations database, POP/DB/MIG/Stock/Rev.2017)
Van Willigen M, Edwards M, Edwards B, Hesse S (2002) Riding out the storm: experiences of the physically disabled during Hurricanes Bonnie, Dennis, and Floyd. Natural Hazards Review 3(3):98–106

Vecchi GA, Soden BJ (2007) Global warming and the weakening of the tropical circulation. J Clim 20(17):4316–4340

Vieira RMSP, Tomasella J, Alvalá RCS, Sestini MF, Affonso AG, Rodriguez DA, Barbosa AA, Cunha APMA, Valles GF, Crepani E, de Oliveira SBP, de Souza MSB, Calil PM, de Carvalho MA, Valeriano DM, Campello FCB, Santana MO (2015) Identifying areas susceptible to desertification in the Brazilian Northeast. Solid Earth 6(1):347–360

Voigt-Graf C, Kagan S (2017) Migration and labour mobility from Kiribati. development policy centre discussion Paper No. 56. Available at SSRN: https://ssrn.com/abstract=2937416 or http://dx.doi.org/10.2139/ssrn.2937416

Walker A (2012) What is Boko Haram?. US Institute of Peace, Washington, DC

Ward ME, Shelley K, Kaase K, Pane JF (2008) Hurricane Katrina: A longitudinal study of the achievement and behavior of displaced students. J Educ Stud Placed at Risk 13(2–3):297–317

Warner K, Hamza M, Oliver-Smith A, Renaud F, Julca A (2010) Climate change, environmental degradation and migration. Nat Hazards 55:689–715

World Bank (2015) South Asia Population, Urban Growth: A Challenge and an Opportunity. Available at: http://go.worldbank.org/K67SR8GMQ0

Part III
Research and Practice: Reviewing Methods and Tools

Chapter 11
The Role of the Physical Sciences in Loss and Damage Decision-Making

Ana Lopez, Swenja Surminski and Olivia Serdeczny

Abstract This chapter reviews the implications of Loss and Damage (L&D) for decision-making with a special focus on the role of the physical sciences for decision support. From the point of view of climate science, the question regarding the estimation of losses and damages associated with climate change can be thought of in terms of two temporal scales: the present and the future. In both cases the aim is to establish the links between human-induced changes in climate and climate variability, the probability of occurrence of extreme meteorological events (e.g., rainfall), and the resulting hazard that causes losses and damages (e.g., flood). We review the approaches used to assess the hazard component of risk, with a special emphasis on identifying sources of uncertainty and the potential for providing robust information to support decision-making. We then discuss tools and approaches that have been developed in the context of Climate Change Adaptation (CCA) to deal with uncertainty from climate science in order to avoid a 'wait and see' mentality for decision-making. We argue that these can be applied to some parts of L&D decision-making, in the same way as suggested for CCA, since the challenges presented by the need to reduce and manage climate change losses and damages are not very different from the ones presented by the need to adapt to climate change and variability. However additional challenges for decision-makers, particularly in the context of the underlying science, are posed by the compensation and burden-sharing components of L&D for climate impacts that are beyond mitigation and adaptation's reach.

Keywords Loss and Damage · Climate decision-making · Uncertainty
Climate change attribution

A. Lopez (✉)
Physics Department and University College, Oxford University, Oxford, UK
e-mail: ana_lopez@fastmail.uk

S. Surminski
Grantham Research Institute on Climate Change and the Environment,
London School of Economics and Political Science (LSE), London, UK

O. Serdeczny
Climate Analytics GmbH, Berlin, Germany

R. Mechler et al. (eds.), *Loss and Damage from Climate Change*, Climate Risk Management, Policy and Governance, https://doi.org/10.1007/978-3-319-72026-5_11

11.1 Introduction

Article 8 of the Paris Agreement calls for action on 'averting, minimising and addressing Loss and Damage associated with the adverse effects of climate change, including extreme weather events and slow onset events.' In response, decisions need to be made—on a wide range of topics and at various levels of governance ranging from the global level, where UNFCCC negotiators need to decide how to take this topic forward, how to allocate funding and to establish possible institutional frameworks around Loss and Damage (L&D), all the way through to the local level, where communities need to understand and manage changing risks.

Despite significant progress in scientific understanding and methodological advances, decision makers face key constraints when making those decisions: limited data, uncertainty about climatic and socio-economic trends, and the complex interplay between climate and human behaviour may seem as insurmountable and lead to inactivity if not addressed properly.

These challenges are well known to those tasked with climate change adaptation and disaster risk management (Watkiss 2015), and a range of decision-support tools have been developed in response. However, assessing and addressing L&D suffers from a further level of complexity: it is a politically charged concept, with blurred conceptual boundaries (e.g., where do climate change adaptation efforts stop and where does the L&D remit start?) and a moral and ethical dimension (see introduction by Mechler et al. 2018; chapters by Wallimann-Helmer et al. 2018; Schinko et al. 2018; James et al. 2018; Botzen et al. 2018 in this book).

The L&D of climate change officially entered the UNFCCC discussions in 2007, but the concept itself has a far longer history. Growing awareness of the projected negative impacts of climate change has been at the core of the emerging mitigation and adaptation efforts. In the early adaptation literature, there was reference to the residual impacts after mitigation and adaptation were carried out. In this context, the idea of L&D associated with extreme events appeared as a consequence of the limits to current levels of adaptation (Smit et al. 2000; Smithers and Smit 1997).

While L&D under the UNFCCC is foremost a political concept determined by legal considerations around climate change, the technical dimension of L&D has its roots in the general risk management methodology, based on a terminology widely applied originally in Disaster Risk Reduction (DRR) and later on in Climate Change Adaptation (CCA). UNFCCC (2012a) explores the terminology in detail—highlighting different approaches to L&D as currently applied to DRR and CCA. Most broadly, 'damage' is seen as the physical impact and 'loss' as monetized values, which could be direct or indirect (economic follow on effects) (UNFCCC 2012a). Here the focus is on categorising, assessing and projecting impacts of events—mainly in the context of disasters, but also in the context of climate change implications for sudden-onset and slow-onset impacts, over a range of time-scales, and including direct and indirect economic losses, as well as so-called non-economic losses such as losses of lives and of eco-system services. In the broader climate change context L&D is often described as the third cost element of climate change, as outlined by Klein et al. (2007) (see also van Vuuren et al. 2011): mitigation costs, adaptation costs and residual damage. In this context addressing L&D is seen as addressing those losses that are likely to occur despite adaptation and mitigation efforts.

This academic exercise of framing L&D (see also chapters by Mechler et al. 2018 and James et al. 2018 in this book) is replicated amongst policy makers—where different interpretations of scope and concept are apparent amongst UNFCCC Parties, as highlighted by Kreft (2012): "Some Parties suggest that L&D is the residual risk when mitigation is insufficient, and when the full potential of adaptation is not met (Norway) while others frame L&D as the residual losses and damages after mitigation and adaptation choices have been made (Gambia). Ghana proposes that the concept of Loss and Damage from the adverse effects of climate be viewed as additional to adaptation focusing on challenges of both identifying and addressing the instances when adaptation is no longer possible. However, Bolivia maintains that Loss and Damage from the adverse effects of climate change concept is beyond adaptation, and as such is additional to adaptation, focusing on challenges of both identifying and addressing the instances when adaptation is no longer possible" (Kreft 2012).

This discourse highlights that stakeholders have different priorities and ambitions for action on L&D. Those can be broadly summarised in three categories of decision goals for L&D (Surminski and Lopez 2014):

- To create awareness about the sensitivity of human and natural systems to climate and the need to respond with appropriate mitigation, adaptation and DRR policies (UNFCCC 2012b).
- To develop risk reduction and risk management responses, with the goal to enhance adaptation to reduce vulnerability and build resilience; in this case the evaluation of climate risk is a necessary component of any adaptation options appraisal. This category has many analogies with CCA and DRR, addressing the assessment of and response to risks.
- To inform discussions on fair burden-sharing and compensation arrangements for L&D. While discussions around compensation underlined debates on L&D particularly in their beginning, they have lost immediate relevance in the official discussions since the Paris decision that stated that L&D would not provide a basis for compensation or liability.

In this chapter we consider how climate science can support those three goals and how uncertainties and limitations arising from the analysis of the climate hazard affect L&D decision-making. In particular, we discuss the role that existing approaches to decision making could play when addressing each of the policy goals embedded in the climate change L&D discussion. We conclude with a commentary and outlook for the on-going discussions about L&D.

11.2 L&D from a Physical Science Point of View—The Challenges of Assessing the Risk

Risk is a function of hazard, exposure and vulnerability. Therefore, any attempt of assessing the risk of losses and damages from climate change needs to incorporate two key components and illustrate their interplay: data on vulnerability and exposure, as well as information on the climatic hazard, including current climatic variability and future, long-term projections of climate change (UNFCCC 2008, 2012a). From a physical science perspective the focus is traditionally on the hazard side of risks, but there is a clear recognition that data needs and limitations for vulnerability and exposure assessments are equally important for understanding climate change risks.

The information about the climate hazard[1] relates to the physical phenomena, such as large cyclonic storms or long-term reductions in precipitation, and their consequences, such as flooding or drought. This hazard information contains the input to estimate the magnitude and frequency of damaging meteorological events in DRR approaches, or to project changes in climate risks to inform CCA. From the physical sciences point of view, there are challenges to estimate the hazard part of the total risk common to all interpretations of L&D.

IPCC's SREX concluded with high confidence that increasing exposure of people and economic assets has been the major cause of long-term increases in economic losses from weather- and climate-related disasters, arguing that the development pathways of a country or community do influence exposure and vulnerability (IPCC 2012). But understanding the 'multi-faceted nature' (IPCC 2012) of both exposure and vulnerability is still a challenge, due to data limitations and the inherent uncertainty in socio-economic trends (GAR 2011). The data required for assessing vulnerability and exposure varies, depending on scope and context. It can include historical loss information, property databases, demographic data, macroeconomic data such as debt and fiscal budgets (UNFCCC 2012a). In addition there are the intangibility aspects of L&D, which are not valued by markets and therefore are often left out of any assessments. The ability to capture direct and indirect losses is also identified as a key challenge as highlighted at the 36th Subsidiary Body for Implementation meeting in May 2012, where it was noted that available estimates on losses typically lack numbers on non-economic losses such as culture and heritage (UNFCCC 2012b). Government asset databases or sectorial disaster loss data are not available in all countries, or they may be very limited in scope, not capturing those intangible impacts (Mechler et al. 2009). This makes assumptions and extrapolations necessary, which add to the degree of uncertainty for L&D assessments. The chapter by Bouwer (2018) in this book discusses in more detail the interplay between exposure and vulnerability and observed and expected losses due to anthropogenic climate change.

---

[1]We note that, while the IPCC AR5 refers to 'physical impacts' as the impacts of climate change on geophysical systems, including floods, droughts, and sea level rise, we use the term 'hazard' instead to refer to the physical impacts.

To evaluate the current and changing likelihood of climatic hazards different sources of information are employed (IPCC 2012, 2013, 2014a, b). Historical records of climate variables, such as temperature or precipitation, are used to estimate the hazard probability under historical climatic conditions. Climate models are used to estimate changes of these variables in the future under different scenarios of greenhouse gasses' emissions or concentrations. Hazard and impact models are then employed to evaluate how changes in climatic variables will produce changes in natural or human systems, e.g., how changes in precipitation patterns will affect flood regimes in a given catchment.

In the rest of this section we briefly describe the information and tools utilised to estimate the current observed hazard probability and its projected changes.

11.2.1 Observed Hazard

Historical records of climate variables must be accurate, representative, homogeneous and of sufficient length if they are to provide robust estimates of current hazard probability. The robustness of the inferred probabilities depends for instance on the record length; short records of precipitation in a particular location do not provide enough information about the extreme precipitation events that might have occurred in the past. Poor quality of data (incorrect records or missing data) can induce large uncertainties in the estimation of current climatic hazards. While data for temperature and precipitation is more widely available, other variables such as soil moisture are poorly monitored, or extreme wind speeds are not monitored with sufficient spatial resolution.

Paleoclimatology can provide information about rare, large magnitude hydrometeorological events in places where long enough observational records are not available and good proxies to estimate the magnitude of past events such as floods or droughts can be found. For instance, instrumental records of floods at gauge stations are limited in spatial coverage and time, with only a small number of gauge stations spanning more than 50 years. Pre-instrumental flood data can provide information for longer periods, however the current availability of this data is scarce particularly in spatial coverage (IPCC 2012). Paleoclimate data can then provide information about a range of climate hazards that have occurred in the remote past, often illustrating the fact that, in many cases, the recent observational records provide very limited information about the range of the unforced natural variability in a particular location (Benito et al. 2004; IPCC 2012). However, paleoclimatology can only provide information in cases where adequate proxies exist, as for instance tree-ring temperature and rainfall reconstructions, paleo coastal surges, etc.; but it is not a viable option for some other variables such as high resolution wind speed.

11.2.2 Projected Changes in Hazard

Projections of changes in future climate are generally derived using General Circulation Models (GCMs) which simulate the response of the climate system to a scenario of future emissions or concentrations of greenhouse gases and aerosols. Even though the physical and chemical processes in the climate system follow known physical laws, its complexity implies that many simplifications and approximations have to be made when modelling them. The choice of approximations creates a variety of physical climate models (IPCC 2013).

There are different sources of uncertainties in climate model simulations, including (anthropogenic and natural) forcing, initial conditions, and model imperfections (both model uncertainty and model inadequacy) (Stainforth et al. 2007). Climate forcing or scenario uncertainty is introduced by the fact that, to simulate future climate, the models are run using different scenarios of anthropogenic forcings that either represent plausible but inherently unknowable future socioeconomic development,[2] or could arise as the result of multiple pathways of socioeconomic development (Meinshausen et al. 2011). Climate model imperfections and initial conditions uncertainties are due to our incomplete knowledge of the climate system, the limitations of computer models to simulate it, and the system's non-linearity (Knutti et al. 2007; Stainforth et al. 2007). To quantify climate model uncertainty a variety of climate models have been developed around the world. For instance, the IPCC AR5 report (IPCC 2013) includes projections from 42 climate models.

The uncertainty in projections of future climate variability is quantified by constructing, for a given climate model, a set of projections that are initialised in slightly different ways (see for instance Deser et al. (2012a, b) for the effect of initialisation in long term projections for a single climate model, and Kirtman et al. (2013) for near term or decadal projections). For each possible forcing scenario, ensembles of different climate models that include various approaches to implementing the components of the climate system, and, within each model, different parameterisations and initialisations, are used to estimate the effect of climate model imperfections and initial conditions uncertainties in the projections of climate change.

The relative contributions to the total uncertainty from these different sources depend on the spatial scale, the lead-time of the projection, and the variable of interest. For instance for precipitation, at spatial scales of the order of 1000 km, internal variability is the main source of uncertainty in climate model projections for many regions in the world for lead times up to three decades ahead, while forcing uncertainty dominates thereafter (Kirtman et al. 2013; Booth et al. 2013; Hawkins and Sutton 2009).

While GCMs simulate the entire Earth with a relatively coarse spatial resolution (e.g. they can capture features with scales of a hundred kilometres or larger), regional climate projections downscaled from GCMs have a much higher resolution

[2]This is the approach used prior to the IPCC AR5 report, see for instance IPCC (2000), Moss et al. (2008).

(simulating features with scales as small as a few kilometres). Downscaling can be accomplished through one of two techniques: 'dynamical' or 'statistical' downscaling (Wilby et al. 2009). 'Dynamical' downscaling refers to the process of nesting high resolution Regional Climate Models (RCMs) within a global GCM (Hewitson et al. 2014; Giorgi et al. 2015) while 'statistical' downscaling relies on using statistical relationships between large-scale atmospheric variables and regional climate (often at meteorological station level) to generate projections of future local climatic conditions. Statistical methods may also include weather generators that simulate weather events and their extremes. Downscaling approaches do not provide magical fixes to possible limitations in the data being downscaled (Kerr 2011). In cases where the large scale GCM signal accurately represents the observed one, downscaling can add value by incorporating features that are absent in GCMs, such as the effect of coastlines and complex orography (Hall 2014). However, when for instance different RCMs driven by the same GCM show a wide range of responses in precipitation (Hewitson et al. 2014), the generation of climate projections using downscaling techniques will often increase the level of uncertainty in the original GCM projections, having significant effects in the estimation of probabilities of occurrence of damaging events in DRR models and climate change risk assessments.

Climate model projections (and their downscaled versions) provide information about climate variables such as temperature, precipitation, sea level, etc. The next step in a climate risk assessment involves understanding how changes in the climate variables will affect natural or human systems. Hazard models are computational models that take as inputs observed or simulated climate variables such as temperature, precipitation, soil moisture content, wind speed, etc., and use them to simulate the variables that are relevant to analyse a particular weather or climate hazard (IPCC 2012, 2014a, b). For instance, extreme rainfall events can cause floods. But to estimate the extent of the flooded area, hydrological and hydraulic models are used to generate the flood footprint for each particular event (Ranger et al. 2011; Jha et al. 2012). Some of the limitations of hazard models are similar to those of climate models: poor representation of the physical processes involved, calibration issues and computational constraints all contribute to compounding the uncertainties in the climate inputs with the uncertainties in the hazard model outputs. This is illustrated, for example, by multi-model assessments of water availability and flood potential, where a large ensemble of global hydrological models is forced by an ensemble of GCMs to estimate climate change impacts on water resources. These studies show that climate and hydrological models contribute to a similar extent to the spread in relative river flows' changes globally (Schewe et al. 2014; Dankers et al. 2014).

An alternative approach to estimate the physical impacts of climate change used when model projections are not available, is the use of 'analogies.' Two types of analogies are possible: spatial analogies whereby another part of the world experiencing similar conditions to those expected to occur in the future is used as a proxy to estimate future impacts in the region of interest; and temporal analogies whereby changes in the past (sometimes obtained from paleo-records) are used to make inferences about changes in the future. This approach has two limitations. Firstly, expert judgment is required to estimate the uncertainty of the projected impacts (Bos et al. 2015; IPCC 2014a, b). Secondly, the applicability of the approach depends on the climate variable and the location; for example Dahinden et al. (2017) show that it is often not possible to find analogues in temperature and precipitation simultaneously. The above discussion refers specifically to the estimation of the hazard component of risk. As already mentioned, the risk is, however, the probability of occurrence of the hazard multiplied by the impacts if these events occur. In the IPCC AR5 'climate change impacts' refer to "the effect on lives, livelihoods, health, ecosystems, economies, societies, cultures, services, and infrastructure due to the interaction of climate changes or hazardous climate events occurring within a specific time period and the vulnerability of an exposed society or system" (IPCC 2014a).

Therefore, the study of 'climate change impacts' requires impacts models that combine projections of climate change with socio-economic scenarios. To this end, the Inter-Sectorial Impact Model Intercomparison Project (ISI-MIP) aims to study the impacts of climate change on flood hazard, food and water availability, health, ecosystems and coastal infrastructure, together with their interactions and uncertainties in order to provide a comprehensive picture of climate change risks (see Schellnhuber et al. (2014) and references therein).

When considering the risk, including exposure and vulnerability, at shorter time scales, in many cases the current natural variability of the climate system and other non-climatic drivers of risks will have a higher impact than the climatic changes driven by changes in atmospheric concentrations of greenhouse gases. For example, in the near term, changes in exposure such as urbanization and building housing developments on flood-prone areas could increase significantly the risk of flooding and damage to the aforementioned infrastructure, independently of climate change. Over longer time scales, it is expected that anthropogenic climate change will often play a more significant role (Oppenheimer et al. 2014).

The above discussion about the estimation of the climate hazard is closely related to, and based on similar discussions in the context of CCA. However, L&D also brings something distinctly unique to the discussion: embedded in the political concept of L&D, at least according to some, is the element of burden sharing and compensation, which could require the estimation of the attributable fraction of losses and damages to human induced climate change. From the physical sciences point of view, and focusing on the question of attribution of the climate hazard or physical impact, it is clear that estimations of changes in its likelihood do not, a priori, have any information about whether or not the changing probability can be attributed[3] to human induced climate change. Approaches that attempt to quantify the attributable component of the changes in the probability of occurrence of meteorological hazards rely heavily on climate models to compare the likelihood of the weather event with and without the influence of anthropogenic emissions of greenhouse gases. However, as already

[3]As defined by the IPCC, detection of climate change is the process of demonstrating that climate has changed in some defined statistical sense, without providing a reason for that change. Attribution of causes of climate change is the process of establishing the most likely causes for the detected change, either natural or anthropogenic, with some defined level of confidence (source: IPCC 2012).

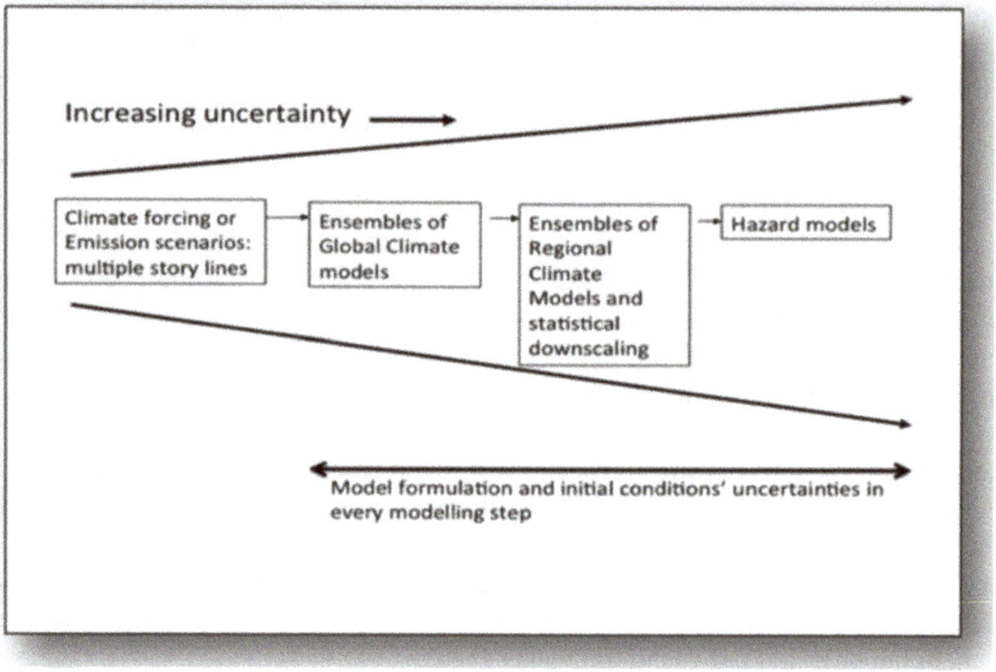

Fig. 11.1 The uncertainty cascade in the modelling chain from climate model forcings to the estimation of the climate hazard (the physical impact of climate change). An estimation of the total risk should include vulnerability and exposure scenarios that, in combination with the climate hazard as inputs for an impact model, outputs the total impact on, for instance, lives, livelihoods, health, ecosystems, economies, societies, cultures, services, and infrastructure

discussed, climate models have significant limitations to simulate the climate system at the scales relevant for extreme meteorological events (Trenberth 2012; Trenberth and Fasullo 2012). Therefore, an evaluation of the climate model skill (Stott et al. 2017) and the statistical reliability of the model-based probabilities (Bellprat and Doblas-Reyes 2016; Weisheimer et al. 2017) should be carried out to ensure robust estimates of attributable changes in climate hazards. For a detailed discussion on attribution we refer the reader to the chapter by James et al. (2018) in this book.

In summary, a comprehensive modelling approach to assess climate change induced hazards requires the combined simulation of all the domains. For flood risk, for instance, it requires the modelling of the atmosphere and ocean, catchment river network, flood plains and indirectly affected areas. As discussed above, and illustrated in Fig. 11.1, considerable uncertainty is introduced in each of the modelling steps involved, including uncertainties about the greenhouse gas concentrations' scenarios, the representation of physical processes in the global climate model, the characterisation of natural variability, the method of downscaling to catchment scales and the hydrological and inundation models' structures and parameterizations.

As a result, the uncertainty associated with a complete modelling chain, from climate forcing and simulation to estimation of hazard probability, is likely to increase in each step, and become particularly large at local scales. In addition, uncertainty estimates are always conditional on the modelling approaches used to obtain them, and do not capture the full uncertainty (Smith and Stern 2011; Stainforth et al. 2007), especially at local scales, where current modelling tools to generate projections cannot produce reliable and robust estimates of future changes (Oreskes et al. 2010; Risbey and O'Kane 2011). This is particularly important in the case of catastrophic changes in the climate system that might occur due to non-linear feedbacks and processes that are not known, or have not been adequately incorporated in the climate models yet.

Nonetheless, the presence of uncertainties in the estimation of hazards, and the fact that in some cases these uncertainties might not decrease in time,[4] should not stop decisions being made. In the next section we discuss some of the decision-making approaches utilised for CCA to deal specifically with this issue.

11.3 Challenges for L&D Decision-Making

L&D—both as a political concept but also in its technical dimension requires decisions to be made at different scales from local to global, and by a range of stakeholders with differing priorities and agendas. These can be broadly grouped into three categories of L&D decision making goals (Surminski and Lopez 2014): creating awareness about the sensitivity of human and natural systems to climate change; developing risk reduction and risk management approaches to enhance adaptation, reduce vulnerability and build resilience; and informing compensation and burden sharing mechanisms.

All three require an understanding of the current and future scale and distribution of climate related L&D. As noted above, decision makers are faced with uncertainties related to hazard, exposure and vulnerability: projections of future weather patterns from different climate models often disagree (Heal and Milner 2014), while socio-economic trends, which influence the impact of climate change, also suffer from inherent uncertainty (IPCC 2012). For some, this may prove as a potentially welcome excuse for inaction, for others this might lead to heated, almost unresolvable disputes about the underlying science. Can this potential paralysation (Dessai et al. 2009) be avoided?

[4]For instance, Knutti and Sedlacek (2013) show that the projected global temperature change from the IPCC AR5 models is very similar to the one reported by the IPCC AR4 models after taking into account the different underlying scenarios. Similarly, spatial patterns of temperature and precipitation change and local model spread are also very consistent despite substantial model development. These authors argue that model improvements often imply more confidence in their projections, but do not necessarily narrow uncertainties.

The ability to make L&D decisions depends on skills and know-how for assessing the risks, and institutional capacity as well as funding to address those risks (UNFCCC 2012a). But given the large uncertainties inherent to the estimation of risk, the use of a decision-making framework that can make the best use of the available information to develop strategies to reduce L&D is also key. Two widely recognised decision-making frameworks have been discussed in the context of CCA: the 'top down or science-driven' and the 'bottom up or policy-driven' frameworks.

In the first framework, the process starts with the generation of climate projections, often downscaled and corrected for possible biases, followed by an analysis of their physical impacts that, combined with vulnerability assessments, are used to design policies and adaptation options to mitigate those impacts. Application of the 'science-driven' approach include, for instance, the Stern Review and the IPCC risk assessments. This approach has been criticised for its heavy reliance on climate projections that are limited in their ability to represent key drivers of extreme events and not generally fit for purpose for decision support (IPCC 2012; Smith and Stern 2011; Stainforth et al. 2007), and for the potential lack of robustness of the projected impacts due to different methodological issues (Hall 2007; Merz et al. 2010; Tebaldi and Knutti 2007). Uncertainty is clearly one of the key challenges for decision-makers, especially when competing with concerns about daily lives. But the uncertainty that comes with this approach does not only stem from climate change; in fact the climate dimension just adds to the uncertainty derived from the wide range of socio-economic and environmental factors considered, often referred to as the 'cascade of uncertainty' (Schneider 1983) or the 'uncertainty explosion' (Henderson-Sellers 1993). Few science-first assessments have been used to evaluate real adaptation options, since the 'uncertainty explosion' often renders the appraisal of adaptation options impracticable (Dessai and Hulme 2007; Wilby and Dessai 2010).

The second framework starts with the adaptation problem itself rather than with climate projections. It is based on risk management approaches that begin by defining the policy or adaptation goal to be addressed (Ranger et al. 2010a, b; Willows et al. 2003). This includes delineating the objective or decision criteria, identifying present and future climatic[5] and non-climatic risks that make the system vulnerable, identifying institutional and regulatory constraints, identifying the possible options,

[5]Modelling capabilities can be used to generate climate projections that, in combination with socio-economic scenarios, result in suitable tools to assess vulnerabilities in different regions including, where possible, the study of vulnerability to changes in frequency of occurrence of extreme events. In the framework of scenario planning as an approach to support strategic decision-making, scenarios are intended to be challenging descriptions of a wide range of possible futures. Therefore, the combination of climate and socio-economic scenarios we refer to cannot be, by construction, representative of the full range of possible futures. On the climate modelling side for example, missing feedbacks and unknown uncertainties in climate models limit the ability to represent all plausible futures. Notwithstanding these constraints, scenarios can still be used as tools to consider a range of possible futures, and their associated consequences. Then, an analysis of the options available could be carried out, and feedback can be provided on what information about the likely futures would be most valuable for decision makers.

and only then (if necessary) appraising their appropriateness against a detailed set of climate projections. In this context, the evaluation of climate risks is just one component of the estimations of all the environmental and social stressors and changes in socio-economic conditions that can induce system failures. Therefore the decision maker is encouraged to think broadly about the interactions of other risks and priorities with the adaptation problem and look for strategies that have co-benefits with other areas such as development and DRR. This approach was adopted in the Thames 2100 Estuary project (Haigh and Fisher 2010) and includes, for instance, community-based adaptation approaches.

Due to the complex, diverse, and context-dependent nature of CCA, it is currently recognised that there is no single approach to adaptation planning, with some evidence suggesting that the links between adaptation planning and implementation are strengthened when both, the science-driven and the policy-driven approaches are combined (Mimura et al. 2014).

The topic of decision-making under uncertainty has received significant attention in the context of CCA (Dessai and Hulme 2007; Gilboa 2009; Lempert 2002; Lempert and Collins 2007; Ranger et al. 2010a, b; and see McDermott 2016 and Heal and Milner 2014 for overviews). Despite the fact that in some cases reliable and robust projections are not possible (in some cases even the sign of change is not known), there are now several decision-making tools that, recognising the inherent uncertainties, are used to develop public policy, particularly in the context of adaptation and flood risk management. See Appendix 1 for an overview of some of the main tools.

Examples include adaptive management and scenario planning. Adaptive management allows for continuous modification of a policy or a strategy to take into account new learning about future trends and impacts. This involves a high degree of learning, experimenting and evaluation throughout the lifetime of the strategy or policy. Scenario planning provides decision makers with a range of different, plausible future scenarios. Policies and strategies can be tested against those scenarios to assess how they may perform. For adaptation decision-making these approaches have been developed into options analysis (Haigh and Fisher 2010; Ranger et al. 2010a, b; Dittrich et al. 2016) and portfolio analysis (Watkiss and Hunt 2016; Dittrich et al. 2016).

Real options analysis was used in the Thames 2100 Estuary project, with extensive sensitivity testing of sea level rise assumptions (i.e. incorporating some elements of robustness-based analyses) (Reeder and Ranger 2010). Gersonius et al. (2013) also applied the real options analysis to urban drainage infrastructure in West Garforth, England.

Alternatively, decision makers can use these different scenarios to identify 'robust' strategies that would work well under most of these scenarios (Lempert and Collins 2007; Hallegatte 2009; Ranger et al. 2010a, b; Fankhauser et al. 2013; Weaver et al. 2013). Robust decision-making was applied to water supply management in California (Groves et al. 2008) and Flood risk management in Ho Chi Minh City Vietnam (Lempert et al. 2013) (see chapter by Botzen et al. 2018).

Other examples of how these strategies have been applied in different countries and sectors include the Dutch Delta Programme, the Louisiana Master Plan for a Sustainable Coast, and the Colorado River Basin Supply and Demand Study (see Lempert and Haasnoot 2017).

Even though these decision-strategies can be of value for L&D decision-making, their application has remained relatively under-explored in this context.

In a broad sense there is clear merit in both science-driven and policy-driven approaches for L&D decision making: scientific assessments are important for all three L&D goals and should underpin and inform the decision process. This is particularly evident for the first L&D goal: identifying the risks and raising awareness heavily relies on the underlying science and the socio-economic scenarios and climate and impacts models used. A top-down or science-driven approach appears most relevant for this, but the adaptation and mitigation pathways are somewhat locked by the climate scenario chosen.

However, planning any policies and measures in response will require from decision makers the need to design flexible adaptation and risk management pathways that allow for periodic adjustments as new information becomes available, and the possibility of changing to new routes when or if incremental adjustments are no longer considered sufficient according to the evidence available at the time (Hallegatte 2009; Hulme et al. 2009; Lopez et al. 2010; Wilby and Dessai 2010; Bhave et al. 2016). Moreover, the planning process will have to consider the fact that the future might involve climate change events that are not predicted, combined with unforeseen technological and societal developments. The 'policy-driven' approach encourages the use of measures that are low regret, reversible, build resilience into the system, incorporate safety margins, employ 'soft' solutions, are flexible, and deliver multiple co-benefits (Hallegatte 2009; Hulme et al. 2009). In this context the second L&D goal shows a strong parallel with climate adaptation planning: how to minimise the climate change risk to tolerable levels, and what are the options to manage what cannot be minimised? Consequently, the challenges presented by the need to reduce and manage climate change losses and damages are not very different to the ones presented by the need to adapt to climate change and variability, and the tools described above seem adequate to address these challenges.

For the third L&D goal of informing discussions on fair burden-sharing and compensation arrangements it is also clear that both approaches are needed.

The estimation of precise information on attribution of damages to the incremental risk caused by anthropogenic climate change requires an estimate of the change in hazard probability that is attributable to anthropogenic climate change. From the point of view of the decision-making frameworks discussed above, this falls within the 'science-driven' approach. Climate simulations are used to estimate the likelihood of the event under current conditions, with the extra requirement of a simulation of the counterfactual world, i.e., an estimation of the likelihood of the event had greenhouse gas concentrations not increased during the last 100 years or so. Some climate scientists argue that the science of attribution of climate events could support decisions related to obtaining compensation for damages caused by attributable natural disasters, since it potentially allows to distinguish between genuine consequences of anthropogenic climate change from climate events that are a result of internal climate variability (Hoegh-Guldberg et al. 2011; Peterson et al. 2012). On the other hand, Hulme et al. (2011) challenges the idea that the science of weather event attribution has a role to play in this context, in particular due to the fact that the estimated changes in attributable risks are based on climate modelling experiments that cannot provide robust answers. However, Huggel et al. (2015, 2016) argue that even though attribution is not necessarily a requirement for L&D policies, it is potentially useful for facilitating a more thematically structured, and constructive policy and justice discussion. The chapter by Wallimann-Helmer (2018) in this book discusses these issues in detail.

For the design and implementation of burden sharing or compensation instruments (technical, financial and capacity building) an estimation of the costs for managing losses and damages is needed. This would rely on a "policy-driven" approach, taking as a starting point what are the societal goals (which values to protect), and then an estimation of the resources needed to do so. Principles to distribute the burden of managing losses and damages include principles that take into consideration the causation of outcomes that need to be managed (e.g. the polluter pays principle) and principles that do not take causation into account (e.g. the ability to pay principle). The information gained through a science-driven approach can help to approximate the portion of the hazard that is of anthropogenic origin, which would inform the discussion on these compensation principles. Importantly, this information may not need to be precise or event-linked: the growing understanding of the *overall likelihood* of anthropogenic footprint in L&D could be enough to justify burden-sharing, for example if big emitters recognise an overall higher responsibility to provide support than low emitters, irrespective of precise event-attribution (see also the chapter by Simlinger and Mayer (2018) on legal issues).

11.4 Conclusions

The different dimensions of L&D of climate change make this a complex topic, with a range of interpretations, approaches and responses being considered, while the political negotiations are in full flow. Reflecting on the current state of discussion we draw the following conclusions.

To date there are no easy answers to the L&D challenges. This is not only due to technical and science limitations, but also due to the political dimension and the uncertainties inherent in this process.

L&D of climate change remains a political concept, developed during the UNFCCC negotiations (see chapter by Calliari et al. 2018), but with its technical roots in CCA and DRR. The 2015 Paris Agreement of the UNFCCC recognises "the importance of averting, minimizing and addressing Loss and Damage associated with the adverse effects of climate change, including extreme weather events and slow onset events" (UNFCCC 2015). This aligns with three goals embedded in the L&D discussion:

- To **create awareness** about the sensitivity of human and natural systems to climate, and the need to respond with appropriate mitigation, adaptation and DRR policies.
- To **plan risk reduction and risk management**, with the goal to enhance adaptation to reduce vulnerability and build resilience.
- To **inform burden sharing** for the costs of managing L&D and compensation arrangements.

Clearly, existing tools and approaches from the fields of CCA and DRR can help responding to L&D.

The first two goals are common to the CCA and DRR discussions, and lessons learnt in those areas can be shared here. The lack of data and knowledge should not be seen as a reason for delaying action—in fact there are a range of existing instruments and tools that can be applied to assess and manage current and future L&D. As described above, within the CCA community, tools and approaches have recently been developed to deal with uncertainty from climate science in order to avoid a 'wait and see' mentality for decision making. In this context, the challenges presented by the need to reduce and manage climate change losses and damages are not very different to the ones presented by the need to adapt to climate change and variability.

The compensation component of L&D, however, offers a different dimension to the climate change discussion. While not explicitly outlined in the official UNFCCC language, this is an underlying aim that has been driving the L&D debate since its beginnings. The focus on compensation for those climate impacts that are beyond mitigation and adaptation's reach poses some additional challenges for decision makers—particularly in the context of the underlying science, as seen in the discussion of attribution (see also chapter by James et al. 2018 in this book).

Importantly, the majority of climate change experts (as reflected by the last chapters of IPCC 2012) seem to have come to the conclusion that the only way to deal with climate change is to take a holistic approach to risk management, using a wide range of approaches to evaluate expected risks and benefits (IPCC 2014a, b). This therefore underlines the importance of comprehensive approaches, incorporating hazard, vulnerability and exposure elements of risk. It also opens up the question of the specific role of L&D under the United Nations Framework Convention on Climate Change, alongside the institutional set up for adaptation under the UNFCCC and for DRR under UNISDR's Sendai Framework. As there are many thematic and technical overlaps between these areas, it is important for those bodies administering this at the UN level to recognize the synergies and avoid duplication. This also applies to other governance levels, from national to local, where far too often disaster risk management and climate adaptation are kept institutionally apart.

Overall, the physical sciences play a key role in informing all aspects of climate change L&D discussions. Climate data is important throughout, while there are some clear shortcomings in terms of accessibility, availability and quality of it. The recognition of limitations and uncertainties in this information is important, particularly for those who will make decisions around L&D. The recognition of these limitations should also extend to the information on exposure and vulnerability, which plays a significant role in determining the eventual losses and damages. Progress is being made with regards to loss assessments and accounting for indirect consequences as well as estimating socio-economic risk drivers (IPCC 2012).

However, the idea of L&D for compensation and burden sharing might trigger increased efforts to dissect the human induced climate change part of the risk. Informing the discussions on how to share the costs for managing L&D relies on two separate steps: (1) estimating the costs of managing L&D, and (2) informing the causation-based principles of the debate. Clearly, the caveats and scientific challenges of attribution that have been outlined here need to be part of such discussions. However, this should not put on hold the efforts to integrate adaptation to climate change with wider development aims and disaster risk reduction, and the search for innovative approaches to share the financial burden of current and future losses and damages.

Appendix

Table on decision tools for understanding and managing climate risks. *Source* Based on McDermott and Surminski (2017)

Decision tool	Benefits	Shortcomings	Applicability	Examples
'Mainstreaming' or 'integration' (OECD 2014; Watkiss and Hunt 2016)	Integrates adaptation into existing policies and decision-making	Requires more time and resources compared to a science-first impact assessment	Useful where emphasis is on understanding the context for an intervention	Applied to climate-resilient development and planning in Columbia and Ethiopia
'Iterative climate risk management', 'Adaptive pathways' or 'Route maps' (Reeder and Ranger 2010; Ranger et al. 2010a, b; Watkiss and Hunt 2011; Fankhauser et al. 2013; Haasnoot et al. 2013; Watkiss 2015)	Considers the timing and phasing of adaptation, and takes account of uncertainty. Ensures that appropriate decisions are taken at the right time, as decisions can be adjusted over time as new evidence is presented. Useful in identifying which types of options to implement first, as well as which options may be warranted to help with future climate change or future decisions. Economic appraisal with this method is flexible as it allows employs tools such as the cost-benefit analysis and the multi-criteria analysis within the framework of uncertainty	Focuses on policy-relevant decisions (i.e. those needed and justified in economic terms. It is difficult to identify risk thresholds	Effective when information on adaptation options is available. Useful under three conditions: (1) the investment decision is irreversible; (2) The decision-maker has some flexibility on when to carry out the investment (single step, or in stages); (3) The decision-maker faces uncertain conditions and by waiting they gain new information regarding the success of the investment (Watkiss 2015)	Long-term water management of the Rhine Delta in the Netherlands. Thames 2100 Estuary project
Cost-benefit analysis (Dittrich et al. 2016; Watkiss and Hunt 2016)	Depending on the availability of reliable data on costs and benefits, this method requires limited technical resources and results can be easily assessed by a non- technical audience (Dittrich et al. 2016)	May produce very misleading policy recommendations as uncertainty not taken into account. Method is of limited use when market prices are not available	Suitable when probabilities are known. Useful when dealing with well-defined problems that involve a limited number of actors who make choices among different mitigation or adaptation options	Berg River Basin, South Africa; Agricultural sector in The Gambia
Cost-effectiveness analysis (Dittrich et al. 2016; Watkiss and Hunt 2016)	Provides the least cost adaptation option that achieves a desired outcome that is quantifiable. Alternative to cost– benefit analysis when monetising benefits is either difficult or controversial (Dittrich et al. 2016). Does not require formalised knowledge about the impact of global warming	Does not consider uncertainty. Does not take account of the impact of specified target on economic efficiency	Useful in determining value for money. Suitable when the benefits of the adaptation options are identical given one metric	Household water deficits in South-East England
Multi-criteria analysis (Dittrich et al. 2016; Watkiss and Hunt 2016)	Combines quantitative and qualitative (monetised and non-monetised) indicators and ranks alternatives based on the weight the decision maker gives to the different indicators. Useful in overcoming some of the limitations of cost-benefit analysis	Does not consider uncertainty	Useful when it is important to weigh up of various decision criteria. Useful where impact of climate change can be monetised	Adaptation options to water scarcity in Spain

(continued)

(continued)

Decision tool	Benefits	Shortcomings	Applicability	Examples
Real options and quasi-option value analysis (Haigh and Fisher 2010; Ranger et al. 2010a, b; Dittrich et al. 2016)	Useful in evaluating the benefits of gaining more information before action is taken. Estimates the value of additional information taking into account the uncertainty surrounding climate change. In contrast to traditional decision-making tools, this method provides flexible strategies along the different climate paths that can be adjusted as new information becomes available	Only relevant where knowledge of true state of climate is available	Can be used where probabilities are known based on current information and are expected to change with availability of new information. Works well for large irreversible investments with long life times and sensitivity to climate conditions	Thames 2100 Estuary project; Urban drainage infrastructure in West Garforth, England
'Robust decision making' or 'info gap' (Lempert and Collins 2007; Groves et al. 2008; Hallegatte 2009; Ranger et al. 2010a, b; Lempert et al. 2013; Weaver et al. 2013)	Provides formalized quantitative analysis under deep uncertainty. It is possible to consider potentially large numbers of 'plausible' climate scenarios. Emphasises the robustness of a decision across a range of potential scenarios	Requires significant analytical or computational resources The absence of probabilities may make this method more subjective, as it becomes easily influenced by the perceptions of stakeholders	Useful in the absence of 'trustworthy probability estimates' (Ranger et al. 2010a, b) Useful in identifying measures that have little sensitivity to different climate change scenarios	Water supply management in California. Flood risk management in Ho Chi Minh City, Vietnam
Portfolio analysis (Watkiss 2015; Watkiss and Hunt, 2016; Dittrich et al. 2016)	It allows a trade-off between the return and the uncertainty of the return of different combinations of adaptation options under alternative climate change projections	It requires assumptions about probabilities of plausible climate change scenarios and associated impacts. Requires data on expected returns, variance, co-variance of return for each option across the range of climate change scenarios. Requires large amount of resources, high degree of specialised knowledge, and is dependent on the availability of quantitative data	This method is only effective if the returns of the adaptation options are negatively correlated and their correlation can be well specified for a long term planning horizon	Local flood management in the UK; Restoration/regeneration of a forest under climate change uncertainty in Canada
Expected utility/Expected value analysis (Ranger et al. 2010a)	Decision-making is based on optimising among several possible future climate outcomes	Knowledge of probabilities required	Useful where probabilities of future climate projections are known and not sensitive to the availability of new information (Ranger et al. 2010a). Useful when uncertainty can be quantified	
Maximin (Ranger et al. 2010a)	Minimises the possible loss for a worst case (maximum loss) scenario for prudency	Knowledge of probabilities required	Applicable where it is not possible to quantify relative confidence of probabilities due to having conflicting probability estimates (knowledge of worst case scenario) or incomplete probability	

References

Bellprat O, Doblas-Reyes F (2016) Unreliable climate simulations overestimate attributable risk of extreme weather and climate events. Geophys Res Lett 43:2158–2164. https://doi.org/10.1002/2015gl067189

Benito G, Lang M, Barriendos M, Llasat MC, Francés F, Ouarda T, Varyl R, Thorndycraft VR, Enzel Y, Bardossy A, Coeur D, Bobée B (2004) Use of systematic, palaeoflood and historical data for the improvement of flood risk estimation. Review of scientific methods. Nat Hazards 31:623–643. https://doi.org/10.1023/B:NHAZ.0000024895.48463.eb

Bhave AG, Conway D, Dessai S, Stainsforth DA (2016) Barriers and opportunities for robust decision making approaches to support climate change adaption in the developing world. Clim Risk Management 14:1–10. https://doi.org/10.1016/j.crm.2016.09.004

Booth BBB, Bernie D, McNeall D, Hawkins E, Caesar J, Boulton C, Friedlingstein P, Sexton DMH (2013) Scenario and modelling uncertainty in global mean temperature change derived from emission-driven global climate models. Earth Sys Dyn 4:95–108. https://doi.org/10.5194/esd-4-95-2013

Bos SPM, Pagella T, Kindt R, Russell AJM, Luedeling E (2015) Climate analogs for agricultural impact projection and adaptation—reliability test. Front Environ Sci. https://doi.org/10.3389/fenvs.2015.00065. Accessed 30 Jan 2016

Botzen W, Bouwer LM, Scussolini P, Kuik O, Haasnoot M, Lawrence J, Aerts JCJH (2018) Integrated disaster risk management and adaptation. In: Mechler R, Bouwer L, Schinko T, Surminski S, Linnerooth-Bayer J (eds) Loss and damage from climate change. Concepts, methods and policy options. Springer, Cham, pp 287–315

Bouwer LM (2018) Observed and projected impacts from extreme weather events: implications for loss and damage. In: Mechler R, Bouwer L, Schinko T, Surminski S, Linnerooth-Bayer J (eds) Loss and damage from climate change. Concepts, methods and policy options. Springer, Cham, pp 63–82

Calliari E, Surminski S, Mysiak J (2018) The politics of (and behind) the UNFCCC's loss and damage mechanism. In: Mechler R, Bouwer L, Schinko T, Surminski S, Linnerooth-Bayer J (eds) Loss and damage from climate change. Concepts, methods and policy options. Springer, Cham, pp 155–178

Dahinden F, Fischer EM, Knutti R (2017) Future local climate unlike currently observed anywhere. Environ Res Lett 12. https://doi.org/10.1088/1748-9326/aa75d7. Accessed 20 Jul 2017

Dankers R, Arnell NW, Clark DB, Falloon PD, Fekete BM, Gosling SN, Heinke J, Kim H, Masaki Y, Satoh Y, Stacke T, Wada Y, Wisser D (2014) First look at changes in flood hazard in the inter-sectoral impact model intercomparison project ensemble. PNAS 111 (9)3257–3261. https://doi.org/10.1073/pnas.1302078110

Deser C, Phillips A, Bourdette V, Teng H (2012a) Uncertainty in climate change projections: the role of internal variability. Clim Dyn 38:527–546

Deser C, Knutti R, Solomon S, Phillips AS (2012b) Communication of the role of natural variability in future North American climate. Nat Clim Change 2:775–779

Dessai S, Hulme M (2007) Assessing the robustness of adaptation decisions to climate change uncertainties: a case study on water resources management in the East of England. Glob Environ Change 17(1):59–72

Dessai S, Hulme M, Lempert R, Jr Pielke (2009) Do we need better predictions to adapt to a changing climate? Eos, Trans Am Geophys Union 90(13):112–113. https://doi.org/10.1029/2009EO130003

Dittrich R, Wreford A, Moran D (2016) A survey of decision-making approaches for climate change adaptation: Are robust methods the way forward? Ecol Econ 122:79–89

Fankhauser S, Ranger N, Colmer J (2013) An independent national adaptation programme for England. Policy brief. Grantham Research Institute on Climate Change and the Environment, London School of Economics

GAR (2011) UNISDR: global assessment report on disaster risk reduction. Switzerland, Geneva, p 2011

Gersonius B, Ashley R, Pathirana A, Zevenbergen C (2013) Climate change uncertainty: building flexibility into water and flood risk infrastructure. Clim Change 116:411–423

Gilboa I (2009) Theory of decision under uncertainty, 1st edn. Cambridge University Press, Cambridge, UK

Giorgi F, Gutowski WJ Jr (2015) Regional dynamical downscaling and the CORDEX initiative. Annu Rev Environ Resour 40:467–490. https://doi.org/10.1146/annurev-environ-102014-021217

Groves DG, Lempert RJ, Knopman D, Berry SH (2008) Preparing for an uncertain future climate in the Inland empire: identifying robust water-management strategies. Rand Corporation, USA

Haigh N, Fisher J (2010) Using a "Real Options" approach to determine a future strategic plan for flood risk management in the Thames Estuary. Draft Government Economic Service Working Paper

Hall A (2014) Projecting regional change. Science 346(6216):1461–1462

Hall J (2007) Probabilistic climate scenarios may misrepresent uncertainty and lead to bad adaptation decisions. Hydrol Process 21:1127–1129. https://doi.org/10.1002/hyp.6573

Hallegatte S (2009) Strategies to adapt to an uncertain climate change. Glob Environ Change 19:240–247. https://doi.org/10.1016/j.gloenvcha.2008.12.003

Haasnoot M, Kwakkel JH, Walker WE, ter Maar J (2013) Dynamic adaptive policy pathways: a method for crafting robust decisions for a deeply uncertain world. Global Env. Change 23(485):498

Hawkins E, Sutton R (2009) The potential to narrow uncertainty in regional climate predictions. Bull Am Meteor Soc 90:1095–1107. https://doi.org/10.1175/2009BAMS2607.1

Heal G, Millner A (2014) Uncertainty and decision making in climate change economics. Rev Environ Econ Policy 8(1):120–137

Henderson-Sellers A (1993) An Antipodean climate of uncertainty. Clim Change 25(3–4):203–224. https://doi.org/10.1007/BF01098373

Hewitson B, Janetos AC, Carter TR, Giorgi F, Jones RG, Kwon W-T, Mearns LO, Schipper ELF, van Aalst M (2014) Regional context. In: Barros VR, CB Field DJ, Dokken MD, Mastrandrea KJ, Mach TE, Bilir M, Chatterjee KL, Ebi YO, Estrada RC, Genova B, Girma ES, Kissel AN, Levy S, MacCracken PR, Mastrandrea LL White (eds) Climate change 2014: impacts, adaptation, and vulnerability. Part B: regional aspects. Contribution of working group II to the fifth assessment report of the intergovernmental panel on climate change. Cambridge University Press, Cambridge, United Kingdom and New York, NY, USA, pp 1133–1197

Hoegh-Guldberg O, Hegerl G, Root T, Zwiers F, Stott P, Pierce D, Allen M (2011) Difficult but not impossible. Nat Clim Change 1:72. https://doi.org/10.1038/nclimate1107

Huggel C, Stone D, Eicken H, Hansen G (2015) Potential and limitations of the attribution of climate change impacts for informing loss and damage discussions and policies. Clim Change. https://doi.org/10.1007/s10584-015-1441-z

Huggel C, Wallimann-Helmer I, Stone D, Cramer W (2016) Nat Clim Change 6:901–908. https://doi.org/10.1038/nclimate3104

Hulme M, Pielke R, Dessai S (2009) Keeping prediction in perspective. Nature 3:126–127. https://doi.org/10.1038/climate.2009.110

Hulme M, Neil O', Dessai S (2011) Is weather event attribution necessary for adaptation funding? Nature 334(6057):764–765. https://doi.org/10.1126/science.1211740

IPCC Nakicenovic N, Swart R (eds) (2000) Special report on emissions scenarios. Cambridge University Press, Cambridge, UK, p 570

IPCC Field CB, Barros V, Stocker TF, Qin D, Dokken DJ, Ebi KL, Mastrandrea MD, Mach KJ, Plattner G-K, Allen SK, Tignor M, Midgley PM (eds) (2012), Managing the risks of extreme events and disasters to advance climate change adaptation. A special report of working groups I and II of the intergovernmental panel on climate change. Cambridge University Press, Cambridge, UK, and New York, NY, USA, 582 pp

IPCC Stocker TF, Qin D, Plattner G-K, Tignor M, Allen SK, Boschung J, Nauels A, Xia Y, Bex V, Midgley PM (eds) (2013) Climate change 2013: the physical science basis. Contribution of working group I to the fifth assessment report of the intergovernmental panel on climate change. Cambridge University Press, Cambridge, United Kingdom and New York, NY, USA, 1535 pp

IPCC Field CB, Barros VR, Dokken DJ, Mach KJ, Mastrandrea MD, Bilir TE, Chatterjee M, Ebi KL, Estrada YO, Genova RC, Girma B, Kissel ES, Levy AN, MacCracken S, Mastrandrea PR, White LL (eds) (2014a) Climate change 2014: impacts, adaptation, and vulnerability. Part A: global and sectoral aspects. contribution of working group II to the fifth assessment report of the intergovernmental panel on climate change. Cambridge University Press, Cambridge, United Kingdom and New York, NY, USA, 1132 pp

IPCC Barros VR., Field CB, Dokken DJ, Mastrandrea MD, Mach KJ, Bilir TE, Chatterjee M, Ebi KL, Estrada YO, Genova RC, Girma B, Kissel ES, Levy AN, MacCracken S, Mastrandrea PR, White LL (eds) (2014b) Climate change 2014: impacts, adaptation, and vulnerability. Part B: regional aspects. Contribution of working group II to the fifth assessment report of the intergovernmental panel on climate change. Cambridge University Press, Cambridge, United Kingdom and New York, NY, USA, pp. 688

James RA, Jones RG, Boyd E, Young HR, Otto FEL, Huggel C, Fuglestvedt JS (2018) Attribution: how is it relevant for loss and damage policy and practice? In Mechler R, Bouwer L, Schinko T, Surminski S, Linnerooth-Bayer J (eds) Loss and damage from climate change. Concepts, methods and policy options. Springer, Cham, pp 113–154

Jha AK, Bloch R, Lamond J (2012) Cities and flooding: a guide to integrated urban flood risk management for the 21st Century. World Bank. https://openknowledge.worldbank.org/handle/10986/2241. License: CC BY 3.0 IGO Accessed 23 Jan 2013

Kerr RA (2011) Vital details of global warming are eluding forecasters. Science 334(6053):173–174. https://doi.org/10.1126/science.334.6053.173

Kirtman B, Power SB, Adedoyin JA, Boer GJ, Bojariu R, Camilloni I, Doblas-Reyes FJ, Fiore AM, Kimoto M, Meehl GA, Prather M, Sarr A, Schär C, Sutton R, van Oldenborgh GJ, Vecchi G, Wang HJ (2013) Near-term climate change: projections and predictability. In: Stocker TF, Qin D, Plattner G-K, Tignor M, Allen SK, Boschung J, Nauels A, Xia Y, Bex V, Midgley PM (eds) Climate change 2013: the physical science basis. Contribution of working group I to the fifth assessment report of the intergovernmental panel on climate change. Cambridge University Press, Cambridge, United Kingdom and New York, NY, USA

Klein RJT, Huq S, Denton F, Downing TE, Richels RG, Robinson JB, Toth FL (2007) Interrelationships between adaptation and mitigation. In: Parry ML, Canziani OF, Palutikof JP, van der Linden PJ, Hanson CE (eds) Climate change 2007: impacts, adaptation and vulnerability. Contribution of working group II to the fourth assessment report of the intergovernmental panel on climate change. Cambridge University Press, Cambridge, UK, pp 745–777

Knutti R, Allen MR, Friedlingstein P, Gregory JM, Hegerl GC, Meehl GA, Meinshausen M, Murphy JM, Plattner GK, Raper SCB, Stocker TF, Stott PA, Teng H, Wigley TML (2007) A review of uncertainties in global temperature projections over the twenty-first century. J Clim 21:2651. https://doi.org/10.1175/2007JCLI2119.1

Knutti R, Sedlacek J (2013) Robustness and uncertainties in the new CMIP5 climate model projections. Nat Clim Change 3:369–373. https://doi.org/10.1038/nclimate1716

Kreft S (2012) Loss & damage overview and summary of party submissions on the role of the convention. A Germanwatch e. V. Paper. http://www.loss-and-damage.net/download/6868.pdf Accessed 29 Jan 2012

Lempert RJ (2002) A new decision sciences for complex systems. Proc Natl Acad Sci 99(10), supp. 3:7309–7313. https://doi.org/10.1073/pnas.082081699

Lempert RJ, Collins MT (2007) Managing the risk of uncertain threshold responses: comparison of robust, optimum, and precautionary approaches. Risk Anal 27(4):1009–1026. https://doi.org/10.1111/j.1539-6924.2007.00940.x

Lempert RJ, Haasnoot M (2017) Decision-making under uncertain climate change: a response, and an invitation, to Bret Stephens, in Society for Decision Making Under Deep Uncertainty

Blog. http://www.deepuncertainty.org/2017/05/09/decision-making-under-uncertain-climate-change-a-response-and-an-invitation-to-bret-stephens/. Accessed 10 May 2017

Lempert RJ, Kalra N, Peyraud S, Mao Z, Tan SB, Cira D, Lotsch A (2013) Ensuring robust flood risk management in Ho Chi Minh City, Policy Research Working Paper 6465, The World Bank. https://doi.org/10.1596/1813-9450-6465

Lopez A, Wilby RL, Fung F, New M (2010) Emerging approaches to climate risk management. In: Fung F., Lopez A, New M (eds) Modelling the impacts of climate change in water resources, Wiley & Sons, Ltd, Chichester, UK. https://doi.org/10.1002/9781444324921.ch5

McDermott TKJ (2016) Investing in disaster risk management in an uncertain climate, World Bank Policy Research Working Paper, WPS7631

McDermott TKJ, Surminski S (2017) How to make climate science useful for the decision-making process? Experiences from the local city-level, forthcoming

Mechler R, Hochrainer S, Kull D, Khan F, Patnaik U, Linnerooth-Bayer J (2009) Increasing resilience to extreme events Options (IIASA, Laxenburg, Austria). http://webarchive.iiasa.ac.at/Admin/PUB/Documents/XO-09-076.pdf. Accessed 12 Feb 2012

Mechler R et al (2018) Science for Loss and damage. Findings and propositions. In: Mechler R, Bouwer L, Schinko T, Surminski S, Linnerooth-Bayer J (eds) Loss and damage from climate change. Concepts, methods and policy options. Springer, Cham, pp 3–37

Meinshausen M, Smith SJ, Calvin K, Daniel JS, Kainuma LT, Lamarque J-F, Matsumoto K, Montzka SA, Raper SCB, Riahi K, Thomson A, Velders GJM, van Vuuren DPP (2011) The RCP greenhouse gas concentrations and their extensions from 1765 to 2003. Clim Change 109:213. https://doi.org/10.1007/s10584-011-0156-z

Merz B, Hall J, Disse M, Schumann A (2010) Fluvial flood risk management in a changing world. Nat Hazards Earth Sys Sci 10:509–527. https://doi.org/10.5194/nhess-10-509-2010

Mimura N, Pulwarty RS, Duc DM, Elshinnawy I, Redsteer MH, Huang HQ, Nkem JN, Sanchez Rodriguez RA (2014) Adaptation planning and implementation. In ref IPCC (2014a)

Moss RH, Babiker WM, Brinkman S, Calvo SE, Carter TR, Edmonds J, Elgizouli I, Emori S, Erda L, Hibbard K, Jones R, Kainuma M, Kellehe J, Lamarque JF, Manning M, Matthews B, Meehl J, Meyer L, Mitchell J, Nakicenovic N, O'Neill B, Pichs R, Riahi K, Rose S, Runci P, Stouffer R, van Vuuren D, Weyant J, Wilbanks T, van Ypersele JP, Zurek M (2008) Towards new scenarios for analysis of emissions, climate change, impacts, and response strategies, Intergovernmental Panel on Climate Change, Geneva, Switzerland, pp 132

OECD (2014) Cities and climate change: national governments enabling local action. OECD

Oppenheimer M, Campos M, Warren R, Birkmann J, Luber G, O'Neill B, Takahashi K (2014) Emergent risks and key vulnerabilities. In: Field CB, Barros VR, Dokken DJ, Mach KJ, Mastrandrea MD, Bilir TE, Chatterjee M, Ebi KL, Estrada YO, Genova RC, Girma B, Kissel ES, Levy AN, MacCracken S, Mastrandrea PR, White LL (eds) Climate change 2014: impacts, adaptation, and vulnerability. Part A: global and sectoral aspects. Contribution of working group II to the fifth assessment report of the intergovernmental panel on climate change. Cambridge University Press, Cambridge, United Kingdom and New York, NY, USA, pp 1039–1099

Oreskes N, Stainsforth DA, Smith LA (2010) Adaptation to global warming: do climate models tell us what we need to know? Philos Sci 77(5):1012–1028. https://doi.org/10.1086/657428

Peterson TC, Stott PA, Herring S (2012) Explaining extreme events of 2011 from a climate perspective, Bull Am Meteor Soc 93(7):041–1061. https://doi.org/10.1175/BAMS-D-12-00021.1

Ranger N, Hallegatte S, Bhattacharya S, Bachu M, Priya S, Dhore K, Rafique F, Mathur P, Naville N, Henriet F, Herweijer C, Pohit S, Corfee-Morlot J (2011) A preliminary assessment of the potential impact of climate change on flood risk in Mumbai. Clim Change 104:139–167. https://doi.org/10.1007/s10584-010-9979-2

Ranger N, Millner A, Dietz S, Fankhauser S, Lopez A, Ruta G (2010a) Adaptation in the UK: a decision making process, Grantham/CCCEP Policy Brief. http://www2.lse.ac.uk/GranthamInstitute/publications/Policy/docs/PB-Ranger-adaptation-UK.pdf. Accessed 29 Jan 2013

Ranger N, Millner A, Lopez A, Ruta G, Hardiman A (2010b) Adaptation in the UK: a decision making process: technical annexes. http://www2.lse.ac.uk/GranthamInstitute/publications/Policy/docs/PB-technical-annexes-rangeretal.pdf. Accessed 29 Jan 2013

Reeder T, Ranger N (2010) How do you adapt in an uncertain world? Lessons from the Thames Estuary 2100 project. World Resources Report, Washington DC

Risby JS, O'Kane TJ (2011) Sources of knowledge and ignorance in climate research. Clim Change 108(4):755–773. https://doi.org/10.1007/s10584-011-0186-6

Schellnhuber HJ, Frieler K, Kabat P (2014) The elephant, the blind, and the intersectoral inter-comparison of climate impacts. PNAS 111:3225–3227. https://doi.org/10.1073/pnas.1321791111

Schewe J, Heinke J, Gerten D, Haddeland I, Arnell NW, Clark DB, Dankers R, Eisner S, Fekete BM, Colón-González FJ, Gosling SN, Kim H, Liu X, Masaki Y, Portmann FT, Satoh Y, Stacke T, Tang O, Wada Y, Wisser D, Albrecht T, Frieler K, Piontek F, Warszawski L, Kabat P (2014) Multimodel assessment of water scarcity under climate change. PNAS 111(9):3245–3250. https://doi.org/10.1073/pnas.1222460110

Schinko T, Mechler R, Hochrainer-Stigler S (2018) The risk and policy space for loss and damage: integrating notions of distributive and compensatory justice with comprehensive climate risk management. In: Mechler R, Bouwer L, Schinko T, Surminski S, Linnerooth-Bayer J (eds) Loss and damage from climate change. Concepts, methods and policy options. Springer, Cham, pp 83–110

Schneider SH (1983) CO_2, climate and society: a brief overview. In: Chen RS, Boulding E, Schneider SH (eds) Social science research and climate change: an interdisciplinary appraisal. Reidel, D., Boston, MA, USA, pp 9–15

Simlinger F, Mayer B (2018) Legal responses to climate change induced loss and damage. In: Mechler R, Bouwer L, Schinko T, Surminski S, Linnerooth-Bayer J (eds) Loss and damage from climate change. Concepts, methods and policy options. Springer, Cham, pp 179–203

Smit B, Burton I, Klein RJT, Wandel J (2000) An anatomy of climate change and variability. Clim Change 45:223–251, and references therein. https://doi.org/10.1007/978-94-017-3010-5_12

Smith LA, Stern N (2011) Uncertainty in science and its role in climate policy. Trans R Soc London A: Math Phys Eng Sci 369(1956):4818–4841. https://doi.org/10.1098/rsta.2011.0149

Smithers J, Smit B (1997) Human adaptation to climatic variability and change. Glob Environ Change 7:129–146. https://doi.org/10.1016/S0959-3780(97)00003-4

Stainforth DA, Allen MR, Tredger ER, Smith LA (2007) Confidence, uncertainty and decision-support relevance in climate predictions. Philos Trans R Soc London A: Math Phys Eng Sci 365(1857):2145–2161. https://doi.org/10.1098/rsta.2007.2074

Stott PA, Karoly DJ, Zwiers FF (2017) Is the choice of statistical paradigm critical in extreme event attribution studies? Clim Change. https://doi.org/10.1007/s10584-017-2049-2

Surminski S, Lopez A (2014) Concept of loss and damage of climate change–a new challenge for climate decision-making? A climate science perspective. Clim Dev 7:267–277

Tebaldi C, Knutti R (2007) The use of multi-model ensemble in probabilistic climate projections. Philos Trans R Soc London A: Math Phys Eng Sci 365(1857):2053–2075. https://doi.org/10.1098/rsta.2007.2076

Trenberth KE (2012) Framing the way to relate climate extremes to climate change. Clim Change 115:283–290. https://doi.org/10.1007/s10584-012-0441-5

Trenberth KE, Fasullo JT (2012) Climate extremes and climate change: The Russian heat wave and other climate extremes of 2010. J Geophys Res: Atmos 117:D17103. https://doi.org/10.1029/2012JD018020

UNFCCC (2008) Compendium on methods and tools to evaluate impacts of, and vulnerability and adaptation to climate change. UNFCCC Secretariat. http://unfccc.int/files/adaptation/nairobi_workprogramme/compendium_on_methods_tools/application/pdf/20080307_compendium_m_t_complete.pdf. Accessed 16 Feb 2014

UNFCCC (2012a) Current knowledge on relevant methodologies and data requirements as well as lessons learned and gaps identified at different levels, in assessing the risk of loss and damage associated with the adverse effects of climate change. United Nations Framework Convention on Climate Change (UNFCCC). Technical paper, FCCC/TP/2012/1. http://unfccc.int/resource/docs/2012/tp/01.pdf. Accessed 23 Jan 2013

UNFCCC (2012b) Report on the expert meeting on assessing the risk of loss and damage associated with the adverse effects of climate change. United Nations Framework Convention on Climate Change (UNFCCC). Subsidiary Body for Implementation (SBI), FCCC/SBI/2012/INF.3. http://unfccc.int/resource/docs/2012/sbi/eng/inf03.pdf. Accessed 29 Jan 2012

UNFCCC (2015) Paris Agreement. FCCC/CP/2015/L.9/Rev.1 https://unfccc.int/resource/docs/2015/cop21/eng/l09r01.pdf. Accessed 24 May 2016

van Vuuren DP, Isaac M, Kundzewicz ZW, Arnell N, Barker T, Criqui P Hilderink H, Hinkel J, Hof A, Kitous A, Kram T, Mechler R, Scrieciu S (2011) The use of scenarios as the basis for combined assessment of climate change mitigation and adaptation. Global Environ Change 21(2):575–591. [N/A]. https://doi.org/10.1016/j.gloenvcha.20https://doi.org/10.11.003

Wallimann-Helmer I, Meyer L, Mintz-Woo K, Schinko T, Serdeczny O (2018) The ethical challenges in the context of climate loss and damage. In: Mechler R, Bouwer L, Schinko T, Surminski S, Linnerooth-Bayer J (eds) Loss and damage from climate change. Concepts, methods and policy options. Springer, Cham, pp 39–62

Watkiss P (2015) A review of the economics of adaptation and climate-resilient development. Centre for Climate Change Economics and Policy Working Paper No. 231, Grantham Research Institute on Climate Change and the Environment Working Paper No. 205

Watkiss P, Hunt A (2011) Method for the UK Adaptation Economic Assessment (Economics of Climate Resilience). Final Report to Defra. May. Deliverable 2.2.1

Watkiss P, Hunt A (2016) Assessing climate-resilient development options. In: Fankhauser S, McDermott TKJ (eds) the economics of climate-resilient development. Edward Elgar, Massachusetts, pp 99–124

Weaver CPRJ, Lempert RJ, Brown C (2013) Improving the contribution of climate model information to decision making: the value and demands of robust decision frameworks. Wiley Interdisc Rev: Clim Change 4(1):39–60. https://doi.org/10.1002/wcc.202

Weisheimer A, Schaller N, O'Reilly C, MacLeod AA, Palmer T (2017) Atmospheric seasonal forecasts of the twentieth century: multi-decadal variability in predictive skill of the winter North Atlantic Oscillation (NAO) and their potential value for extreme attribution. Q J R Meteorol Soc. https://doi.org/10.1002/qj.2976

Wilby RL, Dessai S (2010) Robust adaptation to climate change. Weather 65(7):180–185. https://doi.org/10.1002/wea.543

Wilby RL, Troni J, Biot Y, Tedd L, Hewitson BC, Smith DM, Sutton RT (2009) A review of climate risk information for adaptation and development planning. Int J Climatol 29(9):1193–1215. https://doi.org/10.1002/joc1839

Willows R, Reynard N, Meadowcroft I, Connell R (2003) Climate adaptation: risk, uncertainty and decision-making, Technical Report. In: Willows, RI, Connell RK (eds) UKCIP, Oxford, UK

Chapter 12
Integrated Disaster Risk Management and Adaptation

W. J. Wouter Botzen, Laurens M. Bouwer, Paolo Scussolini, Onno Kuik, Marjolijn Haasnoot, Judy Lawrence and Jeroen C. J. H. Aerts

Abstract This chapter discusses integrated approaches to the management of risks related to extreme weather and climate change. This is done with the Loss and Damage (L&D) mechanism of the UNFCCC in mind. Relevant insights are provided for climate policy negotiators and policymakers on how risk management and adaptation interact with L&D solutions, and vice versa, on how L&D-related activities can support risk reduction and adaptation in vulnerable countries. Particular attention is devoted to how risk management can help society confront the impacts of weather disasters in relation to anthropogenic climate change. A holistic view of risk management is presented by discussing: the state-of-the art of risk assessment methods; (cost-benefit) evaluations of risk management options; household-scale risk reduction strategies; insurance schemes for residual risk and their relations with risk reduction; and the design of adaptation pathways to cope with uncertain timing and intensity of climate change impacts. Each topic is illustrated with concrete case studies. Finally, conclusions are drawn on the links between disaster risk management, climate adaptation and the L&D mechanism.

W. J. Wouter Botzen (✉) · P. Scussolini · O. Kuik · J. C. J. H. Aerts
Institute for Environmental Studies, VU University Amsterdam, Amsterdam, The Netherlands
e-mail: wouter.botzen@vu.nl

W. J. Wouter Botzen
Utrecht University School of Economics, Utrecht, The Netherlands

W. J. Wouter Botzen
Risk Management and Decision Processes Center, The Wharton School, University of Pennsylvania, Philadelphia, PA, USA

L. M. Bouwer · M. Haasnoot
Deltares, Delft, The Netherlands
e-mail: laurens.bouwer@hzg.de

L. M. Bouwer
Climate Service Center Germany (GERICS), Hamburg, Germany

J. Lawrence
New Zealand Climate Change Research Institute, Victoria University of Wellington, Wellington, New Zealand

R. Mechler et al. (eds.), *Loss and Damage from Climate Change*, Climate Risk Management, Policy and Governance, https://doi.org/10.1007/978-3-319-72026-5_12

Keywords Adaptation pathways · Cost-Benefit analysis · Damage mitigation Insurance · Loss&Damage · Risk assessment · Risk management · Protection

12.1 Introduction: Integrated Climate Risk Management in the Loss and Damage Context

The goal of this chapter is to establish the links between the concept of Loss and Damage (L&D) and climate risk management, with relevance to the L&D mechanism under the UNFCCC. Climate risk management is understood to include natural disaster risk reduction and adaptation to climate change (IPCC 2012). L&D was recognised in the 2015 Paris Agreement as a new pillar of climate policy, next to mitigation of greenhouse gas emissions and adaptation (UNFCCC 2015). Its purpose is to address irreversible losses from anthropogenic climate change, and resulting damages beyond what adaptation can avoid. In this context, efforts are currently made by the UNFCCC to propose activities under this pillar as part of the new climate agreement, in order to address L&D. However, various interpretations exist, which are further discussed in the chapter by James et al. (2018); see introduction by Mechler et al. (2018a); and the chapter by Bouwer (2018). For the purpose of this chapter, we will apply the "Risk management perspective" proposed by James et al. (2015) and further operationalised in the chapter by Schinko et al. (2018).

This implies that L&D refers to impacts 'beyond adaptation,' and that adaptation can prevent L&D (ex ante), while other approaches (such as insurance) can help dealing with L&D (ex post). Appropriate measures for risk management include natural disaster risk reduction through engineering solutions or other measures to mitigate risk, and risk transfer mechanisms, such as insurance. Climate risk management in this chapter is narrowed down to include adaptation to anticipated changes in extreme weather risk due to anthropogenic climate change as well as reduction of extreme weather risk beyond adaptation (the adaptation deficit). Climate adaptation according to the IPCC (2012) definition is:

> the process of adjustment to actual or expected climate and its effects. In human systems, adaptation seeks to moderate or avoid harm or exploit beneficial opportunities. In some natural systems, human intervention may facilitate adjustment to expected climate and its effects.

In this definition, adaptation would not include dealing with L&D that occur beyond the prevention of risks, because when L&D occurs, impacts have not been moderated in some way. In this respect L&D solutions can be viewed as addressing the residual risk after adaptation. Natural disaster risk is defined as a function of hazard, exposure and vulnerability. In simplified form this function is often described as follows.

$$\text{Risk} = \text{Hazard} \times \text{Exposure} \times \text{Vulnerability}$$

Hazard is the natural event, in the case of flooding characterised by frequency and intensity (water depth, direction, and flow velocity). Exposure is the set of assets, people and (economic) activities that can be hit by the hazard. Vulnerability indicates the extent to which these assets, people and activities can suffer damage when a hazard occurs. Vulnerability is typically expressed as the mean loss (or the full distribution of losses) for a given intensity of the hazard.

Climate change-related risks, such as weather-related natural disasters, are thus the result of a complex interplay of natural hazards, like storm and flood conditions, and exposure of assets and their vulnerability, i.e. susceptibility to damage (IPCC 2012). While climate change may increase the frequency or intensity of certain natural hazards, exposure and vulnerability are determined by socio-economic development and human decision-making. It is these latter processes, such as population and economic growth in hazard-prone areas that have been the dominant drivers of increases in natural disaster losses in the past (Bouwer 2011; IPCC 2012; see also introduction by Mechler et al. 2018a). Natural hazard risk management can steer these vulnerability and exposure components of risk and traditionally includes all activities aimed at minimising impacts of natural hazards before, during and after an event (Botzen and van den Bergh 2009). Thereby, actions related to anticipated increased risk levels, because of anthropogenic climate change or other drivers, can address the prevention of risk (through adaptation), or the minimisation of impacts during an event (emergency measures), or after the event (clean-up, repair, compensation and rehabilitation). Climate change impacts can be avoided by risk management policies that limit exposure to natural disaster risk, for example by steering development away from hazard-prone areas, by better protecting these developments, and limiting vulnerability of exposed assets, for example through implementing and enforcing building code policies that limit wind or flood damages (Aerts and Botzen 2011; Czajkowski and Simmons 2014).

Integrated risk management takes a holistic view (in the sense that it considers various drivers of risk, and possible mitigation options ranging from structural measures, to emergency management and risk transfer such as insurance). Moreover, it uses a variety of approaches for the assessment of risk and evaluation of options, borrowing methods from natural sciences, engineering, economics, ecology and social sciences. An important cornerstone of successful risk management lies in the application of an assessment of risk, and the analysis of costs (of actions) and benefits (reduced risk) of risk management options in order to identify economically optimal strategies. These analyses show that it often pays off to prevent disastrous damages, or at least prepare for managing these damages when they occur (Mechler 2016). In addition to economic appraisal of risk management options, other considerations can come into play when deciding about the implementation of risk management strategies, such as equity, acceptable risk levels and impacts on the environment.

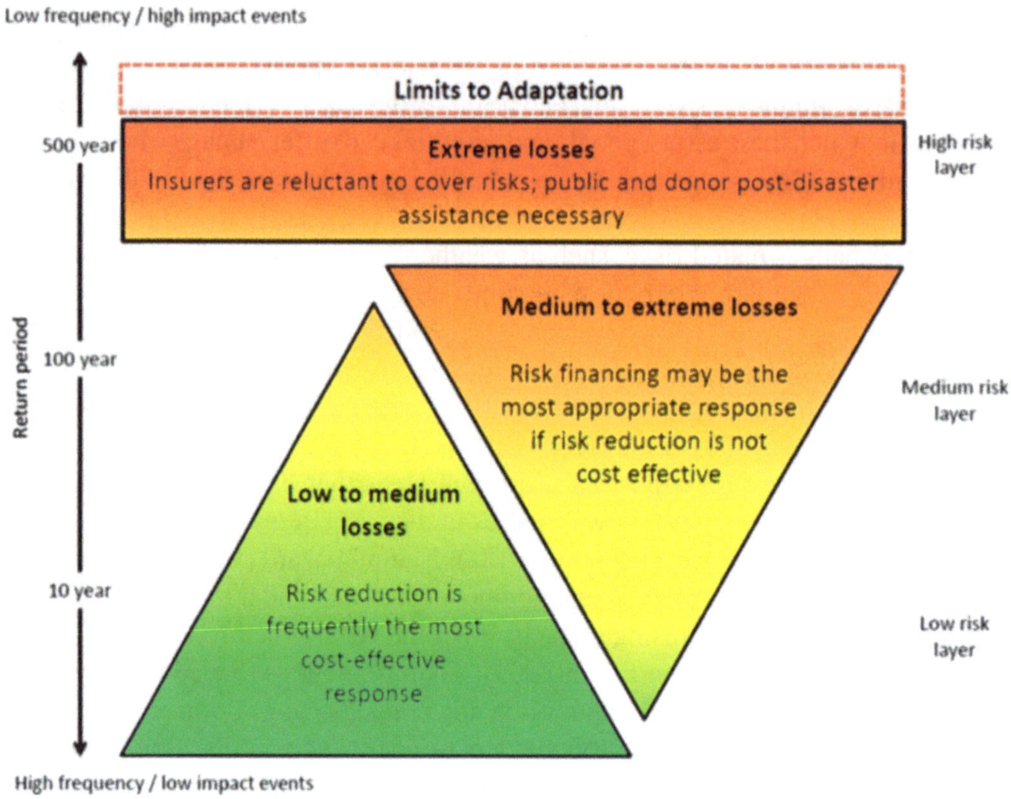

Fig. 12.1 Layered disaster risk management. *Source* Mechler et al. (2014a)

The economic efficiency of actions however depends on the frequency and severity of impacts. For instance, Mechler et al. (2014a) proposed an approach (*risk layering*) where frequent (up to a return period of once in 200 years) events are avoided through risk reduction, while impacts from rare events would need to be covered by risk transfer which includes natural disaster insurance and regional risk pooling mechanisms. Extremely rare losses may not be economically efficient to address with insurance, and may need to partly be compensated by the public sector or the international community (see Fig. 12.1; chapter by Schinko et al. 2018).

Alternatively, public-private partnerships in financial compensation arrangements may be needed for covering such extreme risks (Kunreuther 2015). Applied to L&D from anthropogenic climate change, this means that avoiding the L&D by greenhouse gas mitigation or adaptation will often be a preferred approach, at least to a degree that this is economically efficient, rather than having to address L&D. Moreover, it should be realised that important relations can exist between the way L&D measures are implemented and incentives for adaptation. For example, ill-designed compensation mechanisms that do not provide financial incentives for risk reduction may result in moral hazard effects when investments in natural risk reduction decline because financial compensation for natural disasters from external parties is expected. On the other hand, adequate financial incentives for risk reduction may be integrated in L&D measures, for example, when natural disaster insurance arrangements stimulate risk reduction by their policyholders through risk-based premiums which reward risk reduction activities with premium discounts (Bozen 2013). A further discussion of such incentives related to insurance is provided in the chapter by Linnerooth-Bayer et al. (2018).

Risk reduction and adaptation will have a pertinent influence on the vulnerability of countries to anthropogenic climate change. Various actions exist at present, including:

- National and local public actors addressing natural hazard risk, including planning for increased future risk because of climate change, supported by public sector budgets;
- Private actors reducing their risk and planning for climate adaptation, often supported by (national) public actors;
- International support to reduce natural disaster risk, such as through coordinating activities under the UNISDR and through implement disaster risk reduction actions by donors and International Financial Institutions (IFIs), such as development banks;
- International support to implement climate adaptation actions, including support from funds under UNFCCC and from other donors.[1]

This implies that past impacts from extreme weather and climate events cannot be taken as the norm, because future impacts will be different depending on adaptation efforts that are expected to reduce vulnerabilities. This is already clear from the historical record, as can be seen in the chapter by Bouwer (2018). Also, from an economic perspective adaptation actions and risk reduction need to be considered, and economically efficient adaptation solutions should be implemented, before L&D can be accepted as outcome. The underlying reason is that it is cheaper to make the investment to reduce the impacts than to absorb the impacts in any other way, including mechanisms set up to deal with residual damages, like L&D.

In this chapter, different approaches for risk management and their effects on limiting risk from climate change are discussed. An emphasis is placed on case study insight and actions that avoid damages. Successively, we discuss the following levels of actions:

- Assessment of weather-related disaster risk, as a basis for decision making on risk management;
- Cost-benefit analysis of adaptation strategies in which risk assessment methods are used to evaluate the benefits of adaptation;
- Household-level actions to reduce risk;
- Relations between ex post compensation through insurance and incentives for household risk reduction;
- Adaptation planning approaches including adaptation pathways.

[1]For example see https://www.adaptation-fund.org/projects-programmes/.

The final section provides a synthesis of the different approaches presented in the chapter, and draws conclusions on the links between climate risk management and the L&D mechanism.

12.2 Climate Risk Assessment—Case Studies Jakarta and Ho Chi Minh City

The decisions on adaptation interventions to minimise the impacts of climate change requires the understanding of what is the amount of risk that can or cannot be reduced. The amounts of risk that cannot be reduced (residual impacts) will to some extent be relevant to the L&D mechanism. For risk assessment, two activities are necessary: (1) to quantify the present and future risk in a risk model framework; and (2) to quantify the effectiveness of possible mitigation or adaptation measures in reducing risk.

We present here two recent case studies that apply such assessments for Jakarta, Indonesia, and for Ho Chi Minh City, Vietnam, two Asian megacities that display high vulnerability to natural hazards, in particular floods, and to climate change.

In Jakarta multiple drivers compound the risk of flooding: the huge rate of land subsidence, due to groundwater extraction, sea level rise and change in precipitation patterns, both due to climate change. Following the definition of risk reported in Sect. 12.1. Budiyono et al. (2015) employed a hydrological and hydraulic model to produce maps of river flood. Moreover, they assembled specific exposure and vulnerability data for each land use type, by tapping the expert judgement of local stakeholders. A framework for quantifying flood risk was then build, based on the Damagescanner model of Klijn et al. (2007), which produced results in good agreement with reported flood damages, and estimated current expected annual damage in the order of hundreds of thousand USD per year.

A successive study expanded this modelling framework to project the risk assessment into the future until year 2050 (Budiyono et al. 2016). The hazard modelling incorporated precipitation changes from a combination of four Representative Concentration Pathways (RCP) emission scenarios and five distinct climate models, and a low and a high scenario of sea level rise to explore the probabilities and scenario-dependency of changes in flooding. Furthermore, the effect of the severe land subsidence rates on hazard, and of land use changes on exposure were included. The results show that the probability density function of annual damages shifts to much higher values in the absence of adaptation (see Fig. 12.2). This is primarily due to the effects of land subsidence, but also the result of sea level rise. Climate-change induced changes in maximum rainfall, on the other hand, introduce a large uncertainty in the future damages, as some models and scenarios imply an increase, while others a decrease in hazard. If land use will change according to the government plans, it will have the potential of reducing risk by some 12%. Finally, Budiyono et al. (2017) calculated the risk-reducing potential of a planned upgrade of the polder

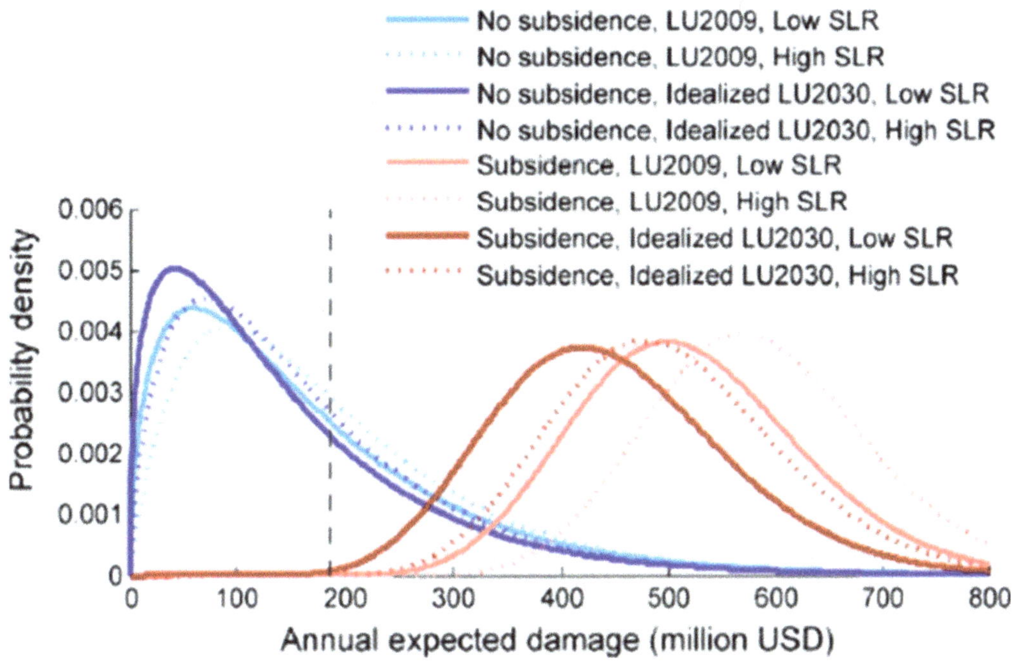

Fig. 12.2 Flood risk in Jakarta measured as annual expected damage. The vertical dashed line represents the present value. The coloured curves represent probability density functions, obtained by fitting gamma distributions to 20 combinations of climate models and emission scenarios, thus each representing the uncertainty in future precipitation extremes. Curves are shown with and without land subsidence, with land use (LU) of year 2009 and LU of 2030, and with low and high sea level rise (SLR). *Source* Modified from Budiyono et al. (2016)

system via construction and rehabilitation of dikes. This is done by cutting the risk curve, also known as the exceedance probability-damage curve, assuming that each polder will provide a standard of protection expressed as the return period of the event it can withstand (e.g., a 50-year flood).

For Ho Chi Minh City, the risk of flooding is quantified under present conditions, and under scenarios of climate and socioeconomic change over the 21st century. This city already suffers regular disruption to livelihoods and business due to seasonal floods, mostly due to storm surges from the South China Sea and heavy precipitation and river discharge.

The assessment includes a number of steps where quantitative information is processed (Fig. 12.3). Following, as for Jakarta, the risk definition in Sect. 12.1, the flood hazard is quantified via hydrodynamic modelling, for four return periods, the exposure is represented by land use and population density maps, and the vulnerability is expressed in vulnerability curves that are specific of the land use. To simulate the future, the framework incorporates: in the flood modelling, projections of sea level rise from regionalised projections relative to two RCP emission scenarios, one of moderate and one of high greenhouse gas emissions; in the impact modelling projections of socio-economic growth from two plausible Shared Socioeconomic Pathway (SSP) scenarios. These pressures are scenario-dependent.

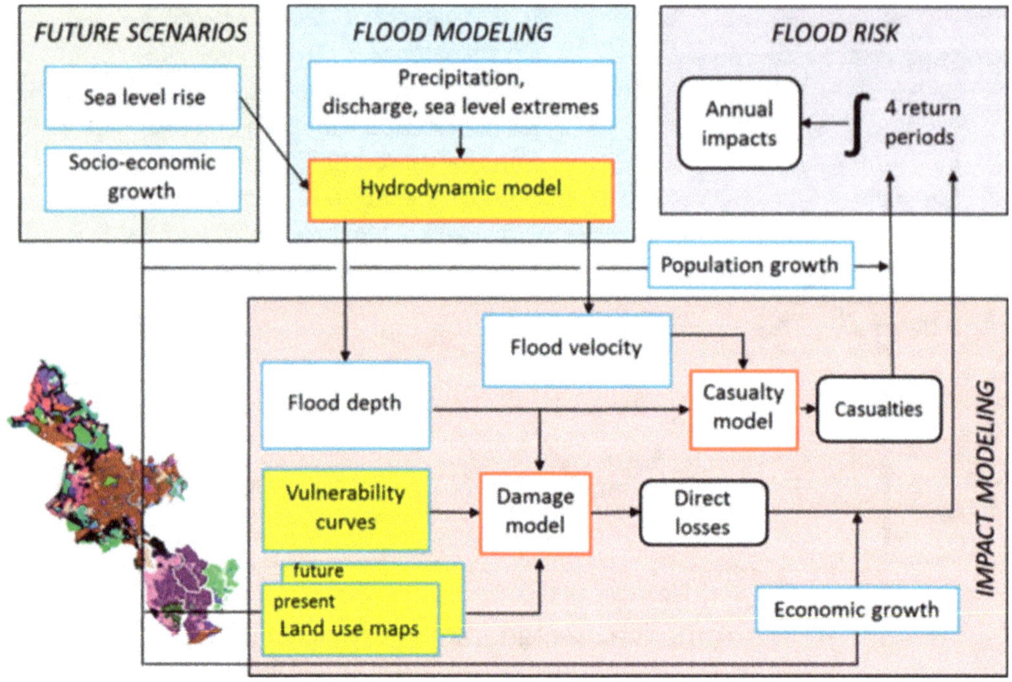

Fig. 12.3 Conceptual framework of the flood risk assessment of Ho Chi Minh City. Yellow boxes indicate the points in the modelling where adaptation measures are implemented. *Source* Modified from Scussolini et al. (2017)

The next step is the modelling of two main impact indicators: the direct economic losses, and the likely casualties. Direct losses include damage to different types of buildings, infrastructure and crops, and are calculated with the Damagescanner model, by combining flood maps and land use maps (for the present and for the future) through the use of vulnerability curves. Casualties are modelled based on the field of flood velocities and depths that is produced by the hydraulic model, and applying empirical relationships to local information on the number people present in Ho Chi Minh City.

The following step is the integration of the impacts of floods of each magnitude across four return periods, to quantity the risk, in terms of average annual impacts. As can be seen in Fig. 12.4 the already large expected annual damage and the potential casualties increase substantially until the year 2050 and 2100, depending on the scenario and if adaptation measures are not taken.

The Ho Chi Minh City case study goes one step further than the Jakarta study by analysing the risk reducing potential of (combinations of) four flood risk management measures. These measures are: the construction of a ring dike around the central districts, the elevation of land in the districts where risk is higher, the retrofitting of residential and commercial buildings by dry-proofing, and spatial reorganisation of land use. These are incorporated in the flood hazard and impact modelling (yellow boxes in Fig. 12.3).

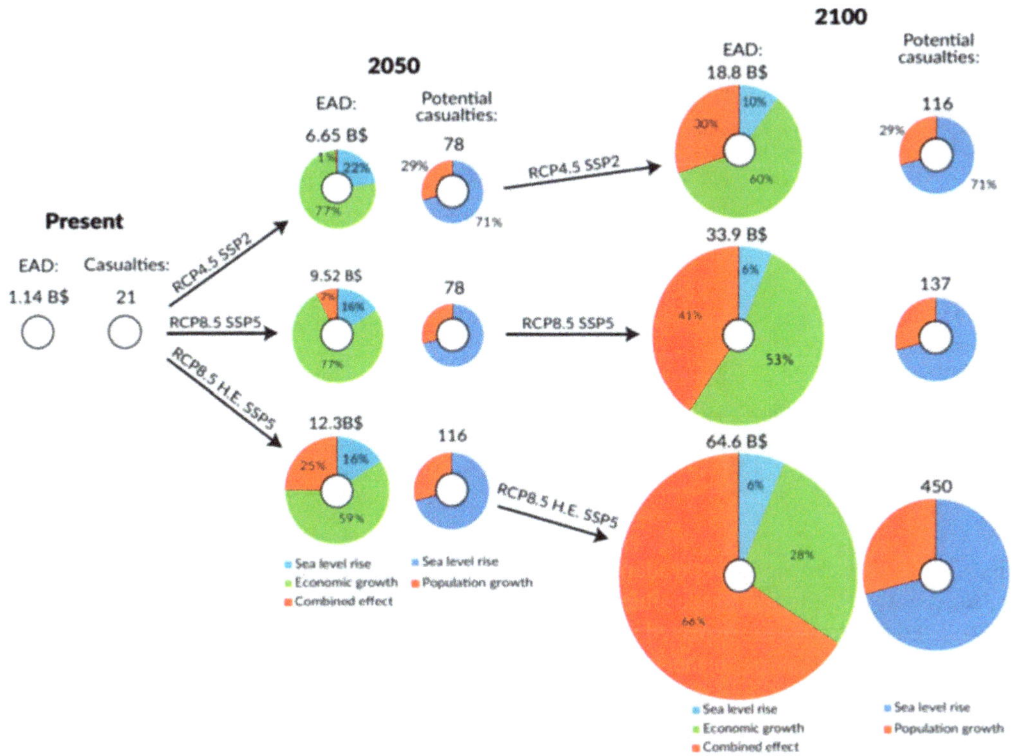

Fig. 12.4 Increase in flood risk (expected annual damage—EAD—and annual potential casualties) of floods in Ho Chi Minh City, from the present to year 2050 and 2100, for three combinations of climate and socio-economic scenarios: RCP4.5 and SSP2, RCP8.5 and SSP5, and the high-end of RCP8.5 and SSP5. The area of the circles is proportional to the intensity of the impacts. The different colours indicate how much of the increase (with respect to the present impacts, in the white circles) is attributed to sea level rise, to economic growth, to population growth, and to the combination of sea level rise and economic growth. *Source* Modified from Scussolini et al. (2017)

The analysis shows that appropriate adaptation can considerably reduce losses and damages (Fig. 12.5), but none of the solutions investigated will reduce impacts to zero, which means that a residual risk remains. The cost-benefit analysis results of these measures are reported in Sect. 12.3. These results can inform decision-making on which adaptation pathway to take.

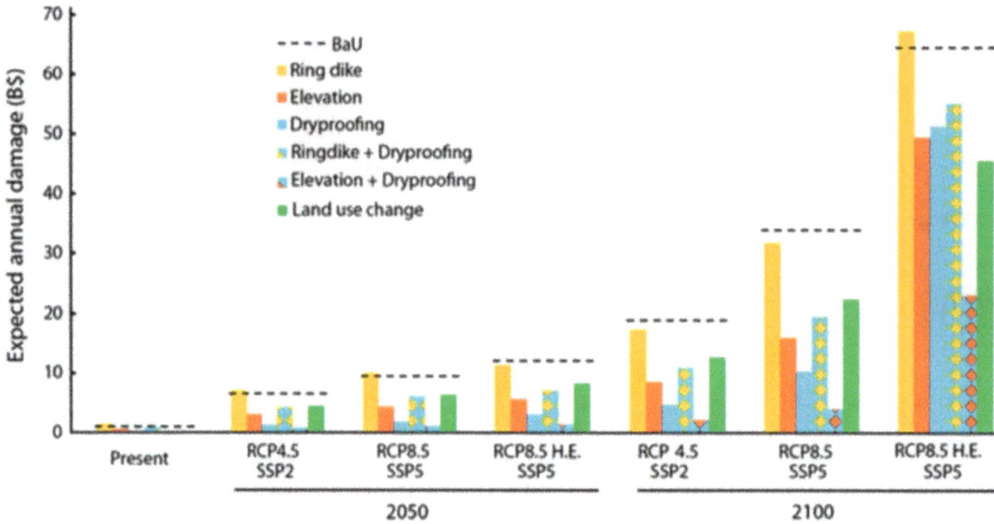

Fig. 12.5 Performance of several adaptation measures and strategies in reducing the future impacts of sea level rise, compared to the situation without adaptation (Business-as-usual, BaU). The risk is displayed in terms of the expected annual damage (not discounted), for the present and for three combinations of scenarios in the years 2050 and 2100: RCP4.5 and SSP2, RCP8.5 and SSP5, RCP8.5 High-End (H.E.) and SSP5. *Source* Modified from Scussolini et al. (2017)

12.3 Cost-Benefit and Multi-criteria Analysis of Risk Management Options—Case Studies from Ho Chi Minh City and The Netherlands

After conducting an assessment of natural disaster risk and identification of risk management options, these options can be appraised using methods like cost-benefit analysis (CBA). CBA is a widely-used tool for prioritising projects, by assessing the project's net benefits to society. In an application to natural disaster risk, CBA can make use of natural disaster risk assessment methods that can estimate the benefits (avoided natural disaster losses) of risk management options. The basic question that is addressed by CBA is: will society as a whole become better off by undertaking this project rather than not undertaking it, or by undertaking instead any of a number of alternative projects? (Mishan 1988). CBA is often used to assess and prioritise risk management options: what are the net benefits to society of this particular option, should we implement it or should we choose any of a number of alternative options, including the one of doing nothing? In CBA all the expected advantages (benefits) and disadvantages (costs) of a project are expressed in money terms, so that they can be compared and the net benefits (benefits minus costs) can be computed.

A CBA of a project ideally identifies all costs and benefits for all parties that are affected by the project over the lifetime of the project. The expected costs and benefits are then valued in monetary terms and the costs and benefits in future time periods discounted by an appropriate discount rate. Finally, the discounted costs and benefits are aggregated into one summary statistic: net present value (NPV), benefit-to-cost ratio (BCR) or internal rate of return (IRR).

Box 12.1 Decision metrics

Net Present Value (NPV): Costs and benefits arising over time are discounted and the difference taken, which is the net discounted benefit in a given year. The sum of the net discounted benefits is the NPV. A fixed discount rate is used for expressing future values in today's terms to represent the opportunity costs of using the public funds for the given project. If the NPV is positive (benefits exceed costs), then a project is considered desirable.

Benefit-to-Cost Ratio (BCR): a variant of the NPV. The total discounted benefits are divided by the total discounted costs. By definition, a benefit-cost ratio of 1 means that the expected discounted benefits of implementing the mitigation equal its costs. Any measure where a BCR is greater than 1 is considered to be cost-effective and should be implemented as the benefits exceed costs and a project thus adds value to society. Any measure with a BCR less than 1 (implying that the upfront cost of mitigation is higher than the expected discounted benefit) should not be implemented. Due to its intuitiveness the BCR is often used.

Internal Rate of Return (IRR): Whereas the former two criteria use a fixed discount rate, this criterion calculates the internal interest rate for which the NPV = 0, which is considered the return of the given project. A project is rated desirable if this IRR surpasses an average return on public capital determined beforehand.

Source Mechler et al. (2014b)

An important benefit category in a CBA of disaster risk reduction measures is the expected value of avoided damage created (defined as the prevented risk). Disasters are low-probability high-impact risks. They follow extreme event distributions which are typically very different from normal distributions. Probabilistic analysis is required to assess the expected flood risk as well as the benefits of risk management options in terms of reduced damages. As an illustration for the case of flood risk management in Ho Chi Minh City, Scussolini et al. (2017) used the risk assessment framework of Sect. 12.2 to estimate the NPV and BCR of different flood risk adaptation strategies, including the construction of a ring dike, and dry-proofing buildings and elevating areas at high risk. Costs and benefits are calculated until the year 2100. To ensure that the BCR ranks the adaptation measures in the same order as the NPV, the BCR was normalised to account for the widely different investment costs of the measures. The results are shown in Fig. 12.6. The flood risk adaptation measures appear to yield benefits that substantially outweigh the costs, except for the ring dike in the high climate change scenario. The ring dike has the lowest BCR and NPV, while the combination of elevation and dry-proofing of buildings has the highest BCR and NPV and is, thereby, the optimal adaptation strategy, from a long-term economic perspective. In evaluating risk management options, the results of CBA can be combined with other (non-economic) considerations and indicators. Economic efficiency is usually considered an important aspect of disaster risk management and adaptation, but often not the only aspect that needs to be considered.

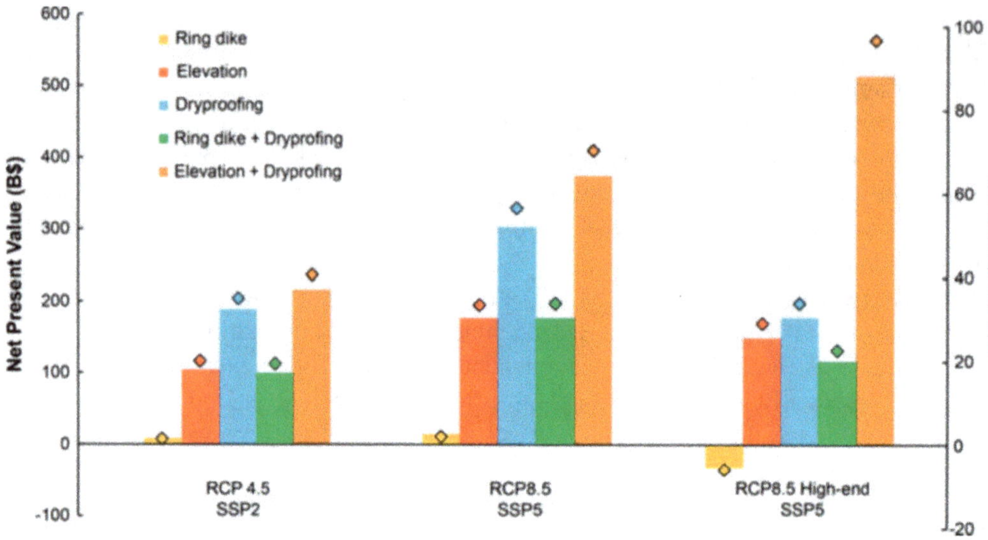

Fig. 12.6 Net Present Value (bars, left axis) and normalised Benefit/cost ratio (diamonds, right axis) of flood risk adaptation measures for Ho Chi Minh City for three combinations of climate change and socio-economic scenarios RCP4.5 and SSP2, RCP8.5 and SSP5, RCP8.5 High-End and SSP5, until the year 2100. Note: discount rate is 2.5%. *Source* Scussolini et al. (2017)

The development of new flood risk protection standards for the Netherlands illustrates the use of CBA in combination with other considerations and indicators (see Box 12.2). The case below also illustrates how the application of CBA in designing region-specific protection standards reduced protection investment costs in comparison to an earlier official proposal for a nation-wide uniform update of the old standards.

There are alternatives to CBA that can be applied. Cost-effectiveness analysis (CEA) is a method that can be applied to identify least-cost options to meet a certain, pre-defined target or policy objective, for example, a certain safety standard. CEA can also be used if the benefits of alternative options are assumed to be similar enough that the choice between options can be made on the cost dimension. The use of CEA is appropriate if the benefits of alternative options are fixed or pre-defined (such as reducing disaster fatalities or losses to a pre-defined level). The advantage of CEA is that it does not require to monetise the benefits of options, such as the monetary benefits of avoiding health or environmental impacts of floods. The disadvantage of CEA is that it cannot determine whether an option is economically efficient, i.e. whether its benefits exceed its costs. Multi-criteria analysis (MCA) is another decision-support method that can be used in certain circumstances. MCA provides a structured way of comparing benefits and costs that are expressed in different units. For example, benefits may be expressed in "number of lives saved" or a qualitative indicator of landscape or environmental quality. MCA is sometimes called a "qualitative CBA." Box 12.2 describes how a combination of BCA and MCA have guided "Room for the River" measures in the Netherlands which have contributed to improving discharge capacities of rivers as well as environmental values. Recently, robust decision-making approaches (RDMA) have gained increasing attention, especially in the context of climate change adaptation (see Watkiss et al. 2015 for a review). RDMA approaches include qualitative and quantitative methods. They are particularly useful to appraise long-term investments in the face of large or "deep" uncertainty about the future. In such circumstances it may not be possible to make optimal decisions (as supported by CBA), but to select options that perform relatively well across a range of possible futures, and thus to minimise regret about an option when the future turns out to be very different than originally envisioned.

Box 12.2 The use of CBA and MCA in flood risk protection policy in the Netherlands

The Netherlands is by its geographical disposition notoriously exposed to extreme flooding. More than half of its land area faces flood risks, putting two-thirds of its population and 70% of its GDP at risk. Flood Protection policy employs a so-called 'multilayer safety approach,' encompassing prevention, spatial solutions (including adaptations to buildings and infrastructure), and crisis management, whereby prevention of flooding receives prominent attention. On the request of the Delta Committee, which was commissioned 1958 after a huge flood, the mathematician Van Dantzig designed an algorithm to determine optimal dike heights based on the equilibrium between marginal investment costs and marginal expected avoided flood damage. The first Delta Act of 1958 included flood protection standards for coastal areas, which were partly based on the work of Van Dantzig (1956). As of the 1970s, safety norms were assigned to rivers and since 1996 all water safety norms have been written in law. This Water Act determines flood protection standards for all dike-ring areas (polders) in the Netherlands. However, the standards of the 1950s did not take account of the possible impacts of climate change and sea level rise.

In response to near flooding events in 1993 and 1995 an alternative approach to flood protection using dikes has been promoted in the Netherlands which entails improving discharge capacities of rivers using land use change, restoration of floodplains and the creation of wetlands. These alternative flood control policies called "Room for the River" create side-benefits, such as ecological, recreational and amenity values. Brouwer and van Ek (2004) applied a CBA and an MCA to appraise the "Room for the River" measures. These evaluations considered the hydrological, ecological, economic and social effects. The extended CBA included monetary benefits of environmental and social benefits of the measures and prevented flood damages. The estimated NPV is €860 million, which favours investing in these measures. Moreover, stakeholder analysis was used to assess effects of these policies on inhabitants, farmers, the environment, water supply companies and recreation. These effects were included in the MCA which also positively evaluated the "Room for the River" measures. In the meantime, most of these measures have now been implemented in practice. A second Delta Committee advised on an update of the flood protection standards in the light of the growth of exposed population and assets, and projected sea-level rise. The Committee upheld the first Delta Committee's risk-based approach and advised that the new standards should be based on three factors: (1) the probability of individual fatalities due to flooding, (2) the probability of large numbers of simultaneous casualties, and (3) economic and other damage (to landscape, to natural and cultural heritage values, to the country's reputation and to society). To achieve this aim, the committee tentatively advised that protection levels for all dike rings should be increased by a factor of ten (e.g., if the current protection level was 1/1,000, it should be increased to 1/10,000).

A cost-benefit analysis to determine optimal protection standards for all dike rings in the Netherlands was initiated by the CBP Bureau for Economic Policy Analysis in 2005 (Eijgenraam et al. 2014). This analysis determined the optimal protection level for a dike ring as that protection level where the marginal protection costs would equate the marginal avoided damages. Damages included direct and indirect economic damage, and loss of life expressed in monetary value through the value of statistical life concept (Bockarjova et al. 2012). With this approach, optimal protection levels were determined for all dike rings in the Netherlands (Kind 2014). It is interesting to note that the investment costs of the economically efficient flood protection standards were estimated to be € 7.8 billion: almost 70% cheaper than the investment costs associated with the advice of the second Delta Committee to increase protection standards everywhere by a factor of ten (Eijgenraam et al. 2014). The Delta Commissioner, appointed in 2010, developed flood protection standards up to the year 2050 and takes the potential effects of climate change on sea level rise and river discharge into account. A number of climate and socioeconomic scenarios have been explored for use in the Delta Programme. The underlying climate scenarios were developed by the Dutch Meteorological Institute KNMI. In the scenario with most climate change, regional sea level rise in 2050 is 35 cm, increasing to 85 cm in 2100. For future river discharge, flood protection policies in upstream countries are relevant. The maximum river discharge of the river Rhine in the Netherlands is presently 'capped' at 16,500 m^3/s, because higher discharge is made impossible by flooding that would occur upstream in Germany. Due to increases in the likelihood of extreme precipitation events, the maximum discharge is assumed to increase to 17,000 m^3/s in 2050 and 18,000 m^3/s in 2100. Similar calculations have been made for the river Meuse. The Delta Programme advocates adaptive management ('adaptive delta management') to address future uncertainties, including the impacts of climate change, in a transparent manner. The Delta Commissioner combined the CPB economic assessment with the other factors that had been suggested by the second Delta committee, In the first place, the standards should offer a common minimum level of protection for each citizen to be protected by dikes or dunes by the year 2050. Secondly, higher standards are offered in locations where there is a risk of large numbers of victims, or of serious damage to vital infrastructure of national importance, or of high economic damage, as indicated by CPB's economic assessment. The new flood protection standards were presented to and adopted by Parliament in 2014. *Source* Kuik et al. (2016)

12.4 Individual (Household) Level Natural Disaster Risk Reduction—Case Studies Germany and Mexico

In addition to public disaster management policy, like the flood protection policy described in Sect. 12.3, private actors including companies and households, can take measures to limit the potential damage of natural disasters. These individual level measures can be an important component of natural disaster risk management when public protection is not economically efficient. Thereby, these measures can contribute to climate change adaptation, and limit the residual risk that has to be dealt with through L&D. Moreover, even when public strategies are in place to limit risk, individual level measures can be a useful complement to minimise damage when public strategies fail and a disaster happens. For example, it has been shown that relatively low-cost measures, like moving furniture to higher floors and placing sand bags in front of doors and window openings, can save substantial damage when floods occur due to failure or overtopping of flood protection infrastructure (Kreibich et al. 2005). Moreover, during construction or renovation of buildings it is usually inexpensive to make structural adjustments to reduce a building's vulnerability to hazards, like through elevation or applying water-resistant materials (Aerts and Botzen 2011).

Although the importance of natural disaster risk mitigation measures at the individual scale is well recognised, relatively few empirical studies have been conducted to estimate the potential damage savings from these measures and their economic desirability (Poussin et al. 2015). Exceptions are the studies described in Box 12.3, which examined this for flood damage mitigation measures in Germany. The German studies (Box 12.3) use mean comparison tests to examine how much flood damage has been saved when particular flood preparedness measures were implemented by households during floods of the river Elbe. The results point toward clear damage savings of up to 50% of some measures.

Even while household level measures to reduce natural disaster risk are cost-effective, this does not mean that many people will voluntarily invest in these measures. This may be due to low awareness about risk and mitigation measures, since damaging natural hazards are often low-probability events that individuals have little experience with. As a result, building codes and zoning policies can be developed to guide the implementation of damage mitigation measures. Zoning regulations are set to control land uses and setting development standards throughout urban areas. Zoning regulations determine (1) what land uses, or combinations of land uses are allowed in the available space, and (2) how land uses utilise space (i.e. conditions for building construction, for instance, including building codes that limit natural disaster risk). In terms of utilising space for especially urban areas, zoning policies and building codes are powerful tools for controlling land use and urban development, and hence (changes in-) future land use (Burby et al. 2000). As such, zoning is increasingly seen as an important tool in climate adaptation and managing changes in weather extremes due to climate change (Aerts and Botzen 2011).

Zoning encompasses the following general policies related to urban development and risk management:

- *Restrictions*: Based on hazard maps and or additional risk information, zoning policies may indicate that in certain areas urban development is not allowed;
- *Conditional development:* Urban development is allowed in risky areas, but only when certain conditions are met, for example, by (a) implementing building codes, (b) homeowners have purchased insurance against natural hazard risk (c) buffer zones are respected: building development is only allowed when appropriate distances between establishments and vulnerable risk areas are maintained.

Box 12.3 Effectiveness of flood damage mitigation measures in Germany

Kreibich et al. (2005) interviewed 1248 households that were affected by the severe Elbe flood in 2002 in Germany in order to assess the level of preparedness of households for flooding, and to estimate the effectiveness of damage mitigation measures that households implemented before and during the flood. Mean comparison tests were conducted to examine how flood damage differs between households who have, or have not, implemented a specific flood damage mitigation measure. Overall, this study shows that the potential gains of implementing mitigation measures at the household level can be substantial. The results show that buildings without a cellar suffer about 24% less building damage and 22% less damage to contents. Water barriers reduced flood damage by about 29%. Stable building foundation or waterproof sealed cellar walls reduced flood damage to buildings by about 24%. The most effective strategies were flood-adapted building use and flood-adapted interior fitting. Flood-adapted building use means that parts of the building that can be flooded (such as the cellar and ground floor) are not used cost-intensively or include expensive constructions, such as a sauna. Flood-adapted interior fitting means that only waterproofed building material and furniture and contents that can be easily moved to higher floors are applied in flood-prone parts of the building. Flood-adapted building use reduced damage to buildings and contents by, respectively, 46 and 48%, while flood-adapted interior fitting saved damage to both buildings and contents by 53%. Placing utility and electrical installation on higher floors reduces flood damage by 36%. These results of the effectiveness of flood mitigation measures in Germany have been confirmed by Kreibich and Thieken (2009) who conducted a similar survey after floods in 2005 and 2006 in the city of Dresden. The results of this survey indicate that household preparedness improved before the 2005/2006 floods, compared with the 2002 Elbe flood, and that this improved preparedness resulted in significantly less flood damage in the events. Kreibich et al. (2011) show that the implementation of low-cost mitigation measures, such as the securing of oil tanks and installation of mobile flood walls, are cost-effective in Germany under a range of flood conditions and discount rates. *Source* (Botzen 2013)

Zoning regulations, and in particular zoning for conditional development, can be further refined in 'building codes' regulations for the development and maintenance of buildings in risk zones. Building codes are meant for the adaptation of building structures to lower their vulnerability to natural hazards. Building codes are anchored in planning law, which is operationalized in legally binding land use- or zoning plans. These zoning plans lay out in which areas building codes will be enforced (for examples of building codes in relation to insurance see Sect. 12.5). Building codes and zoning measures, however, also take quite some time to develop and to process them through all regulatory bodies. In many instances, building codes are not yet assessed against expected increases in risk through, for example, as a result of climate change (e.g. Burby 2006).

In addition to reducing a building's vulnerability to natural disasters, other measures at the individual level can contribute to enhancing an individual's capacity to cope with natural disaster events. As an illustration, Atreya et al. (2017) show how individuals in poor communities in Tabasco, Mexico, take relatively low-cost measures to cope with almost yearly flood events, by protecting belongings, taking emergency preparedness actions and knowing a safe meeting point to evacuate their family during a flood threat. As described in Box 12.4, the implementation of such measures is found to be positively related to community-level policies, such as having flood risk maps available to communicate about risk, and creating early warning systems and shelters. This shows the important role that communities can play in preparing households to cope with natural disaster impacts.

12.5 Natural Disaster Insurance and Incentives for Risk Reduction—Case Study Germany

Financial compensation arrangements, like in the form of aid, public insurance, private insurance, or public-private insurance systems can be designed to provide financial coverage for residual climate change risks (Botzen 2013). The advantage of having an adequate financial compensation system in place is that reimbursement of damage, for example, after a natural disaster, helps people rebuild and limits negative economic consequences.

Box 12.4 Adoption of flood preparedness measures in Tabasco, Mexico

Floods in the Mexican state Tabasco occur frequently, almost on an annual basis. Individual and community level flood preparedness measures are an important way for local households to cope with flood events. The last decade floods have become more severe in this poor region, which suggests that local communities have to improve flood risk management efforts. Atreya et al. (2017) examined flood preparedness decisions in ten communities in Tabasco conducting a survey among 664 households with questions about their flood preparedness decisions. In particular, they focused on the role that community level measures, such as information provision on risk, play in individual decisions to prepare for flooding. Important flood preparedness measures that people take in Tabasco are protecting belongings against flooding, having a safe meeting point to go to during a flood event, and emergency preparedness actions, such as having a family emergency plan of what to do during a flood, first aid training or disaster drills. The figure below shows the percentage of people in these communities who have taken these measures, from which it is apparent that protecting belongings is the most commonly taken measures, while improvements can be made in taking the other measures which are currently taken by fewer people,

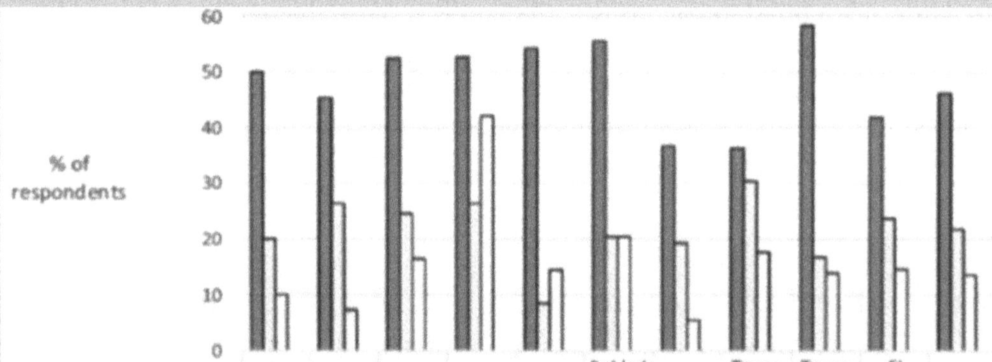

	15 de Mayo	Costitución 1917	El Güiral	El_Piñal	La Esperanza	Poblado Chanero	Pueblo Nuevo	Torno Largo 2da Sección	Torno Largo 4ta Sección	El Pajanol Neuvo Mundo	Total
Protect Belongings	50.0	45.3	52.5	52.6	54.2	55.6	36.7	36.3	58.3	41.8	46.1
Safe Meeting Point	20.0	26.3	24.6	26.3	8.4	20.4	19.3	30.4	16.7	23.6	21.7
Emergency Preparedness	10.0	7.4	16.4	42.1	14.5	20.4	5.5	17.6	13.9	14.5	13.6
Total Households	50	95	61	19	83	54	109	102	36	55	664

Atreya et al. (2017) conducted statistical analyses to examine which factors influence individual flood preparedness decisions. These results show that household preparedness actions are positively related with communities having accessible flood risk maps, early warning systems, and shelters, amongst other factors. This provides insights into community-level flood risk management strategies that can improve individual flood preparedness. For example, very few people (about 8%) currently have access to community's risk maps, while having such knowledge is found to improve individual flood preparedness. Moreover, this can be achieved by better communicating about early warning systems and shelter availability.

It is important to realise that the financial compensation arrangement should be designed so that it is complementary to, and facilitates, the undertaking of cost-effective adaptation measures, and not acts as a substitute or financial disincentive for implementing such measures. A moral hazard effect can arise when individuals prepare less for a risk after they have obtained insurance coverage against the risk. This can occur when policyholders expect to receive compensation from their insurer irrespective of risk reduction efforts and if policyholders receive no financial incentives, like lower premiums, from their insurer to limit risk. This can pose problems for the insurer when due to information asymmetries, the insurer does not observe the heightened risks taken by a particular policyholder. This implies the higher risk is not adequately reflected in a higher risk-based premium. Moreover, such a moral hazard effect is evidently undesirable when climate change increases natural disaster risks since it hampers the implementation of adaptation measures by people covered by insurance.

Hudson et al. (2017) examined the existence of this moral hazard effect using data from samples of households living along the river Elbe in Germany. This is done by estimating relations between flood insurance coverage and the implementation of flood damage mitigation measures, and by estimating whether flood damage outcomes differ between the insured and uninsured, while controlling for a diversity of other relevant explanatory variables. The results show that a moral hazard effect is absent (Hudson et al. 2017). In particular, flood damages of insured households are not significantly higher than those of uninsured households when differences in flood hazard characteristics are accounted for. Moreover, individuals with flood insurance coverage are more likely to have taken specific flood damage mitigation measures than people without flood insurance. These insured individuals did not receive a premium discount for taking flood damage mitigation measures, which implies that other reasons explain why the insured were better prepared for flood risk. The results suggest that behavioural characteristics, like high risk aversion, imply that individuals have preferences for both insurance coverage and risk mitigation.

Although the relations between risk reduction and natural disaster insurance has received little empirical research (see also chapter by Linnerooth-Bayer et al. 2018), the findings by Hudson et al. (2017) do not stand by themselves. Thieken et al. (2006) also observed that individuals with flood insurance coverage in Germany are better prepared for flooding than people without flood insurance. Botzen et al. (2017) find positive relations between having flood insurance coverage and implementing flood-proofing measures among homeowners in flood-prone areas in New York City. Hudson et al. (2017) show that similar positive relations between insurance coverage and risk reduction can be found for windstorm risks in several areas in the U.S. that were impacted by hurricanes Irene, Isaac, and Sandy. These findings are consistent with positive relations between windstorm coverage and windstorm risk reduction activities reported in Carson et al. (2013) and Petrolia et al. (2015).

Additional calls have been made to design natural disaster insurance arrangements in a way that they incentivise risk reduction by policyholders. For instance, insurance could reward investments in damage mitigation measures with premium discounts (Kunreuther 2015). There are few examples of flood insurance arrangements which reward policyholders who elevate their home with lower premiums, like the National Flood Insurance Program in the US (Aerts and Botzen 2011). Nevertheless, most natural disaster insurance systems do not charge risk-based premiums that incentivise risk reduction. Hudson et al. (2016) examine how much additional flood damage mitigation can be achieved when German flood insurance companies start incentivising risk reduction through charging risk-based premiums. For this purpose, they developed an integrated model of flood risk in all main river basins in Germany, the insurance sector, and household flood preparedness behaviour. The results show that the premium incentives for risk reduction limit the expected risk increase that arise from climate change with about 20% on average until the year 2040. These findings suggest that financially rewarding policyholders for taking risk mitigation measures can improve their preparedness for flooding.

In addition to financial incentives provided by insurance, a variety of other mechanisms related to insurance systems can be applied to stimulate natural disaster risk reduction. Insurance systems can be combined with building code and zoning regulations which limit vulnerability and exposure to natural hazards. For example, communities in the U.S. which participate in the National Flood Insurance Program have to limit new construction in floodways and new buildings have to be elevated to the expected water level of the flood that occurs on average once in 100 years (Aerts and Botzen 2011). The French natural disaster insurance system is connected with so-called Risk Prevention Plans which include recommended or compulsory building code and zoning regulations to minimise flood damage (Poussin et al. 2013). Such regulations and standards are useful for setting minimum requirements which are cost-effective for buildings in a specific hazard zone.

12.6 Design of Adaptation Pathways with Policy Makers—Case Studies New Zealand and Bangladesh

There are important challenges for deciding on climate-resilient investment and development pathways under conditions of uncertainty and change, such as anthropogenic climate change. In response to uncertain environmental and socio-economic change, decision makers are urged to develop adaptive plans. A number of approaches that address uncertainty and change have been taken up in practice. These include, real options analysis (Dobes 2008; Ranger et al. 2010), robust decision making (Lempert et al. 2003), iterative risk management (Haasnoot et al. 2011) and strategic planning approaches (Roggema 2009). One of these approaches, Dynamic Adaptive Pathways Planning (DAPP) (Haasnoot et al. 2013), has been used increasingly for implementing climate-resilient pathways for water management, of which the steps are shown in Fig. 12.7.

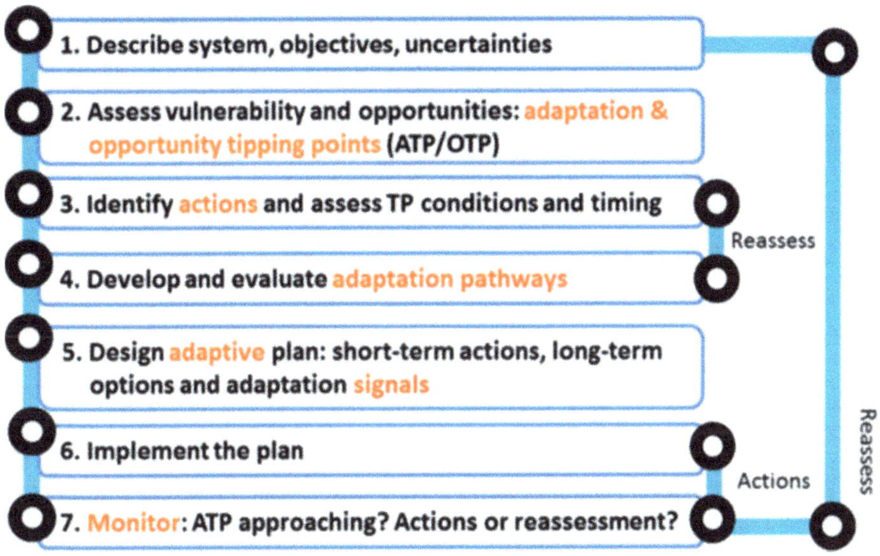

Fig. 12.7 Steps taken in Dynamic Adaptive Pathways Planning (DAPP)

Within the DAPP approach, a plan is conceptualised as a series of actions over time (pathways). The essence is the proactive planning for flexible adaptation over time, in response to how the future actually unfolds. The DAPP approach starts from the premise that policies/decisions have a design life and might fail as the operating conditions change (Kwadijk et al. 2010). A risk assessment can illuminate such adaptation tipping point conditions, as such they can be used to identify up to what changing conditions (e.g. sea level rise) a measure can reach a preferred risk level. Once actions fail, additional or other actions are needed to achieve objectives, and a series of pathways emerge; at predetermined trigger points the course can change while still achieving the objectives. By evaluating different pathways, considering path-dependency of actions and visualising them in a pathways map, an adaptive plan can be designed, that includes short-term actions and long-term options (see Fig. 12.8). Cost-benefit analysis (Sect. 12.3) can be used to evaluate pathways. The plan is monitored for signals that indicate when the next step of a pathway should be implemented or whether reassessment of the plan is needed. It is not only important to identify what to monitor but also how to analyse it. From a policy perspective it seems evident to select signposts that are related to norm or design values, since these are the values upon which the policies are evaluated. However, alternative indicators (i.e. average river flow in summer half year, instead of the 1:10 year return flow)—not necessarily policy related—can be used additionally to get timely and reliable signals for adaptation action. Different levels of assessment are possible to design pathways, from qualitative expert-based pathways to more comprehensive quantitative model-based pathways.

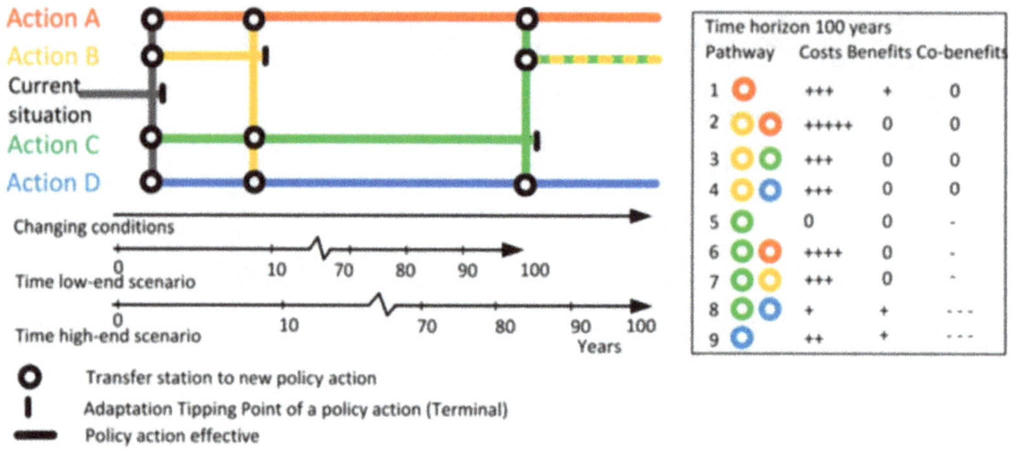

Fig. 12.8 Example of an adaptation pathways map and a scorecard presenting the costs and benefits of the nine alternative pathways presented in the map. An adaptive plan could exist of first implementing action C, monitor the changing condition, and switch to action D if the future unfolds according to the high-end scenario. Action B is potentially a lock-in or regret option, as already after 10 years other actions are needed. If this is the case depends on the amount of the investment compared in relation to the timing of the tipping points and therefore functional lifetime of the action. *Source* Adapted from Haasnoot et al. (2013)

In New Zealand, a combination of serious gaming and development of adaptation pathways were used in a local government flood risk management decision-setting (Box 12.5; Lawrence and Haasnoot 2017) (on gaming see also the chapter by Mechler et al. 2018b). The Sustainable Delta Game (Valkering et al. 2012; http://deltagame.deltares.nl) helped participants learn about decision making under uncertain and changing conditions over time. The game has also been used to discuss climate and climate change uncertainty (Van Pelt et al. 2014). The aim of the exercise on the Dynamic Adaptive Pathways Planning (DAPP) approach was to upgrade the existing flood defence system to 1 in 440 years and maintain that level ('level of service' (LoS)) over at least 100 years. The discharge related to the 440 year standard increasing over time as a result of climate change, with a greater change in the higher emission scenarios. As a result, if the existing system is upgraded only to the current 440 year standard of 2300 cubic meter per second (comics), it will fail to provide the required LoS over 100 years and further actions will be required. The efficacy of five options were evaluated for their ability to maintain the protection level over 100 years, using three climate change scenarios, for meeting development/transport/recreation objectives, the effect of land use planning measures, and comparative costs of staged implementation of options. Each option consisted of a portfolio of measures, and for each portfolio the 'adaptation tipping point' conditions were assessed in terms of the discharge it can accommodate. Three options were taken forward for further evaluation using the DAPP. The figure scorecard (Box 12.5) shows that Pathways 1, 3, 6, and 7 exhibit the best target effect. Option 4 starts to perform unacceptably (not reaching the 1:440 objective) after 40–50 years and thus requires a staged decision to move to Option 2C; Option 2C by itself reaches the target by 2095–2105, and only Option 1 will enable the target to be met going beyond 100 years. The approach of adaptation pathways has been adopted in the national coastal guidance. In Bangladesh, the adaptation pathways were used to develop an adaptive plan inspired by the adaptive delta management approach in the Netherlands. The plan should ensure

> long term water and food security, economic growth and environmental sustainability while effectively coping with natural disasters, climate change and other delta issues through robust, adaptive and integrated strategies, and equitable water governance (Bangladesh Delta Plan, in prep; www.bangladeshdeltaplan.org).

This aim illustrates an important difference in the application of adaptation pathways in the Netherlands and Bangladesh, despite the resemblance in terms of geographic, hydrological, physiographic and climatic vulnerability. While the Bangladesh Delta Plan focuses on *enabling* socio-economic development and food security, the Dutch Delta Plan is oriented at *protecting* the socio-economic system and increasing ecological value of the Dutch water system. In Bangladesh the focus is thus on investments for achieving development goals that should be robust or adaptive under uncertain changing conditions. The difference is also expressed in different criteria that are used to assess risk and evaluate pathways. In addition to flood risk, criteria such as poverty, health, and gender are considered in Bangladesh. Like in the Netherlands, the adaptive plan presents preferred strategies/pathways that exist of short-term (<2030), mid-term (2030–2050) and long-term (2050–2100) strategies. The short-term strategies aim to address present and near future needs and development targets to ensure food and water security in order to become a middle income country. The long-term strategies are based on two iconic end-points, envisioning a delta that is fixed and where water is controlled with dikes and pumps, or a delta that has still dynamics with nature-based solution and land use measures. The Bangladesh Delta Plan pathways are still under construction and need further elaboration to enable implementation. The Bangladesh Planning Commission (2017) published initial results. Regarding disaster risk management for the lower Kulna region, they describe a pathway that starts with construction of sea dykes that may reach acceptable risk levels up to 2050, and can then be combined with a storm surge barrier.

Box 12.5 Adaptation pathways developed for Hutt River City Centre Upgrade Project, New Zealand

Pathway	Main effects		Side effects		
	Relative Costs	Target effects	Social Impacts	Transport impacts	Environ-mental impacts
1	$$$$	++	----	+++	++++
2	$$	+	---	++++	+++
3	$$$$	++	----	++++	++++
4	$	-	0	++	+
5	$$$	+	--	++++	+++
6	$$$$	++	---	+++	++++
7	$$$$$	++	----	++++	++++

The Hutt River City Centre Upgrade Project: the adaptation pathways map shows options, scenarios, decision moments, relative costs of options and potential side effects requiring consideration. Relative impacts are indicated with – and ++; – is negative impact and +positive impact. All pathways except pathway 5 have negative social impacts as land has to be purchased.

Option 1: A 90 m river channel and 50 m berm; right and left stopbanks meets the standard over 100 years in all scenarios; cost $267 m. Option 2C: A 90 m river channel 25 m berm; properties to be purchased; cost of $143 million. Option 4: 70 m river channel; 30 years of flood protection; lower level of protection (2300 cumecs); properties purchased after 20 years; cost $114 m until 2035. Staged option: Option 4 to Option2C will cost an additional $68 million; total cost $182 million).

Source Generated by the Pathways Generator (http://pathways.deltares.nl/) based on (Boffa Miskell Ltd 2015; Infometrics and PS Consulting 2015). *Source* Lawrence and Haasnoot (2017)

12.7 Synthesis

This chapter has discussed integrated approaches to the management of risks related to extreme weather and climate change in the context of Loss and Damage (L&D). We particularly focus on risks from extreme weather, which are expected to increase in frequency and intensity in many regions around the globe. We follow the definition of L&D as strategies that focus on the residual risks that remain after (cost-effective) adaptation strategies have been implemented. Integrated risk management implies that a holistic view is taken in interventions aimed at reducing hazard, vulnerability, and exposure to natural disasters. We discussed a variety of such strategies, like flood-protection aimed at preventing hazards, individual scale damage mitigation measures that reduce vulnerability of buildings to flood impacts which can be formalised in building code regulations, zoning policies that aim to limit (growth in) exposure of properties to natural hazards, and insurance for covering residual risk.

The main conclusions from this chapter can be summarised as follows:

- Risk assessment methods are an important first step in order to identify risk levels on a spatial scale. The mapping of areas with high hazard and risk can guide where risk management strategies may be needed. Estimation of future risk under scenarios of climate change provides insights into the needs for adaptation and L&D measures to limit possible residual risks, as we illustrated for Ho Chi Minh City.
- Cost-benefit analysis allows for a prioritisation of risk management interventions based on economic efficiency criteria. This method allows for identifying economically desirable risk management strategies and adaptation options. The expected reduced risk delivered by a strategy is an important benefit category and can be estimated using a probabilistic natural disaster risk assessment using a variety of scenarios, as our case study of flood risk in Ho Chi Minh City illustrated. Moreover, the case study for the Netherlands showed that a societal cost-benefit analysis can also include important intangible welfare effects, like the prevented loss of life and increased feelings of safety from flood protection. Moreover, multi-criteria analysis can be used for evaluations of risk management strategies with effects that are challenging to express in monetary terms.
- In addition to public natural disaster protection measures it is increasingly recognised that measures taken at the individual scale can be important complements in limiting the impacts of natural disasters. However, few empirical studies have examined the damage savings that these measures can achieve and their economic efficiency. Our case studies for Germany illustrated that in the case of flood, the implementation of household level measures have prevented significant amounts of damage during flood events. Several low-cost measures exist that are cost-effective in flood-prone regions. Moreover, our case study of poor communities in Mexico showed that several low cost-options are available for households to cope with frequent severe flood events, and how the implementation of such options is enhanced by community level actions, like raising risk awareness.

- Although adaptation to climate change will often result in net benefits, completely preventing the expected impacts of climate change on natural disaster risk may not be economically efficient. A residual risk remains to be addressed by L&D options, like financial compensation arrangements which can take the form of aid or a variety of forms of insurance (see also chapter by Linnerooth-Bayer et al. 2018).
- It should be realised that if financial compensation arrangements are part of L&D strategies they should be designed in a way that they stimulate and not hamper the implementation of adaptation measures. Few studies have examined relations between natural disaster insurance and policyholder risk reduction efforts. The studies we described for Germany and other countries show that potential disincentives (moral hazard) to reduce risk from insurance may be minor. Opportunities exist for linking insurance with incentives for risk reduction by rewarding policyholders who limit natural disaster risk with premium discounts and by linking insurance with building code and zoning regulations.
- Even though natural disaster risk assessments and cost-benefit analysis provide important tools for prioritising investments in natural disaster risk management, the uncertainty of climate change impacts complicates adaptation planning. Designing adaptation pathways with policymakers can deal with these uncertainties, as illustrated by the New Zealand case study. The Bangladesh case study shows that risk assessment can be linked to both vulnerability and adaptation pathways to changing conditions, but also to opportunities to enhance socio-economic development.

Acknowledgements The writing of this chapter was co-funded by the Netherlands Organisation for Scientific Research (NWO) through VIDI Grant Nr. 452.14.005 and VICI Grant Nr. 453-13-006, as well as through the Zurich Flood Resilience Alliance.

References

Aerts JCJH, Botzen WJW (2011) Climate-resilient waterfront development in New York City: bridging flood insurance, building codes, and flood zoning. Ann N Y Acad Sci 1227:1–82

Atreya A, Czajkowski J, Botzen WJW, Bustamante G, Campbell K, Collier B, Ianni F, Kunreuther H, Michel-Kerjan E, Montgomery M (2017) Adoption of flood preparedness actions: a household level study in rural communities in Tabasco, Mexico. Int J Disaster Risk Red 24:428–438

Bangladesh Planning Commission (2017) Bangladesh Delta Plan 2100. http://www.bangladeshdeltaplan2100.org

Bockarjova M, Rietveld P, Verhoef ET (2012) Composite valuation of immaterial damage in flooding: value of statistical life, value of statistical evaluation and value of statistical injury. Amsterdam: Tinbergen Institute. TI Discussion Paper

Boffa Miskell Ltd (2015). Hutt river city centre section upgrade project: options evaluation report. Prepared by Boffa Miskell Ltd for Greater Wellington Regional Council, Wellington, 1–58

Bouwer LM (2018) Observed and Projected Impacts from Extreme Weather Events: Implications for Loss and Damage. In: Mechler R, Bouwer L, Schinko T, Surminski S, Linnerooth-Bayer J (eds) Loss and Damage from Climate Change. Concepts, Methods and Policy Options. Springer, Cham, pp 63–82

Botzen WJW, van den Bergh JCJM (2009) Managing natural disaster risk in a changing climate. Environ Hazards 8:209–225
Botzen WJW (2013) Managing extreme climate change risks through insurance. Cambridge University Press, Cambridge and New York, pp 1–432
Botzen WJW, Kunreuther H, Michel-Kerjan E (2017) Flood insurance coverage and flood risk mitigation by policyholders. VU University, Amsterdam and the Wharton School, Philadelphia, Working Manuscript
Bouwer LM (2011) Have disaster losses increased due to anthropogenic climate change? Bull Am Meteor Soc 92(1):39–46
Brouwer R, van Ek R (2004) Integrated ecological, economic and social impact assessment of alternative flood control policies in the Netherlands. Ecol Econ 50:1–21
Budiyono Y, Aerts JCJH, Brinkman JJ, Marfai MA, Ward PJ (2015) Flood risk assessment for delta mega-cities: a case study of Jakarta. Nat Hazards 75:389–413
Budiyono Y, Aerts JCJH, Tollenaar D, Ward PJ (2016) River flood risk in Jakarta under scenarios of future change. Nat Hazards Earth Sys Sci 16:757–774
Budiyono Y, Marfai MA, Aerts JCJH, de Moel H, Ward PJ (2017) Chapter 21—Flood risk in polder systems in Jakarta: present and future analyses. In: Djalante R et al (eds) Disaster risk reduction in Indonesia, disaster risk reduction. Springer. https://doi.org/10.1007/978-3-319-54466-3_21
Burby RJ, Deyle RE, Godschalk DR, Olshansky RB (2000) Creating hazard resilient communities through land-use planning. Nat Hazard Plann Rev 1(2):99–106
Burby RJ (2006) Hurricane katrina and the paradoxes of government disaster policy: bringing about wise governmental decisions for hazardous areas. Ann Am Acad Political Soc Sci 604(1):171–191
Carson JM, McCullough KA, Pooser DM (2013) Deciding whether to invest in mitigation measures: evidence from Florida. J Risk Insur 80(2):309–327
Czajkowski J, Simmons K (2014) Convective storm vulnerability: quantifying the role of effective and well-enforced building codes in minimizing missouri hail property damage. Land Econ 90(3):482–508
Dobes L (2008) Getting real about adapting to climate change: using 'real options' to address uncertainties. Agenda 15:55–68
Eijgenraam C, Kind J, Bak C, Brekelmans R, den Hertog D, Duits M, Roos K, Vermeer P, Kuijken W (2014) Economically efficient standards to protect the Netherlands against flooding. Interfaces 44(1):7–21
Haasnoot M, Middelkoop H, Van Beek E, Van Deursen WPA (2011) A method to develop sustainable water management strategies for an uncertain future. Sustain Dev 199:369–381
Haasnoot M, Kwakkel J, Walker W, ter Maat J (2013) Dynamic adaptive policy pathways: a method for crafting robust decisions for a deeply uncertain world. Glob Environ Change 23:485–498
Hudson P, Botzen WJW, Feyen L, Aerts JCJH (2016) Incentivising flood risk adaptation through risk based insurance premiums: trade-offs between affordability and risk reduction. Ecol Econ 125:1–13
Hudson P, Botzen WJW, Czajkowski J, Kreibich H (2017) Moral hazard in natural disaster insurance markets: empirical evidence from Germany and the United States. Land Economics 93(2):179–208
Infometrics and PS Consulting (2015). Flood protection: option flexibility and its value: Hutt River City Centre Upgrade River Corridor Options Report. Greater Wellington Regional Council, Wellington, 1–31
IPCC (2012) Managing the risks of extreme events and disasters to advance climate change adaptation—Special report of the intergovernmental panel on climate change. In: Field CB, Barros V, Stocker TF, Qin D, Dokken DJ, Ebi KL, Mastrandrea MD, Mach KJ, Plattner GK, Allen SK, Tignorand M, Midgley PM (eds). Cambridge University Press, Cambridge, U.K.
James R, Otto F, Parker H, Boyd E, Cornforth R, Mitchell D, Allen M (2015) Characterizing loss and damage from climate change. Nat Clim Change 4:938–939
James RA, Jones RG, Boyd E, Young HR, Otto FEL, Huggel C, Fuglestvedt JS (2018) Attribution: how is it relevant for loss and damage policy and practice? In: Mechler R, Bouwer L, Schinko T,

Surminski S, Linnerooth-Bayer J (eds) Loss and damage from climate change. Concepts, methods and policy options. Springer, Cham, pp 113–154

Kind JM (2014) Economically efficient flood protection standards for the Netherlands. J Flood Risk Manag 7(2):103–117

Klijn F, Baan PJA, De Bruijn KM, Kwadijk J (2007) Overstromingsrisico's in Nederland in een Veranderend Klimaat. Q4290, WL|delft hydraulics, Delft (in Dutch)

Kreibich H, Thieken AH, Petrow T, Müller M, Merz B (2005) Flood loss reduction of private households due to building precautionary measures: lessons learned from the elbe Flood in August 2002. Nat Hazards Earth Sys Sci 5(1):117–126

Kreibich H, Christenberger S, Schwarze R (2011) Economic motivation of households to undertake private precautionary measures against floods. Nat Hazards Earth Sys Sci 11:309–321

Kreibich H, Thieken AH (2009) Coping with floods in the city of Dresden, Germany. Nat Hazards 51:423–436

Kuik O, Scussolini P, Mechler R, Mochizuki J, Hunt A, Wellman J (2016) Assessing the economic case for adaptation to extreme events at different scales. Deliverable 5.1 of the EU-funded project ECONADAPT. Institute for Environmental Studies, Amsterdam

Kunreuther H (2015) The role of insurance in reducing losses from extreme events: the need for public-private partnerships. The Geneva Papers on Risk and Insurance—Issues and Practice, 1–22

Kwadijk J, Haasnoot M, Mulder J, Hoogvliet M, Jeuken A, Van der Krogt R, Van Oostrom N, Schelfhout H, Van Velzen E, Van Waveren H, de Wit M (2010) Using adaptation tipping points to prepare for climate change and sea level rise: a case study in the Netherlands. Wiley Interdisc Rev: Clim Change 1:729–740

Lawrence J, Haasnoot M (2017) What it took to catalyse uptake of dynamic adaptive pathways planning to address climate change uncertainty. Environ Sci Policy. https://doi.org/10.1016/j.envsci.2016.12.003

Lempert R, Popper S, Bankes S (2003) Shaping the next one hundred years: new methods for quantitative. Long-Term Policy Analysis, RAND, Santa Monica, C.A.

Linnerooth-Bayer J, Surminski S, Bouwer LM, Noy I, Mechler R (2018) Insurance as a response to loss and damage? In: Mechler R, Bouwer L, Schinko T, Surminski S, Linnerooth-Bayer J (eds) Loss and damage from climate change. Concepts, methods and policy options. Springer, Cham, pp 483–512

Mechler R, Bouwer LM, Linnerrooth-Bayer J, Hochrainer-Stigler S, Aerts JCJH, Surminski S, Williges K (2014a) Managing unnatural disaster risk from climate extremes. Nat Clim Change 4(4):235–237

Mechler R, Czajkowski J, Kunreuther H, Michel-Kerjan E, Botzen WJW, Keating A, McQuistan C, Cooper N, O'Donnell I (2014b) Making communities more flood resilient: the role of cost benefit analysis and other decision-support tools in disaster risk reduction. Zurich Flood Resilience Alliance, Zurich

Mechler R (2016) Reviewing estimates of the economic efficiency of disaster risk management: opportunities and limitations of using risk-based cost-benefit analysis. Nat Hazards 81(3):2121–2147

Mechler R et al (2018a) Science for loss and damage. Findings and propositions. In: Mechler R, Bouwer L, Schinko T, Surminski S, Linnerooth-Bayer J (eds) Loss and damage from climate change. Concepts, methods and policy options. Springer, Cham, pp 3–37

Mechler R, McQuistan C, McCallum I, Liu W, Keating A, Magnuszewski P, Schinko T, Szoenyi M, Laurien F (2018b) Supporting climate risk management at scale. Insights from the zurich flood resilience alliance partnership model applied in Peru & Nepal. In: Mechler R, Bouwer L, Schinko T, Surminski S, Linnerooth-Bayer J (eds) Loss and damage from climate change. Concepts, methods and policy options. Springer, Cham, pp 393–424

Mishan EJ (1988) Cost-benefit analysis. An informal introduction, 4th edn. Unwin Hyman, London

Petrolia DR, Hwang J, Landry CE, Coble KH (2015) Wind insurance and mitigation in the coastal zone. Land Econ 91(2):272–295

Poussin J, Botzen WJW, Aerts JCJH (2013) Stimulating flood damage mitigation through insurance: an assessment of the French CatNat system. Environ Hazards 12(3–4):258–277

Poussin JK, Botzen WJW, Aerts JCJH (2015) Effectiveness of flood damage mitigation measures: empirical evidence from french flood disasters. Glob Environ Change 31:74–84

Ranger N, Millner A, Dietz S, Fankhauser S, Lopez A, Ruta G (2010) Adaptation in the UK: a decision-making process. A policy brief. Grantham Institute on climate change and the environment and centre for climate change economics and policy, London

Roggema R (2009) Adaptation to climate change: a spatial challenge. Springer, Cham

Scussolini P, Tran TTV, Koks E, Diaz-Loaiza A, Ho PL, Lasage R (2017) Adaptation to sea level rise: a multidisciplinary analysis for Ho Chi Minh City, Vietnam. Water Resour Res 53(12):10841–10857. https://doi.org/10.1002/2017WR021344

Schinko T, Mechler R, Hochrainer-Stigler S (2018) The risk and policy space for loss and damage: integrating notions of distributive and compensatory justice with comprehensive climate risk management. In: Mechler R, Bouwer L, Schinko T, Surminski S, Linnerooth-Bayer J (eds) Loss and damage from climate change. Concepts, methods and policy options. Springer, Cham, pp 83–110

Thieken AH, Petrow T, Kreibich H, Merz B (2006) Insurability and mitigation of flood losses in private households in Germany. Risk Anal 26:383–395

UNFCCC (2015) Adoption of the Paris Agreement. United Nations Framework Convention on Climate Change (UNFCCC), Paris

Valkering P, Van der Brugge R, Offermans A, Haasnoot M, Vreugdenhil H (2012) A perspective-based simulation game to explore future pathways of an interacting water-society system under climate change. Simulation & Gaming. https://doi.org/10.1177/1046878112441693 or http://deltagame.deltares.nl

van Dantzig D (1956) Economic decision problems for flood prevention. Econometrica 24:276–287

Van Pelt S, Haasnoot M, Arts B, Ludwig F, Swart R, Biesbroek R (2014) Communicating climate (change) uncertainties: simulation games as boundary objects. Environ Sci Policy 45:42–52

Watkiss P, Hunt A, Blyth W, Dyszynski J (2015) The use of new economic decision support tools for adaptation assessment: a review of methods and applications, towards guidance on applicability. Clim Change 132:401–416

Chapter 13
Exploring and Managing Adaptation Frontiers with Climate Risk Insurance

Laura Schäfer, Koko Warner and Sönke Kreft

Abstract This chapter aims to inform the Loss & Damage debate by analysing the degree to which insurance can be used as a tool to explore and manage adaptation frontiers. It establishes that insurance can be used as a navigational tool around adaptation frontiers in three ways: First, by facilitating the exploration of adaptation frontiers by contributing to a framework for signalling the magnitude, location, and exposure to climate-related risks and providing signals when adaptation limits are approached. Second, by supporting actors in moving away from adaptation limits by improving ex-ante decision making, incentivising risk reduction and creating a space of certainty for climate resilient development. Third, by aiding actors in remaining in the tolerable risk space by facilitating financial buffering as part of contingency approaches. However, we also find that insurance against the risks of climate change in market terms possesses several limitations. We therefore suggest the embedding of insurance in a comprehensive climate risk management approach accompanied by other risk reduction and management strategies as key principle for any international cooperation approach to respond to climate change impacts.

Keywords Loss & Damage · Resilience · Climate risk insurance
Comprehensive climate risk management

13.1 Introduction

The idea of adaptation to climatic stressors has emerged as a mainstream risk management strategy to help maintain human-ecological systems in a "safe operating space" (Röckström et al. 2009). However, emerging literature underpinning

L. Schäfer (✉) · S. Kreft
Munich Climate Insurance Initiative (MCII) hosted by United Nations University–Institute for Environmental Security (UNU-EHS), Bonn, Germany
e-mail: schaefer@ehs.unu.edu

K. Warner
United Nations Climate Change Secretariat (UNFCCC), Bonn, Germany

R. Mechler et al. (eds.), *Loss and Damage from Climate Change*, Climate Risk Management, Policy and Governance, https://doi.org/10.1007/978-3-319-72026-5_13

Chaps. 16, 17, and 19 of the IPCC 5th Assessment report (Klein et al. 2014; Chambwera et al. 2014; Oppenheimer et al. 2014) point towards limits in the ability of systems to adapt to climate stressors (Dow et al. 2013a, b; Warner et al. 2013; Adger et al. 2009). There is evidence that poor and vulnerable people and communities already exist and persist at the edges of these boundaries and limits (Islam et al. 2014; Warner et al. 2015; Monnereau and Abraham 2013). They find themselves operating within an adaptation frontier, a "socio-ecological system's transitional adaptive operating space between safe and unsafe domains" (Preston et al. 2014). To successfully navigate adaptation frontiers, these people and communities need tools that allow them to explore the frontier, stay away from adaptation limits and continuously move into safer domains.

As the debate around adaptation constraints, limits, and possible associated losses and damages unfolds, insurance has been promoted as a tool that can help buffer against the disruptive effects of climate variability and climate change (see chapter by Linnerooth-Bayer et al. 2018 in this book; Surminski et al. 2016). Insurance has been a cornerstone in climate impact related discourses of the United Nations Framework Convention on Climate Change (UNFCCC) from its establishment in 1992. Several substantive policy proposals were brought forward resulting in insurance being featured in relevant adaptation and Loss and Damage related decisions and frameworks (compare chapters by Mechler et al. 2018; Linnerooth-Bayer et al. 2018; Schinko et al. 2018 in this book). Insurance is now anchored in major policy arenas as one tool to address the risk of climate change, including the Paris Agreement and the Sendai Framework for Disaster Risk Reduction. Additionally, the topic experienced a boost through the G7's decision to set up a "Climate Risk Insurance Initiative" (InsuResilience) during their 2015 summit in Elmau and the 2017 G20 summit acknowledging a "Global Partnership for Climate and Disaster Risk Finance and Insurance Solution" (G7 2015; G20 2017).

Drawing on research undertaken in the context of the G7 InsuResilience Initiative to assess the potential of insurance to improve risk management for poor and vulnerable communities (Schäfer et al. 2016), this chapter aims to inform the Loss and Damage debate by analysing the degree to which insurance can be used as a tool to explore and manage adaptation frontiers. In a first step, we outline the challenges related to decision making under climate risk and introduce the concept of adaptation frontiers. In a second step, we analyse how decision makers can use insurance in a way to address these challenges and manage adaptation frontiers. In a third step, we discuss limits of insurance as a climate risk management tool and describe principles that enable insurance tools to help move poor and vulnerable people and countries away from adaptation limits into a safer, tolerable risk space.

The chapter concludes that insurance can be used as a navigational tool around adaptation frontiers in three ways: First, by facilitating the exploration of adaptation frontiers by contributing to a framework for signalling the magnitude, location, and exposure to climate-related risks and providing signals when adaptation limits are approached. Second, by supporting actors in moving away from adaptation limits by improving ex-ante decision making, incentivising risk reduction and creating a space of certainty for climate resilient development. Third, by aiding actors in remaining in the tolerable risk space by facilitating financial buffering as part of contingency approaches. However, in order for risk transfer instruments like insurance to approach their potential as risk management tool in developing countries, seven Pro-Poor Principles for climate risk insurance need to be met.

13.2 Decision-Making Under Climate Risks

At the beginning of the 21st century, human activities, primarily their fossil fuel use, have the potential to irreversibly damage the Earth's climate system and transform it rapidly into "a state unknown in human existence" (Barnosky et al. 2012). Science suggests that climate change will cause changes in the "frequency, intensity, spatial extent, duration, and timing of extreme weather and climate events" as the IPCC Special Report on Extreme Events (SREX) concludes (IPCC 2012). This change in climate will lead to "more rapid, larger and more unpredictable changes in risks than have been experienced in the past" (Ranger and Fisher 2012).

Risk is both an analytical and a normative concept. It can be understood as the combination of the probability of an event and its consequences that harm things which human beings value (Klinke and Renn 2002). With the ultimate objective to maintain risks for valued things at a tolerable level, actors apply risk management strategies. They help to identify and evaluate risks, select measures to avoid and prevent them from happening but also to plan for responding and recovering from actual impacts. Risk management measures are used to control risks for things humans value—e.g. livelihoods, ecosystems, cultural assets "with the explicit purpose of increasing human security, well-being, quality of life, and sustainable development" (IPCC 2014). The idea of adaptation to climatic stressors has emerged as a mainstream risk management strategy to help maintain human-ecological systems in a "safe operating space" (Röckström et al. 2009). Effective adaptation means integrating climate change related risks into actors' existing decision-making processes with the aim of maximising the long-term value of today's decisions (Bouwer and Aerts 2006). This includes risk evaluation as a first step to assess potential risk to social objectives and values followed by the decision which risk to actively manage and which not.

Box 13.1 Barriers and limits to adaptation through the lens of risk preferences. Assuming that risk tolerance is socially constructed, Klinke and Renn (2002) suggest that actors evaluate risks based on one of three categories according to which they decide if the risks need to be managed or not: acceptable, tolerable, and intolerable. *Acceptable* risks are low-complex, well understood risks that are deemed so low that no additional efforts for risk reduction are justified (ibid). *Tolerable* risks relate to "activities seen as worth pursuing for their benefit" (Dow et al. 2013a) but where additional efforts to risk reduction are required to keep risk within reasonable levels. Dow et al. (2013a) describe how the scope of risks that fall within this area is heavily influenced by adaptation opportunities and constrains and therefore the categorisation of risks varies spatially, jurisdictionally, and temporally. Constraints may limit the range of available adaptation options creating the potential for residual damages for actors, species, or ecosystems. Within the tolerable risk space, the risk of residual damage may be viewed as an acceptable or tolerable trade-off under some circumstances (de Bruin et al. 2009). *Intolerable* risks go beyond socially negotiated norms and values although adaptation action has been taken (Dow et al. 2013a). At this stage, adaptation options that are practical or affordable to keep valued social objectives or goods within the norm are no longer available. These risks represent threats to core social objectives regarding health, welfare, security, or sustainability (Klinke and Renn 2002; Dow et al. 2013a).

Emerging literature underpinning Chaps. 16, 17, and 19 of the IPCC 5th Assessment report point towards limits in the ability of systems to adapt to climate stressors (Dow et al. 2013a, b; Warner et al. 2013; Adger et al. 2009). Adaptation limits—for example "soft limits" related to institutions and planning processes, and "hard limits" relating to physical characteristics of a system-constitute a point at which existing adaptation options can no longer protect the objectives and needs of actors and systems against intolerable risks (Adger et al. 2009; see also Mechler and Schinko 2016; introduction by Mechler et al. 2018 and chapter by Schinko et al. 2018 in this book). At the limit between tolerable and intolerable risk, the risk must either be accepted, the objective itself must be abandoned, or adaptation must be transformative to avoid intolerable risk (Dow et al. 2013a). Figure 13.1 depicts acceptable, tolerable and intolerable risks, separated by limits of acceptable risk and adaptation limits. The turning space before an adaptation limit is reached, can be described as an *adaptation frontier*. Preston et al. (2014) define it as the "domain between a socio-ecological system's safe operating space and its unsafe operating space". The adaptation frontier is a domain where feasible and affordable adaptation action is still available and has the potential to secure objectives and needs of actors and systems (ibid.) However, the frontier is characterised by uncertainty if the available option is used in an efficient and timely manner which is needed to stay away from adaptation limits (Dow et al. 2013a).

According to Preston et al. (2014) and underpinning literature (Mechler and Schinko 2016; chapter by Schinko et al. 2018 in this book) adaptation can offer two types of benefits to systems on the frontier: On the one hand, reducing the vulnerability of systems to move them away from the edge of the frontier. On the other hand, enhancing resilience, enabling systems to persist despite the continued pres-

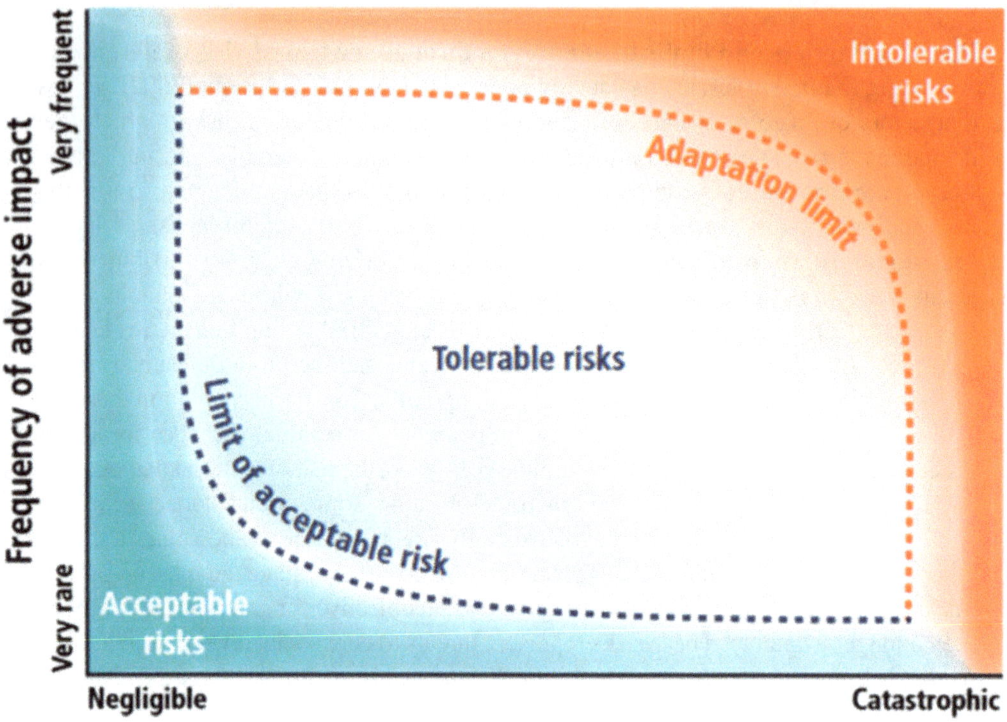

Fig. 13.1 Acceptable, tolerable and intolerable risk. *Source* Dow et al. (2013a)

ence of and exposure to pressures. In the face of potentially growing weather extremes and profound shifts in natural systems driven by climate change, all countries will require pathways that reduce vulnerability and lead to a more climate resilient development. These strategies should complement and facilitate the design of approaches to address longer-term incremental adverse effects of climate change. Increasing comprehensive risk management capacity for dealing with today's extreme climate-related events can provide the basis for managing both current climate variability and long-term shifts in climate patterns. Climate resilient sustainable development pathways run along a spectrum of those things decision makers can plan for and pre-empt, complemented by a suite of contingency measures to help manage climate risks and impacts that have not been accounted for or addressed through planning and risk reduction. This chapter argues that insurance has a role to play across this spectrum.

13.3 Insurance Related Instruments as Navigation Tools for Adaptation Frontiers

Insurance is the transfer of risk of a loss from one entity to another in exchange for a payment which is called premium. The insured person (policyholder) is trading the possibility of a loss for a guaranteed cost to a risk taking entity (the insurer). Insurance works by pooling losses, transferring risk of fortuitous losses and indemnification (Rejda and McNamara 2017). By spreading risks among people and over space and time, insurance-related tools allow to collectively manage losses that would overwhelm individual members of a group, limiting the need for members to take costly individual action. In this arrangement, the premium replaces the "uncertain prospect of losses with the certainty of making small, regular premium payments" (Churchill 2006). In case of a loss which is covered by the insurance policy, the insured holds the right to claim compensation.

Based on these principles, disaster risk insurance is a facilitative mechanism which provides post-disaster financial support against the loss of assets, livelihoods, and lives at an individual, community, national, and regional level. "Climate risk insurance" refers to a special type of disaster insurance, covering losses and damages caused by extreme weather events, which are intensified and increased in frequency by climate change. Climate risk insurance schemes may be both direct and indirect. Direct insurance approaches are those in which the insured benefits directly from transferring risk to a risk taking entity (such as an insurer). In the event the insurance agreement is triggered, the insurance payout is directly transferred to the insured. Indirect insurance approaches are those where the final intended target group benefits indirectly from payments intermediated by an insured government or from being a member of an institution that has insurance (Schäfer et al. 2016; see also chapter by Linnerooth-Bayer et al. 2018 in this book).

This chapter argues that insurance can support people and communities on the frontier of adaptation in several ways, helping them in

- exploring adaptation frontiers by contributing to a framework for signalling the magnitude, location, and exposure to climate-related risks and providing signals when adaptation limits are approached;
- moving away from adaptation limits by improving ex-ante decision making, incentivising risk reduction and creating a space of certainty for climate resilient development;
- remaining in the tolerable risk space by facilitating financial buffering as part of contingency approaches when climate-related risks exceed current capabilities to manage.

In the following, the different roles of insurance in exploring and managing adaptation frontiers are described in detail. It has to be noted, however, that transferring risks in a cost-efficient way through insurance is only one step in a systematic process. The effective management of adaptation frontiers, aimed at enabling climate-resilience development, requires a comprehensive approach to risk management. This approach should involve a portfolio of actions aimed at improving the understanding of disaster risks, reducing and transferring risk as well as responding to and recovering from events and disasters—as opposed to a singular focus on any one action or type of action (see Fig. 13.2).

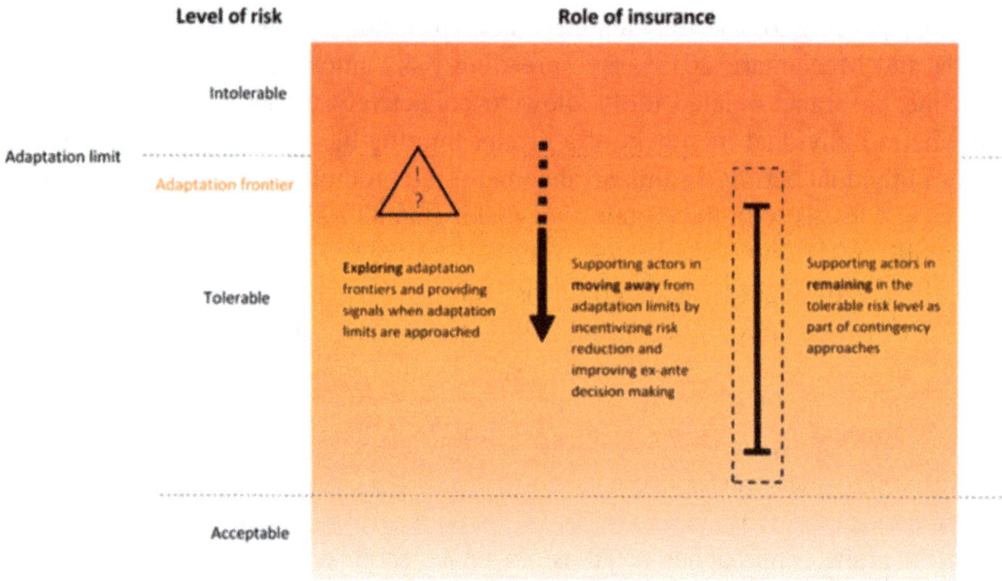

Fig. 13.2 The role ofinsurance in managing adaptation frontiers. *Source* Author's own

13.3.1 Insurance as Part of a Risk Signalling Mechanism

To be able to make informed decisions in a world of increasing climate risks, actors need to explore adaptation frontiers. Therefore, countries and people need reliable information about the magnitude, location, and exposure to climate-related risks as well as signals to determine their leeway regarding adaption limits. Risk transfer tools like insurance can support risk signalling mechanisms in the following two ways.

Catalysing Risk Assessment to Signal the Magnitude, Location and Exposure to Climate-Related Risks

Assessing the risk of losses and damages is a prerequisite for identifying needs and policy priorities. Risk assessment brings attention to the hazard potential, the exposure and vulnerability, and in this way it can raise awareness and expose new options for managing the risks (Warner and Spiegel 2009). Publicly collected and open source data and risk assessments, as well as open source hazard modelling, can contribute meaningfully to national and regional risk-management and investment decisions. However, risk assessments are often not performed in developing countries (Collier et al. 2009). Being the precondition for calculating premium levels for policyholders, risk assessment is a vital part of insurance. Accordingly, insurance can be one way to facilitate regional and international data analysis—such as establishing data standards, methods and data repositories—and can therefore be a catalyst for risk assessment. Thereby, insurance-related tools can help set up a *framework for signalling the magnitude, location, and exposure to climate-related risks.*

At country level, the African Risk Capacity's (ARC) risk modelling and early warning software platform, Africa RiskView, uses satellite-based data to estimate the impact of weather events on vulnerable populations—and the response costs required to assist them—before a hazard season begins, and as it progresses. This instrument provides the hard triggers for ARC's insurance mechanism. But it also allows countries to monitor and analyse rainfall throughout the continent and estimate the impact of weather developments on vulnerable populations in-season, "thus providing ARC Member States and Partners with an innovative early warning tool" (ARC 2015). At micro level we find plenty examples where weather data was collected together with policy holders (e.g. through rain gauges) during the design and set up process of insurance products. This data ultimately contributed to increasing farmers' sensitivity to changing rainfall patterns and helping them develop a better understanding of the likely impact of weather on yields (Sharoff et al. 2015; Hellmuth et al. 2009).

Limits of Insurability as Means to Signal When Adaptation Limits Are Approached
In the context of increasing climate risk, the concept of insurability plays an important role. Vulnerability to rising climate change risks is not only of importance to people but also the insurance industry is vulnerable to rising risks. Increasingly catastrophic losses made private insurance companies in developed countries pull out of some markets, making insurance unavailable for affected households (Botzen and van den Bergh 2008). Herweijer et al. (2009) therefore conclude that "climate change has the potential to threaten the widespread availability and affordability of insurance for people and their property in many regions, that is, the insurability of the risk." Stahel (2003) defines the concept of insurability as the "natural borderline" between the market economy and nation states: risks that cannot be insured need not to be legislated; uninsurable risks, however, have to be dealt with by nation states." Thereby, increasing limits of insurability can provide a strong signal that actors or systems reached the upper end of adaptation frontiers, existing on the edge of adaptation limits. This information could incentivise large scale governmental action to effectively reduce risk and increase insurability in a way that wouldn't be feasible or affordable for individual actors.

13.3.2 Improving Ex-Ante Decision Making with Insurance

Increasing risk of extreme weather events driven by climate change strengthen the need for a more forward-looking approach to disaster risk management, with greater focus on reducing risk before a disaster strikes (Ranger and Fisher 2012). Moving away from purely ex-post responses, actors need to manage risk proactively, before a disaster strikes. This includes reducing risk ex-ante and building long-term resilience against extreme weather events.

Price Signals as Means to Incentivise Risk Reduction?
Insurance can play a role as messenger of climate change impacts through its terms and price signals. Insurance companies have an incentive to 'risk price' as much as possible so that they can accurately predict the probability of a claim, and the

likely cost of that claim. Through the technical risk pricing of contracts, insurance can provide valuable information for societal and economic actors in understanding the risks and how risk cost may be changing. When the risk is priced correctly "the price itself indicates the risk level, which can help people and firms make better-informed decisions about risk taking and risk mitigation investments" (Ranger and Fisher 2012). In an ideal scenario, insurance thereby incentivises risk reduction behaviour, e.g. by making it a prerequisite for reducing premiums or providing the option for people to work for their insurance cover by engaging in community-identified projects to reduce risk and build climate resilience. In this way, insurance could contribute to preventing losses and damages. In a theoretical example, the high costs of insurance against flood would provide an incentive for an actor, wanting to buy a house in a flood prone area, not to buy. Instead, if investing into risk reduction measures directly, this leads to a reduction in premium price and insurance might provide a strong incentive for the actor to invest into risk reduction activities. In this way "insurance can create powerful incentives for people to manage their risk better and reduce losses" (ibid.). However, the evidence on actual insurance schemes incentivising risk reduction is weak. Surminski and Oramas-Dorta (2013) found that only a few already existing schemes show an operational link between risk transfer and risk reduction (Surminski and Oramas-Dorta 2013). Chambwera et al. (2014) moreover show that local and state regulations might undermine incentives to decrease risks, for example by prohibiting fully risk adequate insurance rates.

A Space of Certainty Allowing for Improved Ex-Ante Planning and Decision Making
Insurance-related approaches, in combination with a wide range of others at local, national, regional and international levels, can contribute to creating a space of certainty within which improved ex-ante decision making is possible (Skees et al. 2008; Hoppe and Gurenko 2006). By creating a secure investment environment, insurance instruments can enable productive risk-taking on the part of individuals and governments, and in this way contribute to mitigating disaster-induced poverty traps and foster climate-resilient development.

To limit their exposure, poor households often try to avoid risks. Therefore, they choose activities with lower risk, but also lower returns, and forego income opportunities (Cole et al. 2012). Researchers observed in Tanzania that poorer farmers grew more sweet potatoes (which is a lower-risk, lower-return crop) than richer farmers—resulting in a reduction of up to 25% average earnings (Dercon 1996). To be prepared in the event of a shock, the poor also tend to diversify their income-generating activities, assets or choice of crop or accumulate precautionary savings. While this is certainly a sensible measure to decrease risk, it can also lead to a loss of profits as people cannot afford to specialise in the more profitable options. In general, these informal strategies to manage climate risk usually cover only a small proportion of the loss, so "the poor have to patch together support from various sources" (Churchill 2006). By reducing the residual risk that could not be reduced by measures already taken, insurance can help lessen financial repercussions of volatility and, in the longer-term, help people to adapt to climate change. Insurance represents predictable and manageable costs—the insured party does only pay the insurance premium instead of risking unmanageable costs due to disaster losses. These predictable costs and the security of a payout in case of a disaster create a space of certainty and allow for longer-term planning, investment and development activities. Thereby, insurance can incentivise "positive risk taking" (Mobarak and Rosenzweig 2013), which is essential for innovation and growth. There are first indications that at the micro level, insurance can help to unlock opportunities and may help increase savings, increase investments in higher-return activities and improve credit worthiness (see e.g. Jensen et al. 2015; Cai et al. 2015; Madajewicz et al. 2013; Luxbacher and Goodland 2010). At the macro level, research suggests that insurance may contribute to economic growth by allowing for more effective risk management (Lester 2014; von Peter et al. 2012; Melecky and Raddatz 2011).

We also see that the way risks are currently managed in developing countries is often not effective. The mainly ex-post risk management strategies are not timely and can lead to financial burdens as well as volatility and uncertainty in decision-making. They can ultimately threaten the resilience of poor and vulnerable people, (re-)enforce poverty cycles and impede sustainable development. At the political level we find indications that insurance could help countries to reshape the ways in which risks are managed ex-ante. This can be facilitated by eligibility criteria that insurance companies can define as a precondition for people and countries wanting to purchase their products. These criteria can foster the selection of nationally appropriate risk reduction priorities, and help develop a culture of prevention and resilience. For example, we find indications that requesting contingency planning as eligibility criteria for the ARC has influenced the process of disaster relief programmes in the relevant countries, shifting paradigms away from crisis to risk management. ARC Member States currently pay insurance premiums through national budget processes and receive payouts only for pre-approved contingency plans. Before the countries are allowed to buy ARC insurance policies, they have to submit contingency plans, defining how the money will be used in case of a payout. ARC supports the countries in developing the contingency plans with in-country capacity-building programmes (ARC 2015). By providing incentives for governments to invest in their emergency planning and response capacities, ARC could contribute to shaping a culture of data-driven, prevention-focused risk management in their member countries in the long-term.

However, we have to be cautious about drawing conclusions from these first indications both at micro and macro levels. Evidence with regard to the impact of insurance is scarce as most schemes are still in their early stages of implementation. So far, most of the research is based on small case numbers, the cases and the results being highly context specific. Constant analysis and long-term monitoring and evaluation of project outcomes will be crucial to track potential impacts of insurance in the years to come. We also need to note that in all of the cases examined, it was not insurance alone but the interplay of insurance with other risk management activities and social protection tools that improved opportunities and created incentives. Without this relationship, supporting investment in higher-risk activities might also lead to maladaptation by encouraging people to undertake activities that should be avoided when considering longer-term climatic impacts. This "false sense of security" (Surminski and Oramas-Dorta 2013) might reduce the urgency for risk prevention and reduction, and thereby increase vulnerability to extreme events.

13.3.3 Insurance as a Support Tool for Actors to Remain in the Tolerable Risk Space

Effectively managing increasing climate change risk is a precondition for actors to remain within the tolerable risk space (Mechler and Schinko 2016). Insurance can support risk management strategies ex-post as safety net and buffer for people and countries, particularly for low frequency and moderate to high severity risks.

Providing a Safety Net and Buffer: Insurance as Part of Contingency Strategies
Contingency strategies, managing unexpected shocks from climate stressors which could not have been reasonably anticipated through pre-emptive actions, can provide a key means for actors to remain within the tolerable risk space. These strategies are needed, in addition to planning and pre-emptive undertakings, as some climate-related impact are unforeseeable at the time of planning or the magnitude of climate-related impacts might surpasses estimates. Also, in cases where unforeseen impacts or costs arose from transboundary climate change impacts or responses or impacts were foreseeable, but response actions were economically or technologically unfeasible at the time of planning, contingency approaches are necessary. The strategies should complement and facilitate approaches to address longer-term incremental climate impacts, risks, and vulnerabilities associated with climate change.

Insurance plays an important role as part of contingency strategies. By providing timely finance that improves financial liquidity shortly after a disaster, insurance can play a role as a safety net and buffer for people and countries shortly after an event (Warner et al. 2012). Under these circumstances, insurance can help the insured to better absorb shocks, as they may not have to resort to coping strategies that might impede sustainable development (Okonjo-Iweala and Thunell 2015). Timely and reliable payouts enable households to protect their livelihoods when a disaster strikes: It can help individuals to cover losses and damages, stabilise their income, purchase food and other necessities and avoid costly asset depletion, ultimately allowing people to choose alternative means of coping with negative shocks (Dercon et al. 2005; Barrett et al. 2007; Skees and Collier 2008). There is significant evidence that insurance tools can help people to reduce distress asset sales and to increase food security, both enabling faster recovery after a shock (Greatrex et al. 2015; Bertram-Hümmer and Kraehnert 2015; Reyes et al. 2015; Janzen and Carter 2013). Based on the timely finance, insurance can also help to avoid business interruptions and fiscal deficits and post disaster loans (e.g. CCRIF SPC 2010). By reducing the residual risk that could not be reduced by measures already taken, insurance can help lessen financial repercussions of volatility and, in the longer term, help people to adapt to climate change. Insurance is an adaptation measure when it reduces the *burden* of climate impacts, risks, and vulnerabilities, if not the average loss (Linnerooth-Bayer et al. 2010).

The given examples clearly illustrate how quick and sufficient payouts are key for insurance to realise its potential within a contingency strategy. A poorly designed insurance product that neither covers a sufficient amount of the damage nor provides incentives for risk reduction behaviour might lead to perverse incentives and increases the risk of people slipping (back) into poverty or staying poor. Although we find sufficient examples for quick payouts, there are also cases to be found where timely finance could not be provided by insurance products due to different reasons. Moreover, on the macro level, a fast payout to a government doesn't necessarily convert in timely support for the ultimate beneficiaries, being reliant on slow external processes, for example a sedate humanitarian system. Hence, constantly monitoring errors and challenges as well as learning from them to improve processes is crucial for the success of risk transfer tools like insurance as part of contingency strategies in the long-term.

Insurance for Low Frequency and Moderate to High Severity Risks

There are different layers of risks that risk management measures need to respond to. An efficient risk management system involves assigning an instrument or set of instruments to each layer, consistent with the selected strategy (reduction, retention or transfer). Financial instruments, in combination with risk prevention and reduction measures, should be selected on the basis of frequency and severity of disasters. This suggests that for weather-related risks which happen often (high frequency) but which are less serious (low severity), preventative and risk reduction activities may be the most cost-effective. The costs of preventing these events are typically much lower than the losses that would occur without investments in prevention measures. Alternatively, prevention measures for high-impact, low-frequency events can be far costlier with respect to the losses prevented. These more severe and less frequent risks, which cannot be reduced in a cost-effective manner, could be transferred to private and public insurance markets. Evidence from developed countries shows that insurance instruments have been effective in providing financial compensation for losses from extreme events to avoid the distress caused by the financial aftermath without financial protection (Arent et al. 2014). However, it is important to note that despite adaptation strategies, climate change may bring some residual risks which cannot be transferred to the insurance market cost-efficiently (Warner et al. 2012). Governments also need to adopt approaches to address these residual risks, "the losses and damages that remain once all feasible measures (especially adaptation and mitigation) have been implemented" (ibid). The following Fig. 13.3 illustrates a risk-layering strategy on the basis of the frequency and severity of the event (see also chapter by Schinko et al. 2018).

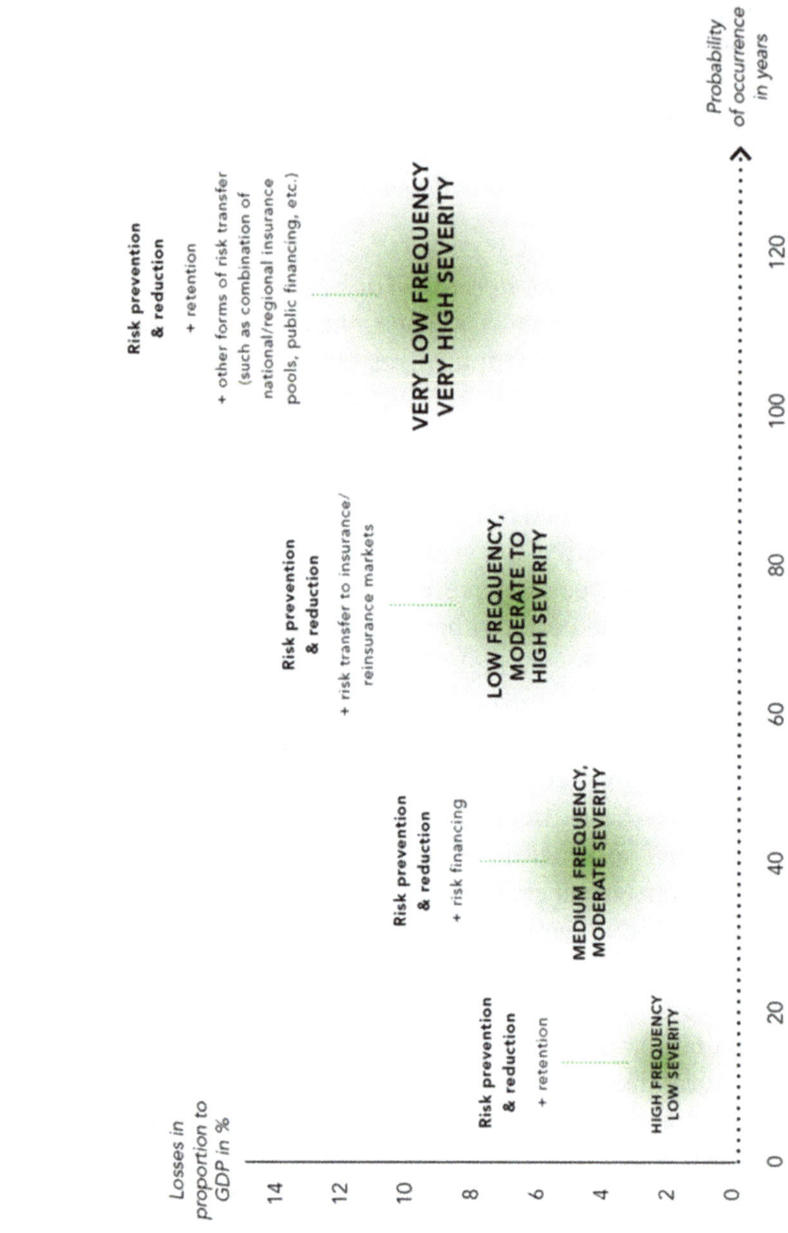

Fig. 13.3 Risk layering. *Source* Schäfer et al. (2016) adapted from Poundrik (2011)

13.4 The Need for Comprehensive Risk Management and the Limits of Insurance: Seven Principles to Design Effective Pro-poor Insurance Products

Section three elaborated on how decision makers can use insurance tools to explore and manage adaptation frontiers. However, in the context of comprehensive planning and pre-emptive activities to manage climate risks, insurance is not a universal remedy for all types of climate impacts, risks, and vulnerabilities associated with climate change. It has limitations with regard to its applicability for some type of risks as it cannot cover all losses and climate change may pose a threat to insurability. These limitations have led to one of the most important insights for how this tool can contribute to addressing the adverse effects of climate change: Insurance should always be embedded in a comprehensive climate risk management system with a focus on risk reduction, and ex-ante planning. A combination of measures that include insurance can reduce maladaptation, and reduce immediate losses and long-term development setbacks from adverse climatic impacts. But beyond comprehensive risk management, there are other factors that need to be met in order for insurance tools to effectively support the risk management efforts of developing countries, a team from the Munich Climate Insurance Initiative (MCII) found. After having dealt with the limits of insurance, this section will describe these factors in detail.

13.4.1 Limits of Insurance

Experience reveals multiple limitations of traditional forms of insurance (Hoff et al. 2005): it is not applicable for all types of risks, does not prevent or reduce the likelihood of direct damage and fatalities from extreme weather events and does not cover all losses. Potential un-insurability associated with increasing frequency and magnitude of extreme weather events poses an additional limitation. Moreover, it is not always the most cost-effective or affordable approach and actor's behaviour towards low probability, high impact events can make the application of insurance approaches challenging.

Insurance Is Not an Appropriate Measure for All Types of Risks

Insurance options can support adaptation and risk resilience for extreme weather events, but are not appropriate for many, usually slower-onset, climate-induced impacts, that happen with high certainty under different climate change scenarios. The losses from long-term, foreseeable risks, such as sea-level rise, desertification and the loss of glaciers and other cryospheric water sources, are estimated to be substantial in the future (IPCC 2012). Even for weather-related events, insurance would be an ill-advised solution for disastrous events that occur with very high frequency, such as recurrent flooding. Resilience-building and prevention in such instances may be cost-effective ways to address these risks.

Insurance Cannot Cover All (Types of) Losses
Insurance can only cover a percentage of losses, and even when policies are in place to offer coverage, basis risk can result in farmers being less protected than they expected to be. Basis risk can be understood as the risk that insurance claims do not adequately reflect the losses incurred; in other words, an individual suffers a loss and does not receive a payment for it because the insurance threshold was not triggered. In this way, even households that are fully insured end up bearing a significant amount of uninsured risk. This is particularly a problem for weather index insurance products (which currently make up the bulk of climate risk insurance schemes) as they pay based on the measure of weather or area yields.

Additionally, we have to note that not all types of losses and damages can be expressed in monetary terms. Insurance cannot address these types of non-economic losses and damages—context-dependent types of losses that don't have market price and cannot be easily given a monetary value. For example, there is no payout that could compensate for the loss of culture, identity or biodiversity, all of which may be results of climate change related events.

Climate Change May Make Some Risks Uninsurable
As climate change will increase the intensity and frequency of extreme weather events, there may come a time when some risks become so severe that they are uninsurable. An increased risk for currently insurable perils, such as crops and livestock, will lead to higher premiums, which might ultimately make the product too expensive for the poor and the actors who pay premiums on behalf of them.

One determinant of increasing premiums is the rising uncertainty about climate related risks. To assess risks and calculate premiums, the insurance industry relies on weather data which are so far based on historical records of hazard occurrences (Herweijer et al. 2009). However, climate change projections include a high level of uncertainty as besides predicting impacts of future extreme events, anticipating future vulnerability, socioeconomic trends and the way complex systems might react to new stressors is challenging (Ranger and Niehoerster 2012). This leads to greater uncertainties of insurers about the frequency and magnitude of future claims. Science indicates that the greater the uncertainty of the probability of an event and the magnitude of losses, the greater will be the insurance premium charged (Kunreuther 1996). However, if premiums "necessary to cover a disaster in a climatically changed world are greater than homeowners and businesses are willing or able to pay, the private insurance market will collapse" (Cousky and Cook 2009). On the other side, if insurers under-price risks, the accumulation of capital may be inadequate to cover losses threatening the solvency of insurers (Herweijer et al. 2009). Insurers therefore have to adjust in particular their underwriting practices that are mostly based on immediate past experience.

It is not known how the private markets would react to rising risk levels in the future, particularly in developing countries. Cousky and Cook (2009) point to the fact that "if risk is increasing over time, such that insurers do not believe they can accurately estimate expected losses, a key condition of insurability is violated." Kunreuther and Michel (2008) therefore conclude that only a requirement by law will make insurers provide coverage for climate-related risk that have a high enough potential for causing catastrophic losses in specific areas.

Behavioural Factors: Why People Don't Insure Against Big Risks
It has often been observed that homeowners don't purchase disaster insurance. While budget constraints are one explanation for this behaviour, another explanation is people's tendency to understate the probability of a rare events and catastrophes for themselves. Kunreuther and Pauly (2004) could show that "people don't insure against low-probability high-loss events even when it is offered at favourable premiums." Due to a pre-disaster "It will not happen to me" perception, people don't feel the need to voluntarily purchase insurance coverage (Hertwig et al. 2004). Kousky and Cooke (2012) conclude that "homeowners, facing a budget constraint and a constraint that their utility with insurance exceeds that without it, may find the required loadings too high to make insurance purchase an optimal decision."

13.4.2 Seven Principles to Design Effective Pro-poor Insurance Solutions

This chapter is based on the observation that poor and vulnerable people and communities already exist and persist at the edges of adaptation limits, operating within adaptation frontiers. To successfully navigate adaptation frontiers, these people and communities need tools that allow them to explore the frontier, stay away from adaptation limits and continuously move into safer domains. So far, this chapter established that insurance can be used as a navigational tool around adaptation frontiers, however has limits that have to be taken into account when applying insurance instruments. Based on these findings, the final part of the chapter examines success criteria for instruments like insurance to approach their potential as risk management tool in developing countries.

In describing these success criteria we make use of an analysis of 18 existing insurance schemes with regard to success factors and challenges for climate risk insurance for the poor and vulnerable, conducted by a team from the MCII. Based on this analysis, the MCII team distilled seven Pro-Poor Principles for Climate Risk Insurance (Schäfer et al. 2016). The principles can aid decision makers and practitioners in reaching poor and vulnerable people with effective insurance solutions. They can guide the design process of new insurance schemes that target the poor and vulnerable in particular by following the suggested steps or help with the identification of existing insurance schemes to be supported by climate risk insurance initiatives. Additionally, the principles can be used to support climate risk insurance practitioners in assessing and/or improving their current operations. The principles are described in Box 13.2 and further discussed below.

Box 13.2 Seven Pro-Poor Principles for Climate Risk Insurance

1. **Facilitating comprehensive-needs based solutions**: Solutions to protect the poor from extreme weather events must be tailored to local needs and conditions. It is imperative to embed insurance in comprehensive risk management strategies that improve resilience.
2. **Offering Client value**: Providing reliable coverage that is valuable to the insured is crucial for the take-up of insurance products.
3. **Ensuring Affordability**: Measures to increase affordability for poor and vulnerable people are paramount to the success of an insurance scheme and also important to satisfy equity concerns.
4. **Maximising accessibility**: Efficient and cost-effective delivery channels that are aligned with the local context are key for reaching scale.
5. **Allowing for Participation, Transparency & Accountability**: Successful insurance schemes are based on the inclusive, meaningful and accountable involvement of (potential) beneficiaries and other relevant local-level stakeholders in the design, implementation and review of insurance products, creating trust and providing a basis for local ownership and political buy-in.
6. **Generating Sustainability**: Safeguarding economic, social and ecological sustainability is crucial for the long-term success of insurance schemes.
7. **Creating an enabling environment**: It is vital to actively build an enabling environment that accommodates and fosters pro-poor insurance solutions.

Comprehensive, Needs Based Solutions

The poor and vulnerable face multiple risks that get in the way of opportunities to reduce poverty. For many of the analysed insurance schemes, the key to success has been offering comprehensive solutions to mitigate weather risks. Three important factors were identified in the analysis of 18 existing insurance schemes: (1) implementing risk, needs, demand and context assessments, (2) linking insurance to ex-ante climate risk management, and (3) fostering locally driven and owned schemes (Schäfer and Waters 2016). The Rural Resilience Initiative (R4) is a good example for this principle. R4 currently reaches more than 37,000 farmers with four integrated risk management strategies: risk transfer, risk reduction, prudent risk taking, and risk reserves. While the risk transfer enables the poorest farmers to purchase a weather index insurance against drought, farmers can pay insurance premiums in cash or through insurance for assets (IFA) schemes that engage them in risk reduction activities. IFA schemes are built into government safety net programmes or World Food Programme food assistance for assets (FFA) initiatives. Additionally, individual or group saving enable farmers to build a financial base. Providing a self-insurance for communities, group savings can be loaned to individual members with particular needs (R4 2015).

Client Value

Ensuring that coverage is reliable and that critical risks are not under-insured is critical for the take up and success of insurance products that target the poor (Schäfer and Waters 2016). Bundling the insurance product, where appropriate, with additional services that are valuable to the client and the active reduction of basis risk, which remains a challenge for index products, were found as effective means to increase client value. SANASA in Sri Lanka is a good example for adding client value through bundling with additional services. The unique part of their index-based crop insurance product is that it is bundled with other covers like accidental death and hospitalisation which catered to various needs of the farmers and offered a good coverage for both production and livelihood risks (Prashad and Herath 2015).

Affordability
Most insurance-related approaches targeting poor and vulnerable people or countries have not been started and performed without some form of financial support, often in the form of premium support (Vivideconomics et al. 2016). Affording risk-based premiums remains a major challenge for this target group, and measures to increase the affordability of products are paramount to the success of insurance schemes. Finding solutions for this challenge is the precondition for establishing solidarity and human-rights-oriented insurance schemes that respond to concerns of equity (Schäfer and Waters 2016). When applied, premium support should always be smart in a way that it's reliable, flexible and long term, that distorts incentives as little as possible, and that makes the client aware of the true risk costs.

Accessibility
Efficient and cost-effective delivery channels that require minimum input but ensure a widespread reach are key for reaching a large client base and scale (Schäfer and Waters 2016). One way to achieve this can be by building on natural aggregators, such as associations, cooperatives, mutuals, federated self-help groups, and savings and credit groups, which have established successful and trusted delivery mechanisms and align the insurance scheme with the local context. Investing in tech-leveraged secure client identification and targeting as well as payment systems to reduce fraud and improve the timeliness of payouts were identified as success factors by the case study analysis. Moreover, it proved successful to utilise social protection programmes, where appropriate, to implement large-scale development of insurance for the poor and vulnerable.

Participation, Transparency and Accountability
Target group ownership and trust are essential for the effective use of insurance as a risk management tool. It is crucial to include the insured and beneficiaries in the design and implementation of insurance solutions and disaster risk reduction activities to ensure products truly work. Participatory approaches to product development can create trust, help with capacity building and make sure that the insurance actually meets the real needs of people at risk, thus creating client value. The case study results showed that it is important to actively support and build partnerships, networks and communication channels that allow for inclusive and meaningful involvement of the poor and vulnerable (Schäfer and Waters 2016). Organisations and structures that have deep roots within the local context are favourable partners. Schemes moreover need to ensure that the design and implementation processes are transparent and accountable. An effective monitoring and evaluation framework that measures out-

puts, outcomes and impacts to ensure that the insurance schemes actually reach and benefit poor and vulnerable people is crucial.

Sustainability
Safeguarding financial, social and ecological sustainability is crucial for the long-term success of insurance schemes. This includes providing a long-term perspective on project planning and financing as setting up insurance schemes is a multi-year effort. Reliable flows of money accompanied by a long-term perspective helps to create a safe environment for key actors to engage in. It also involves making sure that insurance schemes do not incentivise practices that are not environmentally sustainable and incentivising risk reduction and prevention through the design of the insurance scheme, including risk-based premiums. From a social perspective, ensuring the participation and inclusion of women in climate risk insurance policy and programming is key (Schäfer and Waters 2016).

Enabling Environment
An enabling environment is a set of interrelated legal, organisational, fiscal, informational, political and cultural conditions that facilitate the successful development and implementation of an insurance scheme. Although the criteria for an enabling environment will be inevitably contextual, it is vital to actively build an enabling environment that accommodates and fosters pro-poor insurance solutions. Key factors of an enabling environment include capacity-building of key stakeholders, appropriate regulatory framework, strong, long-term partnerships and availability of data and technology (Schäfer and Waters 2016). First, *capacity building* is needed to improve the financial and insurance literacy and risk awareness of the insured, local insurers, distribution channels and governments. In the context of pro-poor insurance solutions it is important to use capacity building tools that respond to the needs of the target group and are suitable to educate clients with low written literacy about the complexity of index insurance. Second, successful insurance schemes need functioning *regulatory and legal frameworks* that govern the market, support the effective functioning of the scheme and allow growth by actively working with national governments and regulatory agencies. Third, *strong, long-term partnerships*, in particular public–private partnerships, which foster a clear allocation of roles is an important component of an enabling environment. The Index-Based Livestock Insurance Project (IBLIP) in Mongolia was first introduced in 2006 and provides herders with insurance through partnering with local private insurance companies. Insurance protects herders from climate-related losses to their livestock. With IBLIP there is a risk-layering approach to holistic risk management, combining self-insurance, market based insurance and a social safety net. Herders only bear the costs of small losses that do not affect the viability of their business; larger losses are transferred to the private insurance industry and the final layer of catastrophic loss is borne by the Government of Mongolia. The combination of the public disaster response product (a social safety net for herders offered by the government) and the private base insurance product (commercial product sold by private companies) proved to be highly successful for IBLIP. Fourth, *freely accessible data and technology* as well as hazard/weather monitoring

infrastructure are essential for effective and efficient design and implementation as well as for ensuring the uptake, distribution and payout of insurance products.

13.5 Conclusions

In this chapter we established that the potential contribution of insurance as a navigational tool around adaptation frontiers can be conceptualised around three different ways: First, through facilitating the exploration of adaptation frontiers by contributing to a framework for signalling the magnitude, location, and exposure to climate-related risks and providing signals when adaptation limits are approached. Second, by supporting actors in moving away from adaptation limits by incentivising risk reduction and creating a space for climate-resilient development. Third, by aiding actors in remaining in the tolerable risk space by facilitating financial buffering as part of contingency approaches. The conceptual debate around adaptation frontiers—including limits to adaptation—has been connected to the UNFCCC Loss and Damage discussions both in political and academic terms (e.g. Dow et al. 2013b). Given the potential contribution that insurance offers, this calls for a comprehensive reflection of insurance as part of the Loss and Damage policy space. Enhancing the international cooperation around the aspect of insurance as a climate risk management tool would allow to move forward several important aspects of the L&D debate, even in the absence of consensus around the different political stands of Parties e.g. the distributive and compensatory justice considerations of increasing climate impacts (Schinko et al. 2018 in this book).

We see, however, that insurance in market terms against the risks of climate change possesses several limitations. Among others these are limited insurability against some climate risks, the inability to cover events on a full loss basis, affordability issues as climate change impacts drive loss expectations. Moreover, reduced insurance demand can be a result of clients discounting rare events psychologically. We therefore suggest the embedding of insurance in a comprehensive climate risk management approach accompanied by other risk reduction and management strategies as key principle for any international cooperation approach to respond to climate change impacts. Moreover, client value, the accessibility, affordability and sustainability of products, participation and transparency, as well as an accommodating enabling environment are key principles described in this chapter. We propose that risk transfer instruments like insurance need to comply with these principles in order to approach their potential as navigational tool around adaptation frontiers for developing countries.

References

Adger WN, Dessai S, Goulden M et al (2009) Are there social limits to adaptation to climate change? Clim Change 93(3–4):335–354

ARC (2015) Accelerating action to resilience. Factsheet. http://www.africanriskcapacity.org/documents/350251/371107/A2R+EN.pdf. Accessed 20 April 2017

Arent DJ, Tol RSJ, Faust E et al (2014) Key economic sectors and services. In: Climate change 2014: impacts, adaptation, and vulnerability. Part A: global and sectoral aspects. In: Field CB et al (eds) Contribution of working group II to the fifth assessment report of the intergovernmental panel on climate change. Cambridge University Press, Cambridge, United Kingdom and New York, NY, USA, pp 659–708

Barnosky AD, Hadly EA, Bascompte SJ et al (2012) Approaching a state shift in earth's biosphere. Nature 486:52–58

Barrett CB, Barnett BC, Carter MR et al (2007) Poverty traps and climate risk: limitations and opportunities of index-based risk financing. IRI Technical Report No. 07-02. http://barrett.dyson.cornell.edu/Papers/WP_Poverty_IRItr0702.pdf. Accessed 24 April 2017

Bertram-Hümmer V, Kraehnert K (2015) Does index insurance help households recover from disaster? Evidence from IBLI Mongolia. DIW Berlin Discussion Papers No. 1515. https://www.diw.de/documents/publikationen/73/diw_01.c.518175.de/dp1515.pdf. Accessed 24 April 2017

Bouwer L, Aerts JCJH (2006) Financing climate change adaptation. Disasters 30:49–63

Botzen WJW, van den Bergh JCJM (2008) The insurance against climate change and flooding in the Netherlands: present, future, and comparison with other countries. Risk Anal 28(2):413–426

Cai H, Chen Y, Fan H et al (2015) The effect of microinsurance on economic activities: evidence from a randomized field experiment. Rev Econ Stat 97(2):287–300

CCRIF SPC (2010) Caribbean Governments receive US$12.8 M insurance payout from CCRIF following passage of Tomas, 17 November. http://www.ccrif.org/news/caribbeangovernments-receive-us128m-insurance-payout-ccrif-following-passage-tomas. Accessed 24 April 2017

Chambwera M, Heal G, Dubeux C, Hallegatte S, Leclerc L, Markandya A, McCarl BA, Mechler R, Neumann JE (2014) Economics of adaptation. In: Climate change 2014: impacts, adaptation, and vulnerability. Part A: global and sectoral aspects. In: Field CB, Barros VR, Dokken DJ et al (eds) Contribution of working group II to the fifth assessment report of the intergovernmental panel on climate change. Cambridge University Press, Cambridge, United Kingdom and New York, NY, USA, pp 945–977

Churchill C (2006) Protecting the poor: a microinsurance compendium. International Labour Organization. http://www.munichre-foundation.org/dms/MRS/Documents/ProtectingthepoorAmicroinsurancecompendium-FullBook.pdf. Accessed 20 April 2017

Cole S, Bastian GG, Vyas S et al (2012) The effectiveness of index based micro-insurance in helping smallholders manage weather-related risks. Working paper: EPPI Centre, Social Science Research Unit. http://r4d.dfid.gov.uk/pdf/outputs/systematicreviews/MicroinsuranceWeather-2012ColeReport.pdf. Accessed 20 April 2017

Collier B, Skees J, Barnett B (2009) Weather index-insurance and climate change: opportunities and challenges in lower income countries. The Geneva Papers 34:401–424

Cousky C, Cook RM (2009) Climate change and risk management challenges for insurance, adaptation, and loss estimation. Discussion paper. Resources for the Future. http://www.rff.org/files/sharepoint/WorkImages/Download/RFF-DP-09-03.pdf. Accessed 20 April 2017

de Bruin K, Dellink RB, Agrawala S (2009) Economic aspects of adaptation to climate change: integrated assessment modelling of adaptation costs and benefits. OECD Publishing, Paris

Dercon S (1996) Risk, crop choice, and savings: evidence from Tanzania. Econ Dev Cult Change 44(3):485–513

Dercon S, Hoddinott J, Tassew W (2005) Consumption and shocks in 15 Ethiopian villages, 1999–2004. J African Econ 14:559–585

Dow K, Berkhout F, Preston BL (2013a) Limits to adaptation to climate change: a risk approach. Environ Sustain 5(3–4):384–391

Dow K, Berkhout F, Preston BL et al (2013b) Limits to adaptation. Nat Clim Change 3:305–307
G7 (2015) Leaders' Declaration G7 Summit, 7–8 June 2015. https://www.g7germany.de/Content/DE/Anlagen/G8_G20/2015-06-08-g7-abschluss-eng.pdf?__blob=publicationFile. Accessed 5 May 2017
G20 (2017) Annex to G20 Leaders Declaration G20 Hamburg Climate and Energy Action Plan for Growth. https://www.g20.org/Content/DE/_Anlagen/G7_G20/2017-g20-climate-and-energy-en.pdf?__blob=publicationFile&v=6. Accessed 23 August 2017
Greatrex H, Hansen J, Garvin S (2015) Scaling up index insurance for smallholder farmers: Recent evidence and insights. CCAFS Report No. 14 Copenhagen: CGIAR Research Program on Climate Change, Agriculture and Food Security (CCAFS). https://cgspace.cgiar.org/rest/bitstreams/38716/retrieve. Accessed 24 April 2017
Hellmuth ME, Osgood DE, Hess U et al (2009) Index insurance and climate risk: Prospects for development and disaster management. Climate and Society 2. Available from https://iri.columbia.edu/wp-content/uploads/2013/07/Climate-and-Society-Issue-Number-2.pdf. Accessed 24 April 2017
Hertwig R, Barron G, Weber EU et al (2004) Decisions from experience and the effect of rare events in risky choice. Am Psychol Soc 15(8):534–539
Herweijer C, Ranger N, Ward R (2009) Adaptation to climate change: threats and opportunities for the insurance industry. The Geneva Papers 34:360–380
Hoff H, Warner K, Bouwer LM (2005) The role of financial services in climate adaptation in developing countries. Vierteljahrshefte zur Wirtschaftsforschung 74(2), 196–207. http://dx.doi.org/10.3790/vjh.74.2.196
Hoppe P, Gurenko E (2006) Scientific and economic rationales for innovative climate insurance solutions. Clim Policy 6(6):607–620
IPCC (2012) Managing the risks of extreme events and disasters to advance climate change adaptation. In: Field CB, Barros V, Stocker TF (eds) A special report of working groups I and II of the intergovernmental panel on climate change. Cambridge University Press, Cambridge, UK, and New York, NY, USA
IPCC (2014) Climate change 2014: impacts, adaptation, and vulnerability. Part A: global and sectoral aspects. In: Field CB, Barros VR, Dokken DJ et al (eds) Contribution of working group II to the fifth assessment report of the intergovernmental panel on climate change. Cambridge University Press, Cambridge, United Kingdom and New York, NY, USA
Islam M, Sallu S, Hubacek K et al (2014) Limits and barriers to adaptation to climate variability and change in Bangladeshi coastal fishing communities. Marine Policy 43:208–216
Janzen S, Carter M (2013) The impact of microinsurance on asset accumulation and human capital investments: evidence from a drought in Kenya. Microinsurance Research Paper 31. http://bit.ly/2gbWzrP. Accessed 24 April 2017
Jensen ND, Barrett CB, Mude A (2015) The favourable impacts of index-based livestock insurance: evaluation results from Ethiopia and Kenya. ILRI Research Brief 52. https://cgspace.cgiar.org/bitstream/handle/10568/66652/ResearchBrief52.pdf?sequence=1. Accessed 25 March 2017
Klein RJT, Midgley GF, Preston BL, Alam M, Berkhout FGH, Dow K, Shaw MR (2014) Adaptation opportunities, constraints and limits. In: Field CB, Barros, VR, Dokken DJ, Mastrandrea MD, Mach KJ, Bilir TE, Chatterjee M, Ebi KL, Estrada YO, Genova RC, Girma B, Kissel ES, Levy AN, MacCracken S, Mastrandrea PR, White LL (eds) Climate change 2014: impacts, adaptation, and vulnerability. Part B: regional aspects. Contribution of working group II to the fifth assessment report of the intergovernmental panel on climate change. Cambridge University Press, Cambridge, United Kingdom and New York, NY, USA, pp 899–943
Klinke A, Renn O (2002) A new approach to risk evaluation and management: risk-based, precaution-based, and discourse-based strategies. Risk Anal 22:1071–1094
Kunreuther HC (1996) Mitigating disaster losses through insurance. J Risk Uncertainty 12(2–3):171–187

Kunreuther HC, Michel-KEO (2008) Climate change, insurability of large-scale disasters, and the emerging liability challenge. http://scholarship.law.upenn.edu/cgi/viewcontent.cgi?article=1283&context=penn_law_review. Accessed 20 March 2017

Kunreuther HC, Pauly M (2004) Neglecting disaster: why don't people insure against large losses? J Risk Uncertainty 28(1):5–21

Kousky C, Cooke R (2012) Explaining the failure to insure catastrophic risks. The Geneva papers on risk and insurance—issues and practice 37(2):206–227

Lester R (2014) Insurance and inclusive growth. Policy Research Working Paper No. 6943. The Word Bank

Linnerooth-Bayer J, Bals C, Mechler R (2010) Insurance as part of a climate adaptation strategy. In: Hulme M, Neufedlt H (eds) Making climate change work for is. Cambridge University Press, Cambridge, pp 340–366

Linnerooth-Bayer J, Surminski S, Bouwer LM, Noy I and R Mechler (2018) Insurance as a response to loss and damage? In: Mechler R, Bouwer L, Schinko T, Surminski S, Linnerooth-Bayer J (eds) Loss and damage from climate change. Concepts, methods and policy options. Springer, Cham, pp 483–512

Luxbacher K, Goodland A (2010) Building resilience to extreme weather: index-based livestock insurance in Mongolia. World Resources Report Case Study. http://www.wri.org/sites/default/files/wrr_case_study_index_based_livestock_insurance_mongolia_pdf. Accessed 21 April 2017

Madajewicz M, Tsegay AH, Norton M (2013) Managing risks to agricultural livelihoods: impact evaluation of the Harita Program in Tigray, Ethiopia, 2009–2012. http://www.oxfamamerica.org/static/media/files/Oxfam_America_Impact_Evaluation_of_HARITA_2009-2012_English.pdf. Accessed 20 April 2017

Mechler R, Schinko T (2016) Identifying the policy space for climate loss and damage. Science 354(6310):290–292

Mechler R et al (2018) Science for loss and damage. Findings and propositions. In: Mechler R, Bouwer L, Schinko T, Surminski S, Linnerooth-Bayer J (eds) Loss and damage from climate change. Concepts, methods and policy options. Springer, Cham, pp 3–37

Melecky M, Raddatz C (2011) How Do governments respond after catastrophes? Natural-Disaster Shocks and the Fiscal Stance. World Bank Policy Research Working Paper No. 5564. http://bit.ly/2eLjDdZ. Accessed 25 April 2017

Mobarak AM, Rosenzweig MR (2013) Informal risk sharing, Index insurance, and risk taking in developing countries. Am Econ Rev: Papers Proc 103(3):375–380

Monnereau I, Abraham S (2013) Limits to autonomous adaptation in response to coastal erosion in Kosrae, Micronesia. Int J Global Warming 5(4):416–432

Okonjo-Iweala N, Thunell L (2015) African countries turn to insurance to safeguard against climate change. The Guardian, 7 October. http://www.theguardian.com/global-development/2015/oct/07/african-risk-capacity-agency-au-climate-changeadaptation-insurance. Accessed 24 April 2017

Oppenheimer M, Campos M, Warren R, Birkmann J, Luber G, O'Neill B, Takahashi K (2014) Emergent risks and key vulnerabilities. In: Field CB, Barros VR, Dokken DJ, Mach KJ, Mastrandrea MD, Bilir TE, Chatterjee M, Ebi KL, Estrada YO, Genova RC, Girma B, Kissel ES, Levy AN, MacCracken S, Mastrandrea PR, White LL (eds) Climate change 2014: impacts, adaptation, and vulnerability. Part A: global and sectoral aspects. Contribution of working group II to the fifth assessment report of the intergovernmental panel on climate change. Cambridge University Press, Cambridge, United Kingdom and New York, NY, USA, pp 1039–1099

Poundrik, S (2011). Disaster Risk Financing: Case Studies. Working Paper No. 23. EAP DRM KnowledgeNotes: Disaster Risk Management in East Asia and the Pacific. Washington, D.C.: The World Bank. Global Facility for Disaster Reduction and Recovery (GFDRR). http://www.documents.worldbank.org/curated/en/324451468026333428/pdf/604560BRI0231R10BOX358322B01PUBLIC1.pdf. Accessed 20 August 2019

Prashad P, Herath R (2015) Introducing index based crop insurance in Sri Lanka and improving client value. http://www.impactinsurance.org/practitioner-lessons/sanasa. Accessed 20 April 2017

Preston B, Dow K, Berhout F (2014) The climate adaptation frontier. Sustainability 5(3):1011–1035

R4 (2015) R4 Rural Resilience Initiative quarterly report, January–March 2015. http://policy-practice.oxfamamerica.org/static/media/files/R4_Report_Jan_Mar15_WEB.pdf. Accessed 20 April 2017

Ranger N, Fisher S (2012) The challenges of climate change and exposure growth for disaster risk management in developing countries. Report produced for the Government Office of Science, Foresight project 'Reducing Risks of Future Disasters: Priorities for Decision Makers'. https://www.gov.uk/government/uploads/system/uploads/attachment_data/file/287434/12-1305-climate-change-exposure-growth-for-disaster-risk.pdf. Accessed 4 March 2017

Ranger N, Niehörster F (2012) Deep uncertainty in long-term hurricane risk: scenario generation and implications for future climate experiments. Glob Environ Change 22(3):703–712

Rejda GE, McNamara MJ (2017) Principles of risk management and insurance, 13th edn. Pearsons, Harlow

Reyes CM, Gloria RAB, Mina CD (2015) Targeting the agricultural poor: The case of PCIC's special programs. http://dirp3.pids.gov.ph/webportal/CDN/PUBLICATIONS/pidsdps1508.pdf. Accessed 24 April 2017

Rockström J, Steffen W, Noone K (2009) A safe operating space for humanity. Nature 461:472–475

Schäfer L, Waters E, Kreft S, Zissener M (2016) Making climate risk insurance work for the most vulnerable. Policy Report No. 1. United Nations University Institute of Environment and Human Security (UNU-EHS), Bonn. http://www.climate-insurance.org/fileadmin/mcii/documents/MCII_PolicyReport2016_Making_CRI_Work_for_the_Most_Vulnerable_7GuidingPrinciples.pdf. Accessed 20 March 2017

Schäfer L, Waters E (2016) Climate risk insurance for the poor and vulnerable. How to effectively implement the pro-poor focus of InsuResilience. http://www.climate-insurance.org/fileadmin/mcii/documents/MCII_2016_CRI_for_the_Poor_and_Vulnerable_full_study_lo-res.pdf. Accessed 20 March 2017

Schinko T, Mechler R, Hochrainer-Stigler S (2018) The risk and policy space for loss and damage: integrating notions of distributive and compensatory justice with comprehensive climate risk management. In: Mechler R, Bouwer L, Schinko T, Surminski S, Linnerooth-Bayer J (eds) Loss and damage from climate change. Concepts, methods and policy options. Springer, Cham, pp 83–110

Sharoff J, Diro R, Mccarney G, Norton M (2015) R4 rural resilience initiative in Ethiopia. http://www.climate-services.org/wp-content/uploads/2015/09/R4_Ethiopia_Case_Study.pdf. Accessed 24 April 2017

Skees JR, Barnett BJ, Murphy AG (2008) Creating insurance markets for natural disaster risk in lower income countries: the potential role for securitization. Agric Financ Rev 68:151–157

Skees JR, Collier B (2008) The Potential of weather index insurance for spurring a green revolution in Africa. Working paper, GlobalAgRisk, Inc. Lexington, Kentucky. https://www.uky.edu/Ag/AgEcon/pubs/resWeatherAGRA04.pdf. Accessed 24 April 2017

Stahel WR (2003) The role of insurability and insurance. The Geneva Papers on Risk and Insurance 28(3):374–381

Surminski S, Oramas-Dorta D (2013) Do flood insurance schemes in developing countries provide incentives to reduce physical risks? Centre for Climate Change Economics and Policy Working Paper No. 139. http://www.cccep.ac.uk/wp-content/uploads/2015/10/WP119-flood-insurance-schemes-developing-countries.pdf. Accessed 20 April 2017

Surminski S, Bouwer LM, Linnerooth-Bayer J (2016) How insurance can support climate resilience. Commentary in: Nat Clim Change 6:333–334

Vivideconomics Surminski Consulting, Consulting Callund (2016) Understanding the role of publicly funded premium subsidies in disaster risk insurance in developing countries. Evidence on Demand, UK

von Peter G, von Dahlen S, Saxena S (2012) Unmitigated disasters? New evidence on the macroeconomic cost of natural catastrophes. BIS Working Papers No. 394. Monetary and Economic Department. http://www.bis.org/publ/work394.pdf. Accessed 25 April 2017

Warner K, Spiegel A (2009) Climate change and emerging markets: the role of the insurance industry in climate risk management. In: Liedtke M (ed) The Geneva Reports. Risk and Insurance Research. The Insurance Industry and Climate Change—Contribution to the Global Debate, pp 83–94

Warner K, Kreft S, Zissener M et al (2012) Insurance solutions in the context of climate change related loss & damage. Policy Brief No. 6. United Nations University Institute of Environment and Human Security (UNU-EHS), Bonn. http://www.climate-insurance.org/fileadmin/mcii/documents/20121112_MCII_PolicyBrief_2012_screen.pdf. Accessed 1 March 2017

Warner K, van der Geest K, Kreft S (2013) Pushed to the limits: Evidence of climate change-related loss and damage when people face constraints and limits to adaptation. Report no. 11. United Nations University Institute of Environment and Human Security (UNU-EHS), Bonn

Warner BP, Kuzdasa C, Yglesiasd MG et al (2015) Limits to adaptation to interacting global change risks among smallholder rice farmers in Northwest Costa Rica. Glob Environ Change 30:101–112

Chapter 14
Integrated Assessment for Identifying Climate Finance Needs for Loss and Damage: A Critical Review

Anil Markandya and Mikel González-Eguino

Abstract This chapter looks at what we can learn about possible Loss and Damage (L&D) and finance needed to address it using economic Integrated Assessment Models (IAMs), which calculate economically optimal responses to climate change mitigation and adaptation in terms of maximising welfare (GDP) a few decades into the future. Interpreting modelled residual damages as unavoided L&D, a few results emerge from the analysis. First, residual damages turn out to be significant under a variety of IAMs, and for a range of climate scenarios. This means that if adaptation is undertaken optimally, there will remain a large amount of damages that are not eliminated. Second the ratio of adaptation to total damages varies by region, so residual damages also vary for that reason. Third, residual damages will depend on the climate scenario as well as the discount rate and the assumed parameters of the climate model (equilibrium climate sensitivity) as well as those of the socioeconomic model (damage functions). These uncertainties are very large and so will be any projections of residual damages in the medium to long term. The chapter raises other aspects that could influence estimates of L&D. An important one is that, since actual adaptation is very unlikely to be optimal, the amount of Loss and Damage may be influenced by the sources from which adaptation and Loss and Damage programs are financed. The level and structure of current limited financial resources is likely to result in adaptation that is significantly below the optimal level and thus result in significant L&D.

Keywords Integrated Assessment Models · Loss and Damage · Residual damage · Adaptation · Mitigation

A. Markandya (✉) · M. González-Eguino
Basque Centre for Climate Change (BC3), Leioa, Spain
e-mail: anil.markandya@bc3research.org

R. Mechler et al. (eds.), *Loss and Damage from Climate Change*, Climate Risk Management, Policy and Governance, https://doi.org/10.1007/978-3-319-72026-5_14

14.1 Introduction

The bulk of the literature on finance for addressing climate change in developing countries relates to mitigation and adaptation measures. The UNEP Emissions Gap Report (2015) and the Adaptation Gap Report (2016) provide a synthesis of the current available finance from different sources for activities under these categories, as well as likely finance needs in the future. There is little documented data on the difference between the adaptation needs and the levels of estimated impacts of climate change. This difference is generally referred to in the economics of climate change literature as the residual damages (Chambwera et al. 2014), and also in some of the literature, as the 'unavoided losses and damages (L&D) from climate change' (see introduction by Mechler et al. 2018). Few estimates of the residual damages using economic modelling exist and there has not been sufficient discussion of the methodological choices and robustness of these model estimates. This chapter presents the underlying analytics and reviews the estimates of total climate change damages as gauged in the economic Integrated Assessment Model (IAM) literature[1] for different mitigation scenarios as a basis for calculating residual damages. It discusses the uncertainties surrounding these estimates and provides interval estimates by region and (where possible) by country for selected countries. Uncertainty, discount rates and other methodological choices play an important role. We discuss these but focus on two important ones: sources of uncertainty inherent to IAM-Equilibrium Climate Sensitivity and damage functions, and how these will increase uncertainty of the damages and residual damages.

It is important to state that, while the damages from climate change are estimated here using IAMs and top-down damage functions, there is a far-reaching debate as to the proper economic methods to use for assessing economic damages and the cost of adaptation. Other methods utilised in the economics of climate change impacts (see Burke et al. 2016) range from improvements in bottom-up estimation of damages (Carleton and Hsiang 2016) to expert elicitation approaches (Pindyck 2016). Particularly, more research is now devoted to represent "non-market" damages such as changes in human health and biodiversity that could be sizeable, but are largely omitted from current estimates (see also Chambwera et al. 2014). Combining the estimates of total damages with those for adaptation, based on the same set of models, the chapter derives a set of estimates of possible L&D for selected dates and under different RCP scenarios. Several issues challenging the robustness of these estimates are discussed in the chapter, including: *ex ante* versus *ex post* losses and damages, non-monetary damages, irreversibility and the role of economic growth in the affected countries. The chapter concludes with a discussion on what the IAM estimates imply for climate finance in the short and medium term, given the mandates and programmes of the main financing institutions, such as the Green Climate Fund.

[1]The economic IAM literature is to be distinguished from a scenario-based IAM literature where models, rather than calculating optimal responses to warming building on economic rationality, project future warming building on key drivers of climate change, including demographic variables, economic output, lifestyle and technology (see e.g. Nakicenovic et al. 2000).

14.2 Estimation of Residual Damages in Economic Integrated Assessment Modelling

14.2.1 IAM-Methods and Models

Economic IAMs are a widely used class of models that explore the economic consequences of different growth paths in the presence of climate change with the objective of maximising social welfare (measured by GDP) over a specific time horizon (Ortiz and Markandya 2009). Several IAMs have been used in this field, with differences that are in part a matter of subjectivity in the modelling design.[2] The IAMs tend to be quite aggregated, with a single measure of output (GDP), which increases over time through capital investment, population growth and technical change. In the model set-up, GDP is reduced as a result of losses or damages caused by climate change. These damages are included through functions that link damages in monetary terms to climate variables such as temperature or precipitation (typically temperature is the variable most commonly used). These functions and monetary damage estimates then feed into the model set-up to calculate the impact of the damages on economic output and growth, globally and for given world regions. Overall, the IAMs select levels of the control variables so as to maximise the discounted present value of welfare (usually represented by GDP or an adjusted version of GDP) over the chosen time horizon (usually 2100 or beyond). The key control variable has been the level of mitigation, but more recently adaptation has been added (the level of adaptation expenditures, which reduce climate-related damages). Levels of the control variables are selected as part of a dynamic welfare maximising exercise (generally in 10 year time steps and often until the year 2100) based on a trade-off between the costs climate change imposes and the reduction it makes to climate-related damages: as long as adaptation costs are smaller than damages avoided, climate change damages are reduced. The damages remaining after the adaptation has taken place are referred to as residual damages.

14.2.2 IAM Mechanics: Relation Between Adaptation Expenditures, Loss and Damage and Residual Costs

Figure 14.1 is a guide to understanding the links between total climate damages, expenditures on adaptation and residual damages. The vertical axis represents the value of damages in monetary terms. They can be thought of as damages in a single period or the present value of damages over the planning horizon. In the latter case additional issues arise about interpretation, which we discuss later. OD is the value of these damages in the absence of any adaptation.

[2]Further see Ortiz and Markandya (2009) for a detailed literature review of previous versions of IAMs for climate change analysis with damage functions mentioned here.

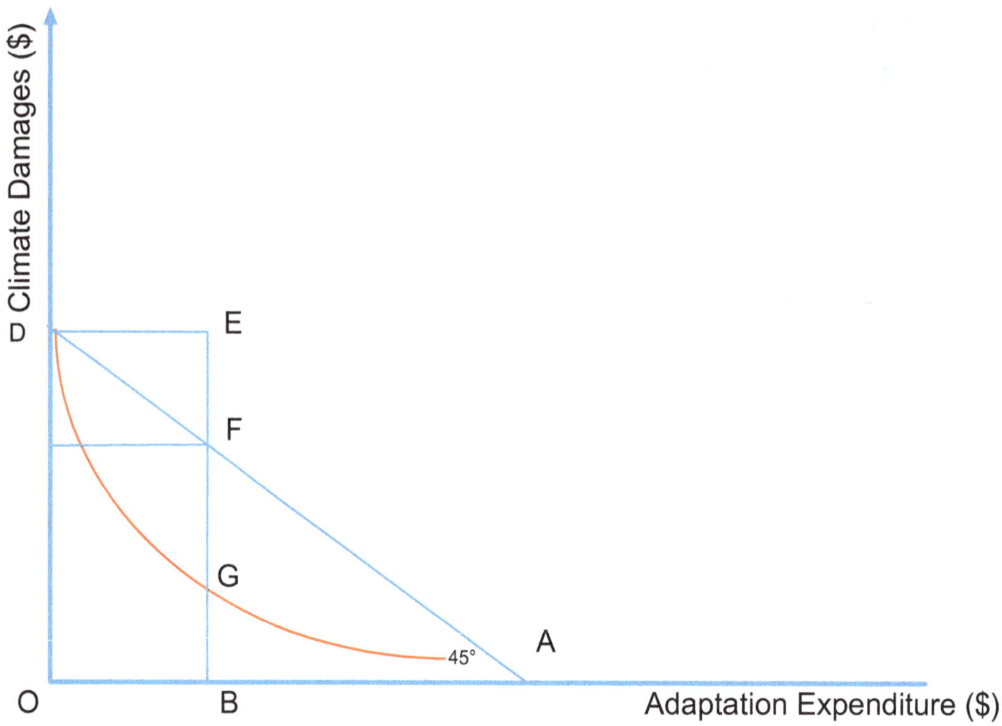

Fig. 14.1 Total damages, residual damages and adaptation expenditures

The horizontal axis measures total expenditure on adaptation, again either in a single period or as the present value over the planning horizon. The curve DA gives the damages corresponding to different levels of adaptation expenditure. It is convex to the origin because initial expenditures on adaptation yield greater reductions in damages than subsequent expenditures. As adaptation expenditure increases each unit generates less reduction than the unit before. It is also important to note that the curve starts with a slope of greater than one in absolute terms. This means that each million dollars spent on adaptation generates a reduction in damages for more than one million dollars. That is another way of saying that investment in adaptation, at least initially, has a cost that is less than the benefit.

The optimal level of adaptation expenditure is given by the distance OB, where the slope of the adaptation curve is equal to -1. Further expenditure would have a cost greater than the reduction in damages, while less reduction on adaptation would not fully exploit the potential net benefits to be gained.

At this optimal level of adaptation expenditure damages fall by the amount EG, leaving a residual damage equal to GB. We can see the net benefits of adaptation as the difference between the reduction in damages (EG) and the cost (OB = EF, by construction). Hence FG is the net benefit from the adaptation. Of course, damages 'beyond adaptation' are still very important—and at the heart of the Loss and Damage debate. With optimal adaptation they are equal to GB, and this could be a very large amount, especially when adaptation is not optimal but even when it is. The above analysis is based on adaptation being undertaken in an optimal fashion. Note that it implies some residual damage and, furthermore, it implies a total cost of climate damage after adaptation that is less than it would be with no action, even after accounting for adaptation expenditures. When adaptation is less than optimal residual damages will be larger.

The above analysis also has a time dimension, which can be simplified by assuming that damages and adaptation expenditures are represented in present value terms. In doing so we abstract from the problem of when the adaptation expenditures are to be made and when the residual damages will occur. The dynamic solution to the adaptation programme is, as we see in the next section, partly a function of the discount rate. The higher the discount rate taken, the less mitigation is undertaken and the greater are total damages likely to be. This implies some more adaptation but the net effect on residual damages, while not totally clear, is likely to be higher than with the lower discount rate. Since there is no agreement on the choice of discount rate there will also not be one on desired adaptation in the future and on residual damages that form the basis of the case for Loss and Damage.

Finally, the choice of adaptation versus residual damages for a given country will be influenced by what is financed internally and what is financed externally. If adaptation is likely to be more fully covered from external funds than compensation for residual damages the incentives will be to go for a higher level than the optimal OB shown in Fig. 14.1. On the other hand, if residual damages are more fully compensated and adaptation has to be financed to a greater degree from internal sources, the incentive will be to aim for a lower level of adaptation than OB. All these factors will play a role in determining how much adaptation actually takes place and how much residual damage arises as a result of climate change.

14.3 Estimating Residual Damages as a Measure of Loss and Damage

14.3.1 Model Set-Up

In this section we provide estimates of residual damages from a range of IAMs, taking account of uncertainty in the damage functions. The basic model ensemble is that of Bosello et al. (2010), which gives perhaps the most detailed time profile for adaptation costs and residual damages from a range of IAMs. The steps involved in making the estimates are the following:

The Base Cases considered are ones in which the temperature increases by 2.5 °C by the end of this century, which is consistent with concentrations stabilising at around 650 ppm (IPCC 2014) and implies moderate success in limiting emissions to the 'low damage' scenario. We can also refer to this as the low emissions scenario. By contrast, in the high emissions/high damage scenario the equivalent temperature increase is around 3.4 °C. In addition, the discount rate, which represents a societal preference for enjoying (consuming) any economic gains today rather than in a distant

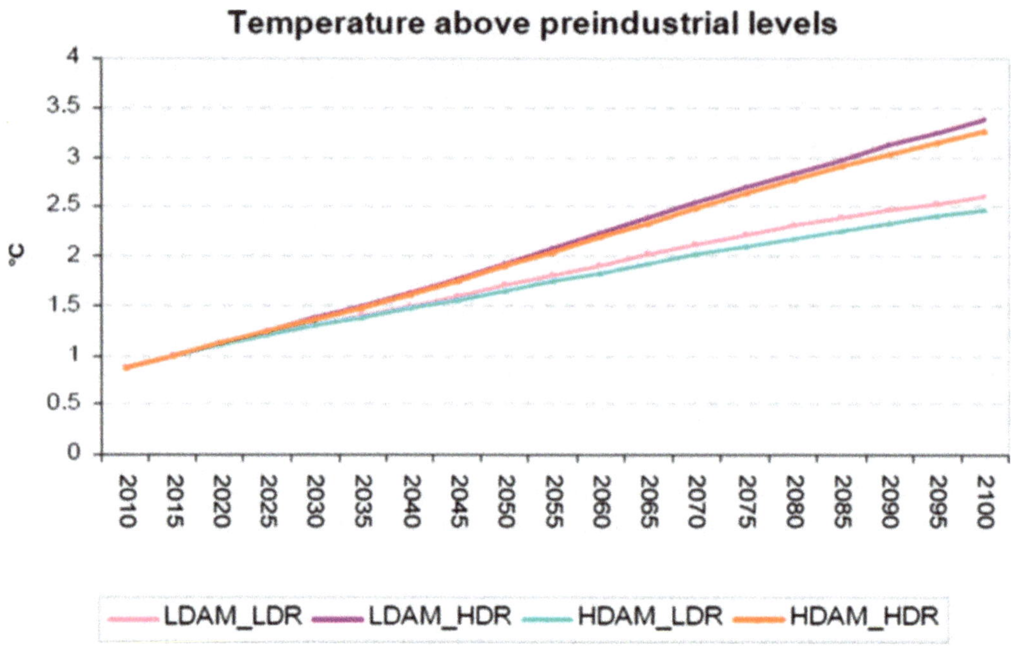

Fig. 14.2 Temperature pathways for low and high damage scenarios

future, specifies the level that future additions to welfare are reduced—a standard procedure in economics, however with heated debate as to the level of discounting (see further below).

Figure 14.2 shows the temperature pathways for four scenarios: (i) low damage/low emissions with a low discount rate (LDAM-LDR), (ii) low damage/low emissions with a high discount rate (LDAM-HDR), (iii) high damage/high emissions with a low discount rate (HDAM-LDR), and (iv) high damage/high emissions with a high discount rate (HDAM-HDR). The high discount rate case is the one where the rate is set initially at 3% and then declines over time as in the IAMs WITCH, DICE and RICE (see Nordhaus and Boyer 2000). The low discount rate is case is the one where the rate is set as 0.1% and then declines as in Stern (2007). To keep the analysis simple we consider only versions (ii) and (iii) of their analysis and use them to calculate residual damages over time. This provides a broad range of estimates.

For these cases Bosello et al. (2010) developed a version of the WITCH model to predict total damages. The model developed by Bosello et al. has 12 world regions (see regions further below in Tables 14.1 and 14.2). The model is run to obtain time profiles to 2100 for total global damages and expenditures on adaptation. Residual damages are only given globally, and in the model the regional share is assumed to be proportional to the regional share of damages. In order to obtain residual damages by region we take figures of total damages by region, which are reported for three IAMs: Nordhaus and Boyer (2000), AD-WITCH and the Bosello et al. (2010) model for the entire period. The average share of these total damages by region is calculated and then applied to the total residual damages by time period as given in Bosello et al. to obtain residual damages by region and time period for each scenario (all

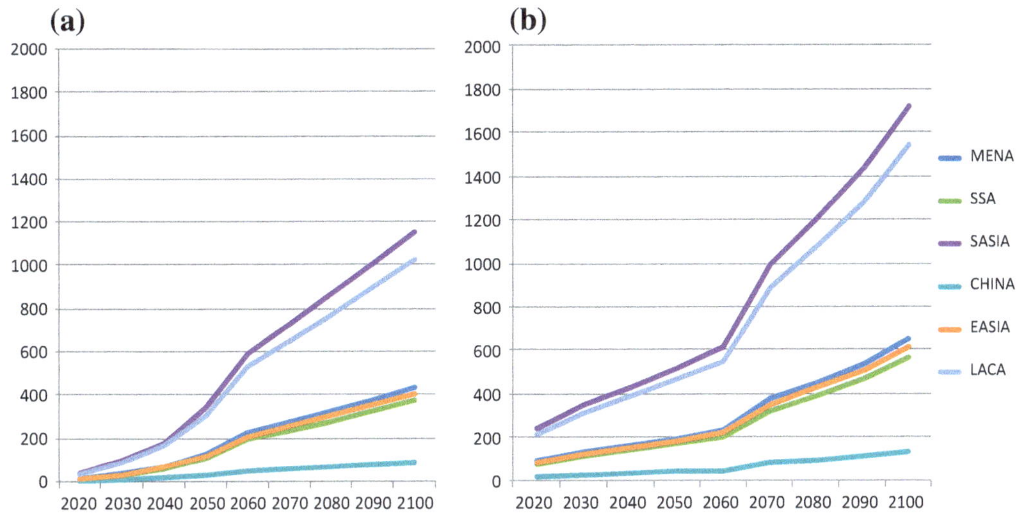

Fig. 14.3 Residual damages estimates for the case of **a**) low damages-high discount rate; **b**) high damages-low discount rate (in billion 2005 US)

estimates are given in billions of USD in 2005 prices). Damages are calculated for 12 regions and for every decade from 2020 to 2100.

14.3.2 Results

The estimates are shown in Tables 14.1 and 14.2. Table 14.1 gives residual damages in the high-damage/low discount rate case and Table 14.2 does the same for the low damage/high discount rate case. As stated, in each case the figures are for the averages of the three IAMs mentioned above. The last column in the two tables gives the range of damages across the three models, reporting the maximum as a percentage of the minimum.[3] Finally the last row of Table 14.1 shows how much damages vary between the high and low damage cases by reporting the high damage as a percent of the low damage. The same information on regional damages is also shown in Fig. 14.3.

The figures show residual damages to vary significantly by region. Since we are interested in those damages that would need to be financed from a possible L&D facility we can focus on the following regions, where the countries belong mainly to the non-Annex I group: MENA, SSA, SASIA, China, EASIA and LACA. Total residual damages for these regions range from $116–435 billion in 2020, rising to $290–580 billion in 2030, $551–1,016 billion in 2040 and 1,132–1,741 billion in 2050. Thus, even in the low damages case the residual cost figures are substantial

[3]There are further variations in damages to consider for a given discount rate and a given temperature profile. These arise from the choice of key parameters of the IAMs and are discussed further in the next section.

Table 14.1 Residual damages across three IAMs: high damages-low discount rate (USD billion 2005)

	2020	2030	2040	2050	2060	2070	2080	2090	2100	Range (*) (%)
USA	78	113	141	169	200	325	391	469	563	8
W. Europe	405	584	730	876	1,038	1,686	2,027	2,432	2,918	79
E. Europe	12	17	22	26	31	50	60	72	86	67
KOSAU	2	2	3	3	4	6	8	9	11	311
CAJANZ	26	38	47	57	67	109	131	157	189	4535
TE	1	2	2	3	3	6	7	8	10	222
MENA	90	130	162	195	231	375	450	540	648	51
SSA	78	112	140	168	199	323	389	467	560	31
SASIA	240	345	431	518	613	997	1,198	1,438	1,725	12
CHINA	19	28	34	41	49	80	96	115	138	118
EASIA	85	122	153	183	217	353	424	509	610	131
LACA	214	308	385	462	548	891	1,070	1,284	1,541	5
Total	1,250	1,800	2,250	2,700	3,200	5,200	6,250	7,500	9,000	

(*) Percentage by which the highest estimate is greater than the lowest estimate over the whole period. *Source* Own calculations based on Bosello et al. (2010)
Note KOSAU-Korea, South Africa; CAJANZ-Canada, Japan, New Zealand; TE-Transition Economies; MENA-Middle East and North Africa; SSA-Sub-Saharan Africa; SASIA-South Asia; EASIA-East Asia; LACA-Latin and Central America and the Caribbean

Table 14.2 Residual damages across three IAMs: low damages-high discount rate (USD billion 2005)

	2020	2030	2040	2050	2060	2070	2080	2090	2100	Range (*) (%)
USA	13	31	59	113	194	238	281	328	375	8
W. Europe	65	162	308	584	1,005	1,232	1,459	1,702	1,946	79
E. Europe	2	5	9	17	30	36	43	50	57	67
KOSAU	0	1	1	2	4	5	6	6	7	311
CAJANZ	4	10	20	33	65	80	94	110	126	4535
TE	0	1	1	2	3	4	5	6	6	222
MENA	14	36	68	130	223	274	324	378	432	51
SSA	12	31	59	112	193	236	280	327	373	31
SASIA	38	96	182	345	594	728	863	1,006	1,150	12
CHINA	3	8	15	28	47	58	69	80	92	118
EASIA	14	34	64	122	210	258	305	356	407	131
LACA	34	86	163	308	531	651	771	899	1,028	5
Total	200	500	950	1,800	3,100	3,800	4,500	5,250	6,000	

(*) Percentage by which the highest estimate is greater than the lowest estimate. *Source* Own Calculations based on Bosello et al. (2010)

and in the high damage case they are more than double for the selected years to 2030. Over time the gap between the low damage and high damage estimates declines but by 2100 the high figure is still 150% of the low damage based residual cost.

The next point to note is the range of residual costs across IAMs. For the three models considered here, the highest estimates are 5–50% greater than the lowest ones, with the exception of two regions: China and East Asia, where the range is much larger—around 100%. This arises because the AD-WITCH model has much higher damage cost estimates for these two regions. Overall, the two sets of figures indicate two things: the fact that if L&D is to be based on residual costs the amounts involved will be significant, but the range of figures is still very wide.

Loss and Damage-Residual Costs Versus Adaptation Costs
It is also instructive to compare the residual costs with the adaptation cost estimates from the same modelling exercise. This will help put L&D figures in context, given the focus on finance for adaptation. To keep the tabulations simple we limit the comparison to the Bosello et al. (2010) model. Tables 14.3 and 14.4 report both adaptation costs and residual costs as percent of adaptation costs. This is done only for the six regions/countries where L&D finance is likely to be an issue.

The tables and figures show that adaptation expenditures are relatively low compared to residual costs, which are 3–20 times higher to start with in 2020, but then decline, so that by 2100 they are 40–400% higher. There are also significant differences in the ratio of adaptation to residual costs across regions and scenarios. For China the difference is smallest, implying a larger share of costs are eliminated by adaptation, while in LACA, SASIA and SSA the ratios are very high, implying a relatively small contribution of adaptation to reducing climate damages. With the exception of estimates for 2020, the difference between residual costs and adaptation costs is greater with the low damage/high discount rate than with the high damage/low discount rate case; it appears that more adaptation is undertaken relative to total damage in the latter than in the former. The same information is also presented in Fig. 14.4.

14.3.3 Implications of Higher Emissions and Greater Climate Impacts on Residual Damages

The analysis presented has focussed on the case where equilibrium temperatures increase by 2.5–3.4 °C, implying some mitigation, but less than is required under the Paris accord. How much difference does it make if a lower reduction in temperature is attained? According to the IPCC AR5 report (Arent et al. 2014) estimates of global annual economic losses for additional temperature increases of ~2 °C are incomplete, but lie in the range of between 0.2 and 2.0% of GDP (±1 standard deviation around the mean) (*medium evidence, medium agreement*). Losses are more likely than not to be greater, rather than smaller than this range (*limited evidence, high agreement*). Additionally, there are large differences between and within countries.

Table 14.3 Adaptation and residual costs for selected regions (high damages-low discount rate)

		2020	2030	2040	2050	2060	2070	2080	2090	2100
Adaptation costs ($billion)	MENA	50	141	252	373	453	655	998	1,360	1,511
	SSA	14	40	71	105	128	185	282	384	427
	SASIA	25	69	123	182	221	319	487	663	737
	CHINA	14	39	70	103	126	181	276	377	419
	EASIA	26	73	131	193	235	339	517	705	783
	LACA	18	50	89	131	159	230	351	478	532
	Total	147	411	735	1,088	1,323	1,911	2,910	3,968	4,409
Residual costs as % of adaptation costs	MENA	191%	98%	69%	56%	54%	61%	48%	43%	46%
	SSA	564%	290%	203%	165%	160%	180%	142%	125%	135%
	SASIA	991%	510%	357%	289%	282%	317%	250%	220%	238%
	CHINA	104%	54%	37%	30%	30%	33%	26%	23%	25%
	EASIA	259%	133%	93%	76%	74%	83%	65%	58%	62%
	LACA	1216%	625%	438%	355%	346%	389%	307%	270%	292%
	Total	488%	251%	176%	143%	139%	156%	123%	109%	117%

Source Based on Bosello et al. (2010)

Table 14.4 Adaptation and residual costs for selected regions (low damages-high discount rate)

		2020	2030	2040	2050	2060	2070	2080	2090	2100
Adaptation costs $billon	MENA	5	10	16	24	151	242	383	554	705
	SSA	1	3	5	7	43	68	108	156	199
	SASIA	2	5	8	12	74	118	187	270	344
	CHINA	1	3	4	7	42	67	106	154	195
	EASIA	3	5	8	13	78	125	198	287	366
	LACA	2	4	6	9	53	85	135	195	248
	Total	15	29	47	71	441	705	1,117	1,617	2,057
Residual costs as % of adaptation costs	MENA	306%	383%	454%	574%	158%	121%	91%	73%	66%
	SSA	902%	1127%	1339%	1691%	466%	357%	267%	215%	193%
	SASIA	1585%	1982%	2353%	2972%	819%	628%	469%	378%	340%
	CHINA	167%	208%	247%	312%	86%	66%	49%	40%	36%
	EASIA	415%	518%	616%	778%	214%	164%	123%	99%	89%
	LACA	1946%	2432%	2888%	3648%	1005%	770%	576%	464%	417%
	Total	781%	977%	1160%	1465%	404%	309%	231%	186%	167%

Source Based on Bosello et al. (2010)

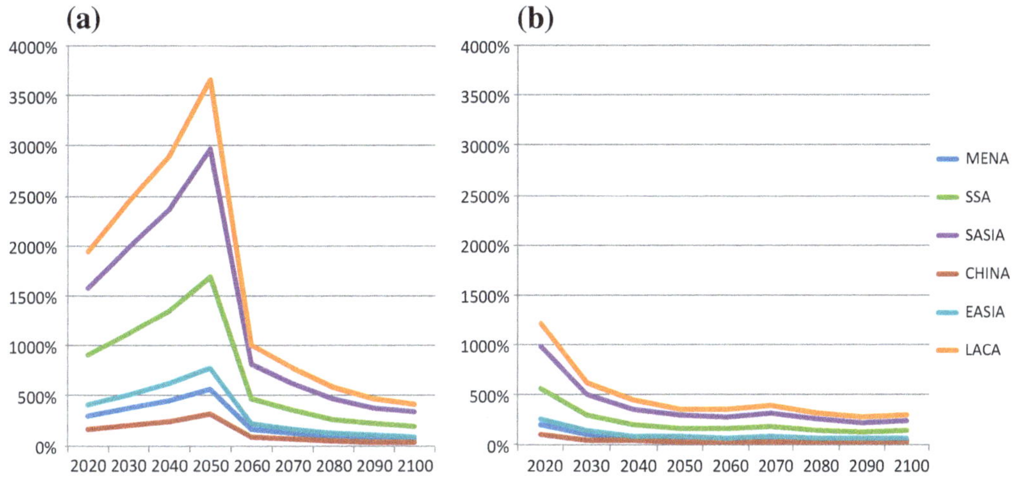

Fig. 14.4 Residual costs as percentage of adaptation costs for the case of **a**) low damages-high discount rate; **b**) high damages-low discount rate (in billion 2005 US)

Losses accelerate with greater warming (*limited evidence, high agreement*), but few quantitative estimates have been completed for additional warming around 3 °C or above.

At a regional level Bosello et al. (2010) find that the effects of increasing temperature are greatest for South Asia, followed by East Asia and Sub Saharan Africa and then by the Middle East (MDE). The sector most sensitive to temperature increases is agriculture, followed by tourism. Costs related to energy decline with temperature in this range (as reduced demand for heating dominates the increased demand for cooling). One can expect therefore a decrease in the temperature target to 2 °C or even 1.5 °C to result in residual costs that are correspondingly lower than the estimates given in Table 14.4.

We conclude this discussion by noting that these estimates are indicative of the results one gets from IAMs. Other models will generate different numbers, but we believe that the broad conclusions drawn from the review carried out here will remain valid. In the next section we focus on two relevant aspects of the IAM literature further to see why the results for climate damages and residual costs can vary so much.

14.4 Discussion of Results

The debate on the costs of climate change and finance generally, as well as specifically for L&D is complex and has several dimensions, many of which are not well informed by the IAM analysis of residual damages. To put the discussion into context, estimates of damages, adaptation costs, L&D and current available finance are worth noting.

The estimates of adaptation costs for developing countries have been estimated in a number of recent IAM studies, summarised in the UNEP Adaptation Gap Report

(UNEP 2016). It states that the current internationally accepted best estimates for adaptation costs are in the US$70 billion to US$100 billion per year range for developing countries by 2050, according to a World Bank (2010) study. This compares with the range of US$147–970 in the Tables 14.3 and 14.4. The UNEP report notes, however, that the World Bank (2010) study is outdated and more recent work based on two IAMs (AD-RICE and AD-WITCH) comes up with estimates of US$200–450 billion (AD-WITCH) and US$570–970 billion (AD-RICE). Thus, our range from the Bosello et al. analysis is similar to that of the UNEP (2016) report.

Other data on costs of adaptation and on L&D damages worth noting are Bond (2016) and Richards and Schalatek (2017), who cite the following estimates:

- UNEP's Adaptation Gap Report (2014) estimates the indicative costs of adaptation and the residual damages (losses and damages) for LDCs at ~USD50 billion/year by 2025/2030 and possibly double this value (USD100 billion/year) by 2050 at 2 °C.
- Baarsch et al. (2015) suggest Loss and Damage costs (not needs) for developing countries of around $400bn in 2030, rising to $1–2 trillion by 2050.
- DARA (2012) estimates these costs to be $4 trillion in 2030.
- AMCEN/UNEP Africa's Adaptation Gap 2 Report (2015) with all cost effective adaptation in Africa losses and damages are estimated at ~USD100bn per year by 2050 for warming below 2 °C, at least double that if warming goes above 4 °C.

These estimates can be compared to the residual damages figures we have given in Sect. 14.2, which range from $20–580 billion in 2030 to $1.1–1.7 trillion in 2050. As Bond (2016) also notes, further work is required on the methodologies and processes for estimating L&D and associated finance needs, as well as non-economic losses. It is in relation to these that the next section addresses some of the key outstanding issues. These include (i) issues relating to the time horizon under consideration and related uncertainty, and (ii) the relationship between adaptation expenditures and L&D.

14.5 Uncertainties in the Estimation of Future Damages from Climate Change in IAMs

Recently, significant debate has emerged about the uncertainties (Pindyck 2013) associated with the quantification of the damages from climate change by IAMs. In the previous section, we provided a range for the residual damages under "standard" climatic conditions. In this section, we show these damages (and, therefore, the residual damages) would change significantly if "tipping points" are considered in the analysis (Lenton et al. 2008, 2012). There is much uncertainty related to these processes and, therefore, they have recently started to be captured in IAM literature in terms of implications for adaptation (Stern 2016) and mitigation (González-Eguino et al. 2016, 2017). We illustrate this through two key sources of uncertainty: the Equilibrium Climate Sensitivity (ECS) parameter and the damage function.

14.5.1 Climate Sensitivity and Damage Functions

Equilibrium Climate Sensitivity (ECS) is one of the key parameters in climate science. ECS is defined as the equilibrium change in global temperature due to a doubling of atmospheric CO_2 over its preindustrial value. This measure is typically characterised as a distribution due to underlying uncertainty in the behaviour of some aspects of the climate system. Studies based on observations, energy balance models, temperature reconstructions and global climate models (GCMs) have concluded that the probability density distribution of ECS peaks at around 3 °C, with a long tail of small but finite probabilities of very large temperature increases. According to the IPCC's Fifth Assessment Report (IPCC 2013), estimates of the ECS indicate that it is *likely* to be in the range of 1.5–4.5 °C (with *high confidence*) and *very* unlikely to be greater than 6 °C (*medium confidence*). The extreme temperature outcomes of the distribution function are sometimes referred to as "fat tails." Some authors (Weitzman 2009, 2012) have proposed that decisions on climate policy should actually be based on trying to avoid extreme outcomes of low probability. The uncertainty range of ECS has not been reduced substantially in the past three decades and it is not expected to be reduced in the near future (Roe and Baker 2007). Typically IAMs use the most likely value for ECS (3 °C as in Sect. 14.3.2), but it is important to perform a sensitivity analysis for different values for ECS.

The other major sources of uncertainty, in this case from climate change economics, is the way in which the damage function from global warming is represented (see Sect. 14.3.1). Damage functions are recognised as being one of the weakest links in the economics of climate change (Pindyck 2013), because it is very difficult to obtain empirical data and because results can be very sensitive to its functional form, particularly when high temperatures are considered. One of the most well-known damage functions is the one used by Nordhaus (DICE[4] model, Nordhaus and Sztorc 2013), which has been recently adopted by the US Environmental Protection Agency (EPA 2010) to provide values for the social cost of carbon. However, in order to capture the possibility of "tipping points" and abrupt climate change, Weitzman (2012) has proposed a different damage function that captures large impacts beyond a 4–6 °C threshold based on an expert panel study involving 52 experts according to which at this temperature change three out of five important tipping points are expected to emerge (see Lenton et al. 2008). These authors mention different processes such as irreversible meltdown of the Greenland ice sheet, disintegration of the West Antarctic ice sheet, reorganisation of Atlantic thermohaline circulation, among others. Some of these processes may have a significant probability of occurring this century for climate conditions involving medium warming (between 2 and 4 °C) and even low

[4]It is important to mention that DICE damage functions include the impacts after adaptation has occurred, so adaptation is already included. Some authors (see, for example, Bruin et al. 2009) have included the possibility of reducing damage through adaptation in IAMs so that they can therefore capture the trade-off between adaptation and mitigation.

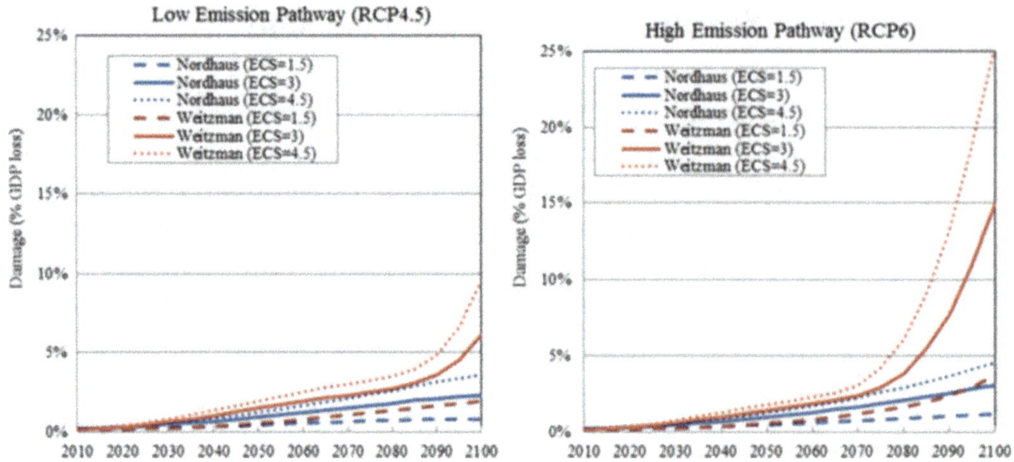

Fig. 14.5 Damage (% GDP) for different damage functions and ECS parameters

warming (<2 °C[5]). Most modellers advise that at higher temperatures the damage functions go beyond their useful limits. Nordhaus, for example, suggests that we have insufficient evidence to extrapolate reliably beyond 3 °C (Nordhaus and Sztorc 2013). However, it is also true that there is a significant risk of temperatures rising above 3 °C in the course of this century.

Figure 14.5 shows the combined effect of the damage when the uncertainty in the ECS and in the damage function choice is considered. We show, using the DICE model, the damage (as % of global GDP) for the Nordhaus and Weitzman damage functions and for three values for the ECS-1.5, 3 and 4.5. The damages are estimated for a low and high emission pathway scenario (RCP 4.5 and RCP 6), which are close to the ones reported in Sect. 14.3.2. We can see that the range of the damages is low before 2050 but then expands substantially at the end of this century. The damage per annum by 2100 in the low emission pathways could be 0.8% in the best case scenario (Nordhaus and ECS = 1.5) and 9.5% in the worst (Weitzman and ECS = 4.5). Similarly, the damage in the high emission pathways could range between 1.2 and 25% in the more extreme situations.

Finally, and although IAMs have been helpful in illustrating the economic damage from climate change under different circumstances (Lenton and Ciscar 2012; Ackerman et al. 2010), these large uncertainties need to be recognised. Although the possibility of crossing a tipping point during this century is far from clear, it must be considered a possibility in any L&D mechanism that could be designed. Similarly, any finance mechanisms implemented will need to be designed in the most flexible manner and considering this extreme situation so when new information is available it can be incorporated quickly as we will analyse in the following section.

[5]This is the case for example of the abrupt loss of Arctic summer sea ice or permafrost thawing (González-Eguino and Neumann 2016; Gonzalez-Eguino et al. 2017).

14.5.2 Time Horizon and L&D Estimates

With respect to the time horizon the following points are relevant: IAMs can help to provide an order of magnitude estimate for the resources that will be necessary to meet losses and damages estimates, but a bottom-up sector-by-sector analysis of existing and projected losses will be necessary. The challenge is to link the two approaches. At present we have the IAM analysis that draws on the bottom-up data in a rather crude way. The current bottom-up analysis for sectors such as agriculture, health etc. is more detailed but does not generally take account of the overall economic profile for the country or region. Uncertainty regarding future damages from climate change is very large in the long-term (2050–2100), especially if some tipping-points are crossed, but more moderate in the near (2020–2030) and medium-term (2030–2050). Thus, the longer the time horizon being considered the greater the uncertainty about the possible level of Loss and Damage. Some of these uncertainties are reduced significantly when mitigation is undertaken but also through adaptation. Previous sections show that low emission mitigation pathways can reduce future damages remarkably and their uncertainty range, and that adaptation measures can reduce residual damages.

In view of these facts one of the first objectives in the near term is for a L&D finance mechanism to get established with the sufficient amount of monetary resources to cover the current existing losses directly attributed to climate change (not to natural variability). In the medium and the long term, it is important that the current design of financing mechanism is flexible enough in order to scale up the financing if and when necessary.

14.6 Conclusions

The aim of this chapter has been to see how much we can learn about possible losses and damages- and finance needed by employing economic IAMs, which are key analytical tools at the heart of economic analysis of the damages caused by climate change and of economically optimal responses to these damages. We interpret modelled residual damages as unavoided L&D.

The current state of knowledge about damages has many gaps and we are not by any means at a stage where the results of these models can form the basis of financial packages of Loss and Damage. On the other hand, a few results stand out as relatively robust and credible, and provide a useful contribution to the Loss and Damage debate.

The first is that residual damages turn out to be significant under a variety of IAMs, and for a range of climate scenarios. This means that if adaptation is undertaken normally, there will remain a large amount of damage that is not eliminated. The figures for that damage vary by region and sector and provide a useful source of likely financial needs. Second the ratio of adaptation to total damages varies by region, so residual damages will also vary for that reason. Third, the residual damage figures will depend on the climate scenario, as well as the discount rate and the assumed parameters of the climate model (equilibrium climate sensitivity) as well as that of the socioeconomic model (damage functions). These uncertainties are very large and no one can make any meaningful projections of residual damages in the medium to long term.

The additional discussion in this chapter raises other aspects that could influence the levels of Loss and Damage. One is the fact that, since actual adaptation is very unlikely to be optimal, the amount of losses and damages may be influenced by the sources from which adaptation and L&D programs are financed.

These findings may seem rather meagre in terms of informing the Loss and Damage debate, but we would contend that they still provide a useful guide to issues that need to be resolved. Certainly, there is scope for much more use of economic tools to understand economically efficient responses to future climate impacts. In the meantime, however, since financial commitments for L&D are unlikely to be determined for more than 5 years ahead at any time, the models should focus on the potential Loss and Damage during that period, taking as given the adaptation programs that are relatively well determined for that period. As new information comes in, climate related damage estimation will improve as will the design of adaptation programs leading to improved use of these tools over time.

References

Ackerman F, Stanton E, Bueno R (2010) Fat tails, exponents, extreme uncertainty: simulating catastrophe in DICE. Ecol Econ 69(8):1657–1665. https://doi.org/10.1016/j.ecolecon.2010.03.013

Arent DJ, Tol RSJ, Faust E, Hella JP, Kumar S, Strzepek KM, Tóth F, Yan D (2014) Key economic sectors and services. In: Field CB, Barros VR, Dokken DJ, Mach KJ, Mastrandrea MD, Bilir TE, Chatterjee M, Ebi KL, Estrada YO, Genova RC, Girma B, Kissel ES, Levy AN, MacCracken S, Mastrandrea PR, White LL (eds) Climate change 2014: impacts, adaptation, and vulnerability. Part A: global and sectoral aspects. Contribution of working group II to the fifth assessment report of the intergovernmental panel on climate change. Cambridge University Press, Cambridge, United Kingdom and New York, NY, USA, pp 659–708

Baarsch F et al (2015) Impacts of low aggregate INDCs ambition: research commissioned by Oxfam. http://policy-practice.oxfam.org.uk/publications/impacts-of-low-aggregate-indcs-ambition-research-commissioned-by-oxfam-582427

BOND (2016) Finance for Loss and damage: marrakech and beyond. Development and Environment Group (DEG) Working Paper

Bosello F, Carraro C, De Cian E (2010) Market and policy driven adaptation. In: Lomborg B (ed) Smart solutions to climate change—comparing costs and benefits. Cambridge University Press, Cambridge, UK

Burke M, Craxton M, Kolstad CD, Onda C, Allcott H, Baker E, Barrage L et al (2016) Opportunities for advances in climate change economics. Science 352(6283):292–293. https://doi.org/10.1126/science.aad9634

Carleton TA, Hsiang SM (2016) Social and economic impacts of climate. Science 353(6304):aad9837. https://doi.org/10.1126/science.aad9837

Chambwera M, Heal G, Dubeux C, Hallegatte, S, Leclerc L, Markandya A, McCarl BA, Mechler R, Neumann JE (2014) Economics of adaptation. In: Climate change 2014: impacts, adaptation, and vulnerability. Part A: global and sectoral aspects. In: Field CB, Barros VR, Dokken DJ, Mach KJ, Mastrandrea MD, Bilir TE, Chatterjee M, Ebi KL, Estrada YO, Genova RC, Girma B, Kissel ES, Levy AN, MacCracken S, Mastrandrea PR, White LL (eds) Contribution of working group II to the fifth assessment report of the intergovernmental panel on climate change. Cambridge University Press, Cambridge, United Kingdom and New York, NY, USA, pp 945–977

DARA (2012) Climate vulnerability monitor (2nd Edition). A guide to the cold calculus of a hot planet. http://daraint.org/wp-content/uploads/2012/09/CVM2ndEd-FrontMatter.pdf

De Bruin KC, Dellink RB, Tol RSJ (2009) AD-DICE: an implementation of adaptation in the DICE model. Clim Change 95(1–2):63–81. https://doi.org/10.1007/s10584-008-9535-5

EPA (2010) social cost of carbon for regulatory impact analysis under executive order 12866 inter-agency, Working Group on Social Cost of Carbon, United States Government. http://onlinelibrary.wiley.com/doi/10.1029/2011JD015804/epdf

González-Eguino M, Neumann M (2016) Significant implications of permafrost thawing for climate change control. Clim Change 136:381–388. https://doi.org/10.1007/s1058

González-Eguino M, Neumann MB, Arto I, Capellán-Perez I, Faria SH (2017) Mitigation implications of an ice-free summer in the Arctic Ocean. Earth's Future 5:59–66

IPCC (2013a) Climate change 2013: the physical science basis. In: Stocker TF, Qin D, Plattner G-K, Tignor M, Allen SK, Boschung J, Nauels A, Xia Y, Bex V and PM Midgley (eds) Contribution of working group I to the fifth assessment report of the intergovernmental panel on climate change. Cambridge University Press, Cambridge, United Kingdom and New York, NY, USA, 1535 pp

IPCC (2014) Climate change 2014. Synthesis report. Summary for policy makers. University Press, Cambridge, Cambridge

Lenton TM, Ciscar J-C (2012) Integrating tipping points into climate impact assessments. Clim Change 117(3):585–597. https://doi.org/10.1007/s10584-012-0572-8

Lenton TM, Held H, Kriegler E, Hall JW, Lucht W, Rahmstorf S, Schellnhuber HJ (2008) Tipping elements in the earth's climate system. Proc Natl Acad Sci 105(6):1786–1793. https://doi.org/10.1073/pnas.0705414105

Mechler R et al (2018) Science for loss and damage. Findings and propositions. In: Mechler R, Bouwer L, Schinko T, Surminski S, Linnerooth-Bayer J (eds) Loss and damage from climate change. Concepts, methods and policy options. Springer, Cham, pp 3 37

Nakicenovic N, Alcamo J, Davis G, de Vries B, Fenhann J, Gaffin S, Gregory K, Grübler A, Jung TY, Kram T, Emilio la Rovere E, Michaelis L, Mori S, Morita T, Pepper W, Pitcher H, Price L, Riahi K, Roehrl A, Rogner H, Sankovski A, Schlesinger M, Shukla P, Smith S, Swart R, van Rooyen S, Victor N, Dadi Z (2000) IPCC special reports: special report on emissions scenarios. Cambridge University Press, Cambridge, UK

Nordhaus WD and P Sztorc (2013) DICE 2013R: Introduction and User's Manual. http://www.econ.yale.edu/~nordhaus/homepage/documents/DICE_Manual_103113r2.pdf

Nordhaus WD and JG Boyer (2000) Warming the world: the economics of the greenhouse effect. The MIT Press

Ortiz RA, Markandya A (2009) Integrated impact assessment models of climate change with an emphasis on damage functions: a literature review, BC3 Working Paper Series 2009–06 (October 2009)

Pindyck RS (2013) Climate change policy: what do the models tell us? J Econ Liter 51(3):860–872. https://doi.org/10.1257/jel.51.3.860

Pindyck RS (2016) The social cost of carbon revisited. w22807. National Bureau of Economic Research. http://www.nber.org/papers/w22807.pdf

Richards J-A, Schalatek L (2017) Financing loss and damage: a look at governance and implementation options. A discussion paper. Boell Foundation

Roe GH, Baker MB (2007) Why is climate sensitivity so unpredictable? Science 318(5850):629–632. https://doi.org/10.1126/science.1144735

Stern N (2007) The economics of climate change. The stern review. Cambridge University Press, Cambridge, UK

Stern N (2016) Economics: current climate models are grossly misleading. Nature 530(7591):407. https://doi.org/10.1038/530407a

UNEP (2016) Adaptation gap report 2016. UNEP, Nairobi

Weitzman ML (2009) On modeling and interpreting the economics of catastrophic climate change. Rev Econ Statis 91(1):1–19. https://doi.org/10.1162/rest.91.1.1

Weitzman ML (2012) GHG targets as insurance against catastrophic climate damages. J Publ Econ Theor 14(2):221–244. https://doi.org/10.1111/j.1467-9779.2011.01539.x

World Bank (2010) Economics of adaptation to climate change: synthesis report. The World Bank Group, Washington, DC, USA, p 136

Part IV
Geographic Perspectives and Cases

Chapter 15
Understanding Loss and Damage in Pacific Small Island Developing States

John Handmer and Johanna Nalau

Abstract Pacific Island states occupy the top categories in the World Risk Index for natural hazards, with Vanuatu consistently at the Number One spot. For some low-lying island states climate change poses an existential threat, and the region is increasingly recognized as the most immediately vulnerable area to potential mass migration and relocation due to climate change. This chapter aims to localise the global debate by focusing on the issue of Loss and Damage in Pacific SIDS. It also provides a commentary regarding the risk and options space in the Pacific SIDS context where many of the livelihood activities are subsistence-based, reliant on the current climate and its variability, and already seriously disrupted by extreme weather events.

Keywords Loss and Damage · Pacific · Adaptation · Disaster risk reduction Relocation · SIDS

15.1 Introduction: Localising Global Loss and Damage Frameworks

Pacific Island states occupy the top categories in the World Risk Index for natural hazards, with Vanuatu consistently at the Number One spot (Birkmann et al. 2011). For some low-lying island states climate change poses an existential threat, and the region is increasingly recognised as the most immediately vulnerable region to potential mass migration and relocation due to climate change (Nurse et al. 2014). This chapter aims to localise the global debate by focusing on the issue of Loss

J. Handmer (✉)
School of Science, RMIT University, Melbourne, Australia
e-mail: j.w.handmer@gmail.com

J. Nalau
Griffith Institute for Tourism (GIFT) and Griffith Climate Change Response Program (GCCRP), Griffith University, Nathan, Australia
e-mail: j.nalau@griffith.edu.au

R. Mechler et al. (eds.), *Loss and Damage from Climate Change*, Climate Risk Management, Policy and Governance, https://doi.org/10.1007/978-3-319-72026-5_15

and Damage in the Pacific Small Island Developing States (SIDS).[1] It also provides a commentary regarding the risk and options space in a PacificSIDS context where many of the livelihood activities are subsistence-based, reliant on the current climate, and seriously disrupted by extreme weather events. We use the case of Tropical Cyclone Pam that hit Vanuatu in March 2015, the first recorded category 5 cyclone in the country, to illustrate some of the points of this global debate. In doing so we take the climate risk and adaptation capacity analysis in IPCC's fifth assessment report (AR5) to another level of detail (for the chapter on the SIDS, see Nurse et al. 2014).

One of the conceptual frameworks to illustrate Loss and Damage (L&D) as integrated into a climate risk management framework has been proposed by Mechler and Schinko (2016) drawing on Nurse et al. (2014) and UNFCCC (2015). This framework has been applied to the group of SIDS globally (see chapter by Schinko et al. 2018). It focuses on current risk exposure and future risk scenarios where the intolerable risk space is seen as being relevant already today and becoming even more critical in the medium to longer term (2030–40 and 2080–2100). We discuss how for some PacificSIDS, there are already cases where communities find themselves impacted by intolerable climate-related risk, and where the risk management options suggested in the graphic are already being deployed (see Fig. 15.2).

Mechler and Schinko's argument is for a broad-based risk management approach including both 'standard' and transformative DRR (Disaster Risk Reduction) and CCA (Climate ChangeAdaptation) actions as well as options. Under their approach, support, including funding, would be allocated on the basis of current needs for dealing with climate variability and change, as well as attribution of losses and damages to anthropogenic climate change. At the global level attribution, for example in regards to sea level rise, can be quantified at high levels of confidence (see IPCC 2014). However, in the Pacific Island countries observed change is a mix of both global as well as local environmental changes, declining crop yield and fish resource reliability, as well as demographic and socio-economic factors. In these country contexts, the options space may also be very constrained, as many people in PacificSIDS have subsistence or semi-subsistence livelihoods, and national economies are very narrowly based. For example, the majority of PacificSIDS base their economies on tourism and foreign aid (Kuruppu and Willie 2015). However, transformative action might be possible and is occurring slowly for example through migrating or travelling to take seasonal work elsewhere, and through remittances.

15.1.1 The South-West Pacific

The South-West Pacific region (see Fig. 15.1 on the South Pacific) is increasingly recognised as the most immediately vulnerable region to potential mass migration and relocation due to climate change impacts (Campbell 2008; McAdam 2012; Weir and

[1]Where the term SIDS is used it is mostly referring to Pacific Small Island Developing States.

Fig. 15.1 Map of the South Pacific. Available at: http://www.scidev.net/global/water/feature/ocean-science-development-sids-facts-figures.html

Virani 2011). Small atoll countries, such as Kiribati and Tuvalu, have provided vivid images of the possible inundation projected for the future (Connell 2011; Mortreux and Barnett 2009). The atoll countries have also been vocal about the plight of island nations (McAdam 2012), in particular in the United Nations Framework Convention on Climate Change (UNFCCC) negotiations through the Alliance of Small Island States (AOSIS) commanding significant media attention.

Recent studies have also emphasised the close linkages between climate change, disasters and conflict in the Pacific, and suggest that relocations due to climate change might become frequent in the region already by the 2040s (Weir and Virani 2011). Fiji announced recently that it had identified 676 coastal communities in need of relocation out of which 42 need to be relocated within the next decade (Fiji News 2014). However, Campbell et al. (2005) also list 86 cases of existing community relocations in the Pacific, which signifies the movement of people historically in the region—note that many of these are partial and local. We now analyse the risk and options space for the South-West (SW) Pacific Island states.

15.2 Charting Out the Loss and Damage Risk Space for Pacific Island States

The risk spaces of most concern globally are those identified as "tolerable" and "intolerable" by Mechler and Schinko (2016). Tolerable risk, as defined here, is a risk level that the affected community is adjusted to, or can adjust to, for example, by (further) implementing sea walls, building codes or style and ecosystem management. Over time, losses associated with the risk and the costs of adjusting and adapting would be expected to rise and could, along with increased frequency of severe disruptive events, lead to risk becoming intolerable.

In the risk space context, a common definition of "intolerable loss" is that it defines an adaptation limit. Dow et al. (2013) define this limit from an actor's (an individual, community or other entity) perspective as "the point at which an actor's objectives cannot be secured from intolerable risks through adaptive actions" (Dow et al. 2013, p. 4). This means that an individual is no longer able to reach his or her objectives in the given context (see also introduction by Mechler et al. 2018). This is in line with Barnett et al. (2015, p. 223) who argue that limits to adaptation "involve irreversible losses of things individuals care about, either due to climate change impacts or as outcomes of climate change policies." Adaptation limits, in other words, are instances where a radical transformation is likely required, which in most cases means addressing loss and damage of those activities, assets and values which people hold important.

In the PacificSIDS, "intolerable" carries the implication of relocation and resettlement given the major biophysical challenges that many of these SIDS face (Nurse et al. 2014). This also includes loss of biodiversity and species specifically needed for traditional practices, such as the disappearance or reduction in kava (Vanuatu, Fiji, Solomon Islands, Samoa), difficulties in cultivating taro and yam (most countries in the Pacific), reduction in species that are used for customary handicrafts (pandanus) and traditional medicine (Melanesian countries, Solomon Islands, Papua New Guinea, Vanuatu and Fiji in particular). The loss and/or contamination of water resources (or significant reduction due to strong El Nino effects) also determine the fate of many remote communities who might not have options to otherwise continue their subsistence-based livelihoods in particular places.

The risk space in some Pacific island states, we argue, could already be at the tolerable/intolerable interface, which is closer to today's reality than a potential scenario that might or might not take place in 2080 (see Table 15.1 and Fig. 15.2). Shortage of water and degradation of agricultural lands is one factor in the relocation of some Solomon Islands communities from a number of provinces to Honiara. Also, low-lying communities such as Ontong Java, Sikaiana and Reef islands and settlements built on water such as Kwai, Ngongosila and Lau are already facing increasing difficulties due to environmental change (Republic of Solomons 2008).

Slow onset processes, such as water and food scarcity (including declining food garden yields), and environmental degradation, which are amplified by natural hazards, can and have triggered relocation. Other factors include a lack of access to

Table 15.1 Loss & Damage concepts applied to the SW Pacific

Concept	Definition	Pacific—risk context	Pacific—option space
Adaptation constraint	Impediment to progress adaptation, which often can be overcome by changes in operational and policy instruments	Lack of alignment between different governance structures, e.g. between customary governance and Westminster systems; lack of capacity in adaptation expertise; lack of funding to implement adaptation actions e.g. community projects, water projects	Changes in operational and policy instruments e.g. closer alignment of customary governance and Westminster systems; increased adaptation capacity; monitoring and evaluation of adaptation activities and 'building back better'
Adaptation limit	Inability to fulfil objectives and goals (in line with intolerable risk space)	Permanent loss of places (atolls, coastal areas), livelihoods (subsistence farming with particular crops e.g. taro, yam); loss of cultural items for ceremonies (kava, palm leaves)	Relocation and resettlement likely away from the most hazardous coastal areas; changes in livelihood types
Avoidable risk	Risks, which can be avoided/reduced due to the implementation of adaptation strategies	Higher temperatures; changes in seasons and impacts on crop quality and timing → impacts on cultural practices and validity of traditional knowledge	Climate resilient crops; increased investments in coastal protection strategies (seawalls, ecosystem-based adaptation); local/in-country relocation; integration of traditional knowledge and Western science
Avoided risk	Risks, which have been avoided/reduced by the implementation of adaptation strategies	Flood risks	Warning systems, building styles, village location
Unavoidable risk	Risks, which cannot be dealt with due to locked in climate change impacts	Sea level rise; contamination of water resources. Increased risk of severe cyclones and droughts	
Tolerable risk	Risks which communities can deal with by implementing strategies	Low level sea level rise and inundation; infrequent storms and storm surge	Building seawalls, strengthening building codes, investing in early warning systems; changing traditional building techniques
Intolerable risk	Risks which (involuntarily) force individuals and communities to leave their places of living or transform their livelihoods	Increased hazards, leaving atolls due to constant and/or permanent inundation; loss of drinking water resources; loss of livelihoods	The focus for low-lying areas is on involuntary relocation & resettlement. In some cases, engineering & structural approaches might be possible; remittances could be used in place of local livelihoods

Sources Based on Dow et al. (2013), Klein et al. (2014), Mechler and Schinko (2016). For discussion of more detailed definitions see the introductory chapter by Mechler et al. (2018)

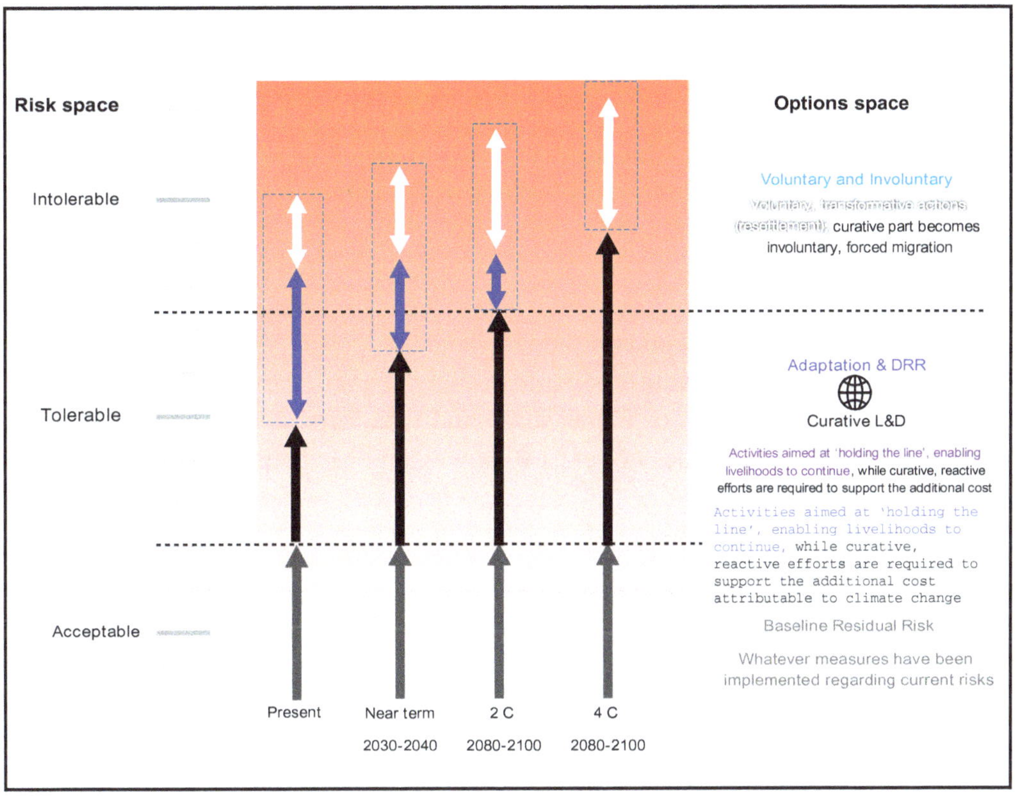

Fig. 15.2 Visualisation of risk and options spaces for the SW Pacific. Drawing on Mechler and Schinko (2016)

services such as health and education. Natural hazards can be the final trigger for the relocation process for communities already suffering from environmental degradation or lack of access to services, who then decide to move (Connell 2011). Commonly identified additional push factors for migration for example in Micronesia include earnings at home, potential earnings abroad, and the costs of migration…poverty and hardship; unemployment; low wages; high fertility; poor health and education services; conflict, insecurity and violence; governance issues; human rights abuse; and persecution and discrimination (Pacific Institute of Public Policy 2010, p. 3).

Much has been written on relocation and climate migrants and refugees in the Pacific context (Barnett and O'Neil 2012; Campbell et al. 2005; McAdam 2012), however much of this discussion has not necessarily fed into the L&D agenda or to research and policy on adaptation limits (Barnett et al. 2015; Nalau and Leal Filho 2018). The concept of adaptation constraints in the Pacific context relates to factors, which currently impede progress in implementing adaptation (Klein et al. 2014). Such constraints could in principle be overcome by, for example, strengthening institutional cooperation and closer alignment of relevant policies and frameworks, such as integrating climate adaptation and disaster risk reduction (Nalau et al. 2016) or increasing the availability and capacity to access relevant information for decision-making (Nalau et al. 2017a).

15.2.1 Attribution

Attribution is particularly complex in the Pacific Island countries due to the scarcity of data and knowledge, which could be used to monitor and understand change. For example, some resource and environmental management practices have been detrimental on the islands and as such are contributing to negative impacts in the form of coastal and catchment erosion. Such practices are not directly the cause of climate change but rather human-induced, and some of these have also long historical roots, e.g. stemming from colonial practices on the islands, such as resource extraction. For estimating L&D linked to anthropogenic climate change, there needs to be a solid understanding how this can or is measured and what proxies can be used in cases where the necessary data does not exist (Conway and Mustelin 2014).

15.3 The Loss and Damage Options Space in the Pacific

Our analysis suggests that the options-policy space may be very constrained—especially when dealing with extreme or intolerable losses and damages (see Table 15.1). Most Pacific Islanders, up to 80% or more in Vanuatu and Solomon Islands, are wholly or partly dependent on subsistence farming and fishing. People depending on subsistence, especially those in remote locations with very limited market economies, cannot simply change their livelihoods. This is the case even though the food gardens can be increasingly unproductive, or unable to provide for changing demands and lifestyles, such as health, education, and technology expenses—with consequent rising food insecurity.

Constraints to adaptation are most obvious in isolated and remote rural areas, however they also exist in urban areas. Increasingly a substantial part of the urban populations in most SW Pacific countries live in informal settlements, characterized as "urban villages" where many of the attributes of rural villages are reproduced (Jones 2016), including food gardens as an essential livelihood strategy. For most people in most Pacific Island countries economic opportunities are very limited, because of "the combination of remoteness, small size, geographic dispersion, and environmental fragility" (World Bank Group 2017). As a consequence, many PacificSIDS have seen only very limited increases in per capita incomes over the past 25 years (World Bank Group 2017). This all acts to limit the options space.

Within this context, we examine what options exist or might need to be developed for SW Pacific Islands states, under the headings of tolerable and intolerable risk (Fig. 15.2). At present there are still tolerable risks, which can be managed largely through better climate changeadaptation, development and disaster risk reduction strategies. The option space can therefore appear to be broad, but is constrained as described above. Tolerable refers here to the circumstances people are dealing with today, while intolerable refers to developing circumstances, but includes cases where people are already faced with the choice of relocation, and decisions that will potentially transform their lives. However, some locations are already experiencing risks generally assumed not to be a problem until 2030–2040. These locations are facing the prospect of forced relocation, but there is still space for voluntary actions, especially in terms of how relocation proceeds.

By 2080–2100, assuming a 2-degree world, however, the options space is already much more limited, whereas in a 4-degree world, it would no longer be possible to pursue voluntary relocation or alternative livelihood strategies in some of the islands. It should be noted that this view does not take account of potential future innovations in the adaptation and options space. There are also differences between sub-regions of Melanesia, Micronesia and Polynesia in the extent that geographical features (e.g., higher mountains) enable some communities and countries to have broader option spaces than others. The figure is nevertheless useful in localising the issue of loss and damage in the SW Pacific context.

15.3.1 Managing Tolerable Risks

It is important to appreciate that many island communities to a greater or lesser extent depend on subsistence farming and fishing for their livelihoods, and endure a significant level of everyday risk for food and livelihoods. Some communities have seasonal food shortages and malnutrition is widespread (Toole 2016). In some areas, such as the "Weather Coast" of Guadalcanal in the Solomon Islands, livelihoods are very marginal with a seasonal "hungry time" (Kastom Gaden/Terra Circle 2005). This is to make the point that even though starvation is not an issue, food security is, and in some areas is a chronic concern. Water security is also an issue, especially on atolls where fresh water is easily contaminated by the sea.

Climate change, demographic change, and changing expectations, are superimposed on top of these existing situations (Khrisnapillai 2017; Kuruppu and Willie 2015)—within the tolerable day-to-day risk and option spaces. A recent extreme event, Cyclone Pam, is used to illustrate some of these issues later in the chapter. Insurance for natural hazards in the Pacific is very limited, with most people having no coverage. The idea of a regional insurance or solidarity pool to support government expenditure in disasters has been raised often. The Pacific Catastrophe Risk Assessment and Insurance Initiative (PCRAFI) was established to provide improved data and understanding of hazards, and now also provides funds to governments in the event of disaster. However, the amounts are very small.

15.3.2 Dealing with Intolerable Risks

There are already cases where communities find themselves impacted by intolerable climate related risk and where risk management options, often only suggested as future possibilities, are already being deployed. In the Pacific, the extent of irreversible loss is prominent as people are abandoning low-lying homes and villages given the increase in storm surges and higher tides, and rising water and food insecurity. Some of the earliest cases of climate change-linked migration in the Pacific are the Carteret Islands (Papua New Guinea) and Vanua Lava in Vanuatu, and the planned relocation of Taro, the provincial capital of Choiseul Province in the Solomon Islands. In this case, we could argue that these communities have to some extent faced an adaptation limit, and that such "intolerable" loss would include irreversible loss where the people and communities have little option but to leave or abandon the places where they currently live and the kinds of lives they lead in that physical environment. Nevertheless, relocation in these cases has been voluntary. In the cases of Taro there is, and for the Carteret Islands there was, considerable planning (even though the relocation is widely seen as a failure). In preparation for much more population movement, Vanuatu, in conjunction with the International Organization for Migration (IOM), has developed a draft National Policy on Climate Change and Disaster-Induced Displacement (Vanuatu & IOM 2017).

The emphasis of options when faced with intolerable risk, is on involuntary relocation (Fig. 15.2). However, transformative action might also be possible through migrating or taking seasonal work elsewhere. Remittances from relatives working elsewhere in Vanuatu or overseas are also a possibility, although currently such opportunities for South-West Pacific islanders are limited. Yet, remittances in particular in the Pacific region are a major source of income and a major enabling factor in how communities can continue to thrive even in difficult circumstances and post-disaster settings (Brown 2015). Aid, remittances, modern communication technology, and local structural engineering and changes can enable communities to reside in places where otherwise they could no longer sustain themselves (Handmer and Mustelin 2013; Jamero et al. 2017).

15.3.3 Case Study: Tropical Cyclone Pam in 2015 as an Example of Coping with Current Risk

Many Pacific Island countries are especially prone to disaster triggered by climate and weather events, for example, Vanuatu has long ranked number one on the World Risk Index (Birkmann et al. 2011; Garschagen et al. 2015). As extreme events in the Pacific are frequent, attribution is more complex. The 2015 Category 5 Tropical Cyclone (TC) Pam was the second most intense tropical cyclone ever in the South Pacific basin (Fig. 15.3).

The lack of baseline data is also relevant here: for example after the cyclone hit, although damage assessments and estimations were done (Government of Vanuatu 2015), providing a clear figure on informal loss and damage was very difficult as the latest population census was done in 2009 and the full extent of asset damage is largely unknown (Barber 2015; Nalau et al. 2017b). Nevertheless, there were significant impacts on most sectors of the economy, in particular food crops, infrastructure and

Fig. 15.3 Damage from tropical cyclone Pam in 2015 in north Efate island, Vanuatu. *Photo* John Handmer

buildings. About 80% of the national housing stock was damaged or destroyed (SPC 2015). Telecommunications ceased functioning in most areas. Infrastructure and food crops were badly damaged, with many tree crops lost. Water supplies were damaged or contaminated with salt water leaving nearly half the population (110,000) in need of clean drinking water (OCHA 2015; Handmer and Iveson 2017).

Given that most of the rural population lives in traditional housing made of palm leaves, bamboo and other local materials, in hard monetary terms losing these structures would amount to little. However, when people's access to income is low and there is much ecosystem damage (Vanuatu 2015); for example on Tanna Island, the assessment of loss and damage becomes much more complex when the houses cannot be rebuilt and the medicinal plants have been lost. In addition, integrating such elements as sense of place into loss and damage assessments is another hurdle when intangible values do not convert easily into monetary forms (see chapter by Serdeczny 2018; Magee et al. 2016).

A recent gap analysis of L&D in Vanuatu (Talakai 2015) found that none of the existing projects, programs or policies explicitly considered risk issues, although there is recognition that the main economic impacts are to tourism and to both formal and informal sector agriculture. Where L&D is considered, it is mostly related to cyclone damages and there are currently no metrics or data to even make statements on slow onset events such as droughts (Talakai 2015). Volcanic ash is one of the prominent concerns across sectors although it is recognized as a non-climatic impact. Some of the risk estimates have been for example informed by the Tropical Cyclone Pam related assessments, e.g., within the tourism sector and by national assessments.

There is a need to recognise where loss and damage occur across sectors and groups: for example, the Post-Disaster Needs Assessment (PDNA) after TC Pam found that 69% of all disaster effects was found in the private sector (private enterprises and individual ownership) with the rest occurring in the public sector. This is clearly a significant finding, which demonstrates the importance of understanding the private formal and informal sector better in the Pacific region. Asset ownership levels and variance therefore could form an important baseline consideration for assessing loss and damage for example from tropical cyclones in the region. The PDNA covered both the formal and informal sectors of the economy.

While TC Pam illustrates the many dimensions of L&D practicalities, from the livelihood point of view it also raises the question of the inter-linkages between an extreme rapid event and slow onset processes, and what these mean in measuring loss and damage. On Tanna island, which was hit the hardest in Vanuatu by TC Pam, the food crops in particular were badly damaged and it took at least a year for them to recover and to support communities again in terms of food security and building materials. This can be partly attributed to El Nino, which strengthened at the time of TC Pam leading to drought conditions with significant decreases in soil moisture and rainfall impeding livelihood and food security recovery. Seedlings planted after TC Pam were not able to grow and produce adequate food crops. Without available vegetables from the gardens, some remote communities, who do not necessarily have access to monetary income, experienced significant food insecurity with increased health problems. Should then, a decline in health status be assessed as losses/damages if inadequate levels of nutrition cause a permanent decline in health of people in the communities? Also, if the same place and same people are hit by a sequence of events in a relatively short timespan, would the loss and damage then be calculated from healthy intact ecosystems or from the already degraded ones after the most recent event?

What this illustrates is the interconnectedness between rapid onset extremes and slow onset processes in creating loss and damage in a particular context. This also poses a dilemma to international mechanisms, which are trying to assess for example the level and scale of loss and damage due to particular impacts and events. In the case of Vanuatu, one could argue that while the PDNA does give some kind of estimate of the damage and loss (which is an underestimation as per the report), it provides a snapshot of the impacts and would require longer term monitoring and reporting that then can be used to determine to what extent loss and damage have become irreversible/permanent, and in which sectors, places and activities (Government of Vanuatu 2015).

15.4 Conclusions

This chapter has situated the discussion of L&D within the context of the Southwest Pacific Small Island Developing States. A key conclusion of this chapter is that limits are being reached already in some locations. Regional and local loss and damage assessments are needed. These could draw on the PDNAs (Post-Disaster Needs Assessments) to create a baseline against which further assessments could be compared, and as such be used to operationalise the L&D mechanisms on the ground. By using the L&D risk and options space as a conceptual framework and metric, countries could provide a national assessment of L&D with respect to activities and communities mapped against risk and option spaces. For example, communities having to involuntarily relocate could be recorded and mapped on the intolerable risk space that could then be part of the L&D reporting process.

Understanding the interaction of rapid onset extremes and slow onset processes is crucial to understanding loss and damage in the Pacific context. Justice dimensions are also fundamental for climate research and policy: for example, most developing and least developed countries do not have the strong long-term scientific evidence base that underpins robust climate policy (Huggel et al. 2016; see chapter by Wallimann-Helmer et al. 2018). There is much effort in the Pacific region devoted to increasing capacity and systems of information and knowledge management, which can aid in addressing some of these issues. However, more needs to be done in order to develop the evidence base for adaptation and L&D.

There is a need for a closer integration of the L&D, disaster risk management and the adaptationcommunities both within and outside the Climate Change Convention. A better understanding, for example, of the concept of 'adaptation limit' can inform the L&D debates while also keeping in mind the difficulties in attribution in particular in contexts where the necessary data is not readily available (Huggel et al. 2016). A more nuanced understanding of where adaptation limits have become a reality, why and how is also essential as decision-making processes might be already taking place due to other stressors than climate change impacts alone (Leal Filho and Nalau 2018; Mortreux and Barnett 2009). The current reliance in the Pacific on hard infrastructures, such as seawalls, also needs re-visiting in identifying how effective such investments are and where these might be better served through ecosystem-based adaptation approaches (Mackey and Ware 2018).

As Moser and Boykoff (2013) also note, it is rarely enough to assess and focus on one type of a risk. Increasingly, attention should be paid on the multitude of risks and changing risk profiles due to particular adaptation actions. In the case of relocation, one approach could be to use destination vulnerability and exposure assessments, which consider new and potentially emerging risks for the community being relocated. Such assessments could include socio-economic, political and cultural dimensions including existing land rights and entitlements, extent of existing services, cultural context, access to labour market and potential for pursuing particular livelihoods, and geophysical risks. Added infrastructure needs in the receiving place need to be also included in such assessments (Aerts 2017). While this sounds scientific and heavily dependent on economic assessments, one should not lose sight of such dimensions such as people's sense of place, that should also be captured at some level and what losing particular places means.

In the Pacific context, understanding the traditional governance arrangements and decision-making processes remains a missing dimension as most of the adaptationscience focuses on the Westminster system of governance (Nalau et al. 2017b). However, adaptation decisions, and decisions regarding L&D, are also very much in the realm of traditional chiefly systems at the community level in countries like Samoa (Brown 2015; Parsons et al. 2017b). Ensuring robust climate risk management, and the availability and robustness of options, needs to ensure that both systems of governance are involved. This also includes the role of Traditional Knowledge and how it together with scientific knowledge can be used to make adaptation more relevant in the Pacific context (Parsons et al. 2016, 2017a; Chambers et al. 2017).

External support to boost the climate risk management options space could usefully take the form of additional opportunities for employment overseas, and support to develop local markets to enhance people's livelihood choices. In the realm of food security, there are a number of strategies and initiatives, which can influence people's opportunities to sustain agriculture-based livelihoods on the islands. Under the frame of climate risk management, investing and experimenting with more climate resistant crops is a strategy, which development agencies, such as GIZ (German agency for international development), have begun to use in order to increase food and livelihood security in Vanuatu. There are also strategies such as drip irrigation, which can potentially transform some of the apparent adaptation limits facing populations today. New technological solutions are forthcoming and hence any discussion on adaptation limits and L&D should also consider those potential innovative approaches that enable communities to thrive under apparent constraints and limits.

Acknowledgements Dr Nalau's contributions were supported by a grant from a private charitable trust.

References

Aerts JCJH (2017) Climate-induced migration: Impacts beyond the coast. Nat Clim Change 7(5):315–316

Barber R (2015) One size doesn't fit all: Tailoring the international response to the national need following Vanuatu's Cyclone Pam. A contribution to the Pacific Regional Consultation for the World Humanitarian Summit Save the Children Australia, CARE International, Oxfam Australia, and World Vision

Barnett J, O'Neill SJ (2012) Islands, resettlement and adaptation. Nat Clim Change 2(1):8–10

Barnett J, Evans LS, Gross C, Kiem AS, Kingsford RT, Palutikof JP, Pickering CM, Smithers SG (2015) From barriers to limits to climate change adaptation: path dependency and the speed of change. Ecol Soc 20(3)

Birkmann JD, Setiadi NJ, Suarez DC, Welle T, Wolfertz J, Dickerhof R, Mucke P, Radtke K (2011) World risk report 2011. United Nations University Institute for Environment and Human Security, Berlin

Brown C (2015) An exploration of climate change adaptation strategies of accommodation providers in Samoa. Masters' Thesis, Master of Science in Environmental Management, University of Auckland

Cambell J, Goldsmith M, Koshy K (2005) Community relocation as an option for adaptation to the effects of climate change and climate variability in Pacific Island Countries (PICs). Final report for APN project 2005-14-NSY-Campbell, Asia-Pacific Network for Global Change Research

Cambell J (2008) International relocation from Pacific Island countries: adaptation failure? Environment, forced migration & social vulnerability. International conference 9–11 October 2008 Bonn, Germany

Chambers LE, Plotz RD, Dossis T, Hiriasia DH, Malsale P, Martin DJ, Mitiepo R, Tahera K, Tofaeono TI (2017) A database for traditional knowledge of weather and climate in the Pacific. Meteorol Appl 24(3):491–502

Connell J (2011) DR16: Small Island states and islands: economies, ecosystems, change and migration. Migration and Global Environmental Change Foresight. Government Office for Science, UK Government

Conway D, Mustelin J (2014) Strategies for improving adaptation practice in developing countries. Nat Clim Change 4(5):339–342

Dow K, Berkhout F, Preston BL (2013) Limits to adaptation to climate change: a risk approach. Curr Opin Environ Sustain 5(3–4):384–391

Fiji News (2014) Sea-level rise threatens 676 communities. http://fijilive.com/news/2014/01/sea-level-rise-threatens-676-local-communities/56298.Fijilive. Accessed 17 Jan 2014

Garschagen M, Hagenlocher M, Kloos J, Pardoe J, Mucke P, Radke K, Rhyner J, Walter B, Welle T (2015) World Risk Report 2015. http://weltrisikobericht.de/wp-content/uploads/2016/08/WorldRiskReport_2015.pdf. Accessed 24 Oct 2017

Government of Vanuatu (2015) Vanuatu post disaster needs assessment—cyclone pam. Vanuatu's Prime Minister's Office, Port Vila, Vanuatu

Handmer J, Mustelin J (2013) Is relocation transformation? Transformation in a changing climate. University of Oslo, 18–21 June, 2013

Handmer J, Iveson H (2017) Cyclone pam in vanuatu: learning from the low death toll. Austr J Emerg Manag 32(2):60–65

Huggel C, Wallimann-Helmer I, Stone D, Cramer W (2016) Reconciling justice and attribution research to advance climate policy. Nat Clim Change 6(10):901–908

IPCC (2014) Climate change 2014 synthesis report—approved summary for policymakers. http://www.ipcc.ch/pdf/assessment-report/ar5/syr/SYR_AR5_SPM.pdf. Accessed 6th June 2016

Jamero ML, Onuki M, Esteban M, Billones-Sensano XK, Tan N, Nellas A, Takagin H, Thao ND, Valenzuela VP (2017) Small-island communities in the Philippines prefer local measures to relocation in response to sea-level rise. Nat Clim Change 7:581–586. https://doi.org/10.1038/nclimate3344

Jones P (2016) The emergence of Pacific urban villages: urbanization trends in the Pacific islands. Asian Development Bank

Kastom Gaden/Terra Circle (2005) People on the edge. http://terracircle.org.au/publications/reports/. Accessed 24 Oct 2017

Khrisnapillai M (2017) Climate-friendly adaptation strategies for the displaced atoll population in Yap. Clim Change Adap Pacific Countries. Springer, Berlin, pp 101–117

Kuruppu N, Willie R (2015) Barriers to reducing climate enhanced disaster risks in least developed country-small islands through anticipatory adaptation. Weather Clim Extremes 7:72–83

Klein RJT, Midgley GF, Preston BL, Alam M, Berkhout FGH, Dow K, Shaw MR (2014) Adaptation opportunities, constraints and limits. In: Field CB, Barros, VR, Dokken DJ, Mastrandrea MD, Mach KJ, Bilir TE, Chatterjee M, Ebi KL, Estrada YO, Genova RC, Girma B, Kissel ES, Levy AN, MacCracken S, Mastrandrea PR, White LL (eds) (2014) Climate change 2014: impacts, adaptation, and vulnerability. Part B: regional aspects. Contribution of working group II to the fifth assessment report of the intergovernmental panel on climate change. Cambridge University Press, Cambridge, United Kingdom and New York, NY, USA, pp 899–943

Leal Filho W, Nalau J (eds) (2018) Adaptation limits: insights and experiences. Springer International Publishing, Berlin

Magee L, Handmer J, Neale T, Ladds M (2016) Locating the intangible: integrating a sense of place into cost estimations of natural disasters. Geoforum 77:61–72

Mackey B, Ware D (2018) Limits to capital works for coastal zone adaptation. In: Leal Filho W, Nalau J (eds) Limits to climate change adaptation. Springer Publishing International, Berlin, pp 301–323

McAdam J (2012) Climate change, forced migration, and international law. Oxford Scholarship, Online May, p 2012

Mechler R, Schinko T (2016) Identifying the policy space for climate loss and damage. Science 354(6310):290–292

Mechler R et al (2018) Science for loss and damage. Findings and propositions. In: Mechler R, Bouwer L, Schinko T, Surminski S, Linnerooth-Bayer J (eds) Loss and damage from climate change. Concepts, methods and policy options. Springer, Cham, pp 3–37

Mortreux C, Barnett J (2009) Climate change, migration and adaptation in Funafuti, Tuvalu. Global Environ Change 19(1):105–112

Moser S, Boykoff M (eds) (2013) Successful adaptation to climate change: linking science and policy in a rapidly changing world. Routledge, Taylor & Francis Group, p 336

Nalau J, Handmer J, Dalesa M, Foster H, Edwards J, Kauhiona H, Welegtabit S (2016) The practice of integrating adaptation and disaster risk reduction in the south-west Pacific. Clim Dev 8(4):365–375

Nalau J, Becken S, Noakes S, Mackey B (2017a) Mapping tourism stakeholders' weather and climate information-seeking behavior in Fiji. Weather Clim Soc 9(3):377–391

Nalau J, Handmer J, Dalesa M (2017b) The role and capacity of government in a climate crisis: cyclone Pam in Vanuatu. In: Leal Filho W (ed) (2017) Climate change adaptation in Pacific countries: fostering resilience and improving the quality of life. Springer, Berlin, pp 151–161

Nalau J, Leal Filho W (2018) Introduction: Limits to Adaptation. In: Leal Filho W, Nalau J (eds) Limits to climate change adaptation climate change management. Springer International Publishing, Berlin, pp 1–8

Nurse LA, McLean RF, Agard J, Briguglio LP, Duvat-Magnan V, Pelesikoti N, Thompkins E, Webb A (eds) (2014) Small Islands. Cambridge University Press, Cambridge, United Kingdom and New York, NY, USA, pp 1613–1654. In: Barros VR, Field CB, Dokken DJ, Mastrandrea MD, Mach KJ, Bilir TE, Chatterjee M, Ebi KL, Estrada YO, Genova RC, Girma B, Kissel ES, Levy AN, MacCracken S, Mastrandrea PR, White LL (eds) (2014) Climate change 2014: impacts, adaptation, and vulnerability. Part B: regional aspects. Contribution of working group II to the fifth assessment report of the intergovernmental panel on climate change. Cambridge University Press, Cambridge, United Kingdom and New York, NY, USA, pp 1613–1654

OCHA (2015) Vanuatu: tropical cyclone Pam Situation Report No. 12 (as of 26 March 2015). United Nations Office for the Coordination of Humanitarian Affairs (OCHA). http://reliefweb.int/sites/reliefweb.int/files/resources/OCHA_VUT_TCPam_Sitrep12_20150326.pdf

Pacific Institute of Public Policy 2010. The Micronesian Exodus. Discussion paper 16, December 2010. http://www.pacificpolicy.org/wp-content/uploads/2012/05/D16-PiPP.pd. Accessed 25 Oct 2012

Parsons M, Fisher K, Nalau J (2016) Alternative approaches to co-design: insights from indigenous/academic research collaborations. Curr Opin Environ Sustain 20:99–105

Parsons M, Nalau J, Fisher K (2017a) Alternative perspectives on sustainability: indigenous knowledge and methodologies. Challenges Sustain 5(1):7

Parsons M, Brown C, Nalau J, Fisher K (2017b) Assessing adaptive capacity and adaptation: insights from Samoan tourism operators. Clim Develop 1–20

Republic of Solomon Islands (2008) National Adaptation Programmes of Action. Ministry of Environment, Conservation and Meteorology, Honiara, Solomon Islands

Schinko T, Mechler R, Hochrainer-Stigler S (2018) The risk and policy space for loss and damage: integrating notions of distributive and compensatory justice with comprehensive climate risk management. In: Mechler R, Bouwer L, Schinko T, Surminski S, Linnerooth-Bayer J (eds) Loss and damage from climate change. Concepts, methods and policy options. Springer, Cham, pp 83–110

Serdeczny O (2018) Non-economic loss and damage and the Warsaw international mechanism. In: Mechler R, Bouwer L, Schinko T, Surminski S, Linnerooth-Bayer J (eds) Loss and damage from climate change. Concepts, methods and policy options. Springer, Cham, pp 205–220

SPC (2015) Tropical cyclone Pam: lessons learned workshop report June 2015. Suva, Fiji; Secretariat of the Pacific Community 66 p. http://reliefweb.int/sites/reliefweb.int/files/resources/tc_pam_lessons_learned_report_final_170316.pdf

Talakai M (2015) Loss and damage gap analysis from climate change: Vanuatu Country Report. June 2015. Secretariat of the Pacific Environmental Programme (SPREP) and GIZ

Toole M (2016) Stunted growth and obesity: the double burden of poor nutrition on our doorstep. The Conversation. https://theconversation.com/stunted-growth-and-obesity-the-double-burden-of-poor-nutrition-on-our-doorstep-50385. Accessed 15 Aug 2017

UNFCCC (2015) Report on the structured expert dialogue on the 2013–2015 review. Decision FCCC/SB/2015/INF.1. http://unfccc.int/resource/docs/2015/sb/eng/inf01.pdf. Accessed 25 Jan 2016

Vanuatu & IOM (2017) Vanuatu Prepares Its Population for Displacement Policy. http://www.pireport.org/articles/2017/07/02/vanuatu-prepares-its-population-displacement-policy. Accessed 24 Oct 2017

Wallimann-Helmer I, Meyer L, Mintz-Woo K, Schinko T, Serdeczny O (2018) The ethical challenges in the context of climate loss and damage. In: Mechler R, Bouwer L, Schinko T, Surminski S, Linnerooth-Bayer J (eds) Loss and damage from climate change. Concepts, methods and policy options. Springer, Cham, pp 39–62

Weir T, Virani Z (2011) Three linked risks for development in the Pacific Islands: climate change, disasters and conflict. Clim Dev 3:193–208

World Bank Group (2017) Pacific possible: long-term economic opportunities and challenges for Pacific Island countries. http://pubdocs.worldbank.org/en/901551487050695687/Pacific-Possible-consult.pdf. Accessed 24 Oct 2017

Chapter 16
Climate Migration and Cultural Preservation: The Case of the Marshallese Diaspora

Alison Heslin

Abstract Potential land loss in Pacific island countries from rising sea levels raises many concerns regarding how nation states will continue to function politically and economically in the event of climate-induced relocation of their populations. This piece expands that conversation, addressing the impacts of relocation on cultural heritage, drawing on data from interviews with migrants from the Marshall Islands to the United States. The study seeks to understand the challenges and opportunities of cultural preservation among the Marshallese diaspora. Marshallese accounts of life in the United States indicate many opportunities for cultural preservation, particularly for those living in communities with large Marshallese populations, while also presenting challenges based on social, economic, and geographic differences between the U.S. and the Marshall Islands. Understanding the means through which Marshallese migrants maintain cultural traditions and the challenges current migrants face, can help us address potentially irreversible, but avoidable losses of cultural traditions in the event of mass displacement.

Keywords Cultural heritage · Migration · Non-economic losses · Marshall islands · Diaspora

16.1 Losses and Damages in the Pacific Islands

For the low-lying islands of the Pacific, climate change poses an existential risk (see also chapter by Handmer and Nalau 2018). In particular, increased sea level and temperature threatens the islands and atolls with floods, erosion, groundwater degradation, and coral reef damage (Nurse et al. 2014). Under the Representative Concentrations Pathway (RCP) scenarios, by 2100 mean sea levels will increase 0.44 m (under RCP 2.6) up to 0.74 m (under RCP8.5) with regional variations that could further increase sea levels in the Pacific (IPCC 2013). Based on these

A. Heslin (✉)
International Institute for Applied Systems Analysis (IIASA), Laxenburg, Austria
e-mail: heslin@iiasa.ac.at

R. Mechler et al. (eds.), *Loss and Damage from Climate Change*, Climate Risk Management, Policy and Governance, https://doi.org/10.1007/978-3-319-72026-5_16

projections, low-lying islands will be severely negatively affected and uninhabitable, necessitating the relocation of their populations within the next 50 years. These impacts will have economic, political, and cultural consequences for the populations of many Pacific nation-states.

With rising seas and increased sea temperatures, islands face challenges to their economic production. Warmer oceans can damage coral reefs, decreasing tourism and fish production (Asian Development Bank 2013; Rosegrant et al. 2016), and changes in rainfall and salt water inundation can affect fresh water lenses and crop production such as copra and taro (Barnett 2011; Patel 2006; Terry and Chui 2012). Additionally, out-migration from the islands removes higher-skilled laborers from the domestic labour pool (Brown and Connell 2004). Politically, the complete relocation of island populations raises questions of sovereignty. Where will the populations move to, how will their governments function outside their national territory, and what rights will island citizens have in new countries (Barnett and Adger 2003)? The short and medium-term projections of climate change raise many such political and economic questions for islands nations. While the challenges related to economic Loss&Damage and political sovereignty are indeed severe and worthy of attention, understandings of climate related Loss&Damage must also take into account non-economic losses, including the effects of climate change on cultural heritage and preservation. Even if existing states agree to host relocated populations, the movement of populations can result in the loss of sacred or culturally significant locations and can affect cultural identity, language, and social structures (see chapter by Serdeczny 2018). Losses of culture or struggles of cultural integration are important for individual and community well-being and can also, in turn, affect the economic and political capacity of the population. Understanding the challenges and opportunities faced by existing Pacific island diasporas offers valuable insight into the potential future of displaced island nations.

16.2 Methods

This study seeks to identify the avoidable and unavoidable risks posed to cultural heritage in the event of displacement. To do so, this study draws on in-depth interviews of members of the Pacific Islands diaspora to understand the ways in which they maintain cultural heritage outside of their country of origin. Using the Marshall Islands (Republic of Marshall Islands, RMI) as a case study for potential relocation of populations, interviews were conducted with Marshallese citizens who had migrated to the United States. The participants answered questions regarding what motivated them to move to the United States, what aspects of life differed markedly from the Marshall Islands, and what challenges and opportunities they faced in adapting to living outside of the Marshall Islands. Participants in the interviews were selected through convenience and snowball sampling, ensuring to include participants from multiple areas of the U.S., not strictly those with large Marshallese diaspora com-

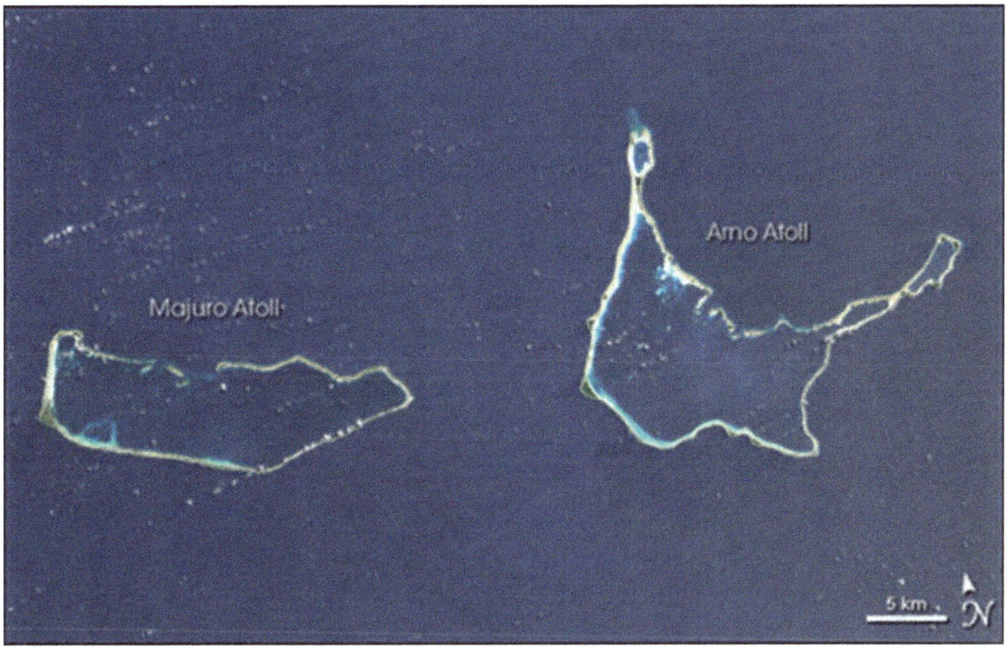

Fig. 16.1 The Republic of the Marshall Islands. *Source* https://visibleearth.nasa.gov/view.phpid=8080

munities. Participants had all lived in the Marshall Islands, and currently lived in multiple locations within the United States, including Arkansas, Washington, and Ohio.

16.3 The Marshall Islands

The Republic of the Marshall Islands presents an important case study for understanding risks to cultural loss for low-lying islands facing relocation in the immediate future. Situated on average just 2 m above sea level, the 29 coral atolls and five coral islands that comprise the Marshall Islands (shown in Fig. 16.1) have little capacity to withstand even minor increases in sea level and tides. In addition to the immediate dangers of increased tides on residents' lives and property, salt-water intrusion threatens already scarce freshwater resources and warmer oceans damage the atolls' protective reefs. In the longer term, the islands face increasingly intolerable risks, leaving limited adaptive options, mainly voluntary resettlement or displacement (see also chapter by Schinko et al. 2018; Mechler and Schinko 2016).

Currently, nearly a third of the population lives outside of the Marshall Islands. These high levels of contemporary migration from the Marshall Islands can help in anticipating future challenges faced by those displaced by sea level rise. The primary destination of movement out of the RMI is the United States, due to the provisions under the Compact of Free Association (COFA). Under the COFA, the

United States has military access to particular Marshallese islands and ocean territory, while Marshallese citizens may live, work, and study in the United States without a visa (U.S. Department of State 2016). As of the 2011 Marshall Islands census, a total of 53, 158 people lived in the Marshall Islands (Economic Policy, Planning, and Statistics Office 2011), while 22, 434 Marshallese lived in the United States. The significant proportion of Marshallese living in the United States occurred rapidly, with fewer than 7,000 Marshallese living the U.S. in 2000, increasing more than threefold by 2010 (Hixson et al. 2012). Marshallese migrants to the U.S. have settled primarily in Hawaii (33% as of 2010), Arkansas (19.3%), and Washington (9.8%).

16.3.1 Challenges

While many relocate to Hawaii, nearly 2/3 of the Marshallese in the U.S. live in geographic locations and climates, which differ markedly from the Marshall Islands, including eastern Washington state and Springdale, Arkansas. With cultural significance tied to a history of ocean navigation (including outrigger canoeing, shown in Fig. 16.2), subsistence from skilled spear-fishing, and handicrafts and local dishes made from tropical crops including banana and coconut, Marshallese face serious challenges of cultural preservation when removed from their island homes. Particularly, those interviewed commented on their families' homes and serene landscape (Fig. 16.3), aspects lacking in the U.S. context. While migrants to the U.S. can still return to the Marshall Islands to visit, they are seldom able to given the price and duration of the flight, with tickets from the mainland U.S. costing up to $2,000 and totalling over 50 h in transit time. Additionally, in the event of further sea-level rise, travel to the Marshall Islands would become infeasible, resulting in the unavoidable loss of the significant physical locations and landscapes described by those interviewed. While damage to the islands would destroy many physical locations with residents have attachments to, migrants to the U.S. did indicate finding particular traditional foods like breadfruit and coconuts from local Latin American grocers, allowing for the continued consumption of traditional foods, particularly for holidays and celebrations. In addition, Marshallese can still send and receive packages fairly easily, as the US postal service operates in the RMI. This allows migrants to the U.S. to receive traditional clothing and handicrafts even while living the abroad. In the absence of continued family ties to the islands, however, this mechanism of cultural preservation would no longer be possible, requiring production of these items outside of the Marshall Islands if materials are accessible.

In addition to geographic differences, Marshallese in the U.S. face a very different social structure than that, which exists on the remote Pacific atolls. Marshallese families generally live in extended family households, lacking linguistic distinctions between mothers and aunts, siblings and cousins. Even when families do live in separate houses, children often move back and forth between households, cared for by parents, aunts, uncles, and grandparents. This fluidity of family and guardian

Fig. 16.2 Outrigger Canoe traditionally used in ocean navigation, Majuro Atoll, Republic of the Marshall Islands. *Photo* A. Heslin

distinctions differs rather sharply from the U.S. norm of single-family households, as well as the legal guardianship afforded to biological parents.

The relocation of Marshallese to particular communities in the U.S., however, does allow for continued community support. Springdale, Arkansas and Seattle, Washington for example, have large Marshallese communities, with Marshallese churches and cultural events. While a location like Arkansas is lacking many of the meaningful geographic components of maintaining island culture, the presence of a large Marshallese community was noted to maintain aspects of the language and culture. Interview respondents in Arkansas and Washington indicated having Marshallese friends in their communities and attending Marshallese celebrations on holidays. The capacity for Marshallese migrants to maintain certain aspects of their culture, including language, religious practices, and holiday celebrations is tied to access to Marshallese communities. Support for these activities and cultural centres can stem the avoidable cultural losses for these activities not explicitly tied to the physical landscape.

Fig. 16.3 Typical landscape, Arno Atoll, Republic of the Marshall Islands. *Photo* A. Heslin

16.3.2 Opportunities

While an involuntary relocation of the Marshall Islands' population would mark a tragic and regrettable failure of the global community in addressing climate change, the established diaspora community in the United States offers some opportunities to the Marshallese community. Marshallese migration to the U.S. has afforded employment and education opportunities not available in the RMI, as evidenced by the large-scale migration that has occurred over the past 20 years. Migration to the U.S. offers an alternative to many challenges faced in the RMI, which include scarce opportunities for employment, with remittances from the U.S. totalling an estimated 25 million dollars in 2015 (Pew Research Center 2016). Additionally, population growth has increased the need for imported foods in the RMI. This reliance on imported food, and the consumption of the least expensive imported options, has caused serious health consequences in the Marshall Islands, with over 20% of the population suffering from diabetes and over two-thirds being overweight or obese (Ichiho et al. 2013; World Health Organization 2016). Migration to the U.S. offers access to additional medical services, though at a substantially higher cost than those in the RMI. One must view the opportunity for additional employment and healthcare within the context of the RMI's history, as many health and economic maladies suffered by Marshallese can be traced back to international involvement in the Marshall Islands—as a location of conflict, recipient of food aid, site of nuclear testing, and base for the U.S. military (Ahlgren et al. 2014).

16.4 Conclusions

Severe damage to the Marshall Islands would result in an irreversible loss of culturally and personally significant locations and activities. The geography of the Marshall Islands is so uncommon, that the possibility for relocating populations to similar landscapes, which would limit the cultural loss, seems almost impossible. While many geographically tied cultural practices face irreversible loss, the sizable and established population base in the United-States provides an opportunity for some cultural preservation outside of the RMI. Marshallese residents in the U.S. can continue to speak Marshallese, eat Marshallese foods, and spend time with the Marshallese communities when living in a city with a Marshallese population. With many established family and friendship ties to people living in the United States, the cultural transition involved in moving could occur more smoothly. Many current Marshallese residents in the U.S. indicate having moved to join family or staying with family when first arriving in the U.S. The possibility of this form of relocation on a larger scale, however, requires the continued terms of the Contract of Free Association, which has allowed for free movement between the two countries since the 1980s. Additionally, should migration become permanent and irreversible, the political circumstances of Marshallese residents in the U.S. would need engagement, as they currently lack guaranteed access to certain federal social programs afforded to U.S. citizens, including Medicaid, as well as representation in government.

References

Ahlgren I, Yamada S, Wong A (2014) Rising oceans, climate change, food aid, and human rights in the Marshall Islands. Health Human Rights J 16(1):69–80

Asian Development Bank (2013) The economics of climate change in the Pacific. Asian Development Bank, Manila

Barnett J, Adger WN (2003) Climate dangers and atoll countries. Clim Change 61(3):321–337

Barnett J (2011) Dangerous climate change in the Pacific Islands: food production and food security. Reg Environ Change 11(1):229–237

Brown RPC, Connell J (2004) The migration of doctors and nurses from South Pacific Island Nations. Soc Sci Med 58(11):2193–2210

Economic Policy, Planning, and Statistics Office (2011) The RMI 2011 census of population and housing summary and highlights only. Majuro, Marshall Islands

Handmer J, Nalau J (2018) Understanding loss and damage in Pacific Small Island developing states. In: Mechler R, Bouwer L, Schinko T, Surminski S, Linnerooth-Bayer J (eds) Loss and damage from climate change. Concepts, methods and policy options. Springer, Cham, pp 365–381

Hixson L, Hepler BB, Kim MO (2012) The native Hawaiian and other Pacific Islander population: 2010. United States Census Bureau

Ichiho HM, Seremai J, Trinidad R, Paul I, Langidrik J, Aitaoto N (2013) An assessment of non-communicable diseases, diabetes, and related risk factors in the Republic of the Marshall Islands, Kwajelein Atoll, Ebeye Island: a systems perspective. Hawaii J Med Public Health 72(5 Suppl 1):77–86

IPCC (2013) Climate change 2013: the physical science basis. In: Stocker TF, Qin D, Plattner G-K, Tignor M, Allen SK, Boschung J, Nauels A, Xia Y, Bex V, Midgley PM (eds) Contribution of working group I to the fifth assessment report of the intergovernmental panel on climate change. Cambridge University Press, Cambridge, United Kingdom and New York, NY, USA, 1535 pp

Mechler R, Schinko T (2016) Identifying the policy space for climate loss and damage. Science 354(6310):290–292

Nurse LA, McLean RF, Agard J, Briguglio LP, Duvat-Magnan V, Pelesikoti N, Tompkins E, Webb A (2014) Small Islands. In: Barros VR, Field CB, Dokken DJ, Mastrandrea MD, Mach KJ, Bilir TE, Chatterjee M, Ebi KL, Estrada YO, Genova RC, Girma B, Kissel ES, Levy AN, MacCracken S, Mastrandrea PR, White LL (eds) Climate change 2014: impacts, adaptation, and vulnerability. Part B: regional aspects. Contribution of working group II to the fifth assessment report of the intergovernmental panel on climate change. Cambridge University Press, Cambridge UK, pp 1613–1654

Patel SS (2006) Climate science: a sinking feeling. Nature 440(7085):734–736

Pew Research Center (2016) Remittance flows worldwide in 2015

Rosegrant MW, Dey MM, Valmonte-Santos R, Chen OL (2016) Economic impacts of climate change and climate change adaptation strategies in Vanuatu and Timor-Leste. Marine Policy 67:179–188

Schinko T, Mechler R, Hochrainer-Stigler S (2018) The risk and policy space for loss and damage: integrating notions of distributive and compensatory justice with comprehensive climate risk management. In: Mechler R, Bouwer L, Schinko T, Surminski S, Linnerooth-Bayer J (eds) Loss and damage from climate change. Concepts, methods and policy options. Springer, Cham, pp 83–110

Serdeczny O (2018) Non-economic loss and damage and the Warsaw international mechanism. In: Mechler R, Bouwer L, Schinko T, Surminski S, Linnerooth-Bayer J (eds) Loss and damage from climate change. Concepts, methods and policy options. Springer, Cham, pp 205–220

Terry JP, Chui TFM (2012) Evaluating the fate of freshwater lenses on atoll islands after eustatic sea-level rise and cyclone-driven inundation: a modelling approach. Global Planet Change 88:76–84

U.S. Department of State (2016) U.S. Relations with Marshall Islands. Bureau of East Asian and Pacific Affairs

World Health Organization (2016) Marshall Islands. Diabetes Country Profiles

Chapter 17
Supporting Climate Risk Management at Scale. Insights from the Zurich Flood Resilience Alliance Partnership Model Applied in Peru & Nepal

Reinhard Mechler, Colin McQuistan, Ian McCallum, Wei Liu, Adriana Keating, Piotr Magnuszewski, Thomas Schinko, Finn Laurien and Stefan Hochrainer-Stigler

Abstract There has been increasing interest in the potential of effective science-society partnership models for identifying and implementing options that manage critical disaster risks "on the ground." This particularly holds true for debate around Loss and Damage. Few documented precedents and little documented experience exists, however, for such models of engagement. *How to organise such partnerships? What are learnings from existing activities and how can these be upscaled?* We report on one such partnership, the Zurich Flood Resilience Alliance, a multi-actor partnership launched in 2013 to enhance communities' resilience to flooding at local to global scales. The program brings together the skills and expertise of NGOs, the private sector and research institutions in order to induce transformational change for managing flood risks. Working in a number of countries facing different challenges and opportunities the program uses a participatory and iterative approach to develop sustainable portfolios of interventions that tackle both flood risk and development objectives in synergy. We focus our examination on two cases of Alliance engagement, where livelihoods are particularly being eroded by flood risk, including actual and potential contributions by climate change: (i) in the Karnali river basin in West Nepal, communities are facing rapid on-set flash floods during the monsoon season; (ii) in the Rimac basin in Central Peru communities are exposed to riverine flooding

R. Mechler (✉) · I. McCallum · W. Liu · A. Keating · P. Magnuszewski · T. Schinko
F. Laurien · S. Hochrainer-Stigler
International Institute for Applied Systems Analysis (IIASA), Laxenburg, Austria
e-mail: mechler@iiasa.ac.at

C. McQuistan
Practical Action, Rugby, UK

P. Magnuszewski
Centre for Systems Solutions, Wrocław, Poland

R. Mechler et al. (eds.), *Loss and Damage from Climate Change*, Climate Risk Management, Policy and Governance, https://doi.org/10.1007/978-3-319-72026-5_17

amplified by El Niño episodes. We show how different tools and methods can be co-generated and used at different learning stages and across temporal and agency scales by researchers and practitioners. Seamless integration is neither possible, nor desirable, and in many instances, an adaptive management approach through, what we call, a *Shared Resilience Learning Dialogue*, can provide the boundary process that connects the different analytical elements developed and particularly links those up with community-led processes. Our critical examination of the experience from the Alliance leads into suggestions for identifying novel funding and support models involving NGOs, researchers and the private sector working side by side with public sector institutions to deliver community level support for managing risks that may go "beyond adaptation."

Keywords Flood risk · Resilience · Science-society partnerships · Boundary objects · Adaptive management · Learning

17.1 Introduction: The 2015 Policy Imperatives and the Implications for the Loss and Damage Debate

International policy as well as local risk and resilience practice are increasingly challenging the scientific community to provide actionable knowledge for identifying acceptable and efficient responses through risk analysis, policy insight and governance studies that help to build resilience. It has been well understood that implementation needs to be multi-scalar involving partnerships between civil society, private sector and government entities (ENHANCE 2016).

17.1.1 Global Policy Imperative-Reducing Risks and Building Resilience

Policy related to climate risk and resilience in recent years has made great strides forward. The *World Conference on Disaster Risk Reduction*, which led to the *Sendai Framework for Action*, demonstrated increasing recognition that a broad-based approach is necessary to incentivise risk reduction, avoid risk creation and generate additional co-benefits that go beyond the direct and indirect gains from reducing risk (UN 2015). The *Sustainable Development Goals* (SDG), passed as well in 2015, constitute a universal set of 17 goals and 169 targets defining development aspiration and ideally transformation in an integrated fashion (UN 2105). A need for transformation is being seen as increasingly relevant for the climate discourse, and at the end of 2015, Paris saw the full endorsement under article 8 of the *Warsaw Loss and Damage Mechanism* (WIM), created at COP19 to "deal with climate-related effects, including residual impacts after adaptation" (UNFCCC 2015).

Demand for broad-based risk and resilience science insight is thus strong with the post 2015 agenda in full swing: the *Sendai Framework for Action* is seeing further implementation at various levels, SDGs are being assessed, mainstreamed and linked to developmental programming and project implementation; the Paris ambition will need to be operationalised in terms of transforming energy and mobility systems towards complete decarbonisation by 2050, as well as strongly supporting climate adaptation (CCA). However, there is robust evidence to suggest that current action and ambition is insufficient to keep climate change at "non-dangerous" levels. Compared to the ambition voiced in the Paris agreement to limit anthropogenically-induced warming to below 2 °C, respectively 1.5 °C, current climate mitigation ambition is projected to lead to significantly greater warming, 3 °C if national pledges are implemented, 4 °C if business as usual is continued, adding to climate-related impacts already experienced across the globe (Climateactiontracker 2018). As discussed in other chapters in this volume (see chapters by Handmer and Nalau 2018; Heslin 2018; Landauer and Juhola 2018) high-level warming would mean pushing some social systems and ecosystems over their adaptation thresholds. As a consequence, there is demand for global evidence to support ramping up efforts for dealing with risks beyond adaptation. This perspective has strong overlaps with the attribution question as laid out in the introduction (chapter by Mechler et al. 2018).

17.1.2 Local Practitioner's Imperative—Learning to Live and Thrive with Floods While Reducing Risk

Calls for assessing and managing risks "beyond adaptation" are being echoed by a practice perspective dealing with severe risks linked to current climate variability already. A key challenge identified and to be addressed by development practitioners working on risk and resilience issues is the nagging feeling that a disaster could wash away generations of hard work by a community in seconds. The limitation for the humanitarian sector is a focus on urgent needs and getting the community back on track, without having the luxury of remaining with the community as they start to rebuild their lives. Thus, the transition from Disaster Risk Preparedness/Management into Community Development, that is ideally sustainable and long-term, is widely recognised as a critical challenge in international development. At the same time, for communities around the world wellbeing is dependent on the ability not only to respond to hazards but also to make the right choices about their future development (see Fig. 17.1 for an example on flood risk).

Large-scale disasters, such as—floods, cannot completely be avoided, but there are measures that can be taken to ensure they do not diminish hard-earned economic and development gains. Learning to live, and thrive, with floods means considering flood risk in planning and investment decisions right from inception, as well as taking steps to protect assets already at risk. It also means planning for response and recovery, which protects and even enhances development and growth potential. Contrary

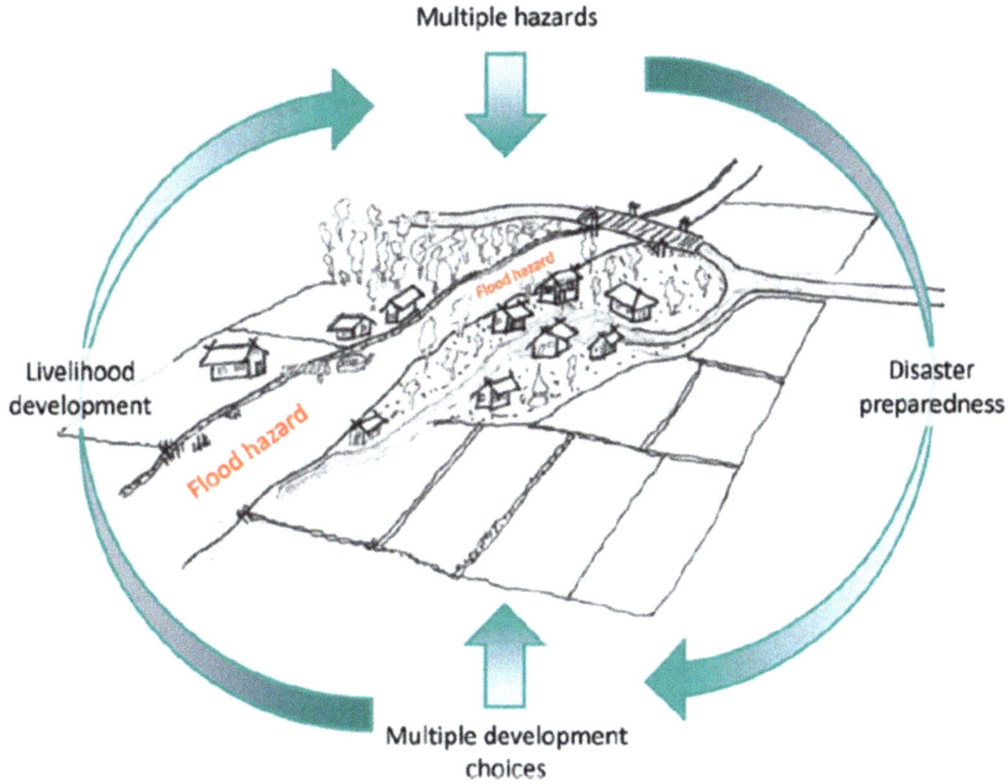

Fig. 17.1 The practice imperative—connecting disaster preparedness and livelihood development. *Figure Source* McQuistan (2015)

to popular belief, judiciously managing flood risk does not have to mean a reduction in economic well-being. Learning to be flood resilient means identifying and taking action where flood risk can be mitigated and development can be enhanced in mutually reinforcing ways (see also Keating et al. 2016a). This involves considering transformational change as part of risk management responses (see chapter by Schinko et al. 2018).

17.1.3 Crafting Effective Science-Society Partnerships that Inform Policy and Practice

How to bring these perspectives together at the different scales that they operate at? In order to inform these policy and practice imperatives there is increasing interest in forging science-society partnership models for effectively managing disaster risks across scales. This particularly holds true for debate around Loss and Damage. We report on one such partnership, the Zurich Flood Resilience Alliance, a partnership launched in 2013 to enhance communities' resilience to flooding at local to global scales. The program brings together the skills and expertise of NGOs, research institutions and the private sector to work to transformation action on managing flood risks. The program uses a participatory and adaptive management approach to develop sustainable portfolios of resilience-building interventions that tackle both flood risk and development objectives in synergy for communities exposed to erosive risks. It has been working in various countries and cases characterised by different challenges and opportunities. The partnership builds its science-society interventions innovatively around a systems perspective for understanding risk and resilience, which takes account of a shifting disaster risk discourse that emphasises disaster resilience as "bouncing forward" and considering transformative approaches (Keating et al. 2016a).

This chapter, reporting and reflecting on the experience of the Alliance in light of the *Loss and Damage* debate, is touching on the following questions: *How to organise such models and partnerships? What are learnings from existing activities? How can learning be upscaled?*

We outline processes and evidence created via a number of case studies conducted as part of the Alliance work. We focus our examination and discussion on two cases, where livelihoods are particularly being eroded by flood risk with amplifications by climate change: (i) in the Karnali river basins in Nepal, communities are facing rapid on-set flash floods during the monsoon season, (ii) in the Rimac basin in Peru communities are exposed to riverine flooding, which periodically is magnified by the El Niño phenomenon.

The chapter is organised as follows: Sect. 17.2 presents the methodological framework underlying the science-society partnership model and our evaluation in this chapter. Section 17.3 presents the Flood Resilience Alliance in some more detail. Section 17.4 outlines methods and models developed, whose applications to the Alliance work and cases is the topic of Sect. 17.5 before Sect. 17.6 finally reflects and derives implications.

17.2 Methodological Framework for Science-Society Partnerships: Implementing a Systems Approach for Dealing with Critical Risks

The methodological framework underlying our further discussion builds on several entry points, which can be aligned using a systems approach. With emphasis on providing useful knowledge for informing sustainability transitions and transformations has come a call to the research community to organise knowledge creation that cuts across scales. As an important key reference, Turnheim et al. (2015) reflect on key analytical traditions and suggests a need for a joint framework and bridging across various approaches. The authors identify 3 dominant research traditions that are of high relevance for the sustainability discourse involving various scales and analytics as well as outcomes and interactions.

1. Coupled human-physical systems modelling to provide broad scenarios for projecting the future along a few decades-applied at global to regional scales;
2. An empirical approach for identifying past and current national patterns and trajectories of change-typically targeting national scales;
3. Locale-specific evidence creation on local initiatives and experimentation taking a backward-looking perspective and often building on heuristics-the local scale.

The literature broadly and the paper specifically emphasise that these methods and models are building on different ontologies and epistemologies. Thus, seamless integration across scales is not possible. Rather, proper boundary processes for effectively aligning these different research traditions are considered conducive in order to provide useful information. Criteria for "usefulness" the following can be generally identified (McNie 2007).

- **Saliency**: Useful information must be salient and relevant to the specific context in which it will be used. Salient information appropriately considers ecological, temporal, spatial, and administrative scales and timeliness.
- **Legitimacy**: Useful information must be legitimate in that those who produce it are perceived to be free from political suasion or bias. This means it is (i) demand driven and involves (experts from) relevant stakeholder groups in the scoping, preparation, peer-review and outreach/communication; (ii) transparent, in that the information is produced and/or transmitted in a way that is open and observable. (ii) builds on relationships between producers and users of the information characterized by mutual trust and respect; (iv) builds social capital through successful relationships and social organization leading to mutual trust, credibility, common rules, norms, reciprocity, and mutual respect.
- **Credibility**: Useful information must be credible and dependable in that it is perceived by the users to be accurate, valid, and of high quality. Peer review is often considered the *sine qua non* of credible information yet in many instances, other types of published information ("grey literature") also can satisfy the credibility criterion.

Importantly, useful information is not only about content, but emerges as the product of an effective process. Useable information needs to have a substantive core in which the information must be useful to the policy maker or actionable for the practitioner. It includes a procedural dimension that provides a mechanism for transmitting knowledge from the scientific community to these different but interdependent worlds. Also, such information provides for agency in terms of social learning and policy-making. We will consider these criteria further on in the discussion.

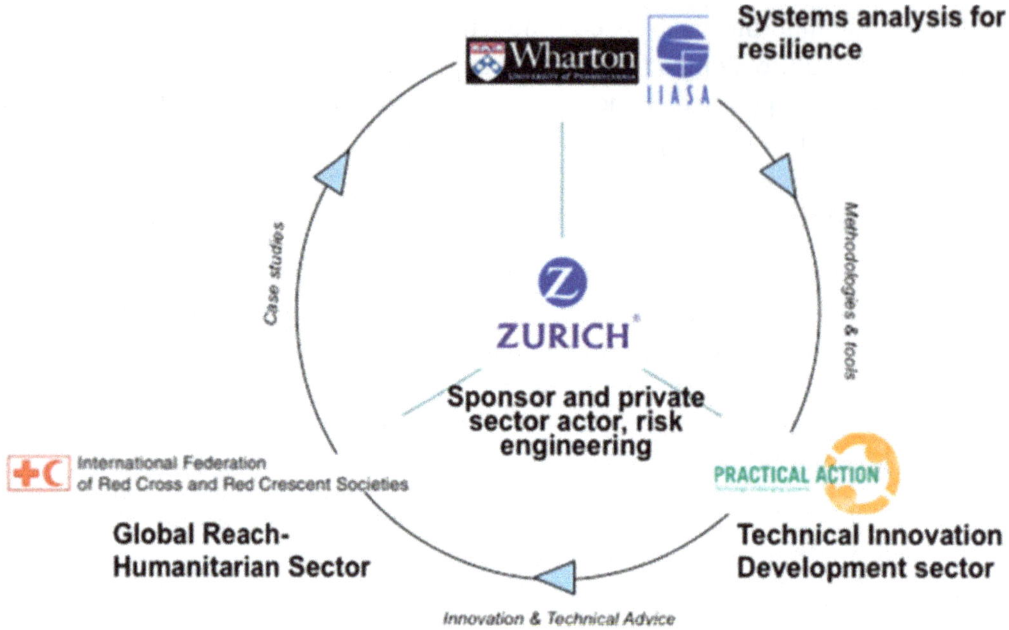

Fig. 17.2 Partners and roles in the Flood Resilience Alliance. *Source* Zurich 2014

17.3 The Zurich Flood Resilience Alliance: A Comprehensive Science-Policy-Practice Partnership

There has been an upspring of partnerships covering the boundary space from science to policy to practice, particularly in relation to disaster risk management, climate adaptation and resilience. The Zurich Flood Resilience Alliance (ZFRA), a unique alliance with leading partners from the development and humanitarian NGO sectors, academia and the private sector has embarked on a journey to help build resilience to flood risk in communities across the globe in order to make a difference for at least 250,000 flood prone households up to mid 2018, households which are often facing erosive risks shaped importantly by climate change. The multi-year initiative set up and co-generated by Zurich Insurance aims to operationalise, measure, and help build the resilience of communities to floods—the most devastating natural hazard globally. This extensive action and research program brings together expertise and skills on risk modeling and systems science as applied by the research partners IIASA and Wharton Business School with risk engineering expertise of Zurich and on-the-ground presence of the International Federation of Red Cross and Red Crescent Societies (IFRC) plus the international development NGO, Practical Action (Fig. 17.2). The Flood Resilience Alliance aims to enhance community flood resilience by exploring innovative ways to reduce risk before a flood strikes. NGO collaborators have used research findings to aid in the design and implementation of interventions to benefit communities.

Focus: Flood Risk

The world is facing increasing risks as globalisation connects people, economies, and ecosystems. Globally, the number of people exposed to floods each year is increasing at a higher rate than population growth. People are drawn to live on flood plains partly because of economic opportunity (World Bank 2013). However, it is increasingly recognised that communities cannot totally avoid risk and that living with risks is the imperative. Future socioeconomic and climatic changes are expected to exacerbate flooding and undermine human wellbeing. Flood risks are increasing, interconnected and interdependent and cannot be enhanced by one stakeholder alone. To date, the development and the disaster risk management (DRM) communities have relied on a mix of interventions to help communities cope with flooding: "hard" interventions like building a dam or flood evacuation routes and, to a much lesser extent, "smart and soft" interventions like land use planning, insurance, and early-warning-systems. Flood-risk management is dominated by single interventions, many of which fail to meet their objectives because they do not consider the wider socioeconomic system within which they operate. In some instances interventions can even be counter-productive in resilience terms, inadvertently undermining development or actually increasing risk in another way.

Focus: A Systems Perspective on Resilience

The engagement in the ZFRA is organised around concepts and methods linked to the notion of resilience. While not a new concept (theory and methods have been developed in the 1970s, importantly coined by thinking on ecological resilience), the resilience discourse has recently been strongly revived, partially also triggered by the aftermath of the global financial crisis. Emphasis in this field has been on identifying synergies with developmental challenges, systemic risks and actions. While some consider resilience the 'new sustainability,' it remains to be seen how this promising, if broad conceptualisation may help to stimulate necessary action on climate change and disaster risks, while seeking to foster an integration of social, ecologic and economic dimensions of sustainability challenges. It is well understood that disasters increasingly impair sustainable development, yet DRM has often looked at corrective measures (rebuilding the status quo and old vulnerabilities), rather than prospective efforts tackling underlying risk drivers, such as unplanned urban sprawl and asset location in harm's way. The concept of resilience provides a chance to take a systems' perspective and tackle prospective risk creation by integrating notions of up-and down-side risk avoidance and management with upside risk taking. Keating et al. (2016a) document the on-going evolution within the extreme event risk management community towards embracing the concept of resilience. The authors also suggest a novel conceptualisation and operationalisation to help jointly tackle the key challenges discussed above, and see resilience as the "ability of a system, community or society to pursue its social, ecological and economic development and growth objectives, while managing its disaster risk over time in a mutually reinforcing way" (Keating et al. 2017).

Fig. 17.3 Flood risk context in the Karnali river basin in Nepal (left panel) and the Rimac river valley in Peru (right panel). *Photo Sources* Practical Action and A. Keating

17.3.1 Joint Boundary Objects: Case Studies for Co-generating Universal Insights

The ZFRA case studies for co-generating insights and implementing sorely needed projects have been carefully chosen. Case studies are generally characterised by severe flood risk and limits to disaster risk management and adaptation interacting with significant development challenges (see Fig. 17.3).

In the Karnali river basins in Nepal, rural communities are facing rapid on-set flash floods during the monsoon season often leading to massive impacts to lives and assets. Therefore Early Warning Systems, improved disaster management coordination between communities and local and national governments, creation of emergency plans and implementation of alternative livelihoods are part of the interventions. In the Rimac basin in Peru, communities are improving their preparedness for the El Niño season by identifying evacuation routes and emergency plans, capacity building of brigades and supporting communities to engage with local governments on DRR planning.

As well, other case studies, not further discussed here, have focussed on Indonesia and Mexico. Along the Ciliwung, Bengawan Solo and Citarum rivers in Indonesia, there is a huge need to improve waste management, reforestation and to connect the impact of upstream behavioural patterns with flooding in downstream communities. In the region of Tabasco in Mexico, communities located in wetlands with flood seasons lasting for over three months have been in need of improved water and sanitation protection, community centres that can also function as emergency shelters, and new livelihood options that can withstand prolonged flood seasons.

The Flood Resilience Alliance is using a participatory and iterative learning approach to identify and develop for the representative ("universal") cases sustainable portfolios of interventions that tackle both flood risk and development objectives in synergy. The strategies communities use to pursue their development and well-being objectives have a profound impact on risk. Likewise, the way a community approaches its disaster risk has a profound impact on development and wellbeing. The trick is to get these two working in a virtuous cycle, rather than undermining each other. Entry points for developing this iterative, cyclical approach are effective community-level processes and a shared vision of adaptive learning discussed in the following.

17.4 Entry Points for Integrating Methods and Models for Putting Flood Resilience into Practice

17.4.1 Participatory Vulnerability Capacity Assessments

For working with communities on implementing DRM activities, the International Federation of the Red Cross (IFRC) and Practical Action use participatory assessment processes to gather, organise and analyse information on the vulnerability and adaptive capacity of communities, which can subsequently be used for joint decision-making. These processes are broadly referred to as Participatory Vulnerability Capacity Assessments (P)VCA. In order to measure vulnerability of communities and households in 1989 Anderson and Woodrow developed the Capacity and Vulnerability Analysis matrix. This largely qualitative, participatory and monitoring approach came to be widely accepted and used by many NGOs in their work on DRM forward (see ActionAid 2005; Davis 2004).

The participatory approaches are particularly valuable in helping to understand the key challenges discussed above namely: (1) The multitude of benefits and local values attached to these; (2) The historical perspective not only in regard to major disasters but also the less intense but recurrent minor shocks and stresses; and (3) Providing an opportunity to link community perceptions including locally-derived knowledge with what science and policy makers are predicting to occur in the future due to existing underlying issues and climate change. This merger of traditional with scientific knowledge adds great value to planning approaches that attempt to consider multiple hazards and accommodate increasing uncertainty.

Overall, VCAs/PCVAs aim to support communities to (i) identify key vulnerabilities of communities; (ii) understand communities' perceived and actual risks; (iii) analyse the resources and capacities available to reduce said risks; and (iv) develop action plans to address identified vulnerabilities and risks. In working with communities on implementing DRR activities, Practical Action has been identifying and estimating the historic and potential natural hazard situation and has been working with communities to estimate the social, environmental and economic losses expected in the area of interest through their PCVA process. These processes are usually completed with the collection of secondary information to provide a baseline of communities' risk to different hazards.

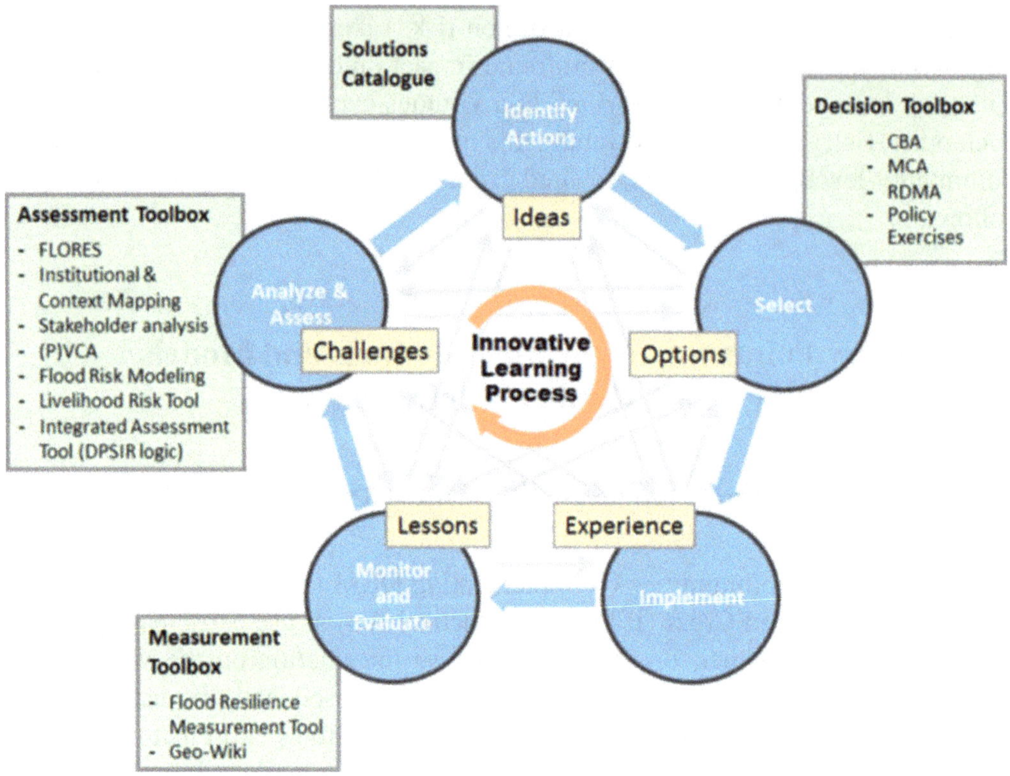

Fig. 17.4 Adaptive management cycle used in the ZFRA to foster Shared Resilience Learning. *Source* IIASA and Zurich 2015

17.4.2 Boundary Processes for the Methodological Framework: Adaptive Management for Shared Resilience Learning

It is well understood that enhancing (flood) resilience is a learning process, which can also be described through an 'adaptive management cycle'. The adaptive management cycle contains the steps required in any process to enhance community flood resilience. In order to link DRM and CCA in practice, the literature has moved towards suggesting a more reflexive-participative approach. Acknowledging the uncertainties and complexities inherent in social–ecological systems impacted by climate-related risks, analysts have started to emphasise iterative and adaptive learning (see, e.g., O'Brien et al. 2012; Mochizuki et al. 2015). Lavell et al. (2012) suggest a learning loop framework that integrates different learning theories, such as experiential learning (Kolb 1984), adaptive management (Holling 1978) and transformative learning (Mezirow 1995). This framework distinguishes three different loops according to the degree that these processes support transformational change of CRM strategies. Figure 17.4 shows the key stages and tools of the learning cycle, which for the Alliance work was termed the "Shared Resilience Learning Dialogue."

Before the cycle is initialised, the first step requires that the organisation(s) driving the development process (including but not limited to NGOs and governments) analyse the situation to identify the development change expected, ensuring that it will address a clear flood risk. The next step is to assess how development and flood risk are linked. This is done together with as many stakeholders as possible. This assessment is designed to explore the current situation, and identify stakeholder's roles and the potential for change. Based on the outcome of this assessment, the organisations select a development plan in line with stakeholders' priorities. This plan will incorporate a suite of solutions to improve community flood resilience. One or more solutions are then chosen as the ones to implement, emphasising a practical ('learning-by-doing') approach.

Those involved in the process monitor and evaluate activities to track how they unfold, test the assumptions upon which the choices were made and see if they deliver results as planned, and to capture lessons that are fed back into assessment. At the centre of the diagram is an iterative learning process, which works cyclically as a loop. This process emphasizes continuous learning and innovation among stakeholders (as opposed to the implementing organisation); the organisation interacts within the 'adaptive' management cycle and ultimately brings about lasting change.

17.4.3 Detecting and Supporting the Management of Risk and Resilience at Scale Around a Learning Framework

For the Loss and Damage discourse and the work reported on in this chapter, we thus propose to employ a learning framework building on risk detection and resilience management. Learning and awareness is fundamental to better understand risk and resilience. The adaptive management framework, as it co-generates insight from local to global scales, can be useful to identify the need for action across time and a scale from incremental (traditional DRR and climate change adaptation) to transformative (fundamentally different livelihood strategies supported by novel policy options), when faced with risks beyond the limits of adaptation. Figure 17.5 links the adaptive learning cycle to a representation of risks today as well as of risks at different levels of warming.

The left panel in exemplary fashion visualises risks and risk tolerance (ranging from acceptable to tolerable to intolerable) for different levels of global warming (complete boxes). The black arrows show the increments to risk with climatic change as a driver. The dashed boxes identify parts of the risk that can further be reduced either by conventional DRR or CCA options (blue-green arrows) or transformative measures as part of responses linked to Loss and Damage (white arrows). The right panel further shows the adaptive management cycle as facilitating single-double and triple-loop learning. It suggests, that in the short-term incremental adjustments to risk and resilience can be taken by (i) monitoring the effectiveness of existing policy

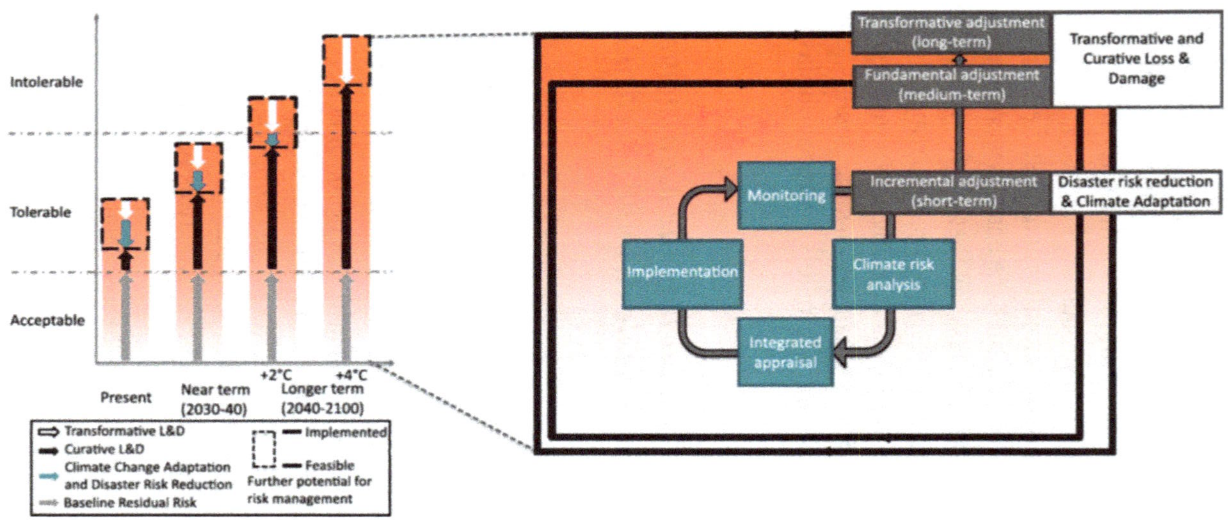

Fig. 17.5 Methodological approach for understanding and learning about risk and resilience. *Source* Mechler and Schinko (2016)

options, scientific evidence regarding climate change, risk and resilience information; (ii) analysis of climate-related risks, such as using flood risk modelling; (iii) appraisals of the resilience of capacities; and (iv) implementation of options and solutions that further build resilience (such as raising flood risk protection). Importantly, going through the incremental adjustment cycle allows for identifying risks beyond standard adaptation calling for fundamental and transformative adjustments. Fundamental adjustment options may be to provide more room for the river, so peak floods levels can be absorbed. Transformative adjustments may involve resettling flood-prone households.

In this fashion, the loop-learning framework sets out a continuous process for identifying and generating sequential adjustment to changing risk and resilience conditions, which benefits the communities at risk as well as, if projected for levels of global warming, provides insight regarding the stresses imposed by climate change, thus underlining the need for stringent mitigation efforts and support for resilience building.

17.5 Application of Methods and Models

We now turn to presenting some of the methods and tools used for the Alliance's *Shared Resilience Learning Dialogue*. As laid out, the Alliance is working with communities in Mexico, Nepal, Indonesia, and Peru in order to design advanced modelling techniques that are robust, user-driven, and user-friendly. The work and findings aim at not only helping communities directly at risk, but also eventually supporting local, national, and international policymakers, NGOs, and donors worldwide to mainstream risk reduction against multiple natural hazards.

17.5.1 Understanding Risk: Risk Geo Wiki and Crowdsourcing

Communities need flood-related risk information to prepare for and respond to floods—to inform risk reduction strategies and strengthen resilience, improve land use planning, and generally prepare for the case when disaster strikes. But across much of the developing world, data are sparse at best and not fit for the purpose for understanding the dynamics of flood risk. The IIASA Risk Geo-Wiki online platform provides for a risk crowdsourcing approach and acts not only as a repository of available flood-related spatial information, but also provides for two-way information exchange. The platform provides digital technology in terms of crowdsourcing and citizen science in order to integrate local/traditional knowledge and expert-sourced knowledge to better understand flood vulnerability of households and communities, scaling up community-level information to river basin level and

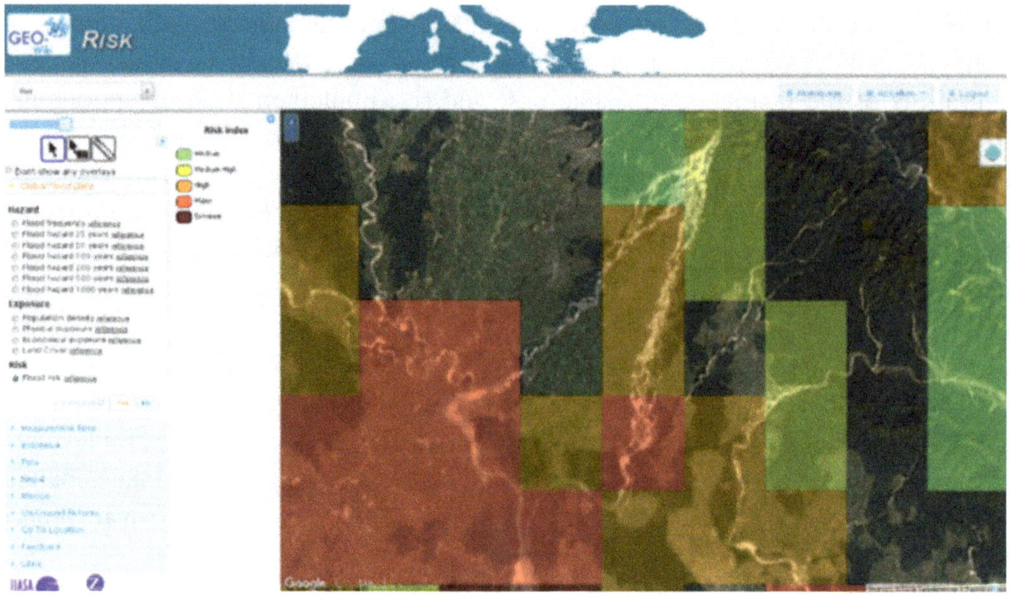

Fig. 17.6 Screenshot of Risk Geo-Wiki. Modelled global flood risk data overlaid on satellite imagery at the regional level for the Karnali, Nepal

more. The portal is intended to be of practical use to community leaders and NGOs, governments, academia, industry and citizens who are interested in better understanding the information available to strengthen flood resilience. This is particularly useful for communities and in locations where accurate topographic maps are not available or the elevation mapping is so course that flood inundation modelling for examples is meaningless.

As a starting point, a variety of global expert-sourced flood datasets (e.g., the GLOFRIS model, Ward et al. 2013) included in the Risk Geo-Wiki can be displayed exhibiting an estimate of flood hazard, exposure and risk based on various flood frequencies/return periods—see Fig. 17.6 for a view of the Karnali basin. This information is a starting point for global and regional analyses to conduct risk-based analysis and broadly identify hotspots.

However, as this figure shows, global expert-based modelled data is by necessity coarse in terms of spatial resolution and often not directly applicable to community level needs. Hence, what is needed is the ability to capture local community level information in a global context.

As introduced, Participatory Vulnerability and Capacity Assessment is a widely used tool to collect community level disaster risk and resilience information and to inform DRR strategies, yet it is not linked to digitised information and broadly available. The Risk Geo-Wiki effort has developed a general methodological approach that combines community-based participatory mapping processes, which have been widely used by governments and non-government organisation in the fields of natural resources management, disaster risk reduction and rural development, with emerging internet-based collaborative digital mapping techniques. The project digitised a set

Fig. 17.7 Community and NGO members mapping into OpenStreetMap with mobile devices in the Karnali basin, Nepal. *Photo Source* W. Liu

of existing maps on disaster risk and community resources where the locations of, for example, rivers, houses, infrastructure and emergency shelters are usually hand-drawn by selected community members. Such maps provide critical information used by local stakeholders in designing and prioritising among possible flood risk management options. Communities in Nepal, Peru, and Mexico have uploaded data to the site and are working on developing it further. For local communities who have uploaded spatial information to the site, it allows them to visualise their information overlaid upon satellite imagery or OpenStreetMap (OSM) (Fig. 17.7).

In collaboration with Practical Action, IIASA researchers worked side-by-side with in-country professionals and communities to demonstrate the value and potential of this general participatory and collaborative digital mapping approach in the flood-prone lower Karnali River basin in Western Nepal. As Fig. 17.8 shows, the new digital community maps are richer in content, more accurate, and easier to update and share than conventional hand-drawn VCA maps. The process engaged a wide range of stakeholders to generate geographic information on resources, capacities and flood risks of pilot communities based on their local needs. This approach, as an inclusive form of risk knowledge co-generation, can make important contribution to evidence-based understanding of disaster risk and thus enhance disaster resilience at all levels. The work has since been taken forward with the collaborators to map communities in Western Nepal, Peru and the Tabasco region in Mexico.

Fig. 17.8 Conventional hand-drawn community risk map, capacity map, and social map versus digital community map produced via a participatory and collaborative mapping approach. *Source* Liu et al. (2018)

17.5.2 Measuring Resilience

Comprehensive risk information is one starting point for guiding disaster risk reduction actions that build resilience. In this regard, a proper understanding of risk in qualitative and quantitative terms is essential, but has not sufficiently permeated resilience research and resilience building to date. Arguably, this is why there has been little concrete, measurable progress on the ground. The resilience measurement initiative of the ZFRA around developing the Flood Resilience Measurement Framework for Communities (FRMC) has been focused on benchmarking and tracking the underlying sources of resilience and the long-term outcomes (see Keating et al. 2017). For the flood-prone communities involved in the study, this means shedding light on why one community may fare better than another in the same disaster, despite seemingly identical levels of development and vulnerability. With the information and resources acquired in this work, communities will not just be able to bounce back after a disaster. They will be able to actually bounce forward in terms of making progress on important development objectives. The tool will help communities and development partners review available options and make judgements on how to build resilience, helping communities with limited resources decide what to invest in, such as increasing and strengthening livelihoods, investing in preparedness measures or building requisite DRR infrastructure.

The FRMC approach to measuring resilience involves measuring the sources of resilience pre and post-disaster, operationalised around key capacity indicators of a community's socio-economic system (Fig. 17.9). The resilience framework, building on detailed literature review aligns resilience systems thinking (Bruneau 2006) with the Sustainable Livelihoods Approach (SLA) adopted by development agencies for broadly tracing achievement of development objectives in communities (DFID 1999). Overall, the approach consistently considers communities' assets, interactions and interconnections across, what we call, 5 capitals (or capacities): human, natural, social, physical and financial. The measurement of capital groups builds on a set resilience sources, overall, for the 5 classes there are a total of 88 sources of resilience in this so-called 5C-4R framework. Sources are qualitatively graded from A-D based on available data depending on context and need, e.g. from household surveys, community focus group discussions, expert informants, and other third-party sources. To assure validity of measurement, sources are assessed and graded by specially trained NGO experts embedded in the respective communities, while data are collected globally via an integrated mobile and web-based system. Building on measuring potential resilience of a community, projecting actual outcomes of resilience after an event considers observed impacts (losses and time for getting back to 'normal').

The measurement framework has been rolled out globally, and in addition to the 4 case locations of the ZFRA, other NGOs have been enlisted as additional boundary partners to the ZFRA, contributing data from communities in Afghanistan, East Timor, Indonesia, Haiti and the United States amounting to more than 100 currently graded communities with more than 1 million data points.

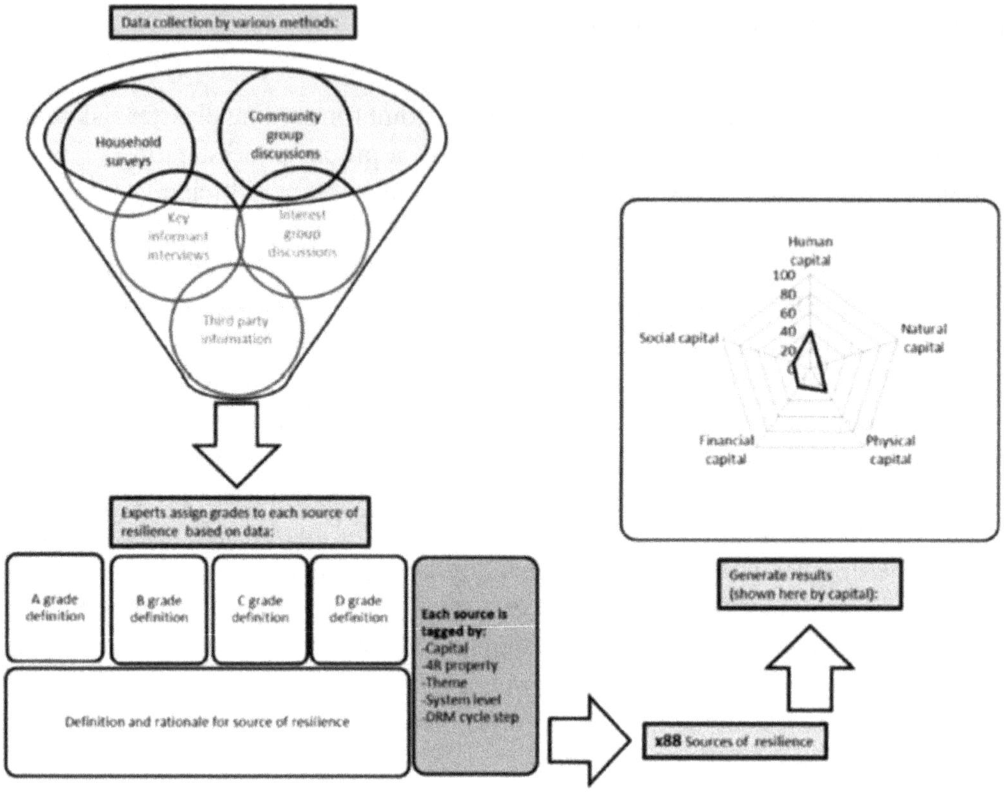

Fig. 17.9 Zurich Flood Resilience Measurement Framework implementation process. *Source* Keating et al. (2017)

The FRMC framework is meant to consistently measure dynamic progress (or lack thereof) over time given internal and external resilience determinants. It can also be applied at a fixed point in time, as done for Nepal in order to statically assess and compare resilience with average resilience across all communities (see Fig. 17.10).

17.5.3 *Towards Truly Informing Decision-Making: Decision-Support Techniques*

Resilience is generally built by implementing efficient, effective and acceptable measures. There are a variety of decision-support tools for evaluating such options (see Table 17.1). Ultimately, economic efficiency underlying Cost-Benefit-Analysis is only one decision-making criterion of relevance for prioritising DRR flood risk reduction investments. Decisions on investments to increase flood risk resilience are likely to be made based on a number of criteria, some of which are more or less transparent (Mechler 2016). Criteria such as risk-effectiveness, robustness, equity and distributional concerns, and acceptability have been found to be key for deciding on implementing DRR projects. There are other decision support techniques such as

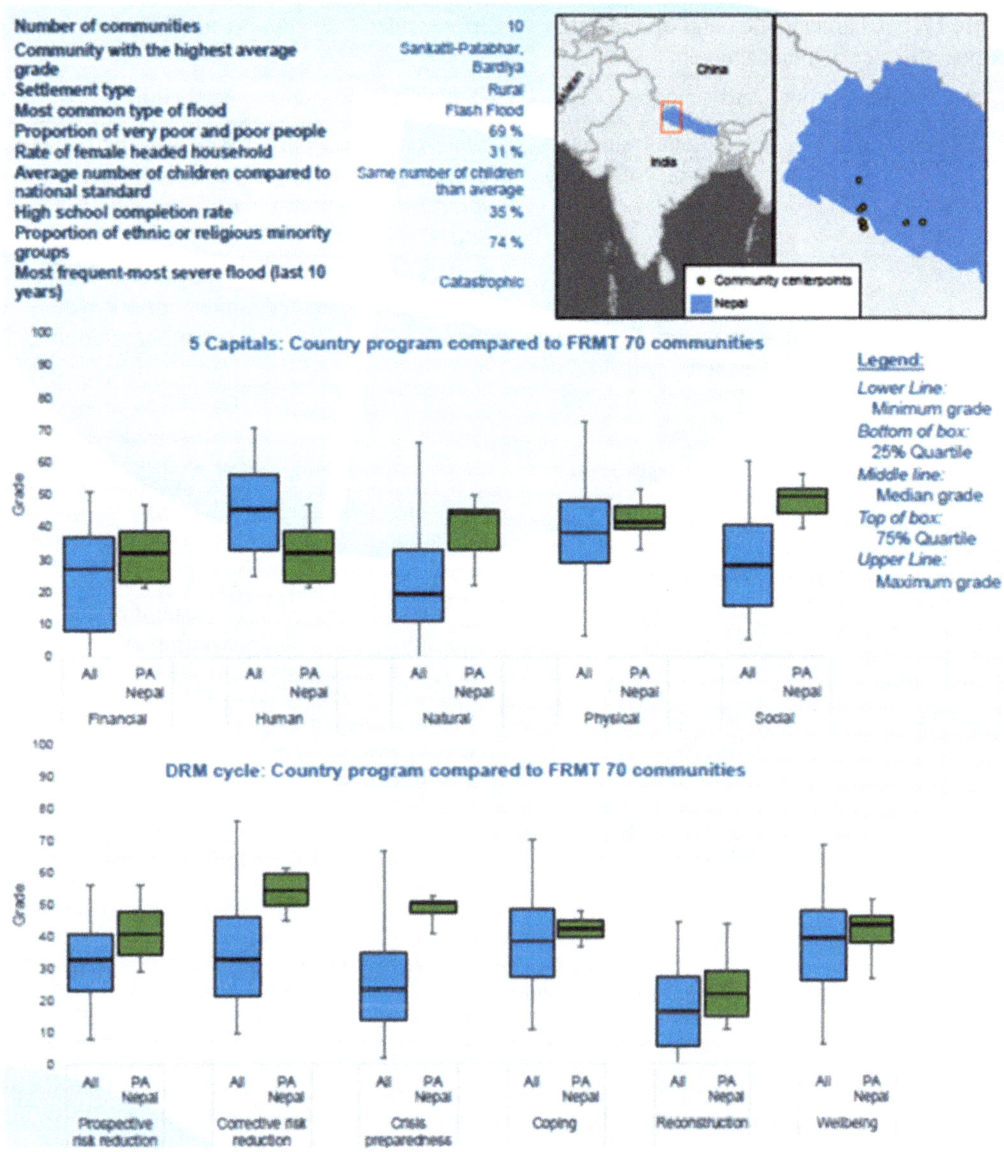

Fig. 17.10 Measuring resilience in Nepal as compared to the global measurement. *Source* Laurien 2017

cost-effectiveness analysis (CEA), multi-criteria analysis (MCA), robust decision-making and serious gaming approaches that can be used to measure achievement of these criteria. These tools can be used to make a more comprehensive case for DRR. As a challenge, they do not lead to easily communicable metrics for presenting the results, such as benefit-cost ratios. These tools inform various types of decisions in many different contexts, including project appraisal, evaluation, informational/advocacy studies and iterative decision-making. Table 17.1 summarises the key advantages, challenges and applicability of CBA, CEA, MCA, robust and gaming approaches. The table illustrates that no tool is perfect for each and every situation.

Table 17.1 Characteristics and applicability of different decision-support tools for ex-ante and ex-post disaster risk management

Decision support tool	Advantages	Challenges	Application
CBA	Rigorous framework based on comparing costs with benefits	Need for monetising all benefits, difficulty in representing plural values	Well-specified *hard-resilience* projects with economic benefits
CEA	Ambition level fixed, and only costs to be compared. Intangible benefits part. loss of life do not need be monetised	Ambition level needs to be fixed and agreed upon	Well-specified interventions with important intangible impacts, which should not be exceeded (loss of life etc.)
MCA	Consideration of multiple objectives and plural values	Subjective judgments required, which hinder replication	Multiple and systemic interventions involving plural values
Robust approaches	Addressing uncertainty and robustness	Technical and computing skills required	Projects with large uncertainties and long timeframes
Gaming/Policy Exercise	Truly engaging stakeholders to inform decisions	Extensive facilitation skills and ability to manage complexity of social interactions	Community level interactions to inform decisions with stakeholders and decision-makers

Note CBA Cost benefit analysis; *CEA* Cost-effectiveness analysis; *MCA* Multi-criteria analysis

Each has its strengths and weaknesses and is suited to different decision-making contexts.

These methods and metrics mostly require some expert facilitation. However, the information-action gap inherent in providing expert input to working with local, national and international stakeholders for selecting options is well known. Failures to produce useful insight often resulted from over-reliance on biophysical data and inadequate appreciation of the diversity of ways decisions are made at all levels of society. Yet, understanding and analysis of complex policy issues is often hampered by the high costs of gathering data about how various members of society actually think and decide about such issues. Similarly, scientists and policy makers often must invest years to gain experience critical to managing systems that change and evolve without undertaking real risk (Sterman 1994). This raises the question: How can we lower the costs of learning through experience? "Serious gaming" and policy exercises (also known as Open Simulations) have emerged to fill this gap (Duke and Geurts 2004). Such exercises use social simulation tools that combine computational models and participation of real actors. Particularly when actions are contested and broad participation in knowledge co-generation and decision-making is required (as is the case for the Loss and Damage discourse), serious gaming approaches become relevant and have been tested and applied in the ZFRA work (see Box 17.1 on serious gaming objectives).

Box 17.1 Objectives of serious gaming to support resilience assessment and building through engagement

- *Demonstrating the benefits of ex ante disaster risk reduction and preparedness.* The game can be used in case studies to test responses of different actors to policy innovations thereby helping to improve them by reducing potential negative side effects. Games can especially draw attention to the 'invisible' indirect and intangible impacts.
- *Fostering flood risk protection through enhancing participatory decision-making.* The game can help stakeholders to build flood resilience buy-in. As a tool it has unique potential to change how people perceive and understand resilience. Through intellectual and emotional engagement in an interactive environment, stakeholders may start to see how important flood resilience becomes for their security and livelihoods. It will also contribute to building social capital by increasing trust and collaboration.
- *Knowledge dissemination and outreach.* Games, by engaging participants, can become a very successful dissemination instrument—with broader outreach than traditional reports. The games developed in the project for stakeholders can be later used for disseminating project insights to broader audience.
- *Supporting the integrated assessment for flood resilience.* Decision-making rules are of the most difficult modelling tasks (either in system dynamics or agent-based models). Gaming exercises can provide a better understanding of decision making of actors that can influence flood resilience. Because they provide context and engage participants emotionally, they are more reliable than questionnaires in eliciting stakeholder responses in a way that can be translated into modelling language.

These exercises mediate collaboration between actors and scientists in analysing how problems emerge in complex systems and where points of intervention may lie. Because they are experienced as something that feels real, more information is retained, learning is faster, and an intuition is gained about how to make real decisions and improve policies. Ideally, if the right actors can be brought together gaming allows the exploration of real issues and provides a neutral platform for different stakeholders to understand conflicting opinions and perspectives in a safe space. The sophistication of the approach allows even non-trained actors to engage in highly complex decisions.

The focus of using policy exercises for the ZFRA, conducted in collaboration with the Centre for Systems Solutions (CRS) in Wroclaw, Poland, has been to apply simulation games and policy exercises to support the activities in the Flood Resilience project. A Flood Resilience Game has been developed, which is a board-game played by 8–16 players, who each take on a role as a member of a flood prone community. Direct interactions between players create a rich experience that can be discussed and analysed in structured debrief sessions. This allows players to explore vulnerabilities, risks and capacities—citizens, local authorities and NGOs together—leading to an advanced understanding of interdependencies and the potential for working together. The game draws on research on the complex challenges of reducing flood risk and fostering sustainable development. It allows players to experience, explore, and learn about the flood risk and resilience of communities in river valleys. Players experience the simulated impacts of flood damage on housing and infrastructure, as well as

Fig. 17.11 Application of the Flood Resilience Game provoking discussion at an NGO workshop in Jakarta

indirect effects on livelihoods, markets, and quality of life. It lets them experience the effects on resilience of investments in different types of "capital"—such as financial, human, social, physical, and natural (see Fig. 17.11).

Finally, players can explore the complex outcomes on the society, environment and economy from different long-term development pathways. This highlights the types of decisions needed to avoid creating more flood risk in the future, incentivising action before a flood through enhancing participatory decision-making. Overall, the learning generated in these interactions in a "safe-space" environment provides a platform for subsequently exploring real-life decisions.

17.5.4 A Systems Model for the Integrated Assessment of Resilience

As an effort to support the development of the gaming approach as well as provide an integrated perspective on flood resilience, the Flood Resilience System Framework and Model (FLORES) has been designed to help provide a first step towards understanding the complexity of the community decision context. The first version of the system dynamics model developed is based on successful collaboration between IIASA and Soluciones Practicas (Peru).[1] The knowledge and experience of Soluciones Practicas' staff has been critical to develop a model that helps to answer

[1] Soluciones Practicas is the Practical Action country organisation for Peru.

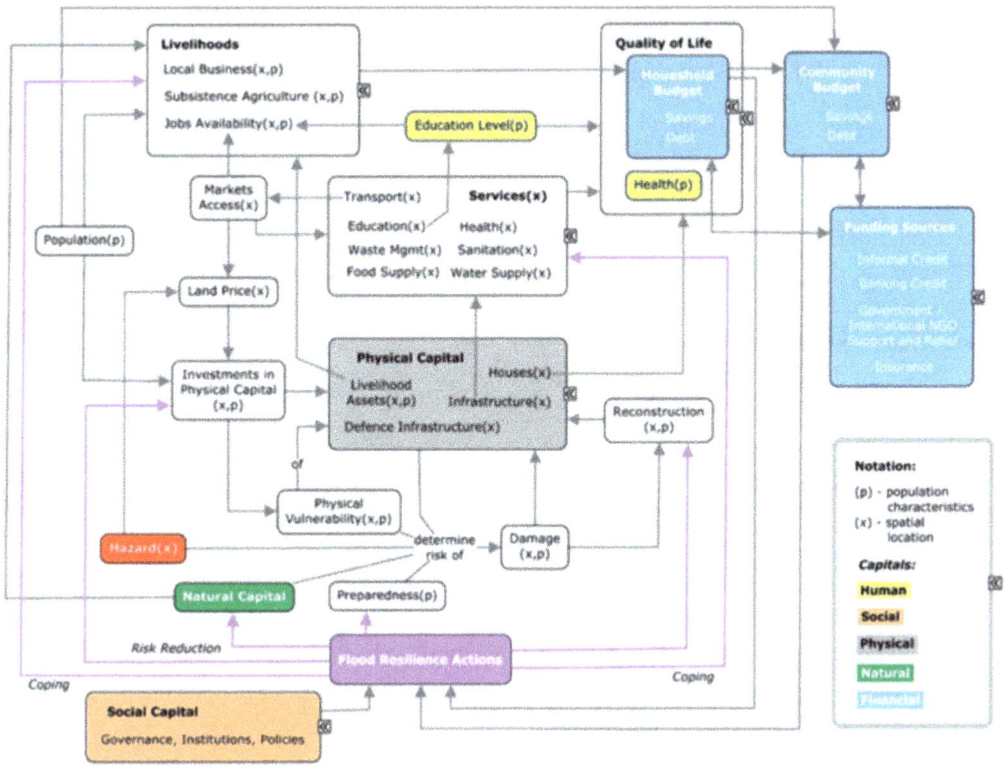

Fig. 17.12 Flood Resilience Systems Framework (FLORES)—a simplified view

strategic questions about improving flood resilience in the Rimac river valley in Peru. FLORES enables users to visualise this complexity to start to learn about how the system behaves, thus helping to unwrap the layers of complexity associated with community-level resilience.

The main purpose of the model has been to explore the medium to long-term dynamics of risk and options for risk management (that is to say: potential hazards and conditions of vulnerability and capacities) of the vulnerable communities with respect to hazardous events (here: huaycos and floods in the Rimac Valley). This perspective has been fundamentally underlying the development of a more comprehensive resilience framework and dynamic model for understanding the relationships. The framework has been discussed and further co-generated with local experts and stakeholders in the Rimac basin in Peru in a workshop setting (see Box 17.2 and Fig. 17.12).

In the case of the Rimac Valley river basin system, community members voiced demand for information that helps to understand how trends in El Nino patterns, climate change, economic development and migration interact with land use, building (new settlements) and transportation in hazard zones and disaster risk reduction activities over a time horizon of 20–50 years. This means different scenarios need to be developed to see how the system will evolve under different policy choices. The system dynamics modelling developed is meant to support interactive simulations (policy exercises), which, in later stages of the community interactions may inform the evaluation and selection of options and solutions.

Box 17.2 The Systems dynamics model FLORES investigates the following problems

- Modelling medium to long-term dynamics of risk (that is to say: potential hazards and conditions of vulnerability and capacities) of the Rimac Valley communities with respect to huaycos and floods.
- Exploring the effects of damages (direct impacts on housing and infrastructure) and losses (indirect impacts) on livelihoods, markets and quality of life, using different modelling scenarios.
- Investigating the influence of different disaster management capacities: emergency preparedness, response, reconstruction, exposure, physical vulnerability (fragility) and risk reduction measures on flood/huayco resilience of communities in the Rimac Valley.
- Analysing the social and economic effects of the El Nino disturbance (including possible migrations) within different climatic and policy scenarios.
- Analysing the effects of institutional arrangements (formal but also informal including illegal settlements, building and transportation) on flood resilience of the Rimac Valley communities.
- Identifying medium-long-term development pathways that avoid creating a flood risk catastrophe (*prospective* risk reduction).

The model is planned to be further used by Soluciones Prácticas staff to explore the critical variables and long-term drivers of resilience and change, and how these interact to produce risk and development outcomes. This might assist in identifying critical entry points (intervention options) for project planning, and to produce advocacy materials/messages to be used in engaging with the disasters and development sectors in Peru. The model has a relatively user-friendly interface and can be computed very quickly, which makes it possible to use it in a workshop setting together with disaster experts or other stakeholders to analyse different scenarios, as well as modify assumptions to produce and examine new scenarios and/or policy options. Modelling workshops can support experts and policy makers to understand the problem space, and develop new, evidence-based policies addressing long-term challenges. Based on the developed model, a policy exercise can be developed where a group of stakeholders can examine step by step the consequences of their decisions, resulting both from the biophysical dynamics and social interaction.

17.5.5 Understanding Past Impacts for Projecting Future Risk: Forensics and Scenario Analysis

Projecting future risk and resilience requires a good understanding of observed events and factors driving impacts. Disaster forensics, the study of root causes, has seen increasing attention; as a key work element the Flood Resilience Alliance over the last few years developed and applied its forensic approach, termed Post-Event Review Capability (PERC) to an increasing number of flood disasters around the world[2] (Venkateswaran et al. 2015; Keating et al. 2016b; Zurich 2014a, b, 2015a, b). The point of departure for disaster forensics, an inter- and transdisciplinary research effort, has been the understanding that the wealth of disaster risk information available has not been sufficiently effective to help halt the increase in risk. A number of propositions have been suggested by forensics to work towards actionable information to reduce risk and build resilience-all of which are of fundamental importance for the *Loss and Damage Debate* (see IRDR 2011): (i) *Risk reduction*: More probing research coupled with actors' roles visibility and transparency will lead to increased investment into risk reduction; (ii) *Integration*: More integrated (inter-and transdisciplinary) and participatory research will produce more useful and effective results; (iii) *Identification and Communication of Risk Management Roles*: More effective and sustained communication of findings is required.

One entry point for taking retrospective disaster forensics forward to inform Loss and Damage tackled in the Alliance has been to explore its integration with prospective scenario analysis. Scenario analysis is a technique and structured process for projecting out key variables of interest (in this case disaster risk and resilience) as a function of its drivers based on shared narratives about future socio-economic development and other inputs. Scenario analysis has been widely used for global problems (e.g., IPCC climate scenarios) as well as applied in local-participatory context to explore solutions to local problems (Notten et al. 2003). It has neither been widely used for problems related to disaster and climate-related risks nor applied in forensics studies. Building on substantial forensics work undertaken in the Alliance, we tested a forensics approach for understanding and dealing with the impacts brought about by the El Nino Phenomenon in Peru in 2016/17 (see French and Mechler 2017).

The El Nino Phenomenon generally and particularly in Peru has brought about large disaster impacts about the affected. Impacts are recurrent and highly variable, with a cycle of 7–14 years. Other hazards interact and recently a so-called coastal El Nino hit Peru leading to major devastation (Fig. 17.13). The forensics work, building on other PERC and disaster forensics studies (Venkateswaran et al. 2015; Keating et al. 2016b), and utilising desk-based research and analysis, semi-structured and unstructured key-informant interviews, empirical risk analysis and risk modelling, took the large uncertainty associated with El Nino as a point of departure in order to better understand the history and future evolution of El Niño impacts and linked DRM efforts in Peru. The research has been building on empirically grounded insights and

[2] see www.floodresilience.net/solutions/collection/perc.

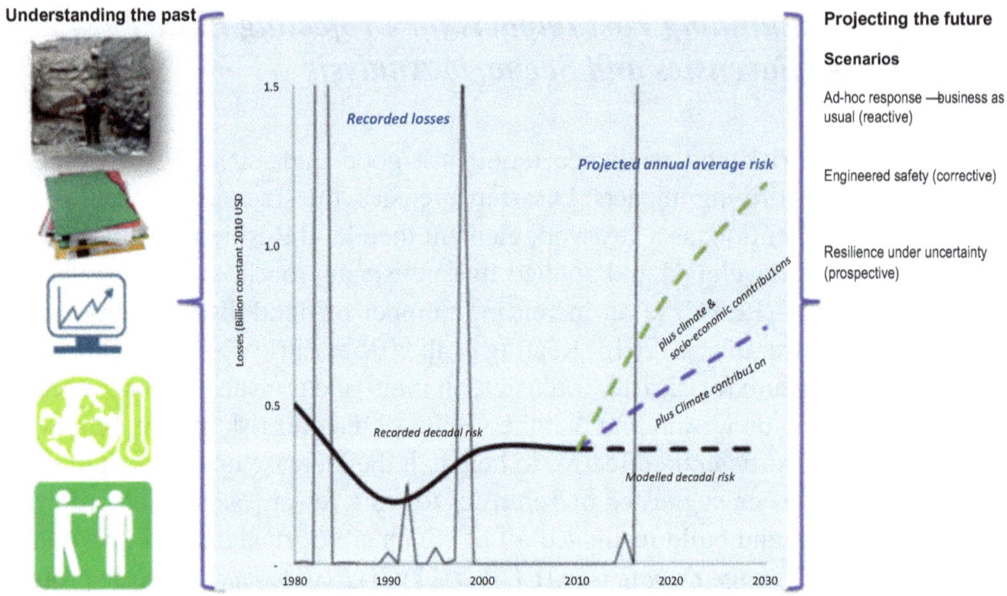

Fig. 17.13 Prospective forensics for projecting flood risk in Peru. *Source* French and Mechler (2017)

learning from past experience in order to identify future resilience pathways. It went beyond analysing the discrete events of 1997–98 and 2015–16 to understand the evolution of the key risk drivers hazard, exposure and particularly vulnerability over the past and the future using a scenario approach. This forward-looking analysis, termed projective forensics, thus linked retroactive PERC assessment with a future-oriented scenario approach for risk and resilience building for flood risk in Peru. As guiding question the team asked was: *Given the risk drivers and actions implemented or considered, how would future risk in Peru evolve over the short to medium-term horizon-up to 2030 as compared to today and what additional actions to take?*

Building on risk projections given by a prominent flood risk model (Ward et al. 2013) to also consider the socio-economic portion, trends identified in the past were used to project the future using different scenarios as detected locally: (i) *Ad hoc response* (reactive)-only prioritising DRR when an event is predicted/imminent; (ii) *Engineered safety* (corrective)-investing in hard infrastructure projects; and (iii) Resilience *under uncertainty* (prospective)-investing heavily in planning, zoning and relocation. As shown in Fig. 17.13, future risk associated with these pathways differs markedly. None of these scenario projections is likely to exactly see implementation, yet they provide a projection space, and thus may, as one application, support gameful policy exercises, help to identify and motivate further actions today and in the short-medium-term for building resilience.

17.6 Reflections and Implications: Providing Insight at Scale for Detecting and Managing Erosive Risk

Our reflection on the ZFRA experience started out by asking how analytical methods and tools can be co-generated and used by experts, practitioners and those at risk in order to build resilience against climate-related hazards (here flooding). Employing an adaptive management learning framework (the *Shared Resilience Learning Dialogue*) as the boundary process for integration, we presented a variety of different demand-driven tools and methods co-generated and used at different learning stages and across temporal and agency scales in this science-society partnership. Figure 17.14 graphically charts out the various tools and methods across time and agency scales. Many tools focus on present and future insight, while PVCA provides evidence on past identification of hazards and risks, and the forensic scenarios work from the past to projecting the future. Community-level tools, such as PVCA, crowdsourcing, resilience measurement 'speak' to efforts positioned at higher agency levels, such as the Risk Geo-Wiki and flood risk modelling. Gaming exercises and the FLORES model are nested between scales as potential connectors between global and local insight. Seamless integration of the tools and methods is often not possible, but the *Shared Resilience Learning Dialogue* generated throughout the partnership provides the boundary process that connects the different tools and methods, and particularly links these up with community-led processes.

The Zurich Flood Resilience Alliance is further gaining knowledge and experience to use these tools to enhance community flood resilience. The tools outlined here are being refined in joint collaboration with partners Practical Action, IFRC and Zurich insurance and other boundary partners working with the Alliance. The tools are compatible with, and being applied in conjunction with established community

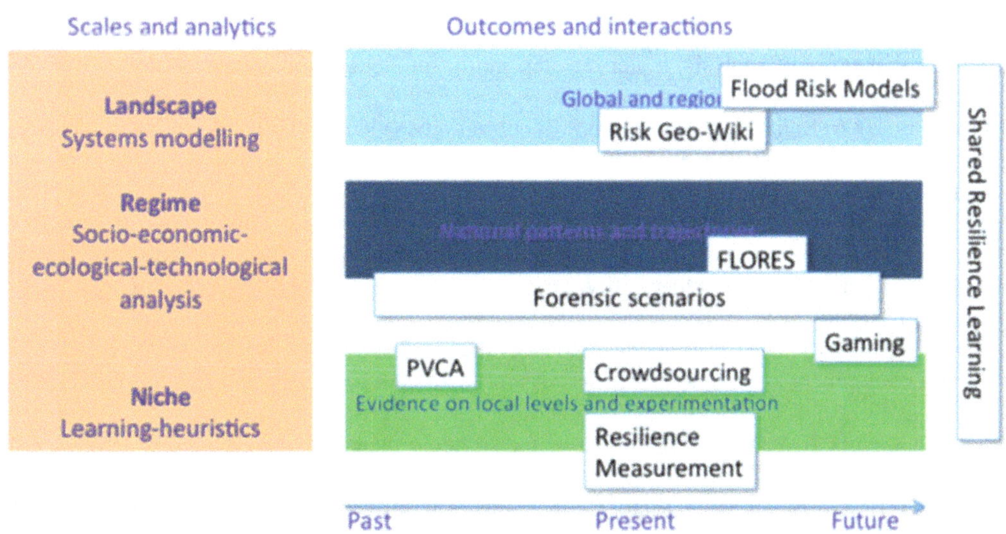

Fig. 17.14 Tracing methods and tools developed in the Zurich Flood Resilience Alliance in time and space connecting risk and resilience research with practice

initiative process-based tools such as vulnerability and capacity assessment, participatory capacity and vulnerability analysis, stakeholder mapping, hazard mapping and vulnerability assessments, household economic analyses, political economic analysis, etc. The ZFRA case studies all deal with marginal communities that have to face erosive flood-related risk in Nepal, Peru, Mexico and Indonesia. The charge is to support incremental with fundamental and transformative adjustments across the risk spectrum to support DRR and CCA practice as well as Loss and Damage policy debate. Global policy, such as on Loss and Damage is increasingly faced with demands for local, i.e. subnational to community-level engagement to deliver "on the frontlines of climate change." The partnership model described shows one effective model for doing so. It also shows that seamless integration of tools and methods across partners is neither feasible nor desirable. It is not fully feasible, as partners follow different theories of change building on differences in ontological perspectives. It is not desirable as these differences in worldviews are mutually enriching and conducive for action at appropriate scales (local to global). The lack of seamless integration can be effectively dealt with by the adaptive learning approach implemented through the Shared Resilience Learning. Continuous learning for partners and stakeholders allows for identifying options and solutions that work across scale, are acceptable, efficient and above all, effective for those dealing with increasing risks from climate change now and in the future.

Acknowledgements Funding by the Z Zurich Foundation through the Zurich Flood Resilience Alliance Program is gratefully acknowledged. We particularly thank Michael Szönyi for helpful comments.

References

ActionAid (2005) Participatory vulnerability analysis, a step-by-step guide for field staff. Anticipatory vulnerability analysis, a step-by-step guide for field staff. Johannesburg: Action Aid International

Bruneau M (2006) Enhancing the resilience of communities against extreme events from an earthquake engineering perspective. J Secur Educ 1(4):159–167

Climateactiontracker (2018) Climate analytics. New Climate Institute, Ecofyys. Climateactiontracker.org

Davis I (2004) Progress in analysis of social vulnerability and capacity. In: Bankoff G, Frerks G, Hilhorst D (eds) Mapping vulnerability: disasters, development and people. Earthscan, London, UK, pp 128–144

DFID (1999) Sustainable livelihoods guidance sheets. London, UK: Department of International Development. http://www.eldis.org/vfile/upload/1/document/0901/section2.pdf. Accessed 23 Jan 2018

Duke RD, Geurts JLA (2004) Policy games for strategic management. Dutch University Press, Amsterdam

ENHANCE (2016) Novel Multi-Sector Partnerships in Disaster Risk Management. Results of the ENHANCE project. In: Aerts J, Mysiak J (eds) EU FP7 project ENHANCE, pp 346

French A, Mechler R (2017) Managing El Niño risks under uncertainty in Peru: Learning from the past for a more disaster-resilient future. Laxenburg, Austria, International Institute for Applied Systems Analysis. http://pure.iiasa.ac.at/id/eprint/14849/

Handmer J, Nalau J (2018) Understanding loss and damage in Pacific Small Island developing states. In: Mechler R, Bouwer L, Schinko T, Surminski S, Linnerooth-Bayer J (eds) Loss and damage from climate change. Concepts, methods and policy options. Springer, Cham, pp 365–381

Heslin A (2018) Climate migration and cultural preservation: the case of the marshallese diaspora. In: Mechler R, Bouwer L, Schinko T, Surminski S, Linnerooth-Bayer J (eds) Loss and damage from climate change. Concepts, methods and policy options. Springer, Cham, pp 383–391

Holling CS (1978) Adaptive environmental assessment and management. JohnWiley and Sons, Chichester

IIASA and Zurich Insurance (2015) Turning knowledge into action: processes and tools for increasing flood resilience. Zurich, Switzerland

IRDR (2011) Forensic Investigations of Disasters: The FORIN Project. IRDR FORIN Publication No. 1, Integrated Research on Disaster Risk, Beijing

Keating A, Campbell K, Mechler R, Magnuszewski P, Mochizuki J, Liu W, Szoenyi M, McQuistan C (2016a) Disaster resilience: what it is and how it can engender a meaningful change in development policy. Develop Policy Rev 35(1):65–91

Keating A, Venkateswaran K, Szoenyi M, MacClune K, Mechler R (2016b) From event analysis to global lessons: disaster forensics for building resilience. Nat Hazards Earth Sys Sci 16:1603–1616

Keating A, Campbell K, Szoenyi M, McQuistan C, Nash D, Burer M (2017) Development and testing of a community flood resilience measurement tool. Nat Hazards Earth Sys Sci Discuss 17(1):77–101. https://doi.org/10.5194/nhess-17-77-2017

Kolb DA (1984) Experiential learning: experience as the source of learning and development. Prentice-Hall, Englewood Cliffs

Landauer M, Juhola S (2018) Loss and damage in the rapidly changing arctic. In: Mechler R, Bouwer L, Schinko T, Surminski S, Linnerooth-Bayer J (eds) Loss and damage from climate change. Concepts, methods and policy options. Springer, Cham, pp 425–447

Lavell A, Oppenheimer M, Diop C, Hess J, Lempert R, Li R, Muir-Wood R, Myeong S (2012) Climate change: new dimensions in disaster risk, exposure, vulnerability, and resilience. In: Field CB, Barros V, Stocker TF, Qin D, Dokken DJ, Ebi KL, Mastrandrea MD, Mach KJ, Plattner GK, Allen SK, Tignor M, Midgley PM (eds) Managing the risks of extreme events and disasters to advance climate change adaptation. A special report of working groups I and II of the intergovernmental panel on climate change (IPCC). Cambridge University Press, Cambridge and New York, pp 25–64

Liu W, Dugar S, McCallum I, Thapa G, See L, Khadka P, Budhathoki N, Brown S, Mechler R, Fritz S, Shakya P (2018) Integrated participatory and collaborative risk mapping for enhancing disaster resilience. ISPRS International Journal of Geo-Information 7(2):68. https://doi.org/10.3390/ijgi7020068

McNie E (2007) Reconciling the supply of scientific information with user demands: an analysis of the problem and review of the literature. Environ Sci Policy 10:17–38

McQuistan C (2015) Why technology justice is critical for the climate negotiations. Delivering on loss and damage. Technology Justice Policy Briefing, 4. Practical Action: Rugby, UK

Mechler R (2016) Reviewing estimates of the economic efficiency of disaster risk management: opportunities and limitations to using risk-based Cost-Benefit Analysis. Nat Hazards. https://doi.org/10.1007/s11069-016-2170-y

Mechler R, Schinko T (2016) Identifying the policy space for climate loss and damage. Science 354(6310):290–292

Mechler R et al (2018) Science for loss and damage. Findings and propositions. In: Mechler R, Bouwer L, Schinko T, Surminski S, Linnerooth-Bayer J (eds) Loss and damage from climate change. Concepts, methods and policy options. Springer, Cham, pp 3–37

Mezirow J (1995) Transformation theory in adult learning. In: Welton MR (ed) In defense of the life world. State University of New York Press, Albany, pp 39–70

Mochizuki J, Vitoontus S, Wickramarachchi B, Hochrainer-Stigler S, Williges K, Mechler R, Sovann R (2015) Operationalizing iterative risk management under limited information: fiscal and economic risks due to natural disasters in Cambodia. Int J Risk Sci. 6(4):321–334

Notten P, Rotmans J, van Asselt M, Rothman D (2003) An updated scenario typology. Futures 35(5):423–443

O'Brien K, Pelling M, Patwardhan A, Hallegatte S, Maskrey A, Oki T, Oswald-Spring U, Wilbanks T, Yanda PZ (Lead authors), Mechler R et al (Contributing authors) (2012) Toward a sustainable and resilient future. In: Field CB, Barros V, Stocker TF, Qin D, Dokken DJ, Ebi KL, Mastrandrea MD, Mach KJ, Plattner G-K, Allen SK, Tignor M, Midgley PM (eds) Managing the risks of extreme events and disasters to advance climate change adaptation. A special report of working groups I and II of the intergovernmental panel on climate change (IPCC). Cambridge University Press, Cambridge and New York, pp 437–486

Schinko T, Mechler R and S Hochrainer-Stigler (2018) The Risk and Policy space for Loss and Damage: Integrating Notions of Distributive and Compensatory Justice with Comprehensive Climate Risk Management. In: Mechler R, Bouwer L, Schinko T, Surminski S, Linnerooth-Bayer J (eds) Loss and Damage from Climate Change. Concepts, Methods and Policy Options. Springer, Cham, pp 83–110

Sterman JD (1994) Learning in and about complex systems. Sys Dyn Rev 10(2–3):291–330

Turnheim B, Berkhout F, Geels F, Hof A, McMeekin A, Nykvist B, van Vuuren D (2015) Evaluating sustainability transitions pathways: bridging analytical approaches to address governance challenges. Glob Environ Change 35:239–253

UN (2015) Transforming our world: the 2030 agenda for sustainable development, A/RES/70/1. http://www.refworld.org/docid/57b6e3e44.html

UNFCC-United nations framework convention on climate change (2015) Adoption of the Paris Agreement. Decision FCCC/CP/2015/L.9

Venkateswaran K, MacClune K, Keating A, Szoenyi M (2015) Learning from disasters to build resilience: a simple guide to conducting a post event review. ISET-International & Zurich Insurance Group

Ward P, Jongman B, Sperna F, Weiland A, Bouwman A, van Beek R, Bierkens M, Ligtvoet W, Winsemius H (2013) Assessing flood risk at the global scale: model setup, results, and sensitivity. Environ Res Lett 8:044019

World Bank (2013) World development report 2014. Risk and opportunity. Managing risk for development. World Bank, Washington DC

Zurich Flood Resilience Alliance (2014a) After the storm: how the UK's flood defenses performed during the surge following Xaver. Zurich Insurance Group: Zurich, Switzerland

Zurich Flood Resilience Alliance (2014b) Central European floods 2013: a retrospective. Zurich Insurance Group, Zurich, Switzerland

Zurich Flood Resilience Alliance (2015a) Balkan floods of May 2014: challenges facing flood resilience in a former war zone. Zurich Insurance Group: Zurich, Switzerland

Zurich Flood Resilience Alliance (2015b) Morocco floods of 2014: what we can learn from Guelmim and Sidi Ifni. Zurich Insurance Group: Zurich, Switzerland

Chapter 18
Loss and Damage in the Rapidly Changing Arctic

Mia Landauer and Sirkku Juhola

Abstract Arctic climate change is happening much faster than the global average. Arctic change also has global consequences, in addition to local ones. Scientific evidence shows that meltwater of Arctic sources contributes to sea-level rise significantly while accounting for 35% of current global sea-level rise. Arctic communities have to find ways to deal with rapidly changing environmental conditions that are leading to social impacts such as outmigration, similarly to the global South. International debates on Loss and Damage have not addressed the Arctic so far. We review literature to show what impacts of climate change are already visible in the Arctic, and present local cases in order to provide empirical evidence of losses and damages in the Arctic region. This evidence is particularly well presented in the context of outmigration and relocation of which we highlight examples. The review reveals a need for new governance mechanisms and institutional frameworks to tackle Loss and Damage. Finally, we discuss what implications Arctic losses and damages have for the international debate.

Keywords Arctic · Climate risk · Adaptation · Vulnerability · Indigenous people · Communities · Policy

---

M. Landauer (✉)
Arctic Centre, University of Lapland, Rovaniemi, Finland
e-mail: mia.landauer@ulapland.fi; landauem@iiasa.ac.at

M. Landauer
Risk and Resilience Program and Arctic Futures Initiative, International Institute for Applied Systems Analysis (IIASA), Laxenburg, Austria

S. Juhola
Ecosystems and Environment Research Programme, University of Helsinki, Helsinki, Finland

S. Juhola
Department of Thematic Studies, Linköping University, Linköping, Sweden

S. Juhola
Helsinki Sustainability Science Institute (HELSUS), Helsinki, Finland

R. Mechler et al. (eds.), *Loss and Damage from Climate Change*, Climate Risk Management, Policy and Governance, https://doi.org/10.1007/978-3-319-72026-5_18

18.1 Introduction

Dangerous climate change increases the need for emergency preparedness mechanisms, disaster risk responses, and climate adaptation strategies in case of losses and damages. To avoid dangerous climate change, the United Nations Framework Convention on Climate Change (UNFCCC) has called for action within a

> time frame sufficient to allow ecosystems to adapt naturally to climate change, to ensure that food production is not threatened and to enable economic development to proceed in a sustainable manner (UNFCCC 1992, Article II).

Crowley (2011) has criticised this Article II because it does not consider the international human rights principles when interpreting what "dangerous" climate change means. For example, the ability of ecosystems to recover naturally has already been compromised in many places in the Arctic, and these changes are threatening food security and traditional livelihoods already, especially those of indigenous peoples. Liability and compensation are under debate in international climate policy discussions (Huggel et al. 2015). Financing mechanisms to support adaptation or transformative actions can be provided from local, national, regional and international sources. However, this requires consensus between responsible parties and potential beneficiaries. It is also problematic that losses and damages cannot always be compensated by technical or financial support, if they include, for example, loss of culture and tradition. In these international debates, little attention and support has been given to Arctic vulnerable communities so far. These communities have to find ways to deal with rapidly changing environmental conditions, either by adapting or taking actions that can lead to social impacts similarly to global South, such as outmigration (e.g. Wolsko and Marino 2016).

Arctic climate change is happening much faster than the global average (Arctic Climate Impact Assessment 2005; IPCC 2007; AMAP 2017). According to AMAP (2017: 3), "*The Arctic … has been warming more than twice as rapidly as the world as a whole for the past 50 years*". The Arctic has often been referred to as "the canary in the coalmine" (Chinowsky et al. 2010), "climate hotspot" (Hare et al. 2011), or "harbinger of change" (Carmack et al. 2012). The Arctic represents a place where the impacts of climate change are already visible. Both scientific evidence (e.g., attribution studies and vulnerability analyses of Arctic communities, including the most recent reports of the IPCC) and traditional knowledge (e.g., indigenous discourses and field observations of Arctic residents) indicate that climate change has severe impacts on the Arctic and risks and impacts also have global consequences. Recent scientific evidence shows that meltwater of Arctic sources contributes to sea-level rise significantly while accounting for 35% of current global sea level rise (AMAP 2017).

According to Carmack et al. (2012) examining the Arctic is particularly important for four reasons. First, understanding change in the Arctic may reveal lessons of how change happens in complex systems and improve our understanding how to deal with these. Second, changes already taking place in the Arctic are likely to have irreversible impacts regionally and locally, leading to limited possibilities of communities to adapt, and significant consequences to the global economy as well. Globally, Arctic climate change has been estimated to cost between 9 and 70 trillion U.S. dollars over the period 2010–2100 (AMAP 2017:13). Third, climate change is advancing faster in the Arctic than anywhere else, and finally, responses to climate change through adaptation are manifold, and can be tested in the Arctic in the face of rapidly approaching tipping points.

In this chapter, we examine what "dangerous climate change" means in the Arctic context, by identifying critical risks and impacts in the region in general, and then presenting cases from the literature that are beyond Arctic communities' capacity to adapt, in particular. The examples provide evidence on Arctic regions' need for institutional support to cope with the consequences of climate change, despite being part of developed countries. So far, neither the United Nations Climate Change Conference of the Parties (COP) nor the subsidiary bodies under the UNFCCC have discussed Arctic climate changes in detail (Duyck 2015a, b). Yet, changes already affect Arctic communities, questioning whether they are in fact bearing a "disproportionate or under abnormal burden" (cf. UNFCCC, Article II). Examples of losses and damages more broadly are climate change affecting critical infrastructure and traditional livelihoods (Bronen 2015) as these harms can affect societies across generations (Sejersen 2012; Himes-Cornell and Hoelting 2015). Similar actual and potential losses and damages are under discussion in developing countries too. Their capability to adapt to change or transform their livelihoods to something that still allows them to maintain their land, livelihoods and culture, is critical to affected communities. If this is not possible, and the residents have to leave and abandon their livelihoods, they are faced by Loss and Damage in its "narrow" sense. Thus, we review Arctic studies to understand what losses and damages mean in the Arctic context, what are global consequences of Arctic change, and what implications these changes have for the international Loss and Damage debate.

18.2 Rationale for Including the Arctic in the Loss and Damage Debate

Internationally, the debate on Loss and Damage has predominantly concentrated on discussing the risks and impacts of climate change on developing countries so far. International climate negotiations have been the main arena and as other chapters in this volume show, a consensus on the definition of Loss and Damage is yet to emerge (Mechler and Schinko 2016; see introduction by Mechler et al. 2018; chapter by James et al. 2018). A broad definition in the literature makes a distinction between avoidable, unavoided and unavoidable impacts of climate change, where "irreversibility" refers to 'losses' and "impacts that can be alleviated" refer to 'damages' (see Mechler and Schinko 2016: 290). In essence, this means that Loss and Damage can be narrowly defined as the "residual, adverse impacts of climate change beyond what can be addressed by mitigation and adaptation" (see Huggel et al. 2015: 454). Here, we employ this definition of Loss and Damage related to climate change impacts that are unavoidable.

18.2.1 Little Responsibility of Emissions

On a global scale, Arctic traditional and indigenous lifestyles have hardly contributed to greenhouse gas emissions, although traditional livelihoods of the Arctic communities take place in high-emitting first world countries, and fossil fuels extracted from Arctic regions contribute to global GHGs and serve all countries (Pechsiri et al. 2010). Global mitigation responsibility of all countries, developed countries, emerging economies and developing countries, is not only important to reduce vulnerability of communities of global South but also of the Arctic communities. This has been shown by empirical evidence in the IPCC 4th assessment synthesis report (IPCC 2007).

18.2.2 Identifying the Most Vulnerable by Following Human Rights Principles

From the climate justice point of view (see chapter by Wallimann-Helmer et al. 2018), and as considered by Inuit political leaders (see Ford 2009; Crowley 2011), climate change is primarily a human rights issue because it puts the ecosystem services-based traditional livelihoods at risk, and leads to social and economic impacts in Arctic communities (Maldonado et al. 2013). Marginal livelihoods, especially those located in Arctic coastal areas, face both slow-onset and extreme events that heavily affect critical infrastructure, and cause harm to local and traditional livelihoods (Huggel et al. 2015). Some traditional ways of living, for example, can no longer be practiced due to changes in sea ice conditions (Sejersen 2012; Shearer 2012; Bronen and Chapin III 2013; Bronen 2015). Yet, international roles and responsibilities to deal with Loss and Damage are not clear, and current national level legal frameworks seem not to provide "optimal" solutions to support adaptation of vulnerable Arctic communities—and in fact, even limit adaptation in many ways. According to the International Commission on Intervention and State Sovereignty, nation state governments have the responsibility to enhance protection of vulnerable groups, minorities, and support work to advance human rights (ICISS 2001, cited in Bronen 2015). But still, the UNFCCC Parties are not meeting their international legal obligations under the Article II (see Crowley 2011; chapter by Simlinger and Mayer 2018).

18.2.3 Unequal Distribution of Risks and Limits to Adaptation

In the current Loss and Damage debate of the UNFCCC, the global North is considered to have high responsibility and liability for dealing with climate-related risks affecting vulnerable communities in the South. In general, countries in the global North are considered to have high adaptive capacity, due to national and regional financial and technological resources that should also support sustainable transformation of societies. But as the case in many southern regions too, neither are climate-related risks distributed equally among the population and geographically in the northern circumpolar region, nor do those in need necessarily have access to these resources (Larsen et al. 2014). Also, considering unforeseen future conditions, Arctic ecosystems cannot adapt to climate change naturally, and this hampers the provision of ecosystem services, which provide the basis for traditional livelihoods (White et al. 2007; Larsen et al. 2014). Climate change forces people to make choices and face situations that lead to radical, but not necessarily sustainable transformations of society (Sejersen 2012). Marino (2012) has pointed out that federal, state and local authorities in the US identify today nearly all 200 Alaskan native villages as being "under threat" or "immanent threat" due to erosion and/or flooding. To tackle these kinds of challenges Arctic communities would need decision-making power, access to information and financial resources. One example is relocation actions, which are costly and require careful planning in order to lead to positive outcomes (Lopez-Carr and Marter-Kenyon 2015). Especially Arctic populations in remote locations need institutional and financial support and assistance in adaptation planning (Ford 2009; Dengler et al. 2014) to be able to successfully implement adaptation actions that should end up with positive outcomes—forced or poorly planned relocation actions cannot be considered as such.

18.3 Review of the Impacts of Climate Change and Vulnerability in the Arctic

We conducted a systematic literature review of Arctic scientific studies found mainly in *Scopus* database. Out of 3,473 Arctic studies we found 164 studies addressing issues related to risks and impacts of climate change that relate to losses and damages more broadly. Categories of these can be found in Table 18.1. We could also identify examples that fit the narrow definition of Loss and Damage, while providing examples of climate risks and impacts that are 'beyond adaptation.' Instead of trying to identify all examples that belong to the "narrow" category, we selected examples from the literature that have been found particularly relevant for the global South and developing countries, and are also discussed in the international Loss and Damage debate: relocation and outmigration. For instance, climate-induced migration is explicitly covered in the United Nations Climate Change Convention (UNFCCC) conferences, the Conference of the Parties (COP), and the Executive Committee on the Warsaw International Mechanism on Loss and Damage (WIM), which has a mandate to establish a migration facility.

Based on the literature review, the impacts of climate change can be divided into a number of different types from ecological to socio-cultural and economic, whereby joint impacts can also reinforce each other. For example, there are biophysical impacts when changes in climate affect the biogeochemical cycles in the Arctic and change the prevailing conditions in the region, which in turn affects the ability of Arctic communities to engage in economic, social and cultural activities. Alternatively, there are socio-economic developments that can amplify ecological impacts through new migration patterns or use of natural resources, for example. Impacts can also be described as local, regional or global, with the first two being climate change impacts happening in the Arctic and the third impacts that occur elsewhere but have consequences in the Arctic and vice versa.

Table 18.1 Categories of Arctic studies focusing on risks and impacts of climate change (N=164). Especially the climate-induced relocation and migration studies provide indications of Arctic Loss and Damage

Categories	Number of studies
Dangerous climate change: risks, hazards, disasters, extreme events	13
Infrastructure impacts and costs	6
Climate-induced relocation and migration	18
Vulnerability, resilience, impacts, adaptation	70
Human rights, equity, climate justice, gender issues, generations	8
Research tools and methods: monitoring, assessments, use of traditional knowledge in research	27
Human health impacts	22
Total	**164**

Research on socio-economic impacts has also shown that biophysical changes are impacting anthropogenic activities in the Arctic directly, but also indirectly through increased economic interests, such as in mineral exploitation and other industrial developments, affecting traditional land use and causing pollution. There are number of strands in the impacts and vulnerability literature and many of these categories touch upon the topics included in the international Loss and Damage debate, which we place in seven loosely defined categories (Table 18.1). The classification is based on the main focus of the studies as indicated by title, abstract and keywords. Studies modelling the changes or impacts of climate change focus on the Arctic as a whole. Smaller scale ecological or biological studies tend to be site-specific with varying considerations given to their generalisability across areas. The majority of studies that address socio-economic aspects, either through vulnerability or adaptation, tend to consider a specific community or country. As part of these studies, North American analyses were very well represented whereas there were fewer studies from the Nordic Arctic (Finland, Sweden, Norway) and Siberia (Russia).

Figure 18.1 presents these Arctic studies as a "keyword mining" visualisation made by means of VOSviewer software. The term map is based on a text corpus option to visualise the main topics found in the articles. The figure shows the essential keywords most frequently encountered terms related to Arctic climate impacts and risks topic, extracted from the article titles and abstracts. 83 terms that met the threshold of appearance 10 times were selected. The size of the circles indicates frequencies of keywords. Circle colours indicate close relatedness of the terms (substance-wise). The terms marked with the same colour form a cluster of related terms that can be seen as a topic. Lines express co-occurrence of the terms between the clusters either in the article title, or abstract, or both.

As can be seen from the terms that emerged, much focus has been placed on research into impacts related to infrastructure and vulnerability. Both of these have implications for the debate on Loss and Damage, even though the debate itself has largely been ignored in the context of the Arctic. Studies have centred on identifying the impacts of climate change on Arctic societies in terms of both infrastructure and socio-economic conditions, and their ability to adapt. These analyses can be used to identify to what extent communities are able to adapt or whether they will experience losses and damages arising from impacts that they are not able to adapt to.

18.3.1 Biophysical Impacts

Since the publication of the Fourth Assessment Report of the Intergovernmental Panel on Climate Change (IPCC), it has been recently estimated that the decrease of Arctic sea ice is more rapid than according to previous estimations (Hare et al. 2011) and the Arctic melting will significantly affect sea level rise globally (AMAP 2017). Climate change effects on sea ice-based ecosystems are likely to have significant consequences, including possible extinction of some species (Johannessen and Miles 2011). Another significant long-term trend in the Arctic areas is the thaw of the

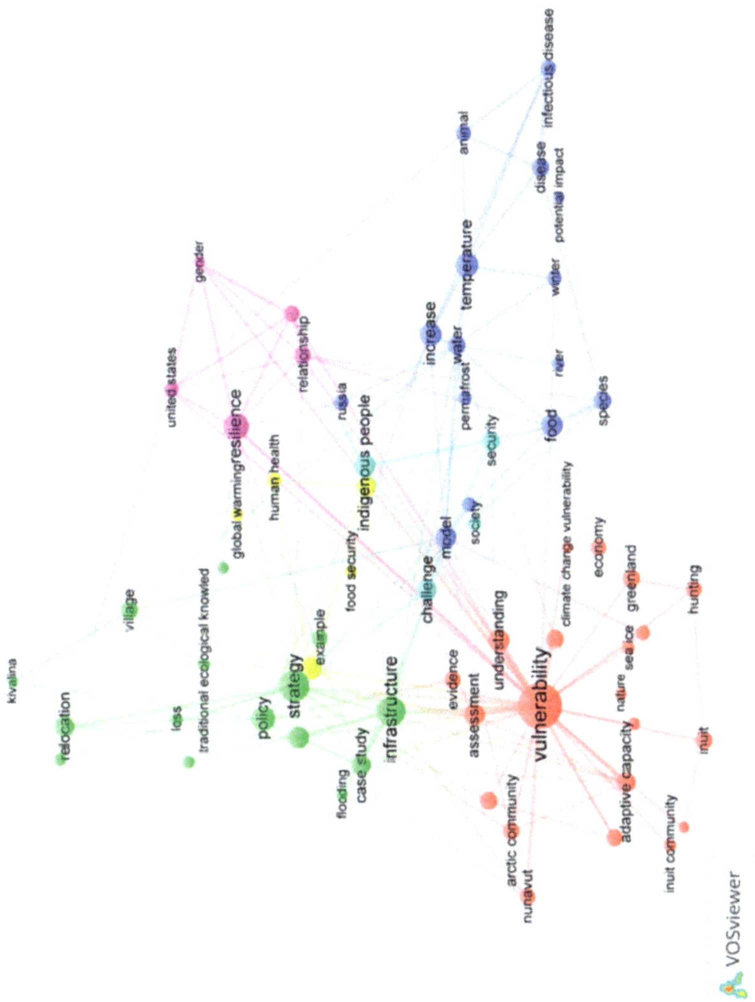

Fig. 18.1 VOSviewer visualisation of Arctic literature sample (N = 164). Created by Maria Söderholm

permafrost, which contributes to the slow release of carbon in the atmosphere (Schuur and Abbott 2011), resulting in global consequences.

It is worth noting that not all biophysical impacts are uniform and that the Arctic covers many different types of landscapes and societies. There is a shift from tundra to continental climate in Alaska, Canada and North-Eastern Russia and a shift from continental to temperate climate in North America: these are examples of a global decrease in cold areas and in Alaska and Siberia, which are on top facing the risk of desertification (Spinoni et al. 2015). Other Arctic areas, such as western Siberia, are facing hydrological risks and permafrost thaw causing floods and mudflows and increasing the risks to industry and urban centres (Zemtsov et al. 2014).

There are slow-onset events, such as tundra decline, tundra shrubification, permafrost thaw, tree line advance, deforestation, loss of palsa mires in Nordic Arctic; the Arctic region is also facing albedo changes and diminishing sea ice, soil and coastal erosion, sea-level rise, and desertification. Further direct impacts are extreme events, such as storms and wildfires, floods, and landslides. It is estimated that increases in precipitation will affect snow events in Alaska and increase the likelihood of avalanches and landslides in the mountainous areas (Hansen et al. 2014). All these biophysical impacts can be disruptive to wildlife and ecosystems, and the provision of ecosystem services, and cause serious damage to people and critical infrastructure also, as well as emergency preparedness systems and monitoring systems (Crowley 2011). They can also cause impacts on (traditional) food and water security (White et al. 2007), but also tourism (Lemelin et al. 2012). Arctic livelihoods and lifestyles are closely connected to the environment, and dependent on the prevailing conditions of ecosystem services. For example, risks associated with loss of sea ice and its consequences on practicing traditional activities, such as seal hunting and ice fishing, are increasing and local communities have to adapt to these changes (Giles et al. 2013), and if adaptation is not possible, try to move away.

18.3.2 Socio-economic Impacts

Further reading of the literature reveals that there are studies that focus on understanding and mapping socio-economic vulnerability of Arctic communities, societies, culture and lifestyles. Among these are studies that approach vulnerability within a specific sector and focus on modeling or providing cost estimates related to climate change impacts and adaptation. We also found several studies indicating health impacts driven by climate change. For example, hydrological cycle changes are an example of emergent changes that cause lack of ice for long periods of time in Russia. This has health consequences because the people cannot access health services and also the "social fabric" is being affected, according to Amstislavski et al. (2013).

The literature also shows evidence of socio-cultural consequences of climate change in the case of relocation and climate-induced migration. These studies indicate that across the Arctic regions, and especially in the coastal areas, climate change increases the vulnerability of local and indigenous communities. It has already led to outmigration ("climigration") and related cultural loss and demographic changes in the region. The interest in studying the Arctic from the perspectives of climate justice, intra- and intergenerational issues has been growing, particularly in terms of relocations and human rights. As outmigration and relocation can have multiple negative consequences, the question remains whether these actions should be considered as adaptation, or whether they are rather 'beyond adaptation,' i.e. related to Loss and Damage given that currently outmigration and relocation are key issues of the international Loss and Damage debate.

18.3.3 Economic Models and Impact Analyses

Economic models and impact studies place emphasis on estimating potential local impacts and costs (or costs and benefits) associated with climate change, mainly in the context of Alaska, although there are some Nordic studies as well. These studies focus on a variety impacts, such as coastal erosion (Radosalvjevic et al. 2015) and temperature changes (Chinowsky et al. 2010). Many of the studies model the impacts on infrastructure, for which the costs of climate change are likely to increase significantly as conditions change (Instanes 2006; Larsen et al. 2008; Hatcher and Forbes 2015). Arctic infrastructure is already tailored to specific conditions and now maintenance and replacement costs under any adaptation scenario is likely to increase about 10% (Chinowsky et al. 2010), so adaptation might technically be possible, but it is too expensive. A number of economic studies estimates potential damages either through modeling or by analysing historical events and its costs. It is argued that there is a continuous need to monitor and develop responses through emergency management (Brunner et al. 2004). Immediate impacts and related costs due to damage on critical public infrastructure have been estimated and modeled with an economic point of view towards losses and damages (e.g. Instanes 2006; Larsen et al. 2008; Ford and Pearce 2010; Chinowsky et al. 2010; Karvetski et al. 2011; Radosavljevic et al. 2015). So, it is very simple to understand that if costs are exceedingly high and financial resources not available, adaptation is not possible; the residual risks and impacts remain 'beyond adaptation,' and thus belong under the narrow definition of Loss and Damage.

18.3.4 Societal Impacts

We also found studies that focus on understanding the socio-economic and cultural vulnerabilities of Arctic communities in-depth. These studies provide a socio-cultural angle on climate impacts, and include non-monetary impacts, such as loss of culture and tradition. These are often case studies of specific communities undertaken with ethnographic methods (e.g. Carothers et al. 2014). Many contributions in this field focus on the role that traditional/indigenous knowledge has played in adaptation of Arctic peoples in the past, yet find that the knowledge now is eroding, and affecting their culture and traditions. We also found a strand of literature that takes a more critical view on conceptualising vulnerability by stressing the historical background, which reinforces current vulnerability and places barriers to adaptation in the future. For example, due to a multitude of changes in the past and currently, traditional knowledge has had to make place for wages, hunting regulations, for example, due to colonialism in the past and due to ongoing industrial developments today (Cameron 2012).

However, studies which take into account traditional knowledge now seem to have gained more importance in research to better understand Arctic change and adaptation to it (e.g. Riedlinger and Berkes 2001; Maynard et al. 2010; Douglas et al. 2014; Cuerrier et al. 2015; Vinyeta and Lynn 2013; Golden et al. 2015). Also, special attention in this literature has been placed on recognising the impacts to indigenous communities and institutional frameworks related to strategies to deal with the impacts, such as community-based adaptation strategies and participatory planning (Tremblay et al. 2008; Hovelsrud and Smit 2010; Pearce et al. 2012; Champalle et al. 2015). As a matter of fact, the resources of indigenous communities to increase adaptive capacity have been diminishing due to reduced possibilities to make decisions and practice traditional ways of living (Roberts and Andrei 2015) and consequently, studies on outmigration (or "climigration") and (forced) relocations have started to emerge (Table 1).

The focus on vulnerability due to climate impacts has indeed drawn some critique for its narrow view. Many studies are considered to ignore the colonial legacy in the Arctic and its effects in terms of inducing social change with negative implications (Cameron 2012; Whyte 2016). So, there are also new social, political and economic settings emerging and "blocking" the traditional ways to adapt to changes, as traditional livelihoods are now being regulated from "outside," such as changes in governance of resource use, land use, and land ownership. It has been proposed that more public participation, co-management and self-governance of local communities is needed in decision-making and planning, and new (participatory) governance mechanisms to tackle the transformation of the Arctic region (Nuttal 2007; Bronen and Chapin III 2013). Ford et al. (2007) have argued that without financial support provided by larger-scale actors, such as the UNFCCC, for example Inuit communities and regions cannot successfully adapt. Indigenous peoples often have limited decision-making power, and both environmental and social changes are more rapid than they have been before. Integrated understanding of science, people, and cross-scale information networks to increase Arctic resilience is needed to respond to the rapid changes (Carmack et al. 2012) and identify what remains beyond adaptation, i.e. Loss and Damage, and why.

In summary, this reviewed literature shows that many kinds of risks and impacts on societies can already be seen in the Arctic, and some of them fall under the "narrow" category of Loss and Damage, in the literature typically defined as the "residual, adverse impacts of climate change beyond what is addressed by mitigation and adaptation" (see Huggel et al. 2015: 454). Climatic changes affect societies that are already much more vulnerable than the general population in these developed countries. Arctic societies need to find options to tackle drivers of environmental, economic, social and cultural transformation, but at the same time they also have to find ways to deal with the residual losses and damages that are 'beyond adaptation' to climate change. In the next section we delve deeper into these ways by providing examples.

18.4 Loss and Damage in the Context of the Arctic

Throughout the history, Arctic ecosystems and dependent local and indigenous communities with varying needs, perceptions and values, have been adapting to climate variability. However, due to rapid climate change and global change, limits to adaptation have started to emerge. The Arctic literature show limits to adaptation due to institutional, political, organisational and jurisdictional factors hindering implementation of adaptation to climate impacts, leading to Loss and Damage. The threshold of adaptation also depends on current socio-economic, cultural and political settings. A schematic depiction is shown in Fig. 18.2. The Arctic examples of relocation and migration show very well that due to negative societal and cultural impacts related to these actions, they can be considered as being 'beyond adaptation,' i.e. Loss and Damage.

Inadequate institutional and financial frameworks to deal with Loss and Damage are considered to imply important challenges (Lopez-Carr and Marten-Kenyon 2015). This becomes clear throughout the Arctic examples, albeit mainly from North America (Alaska) that highlight the need for new governance mechanisms and institutional frameworks to tackle climate change. One problem is, that sometimes not all types of impacts are included in jurisdictional frameworks. For example, in case of (climate change related) disaster mitigation, Bronen and Chapin III (2013) think that one factor considering gaps in post-disaster and hazard mitigation statutory framework is erosion. Even though it is one of the most significant climate change related hazards in the region, it is not included in the official lists of major disasters, such as in the Stafford Act in the US. Shearer (2012) studied climate adaptation assistance in Kivalina, Alaska and found that indigenous communities face intra-national inequalities while not receiving adaptation assistance, which is only available to formal state actors. Another problem is insufficient allocation and availability of financial resources. Bronen and Chapin III (2013) also found that resources are allocated for rebuilding homes as part of the post-disaster recovery measures only in their current location, not in a new location. This creates a problem if the land is lost for good, such as in the case of coastal erosion or sea level rise (see also Bronen 2015). Full integration of hazard mitigation planning into comprehensive risk assessments is considered expensive, and time intensive. Also, allocation of funding is based on cost-benefit ratios which means that for example Alaskan communities, such as in Newtok cannot compete for hazard mitigation funds due to their remote location and low population density, which equals to high costs and low benefits (Bronen and Chapin III 2013). These kinds of barriers (more examples in Table 18.2) represent drivers of Loss and Damage because they hinder implementation of adaptation.

They act as limits to adaptation and can thus lead to Loss and Damage because they prevent communities from taking action. Interpreted in this way, Loss and Damage can arise not only from climate impacts per se, but also from the socio-economic constraints that hinder adaptation of local communities.

In the next subsection, we present examples of relocation and outmigration in the Arctic showing examples when adaptation in situ is not possible and leads to (forced) relocation and outmigration and can cause societal and cultural Loss and Damage. These examples provide evidence that with insufficient institutional, organisational and jurisdictional support relocation and migration actions cannot be considered as adaptation.

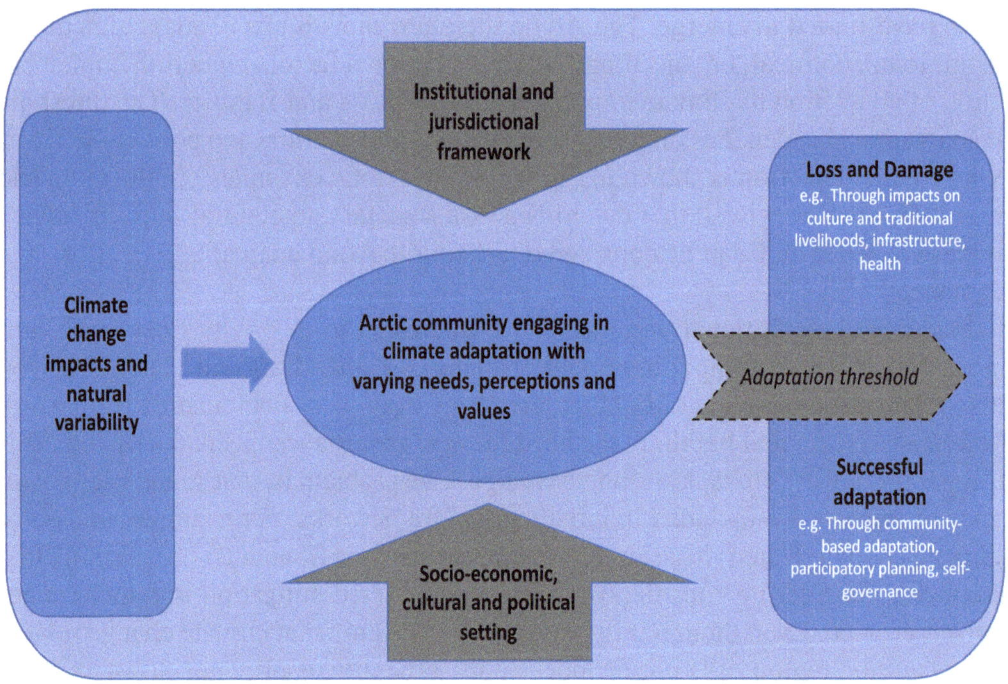

Fig. 18.2 Institutional and jurisdictional framework, as well as socio-economic, cultural and political settings affect adaptation threshold of Arctic communities, and can be drivers of Loss and Damage

Table 18.2 Examples limiting Arctic communities to adapt to climate change

Examples preventing adaptation or leading to negative consequences of adaptation actions	Author (publication year)
Inadequate institutional and financing mechanisms such as federal funding procedures for disaster prevention and recovery	Bronen (2015)
Disabilities to determine and evaluate when preventive actions needed	Bronen (2015)
Slow implementation of actions or statutory and institutional barriers in implementation	Bronen (2015)
Lacking governance framework for the evaluation of risks and impacts	Bronen (2015)
Government funding does not reach Arctic communities	Lopez-Carr and Marten-Kenyon (2015)
Inequity and injustice related to current actions	Kingston and Marino (2010)
Mis- and under-representation of local voices in political arenas	Marino (2012)
Lack of adaptation assistance when only available for formal state actors	Shearer (2012)
Inadequate accommodation of climate change scenarios into disaster risk protocols	Marino (2012)
Unclear responsibilities of government or lacking government body to implement actions	Shearer (2012)
Lack of preventive disaster programs and funds	Shearer (2012)
Missing international support regarding capacity building for adaptation actions	Marino (2012), Shearer (2012)
Traditional and indigenous knowledge not considered in planning actions	Shearer (2012)
Lacking networks of multiple and diverse organisations to build adaptive capacity and balance between different interest groups	Bronen (2015)
Migration strategies not considered in disaster risk reduction and adaptation programs	Dengler et al. (2014)
Difficulties to monetise loss of health and social cohesion	Dengler et al. (2014)
Unclear or inadequate allocation of funding for disaster mitigation (for example, erosion not included, although it can be one of the most significant hazards in some regions)	Bronen and Chapin III (2013)
Full integration of hazard mitigation planning into comprehensive risk assessments is considered too expensive and time intensive	Bronen and Chapin III (2013)
Allocation of funding often based on cost-benefit ratios which leaves out remote communities with low population densities (seen as high costs and low benefits)	Bronen and Chapin III (2013)

18.4.1 Relocation and Outmigration as Adaptation or Part of Loss and Damage?

At the moment, it is yet unclear to whether relocation is considered to be an adaptation measure and thus it would be integrated in states' adaptation strategies, or whether it is something that needs to be undertaken separately when impacts are beyond adaptation, i.e. part of the Loss and Damage agenda. As can be seen from above, many Arctic regions are highly vulnerable to climate change and there are places where adaptation is not possible for local communities. However, they are forced to abandon their livelihoods and traditional residential areas due to increased risks and lack of governance mechanisms and resources to manage risks. Bronen (2015) argues that nation states are required to protect vulnerable populations from climate change impacts within its jurisdiction. But the literature reveals that nation states have often failed to do so: relocation is considered a massive challenge for governments. Our review shows that both perspectives on relocation can be found in the literature. Relocations due to colonisation and natural disasters have been experienced in the Arctic throughout the history, but now climate change also plays a more intense role as a driver of relocations and outmigration. Several studies have found that independent of the drivers of change, relocations will have effects on culture, and maintenance of tradition. We illustrate the challenges of relocation by presenting an example from the Alaskan village *Kivalina*, see Box 18.1.

Similar issues have been experienced in the other Alaskan regions *King Island* and *Shishmaref,* that are also at risk of climate change and need to consider relocation. Relocation can also lead to a sense of loss of place and have emotional impacts as found in the study based on King Islanders' experiences (Kingston and Marino 2010). In the case of Shishmaref, Marino (2012) found that colonial history and historical inequity is linked to contemporary exposure to hazards and vulnerability of climate change. The author also identified mis- and under-representation of local voices in political arenas to discuss relocation planning. According to Bronen (2015), permanent relocation can be considered as one adaptation strategy only if culture and traditions can be secured in the long-term, so the implementation of it requires new governance tools. Currently existing institutional mechanisms are often considered inadequate and unable to determine when preventive relocation is needed and how it should be organised (Bronen 2015; see Box 18.1). Some disaster risk reduction and adaptation programs do not necessarily consider migration strategies at all (Dengler et al. 2014). Given that it appears that existing mechanisms, i.e. adaptation, is insufficient, one could label this as part of Loss and Damage.

Box 18.1 Why is community relocation so challenging: Example from Kivalina, Alaska

Kivalina is a village in the Northwest Arctic Borough in Alaska, the United States. It has about 400 inhabitants (mostly Inupiats) that are now being forced to relocate due to risks of rising sea levels and coastal erosion and also impacts of permafrost thaw and heavy snowstorms (Gregg 2010; Washington Post 2015; NOAA 2017).

The village has been planning relocations for 20 years already, detailed in the Kivalina Relocation Master Plan published in 2006. Despite this, potential relocation options have not been considered suitable, due to high costs, social and cultural objections or because the sites under discussion are geotechnically inappropriate (Gregg 2010). Efforts to respond to climate impacts through adaptation have been made: such as building a rock revetment to postpone the relocation in 2010. The decision on relocation is to be made in the upcoming decade (NOAA 2017). Difficulties in financing relocation is a common problem. In Kivalina, relocation has been estimated to cost between 95 and 125 million US dollars (IAW 2009 cited in Lynn and Donoghue 2011).

The Alaskan ecosystem services-based communities have been able to adapt to changing conditions in the past, but institutional, financial and political barriers have hindered local communities to participate in decision-making—examples of these are lacking government agency in charge of relocation, and funding allocated to disasters (e.g. for rebuilding) but not for relocation (ADN 2016).

Forced relocation can lead to cultural damage, such as loss of traditional livelihoods (Lynn and Donoghue 2011). It is hard to put a price to cultural loss, but efforts have been made to maintain the culture and traditions of Kivalina residents, despite relocation. This is done, for example, by creating projects that enable the communities to share thoughts about local ways of life and locate, connect and educate new relocation partners and networking with global community to shape the discourse on climate displacement (see: www.relocate-ak.org).

Fig. 18.3 Risk and Indigenous Peoples in Alaska

In the following examples from the literature, insufficient allocation of funding is driving Loss and Damage. Lopez-Carr and Marten-Kenyon (2015) studied management of climate-induced resettlements in the United States' territory of the Arctic and found that although governments have spent considerable amounts of money on erosion control nationally, funding has not reached the Arctic communities. Also in the case of Kivalina, financing coastal erosion protection has failed, and at the same time tens of thousands of people in Alaska's native villages are under threat due to damages to water supply and waste-storage systems that affect food and water security (ibid.). Whether the discussion is about climate refugees or climate migrants, there is a need for an effective institutional framework to reduce bureaucracy to allocate resources, access funding and provide technical assistance at the community level (Dengler et al. 2014).

In countries like the United States, governments have resources for disaster preparedness, insurance payouts and infrastructure repairs, but there is no governance framework to evaluate climate change risks and impacts and the needs for relocation actions (Bronen 2015). Dengler et al. (2014) state that lacking access to finance creates one of the main constraints for communities to take action and leads to inability to take lead on disaster risk responses. For example, building of new infrastructure, which is considered very costly especially in remote locations such as in the Arctic, is difficult. Sometimes resources are being allocated to technical solutions rather than solutions where potential and obstacles for organised relocation, and other measures are considered more holistically and sustainably, as revealed by the literature review.

Other challenges are the difficulties to monetise loss of health or social cohesion, and excluding indigenous knowledge in planning of disaster risk and adaptation schemes. Furthermore, inequity and injustice in climate risk governance characterise Loss and Damage from climate change. This is already known from developing countries experience (see chapters by Wallimann-Helmer and Serdeczny 2018).

18.5 Concluding Remarks

In this chapter, we reviewed the Arctic risk, vulnerability and impacts literature in order to find evidence that losses and damages are distributed across very different geographical areas and affect vulnerable communities in the Arctic as well. The role of the Arctic has changed due to climate change: enormous resources have become available and land and sea transport has become easier due to less ice and snow, and better technology to access the areas and natural resources (oil and gas, and minerals, for instance). The Arctic has become a common good, serving various needs of the global community. But Arctic indigenous communities are among the least responsible for climate change and they are facing harm caused by economic developments, those that are mainly driven by climate change directly, and indirectly by easier access to natural resources at the same time, leading to environmental and social impacts (Maldonado et al. 2013).

Why should we include the Arctic region in the Loss and Damage debate? One answer is that if socio-economic indicators were compared between Inuit regions and Small Island Developing States, also many of the Inuit regions would be considered as "developing" regions and should gain assistance from the UNFCCC for instance in form of an international fund (Ford 2009). In Kivalina, Alaska, the communities are considered as first victims of climate change, facing also migration pressures and displacement, which can lead to political instability, and cultural loss, similar to examples from developing regions such as the Maldives (Wolsko and Marino 2016). Because of direct impacts and relocations, other, indirect impacts have increased, such as post-traumatic disorders affecting health and wellbeing. Even though the people can survive disasters by relocation, there are still differences between individuals regarding how well, if at all, they can adapt, due to differences in health, cultural integrity and sense of place (ibid.) Although sometimes seen as an adaptation strategy, outmigration has caused problems because young generations are "pushed" away from their land, and traditional livelihoods are eroding (Himes-Cornel and Hoelting 2015). In other cases, such as shown in Newtok, Alaska, relocation planning has been going on for so long that one generation has experienced it, but still it has not lead to implementation of relocation actions (Bronen and Chapin III 2013). The case of Kivalina shows clearly that, although the community is located within a developed country, it is vulnerable, but it is not getting the assistance it would need from the state and internationally. There are examples showing that, once relocated, there is no turning back. This is when the land has been literally lost due to sea level rise, for example.

As found in many local studies from the Arctic, the current institutional and financial frameworks are insufficient to tackle the consequences of climate risks and impacts, leading to Loss and Damage. Furthermore, inclusion of local communities in planning and decision-making is lacking (Marino 2012; Lopez-Carr and Marten-Kenyon 2015). It is also problematic that indigenous communities are not always considered as part of nation states and thus, do not enjoy the same rights as the general population, which raises questions around ethical aspects (see Huggel et al. 2015). We found several legitimacy and justice issues that support our argument that Arctic Loss and Damage should be discussed in the international climate policy arena. This includes (re-) interpretation of human rights principles, identification of roles and responsibilities, liability, and compensation mechanisms, as well as a need for international institutional support to reduce limits to adaptation. There is a lack of a proper international institutional framework and lack of local capacity to organise relocation (e.g. Dengler et al. 2014; Maldonado et al. 2013). On the other hand, forced relocation is one consequence of weak risk governance mechanisms, but relocations represent actions that could be supported nationally and internationally to respond to climate risks if guided by international actors and implemented by Arctic communities themselves, who have the local knowledge to reduce negative consequences to culture and society.

Lack of financial resources is one of the main factors why relocation or building new infrastructure cannot be implemented. The costs of relocation or rebuilding and new technology in the Arctic are very high considering the remote location and other construction-related difficulties. Furthermore, some indigenous communities do not even have cash economies. Although economic losses have been calculated for Arctic villages and cities, and adaptive climate cost models have been created (e.g. Chinowski et al. 2010) regarding damages to physical assets such as infrastructure (e.g. Larsen et al. 2008; Chinowsky et al. 2010), more information on costs of relocations, health impacts and especially non-economic losses is needed (Roberts and Andrei 2015). In addition to financial and technical issues the remaining question is social justice: how to maintain viability of the communities and how viability is actually perceived by different communities (Sejersen 2012).

According to Duyck (2015a, b), the UNFCCC has not yet considered Arctic vulnerability issues in the international debate on Loss and Damage, and this was still the case in 2018. Thus, the responsibility of Arctic states themselves should be clarified: they should make sure the voices of Arctic vulnerable communities will be heard and communicated in international climate policy negotiations. Also, Arctic States and the Arctic Council should clarify and improve their national communications and the statements from ministers at UNFCCC deliberations. So far, Arctic states have not sufficiently considered Arctic Loss and Damage issues, and the Arctic Council has not been represented sufficiently in the Arctic states' documents and statements presented to international bodies (ibid.).

Based on the empirical evidence of Arctic literature, we consider that the international Loss and Damage debate should include the Arctic as an example when considering what "vulnerable" and "dangerous climate change" means and what should be taken into account when trying to reduce vulnerability. For example, non-economic losses and ways to measure these are also relevant to the Arctic, such as loss of sense of place and belonging (Roberts and Andrei 2015), and loss of culture and traditions, but they are not adequately considered in the current international Loss and Damage debate. If the international human rights principles lense were to be used to define the vulnerable, then violations of these rights regarding Arctic indigenous communities would be evident, based on the results of our literature review. More in-depth local level studies are needed to examine in detail what is perceived as "dangerous climate change". According to Sejersen (2012), the ways Arctic societies perceive transformations in society and seek for opportunities to adapt to change are very heterogeneous; this is owing, among others, to different histories of colonialism or different types of livelihoods practiced in the Arctic, but also due to different values and perceptions, as well as cultural backgrounds.

Under the conditions of rapid change in the Arctic, current institutions and government mechanisms are not found sufficient to deal with these multiple challenges and dynamics of change: climate change, deterioration of environment, pressure of new industries and businesses entering the Arctic region, and intra- and inter-generational changes for example when outmigration causes unbalanced age and gender populations in remaining communities. Furthermore, the climate refugee problem can first be seen locally (local responsibility to tackle with), but it will have international consequences (global responsibility) and needs international attention and rethinking of relocation policies.

It has been argued that in order to understand limits to adaptation, the traditional instrumental and management-oriented view of adaptation in social systems should be revisited (Sejersen 2012). Nowadays, climate change is used as a platform to address issues of justice, development and self-determination, which are issues already known from the past, where, however, scales, causations, and agency differed as pointed out by Sejersen (2012). In case of adaptation (whether due to climate change or other changes), the focus is on moving from "how to adapt", to "who to become" when adapting (ibid:195). One question should be added to this list: what happens 'beyond adaptation'? But what these changes and impacts of climate change in the Arctic mean globally is still unknown to many. What we know is that more knowledge and resources to deal with climate change impacts faced by vulnerable communities is needed and learning from the Arctic could be a forerunner case for the international debate on Loss and Damage.

Acknowledgements We would like to thank Information Specialist M.Sc. Maria Söderholm from Aalto University (Finland) for her support in the main data collection procedure for the systematic literature review, and Library Manager Dr. Michaela Rossini from IIASA (Austria) for additional support in data collection.

References

ADN (Alaska Dispatch Publishing) (2016) Behind Obama's $400 million budget request to relocate entire Alaska villages. https://www.adn.com/rural-alaska/article/behind-obamas-400-million-budget-request-relocate-entire-alaska-villages/2016/02/10/. Accessed 30 July 2018

AMAP (2017) Snow, water, ice and permafrost in the Arctic. Summary for policy-makers. Arctic Monitoring and Assessment Programme (AMAP) report. https://www.amap.no/documents/doc/Snow-Water-Ice-and-Permafrost.-Summary-for-Policy-makers/1532. Accessed 30 July 2018

Amstislavski P et al (2013) Effects of increase in temperature and open water on transmigration and access to health care by the Nenets reindeer herders in northern Russia. Int J Circumpolar Health 72(1):21183

Arctic Climate Impact Assessment (2005) Arctic climate impact assessment scientific report. Cambridge University Press, Cambridge. http://amap.no/acia/. Accessed 30 July 2018

Bronen R (2015) Climate-induced community relocations: using integrated social-ecological assessments to foster adaptation and resilience. Ecol Soc 20(3):36

Bronen R, Chapin FS (2013) Adaptive governance and institutional strategies for climate-induced community relocations in Alaska. Proc Natl Acad Sci 110(23):9320–9325

Brunner RD et al (2004) An Arctic disaster and its policy implications. Arctic 57(4):336–346

Cameron ES (2012) Securing Indigenous politics: a critique of the vulnerability and adaptation approach to the human dimensions of climate change in the Canadian Arctic. Glob Environ Change 22(1):103–114

Carmack E et al (2012) Detecting and coping with disruptive shocks in Arctic marine systems: a resilience approach to place and people. Ambio 41(1):56–65

Carothers C et al (2014) Measuring perceptions of climate change in northern Alaska: pairing ethnography with cultural consensus analysis. Ecol Soc 19(4):27

Champalle C et al (2015) Prioritizing climate change adaptations in Canadian Arctic communities. Sustainability 7(7):9268–9292

Chinowsky PS et al (2010) Adaptive climate response cost models for infrastructure. J Infrastruct Sys 16(3):173–180

Crowley P (2011) Interpreting 'dangerous' in the United Nations framework convention on climate change and the human rights of Inuit. Reg Environ Change 11(1):265–274

Cuerrier A et al (2015) The study of Inuit knowledge of climate change in Nunavik, Quebec: a mixed methods approach. Human Ecology 43(3):379–394

Dengler S et al (2014) Climate refugees in a developed country: the case of Newtok, Alaska. In: Proceedings of the 5th international disaster and risk conference: Integrative risk management—the role of science, technology and practice, IDRC Davos 2014, pp 167–170

Duyck S (2015a) The Arctic voice at the UN climate negotiations: interplay between Arctic & climate governance. http://hdl.handle.net/1946/21031. Accessed 30 July 2018

Duyck S (2015b) What role for the Arctic in the UN Paris climate conference (COP-21)? In: Heininen L et al (eds) Arctic Yearbook 2015. https://www.joomag.com/magazine/arctic-yearbook-2015/0357456001446028961?short. Accessed 30 July 2018

Douglas V et al (2014) Reconciling traditional knowledge, food security, and climate change: Experience from Old Crow, YT, Canada. Progr Community Health Partnerships: Res Educ Action 8(1):21–27

Ford JD (2009) Dangerous climate change and the importance of adaptation for the Arctic's Inuit population. Environ Res Lett 4(2):024006

Ford J et al (2007) Reducing vulnerability to climate change in the Arctic: the case of Nunavut. Canada. Arctic 60(2):150–166

Ford JD, Pearce T (2010) What we know, do not know, and need to know about climate change vulnerability in the western Canadian Arctic: a systematic literature review. Environ Res Lett 5(1):014008

Giles AR et al (2013) Adaptation to aquatic risks due to climate change in Pangnirtung, Nunavut. Arctic 66(2):207–217

Golden DM et al (2015) "Blue-ice": framing climate change and reframing climate change adaptation from the indigenous peoples' perspective in the northern boreal forest of Ontario, Canada. Clim Develop 7(5):401–413

Gregg RM (2010) Relocating the village of Kivalina, Alaska due to coastal erosion. http://www.cakex.org/case-studies/relocating-village-kivalina-alaska-due-coastal-erosion. Accessed 30 July 2018

Hansen BB et al (2014) Warmer and wetter winters: characteristics and implications of an extreme weather event in the High Arctic. Environ Res Lett 9(11):114021

Hare WL et al (2011) Climate hotspots: key vulnerable regions, climate change and limits to warming. Reg Environ Change 11(1):1–13

Hatcher SV, Forbes DL (2015) Exposure to coastal hazards in a rapidly expanding Northern Urban Centre, Iqaluit, Nunavut. Arctic 68(4):453–471

Himes-Cornell A, Hoelting K (2015) Resilience strategies in the face of short-and long-term change: Out-migration and fisheries regulation in Alaskan fishing communities. Ecol Soc 20(2):9

Hovelsrud GK, Smit B (2010) Community adaptation and vulnerability in Arctic regions. Springer, Cham, p 353

Huggel C et al (2015) Potential and limitations of the attribution of climate change impacts for informing loss and damage discussions and policies. Clim Change 133(3):453–467

ICISS [International Commission on Intervention and State Sovereignty] (2001) The responsibility to protect. International Development Research Centre, Ottawa, Canada. http://responsibilitytoprotect.org/ICISS%20Report.pdf. Accessed 30 July 2018

Instanes A (2006) Impacts of a changing climate on infrastructure: buildings, support systems, and industrial facilities. In: 2006 IEEE EIC climate change conference May 2016. IEEE, pp 1–4

IPCC (2007) Climate change 2007: synthesis report. In: Core Writing Team, Pachauri RK, Reisinger A (eds) Contribution of working groups I, II and III to the fourth assessment report of the Intergovernmental Panel on Climate Change. IPCC, Geneva, Switzerland, 104 pp

James RA, Jones RG, Boyd E, Young HR, Otto FEL, Huggel C, Fuglestvedt JS (2018) Attribution: how is it relevant for loss and damage policy and practice? In: Mechler R, Bouwer L, Schinko T,

Surminski S, Linnerooth-Bayer J (eds) Loss and damage from climate change. Concepts, methods and policy options. Springer, Cham, pp 113–154

Johannessen OM, Miles MW (2011) Critical vulnerabilities of marine and sea ice–based ecosystems in the high Arctic. Reg Environ Change 11(1):239–248

Karvetski CW et al (2011) Climate change scenarios: risk and impact analysis for Alaska coastal infrastructure. Int J Risk Assess Manag 15(2–3):258–274

Kingston D, Marino E (2010) Twice removed: King Islanders' experience of "community" through two relocations. Human Organ 69(2):119–128

Larsen PH et al (2008) Estimating future costs for Alaska public infrastructure at risk from climate change. Glob Environ Change 18(3):442–457

Larsen JN et al (2014) Polar regions. In: Barros VR et al (eds) Climate change 2014: impacts, adaptation, and vulnerability. Part B: regional aspects. contribution of working group II to the fifth assessment report of the Intergovernmental Panel on Climate Change. Cambridge University Press, Cambridge, United Kingdom and New York, NY, USA, pp 1567–1612

Lemelin RH et al (2012). Résilience, appartenance et tourisme à Nain, Nunatsiavut. Études/Inuit/Studies, pp 35–58

López-Carr D, Marter-Kenyon J (2015) Human adaptation: manage climate-induced resettlement. Nature 517(7534):265–267

Lynn K, Donoghue A (2011) Climate change: realities of relocation for Alaska native villages. http://tribalclimate.uoregon.edu/files/2010/11/AlaskaRelocation_04-13-11.pdf. Accessed 30 July 2018

Maldonado JK et al (2013) The impact of climate change on tribal communities in the US: displacement, relocation, and human rights. Clim Change 120(3):601–614

Marino E (2012) The long history of environmental migration: assessing vulnerability construction and obstacles to successful relocation in Shishmaref, Alaska. Global Environ Change 22(2):374–381

Maynard NG et al (2010) Impacts of Arctic climate and land use changes on reindeer pastoralism: indigenous knowledge and remote sensing. Eurasian Arctic land cover and land use in a changing climate. Springer, Netherlands, pp 177–205

Mechler R, Schinko T (2016) Identifying the policy space for climate loss and damage. Science 354(6310):290–292

Mechler R et al (2018) Science for loss and damage. Findings and propositions. In: Mechler R, Bouwer L, Schinko T, Surminski S, Linnerooth-Bayer J (eds) Loss and damage from climate change. Concepts, methods and policy options. Springer, Cham, pp 3–37

NOAA (2017) US Climate Resilience Toolkit. https://toolkit.climate.gov/case-studies/relocating-kivalina. Accessed 30 July 2018

Nuttall M (2007) An environment at risk: Arctic indigenous peoples, local livelihoods and climate change. In: Arctic alpine ecosystems and people in a changing environment. Springer, Berlin, Heidelberg, pp 19–35

Pearce et al (2012) Climate change adaptation planning in remote, resource-dependent communities: an Arctic example. Reg Environ Change 12(4):825–837

Pechsiri JS et al (2010) A review of the climate-change-impacts' rates of change in the Arctic. J Environ Protect 1(01):59

Radosavljevic B et al (2015) Erosion and flooding—threats to coastal infrastructure in the Arctic: a case study from Herschel Island, Yukon Territory, Canada. Estuaries and Coasts 1–16

Riedlinger D, Berkes F (2001) Contributions of traditional knowledge to understanding climate change in the Canadian Arctic. Polar Record 37(203):315–328

Roberts E, Andrei S (2015) The rising tide: migration as a response to loss and damage from sea level rise in vulnerable communities. Int J Global Warming 8(2):258–273

Schuur EA, Abbott B (2011) Climate change: high risk of permafrost thaw. Nature 480(7375):32–33

Sejersen F (2012) Mobility, climate change, and social dynamics in the Arctic: the creation of new horizons of expectation and the role of community. Climate change and human mobility: global challenges to the social sciences. Cambridge University Press, Cambridge, UK, pp 190–213

Serdeczny O (2018) Non-economic loss and damage and the Warsaw International Mechanism. In: Mechler R, Bouwer L, Schinko T, Surminski S, Linnerooth-Bayer J (eds) Loss and damage from climate change. Concepts, methods and policy options. Springer, Cham, pp 205–220
Shearer C (2012) The political ecology of climate adaptation assistance: Alaska Natives, displacement, and relocation. J Political Ecol 19:174–183
Simlinger F, Mayer B (2018) Legal responses to climate change induced loss and damage. In: Mechler R, Bouwer L, Schinko T, Surminski S, Linnerooth-Bayer J (eds) Loss and damage from climate change. Concepts, methods and policy options. Springer, Cham, pp 179–203
Spinoni J et al (2015) Towards identifying areas at climatological risk of desertification using the Köppen-Geiger classification and FAO aridity index. Int J Climatol 35(9):2210–2222
Tremblay M et al (2008) Climate change in northern Quebec: Adaptation strategies from community-based research. Arctic, pp 27–34
UNFCCC (1992) United Nations framework convention on climate change. https://unfccc.int/resource/docs/convkp/conveng.pdf. Accessed 30 July 2018
Vinyeta K, Lynn K (2013) Exploring the role of traditional ecological knowledge in climate change initiatives. General Technical Report PNW-GTR-879. May 2013. United States Department of Agriculture. Forest Service. Pacific Northwest Research Station. http://www.fs.fed.us/pnw/pubs/pnw_gtr879.pdf. Accessed 30 July 2018
Wallimann-Helmer I, Meyer L, Mintz-Woo K, Schinko T, Serdeczny O (2018) Ethical challenges in the context of climate loss and damage. In: Mechler R, Bouwer L, Schinko T, Surminski S, Linnerooth-Bayer J (eds) Loss and damage from climate change. Concepts, methods and policy options. Springer, Cham, pp 39–62
Washington Post (2015) The remote Alaskan village that needs to be relocated due to climate change. https://www.washingtonpost.com/news/energy-environment/wp/2015/02/24/the-remote-alaskan-village-that-needs-to-be-relocated-due-to-climate-change/?utm_term=.b673a18e47a4. Accessed 30 July 2018
White DM et al (2007) Food and water security in a changing Arctic climate. Environ Res Lett 2(4):045018
Whyte K (2016) Indigenous peoples, climate change loss and damage, and the responsibility of settler states. Climate change loss and damage, and the responsibility of settler states (April 25, 2016). http://papers.ssrn.com/sol3/papers.cfm?abstract_id=2770085. Accessed 30 July 2018
Wolsko C, Marino E (2016) Disasters, migrations, and the unintended consequences of urbanization: what's the harm in getting out of harm's way? Popul Environ 37(4):411–428
Zemtsov VA et al (2014) Hydrological risks in Western Siberia under the changing climate and anthropogenic influences conditions. Int J Environ Stud 71(5):611–617

Part V
Policy Options and Other Response Mechanisms for the L&D Discourse

Chapter 19
Towards Establishing a National Mechanism to Address Losses and Damages: A Case Study from Bangladesh

Masroora Haque, Mousumi Pervin, Saibeen Sultana and Saleemul Huq

Abstract This chapter presents a case study of setting up a national mechanism to address losses and damages in Bangladesh—a highly climate vulnerable country facing significant losses and damages, putting its domestic resources and expertise together to respond in a way that looks ahead and beyond the conventional responses to climate change. The efforts underway to establish the national mechanism build upon existing institutions and frameworks and are an example of collaboration across ministries, and a break-away from working in silos. The proposed mechanism is an attempt to embed climate change perspectives into disaster policymaking, to address the gaps in the current policy framework and to design a comprehensive system to for a stronger response to losses and damages from climate impacts. A national mechanism to address losses and damages not only responds to the needs within the country, it also reaffirms Bangladesh's commitment to the national targets and indicators within the Sendai Framework for Disaster Risk Reduction 2015–2030. Furthermore, the functions of the national mechanism replicate the work areas of the

M. Haque (✉) · S. Huq
International Centre for Climate Change and Development (ICCAD), Dhaka, Bangladesh
e-mail: masroora.haque@icccad.net

M. Pervin
United Nations Development Programme, New York, USA

S. Sultana
Bangladesh Climate Change Trust, Dhaka, Bangladesh

R. Mechler et al. (eds.), *Loss and Damage from Climate Change*, Climate Risk Management, Policy and Governance, https://doi.org/10.1007/978-3-319-72026-5_19

WIM, signalling Bangladesh's commitments to the Paris Agreement. For a resource constrained LDC country, the efforts made by researchers, the development community and policymakers show resourcefulness, proactiveness and agency that can be replicated in countries facing similar vulnerabilities and resource constraints.

Keywords Loss and Damage · Sea level rise · Cyclones · Flooding · National policy · Disaster risk reduction · Adaptation · Technical committee

19.1 Introduction

Despite being heavily impacted by climate change, Bangladesh has made laudable strides in enacting laws, policies and procedures to deal with climate related hazards. The geographically small nation has been historically prone to heavy rainfall, floods, cyclones and river erosion due to its geographical location, low-lying topography and tropical climate. Bangladesh now ranks as the 6th most affected by human induced climate change according to Kreft et al. (2017). Given the country's high population density and multidimensional poverty, this risk is further exacerbated (Wright 2014). Hijoka et al. (2014) finds food productivity and food security especially threatened by climatic stressors such as heavy rainfall leading to floods, sea level rise and heatwaves. Floods cause high human and material losses, sea level rise threatens the coastal region's ability to produce rice, and heat stress has already reached critical levels unsuitable for rice production. Increased frequency and intensity of heat waves increases the spread of infectious diseases such as cholera, increases mortality and morbidity among poor and vulnerable populations.

Faced with the increasing impacts of climate change and recognising that gains in development and poverty alleviation could be severely hampered by climate change, all levels of the Bangladeshi government are committed to reducing vulnerability and building the resilience of its people. Disaster risk reduction falls under the purview of the Ministry of Disaster Management and Relief (MODMR) and climate change adaptation under the Ministry of Environment and Forests (MOEF). Responding to disasters and implementing adaptation programs also involve related ministries such as Agriculture, Health and Finance. The MODMR and the MOEF have established policies and procedures to deal with their respective portfolio and responsibilities and both ministries have committed significant domestic resources. Civil society, NGOs, community organisations, researchers, academics, development practitioners are active contributors in generating knowledge and implementing adaptation and disaster risk reduction strategies.

However, despite the success and competencies in dealing with climate-related risks, losses and damages from climate change are projected to increase and gaps exist in the current policy and response framework that needs to be addressed proactively. This chapter is a case study of the efforts of the Bangladesh government and experts collaborating to address losses and damages from climate change by establishing a new mechanism from current domestic institutional arrangements and resources. The proposed new mechanism will be a centralised framework for accounting, coordinating, disbursing finance, monitoring and evaluating programs that address losses and damages from climate change. The proposed mechanism will facilitate and incorporate climate induced losses and damages into both climate and disaster policies and address these losses and damages for a more comprehensive and long-term response to climate change.

This chapter is divided into four parts: (i) A discussion of the losses and damages facing Bangladesh from various climatic hazards; (ii) A presentation of policies and procedures of MoDMR including the national plan, laws governing disaster management and the procedures immediately following a disaster; as well as (iii) An elaboration of the policies of the MoEF including the laws, institutions and strategic plans that govern climate change within the ministry; and (iv) Reflection on current efforts undertaken by the government, researchers, experts and NGOs towards establishing a national mechanism to address loss and damage.

19.2 Losses and Damages from Climate-Related Hazards Facing Bangladesh

Bangladesh is affected by both slow- and rapid-onset climatic events and experiences, among others flooding, cyclones, drought, sea-level rise, shifting patterns in rainfall and rising temperatures (see Fig. 19.1 for a multi-hazard map). The following captures the evidence on observed and projected losses and damages[1] faced by the country.

Flooding

Being the most common climatic hazard facing the country, floods inundate nearly 25% of the country every year and a severe flood occurs every 4 or 5 years submerging over 60% of the country (Nishat et al. 2013; see Fig. 19.2). Floods result in loss of lives, crops, homes and damage to infrastructure and assets. Observed data from the Bangladesh's Meteorological Department show that rainfall is becoming increasingly erratic. With increasing global temperatures above 2 °C, rainfall could increase with a significant impact on flood levels (Mirza 2002).

On the other hand, Nishat et al. (2013) posit that over the years the death toll from extreme events including cyclones and flooding has decreased, as has the severity of

[1]Although many definitions of losses and damages exist, for the purpose of this chapter, we first break down the conc ept into the two terms: losses and damages (for definitions, see also see chapter by Mechler et al. 2018). We define losses as impacts that "are lost forever and cannot be brought back once lost, "and damages as harm to something "that can be repaired, such as a road or building or embankment." (Durand and Huq 2015). This approach highlights the different implications of the two types of impacts, and may create a policy space to enable different supportive responses. When we tie these two concepts together, Durand and Huq's definition of losses and damages holds when the costs of adaptation are not recuperated; or when adaptation efforts are ineffective, maladaptive in the long term or altogether impossible. Warner and Van der Geest and Warner's (2015) definition, "the negative effects of climate variability and climate change that people have not been able to cope with or adapt to," is also relevant in our understanding of the issue.

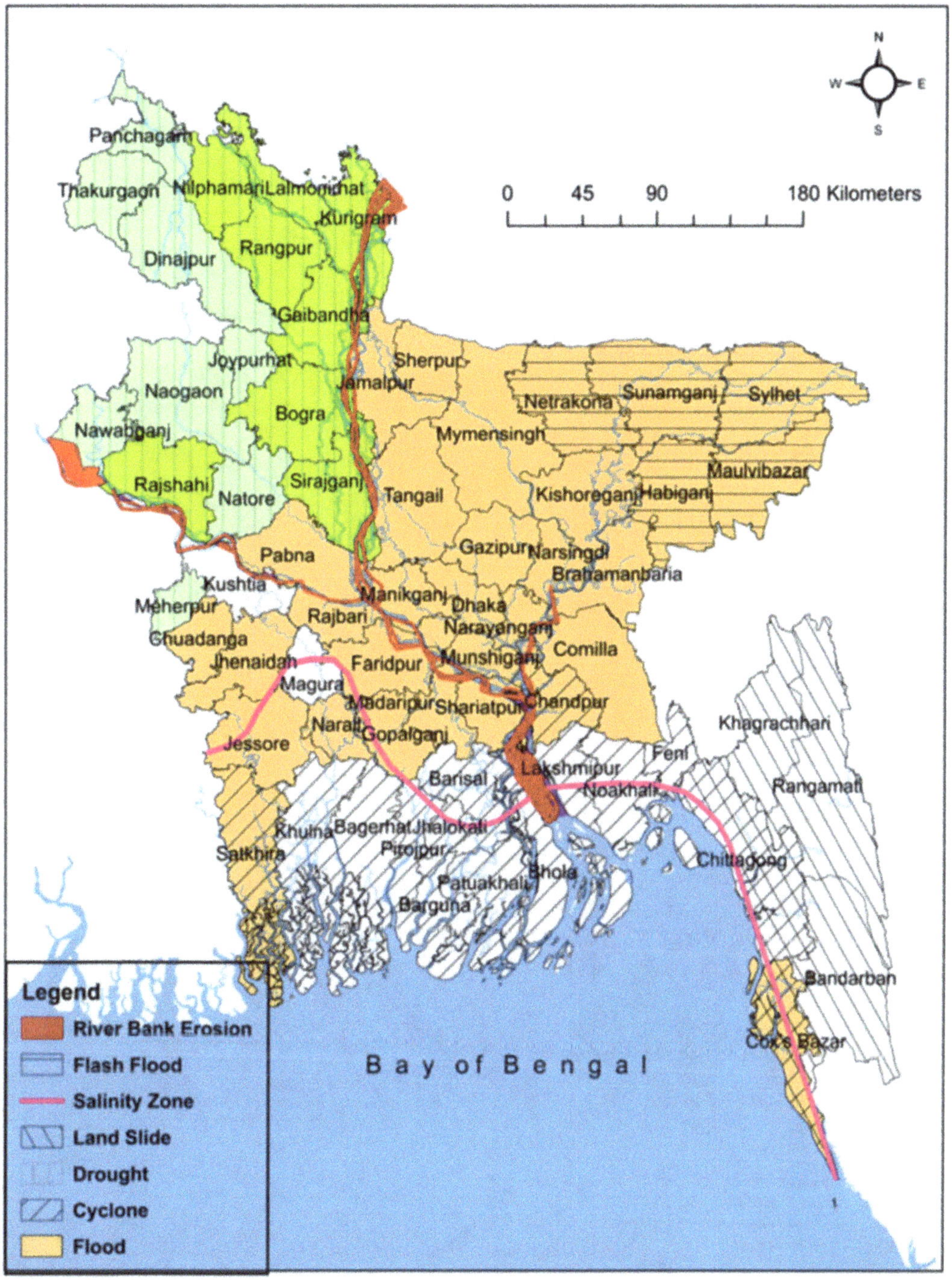

Fig. 19.1 Multi-hazard map of Bangladesh. *Source* Huq et al. (2016)

general impacts (see also chapter by Bouwer 2018). This can be attributed to better macroeconomic performance, increased resilience of the poor, the implementation of protective infrastructure and generally better disaster management (see Fig. 19.3 for an example of riverine flood protection).

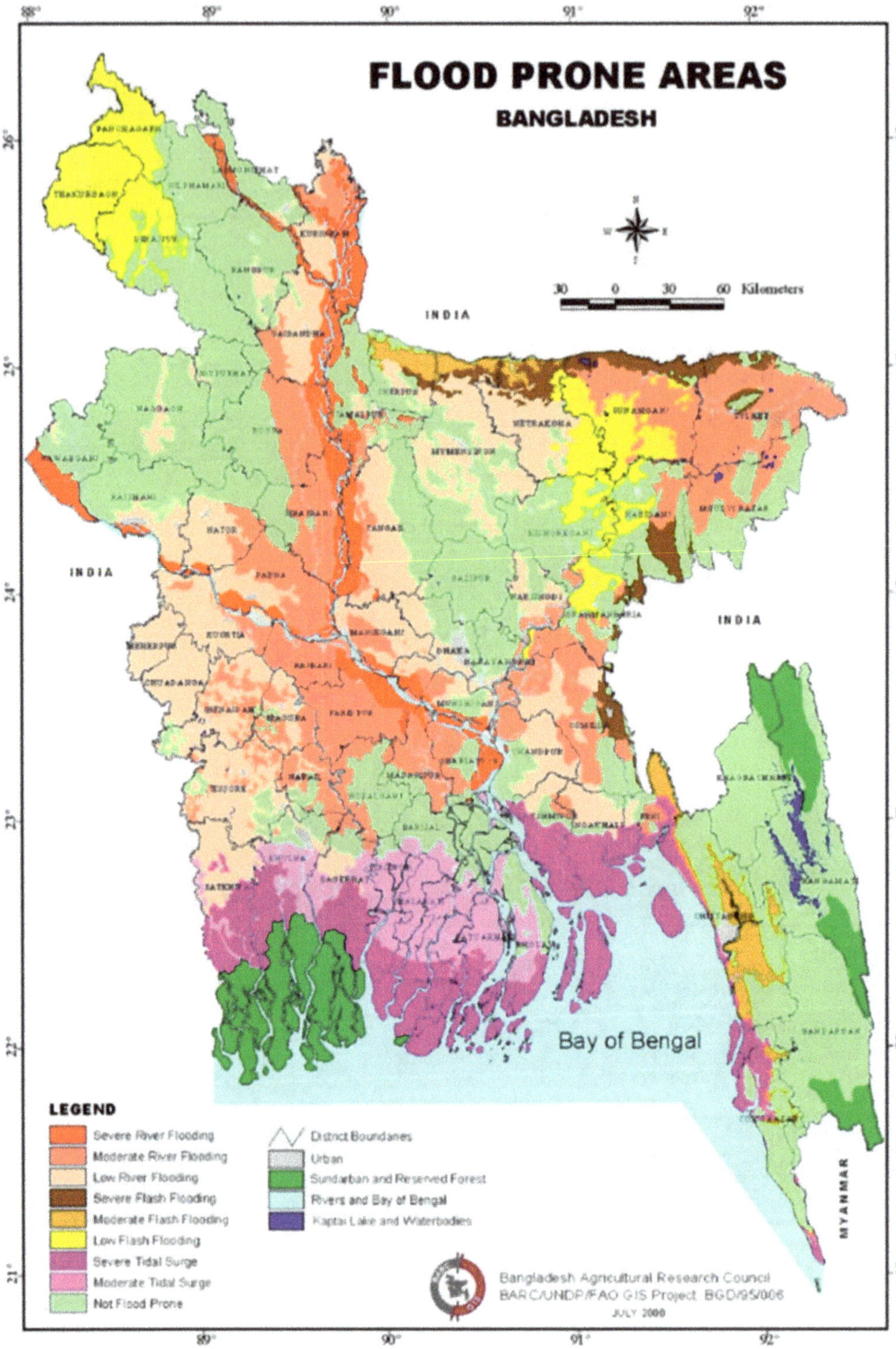

Fig. 19.2 Areas at risk of flooding in Bangladesh. *Source* Bangladesh Agricultural Research Council 2000

Fig. 19.3 River embankment in Bangladesh. *Source* Bangladesh Climate Change Trust

Cyclones

Cyclones cause untold damage to livelihoods, property and livestock of the most vulnerable people (World Bank 2010). One severe event occurs every 3 years according to the Bangladesh Climate Change Strategy and Action Plan (BCCSAP). Cyclone Sidr, which hit the Southern coast in 2007, caused total economic losses of USD 1.7 billion, or about 1.2% of annual GDP in Bangladesh (GoB 2008). The country lost an estimated 6% of GDP to storms from 1998 to 2009 (Wright 2014). Although the death toll from cyclones has been reduced significantly, the destruction, both economic and non-economic, is still prevalent today.

Drought

Most prevalent in the northwest of Bangladesh, drought has often caused famine in the region. The past 50 years have seen about 20 drought periods with almost roughly 23.000 sq. km of land affected by drought each year during the second dry season occurring between June to October (Nishat et al. 2013). Droughts affect about 47% of the land and 53% of the population.

Sea Level Rise

Rising sea levels impact the agricultural productivity of arable land and has an impact on livelihoods of people living in the coastal region of Bangladesh. The IPCC reports that approximately 27 million people are estimated to be at risk from sea level rise by the year 2050 in Bangladesh. According to Rabbani et al. (2013), sea levels at the coast of the Bay of Bengal, which lines the Southern coast of Bangladesh, have already risen by an average of 2.5 mm per year since 1950 and by an average of 5.3 mm per year from 1977 to 2002. The authors also cite projections that show that by 2030 sea levels could rise by a further 30 cm and by 2050 by 50 cm. Further projections show that by 2080 about 43 million people would be affected with a 62 cm rise in sea level inundating about 16% of the country.

Overall Picture of Losses and Damages in Bangladesh
The climatic impacts mentioned above translate to tangible and intangible losses and damages for the country. The World Bank (2011) estimates that climate change will lower the nation's agricultural GDP by 3.1% per year, for a cumulative $36 billion in losses between 2005 and 2050. An Asian Development Bank report (2014) states that Bangladesh would suffer yearly economic costs equivalent to 2% of its GDP by 2050, widening to 9.4% by 2100. The report goes on to explain that a mix of floods, cyclones, heat stress, drought and shorter growing seasons could threaten agricultural livelihoods and food security in the country. Hijoka et al. (2014) suggest Bangladesh would see a net increase in poverty of about 15% by 2030. Alongside obvious economic losses and damages, research in affected communities also reveal non-economic losses and damages (NELD) such as loss of biodiversity, cultural norms and practices, physical and psychological wellbeing, education and loss of ecosystem services (Andrei et al. 2014).

19.3 Linking Climate Adaptation and Disaster in the Context of Losses and Damages

Given these climate-induced losses and damages faced by the country, the impacts on food security and development are evident. Reducing poverty, increasing growth and graduating to middle income status by 2021 is of utmost importance to the Bangladesh government. Since 1991 and 2005 Bangladesh has made steady gains in economic growth and reduced poverty levels by 19% (Government of Bangladesh 2009). The Bangladesh Climate Change Strategy and Action Plan states that the severity and frequency of storms, floods, cyclones and drought will increase in the future stymying the country's economic growth and potentially hindering poverty reduction. Disaster risk reduction and climate adaptation are united in their mutual interest in addressing losses and damages arising from climatic events (Shamsuddoha et al. 2013). Linking climate adaptation and disaster risk reduction results in a stronger response to the climatic hazards facing the country when theory and practice are combined to address losses and damages faced by the country (Ibid). Bangladesh has made great strides in developing appropriate disaster management and climate policies and the following section highlights the policies, laws, frameworks and institutions that govern these two domains.

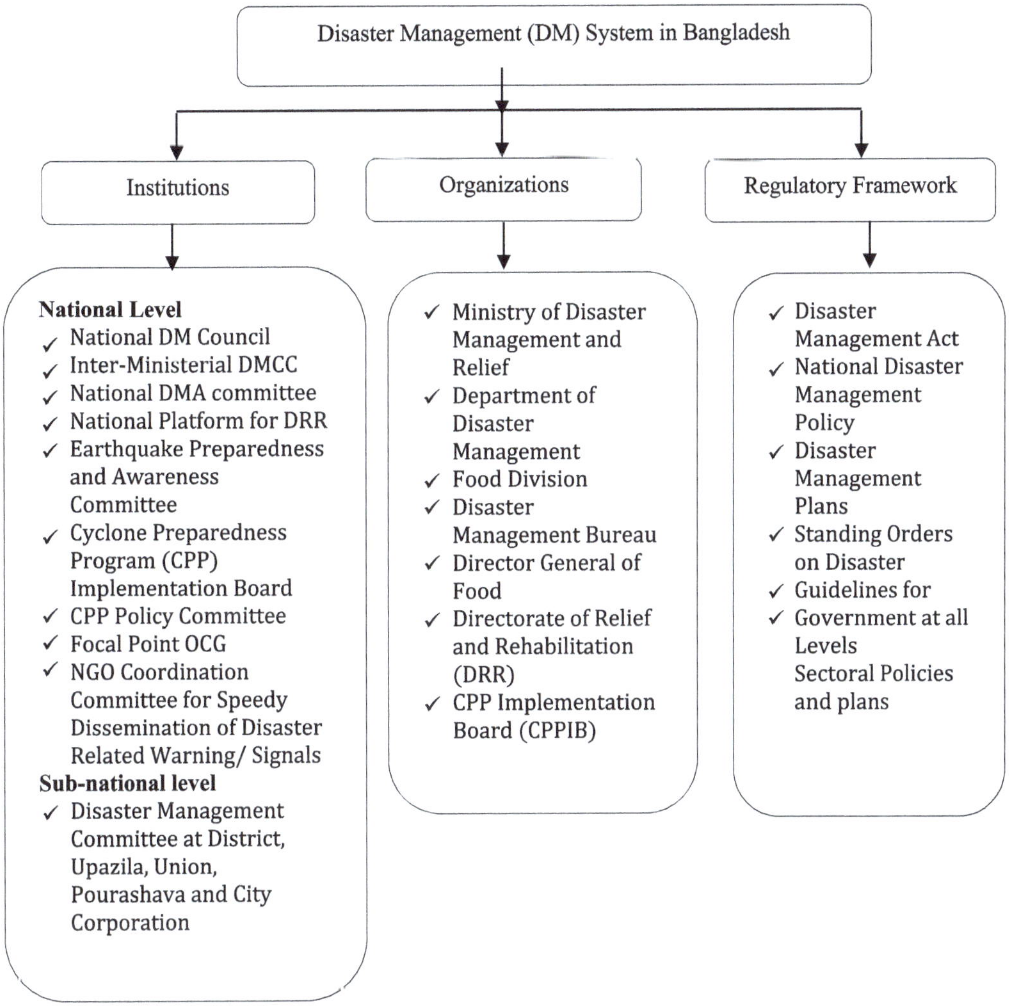

Fig. 19.4 Institutions, policy frameworks and organisations comprising the disaster management system in Bangladesh

19.3.1 Policies and Procedures Governing Disaster Management and Relief

Disaster risk reduction (DRR) policies in Bangladesh are well established and involve institutions at the national and sub national levels involving both political and regulatory institutions (Ibid) (see Fig. 19.4).

At the political level, the National Disaster Management Council (NDMC), led by the Prime Minister, formulates national policies. The Inter-Ministerial Disaster Management Coordination Committee (IMDMCC), led by the Minister of Disaster Management and Relief, conducts implements, coordinates and supervises the work of those implementing relevant policies. At the regulatory level, the Ministry of Disaster Management and Relief (MoDMR) is the primary governing body that aims to pursue comprehensive risk reduction policies and ensure food security to affected communities during disasters (MoDMR 2014). The ministry's main functions include: (i) Formulating the laws, policies and action plans for disaster risk reduction, emergency response and disaster management; (ii) Preparing policies and plans for urgent humanitarian assistance and rehabilitation program, preparation and preservation of all social safety net program; (iii) Preparing disaster risk reduction plans, undertaking activities for training and research, and coordination, monitoring and evaluating activities among local, regional and international development partners; (iv) Undertaking humanitarian assistance to ensure food security through the implementation of food for work program (FFW), gratuitous relief (GR) and vulnerable group feedings program (VGF); and (v) Ensuring employment for the ultra-poor during lean period of the year to reduce poverty risk and vulnerability.

The Department of Disaster Management (DDM) is the technical arm of the MoDMR which delivers and implements interventions on the ground. The DDM ensures that disaster risk reduction (DRR) considerations are mainstreamed into the policies, plans and programmes of related ministries and departments. It further coordinates research, capacity building, and awareness raising on DRR related activities (Shamsuddoha et al. 2013). Key development policies and plans of the government such as the Bangladesh Perspective Plan 2010–2021, Sixth Five Year Plan 2011–2015 and National Sustainable Development Strategy (NSDS) emphasise implementing the National Plan on Disaster Management (NPDM) in line with the national plan. The Seventh Five Year Plan 2016–2020 calls for building resilience of the poor and reducing their exposure and vulnerability to geo-hydro-meteorological hazards, environmental shocks, man-made disasters, emerging hazards and climate related extreme events.

The Disaster Management Act of 2012 aims to mitigate the overall impacts of a disaster and reduce vulnerability. The Act governs post disaster rescue and rehabilitation programs, humanitarian assistance to enhance the capacity of poor and disadvantaged, programs undertaken by various government and non-government organisations (GoB 2012). The aim of Disaster Management Policy is to strengthen the capacity of the Bangladesh disaster management system to reduce unacceptable risk and improve response and recovery management at all levels. It makes references to relevant sector policies, operational guidelines and procedures.

The Standing Order on Disaster (SOD) was first issued in 1997 to act as a guidebook during an emergency for concerned ministries, departments, line agencies, local government bodies and communities to understand and perform their duties and responsibilities during a disaster. The SOD has been revised in 2010 to include sector development plans, and those having emergency management responsibilities to prepare their own contingency plans and train their staff accordingly. Moreover, to maintain coordination amongst the concerned ministries, departments, line agencies, local government bodies (LGD) and communities, the government has formulated a set of mechanisms for council and committees from national down to the grass-root levels. Established by the National Disaster Management Council, the National Plan for Disaster Management 2010–2015 (NPDM) aims to reduce the risk of people, especially the poor and the disadvantaged, from the effects of natural, environmental and human induced hazards. The plan puts in place an efficient emergency response system capable of handling large scale disasters and has been embedded in government high level policy and operation documents.

The Disaster Management Bureau (DMB) performs specialist functions and ensure coordination with line departments/agencies and NGOs by convening meetings every three months with teams of the Disaster Management Training and Public Awareness Building Task Force (DMTATF), the Focal Point Operational Co-ordination Group on Disaster Management (FPOCG), the NGO Co-ordination Committee on Disaster Management (NGOCC), and the Committee for Speedy Dissemination of Disaster Related Warning Signals (CSDDWS). Coordination at district, thana and union levels (sub national levels) are done by the respective District, Sub-district (Thana) and Union Disaster Management Committees. The DMB will render all assistance to them by facilitating the process. Inter-related institutions, at both national and sub-national levels have been created to ensure effective planning and coordination of disaster risk reduction and emergency response management.

19.3.2 History of Damage Assessment and Current Practices

After Cyclone Sidr in 2007, the Local Consultative Group (the forum for development dialogue and donor coordination) agreed to conduct a Joint Damage-Loss and Needs Assessment (JDNLA). This assessment identified priority areas to support the Government of Bangladesh in cyclone recovery efforts and recommended interventions for a long-term disaster management strategy. Based on the assessment, a 15-year long-term strategic plan of action was developed supported by the World Bank. A Damage-Loss and Needs Assessment (DNA) cell was established within the DMB to provide emergency relief, rehabilitation, and reconstruction for victims of natural disasters. The cell is responsible for strengthening the existing data collection by using a standardised template (FORM-D) and to build the capacity of relevant agencies and administrative levels to conduct DNA. In 2011, after the cyclone Mahasen, the Department of Disaster Management gradually shifted to a formal damage and loss assessment in the name of Joint Needs Assessment (JNA). The JNA approach has embedded in it a national coordination mechanism and has the buy-in of a broad range of stakeholders including the DDM and MoDMR. The JNA initiative is now managed by CARE for the humanitarian community in Bangladesh with ACAPS working as a key partner providing technical inputs and assessment coordination. DDM in partnership with INGOs, CDMP II and other government departments developed loss and damage resource maps using the 4 W (what, where, when, and who) database to make disaster information and assessments more available.

According to Shamsuddoha et al. (2013), under the MoDMR, the Comprehensive Disaster Management Programme (CDMP), one of the largest initiatives ever implemented in the country to deal with disaster management, is "currently undertaking efforts to "harmonise" DRR and CCA in its work to reduce disaster risk. In addition,

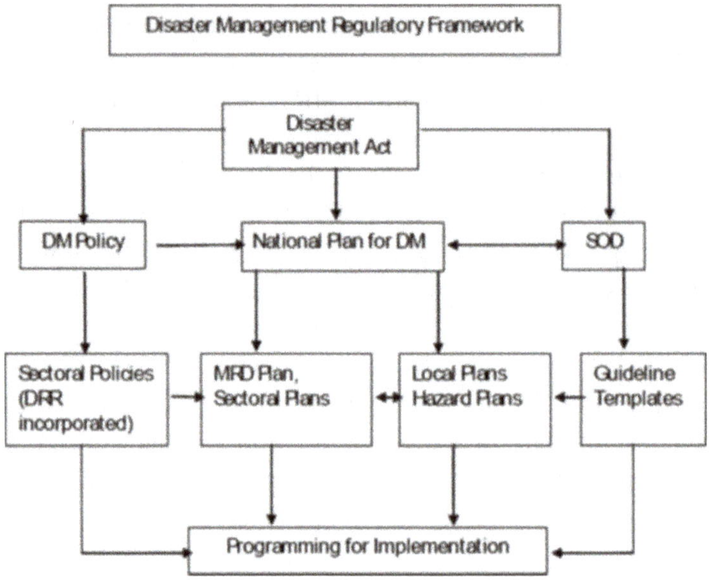

Fig. 19.5 Disaster Management Regulatory Framework of Bangladesh. *Source* Shamsuddoha et al. (2013)

the CDMP has begun to recognise the importance of addressing loss and damage in its agenda" (p. 15).

The Local Disaster Risk Reduction Fund (LDRRF), a component of CDMP provides some resources and financial support to the most vulnerable communities affected by a climatic disaster. Approximately USD 5 million was disbursed to local governments in the 2013–2014 fiscal year from this fund. In addition to the LDRRF, the MoDMR also runs several social safety net programs meant to support climate affected communities such as Food For Work (FFW), Test Relief, Bridge and Culverts (FFW), Execution of Risk Reduction Programme, Relief and Rehabilitation Programme, Vulnerable Group Feeding (VGF) and Vulnerable Group Development (VGD). Other disaster and relief related programmes include the National Relief Fund and Prime Minister's Relief Fund (Huq et al. 2016) (Fig. 19.5).

19.3.3 Climate Change Policies in Bangladesh

Bangladesh was an early mover amongst Least Developed Countries (LDCs) to create a National Adaptation Programme of Action (NAPA) and a dedicated national policy on climate change. Stemming from the NAPA process, the Ministry of Environment and Forests, along with DFID and other partners, formulated the Bangladesh Climate Change Strategy and Action Plan (BCCSAP) in 2009. The document guides climate change policies, programs and projects in the country and is in line with the government's vision to eradicate poverty and achieve economic prosperity for its people. The document stresses,

We will achieve this through a pro-poor, climate resilient and low-carbon development, based on the four building blocks of the Bali Action Plan—adaptation to climate change, mitigation, technology transfer and adequate and timely flow of funds for investment, within a framework of food, energy, water and livelihoods security (BCCSAP 2009, p. 2).

The BCCSAP identifies six thematic areas of work where interventions to adapt and mitigate climate change are to be focused: (1) food security, social protection and health; (2) comprehensive disaster management; (3) infrastructure; (4) research and knowledge management; (5) mitigation and low-carbon development; (6) capacity building and institutional strengthening. There are 44 programs identified under these six areas. Although there is no holistic mention of addressing Loss and Damage in the way it is defined in this chapter, the pillar on Comprehensive Disaster Management lends some scope for synergies. The document does identify a programme for risk management against loss of income and property under the comprehensive disaster management theme. One of the programs of the Comprehensive Disaster Management theme is to manage risk against loss of income and property. The objective of this program is "to put in place an effective insurance system for risk management against loss of income and property" (BCCSAP 2009). The program promotes working with NGOs and insurance companies on three action areas:

1. Devise an effective insurance scheme for losses in property due to climate change impacts
2. Develop an effective insurance scheme for loss of income from various sources to persons, households and enterprises
3. Pilot the insurance schemes and if successful, establish insurance systems for lowering risk of adverse impact of climate change (Ibid).

Climate migration and displacement is an action area of the work plan of the Warsaw International Mechanism (WIM). The BCCSAP makes several references to migration, cautioning that displacement of millions of people, livelihoods and long-term health of the population will be affected under the worst-case scenario.

19.3.4 Government Funds to Support the Climate Change Strategy and Action Plan (BCCSAP)

To fund the projects and activities under the BCCSAP, two funds were established by the government in 2010, the Bangladesh Climate Change Trust Fund (BCCTF) from the government's own resources and the Bangladesh Climate Change Resilience Fund (BCCRF) from donor funding and managed by the World Bank.

The Bangladesh Climate Change Trust
Climate change work in the government, falls under the jurisdiction of the Ministry of Environment and Forests (MOEF). The Climate Change Unit (CCU) under the MoEF coordinates and facilitates the implementation of the BCCSAP under the overall guidance of the National Environment Committee chaired by the Prime Minister and the National Steering Committee on Climate Change (Shamsuddoha et al. 2013). The CCU's main objective is to use the trust fund, provide management, administrative and monitoring support to the trustee board and its technical committee. In 2010, the government enacted the Climate Change Trust Act to conduct the functions of the BCCTF according to the Bangladesh Climate Change Trust Annual Report 2014–2015. The Bangladesh Climate Change Trust (BCCT) and its functions are governed by a 17-member Trustee Board which is the highest decision-making body for the Fund. It comprises of the minister of Ministry of Environment and Forests as the chair and 16 other members including 10 ministers/state ministers, cabinet secretary, governor of the central, finance secretary, member of Planning Commission and two experts appointed by the government. The secretary, Ministry of Environment and Forests, acts as the board's member-secretary (Ibid). To assist the trustee board, there is a technical committee headed by the Secretary, Ministry of Environment and Forests. It committee comprises thirteen members including experts/representatives from the Planning Commission, Department of Environment, Department of Forest, and Centre for Environmental and Geographic Information Services (CEGIS) and social organisations/NGOs working on climate change. The technical committee provides recommendations to the trustee board on the different projects submitted for approval.

According to the 2014-105 Annual Report of the Bangladesh Climate Change Trust, specific functions of the BCCT include overall management of the trust fund; to provide administrative support to the trustee board and the technical committee; to send project proposals to the technical committee (after preliminary screening) and to place the proposals to the trustee board after the recommendation from the technical committee; implementing the decision of the trustee board; and monitoring and evaluation of projects.

The Bangladesh Climate Change Trust Fund (BCCTF)
The Trust Fund created in fiscal year 2009–10 specifically funds the 44 programs specified under the six thematic areas of BCCSAP. 66% of the funding from the trust fund is utilised in the projects and 34% is held in reserve in a fixed deposit account (Ibid). About 77% of all climate finance projects in Bangladesh are financed from the domestic budget (Faruque and Khan 2013). The Government of Bangladesh has to date allocated BDT 3100 crore (US$400 million approximately) to BCCTF during the last eight fiscal years (Table 19.1).

Table 19.1 Annual allocations to the trust fund are as follows (BCCT)

Fiscal year	Allocation (BDT in crore)	Allocation (USD in millions, approximate figures)
2009–2010	700	902
2010–2011	700	902
2011–2012	700	902
2012–2013	400	515
2013–2014	200	258
2014–2015	200	258
2015–2016	100	129
2016–2017	100	129
Total	3100	399

Source Bangladesh Climate Change Trust Fund

As per Climate Change Trust Act, 2010, a maximum of 66% of the allocated amount can go towards the projects. The remaining 34%, approximately totaling USD 135 million or BDT 1054 crore, is kept in a fixed deposit account in various private and public banks. One of the reasons why the government has kept a certain portion in reserve is that in the future the interest can create the possibility of funding climate change projects without allocating an amount from the annual budget. As of July 2016, 431 projects have been undertaken—368 projects are being implemented by the government, semi-government and autonomous agencies, 63 projects are being implemented by NGOs. A GCF accredited national organisation called the Palli Karma-Sahayak Foundation (PKSF) manages the portion of funds that goes towards NGOs. Projects have to satisfy the environmental and social safety standards as recommended by the technical committee in order to receive funding from the BCCTF. Major projects under the BCCTF include construction of coastal sea dykes, embankments, river protection work; development of cyclone resilient houses and multipurpose cyclone shelters in vulnerable areas; establishing agro-met stations; water supply for irrigation; excavation/re-excavation of canals and construction of drains at different rural municipalities; afforestation projects to protect coastal areas and conserve biodiversity; biogas plants; improved cook-stoves; solar home systems are mitigation projects funded from the trust fund. In the fiscal year 2014–15 the Ministry of Local Government and Engineering department was awarded the highest number of projects, followed by the Ministry of Water Resources (see Fig. 19.6).

The financial management and accounting procedures are maintained in strict adherence to existing government financial rules. BCCTF has been audited by the Office of the Comptroller and Auditor General and no objection has been received. There is an Internal Audit Committee headed by the Secretary of BCCT that audits all files with financial implications and adopts corrective measures. The external audit is done by the Office of the Comptroller and Auditor General of Bangladesh as per the direction of Climate Change Trust Act of 2010.

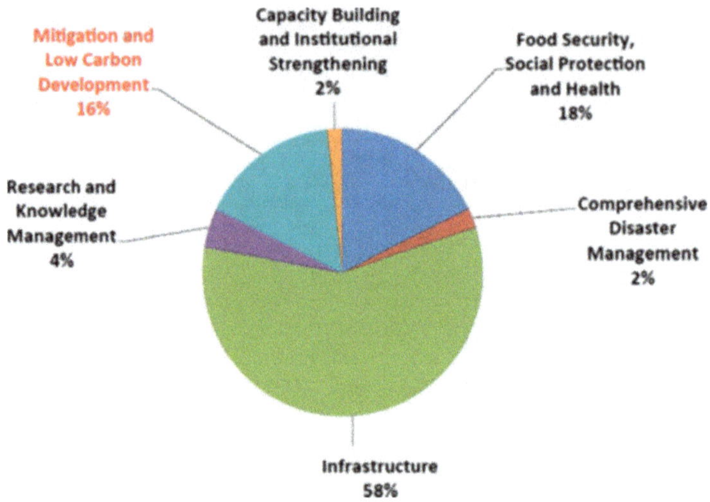

Fig. 19.6 Allocation of funding for projects by the Bangladesh Climate Change Trust Fund (BCCTF). *Source* Kamruzzaman (2015)

The monitoring of projects funded by the BCCTF are the responsibility of the concerned implementing ministries. The Monitoring and Evaluation Branch in BCCT also receives monthly progress report from the project directors, sends inspection team for field visits, and convenes regular monitoring meetings with Project Directors. Headed by the Managing Director of the Trust, there is also a Monitoring Committee that analyses the monitoring reports and puts forward its recommendation for proper implementation of the projects. According to the Trust's website, local administration is involved in the monitoring process to ensure local oversight. The administrative officers and elected representatives also discuss these projects in the district coordination meetings. Completed projects are evaluated by the Implementation Monitoring and Evaluation Division (IMED) of the Ministry of Planning.

19.4 Towards Establishing a National Mechanism to Address Climate Induced Losses and Damages in Bangladesh

Both economic and non-economic losses and damages from climatic events are being experienced in Bangladesh currently, with the impacts expected to grow according to future projections. As explained in the first section of this chapter, climatic events are changing their patterns, frequency and intensity, which is expected to negatively affect the country's economic growth, food security and public health. The main gap that exists in the current climate-related policy framework in Bangladesh is a lack of legislative, institutional and policy-related mechanism that explicitly address climate induced losses and damages. A system that documents or accounts for the extent of losses and damages, both monetary and non-monetary and provides for longer term support does currently not exist. Losses and damages affecting the most vulnerable communities are addressed tangentially and disparately organised through MoEF and MoDMR. To respond to the experienced and future losses and damages a proactive and robust system of collecting evidence, proving support to communities whose livelihoods, assets and quality of life have been most affected by climate change is much needed.

Over the years, Bangladesh has well established, but separate laws, institutions, rules and procedures to respond to climatic events. DRR and adaptation share a common mandate to reduce vulnerability and enhance the resilience of affected populations. Policy makers in the MoDMR and MoEF are both concerned with protecting lives, livelihoods, food security and minimising of losses and damages of the most at-risk populations. Despite these commonalities, the disaster and climate change policy realms in Bangladesh operate in silos, with little collaboration or cooperation. Shamsuddhoa et al. (2013) highlights that "bureaucratic demarcation of responsibility" and "institutional silos" of climate adaptation and DRR policy-making hinder cross-sectoral cooperation. To address losses and damages more effectively and efficiently, climate adaptation approaches and perspectives need to be integrated into DRR policy-making.

The competency and success of disaster reduction strategies in Bangladesh have focused on immediate response and relief. There is an expressed need for communities on the frontlines to adapt and receive support for the impacts of climate change that they cannot adapt to. Long term support to rebuild and build back better requires the integration of DRR and climate adaptation approaches and perspectives. According to Shamshuddoha et al. (2013), "the incorporation of DRR expertise in implementation could help to increase the pace at which CCA efforts move from planning to action DRR can also learn from the long-term perspectives of CCA in order to ensure that DRR activities align with shifting climatic realities, and not just historical experience" (p. 27).

Slow onset events, salinity intrusion, increased intensity of cyclones and non-economic losses and damages are not accounted for in the current national policies of the MoDMR. There is currently no provision in the legislative framework in either MoDMR and MoEF that address slow onset events such as sea level rise and non-economic losses and damages. Different projections show various scenarios of inundation and the population affected under sea-level rise and there is a need to systematically understand, document and prepare for this hazard. Non-economic losses and damages have not received mention in policy frameworks and procedures, but evidence shows that there are profound psychological, environmental, social and cultural impacts of losses and damages from a variety of climatic stressors. Current disaster preparedness procedures do not take into account future climate projections and the systems that need to be put in place so that losses and damages are minimised in the future.

The above highlight the need to address the gaps in the current policy and legislative framework and build a more robust response to climate-induced losses and damages. Efforts are now underway in Bangladesh to bring policy-makers in MoDMR and MoEF in coordination with one another to build a national mechanism that addresses losses and damages more holistic and comprehensive manner. A scoping paper (Huq et al. 2016) on developing a national mechanism offers a framework to address Loss and Damage and documents the current efforts being undertaken to establish such a system. According to Huq et al. (2016), to develop local, national and international policy and institutional frameworks to address Loss and Damage, it is first essential to identify, measure and characterise losses and damages faced in Bangladesh. Understanding and quantifying losses and damages experienced from various climatic events, taking into account the social, economic and geographical contexts in which they occur is the first step towards building a national mechanism. The scoping paper argues for a centralised mechanism that facilitates the coordination between MoDMR and MoEF, disburse financing, monitor and evaluate programs to address climate induced losses and damages in Bangladesh.

Over the years, Bangladeshi policymakers and practitioners have acquired knowledge and expertise on disaster management and climate adaptation, making them highly capacitated to plan, strategise and execute climate policies. Both the political/bureaucratic and technical spheres involved in the climate and disaster sector are motivated and committed to preventing the worst of climate impacts impeding the development of the nation. The Bangladesh delegation is an active member of the LDC negotiating bloc in the UNFCCC. Moreover, a senior bureaucrat of the MoEF currently sits on the Executive Committee of the Warsaw International Mechanism on Loss and Damage (WIM).

In 2012 the Government of Bangladesh initiated the "Loss and Damage in Vulnerable Countries Initiative," a pioneering study on understanding the issue. The initiative commissioned a number of studies on losses and damages, which brought together climate change researchers, academics, practitioners and NGOs and deepened their knowledge, capacity and expertise on this issue. The initiative created awareness, understanding and a systematic body of work that laid the foundation for an intellectual and practical understanding of losses and damages.

The human and institutional capacity and common mandate of the MoEF and MoDMR to reduce vulnerability and build resilience means that there is much potential to establish a mechanism to address climate Loss and Damage. This reserve fund of approximately USD 135 million or 34% of the Bangladesh Climate Change Trust Fund creates a financial resource base to setup such a mechanism with domestic resources. Huq et al. (2016) recommends developing the national mechanism on Loss and Damage based on the country's current adaptation and disaster risk finance frameworks. This section further highlights the current efforts being undertaken in the country to establish such a national mechanism to account for climate induced losses and damages more holistically looking inward at the competencies that already exist in the country.

19.4.1 Unpacking the Warsaw International Mechanism on Loss and Damage in the National Context of Bangladesh

On February 16, 2016, the MoDMR hosted a workshop on Loss and Damage supported by the Climate and Development Knowledge Network (CDKN), Action Aid Bangladesh, C3ER and NACOM in Dhaka. The event was primarily targeted towards MoDMR staff and aimed at helping staff understand how national mechanism to address Loss and Damage could form part of the disaster risk reduction strategy (Khan 2016). The workshop brought together the minister of MoDMR, senior bureaucrats, policymakers, field professionals from MoMDR along with civil society, researchers and experts working on DRR and loss and damage to start discussions on how the WIM can be translated at the national level. The workshop identified gaps, synergies and opportunities in addressing losses and damages within the MoDMR's DRR framework and the way forward on establishing a national mechanism. Highlights of the discussions included Strengthening the assessments of key sectors impacted by climate disasters by modifying current disaster assessments conducted by MoDMR through various scientific tools; Improving coordination and monitoring among relevant institutions and ministries to address and account for loss and damage; Establishing a national coordination cell and a legal framework to implement climate induced loss and damage related policies; The need for adequate financial support to conduct research, gather and quantify data on loss and damage. The workshop was a first step to bring on board key stakeholders to understand and agree on establishing a national system/mechanism to deal with climate induced losses and damages. The Ministry of Disaster Management and Relief has agreed to lead the process of the mechanism with input and support from the Ministry of Environment and Forests, Ministry of Land, Ministry of Water Resources.

19.4.2 National Consultations

Following the aforementioned workshop on loss and damage, four sub national consultations took place in the Sylhet, Rangpur, Khulna and Chittagong districts with relevant stakeholders including the Deputy Commissioners of MoDMR of those regions in September 2016 (Huq et al. 2016). These nationwide consultations took stock of the current practices to address losses and damages from disasters, possible responses when climatic events are intensified and the support needed from the national level to aid the local level to respond more effectively. Since climate impacts are experienced at the local level, these regional consultations were extremely valuable in gathering the local level's insight on how the mechanism should be devised (Huq et al. 2016). Recommendations from the regional consultation included:

- A need for DRR responses within the MoDMR to include protection of assets and livelihoods of those affected by climatic disasters;

- A need for enhanced coordination at the local level;
- Establishment and maintenance of a comprehensive database of people and assets. Related to the database, a pre-assessment mechanism is recommended;
- Education and awareness of climate induced losses and damages;
- Human and financial resources dedicated to build capacity of local government to deal with increased frequency of disasters or a large scale single event (Ibid).

Following the regional consultations, a national consultation took place in October 2016, organised jointly by CARE Bangladesh and Action Aid Bangladesh with key MoDMR policymakers including the Director General of the Department of Disaster Management in Dhaka. The consultation presented the findings of the field-level consultations along with discussions on taking the mechanism forward. Several areas of further research emerged from the consultation which look to better understand Loss and Damage in the country and the information needed to build a holistic national mechanism. The central recommendation that emerged from this consultation was that the Government of Bangladesh should consider setting up a national mechanism on Loss and Damage through a new technical team with specific terms of references. Also presented at the consultation was a scoping study which articulated the details on the process of establishing a national mechanism on losses and damages prepared by ActionAid Bangladesh, CARE Bangladesh, the International Centre for Climate Change and Development and Nature Conservation Management. The study included proposed functions and activities of the national mechanism and an institutional structure comprising of a national steering committee and a technical working group to oversee the development of the mechanism.

19.4.3 National Steering Committee and Technical Working Group

The scoping study proposed to establish a national steering committee comprising of high level policy makers and relevant experts to oversee the development of the mechanism. The mandate of the steering committee would be to formulate positions for the UNFCCC negotiations on Loss and Damage, make decisions on national policy for Loss and Damage and oversee, approve and monitor the work of the technical working group (Huq et al. 2016) (see Fig. 19.7).

The scoping study also recommends forming a technical working group comprising of sector experts to conduct specific activities. The tasks of the working group include: to provide technical guidance/recommendations to national steering committee; to identify thematic areas and activities of the national mechanism; to develop a work plan to implement the activities of the thematic areas identified; to recommend a panel of experts, approving their work plan and monitoring and evaluating the of implementation work plans.

Fig. 19.7 Proposed functions of the national mechanism to address climate induced loss and damage. *Source* Huq et al. (2016)

19.5 Conclusions

This chapter highlighted the case of Bangladesh, a highly vulnerable country facing significant losses and damages, which is putting its domestic resources and expertise together to respond in a way that looks ahead and beyond the conventional responses to climate change. The actions taken to establish a national mechanism to address losses and damages builds upon existing institutions, mechanisms and frameworks and is an example of collaboration across ministries, departments and a break away from working in silos. Working towards a holistic mechanism embodies a systematic approach to understanding the different perspectives of relevant stakeholders, where the gaps lie and crafting a system to address the gaps for a stronger response to loss and damage from climate impacts. The coordination of the work through the Ministry of Disaster Management and Relief (MoDMR) and Ministry of Environment and Forests (MoEF) signify that the issue of climate change has broader acceptance and recognition among policymakers in the Bangladesh. Recognising that climate change is not just an environmental issue, but it has implications on the work of the disaster community, MoDMR's activities described above signifies an acceptance of responsibility to respond to Loss and Damage from climate change. Moreover, establishing the mechanism will significantly aid in much needed coordination and collaboration between MoDMR and MoEF. As of April 2018, the Government of Bangladesh has formed an inter-ministerial committee headed by MoDMR to develop a 2-year pilot phase for exploring the National Mechanism on Loss and Damage. A concept note has already been developed and a detailed workplan for the 2-year pilot phase is being developed. The government of Bangladesh intends to make a public announcement of the National Mechanism on Loss and Damage at COP24 in December 2018.

A national mechanism to address Loss and Damage not only responds to the needs within the country, it also reaffirms Bangladesh's commitment to the national targets and indicators within the Sendai Framework for Disaster Risk Reduction 2015–2030. Furthermore, the functions of the national mechanism replicate the work areas of the WIM, signalling Bangladesh's commitments to the Paris Agreement. For a resource constrained LDC country, the efforts made by researchers, the development community and policymakers display a resourcefulness and creativity that can be replicated in countries facing similar vulnerabilities and resource constraints.

References

Andrei S, Rabbani G, Khan HI, Haque M, Ali DE (2014) Non-economic loss and damage caused by climatic stressors in selected Coastal Districts of Bangladesh. http://gobeshona.net/publication/non-economic-loss-damage-caused-climatic-stressors-selected-coastal-districts-bangladesh/. Accessed 7 June 2017

Asian Development Bank 19 August 2014. Bangladesh Could See Climate Change Losses Reach Over 9% Of GDP—Report. Asian Development Bank [online]. https://www.adb.org/news/bangladesh-could-see-climate-change-losses-reach-over-9-gdp-report

Bangladesh Agricultural Research Council (2015) Areas at risk of flooding in Bangladesh. http://www.thebangladesh.net/flood-maps-of-bangladesh.html#map-2. Accessed 7 April 2018

Bouwer LM (2018) Observed and projected impacts from extreme weather events: implications for loss and damage. In: Mechler R, Bouwer L, Schinko T, Surminski S, Linnerooth-Bayer J (eds) Loss and damage from climate change. Concepts, methods and policy options. Springer, Cham, pp 63–82

Durand A, Huq S (2015) Defining loss and damage: key challenges and considerations for developing an operational definition. In: The International Centre for Climate Change and Development. ICCCAD www.icccad.net/wp-content/uploads/2015/08/Defininglossanddamage-Final.pdf. Accessed 7 June 2017

Faruque DA, Khan MI (2013) Loss and damage associated with climate change: the legal and institutional context in Bangladesh. In: Loss and damage in vulnerable countries initiative. Available via www.lossanddamage.net, www.loss-and-damage.net/download/7114.pdf. Accessed 7 June 2017

Government of Bangladesh (GOB (2008) Cyclone Sidr in Bangladesh Damage, Loss, and Needs Assessment for Disaster Recovery and Reconstruction. Available via Reliefweb. http://reliefweb.int/report/bangladesh/cyclone-sidr-bangladesh-damage-loss-and-needs-assessment-disaster-recovery-and. Accessed 7 June 2017

Government of Bangladesh (2009) Bangladesh Climate Change Strategy and Action Plan. Available via Climate Change Cell. www.climatechangecell.org.bd/Documents/climate_change_strategy2009.pdf. Accessed 7 June 2017

Government of Bangladesh (GoB) (2010) Standing Order on Disasters. Available via Local Consultative Group. www.lcgbangladesh.org/DERweb/doc/Final%20Verion%20SOD.pdf. Accessed 7 June 2017

Government of Bangladesh (GoB) (2012) Bangladesh Disaster Management Act. Available via EMI. http://emi-megacities.org/?emi-publication=bangladesh-disaster-management-act-of-2012. Accessed 7 June 2017

Government of Bangladesh (GoB) (2014) Bangladesh Climate Change Trust Fund: Fund use guidelines. Available via http://www.bcct.gov.bd/index.php/projects/fund-use-guidelines. Accessed 7 June 2017

Government of Bangladesh (GOB) (2015) Climate Change Trust Annual Report 2014–2015. http://www.bcct.gov.bd/index.php/publications-downloads. Accessed 7 June 2017

Hijioka Y, Lin E, Pereira JJ, Corlett RT, Cui X, Insarov GE, Lasco RD, Lindgren E, Surjan A (2014) Impacts, adaptation, and vulnerability. Part B: Regional aspects. Contribution of working group II to the fifth assessment report of the intergovernmental panel on climate change

Huq S, Kabir F, Khan MH, Khan MHI, Hossain T, Hossain JB, Pasternak L, Nasir N, Hadi T, Mahmud S, Mahid Y (2016) National mechanism on loss and damage in Bangladesh: Scoping Paper. Available via Scribd. https://www.scribd.com/document/329856845/Bangladesh-loss-and-damage-proposal. Accessed 7 June 2017

Kamruzzaman M (2015) National Climate Finance: Performance of Bangladesh Climate Change Trust Fund [PowerPoint Presentation]. Gobeshona Conference for Climate Change Research in Bangladesh. Available via http://gobeshona.net/wp-content/uploads/2014/09/National-Climate-Finance-Performance-of-Bangladesh-Climate-Change-Trust-Fund.pdf. Accessed 9 April 2018

Khan MH 16 April 2016. FEATURE: Unpacking Warsaw International Mechanism on Loss and Damage in the National Context of Bangladesh. Climate and Development Knowledge Network [online] Retrieved from https://cdkn.org/2016/04/feature-unpacking-warsaw-international-mechanism-loss-damage-national-context-bangladesh-2/?loclang=en_gb

Kreft S, Eckstein D, Melchior (2017) Global climate risk index: who suffers most from extreme weather events? Weather-related loss events in 2015 and 1996 to 2015. Available via https://germanwatch.org/en/12978. Accessed 25 October 2017

Mechler R et al (2018) Science for loss and damage. Findings and propositions. In: Mechler R, Bouwer L, Schinko T, Surminski S, Linnerooth-Bayer J (eds) Loss and damage from climate change. Concepts, methods and policy options. Springer, Cham, pp 3–37

Minister of Disaster Management and Recovery (MoDMR) (2014). http://www.modmr.gov.bd/. Accessed 7 June 2017

Mirza MM (2002) Global warming and changes in the probability of occurrence of floods in Bangladesh and implications. Glob Environ Change 12(2):127–138

Nishat N, Mukherjee N, Roberts E, Hasemann A (2013) A range of approaches to address loss and damage from climate change impacts in Bangladesh. In: Loss and damage in vulnerable countries initiative. Available via www.lossanddamage.net, www.loss-and-damage.net/4825. Accessed 7 June 2017

Rabbani G, Rahman S, Faulkner L (2013) Impacts of climatic hazards on the small wetland ecosystems (ponds): evidence from some selected areas of coastal Bangladesh. Sustainability 5(4):1510–1521

Shamsuddoha M, Roberts E, Hasemann A, Roddick S (2013) Establishing links between disaster risk reduction and climate change adaptation in the context of loss and damage: policies and approaches in Bangladesh. In: Loss and damage in vulnerable countries initiative. Available via www.lossanddamage.net, www.loss-and-damage.net/download/7096.pdf. Accessed 7 June 2017

Van der Geest K, Warner K (2015) Editorial: loss and damage from climate change: emerging perspectives. Int J Global Warming 8(2):133–140

World Bank (2010) Economics of adaptation to climate change synthesis report. Available via The World Bank Group. Available via https://siteresources.worldbank.org/…/EACC_FinalSynthesisReport0803_2010.pdf. Accessed 7 June 2017

World Bank (2011) Vulnerability, risk reduction and adaptation to climate change. Available via http://www.worldbank.org/en/results/2016/10/07/bangladesh-building-resilience-to-climate-change. Accessed 22 September 2017

Wright H (2014) What does the IPCC say about Bangladesh? In The International Centre for Climate Change and Development. Available via ICCCAD. www.icccad.net/wp-content/uploads/2015/01/IPCC-Briefing-for-Bangladesh.pdf. Accessed 7 June 2017

Chapter 20
The Case of Huaraz: First Climate Lawsuit on Loss and Damage Against an Energy Company Before German Courts

Will Frank, Christoph Bals and Julia Grimm

Abstract The civil law case brought forward in 2016 by the Peruvian Saúl Luciano Lliuya with the support of the NGO Germanwatch against the German energy company RWE is the first climate lawsuit in Germany. It addresses the question whether and how the biggest greenhouse-gas emitters, such as energy suppliers, may be held liable for losses and damages caused by climate change. Specifically, the plaintiff sued the company for a contribution to safety measures that help avoid the outburst of a glacial lagoon fuelled by glacial retreat linked to anthropogenic climate change. The requested support for necessary risk management measures at the lake to reduce the risk of flooding are commensurate with the causal contribution of the company's share in historical CO_2 emissions, approximately 0.5%. After having been rejected by a district court in November 2017, the Court of Appeals accepted the case and took it forward to the evidentiary phase. This decision marks the first time that a court acknowledged that a private company is in principal responsible for its share in causing climate damages. The lawsuit has raised the issue of responsibility of large energy companies, and other emitters of greenhouse gas emissions, for climate change in terms of liability for nuisance caused to private property. The acceptance of the case and its entering into the evidentiary phase has written legal history and

W. Frank · C. Bals · J. Grimm (✉)
Germanwatch e.V., Bonn, Germany
e-mail: grimm@germanwatch.org

R. Mechler et al. (eds.), *Loss and Damage from Climate Change*, Climate Risk Management, Policy and Governance, https://doi.org/10.1007/978-3-319-72026-5_20

the case may act as a model for lawsuits in other countries. Comparable legal bases for similar cases exist in numerous countries around the world. The decision thus may have implications for the responsibility of great emitters all around the globe in terms of communicating the relevant litigation risks to shareholders and building adequate financial reserves.

Keywords Litigation · Civil law · Glacial lake outburst flooding · Causation Peru · Huaraz

20.1 The Case of Huaraz and Its Civil Law Dimension

Loss and Damage caused by climate change has a civil law dimension (see book chapter by Simlinger and Mayer 2018). The case of Saúl Luciano Lliuya brought forward in 2016 against the German energy utility RWE is the first climate lawsuit in Germany that addresses the question if greenhouse gas emitters, such as big energy suppliers, may be held liable proportionally for safety measures necessary to protect others against the dangers to life and property caused by the consequences of climate change, such as through the accelerated retreat of glaciers and rising water levels of glacial lagoons.

The plaintiff, Saúl Luciano Lliuya, who lives in the Andean city of Huaraz in Peru, owns a house just below Palcacocha Glacier Lake (see Fig. 20.1). Global warming has led to dangerous increases in the lake's volume. At any time, a glacial ice avalanche may cause a glacial lake outburst flood (GLOF) from the lake (Rivas et al. 2015). Saúl Luciano Lliuya's family and house along with large parts of the city of Huaraz are at risk of being hit by such a wave. There are precedents of GLOFs causing death and destruction in the region: since 1941 such disasters have killed more than 30,000 people in the Cordillera Blanca region (Carey 2005). To ensure protection from the hazard, water levels of the glacier lake need to be reduced by upgrading the pumping system and strengthening the current protective moraine dam (see Fig. 20.2).

The intent of Saúl Luciano Lliuya's climate lawsuit, brought forward in 2016 against the German energy company RWE, is to get the company to make a contribution to safety measures at the lake in order to reduce the risk of flooding. This contribution is to be commensurate to the causal contribution of the company's share in historical CO_2 emissions, approximately 0.5% (Heede 2014). As an affected landowner, Saúl Luciano Lliuya bases his claim against RWE on § 1004 of the German Civil Code (BGB 2002), which reads as follows:

> If the ownership is interfered with by means other than removal or retention of possession, the owner may require the disturber to remove the interference. If further interferences are to be feared, the owner may seek a prohibitory injunction.

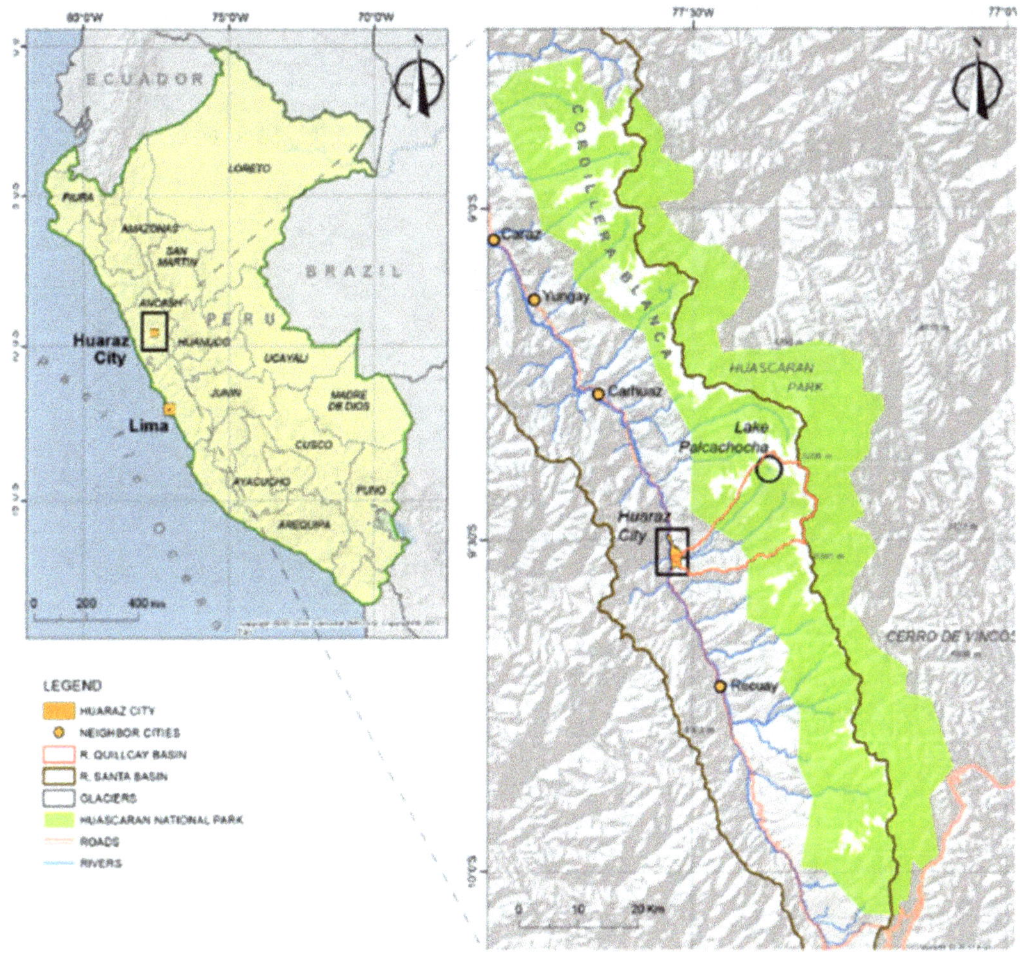

Fig. 20.1 Location of Lake Palcacocha and the city of Huaraz. *Source* Rivas et al. (2015)

20.2 The Question of Causality

For any claim based on § 1004 BGB a legally relevant causal link has to be established between the respective activity of the defendant and the nuisance suffered by the plaintiff. The claim asserts that such a causal link can be established between CO_2 emissions generated by the power plants operated by RWE and the imminent harm to the claimant's property. In German Civil Law the test for causality is the "conditio sine qua non" rule: Accordingly, causality is established if a certain consequence had not occurred fully or partially "but for" the said activity. Additionally, the principle of "adequacy" has to be fulfilled. Consequences which are so unlikely that their occurrence reasonably cannot be anticipated, are not imputed.

Causality in the Huaraz Case is strongly linked to scientific confidence as established e.g. by the assessments of the International Panel of Climate Change (IPCC 2013; Cramer et al. 2014). As shown in Fig. 20.3 of the IPCC Report of 2014, building on its detection and attribution framework (Cramer et al. 2014), the IPCC assigned *high confidence* that glacial retreat in South America is linked to anthropogenic climate change (item 1 in the figure; Magrin et al. 2014).

Fig. 20.2 Palcacocha Glacier Lake with the provisional pumping system in need of upgrading. *Source* Noah Walker-Crawford 2016

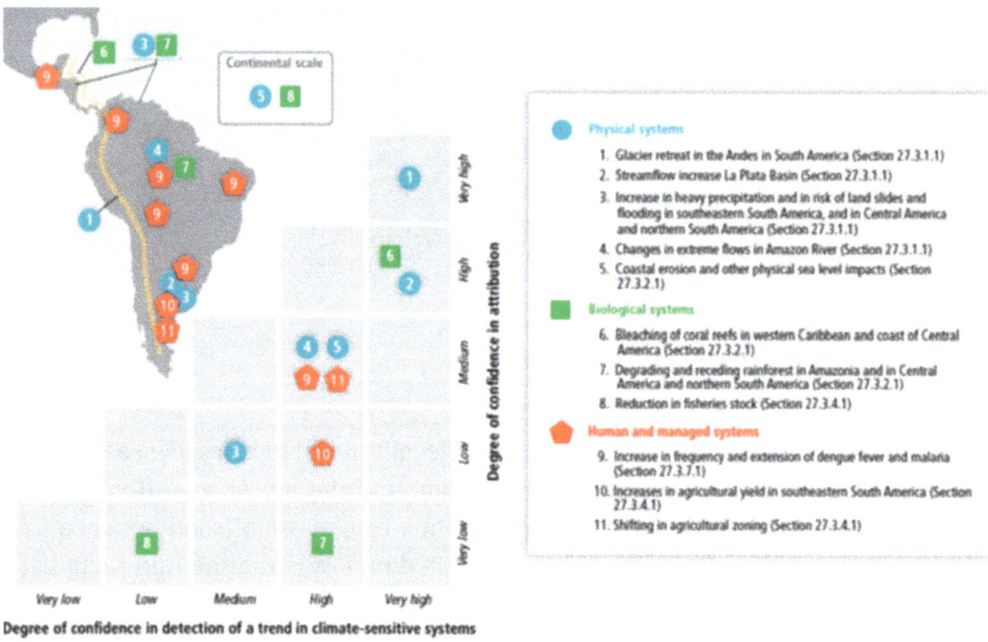

Fig. 20.3 Detection and attribution for climate impacts in Central and South America. *Source* Magrin et al. (2014) (IPCC 5th assessment report)

20.3 The Ruling

The First-Instance Judgement

In late 2016, the district court of Essen dismissed the case in the first instance denying the existence of legally-relevant causation between the greenhouse gas emissions by RWE and the endangerment of the claimant's property. Basically, the court argued that the processes of climate change and its consequences are so complex that it is virtually not possible to prove an individual causal link between CO_2 emissions of single emitters and specific climate change impacts. The court further argued, with reference to the principle of "adequacy", that there are many contributors to the overall greenhouse gas burden in the atmosphere, and consequently the share of a single emitter is irrelevant for the specific climate change impacts caused.

The Appeal

In the appeal lodged with the next-higher instance, the Higer Regional Court of Hamm, North Rhine-Westphalia, the claimant asserted that the lower court misjudged the issues concerning causality. He argued that there is a scientifically provable causal chain between CO_2 emissions from RWE's emissions and the increasing danger to the claimant's property being exposed to a possible outburst flood caused by a glacial ice avalanche. This causal chain can be established around four clearly definable steps: (1) A certain definable proportion of CO_2 emissions from RWE power plants end up in the atmosphere. They contribute to higher concentrations of greenhouse gases in the entire atmosphere—irrespective of the origin of emissions—as described by physical laws (Cubasch et al. 2013); (2) Due to the increasing concentrations of greenhouse gases, radiative forcing in terms of the absorption of solar radiation increases, which correlates with an increase in average global temperature. In the Peruvian Andes, specifically, this has led to regional warming and no other reasons have been observed for the rise in average temperature (Magrin et al. 2014); (3) Increased temperature leads to accelerated glacial retreat and heavily increases the probability of glacial ice avalanches (Magrin et al. 2014); (4) Due to accelerated glacial melting the glacial lake's volume increases which consequently further raises the risk of harm to the claimant's property by an outburst flood caused by glacial ice avalanches. Additionally, the claimant—referring to the principle of adequacy, as used by the court, asserted that the contribution of RWE, the largest emitter in Europe to climate change, is not as low as not too carry weight. Accordingly, the claimant demanded a contribution from RWE to risk management measures at the lake commensurate with the company's contribution to global CO_2 emissions. The claimant asserted that there is no legal reason why a large emitter, such as RWE, should be exempt from its climate-related legal responsibilities, and that a big emitter should not be treated like the numerous collectively irresponsible small emitters, whose individual contributions to climate warming are indeed not measurable.

The Decision to Accept the Case
On November 13th 2017, the Higher Regional Court of Hamm in North Rhine-Westphalia accepted the case Lliuya against RWE. This decision marks the first time that a court acknowledged that a private company is in principal responsible for its share in causing climate damages. This applies if concrete damages or risks to private persons or their property can partly be assigned to the activities of the relevant company. On November 30th 2017, the case formally entered into the next stage—the taking of evidence. Now that the court accepted the legal argument of this case, the task for the plaintiff is to provide evidence for his claim before the court. The following questions play a central role and will need to be addressed in the hearing

- Is Saúl Luciano Lliuya's home in fact acutely endangered by a glacier outburst flood?
- Do RWE's historical emissions really amount to half a percent of global emissions since the beginning of industrialisation—and if not, to how much?
- Is there proof that these emissions contributed to accelerated glacier melting and the risk of flooding in Huaraz?

20.4 The Outlook

The lawsuit raises the issue of responsibility of large energy companies for climate change in terms of liability for nuisance and losses and damages. It may act as a model for similar lawsuits in other countries. The acceptance of the case and its entering in the evidentiary phase itself has already written legal history, says lawyer Roda Verheyen:

The OLG Hamm confirmed its vote of the oral hearing on November 13th 2017: Major emitters of greenhouse gases can be held liable for protective measures against climate damages. The decision establishes a solid argument for legally relevant causality in cases that were not accepted before, notably in reference to a negative ruling of the Federal Supreme Court on acid rain in 1987. Now we can prove in a concrete case that RWE contributed and continues to contribute to the risk of a local glacier outburst flood in Huaraz (Germanwatch 2017).

Beside the claimant's concrete concern about climate change impacts in Huaraz, the lawsuit, which is financially supported by the Foundation Zukunftsfähigkeit and technically supported by the NGO Germanwatch, qualifies as a legal test case. It addresses responsibility of energy suppliers with regard to bearing the social costs of using fossil fuels, costs which have been largely externalised. In addition to confirming the need for political solutions with regard to climate change induced Loss and Damage, the case has also shown to investors that they ought to consider the potential costs of legal liabilities in their energy investment decisions. These costs may fall on large emitters, effectively serving as a disincentive to continuing investing in fossil fuel-based energy production.

Similar legal rules—from which climate responsibility of big greenhouse gas emitters may follow—exist in other countries around the world. The decision in the Huaraz Case will thus have implications for great emitters all around the globe in terms of them having to communicate the relevant litigation risks to shareholders and building adequate financial reserves. Investors will have to take those risks into account when taking investment decisions.

Of course, we do not consider it a long-term solution that the most vulnerable people around the world exposed to climate change related losses and damages have to file legal actions in order to defend their rights. Germanwatch thus emphasises the need for acting on responsibility and expects, as a consequence of litigation action, a strengthening of political will to protect affected people and hold big emitters accountable (Schäfer et al. 2018).

References

Bürgerliches Gesetzbuch [BGB] [Civil Code] (2002) Bundesgesetzblatt, Part I, 2002-01-08, No. 2, pp. 42–341, ISSN: 03411095

Carey M (2005) Living and dying with glaciers: people's historical vulnerability to avalanches and outburst floods in Peru. Global Planetary Change 47:122–134. https://doi.org/10.1016/j.gloplacha.2004.10.007

Cramer W, Yohe G, Auffhammer M, Huggel C, Molau U, Da Silva Dias MAF, Solow A, Stone D, Tibig L (2014) Detection and attribution of observed impacts. In: Field CB et al (eds) Climate change 2014: impacts, adaptation, and vulnerability. Contribution of working group II to the fifth assessment report of the intergovernmental panel on climate change, Chap 18. Cambridge University Press, Cambridge, UK, and New York, NY, USA, pp 979–1037

Cubasch U, Wuebbles D, Chen D, Facchini MC, Frame D, Mahowald N, Winther JG (2013) Introduction. In: Stocker TF, Qin D, Plattner GK, Tignor M, Allen SK, Boschung J, Nauels A, Xia Y, Bex V, Midgley PM (eds) Climate change 2013: the physical science basis. Contribution of working group I to the fifth assessment report of the intergovernmental panel on climate change. Cambridge University Press, Cambridge, United Kingdom and New York, NY, USA, pp 119–158

Germanwatch (2017) Historic breakthrough with global impact in "climate lawsuit." Germanwatch. https://germanwatch.org/en/14795. Accessed 28 Jan 2018

Heede R (2014) Tracing anthropogenic carbon dioxide and methane emissions to fossil fuel and cement producers, 1854–2010. Clim Change 122(1–2):229–241

IPCC (2013) Climate change 2013: the physical science basis. In: Stocker TF, Qin D, Plattner G-K, Tignor M, Allen SK, Boschung J, Nauels A, Xia Y, Bex V, Midgley PM (eds) Contribution of working group I to the fifth assessment report of the intergovern-mental panel on climate change. Cambridge University Press, Cambridge, United Kingdom and New York, NY, USA, 1535 pp

James RA, Jones RG, Boyd E, Young HR, Otto FEL, Huggel C, Fuglestvedt JS (2018) Attribution: how is it relevant for loss and damage policy and practice? In: Mechler R, Bouwer L, Schinko T, Surminski S, Linnerooth-Bayer J (eds) Loss and damage from climate change. Concepts, methods and policy options. Springer, Cham, pp 113–154

Magrin G, Marengo J, Boulanger J-P, Buckeridge M, Castellanos E, Poveda E, Scarano F, Vicuña S (2014) Central and South America. In: Climate change 2014: impacts, adaptation, and vulnerability. Part B: regional aspects. In: Barros VR et al (eds) Contribution of working group II to the fifth assessment report of the intergovernmental panel on climate change. Cambridge University Press, Cambridge, United Kingdom and New York, NY, USA, pp 1499–1566

Rivas DS, Somos-Valenzuela MA, Hodges BR, McKinney DC (2015) Predicting outflow induced by moraine failure in glacial lakes: the Lake Palcacocha case from an uncertainty perspective. Nat Hazards Earth Sys Sci 15:1163–1179. https://doi.org/10.5194/nhess-15-1163-2015

Schäfer L, Künzel V, Bals C (2018) The significance of climate litigation for the political debate on Loss&Damage. Germanwatch Bonn

Schinko T, Mechler R, Hochrainer-Stigler S (2018) The risk and policy space for loss and damage: integrating notions of distributive and compensatory justice with comprehensive climate risk management. In: Mechler R, Bouwer L, Schinko T, Surminski S, Linnerooth-Bayer J (eds) Loss and damage from climate change. Concepts, methods and policy options. Springer, Cham, pp 83–110

Simlinger F, Mayer B (2018) Legal responses to climate change induced loss and damage. In: Mechler R, Bouwer L, Schinko T, Surminski S, Linnerooth-Bayer J (eds) Loss and damage from climate change. Concepts, methods and policy options. Springer, Cham, pp 179–203

Chapter 21
Insurance as a Response to Loss and Damage?

JoAnne Linnerooth-Bayer, Swenja Surminski, Laurens M. Bouwer, Ilan Noy and Reinhard Mechler

Abstract This chapter asks whether insurance instruments, especially micro-insurance and regional insurance pools, can serve as a risk-reducing and equitable compensatory response to climate-attributed losses and damages from climate extremes occurring in developing countries, and consequently if insurance instruments can serve the preventative and curative targets of the Warsaw International Mechanism for Loss and Damage (WIM). The discussion emphasises the substantial benefits of both micro-insurance programs and regional insurance pools, and at the same time details their significant costs. Beyond costs and benefits, a main message is that if no significant intervention is undertaken in their design and implementation, market-based insurance mechanisms will likely fall short of fully meeting WIM aspirations of loss reduction and equitable compensation. Interventions can include subsidies and other types of support that make insurance affordable to poor clients; interventions can also enable public-private arrangements that genuinely catalyse risk reduction and adaptation. Many such interventions are already in place, and the chapter highlights two potential success stories for insurance instruments serving the most vulnerable: the African R4 micro-insurance program and the African Risk Capacity (ARC) regional insurance pool. While support to these and other insurance programs continues to be framed as humanitarian aid based on the principle of solidarity, discussions on the G7 initiative to insure vulnerable households, as

J. Linnerooth-Bayer (✉) · R. Mechler
International Institute for Applied Systems Analysis (IIASA), Laxenburg, Austria
e-mail: bayer@iiasa.ac.at

S. Surminski
Grantham Research Institute on Climate Change and the Environment, London School of Economics and Political Science (LSE), London, UK

L. M. Bouwer
Deltares, Delft, Netherlands
e-mail: laurens.bouwer@hzg.de

I. Noy
Victoria University of Wellington, Wellington, New Zealand

L. M. Bouwer
Climate Service Center Germany (GERICS), Hamburg, Germany

R. Mechler et al. (eds.), *Loss and Damage from Climate Change*, Climate Risk Management, Policy and Governance, https://doi.org/10.1007/978-3-319-72026-5_21

well as on ARC's initiative to link international payments to climate risks, raise the question whether the narrative will evolve from solidarity to responsibility based on the principle of developed country accountability.

Keywords Risk transfer · Financial instruments · Climate change · Catastrophic loss · Safety nets · Disaster risk reduction · Equity · Liability · Compensation

21.1 Introduction

Insurance has played a central role in discussions on adapting to the impacts of climate change, dating back to the early 1990s, when the Alliance of Small Island States (AOSIS) proposed a global insurance fund to compensate small islands for sea-level rise (see introduction by Mechler et al. 2018). Taking stock of this history, as well as the accumulated experience with catastrophe insurance instruments, this chapter asks if insurance mechanisms can help serve the intent of the Warsaw International Mechanism for Loss and Damage (WIM) and Article 8.1 of the Paris Agreement of 'averting, minimising and addressing loss and damage associated with the adverse effects of climate change, including extreme weather events and slow onset events…" (UNFCCC 2015, Article 8). The focus is on weather and climate extremes, including droughts, floods, windstorms and other hazards impacted by anthropogenic climate change, which occur in particularly vulnerable developing countries.

Although the precise intentions of the WIM are still unclear, and especially its distinction from climate adaptation (see chapters by Mechler et al. 2018; Schinko et al. 2018), the WIM Executive Committee (2016) emphasises the role of insurance in furthering climate risk management, or more specifically its role in proactively reducing and transferring risks. In addition, and importantly, discussions on Loss and Damage (L&D) and the WIM have extended to adaptation limits and 'beyond adaptation' (Schäfer et al. 2018). According to the UNFCCC, loss and damage "includes, and in some cases involves more than, that which can be reduced by adaptation" (Decision 2/CP.19, UNFCCC 2014). This has been interpreted by many WIM commentators, and especially developing country parties, to suggest compensation for climate-attributed losses and damages experienced by the most vulnerable communities (see Mace and Verheyen 2016). A legal obligation to compensate for residual loss and damage (the climate-attributed losses and damages that remain once all cost-effective and socially/politically feasible measures have been implemented (UNFCCC 2012) is ruled out in the Paris Agreement (Paragraph 52), yet not for the broader debate, where residual losses and damages resulting from climate-related extremes raise ethical issues concerning retribution or (non-legally binding) compensation (see also Simlinger and Mayer 2018). In line with the discussion in Mechler and Schinko (2016) and the chapter by Schinko et al. (2018) we refer to risk reduction and (non-legally binding) compensation as preventative and curative responses, respectively, and explore the role of insurance instruments in promoting these responses.

In simple terms, insurance allows one party (the insured or policyholder) to transfer the risk of future economic losses to a second party (the insurer) willing to bear this risk for the payment of a premium. By transferring the risk *ex ante*, insurance clients are guaranteed payments for the agreed upon losses and damages from events *ex post*. In this way insurance, as one of a number of *risk financing* instruments, provides reimbursement in return for the payment of a premium such that households, businesses, governments and whole regions can recover in a timely way from the damages from extreme events. In addition, many argue that insurance goes beyond post-disaster reimbursement to pro-actively prevent damages from occurring (see chapter by Schäfer et al. 2018). By 'pricing' risk and requiring preventative measures, insurance provides (in theory) incentives or conditions for clients to adopt damage-reducing behaviour and make investments to reduce their risks.

Insurance thus appears to serve the goals of disaster risk reduction (DRR) as well as post-disaster reimbursement. If insurance payouts are viewed as compensation for losses and damages, insurance serves as a preventative and curative instrument, therefore responding to WIM aspirations as (differently) voiced by developed and developing country parties (see chapter by Calliari et al. 2018). It is not surprising, then, that insurance has figured so prominently in the L&D discussions and work plan. However, while these insurance characteristics have motivated the discussions on insurance as a tool to address climate-attributed losses and damages, they raise questions essential to the WIM deliberations. Most fundamentally, can insurance be viewed as an equitable curative measure for climate-attributed impacts and risks incurred by poor communities in vulnerable countries? This in turn raises questions concerning burden sharing: How are premiums determined and who pays them? Another central question concerns the disaster-risk-reduction (DRR) potential of insurance. Are insurance instruments, as they are currently practiced, effective in encouraging prevention and risk reduction by incentivising or requiring adaptation and resilience investments?

By examining these and other questions, this chapter explores the extent to which insurance—provided through private markets or public institutions—can meet the differentiated WIM ambitions of reducing and compensating for Loss and Damage. The discussion focuses on recent evidence from micro-insurance and regional sovereign insurance pools as these are the most common types of catastrophe insurance currently operating in developing countries, which has given them a particular standing the L&D discussions.

After an overview of catastrophe insurance and its role for loss and damage from climate change (Sect. 21.2), the discussion turns to the benefits and costs of insurance (Sect. 21.3), before it examines insurance as a tool for preventing the economic impacts from extreme weather events (Sect. 21.3) and for reimbursing the residual loss and damage (the curative aspect) (Sect. 21.4) with examples from micro-insurance programs and regional insurance pools. The chapter concludes (in Sect. 21.5) that *insurance instruments based on the 'mutuality principle' (premiums reflect risk plus markup or 'load') will fall short of meeting the 'preventative' and 'curative' aspirations underlying the WIM and Paris Agreement; however, insurance based on the 'solidarity' and 'accountability' principles accompanied by significant outside interventions can indeed support WIM objectives.*

21.2 Insuring Climate Risks: An Overview

21.2.1 Brief History

Reference to insurance was first made by the Alliance of Small Island States (AOSIS), which suggested in 1991 that an international insurance pool funded by industrialised parties be established to compensate small-island and low-lying developing nations for impacts resulting from sea level rise (INC 1991; chapter by Mechler et al. 2018). The insurance mechanism proposed by AOSIS was not aimed at establishing private sector risk transfer, but geared towards a compensation fund to address L&D from sea level rise. As such, it was not strictly insurance in a technical sense, but a compensation mechanism (Linnerooth-Bayer et al. 2003). What remained from these early discussions is reflected in Article 4.8 of the UNFCCC, which calls upon Parties to "consider" actions, including those related to insurance, to meet the specific needs and concerns of developing countries with respect to the adverse impacts of climate change (United Nations 1992). In subsequent years, AOSIS as well as other organisations, such as the Munich Climate Insurance Initiative (MCII), developed proposals for the use of insurance mechanisms to address climate change impacts and risks (AOSIS 2008; MCII 2008). Notably, both the AOSIS and MCII proposals brought a compensatory or curative mechanism for loss and damage in through the back door by including a risk layer in the insurance arrangement that would be fully financed by developed countries; although not differentiating between climate-change attributed impacts and other risk drivers. In addition, both proposals called for increased financing for DRR projects as part of a holistic climate risk management approach. The proposals informed the negotiating text at COP 15 in Copenhagen in 2009, and went on to influence negotiations on the L&D mechanism at COP 19 in Warsaw in 2013. Subsequently, insurance has featured prominently on the WIM agenda, most notably on the workplans of the WIM executive committee (ExCoM) (UNFCCC 2014, 2016).

Recognition of insurance as a potent response to climate risk has been subsequently underscored by the G7 InsuResilience initiative, and recently upgraded to the G20 and V20 partnership (most vulnerable 20 countries), which ambitiously aims at insuring 400 million currently uninsured people in vulnerable countries by 2020 (G7 2015; InsuResilience 2017). Interestingly, these efforts to enhance the role of insurance in addressing disaster and climate risks in developing countries occur predominantly outside the UNFCCC's L&D discussions and are increasingly presented as part of broader development support.

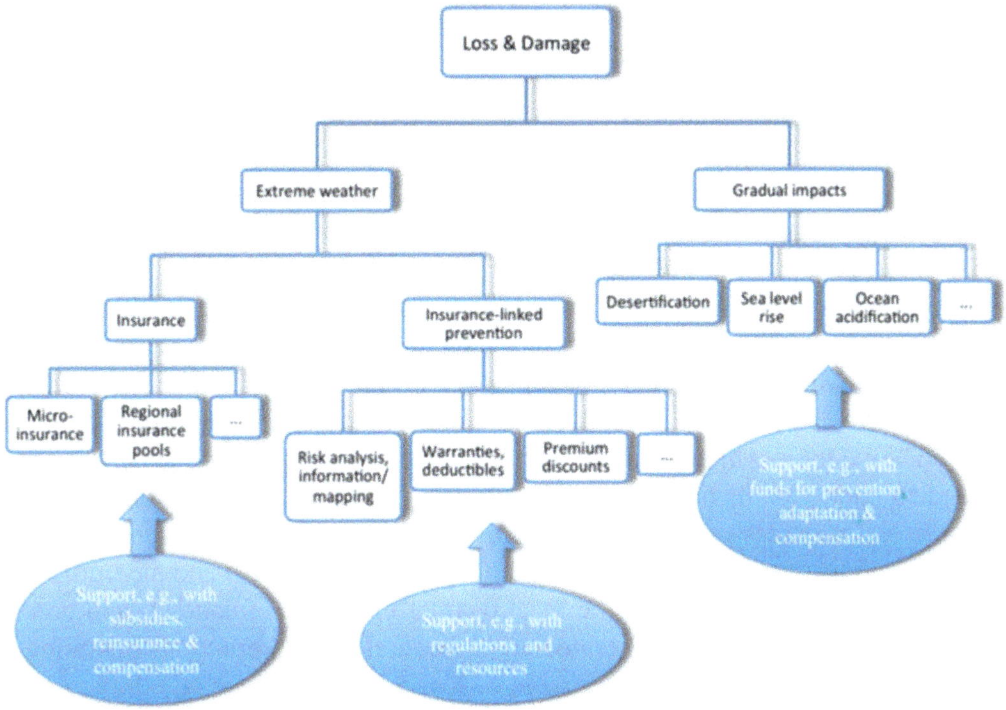

Fig. 21.1 Overview of 'risk management applications' of insurance, in the context of loss and damage . Adapted from Warner et al. (2012)

21.2.2 Can Insurance Cover All Loss and Damage from Climate Change?

It should be emphasised that insurance cannot provide financial protection against all impacts from climate change (Warner et al. 2009). As shown in Fig. 21.1 insurance is an instrument for financing the recovery from extreme and non-gradual climate events, like floods, windstorms and droughts, but is not suited for managing the damage caused by slow-moving or gradual changes that include, among other impacts, sea-level rise, desertification, loss of habitat, loss of biodiversity, erosion, ocean acidification and glacial retreat (chapter by Bouwer 2018). At the same time, these slow climatic changes can become manifest through insurable rapid-onset events, for example, sea-level rise exacerbates storm surge levels and coastal flooding. Equally difficult to insure are small-scale events for which damages are mostly expressed in the cumulative wear-and-tear of assets and infrastructure (Moftakhari et al. 2017). Insurance thus has clear limitations, as it can only cover those events that are sufficiently random and infrequent in their occurrence. Finally, as shown in Fig. 21.1, the range of loss events (rapid-onset to gradual) is accompanied by a range of policy support instruments for risk reduction or reimbursing impacts—from support for insurance instruments (e.g., public subsidies or reinsurance) or insurance-linked prevention, to reparations for gradual onset impacts.

21.2.3 Spectrum of Ex Ante and Ex Post Financing Instruments

Insurance is not the only measure to ensure post-disaster financial resources, and in some contexts other mechanisms can be more appropriate and cost-effective. It is therefore important not to view insurance as a stand-alone solution but consider if and how it can be part of a holistic climate risk management approach. In contrast to wealthy countries, insurance mechanisms for providing catastrophe cover are still in their infancy in the developing world. The percentage of losses from natural hazards covered by private or public insurance in 2014 in the US and Europe were 42 and 34%, respectively, compared to only 1.4% in Africa and 12.5% in Asia (Swiss Re 2015). The extent to which insurance can be offered is risk and country-specific and dependent mainly on income.

Table 21.1 provides an overview of financial instruments and arrangements available to cover disaster risks facing (i) households, farms and small and medium sized enterprises (SMEs) operating at the local or micro scale, (ii) financial- and donor-organisations operating at the intermediary scale, and (iii) governments operating at the national or macro scale.

Table 21.1 Examples of risk financing arrangements at micro, intermediary and macro scales

	Micro-scale Households/SMEs/Farms	Intermediary-scale Insurers/financial institutions/donor organisations/NGOs/Agro-Businesses/Cooperatives	Macro-scale Governments
Insurance instruments	Indemnity–based property, crop & life insurance, index-based (parametric) property, livestock & crop insurance, weather hedges, national insurance programs	Indemnity and parametric insurance for NGOs, co-ops, Re-insurance for direct insurance providers, catastrophe bonds, sidecars	Sovereign risk transfer (e.g., sovereign re-insurance, catastrophe bonds, sidecars), contingent credit, regional catastrophe insurance pools
Solidarity	Government assistance, humanitarian aid	Government guarantees/bail outs	Bi-lateral and multi-lateral assistance, EU solidarity fund
Savings and credit	Savings, micro-savings, micro-credit, fungible assets, food storage, money lenders	Emergency liquidity funds	Reserve funds, post-disaster credit
Informal risk sharing	Kinship and other mutual arrangements, remittances		Diversions from other budgeted programs

Source Adapted from Linnerooth-Bayer et al. (2010)

Lacking insurance, vulnerable households and other local actors have traditionally financed post-disaster recovery with a combination of savings and credit, informal kinship arrangements, government relief and international donor support. Savings can take the form of stockpiles of food, grains, seeds and marketable assets, which serve to smooth consumption during crises. The most common form of assistance is remittances, which are more than three times the size of official development assistance (World Bank 2016), and can be a significant contribution to post-disaster recovery. Banks, insurers and other monetary financial institutions (MFIs), as intermediary-scale actors, can also protect their post-disaster liquidity by purchasing reinsurance, relying on bail outs from the government, or support from institutions like the African Emergency Liquidity Facility (OMTRIX 2005) or the World Bank.

Governments as national operators can meet their obligations to repair public infrastructure and support needy households with *ex post* and *ex ante* instruments. Typically, and as detailed in Table 21.2, public authorities seek financing after disasters occur, for instance, by issuing tax increases, re-allocating funds from other budgeted activities, or borrowing through issuing bonds. Governments of highly exposed countries may also rely on assistance from the international community. An example of the latter is the significant support provided by the World Bank, and in Europe the European Union Solidarity Fund provides post-disaster support to governments to support their recovery (Hochrainer-Stigler et al. 2017).

In addition to these *ex post* instruments, governments increasingly anticipate disaster events with *ex ante* financing or risk transfer as shown in Table 21.2. Risk financing at sovereign level includes a wide range of tools such as national reserve funds, sovereign insurance (also offered through regional pools), and credit and capital market products, such as catastrophe bonds, where bond purchasers agree to forfeit interest or principle if a pre-defined hazard or disaster occurs (see Cardenas et al. 2007). Such a catastrophe bond (150 Million USD), for example, was triggered by the 2017 Oaxaca earthquake (ARTEMIS 2017b). Insurers make use of other types

Table 21.2 Financing instruments for protecting government budgets

Financial and budgetary instruments		
Goal	Ex ante instrument *[arranged before a disaster]*	Ex post instrument *[arranged after a disaster]*
Risk retention *[changing how or when one pays]*	Contingency fund or budget allocation	Budget reallocation
	Line of contigent credit	Tax increase
		Post-disaster credit
Risk transfer *[removing isk from the balance sheet]*	Traditional insurance or reinsurance Indexed insurance, reinsurance, or derivatives	Discretionary post-disaster relief
	Capital market instruments	

Source Clarke and Dercon (2016)

of alternative instruments, such as reinsurance sidecars, where investors act directly as reinsurers, and risk swaps, options and loss warranties. Most of these alternative instruments provide an opportunity for investors in the capital markets to take a more direct role in providing insurance and reinsurance protection.

21.2.4 Types of Insurance

Insurance, whether for health, unemployment or climate-related disasters, is a central feature of most wealthy countries; yet, institutional arrangements can differ significantly depending particularly on the degree of private-market responsibility. In this discussion, we distinguish between private-market insurance, public-private insurance arrangements, and public assistance. Private-market insurers underwrite the risks, and clients are asked to pay their full or close-to-full risk-based premium, albeit often with cross-subsidies from low-risk to high-risk clients that keep the premiums affordable (e.g., flood insurance in Germany, Norway and the U.K.). At the other end of the spectrum is public assistance, which can take the form of a catastrophe reserve fund financed from general taxes (e.g., in Austria) from which loss reimbursement can be legally binding (e.g., earthquake relief in Italy) or non-legally binding and ad hoc (e.g., in Hungary). In between these two ends of the spectrum are many public-private arrangements. Public institutions are active, for instance, in underwriting insurance (e.g., the US National Flood Insurance Program), providing subsidies and other support to private insurance programs (e.g., the Austrian crop insurance system), or supporting commercial insurers with reinsurance arrangements (e.g., the French all-hazard insurance system).

Insurance can be indemnity-based, where products are written against actual losses, or parametric, where products are written against a physical index (e.g., soil moisture), that is, against events that cause loss, not against the loss itself. A parametric instrument disburses funds based on a triggering event that reaches a pre-determined threshold of a quantifiable measure (for example, wind speed or precipitation), which importantly is not conditional on an on-site loss assessment. Semi-parametric schemes are also written, where the trigger is a combination of a hazard and its calculated/modelled impact based on known exposures and vulnerabilities (Molini et al. 2007).

Because they target the most vulnerable in the developing world and have featured prominently in the L&D discussions, two types of insurance are highlighted in this chapter: (1) micro-insurance that offers cover to households, farms and SMEs, and (2) regional sovereign risk pools providing support for national governments. The intent of micro-insurance is to make insurance accessible by avoiding the high costs of traditional insurance in order to service resource-poor markets, usually by offering limited cover and greatly reducing transaction costs (Mechler et al. 2006). The intent of regional sovereign risk insurance pools, including those already formed in the Caribbean, Pacific Islands and Africa, is to ensure needed and timely liquidity post-disaster.

21.3 The Benefits and Costs of Insurance

21.3.1 Benefits of Insurance

The central feature of insurance is its risk-pooling capacity. By pooling risks from a sufficiently large and independent number of individual households, farms, businesses and even sovereign states, insurance collectively reduces loss volatility (mathematically speaking, the variance of losses) and in this way can guarantee post-disaster liquidity to those individuals at risk (Kunreuther 1998). The assurance of post-disaster liquidity, in turn, can reduce impacts, including disaster-induced bankruptcy, hunger, selling of productive financial assets or taking kin out of school with long-term impacts on human capital formation. If correctly implemented insurance thus delivers risk pooling over space and time; faster and more efficient reconstruction; certainty about post-disaster support; and can reduce immediate welfare losses and consumption reductions (Brainard 2008; von Peter et al. 2012).

An important advantage of insurance over many other types of risk financing is the timeliness of the post-disaster payments. A study by Clarke and Hill (2013) suggests that rapid payouts and prompt assistance to affected populations can reduce the impact of disasters and enable poor and vulnerable people to recover more quickly. Examining experience of pro-poor insurance instruments shows that they have been an effective risk management tool in terms of providing timely payments post-event (Arent et al. 2017). Moreover, an insurance contract can be a more secure and timely means of coping with disasters than dependency on ad hoc and often delayed generosity of governments and donors. To add to these benefits, insurance can render clients more creditworthy, and in so doing promote investments in productive assets and higher-risk/higher-yield activities, in turn reducing disaster-related poverty traps (Hallegatte et al. 2016).

Turning to governments, sovereign disaster risk financing instruments including insurance pools aim at protecting public budgets in the wake of disasters. Due to limited tax bases, high indebtedness and low uptake of insurance, many highly exposed developing countries cannot fully recover by simply relying on limited external donor aid. Ex post liquidity through insurance enables governments to provide relief to the most vulnerable and to invest in reconstruction and recovery, thus reducing long-term losses and development setbacks from disasters. Sovereign risk transfers can also indirectly benefit households and other victims of disasters. With internationally backed risk-transfer programs, developing country governments will rely less on debt financing and international donations, and assured funds for repairing critical infrastructure can attract foreign investment. Finally, and importantly, insurance instruments may provide incentives to reduce risk (Newsham et al. 2011; Heltberg et al. 2009a, b), but only if they do not encourage behaviour that neglects to reduce risks in a cost-effective way, a common concern in insurance applications often referred to as 'moral hazard.' The preventative capacity of insurance instruments is the topic of Sect. 3, where we examine their risk-reduction potential in practice.

21.3.2 Costs of Insurance

While there are substantial benefits provided by privately or publicly offered insurance, the costs of insurance are considerable. The average financial cost of insurance generally surpasses average losses, meaning that un-subsidised insurance premiums are greater than what the client expects to lose. For this reason, clients should carefully consider the costs and benefits, and rely on insurance only after considering the alternatives, or in the words of Vaughan and Vaughan (2008, p. 62), only as a last resort. *Indeed, without outside subsidies and other forms of support policyholders can expect, on average, a higher financial burden in the long run with insurance than without it*. That insurance results, on average, in greater costs to those insured is often not appreciated and needs further explanation.

The insurance premium tends to be inflated above the 'actuarially fair value' or 'pure premium' (expected losses) due to the fact that on top of the annual expected losses a risk premium is charged. As shown in Fig. 21.2, the risk premium is determined by two factors: expense load and risk load (Pollner 2000). Additionally, in the case of private insurance a profit margin is charged. In general terms the *expense load* reflects the costs of the insurer doing business, and the *risk load* includes the cost of holding capital, reinsurance and of assuming uncertain contracts for high-level risks. The risk load distinguishes catastrophe insurance from other types of insurance, like life and health, since insurers covering catastrophic risks must be prepared to pay claims for disasters that affect whole regions or countries at the same time (co-variate risk). Still, if insurers are sufficiently diversified, the risk load will not only insulate them from large losses at one time, but will also in the long run result in significant profits.

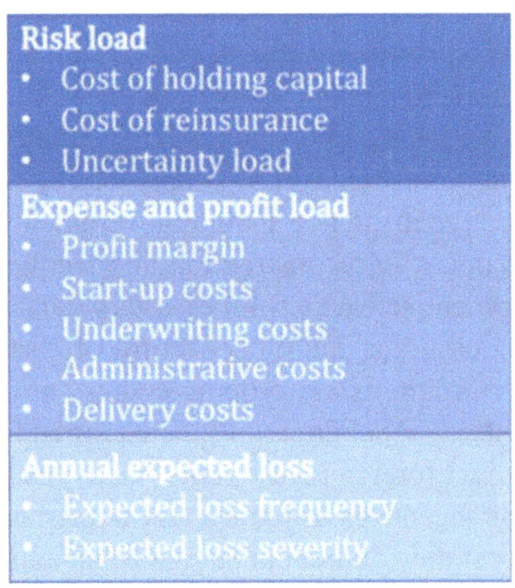

Fig. 21.2 Costs contributing to catastrophe insurance premium *Source* Adapted from Cummins and Mahul (2009)

The ratio of the premium paid versus the coverage obtained gives an indication of the insurance cost, particularly when comparing insurance to other risk financing tools. Using this ratio, Ghesquiere and Mahul (2010) found that risk transfer is very costly compared to most other financial instruments (Ghesquiere and Mahul 2010; Clarke and Dercon 2016). As a case in point, in the Caribbean region annual insurance premiums (paid mostly by businesses) were estimated to represent about 1.5% of GDP during the period 1970–1999, while average losses per annum (insured and uninsured) accounted for only about 0.5% of GDP (Auffret 2003).

If insurance premiums cost clients on average more than their anticipated losses, and in the case of co-variant catastrophic events significantly so, why do households, businesses and governments insure? This question is particularly pertinent for resource-poor households and governments, where premium payments can have high opportunity costs. The textbook rationale for purchasing insurance, verified by evidence on insurance penetration, is based on the concept of "risk aversion". Risk-averse persons and entities (generally people who cannot cope with large losses) are willing to pay more than they expect to lose on average to avoid catastrophic losses. Households and farms in developing countries are likely to be highly risk averse since large losses can threaten livelihoods and lives (and thus have severe costs and other implications beyond the sheer financial loss). The same holds for the public sector since disasters can significantly affect development if governments do not have the means for rapid reconstruction and relief efforts (Mechler 2004).

For middle- to high-income earners in developed as well as developing countries an insurance value proposition can often be discerned as shown by substantial insurance demand, yet it is pertinent to ask how insurance mechanisms can serve resource-poor clients facing high risk? As current programs demonstrate, insurance premiums are made affordable by targeting higher income clients, implementing cross subsidies, limiting coverage, providing outside support and forming partnerships (Linnerooth-Bayer et al. 2010). Whereas most discussions focus largely on making insurance affordable, it should be recognised that it may not be advisable from a benefit-cost perspective. Indeed, reliance on alternative financial arrangements, like donor solidarity, savings, credit and remittances, can be considerably less costly than insurance, and these arrangements can work reasonably well for low-loss events (Cohen and Sebstad 2003). However, they can be unreliable and inadequate for covariate and catastrophic shocks that place a significant financial strain on whole communities, regions and governments. *Insurance theory and recent cost-benefit assessments indicate that insurance and other risk financing instruments are mainly advisable, and viable, for large and residual risks that cannot be reduced or retained otherwise.*

21.4 Preventative Response: Does Insurance Support the Risk-Reduction Response to the WIM?

Many analysts argue that insurance can go beyond enabling *ex post* relief, reconstruction and recovery, to be an *ex ante* tool for promoting risk reduction (Kunreuther 1996; Kunreuther and Michel-Kerjan 2009; Crichton 2008; Botzen 2013). According to the chapter by Schäfer et al. (2018): "Insurance spurs transformation by helping countries reshape the way risks are managed. It does so by encouraging risk reduction, catalysing risk assessment, and driving more structured decision-making around ex-ante risk". Despite these claims, some commentators, including NGOs and parties to the UNFCCC, remain sceptical that insurance goes beyond risk spreading to risk reduction, and worry that insurance can even lead to a false sense of security or moral hazard if the insured, by not bearing the full costs of risky decisions, take on more risk (Vellinga et al. 2001; UNFCCC 2008). Moral hazard is widely recognised, and insurers address it through the design of insurance products by using deductibles or parametric products; however, questions remain whether insurance products lead directly to risk reduction. According to the Intergovernmental Panel on Climate Change (IPCC), insurance can "directly provide incentives for reducing risk, yet the evidence is weak and the presence of many counteracting factors often leads to disincentives…" (Chambwera et al. 2014).

Building on Surminski and Eldridge (2015) and Surminski (2014), Lorant et al. (*forthcoming*) identify ways in which the contractual elements and ancillary mechanisms of insurance can (in concept) encourage risk reduction. After surveying the developed-country practices of flood insurers, the authors note the disappointing evidence of a strong link between insurance and DRR and suggest ways that insurers can contribute more effectively, for example, making better use of hazard maps, monitoring household risk improvements, rewarding risk mitigation with premium discounts, inserting conditions or warranties into contracts, and developing protocols that will better link risk inspections of large facilities with underwriting practices. Beyond these design changes, there is evidence that public insurers invest more in preventative risk reduction than their private insurer counterparts (Schwarze and Croonenbroeck 2017; Ungern-Sternberg 1996). The evidence on the insurance-DRR link for the on-going work under the WIM is *that indemnity-based insurance as practiced in wealthy countries may need adapting if it is to be applied as an* instrument *to foster reduction of loss and damage in developing countries*. A similar conclusion was reached by the IPCC, where authors confirmed that risk-financing mechanisms contribute to increasing resilience, but that major design changes would be needed to avoid providing disincentives for DRR (Chambwera et al. 2014). As we witness in wealthy countries, *progress will be slow and patchy without public and private commitment to shaping insurance systems such that they foster practices that lead to investment in disaster risk reduction practices.*

21.4.1 The Experience of Micro-insurance in Promoting Risk Reduction

The message that insurance practices will require reform if they are to better promote risk reduction holds not only for indemnity-based systems in wealthy countries, but also for parametric micro-insurance systems that are increasingly targeting resource-poor clients in the developing world (for reviews, see Linnerooth-Bayer et al. 2012; Mechler et al. 2006; Schäfer and Waters 2016). Already in 2010, there were a reported 36 parametric weather insurance programs, including 28 addressing individual farmers/herders, residents of informal settlements, village or cooperative risk (Hazell et al. 2010), with many other programs having appeared since then (Schäfer and Waters 2016).

Parametric systems are notable for the absence of moral hazard. The insured remain motivated to reduce their losses and damages because insurance disbursements, if they are triggered, are not based on actual losses. For example, a farmer with a parametric insurance contract, which pays out if rainfall falls below a pre-defined level, can gain doubly by planting drought-resistant crops since the farmer will have less losses and still receive a pay-out. Beyond the elimination of moral hazard, the literature on parametric micro-insurance makes little reference to specific risk-reduction requirements, for example, in the form of conditions or warranties, and there are few accounts of micro-insurers informing clients of hazards or advising them on risk-reduction activities.

One notable positive exception is the R4 Rural Resilience Initiative (R4) that offers micro-insurance for drought risk to food-insecure communities in Ethiopia, Senegal, Malawi and Zambia (see Box 21.1). R4 currently reaches over 40,000 farms through a combination of its four risk-management strategies: The first, R1, promotes improved resource management (risk reduction); R2 supports microcredit (prudent risk taking;); R3 is insurance (risk transfer); and R4 is savings (risk reserves). The most unique and interesting feature of this initiative is its direct link to the reduction of crop loss from drought. In lieu of paying aa premium, cash-constrained farmers can opt to participate in an insurance-for-assets (IFA) plan, whereby they pay the premium through their labour on projects that reduce risk in the community, such as field irrigation projects and tree planting (World Food Programme and Oxfam America 2016). It should be noted, however, that the R4 Program operates with generously subsidised premiums, even to those not participating in insurance-for-assets, and cannot be compared to a market-based insurance program.

R4 is exemplary by providing a proven insurance system design that promotes DRR, especially since the risk management experiences of most micro-insurance programs suggest that they could become a more powerful DRR tool with carefully designed interventions by governments or donors. Importantly, the ability of those most vulnerable to reduce their own risk and to change their behaviour may be very limited or not feasible unless supported by donors.

Box 21.1 R4 Rural Resilience Initiative for drought risk management
Countries: Ethiopia, Senegal, Malawi, Zambia
Partners: farmers, local relief society, insurers, reinsurers, rural banks, university, government and donors
Policy holders: 40,000 Smallholder farmers' livelihoods in
drought-prone regions with a sum insured of USD 2.2 million, premiums of USD 370,000, and payouts USD 450,000 (2015)

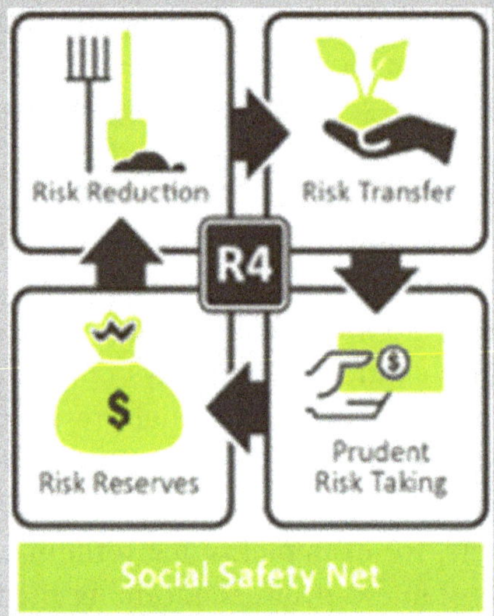

Fig. 21.3 The R4 Rural Resilience Initiative

Integrated risk management framework
- Improved resource management (risk reduction)
- Individual/group savings (risk reserves)
- Microinsurance (risk transfer)
- Microcredit (risk taking)

Insurance-for-work program to supplement the government's "food and cash for work" Productive Safety Net Programme (PSNP)
Work program includes projects for reducing risk and building climate resilience, such as improved irrigation or soil management.
Source World Food Program & Oxfam America 2016; World Food Programme 2017

21.4.2 The Experience of Regional Risk Pools in Promoting Risk Reduction

The first of three regional sovereign risk pools, the Caribbean Catastrophe Risk Insurance Facility (CCRIF), was created in 2007 as a multi-government disaster risk pooling arrangement with the aim of providing sovereign insurance coverage for hurricanes and earthquakes to its participating member countries (UNISDR 2017). A second regional pool, Africa Risk Capacity (ARC) was established in 2012 as a specialised agency of the African Union to help member states improve their capacities to better plan, prepare and respond to natural disasters (Wilcox 2014). Recently, a third regional sovereign risk pooling arrangement has been created for the Pacific island states, the Pacific Catastrophe Risk Assessment and Financing Initiative (PCRAFI) (World Bank 2017). In all three cases, disbursements from the pool go to participating governments for the purpose of supporting their post-disaster relief and reconstruction efforts, although only one of the pools (ARC) makes requirements on how the disbursements are used by requesting its members to provide details about contingency management and disbursement when they join the pool.

A key feature of all three pools is the parametric nature of the insurance contract, which, as discussed for micro-insurance, makes payments faster and the claim process less costly than traditional indemnity-based insurance products for which claims are paid based on assessments of loss through on-site verification. Fast payment of claims is especially critical. Intervening quickly after a disaster can provide governments with funds that support households and prevent the adoption of damaging coping strategies (such as selling off or slaughtering livestock). A benefit-cost analysis carried out on the ARC shows that getting aid to households in the critical three months after harvest can result in economic gains of over USD 1,200 per household assisted (Clarke and Hill 2013). CCRIF announced that its payouts to Caribbean governments due to the impacts of Hurricane Irma, which devastated many island states in September 2017, will reach $31.2 million, and the facility has now passed $100 million of payouts to members since its launch. All of the $100 million of payouts were made to members within 14 days of the catastrophe events that triggered their parametric insurance policies (ARTEMIS 2017a).

Advancing ex ante risk management is also important in all three regional programs, especially with respect to developing the knowledge base on which disaster risk reduction and management policy can be pursued. Each pool makes an effort, paid for by donors, to measure and quantify disaster risk in the relevant region by examining not only the hazard but also exposure and vulnerability using detailed mapping, data and modelling tools developed explicitly for this purpose. An example is ARC's modelling platform called African Risk View. It provides modelling input to ARC for insurance purposes, but also aims to be a financial early warning tool, supporting government decision-makers with cost estimates before and during a drought season. As such it can trigger early action and risk reduction measures. The models and quantification of risk constitute major progress as private markets and the governments of the region were not supplying this information previously. If combined with technical assistance and capacity building these advances in risk information can lead to a culture of risk management across governments, potentially inducing a more anticipatory approach to risk (Vivid Economics et al. 2016).

ARC is currently preparing for the launch of an additional tool, the Extreme Climate Facility (ARC-XCF), which aims to address adaptation and resilience shortfalls in African countries in the face of climate change. XCF is designed to take account of increasing risk of extreme weather event activity in order to disperse funds to be used to invest in risk-reduction activities (Wilcox 2014, see Box 21.3). This tool, requested by ARC member countries, offers an interesting approach to linking the risk transfer structure of ARC to climate adaptation and risk reduction investment.

Notwithstanding the paramount importance of assessing risks to countries in the pool and providing timely post-disaster funds, the regional pools have put into place very few explicit incentives or funds for reducing disaster risks. There are some requirements with regard to usage of pay-outs and emergency management, yet as shown in the case of ARC, there are no conditions for proven disaster and climate risk reductions. CCRIF has a disaster risk management function, but it focuses on reducing downstream losses after a disaster has occurred by providing immediate liquidity. In practice, then, beyond the data collection and modelling aspects (though only the ARC provides open source risk data), there is very little evidence that the regional pools shape DRR and climate adaptation policy in their member countries.

To conclude, it appears that more can be done to design regional sovereign risk pools that contribute to the preventative aspiration of the WIM, although the proposed ARC XCF offers an interesting proposition for this purpose. Design reform of the pools might include a requirement for detailed contingency plans for pre-disaster risk reduction and (in the case of CCRIF and PCRAFI) making risk data open source. The implementation of these plans could be made a requisite for continued membership in the pool.

21.5 Curative Response: Does Insurance Promote the Equitable Compensation Response T the WIM?

The WIM extends beyond aspirations for disaster risk reduction to include climate-attributed loss and damage that cannot be effectively reduced. This has raised aspirations especially among highly vulnerable developing countries that a form of (legally non-binding) compensation for residual climate impacts may be in the offing. The question in this section is *whether insurance, by reimbursing loss and damage from climate disasters, contributes to the 'equitable compensation' or curative aspirations for the WIM?*

At the outset, it is worth emphasising that financial instruments, including insurance, are not neutral as to how disaster costs are shared. Risk-based instruments that require premiums or payments from those in the insurance program can shift responsibility to vulnerable households and communities and away from social institutions that may have previously aided reconstruction; in contrast, informal or public mechanisms, like remittances or reserve funds, share losses usually across family members and taxpayers. For insurance programs, it should be asked if the insured, themselves, pay the risk-estimated premium thus putting the full burden on their own at-risk communities (and at the same time providing incentives for them to reduce their risks). Alternatively, are there arrangements, like cross subsidies, that allocate this burden differently within the risk pool, or are there arrangements, like transfer payments, that allocate the burden at least partially to those outside the risk pool?

21.5.1 Equity Principles in the Compensation of Loss and Damage

The essential question for the L&D discussions is then "who pays the premium?" To address this question in Box 21.2 we distinguish three principles of fundamental importance for organising insurance arrangements, each principle building on a different view of equity. Private market-based insurance, unless it is subsidised from outside or within the pool, operates on the principle of mutuality and thus does not share losses beyond the at-risk insured community. Private insurers may deviate from the mutuality principle with premium cross-subsidies, e.g., by charging their wealthy, lower-risk clients higher premiums to make policies affordable to low-income clients in high-risk locations. Sometimes this means a flat or undifferentiated premium that helps high risk (and often less wealthy) clients and avoids the costs and administrative burdens associated with differentiated premiums. In some cases, regulation dictates how private insurers can set premiums, usually to safeguard affordability. In India, for example, commercial insurers are required to offer 'pro-poor' policies, which they finance by charging their wealthy clients a higher rate. Without these forms of subsidy in a mutuality-based system the policyholders, themselves, can expect (in the long term) to pay premiums that are approximately equivalent to their received claim payments (actuarially fair premiums), plus significant additional costs (loads shown in Fig. 21.2). *Thus, in an insurance system based on mutuality, there is no reimbursement to the victims of disasters (on average) outside of what they, themselves, contribute in premiums; in other words, the at-risk community finances its own curative measures*. This is an important and often misunderstood feature of the insurance mechanism, and arguably disqualifies commercial insurance as a curative measure as intended by the WIM.

Solidarity can take many forms, including subsidised or cross-subsidised premiums, reinsurance or other forms of assistance that reduce premiums paid by the most vulnerable. It is the fundamental principle underlying pre-disaster assistance and post-disaster humanitarian relief and reconstruction (see Schinko et al. 2018). Support can come from, among others, governments, NGOs, financial institutions or international development organisations. Indeed, almost all micro-insurance programs and macro-level pools operating in developing countries receive some type of donor or government support (Vivid Economics et al. 2016). Importantly, solidarity, in contrast to accountability, need not appeal to a causal relationship between historical greenhouse gas emissions and loss and damage, or culpability on the part of those providing support for insurance instruments.

Box 21.2 Three equity principles for organising insurance

Mutuality

Mutuality is at the core of the insurance concept, according to which the insured participate in a disaster pool according to their risk class (and pay a risk-based premium). The pool then pays those insured in accordance with the scale of their losses. Mutuality is the primary principle underlying private, market-based insurance; clients enter the pool usually voluntarily, and pay according to the best estimate of the risk they bring with them. While insured agents receive payments from the pool depending on their losses, in the long run (and on average) they pay their own reimbursement, and more, since the premium is based on expected loss plus the additional insurance loads shown in Fig. 21.2. According to this principle, there are no transfer payments within the pool or from outside the pool (Wilkie 1997).

Solidarity

Solidarity is a profoundly different concept in that losses are paid according to need, and contributions to the pool are not made fully in accordance with the risks that the applicants bring with them, but perhaps partly according to ability to pay, or just equally. Solidarity can result from cross subsidies among those in the pool. It can also take the form of payments by those not in the pool, for example, aid agencies can subsidise micro-insurance schemes. Importantly, solidarity is based on the concept of voluntary transfers for humanitarian or other grounds; there is no underlying notion of liability. The concept of solidarity thus corresponds to the concept of distributive justice discussed in Wallimann-Helmer et al. (2018).

Accountability

Accountability as a concept differentiates itself from the solidarity principle in one important aspect; here, it is motivated by a perceived ethical or legal obligation for compensating those experiencing climate-attributed losses and damages. Accountability links an actor's actions with outcomes, either causally or legally (Honoré 2010) where the allocation of responsibility is based on causation and (often but not always) fault or negligence. Being accountable not only means being responsible for climate-attributed impacts and risks but also ultimately being answerable for them.

A far more controversial and potent principle to underlie support for insurance instruments is *accountability* for loss and damage, which mirrors the "polluter-pays principle" that is invoked across many environmental issues. *Accountability* invokes questions of attribution (James et al. 2018) as well as some degree of culpability or fault. Both can be difficult to assign to state and other actors since the science is not sufficiently precise to estimate increased risk of losses and damages due to emissions of greenhouse gases, and fault for emissions can be questioned due to historical knowledge and other factors (Burkett 2014). The assignment of accountability for losses and damages, and ultimately responsibility, has been understandably resisted because of fears of legal liability. Indeed, the Paris Agreement explicitly rejects that the treaty provide a basis for liability or compensation (Simlinger and Mayer 2018). Yet, as Lees (2016) argues, the refusal to contemplate liability should not lead to a refusal to contemplate the allocation of ethical responsibility—what he refers to as a responsibility allocation mechanism. Indeed, recognition of ethical responsibility, as differentiated from legal liability, may be necessary, if not essential, for motivating even voluntary support for insurance instruments on the scale contemplated by the L&D discussions.

Principles of solidarity and accountability are strongly voiced in the Framework Convention on Climate Change (UNFCCC), which states that parties should act to protect the climate system "on the basis of equality and in accordance with their common but differentiated responsibilities and respective capabilities" (United Nations 1992). A fundamental element of this principle, which is restated in the preamble to the Paris Agreement, is the need to take account of the different circumstances, particularly each State's contribution to the problem and capacity to remedy it (Decision 3/CP.19). The WIM, likewise, refers to the need to take account of differentiated responsibility (accountability) for losses and damages (Lees 2016). *The principles set out in the UNFCCC and Paris Agreement suggest that those bearing responsibility for losses and damages, and those most capable of addressing it, should bear some obligation to contribute to insurance premiums for climate-attributed risks in highly vulnerable countries.* In fact, many developing country Parties and NGOs have advocated the accountability principle. The submission of CARE to the current WIM work plan is illustrative:

> …(WIM) should apply principles of global equity, including taking into account a "polluter pays"-based approach to generating finance for addressing loss and damage from countries, companies and institutions who significantly contribute to the causes of climate change through fossil fuel emissions (CARE International 2017).

Invoking responsibility/accountability in the discourse on developed country support (but avoiding legal liability) changes the paradigm of post-disaster support from 'charity' to 'amends', which has significance in terms of allocating funds beyond humanitarian assistance budgets. Arguably, a responsibility-based discourse can change the motivation for assisting victims of climate-attributed impacts and risks—so essential to implementing the Paris Agreement and maintaining its voluntary, cooperation-focused approach (see chapter by Schinko et al. 2018).

21.5.2 Experience of Micro-insurance for Equitably Allocating the Impacts and Risks Burden

Almost without exception micro-insurance schemes that serve the resource-poor are subsidised either by national taxpayer funds or, more often, by international donors, international financial institutions, NGOs and official development assistance (Mechler et al. 2006; Schäfer and Waters 2016). Few private insurers are optimistic about the prospects of providing non-subsidised insurance to clients below the poverty level (Swiss Re 2012).

As one example, India's National Agricultural Insurance Scheme (NAIS), globally the largest micro-insurance crop program, targets mainly middle-income farmers and is heavily subsidised by Indian taxpayers (Mechler et al. 2006). As another example, the pro-poor R4 initiative discussed above is made possible by the significant support it receives from NGOs and donors as well as its reliance on funds (in Ethiopia) from Ethiopia's Productive Safety Net Program and the World Food Programme. An innovative micro-insurance program for herders in Mongolia is affordable and viable to insurers due to its layered system of responsibility and payment, including herders (who retain small losses or the lowest risk layer), the private insurance industry (risk-based premium payments for the middle layer of risk) and taxpayers (for the highest risk layer). In addition to subsidies, micro-insurance is typically made affordable by greatly reducing the cover offered. A micro-insurance program in Bangladesh, *Proshika*, that insures savings against natural disasters limits claims to twice the amount in the client's savings account (Mechler et al. 2006). Similarly, a micro-insurance project in Malawi was made affordable by limiting cover to the cost of the hybrid seeds, which protects the banks against defaults for their seed loans, but does not protect households against drought losses (Linnerooth-Bayer et al. 2009).

The extensive support for micro-insurance falls thus solidly under the insurance principle of *solidarity*, where contributions to the pool are made, not in accordance with the risks that applicants bring to the pool, but typically according to their ability to pay the premium. Climate-attributed impacts and risks will likely continue to be framed as a humanitarian issue invoking solidarity, and not as an issue invoking accountability or liability.

21.5.3 Experience of Regional Insurance Pools for Equitably Sharing the Impacts and Risk Burden

The question addressed in this section is to what extent the regional insurance pools (CCRIF, ARC and PCRAFI) provide their members with an equitable *curative* respons*e* to climate-attributed losses and damages, keeping in mind that the pools provide cover to governments, which in turn (and in varying degrees) provide post-disaster support to vulnerable households, farms and SMEs. By 'equitable' we again refer to the three principles relevant to insurance: *mutuality, solidarity and accountability*. We ask, thus, who pays the price for membership in the risk pools, and based on which equity principle?

All pools have received donor support, mostly through capitalisation, payment of operational expenses, direct premium support or capacity building. While the premiums are therefore less than would be required without outside support, in the case of ARC and CCRIF the relative premiums (the proportion each member country pays to the pool) tend to be based on risk levels (i.e., there are no cross subsidies). The pools are thus based on *solidarity* from the outside, but *mutuality* in determining the relative payments from members. For ARC, all insured countries pay premiums based on risk estimates, while for setting up and operating the pools support comes from donor organisations. In other words, donors contribute to reducing some of the loads on the insurance premium. ARC's non-profit mutual insurance company (not necessarily meaning the premiums are based on mutuality) is capitalised by financial and development institutions, including the German Development Bank and the UK Department for International Development (DFID), which means that premiums are indirectly supported through a solidarity principle. For ARC, thus, there are elements of *mutuality* in setting country-specific trigger points and caps, which largely determine premiums, and also elements of *solidarity* given substantial donor support.

The PCRAFI, in contrast, bases premiums largely on ability-to-pay of its member countries rather than a calculated risk. This means there are substantial cross subsidies across member states. In addition, multiple development partners and IDA credit have contributed to the establishment of the pool as well as to premium support. The PCRAFI is thus based primarily on the principle of *solidarity* in terms of both outside- and inside-pool support.

Interestingly the principle of *accountability* has not been invoked in justifying the contributions of the donor community to these systems, even though climate change is a concern to all regional pools. However, not surprising after the devastating 2017 Hurricanes Harvey and Irma, the attribution of the covered hazards to climatic change is under investigation for CCRIF and the other pools. More specifically, as an innovative proposition, ARC is setting up an Extreme Climate Facility (XCF) that would be capitalised by the international community if trends in extreme weather are found attributable to climate change (Wilcox 2014). Thus, the XCF can be considered a manifestation of climate change risk, although there is no direct discussion of this facility extracting payments based on greenhouse emissions from wealthy countries, and thus no direct appeal to the *accountability* principle.

Box 21.3 The Extreme Climate Facility (XCF) of the African Risk Capacity (ARC)

Function

Additional financing for countries already managing their current weather risks through ARC.

Data-driven modus operandi

Payments to countries will be entirely data-driven over a 30 year period—if there is no significant *increase in extreme events over current climatology, then no payment is made.*

Climate Adaptation

Countries must use payments to invest in DRR or climate change adaption measures specified in pre-defined country level adaptation funds.

Scale

Payment size would increase with extreme event number and magnitude over and above a pre-specified threshold, corresponding to the degree of confidence that extreme events are increasing due to climate change.

Action focus

Leveraging ARC's existing infrastructure, XCF will ensure that countries and the international community properly monitor climate shocks and are financially prepared to undertake greater adaptation measures should their frequency and intensity increase.

Source Wilcox (2014)

21.6 Summary: The Evolving Insurance Narrative

This chapter has asked whether insurance instruments, and particularly micro-insurance and regional insurance pools, can serve as a risk-reducing and equitable compensatory response to climate-attributed losses and damages from weather extremes occurring in developing countries, and consequently if insurance instruments can serve the preventative and curative targets of the WIM and the Paris Agreement? As background, the chapter recognises that insurance, by dealing exclusively with residual, sudden-onset event risks, can be only one part of the L&D response.

The discussion has emphasised the substantial benefits of both micro-insurance programs and regional insurance pools: micro-insurance for providing post-disaster relief and reconstruction and also pre-disaster security (so important for adaptation and escaping poverty); regional insurance pools for decreasing the costs of reinsurance for governments and enabling early disbursement of emergency relief that saves lives, reduces distressed productive asset sales and mitigates disaster-induced poverty traps. The discussion has also emphasised the significant costs of insurance, noting that insured households and governments will on average pay considerably more for climate insurance than they expect to lose from extreme climate events.

Notwithstanding the benefits and costs, the discussion has examined insurance instruments for their role in meeting the curative and preventative aspirations for the WIM—equitably compensating for residual climate-attributed impacts providing strong incentives or directives for reducing risks. *A main message from this discussion is that absent significant intervention in their design and implementation, insurance mechanisms as currently implemented will likely fall short of fully meeting WIM aspirations as (differently) expressed by developed and developing country Parties.* This message is detailed in Table 21.3, which provides the mechanisms by which insurance can in principle support WIM responses.

Recent experience shows that with some important exceptions indemnity and parametric programs (mainly public-private partnerships), beyond pricing risk and reducing moral hazard, have few explicit incentives or requirements for risk reduction, even if their potential is promising. Reforming insurance programs for improved loss reduction can build on recent successful experiences, particularly evidence of significant risk-reduction activities on the part of public insurers compared to their private insurer counterparts, and innovations and developments in risk pricing and engineering, along with more targeted use of limits, deductibles and warranties. Still, as we witness in wealthy countries, *progress will be slow and patchy without public and private commitment to shaping insurance systems such that they foster practices that lead to investment in disaster risk reduction practices.*

A similar message emerges regarding the *curative* aspirations for the WIM. Insurance based on the principle of mutuality (typically private, market-based insurance), unless subsidised or otherwise supported, does not share risk beyond the at-risk insured community. *There is thus no reimbursement of losses to the victims of disasters (on average) outside of what policyholders, themselves, contribute in premiums, which disqualifies mutuality-based insurance as a curative mechanism meeting vul-*

Table 21.3 An overview of preventative and curative functions of climate risk insurance

Function	Mechanism	Evidence	Main messages
Preventative	Insurance provides incentives and prescriptions to reduce risks by: (i) setting premiums to reflect risk, (ii) providing information on risks and their reduction, and (iii) making use of deductibles and warranties	Experience with private flood insurance in developed countries shows little evidence of these measures, whereas limited evidence shows that public insurers may perform better Moral hazard can be a dominating factor in indemnity-based insurance systems, but is avoided in parametric systems	Far-reaching changes in institutional design and regulation of insurance may be necessary for insurance to contribute to disaster loss prevention Lessons can be learned from some exemplary insurance and micro-insurance projects
	Timely payments help avoid follow-on loss and damage	Good evidence from micro-insurance and regional insurance pools	For reducing indirect (downstream) impacts and risks, insurance may be advantageous compared to other forms of relief
Curative	Insurance provides compensation for losses and damage	Insurance based on the mutuality principle lacks any victim compensation from those outside the insurance pool; the solidarity principle can be invoked for providing humanitarian-based compensation generally, and the attribution principle for non-legally binding compensation for climate-attributed impacts and risks The solidarity principle is generally the basis for donor-supported micro-insurance and regional insurance pools Of interest is one proposed scheme in Africa for non-binding attribution-based support	The L&D deliberations are an opportunity to 'nudge' the narrative underlying international support for pro-poor insurance instruments from 'solidarity' (humanitarian aid) to accountability (non-legally binding compensation)

nerable country aspirations for the WIM. Mutuality, however, is not a feature of most donor-supported micro-insurance and regional insurance pools.

A challenge with the *solidarity* principle, if premiums are subsidised, is the lessened incentive for policyholders to reduce their risk. In meeting this challenge, international financial institutions, development agencies and other donors will need to reconcile the contending equity and preventative objectives in their support of climate insurance programs. This is foremost a challenge in designing "smart" insurance programs that are considered equitable and at the same time provide incentives or directives to their clients to reduce risks.

Two often cited success stories for insurance instruments serving the most vulnerable the African R4 micro-insurance program and the African Risk Capacity (ARC) regional insurance pool, go a long way in combining these goals. Neither is a commercial insurance enterprise; neither is (fully) characterised by risk-based premiums; and both are highly subsidised. The R4 program's success has been attributed in large part to its close connection with public safety net programs in the participating countries, and the ARC can attribute its success largely to its required disbursement plans. As evidence of extreme climate-attributed impacts and risks becomes more widely available and accepted, ARC's innovative XCF program may serve as a conduit for institutionalising donor support in the form of increased pool capitalisation.

The provision of support to regional insurance pools and micro-insurance programs continues to be framed as humanitarian aid, not invoking accountability or liability for climate-attributed loss and damage. Indeed, support for insurance programs has come mainly from development and financial organisations, such as the World Bank, national development partners, and international NGOs, with emphasis on the potential role of insurance in supporting poverty reduction in the face of climate and disaster risks. In other words, the narrative for support has been framed as a humanitarian and development issue.

The insurance discourse may, however, be changing. This is perhaps most apparent in discussions on the recent G7 Initiative on Climate Risk Insurance (InsuResilience), which has the ambitious goal of increasing access to direct or indirect climate insurance coverage for up to 400 million of the most vulnerable people in developing countries by 2020 (G7 2015; InsuResilience 2017). While InsuResilience does not officially commit to any specific equity principle, there are a number of voices that raise this aspect. One example is the Munich Climate Insurance Initiative (MCII), a close advisor to InsuResilience. MCII is forthright about the need to ground financial support in ethical claims of accountability and also capability. In the words of this NGO (whose members include insurers, NGOs and researchers), InsuResilience should provide technical and financial support to the set-up and maintenance of risk facilities and pools, the capitalisation of national and regional risk pools and other forms of co-financing premiums. This support should follow the principles of "capability, including sharing the risks imposed by climate change and responsibility for climate change impacts" (Schäfer and Waters 2016). The G7 initiative has thus unleashed a broad-ranging discussion on who should pay for insurance, sovereign risk transfer and social protection systems in light of climate change. In a commentary in Nature Climate Change, Surminski and colleagues (2016) explicitly raise this issue:

> As the intensity and frequency of climate extremes increase, is it fair to shift responsibility on to those who are the least responsible for climate change, the least able to shoulder the premiums, and in many cases the least able to reduce their losses?

As the recent G20/V20 Global Partnership on InsuResilience (launched at COP23) shows, the need for donor support is increasingly accepted by the development finance community. Importantly, this financial support should be 'smart', understood as reliable, flexible, minimise incentive distortions, and make the recipients aware of the true cost of the covered risk (Schäfer and Waters 2016). In this way, subsidised insurance can be linked to risk reduction (Hill et al. 2014; Vivid Economics et al. 2016). As a concrete proposal, Kunreuther and Michel-Kerjan (2009) have argued that the subsidy should take the form of an insurance voucher so that the recipient is aware of the unsubsidised premium. In addition, donor support should be conditional by requiring contingency and disbursement plans (Schäfer and Waters 2016; Surminski et al. 2016). A suggestion recently iterated by Schäfer and Waters (2016) is that smart premium support should cover only part of the premium, for example, only the markup (the risk and expense loads) while the beneficiary pays just the actuarial fair value or pure premium.

The message this chapter holds for the L&D discussions is to advise caution about relying on the market, alone, to provide insurance for fulfilling aspirations for the WIM, and to recognise the criticality of international and public intervention in climate insurance provision. Interventions can include subsidies, technical assistance, capitalisation of insurance programs, provision of reinsurance and other types of support that make insurance affordable to resource-poor and climate-sensitive clients; interventions can also enable regulatory regimes and public-private arrangements that exploit the potential for insurance to genuinely catalyse risk reduction far beyond what has been accomplished by commercial insurers thus far. It is therefore important to continue developing "smart" regional or national programs that explicitly combine insurance with loss prevention and that address the emerging equity issues as climate change impacts the most vulnerable and least responsible. The WIM Executive Committee continues to contemplate subsidies for pro-poor insurance programs (Executive Committee to the WIM 2016), a measure that will grow in importance if the insurance narrative continues to evolve from solidarity-based humanitarian assistance to accountability for climate-attributed impacts.

References

Alliance of Small Island States (AOSIS) (2008) Proposal to the AWG-LCA multi-window mechanism to address loss and damage from climate change impacts

Arent DJ, Tol RSJ, Faust E, Hella JP, Kumar S, Strzepek KM, Tóth FL, Yan D (2014) Key economic sectors and services. In: Field CB, Barros VR, Dokken DJ, Mach KJ, Mastrandrea MD, Bilir TE, Chatterjee M, Ebi KL, Estrada YO, Genova RC, Girma B, Kissel ES, Levy AN, MacCracken S,

Mastrandrea PR, White LL (eds) Climate change 2014: impacts, adaptation, and vulnerability. Part A: global and sectoral aspects. Contribution of working group II to the fifth assessment report of the intergovernmental panel on climate change. Cambridge University Press, Cambridge, United Kingdom and New York, NY, USA, pp 659–708

ARTEMIS (2017a) CCRIF parametric payouts on Hurricane Irma reach $31.2 m, Sept 20. http://www.artemis.bm/blog/2017/09/20/ccrif-parametric-payouts-on-hurricane-irma-reach-31-2m/. Accessed 30 Sep 2017

ARTEMIS (2017b) AIR puts M8.1 Chiapas, Mexico quake industry loss at up to $1.13bn, Sept. 20. http://www.artemis.bm/blog/2017/09/20/air-puts-m8-1-chiapas-mexico-quake-industry-loss-at-up-to-1-13bn/

Botzen WJW (2013) Managing extreme climate change risks through insurance. Cambridge University Press, Cambridge

Bouwer LM (2018) Observed and projected impacts from extreme weather events: implications for loss and damage. In: Mechler R, Bouwer L, Schinko T, Surminski S, Linnerooth-Bayer J (eds) Loss and damage from climate change. Concepts, methods and policy options. Springer, Cham, pp 63–82

Brainard L (2008) What is the role of insurance in economic development?. Zurich Government and Industry Affairs thought leadership series, Zurich Insurance, Zurich

Burkett M (2014) Loss and damage. Clim Law 4(1–2):119–130

Calliari E, Surminski S, Mysiak J (2018) Politics of (and behind) the UNFCCC's loss and damage mechanism. In: Mechler R, Bouwer L, Schinko T, Surminski S, Linnerooth-Bayer J (eds) Loss and damage from climate change. Concepts, methods and policy options. Springer, Cham, pp 155–178

Cardenas V, Hochrainer S, Mechler R, Pflug G, Linnerooth-Bayer J (2007) Sovereign financial disaster risk management: the case of Mexico. Environ Hazards 7:40–53

CARE International (2017) Submission on the 5 year work plan of the Warsaw International Mechanism for Loss and Damage, 28 February. http://careclimatechange.org/wp-content/uploads/2017/03/CARE-Submission-on-the-5year-work-plan-of-the-WIM.pdf

Chambwera M, Heal G, Dubeux C, Hallegatte S, Leclerc L, Markandya A, McCarl BA, Mechler R, Neumann JE (2014) Economics of adaptation. In: Field CB, Barros VR, Dokken DJ, Mach KJ, Mastrandrea MD, Bilir TE, Chatterjee M, Ebi KL, Estrada YO, Genova RC, Girma B, Kissel ES, Levy AN, MacCracken S, Mastrandrea PR, White LL (eds) Climate change 2014: impacts, adaptation, and vulnerability. Part A: global and sectoral aspects. contribution of working group II to the fifth assessment report of the intergovernmental panel on climate change. Cambridge University Press, Cambridge, United Kingdom and New York, NY, USA, pp 945–977

Clarke D, Hill R (2013) Cost-benefit analysis of the African risk capacity facility, IFPRI Discussion Paper 01292, International Food Policy Research Institute, Washington DC, USA

Clarke D, Dercon S (2016) Dull disasters. How planning ahead will make a difference. Oxford University Press, Oxford

Cohen M, Sebstad J (2003) Reducing vulnerability: the demand for microfinance. A synthesis report. Micro Save-Africa, Nairobi

Crichton D (2008) Role of insurance in reducing flood risk. The Geneva Papers on Risk and Insurance Issues and Practice, 33:117–132. https://doi.org/10.1057/palgrave.gpp.2510151

Cummins J, Mahul O (2009) Catastrophe risk financing in developing countries: principles for public intervention—overview. Washington, DC, The World Bank. http://gfdrr.org/docs/Track-II_Catrisk_financing_Overview_booklet.pdf. Accessed 27 May 2017

G7 (2015) Leaders' Declaration G7 Summit, 7–8 June 2015. Available from https://sustainabledevelopment.un.org/content/documents/7320LEADERS%20STATEMENT_FINAL_CLEAN.pdf. Accessed 27 Jan 2017

Ghesquiere F, Mahul O (2010) Financial protection of the state against natural disasters: a primer. Policy Research working paper WPS 5429. World Bank, Washington, DC

Hallegatte S, Vogt-Schilbac, Bangalore M, Rozenberg J (2016) Unbreakable: building the resilience of the poor in the face of natural disasters. Climate change and development series. Washington,

D.C.: World Bank Group. http://documents.worldbank.org/curated/en/512241480487839624/Unbreakable-building-the-resilience-of-the-poor-in-the-face-of-natural-disasters. Accessed 30 May 2017

Hazell P, Anderson J, Balzer N, Hastrup Clemmensen A, Hess U, Rispoli F (2010) The potential for scale and sustainability in weather index insurance for agriculture and rural livelihoods. International Fund for Agricultural Development and World Food Programme, Rome

Heltberg R, Siegel P, Jorgensen S (2009) Addressing human vulnerability to climate change: towards a 'No-Regrets' approach. Glob Environ Change 19(1):89–99

Heltberg, R, Siegel P, Jorgensen S (2009b) Social policies for adaptation to climate change. In: Mearns R, Norton A (eds) Social dimensions of climate change: equity and vulnerability in a warming world. Washington, DC, The World Bank

Hill VR, Gajate-Garrido G, Phily C, Dalal A (2014) Using subsidies for inclusive insurance: lessons from agriculture and health. Microinsurance Paper No. 29. International Labour Organization. http://www.impactinsurance.org/sites/default/files/MP29.pdf. Accessed 27 May 2017

Hochrainer-Stigler S, Linnerooth-Bayer J, Lorant A (2017) The European union solidarity fund: an assessment of its recent reforms. Mitig Adapt Strat Glob Change 22(4):547–563. https://doi.org/10.1007/s11027-015-9687-3

Honoré A (2010) Causation in the law. In: Zalta EN (ed) Stanford encyclopedia of philosophy. Stanford University (online), Stanford, pp 1–22

INC (Intergovernmental Negotiating Committee for a Framework Convention on Climate Change) (1991) Preparation of a Framework Convention on Climate Change. Set of informal papers provided by delegations, related to the preparation of a Framework Convention on Climate Change. Addendum 3, A/AC.237/Misc.1/Add.3 A/AC.2, United Nations Office at Geneva

InsuResilience (2017) Joint Statement on the InsuResilience Global Partnership. 14 November 2017. Bonn

James, RA, Jones, RG, Boyd, E, Young, HR, Otto, FEL, Huggel, C and JS Fuglestvedt (2018) Attribution: how is it relevant for loss and damage policy and practice? In: Mechler R, Bouwer L, Schinko T, Surminski S, Linnerooth-Bayer J (eds) Loss and damage from climate change. Concepts, methods and policy options. Springer, Cham, pp 113–154

Kunreuther H (1996) Mitigating disaster losses through insurance. J Risk Uncertainty 12:171–187. https://doi.org/10.1007/BF00055792

Kunreuther H (1998) Insurability conditions and the supply of coverage. In: Kunreuther H, Roth RJ (eds) Paying the price: the status and role of insurance against natural disasters in the United States. Washington DC, Joseph Henry Press, pp 17–50

Kunreuther H, Michel-Kerjan E (2009) At war with the weather: managing large-scale risks in a New Era of catastrophes. MIT Press Books, Cambridge, MA

Lees E (2016) Responsibility and liability for climate loss and damage after Paris. Clim Policy 17(1):59–70

Linnerooth-Bayer J, Mace MJ, Verheyen R (2003) Insurance-related actions and risk assessment in the context of the UNFCCC. Background paper for UNFCCC workshop on Insurance-related Actions and Risk Assessment in the Framework of the UNFCCC, 11–15 May 2003, Bonn, Germany

Linnerooth-Bayer J, Mechler R, Bals C (2010) Insurance as part of a climate strategy. In: Hulme M, Neufeldt H (eds) Making climate change work for us: European perspectives on adaptation and mitigation strategies. Cambridge University Press, Cambridge

Linnerooth-Bayer J, Hochrainer-Stigler S, Mechler R (2012) Mechanisms for financing the costs of disasters, Foresight project 'Reducing Risks of Future Disasters: Priorities for Decision Makers', UK Government Office of Science, London. http://www.bis.gov.uk/assets/foresight/docs/reducing-risk-management/supporting-evidence/12-1308-mechanisms-financing-costs-of-disasters.pdf. Accessed 5 Feb 2018

Linnerooth-Bayer J, Suarez P, Victor M, Mechler R (2009). Drought insurance for subsistence farmers in Malawi. Nat Hazards Observer 33(5):1–8

Lorant A, Linnerooth-Bayer J, Hanger S Insurance and climate risk reduction: from concept to practice? IIASA Working Paper, Laxenburg, Austria, forthcoming

Mace M, Verheyen R (2016) Loss, damage and responsibility after COP21: all options open for the paris agreement. Rev Eur Compar Int Environ Law 25(2):197–214

Mechler R, Linnerooth-Bayer J, Peppiatt D (2006) Disaster insurance for the poor? A ProVention/IIASA study. A review of microinsurance for natural disaster risks in developing countries. Provention consortium, Geneva

Mechler R, Bouwer LM, Linnerooth-Bayer J, Hochrainer-Stigler S, Aerts JCJH, Surminski S, Williges K (2014) Managing unnatural disaster risk from climate extremes. Nat Clim Change 4(4):235–237. https://doi.org/10.1038/nclimate2137

Mechler R, Schinko T (2016) Identifying the policy space for climate loss and damage. Science 354(6310):290–292. https://doi.org/10.1126/science.aag2514

Mechler R (2004) natural disaster risk management and financing disaster losses in developing countries. Verlag für Versicherungswirtschaft, Karlsruhe

Mechler R et al (2018) Science for loss and damage. Findings and propositions. In: Mechler R, Bouwer L, Schinko T, Surminski S, Linnerooth-Bayer J (eds) Loss and damage from climate change. Concepts, methods and policy options. Springer, Cham, pp 3–37

Moftakhari HR, Agha Kouchak A, Sanders BF, Matthew RA (2017) Cumulative hazard: the case of nuisance flooding, Earth's Future, 5. https://doi.org/10.1002/2016ef000494

Molini V, Keyzer M, van den Boom B, Zant W (2007) Creating safety nets through semi-parametric index-based insurance: a simulation for Northern Ghana, MyIdeas. https://ideas.repec.org/p/ags/eaa101/9263.html. Accessed 27 Jan 2017 l

Munich Climate Insurance Initiative (MCII) (2008). Insurance Instruments for Adapting to Climate Risks: A proposal for the Bali Action Plan, Version 2.0. MCII Submission to the 4th session of the Ad Hoc Working Group on Long-Term Cooperative Action under the Convention (AWG-LCA 3). Poznan 1–13 December, 2008. www.climate-insurance.org/upload/pdf/MCII_submission_Poznan.pdf. Accessed 27 May 2017

Newsham A, Davies M, Béné C (2011) Making social protection work for pro-poor disaster risk reduction and climate change adaptation. background paper. Institute of Development Studies, Brighton

OMTRIX (2005) A fund to support micro-finance institutions in case of emergency (ELF). Costa Rico, San Jose

Oxfam International Four simple strategies which are helping Ethiopian farmers adapt to climate change. https://www.oxfam.org/en/ethiopia/four-simple-strategies-whichare-helpingethiopian-farmers-adapt-climate-change. Accessed 6 Oct 2017

Pollner J (2000) Managing catastrophic risks using alternative risk financing & insurance pooling mechanisms. World Bank, Washington DC

Re Swiss (2012) Microinsurance—risk protection for 4 billion people, SIGMA 6/2012. Swiss Re, Zurich

Schäfer L, Waters E (2016) Climate risk insurance for the poor and vulnerable. How to effectively implement the pro-poor focus of InsuResilience. http://www.climateinsurance.org/fileadmin/mcii/documents/MCII_2016_CRI_for_the_Poor_and_Vulnerable_fullstudy_lo-res.pdf. Accessed 20 March 2017

Schäfer, L, Warner, K, Kreft S (2018) Exploring and managing adaptation frontiers with climate risk insurance. In: Mechler R, Bouwer L, Schinko T, Surminski S, Linnerooth-Bayer J (eds) Loss and damage from climate change. Concepts, methods and policy options. Springer, Cham, pp 317–341

Schinko T, Mechler R, Hochrainer-Stigler S (2018) The risk and policy space for loss and damage: integrating notions of distributive and compensatory justice with comprehensive climate risk management. In: Mechler R, Bouwer L, Schinko T, Surminski S, Linnerooth-Bayer J (eds) Loss and damage from climate change. Concepts, methods and policy options. Springer, Cham, pp 83–110

Schwarze R, Croonenbroeck C (2017) Economies of integrated risk management? An empirical analysis of the Swiss public insurance approach to natural hazard prevention. Econ Disaster Clim Change 1:167–178

Simlinger F, Mayer B (2018) Legal responses to climate change induced loss and damage. In: Mechler R, Bouwer L, Schinko T, Surminski S, Linnerooth-Bayer J (eds) Loss and damage from climate change. Concepts, methods and policy options. Springer, Cham, pp 179–203

Surminski S (2014) The role of insurance in reducing direct risk: the case of flood insurance. Int Rev Environ Res Econ 7(3–4):241–278

Surminski S, Eldridge J (2015) Flood insurance in England: an assessment of the current and newly proposed insurance scheme in the context of rising flood risk. J Flood Risk Manag

Surminski S, Bouwer LM, Linnerooth-Bayer J (2016) How insurance can support climate resilience. Nat Clim Change 6:333–334. https://doi.org/10.1038/nclimate2979

Swiss Re (2015) Natural catastrophes and man-made disasters in 2013, Sigma No 1/2014

UNFCCC (2008) Ideas and proposals on the elements contained in paragraph 1 of the Bali Action Plan Submissions from Parties, Addendum, Part I. http://unfccc.int/resource/docs/2008/awglca4/eng/misc05a02p01.pdf. Accessed 5 Feb 2018

UNFCCC (2012) A literature review on the topics in the context of thematic area 2 of the work programme on loss and damage: a range of approaches to address loss and damage associated with the adverse effects of climate change note by the secretariat. Bonn, Germany

UNFCCC (2014) Decision 2/CP.20, paragraph 1. https://unfccc.int/files/bodies/election_and_membership/application/pdf/decision_2_cp20_loss_and_damage_committee.pdf. Accessed 27 Jan 2017

UNFCCC (2015) Paris Agreement. http://unfccc.int/files/essential_background/convention/application/pdf/english_paris_agreement.pdf. Accessed 24 June 2017

UNFCCC (2016) FCCC/SB/2016/3. http://unfccc.int/resource/docs/2016/sb/eng/03.pdf. Accessed 27 Jan 2017

UNISDR (2017) Caribbean Catastrophe Risk Insurance Facility, the (CCRIF SPC), Prevention Web, http://www.ccrif.org. Accessed 5 Feb 2018

United Nations (1992) United Nations Framework Convention on Climate Change, New York

United Nations Office for Disaster Risk Reduction (UNISDR) (2017) Terminology. https://www.unisdr.org/we/inform/terminology. Accessed 4 Jun 2017

Vaughan E, Vaughan T (2008) The fundamentals of risk and insurance. Wiley, New Jersey

Vellinga PV, Mills E, Bowers L, Berz G, Huq S, Kozak, L, Palutikod J, Schanzenbacher, Soler G, Dlugolecki A (2001) Insurance and other financial services. Climate change 2001: impacts, vulnerability, and adaptation. Working group II. none: none.—Report Number: LBNL-47924

Vivid Economics, Surminski Consulting and Callund Consulting (2016) FINAL REPORT: understanding the role of publicly funded premium subsidies in disaster risk insurance in developing countries. UK Department for International Development

von Peter G, von Dahlen S, Saxena S (2012) Unmitigated disasters? New evidence on the macroeconomic cost of natural catastrophes. BIS Working Papers No 394. Bank for International Settlements

von Ungern-Sternberg T (1996) The limits of competition: housing insurance in Switzerland. Eur Econ Rev 40(3–5):1111–1121

Wallimann-Helmer I, Meyer L, Mintz-Woo K, Schinko T, Serdeczny O (2018) The ethical challenges in the context of climate loss and damage. In: Mechler R, Bouwer L, Schinko T, Surminski S, Linnerooth-Bayer J (eds) Loss and damage from climate change. Concepts, methods and policy options. Springer, Cham, pp 39–62

Warner K, Ranger N, Surminski S, Arnold M, Linnerooth-Bayer J, Michel-Kerjan E, Kovacs P, Herweijer C (2009) Adaptation to climate change: linking disaster risk reduction and insurance, United Nations International Strategy for Disaster Reduction Secretariat (UNISDR), Geneva. http://www.microinsuranceconference.com/dms/MRS/Documents/Microinsurance/MIC_Agriculture_Bibliography/9654_linkingdrrinsurance.pdf. Accessed 27 Jan 2017

Warner K, van der Geest K, Kreft S, Huq S, Kusters K, de Sherbinin A (2012) Evidence from the frontlines of climate change: Loss and damage to communities despite coping and adaptation. Loss and Damage in Vulnerable Countries Initiative. Policy Report. Report No. 9. Bonn: United Nations University Institute for Environment and Human Security (UNU-EHS)

Wilcox R (2014) ARC Extreme Climate Facility (XCF). Presentation at 5th International Disaster & Risk Conference IDRC Davos

Wilkie D (1997) Mutuality and solidarity: assessing risks and sharing losses. Philos Trans Roy Soc London B: Biol Sci Lond B 352(1357):1039–1044. https://doi.org/10.1098/rstb.1997.0082

WIM Executive Committee of the Warsaw International Mechanism (2016) Submission to the Standing Committee on Finance (SCF) for inputs related to its 2016 fourth forum on "financial instruments that address the risks of loss and damage associated with the adverse effects of climate change". http://unfccc.int/adaptation/workstreams/loss_and_damage/items/8805.php

World Bank (2016) Migration and Remittances Factbook 2016, World Bank Group's Global Knowledge Partnership on Migration and Development (KNOMAD) initiative: Washington D.C

World Bank (2017) PCRAFI Facility: phase II: enhancing the financial resilience of Pacific island Countries against natural disaster and climate risk, Global Facility for Disaster Risk Reduction http://pubdocs.worldbank.org/en/178911475802966585/PCRAFI-4-pager-web.pdf. Accessed 5 Dec 2017

World Food Programme (2017) The R4 Rural Resilience Initiative. https://www.wfp.org/climatechange/initiatives/r4-rural-resilience-initiative

World Food Programme and Oxfam America (2016) Joint Submission by the World Food Programme and Oxfam International to the UNFCCC Standing Committee on Finance. https://unfccc.int/files/cooperation_and_support/financial_mechanism/standing_committee/application/pdf/scf_forum_joint_oxfam_wfp_submission_2_29_2016.pdf. Accessed 20 Mar 2017

Chapter 22
Technology for Climate Justice: A Reporting Framework for Loss and Damage as Part of Key Global Agreements

Marc van den Homberg and Colin McQuistan

Abstract Technology plays a critical role in the ability to retain, reduce or transfer climate risk or address impacts. However, vulnerable communities do not fully benefit from existing technology, whereas they are disproportionally impacted by climate change. This chapter assesses how technology can shape limits to adaptation and how to report on this injustice as part of key global agreements. We develop an access, use and innovation of technology framework. As a case on a relevant technology, we test it on transboundary early warning systems in South Asia. We find that only a limited set of the state-of-the-art technologies available globally is accessed and used. Insufficient capacity and funding result in the bare minimum, largely copycat type of technology. As climate change progresses, demands on technology increase, whereas, if no action is taken, the technology remains the same widening the adaptation deficit. A better understanding of the crossover from disaster risk reduction to climate adaptation and the emerging policy domain of loss and damage allows trade-offs in terms of reducing risks through greater investment in technologies for adaptation versus absorbing risks and then financing curative or transformative loss and damage measures. We argue that attention to especially distributive, compensatory and procedural climate justice principles, in terms of distributing technology, building capacity and providing finance, can help to motivate support for widening the technology spectrum available to developing countries. We

M. van den Homberg (✉) · C. McQuistan
Practical Action, Rugby, UK
e-mail: marcjchr@gmail.com

C. McQuistan
e-mail: colin.mcquistan@practicalaction.org.uk

R. Mechler et al. (eds.), *Loss and Damage from Climate Change*, Climate Risk Management, Policy and Governance, https://doi.org/10.1007/978-3-319-72026-5_22

propose as part of comprehensive risk management that, first, an inventory should be developed how of technologies shape soft and hard adaptation limits. Second, technology for climate justice might be included in the adaptation communications to support reporting on the expected and experienced impact of measures on loss and damage, at a sufficiently disaggregated level. Third, soft adaptation limits should be levelled by making technology research, innovation and design equitable between those countries having capacity and those not, recognising the commitment to leave no one behind.

Keywords Loss and damage · Flood early warning systems · Adaptation Climate risk management · Climate justice · Sendai framework for DRR Sustainable development goals · Paris agreement

22.1 Introduction: Unequal Impact of Climate Change and the Role of Key Global Agreements

Although anthropogenic climate change is a global phenomenon, its impacts are neither equally distributed over developing and developed countries nor between the rich and the poor. The poor face greater impacts when exposed to natural hazards than the non-poor (Hallegatte et al. 2016). There is evidence that adaptation capacity is and will be exceeded in various instances, requiring attention to loss and damage (L&D) (see book chapters by Handmer and Nalau 2018; Heslin et al. 2018; Haque et al. 2018; Landauer and Juhola 2018; and the introduction by Mechler et al. 2018). This inequality places the impacts of climate change (and climate variability) and the burden of climate action disproportionately on the most vulnerable (IPCC 2014). At the same time, those developing countries and poor communities that will be most heavily affected by the impacts of climate change have contributed the least (in terms of greenhouse gas emissions) to the problem (Clark 2011). This latter aspect has been discussed under the concept of Climate Justice in the domain of climate change impacts and mitigation. Climate justice is a term used for framing climate change as an ethical and political issue, rather than one that is purely environmental or physical in nature. This is done by relating the effects of climate change to concepts of justice, particularly environmental justice and social justice (see chapter by Wallimann-Helmer et al. 2018). This chapter focuses on the unequal dimensions of climate justice and, more particularly, it asks how technology can address climate risks for the most vulnerable in a just way, and where the practical limits are to what technology can achieve.

Fig. 22.1 Community information board in the Banke and Bardia district in Nepal explaining appropriate flood mitigation measures and the community-based early warning system

More specifically, we aim to disentangle the relationship between technology and loss and damage, adaptation and disaster risk management from a climate justice perspective through three guiding questions (1) *How can the role of technology in reaching climate justice for vulnerable and poor communities be assessed?* (2) *How is technology shaping adaptation limits, thereby reducing losses and damages?* (3) *What are the current transparency mechanisms of key global agreements (and related regional, national and local ones) with relevance for climate change and how do these cover losses and damages and unveil technology (in)justice?* We use an exploratory and mostly qualitative research design to address these research questions. We combine desk research of scientific literature, an analysis of the reporting that is available on the global agreements (retrospectively) and an analysis of what will be reported in the future (forward-looking), national and local level documents in relation to disaster risk management on floods (the dominant climate-related risks globally) as well as a case study. The case study investigates transboundary flood community-based early warning systems (EWS) that are operational in the Brahmaputra river basin (Bangladesh–India) and in the Karnali river basin (India–Nepal; Fig. 22.1 shows community information on such an EWS in Nepal).

The chapter structure is as follows. Section 22.2 addresses research question (1) and presents five components to characterise the role technology plays in reaching climate justice. Section 22.3 categorises how technology can shape adaptation limits (research question 2). Section 22.4 shows how the plethora of reporting and reviewing mechanisms of the key global agreements and their regional, national and local counterparts cover loss and damage only to a limited extent and do not adequately unveil injustices (research question 3). Section 22.5 brings the results of these three sections together in a coherent framework that can be used to assess technology for climate justice in global agreements and applies it to a case study on EWS. The case study demonstrates far from equitable access to early warning and early action information, as well as untapped technology and innovation potential. Section 22.6 shows how the framework can be used to guide action. We identify windows of opportunities to include technology for climate justice more strongly into the crossover from adaptation to L&D in the climate agreement, but also to make sure there is a linkage to the other key global agreements.

22.2 Technology for Climate Justice

Climate justice is an umbrella term bringing together distributive and compensatory (see chapters by Wallimann-Helmer et al. 2018; Schinko et al. 2018), retributive, transitional[1] (Klinsky and Brankovic 2018) and procedural justice (Tomlinson 2015; Walker 2009) perspectives. Climate justice has spatial and temporal dimensions. As an example, distributive justice is based on an inter-generational or an intra-generational perspective, and compensatory justice on a retrospective one. We indicate how different justice dimensions could influence the means of implementation of the Paris Agreement through backward-, forward- and both backward- and forward-looking actions in Fig. 22.2. Mitigation and adaptation are often discussed under one and the same heading of climate justice, whereas there are clear distinctions between what climate justice means in terms of duties for these two pillars (see chapter by Wallimann-Helmer et al. 2018). Climate justice aims to address inequalities and is hence key for the L&D debate. We focus on the role that technology could play in delivering climate justice. Technology and innovation are important enablers for climate actions. In addition, technology can be seen as a way to overcome political sensitivities. For example, a technological innovation process makes use of equitable procedures that engage all stakeholders in a non-discriminatory way, a form of procedural justice (Walker 2009).

Disaster risk reduction (DRR), climate change adaptation (CCA) and L&D strategies can minimise current and future losses and damages by protecting people, properties and ecosystems against climate-related stressors for flood risk (see box 22.1). Even though these strategies comprise a plethora of different hard and soft risk management measures, technology plays a crucial role. Inadequate or inappropriate technology reduces the range of available options as well as their effectiveness in reducing or avoiding risk from increasing rates or magnitudes of climate change (IPCC 2014). In terms of climate justice, access to technology and its benefits are not fairly shared.

[1] A way to recognise and at least partially remedy past injustices while also building a sense of cooperation. It helps to overcome tension about the ideal relationship between responsibility for past and future action and avoids the liability debate (Walker 2009; Klinsky and Brankovic 2018).

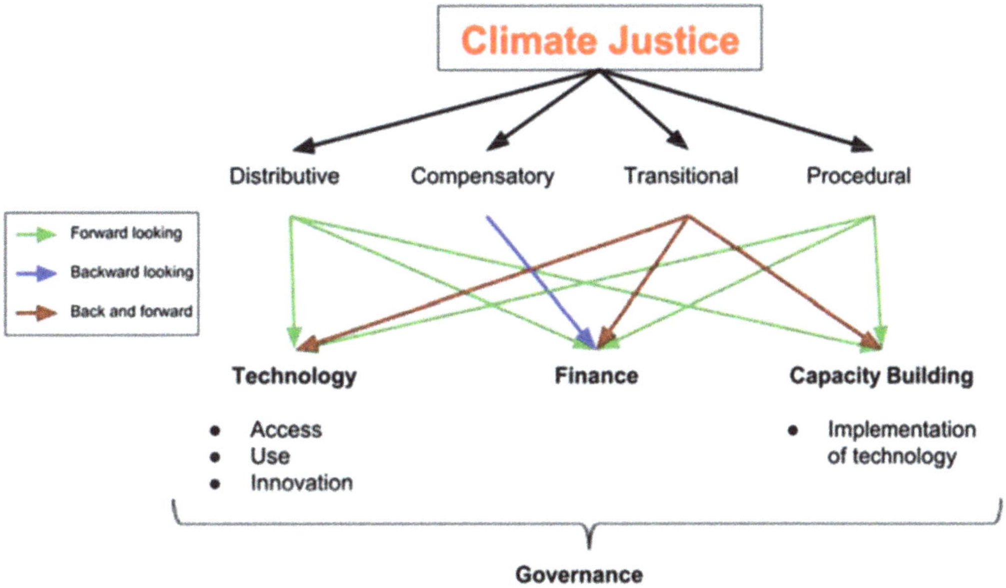

Fig. 22.2 Overview of underlying climate justice principles and means of implementation

Box 22.1 Importance of technology to reduce flood risk

Our examination focuses on flood risk, as hydro-meteorological hazards cause the largest economic, social and humanitarian climate-related losses. Between 1980 and 2013, global direct economic losses due to floods exceeded $1 trillion (2013 values), and more than 220,000 people lost their lives (Winsemius et al. 2015). In 2016, the high number of flood events, including river flooding and flash floods, was exceptional and accounted for 34% of overall losses, compared with an average of 21% over the past 10 years (Munich Re NatCatService 2017). Globally, economic losses due to flood events have increased, due to the expansion of population and property in floodplains (IPCC 2012) resulting from poorly planned socio-economic activities. Climate change increases the frequency and aggravates the severity of many of these hazards (IPCC 2014). In Asia and the Pacific, 32% of the economic losses from natural disasters in 1970–2013 were due to floods (UNESCAP 2015). Calculations for Bangladesh predict, for example, an average increase of flooded area of 3% in 2030 and 13% by 2050, combined with an increase of inundation depth in most areas that are currently already at risk, exposing 22% more of the population (World Bank 2010).

There are several frameworks developed by international organisations and Non-governmental organizations (NGOs) to describe the transfer and diffusion of climate technologies. As one example, UNEP developed a framework to identify and analyse these barriers as part of technology needs assessments (as we will discuss in Sect. 22.4) (Boldt et al. 2012). They identified four key groups of barriers (or enabling environments). Klein et al. (2014) used four key considerations for technology as an adaptation constraint that are closely related to the barriers. For example, access is directly linked to the economic and financial conditions. The effectiveness

Table 22.1 Practical Action's framework for technology justice with five components

Technology justice component	Description
Access	Equitable access to services
	Equitable access to technology and knowledge
Use	Technology use can have a negative impact on future generations and a negative impact on certain groups in society, while beneficial to others. Sustainable, intergenerational use should be promoted and enabled
Technological innovation and implementation	Considerable untapped potential in implementing and developing technology to push the limits of what can be managed and absorbed by the poor and vulnerable. Unfortunately, technological development and innovation are focused on creating new markets or exploiting existing markets for those who can afford to pay. Investments therefore focus on high tech technologies. Ideally, innovation and implementation of technologies is driven by the most pressing social and environmental challenges and with the equitable involvement of the poor and vulnerable
Governance	Governance should enable access to the technology and knowledge that is required, promote the use of inclusive technologies and curb those that adversely affect the environment
Finance	Adequate and well targeted finance from different sources funds technology access, use, innovation and governance prioritised to respond to the critical loss and damage challenges

in managing climate risk links to research and technological capacity but also to the social acceptance of a new technology. Both frameworks have a multi-stakeholder perspective and show that it is never about a straightforward transfer of technology. If that is done, like with agricultural machinery (Trace 2016) or advanced flood modelling software, chances are very high the technology is abandoned and not used. As an NGO example, the technology justice framework launched by Practical Action (Practical Action 2016) rethinks the role of technology from the perspective of the poor and vulnerable (Trace 2016) and consists of three components: Access, Use and Innovation. We complement these with Governance and Finance (see Table 22.1), creating five components that are closely linked to the three Paris means of implementation.

Access to Services and Access to Technology and Knowledge is Not Equal

The poor have almost always more limited access to basic services such as water and energy, but also to disaster-related services such as early warning and climate information (Raworth 2012). In addition, developing countries and, within those countries, the poor more than the rich have limited access to technology and knowledge (Traces 2016). In the case of an EWS, further discussed below, even if vulnerable communities receive early warning information, they often lack access to the knowledge required for early action (Cumiskey et al. 2014). Christiansen et al. (2011) extracted about 165 unmet technological needs related to adaptation (and mitigation) from technology needs assessments carried out in developing countries. Examples include applications to agriculture in Cambodia and Bangladesh and coastal zones in Thailand. In many of these cases patents and other forms of intellectual property protection constrain technology transfer, especially from developed to developing countries (Klein et al. 2014). Between 2008 and 2010, 262 patents were published making specific claims to abiotic stress tolerance (such as drought, heat, flood, cold and salt tolerance) in plants. Just six corporations, including DuPont, BASF and Monsanto, control 77% of these patents in relation to climate-ready crops (ETC Group 2010). National Meteorological and Hydrological Services (NMHS) in developing countries do not have access to the same level of knowledge and technology as developed countries. For example, digital elevation model data at sufficiently high resolution, required for more accurate flood risk modelling, is usually not affordable (Simpson et al. 2015).

Use of Technology is Unjust
Technologies are often used in unsustainable ways, depleting resources and stacking up problems for future generations (Practical Action 2016). For example, industrialised agriculture leads to biodiversity loss, thereby limiting the options available to farmers to respond to climate-induced shocks and stresses. In some circumstances, the use of technologies to reduce short-term risk and vulnerability can contribute to increased vulnerability to extreme events for future generations (Etkin 1999; Moser 2010). This was seen in the impacts of Hurricane Katrina, where a flood defence system enabling construction in a floodplain decades before failed, with catastrophic consequences for the population of New Orleans in 2005 (Freudenburg et al. 2008; Link 2010). Flood protection levees are known to eliminate overbank flooding, causing diminished sediment accumulation and eventual wetland loss, whereas wetlands are beneficial as a natural buffer for hurricanes (Turner et al. 2006).

Technological Innovation and Implementation for the Most Vulnerable
Technological innovation and implementation is rarely driven by the most pressing social and environmental challenges. Technology justice argues for the involvement of the poorest and most vulnerable so that technologies deliver impacts on our biggest human challenges and are not driven by a profit motive alone (Practical Action 2016). It requires looking into how technologies can empower vulnerable communities and which corresponding capacities they need to best utilise and further innovate these technologies. This requires a critical examination of not only how technology reduces vulnerability but also how the use of some technologies can increase vulnerability to disasters, for example by degrading the local environment or by creating a false sense of security.

Governance Mechanisms to Enable Access
Appropriate governance enables access to the technology and knowledge that is required, promotes the use of inclusive technologies and curbs those that adversely affect the environment (Practical Action 2016). Governance mechanisms should ensure that there is a coherence between the global and national/local policies and that technologies required for implementing climate risk management (CRM) are considered in national and local public investments. Governance mechanisms are

directly related to the ownership and institutional arrangements around the use of technology (or orgware, as we will introduce in the next section).

Financial Support is Essential

The tragedy is that the poor and vulnerable are usually more exposed to natural hazards, but not in a position to invest in technology that could potentially reduce their exposure (Hallegatte et al. 2016). Similarly, at a national level, the least developed countries will in many cases have to apply their limited funds to deal with the losses and damages incurred, rather than to invest in adaptation. International climate change financing mechanisms are increasingly charged with addressing this funding gap, but currently at low levels. In addition, economic valuations such as cost-benefit analysis that are used to justify expenditures inter- and intra-nationally are not well designed to consider the poor and vulnerable in an equitable way, as, in absolute terms, the asset loss will be higher in the richer and more wealthy areas than in poorer areas (Hallegatte et al. 2016).

This shows that developing countries have severely lower institutional and technological capacities to pursue climate-resilient development pathways (IPCC 2014) as compared to developed countries. *Technology for climate justice requires rethinking access, use, innovation, finance and governance from the perspective of the poor and vulnerable and making sure there is justiceand equity in these components*. The transfer and diffusion of technologies for risk management can be assessed against the technology justice components at the global, regional, national and local level, to which we turn after describing the spectrum of technologies for dealing with climate-related risks.

22.3 Technologies for Public and Private Actions to Address Loss and Damage

Technology involves hardware, software and orgware (Christiansen et al. 2011; Boldt et al. 2012). Hardware refers to the tangible aspects such as capital goods and equipment and includes flood resistant crops and new irrigation systems. Software refers to the capacity and processes involved in the production and use of the hardware and ranges from know-how (e.g. manuals and skills, awareness-raising, education and training) and experience to practices (e.g. agricultural management, cooking and behavioural practices). Adaptation methods and practices that may not normally be regarded as technologies, such as insurance schemes or crop rotation patterns, may also be characterised as software (UNFCCC 2006). Orgware is equally important from an implementation point of view and relates to the ownership and institutional arrangements of the community or organisation where the technology will be used. It includes those organisations involved in the adoption and diffusion process of a new technology.

Adaptation measures either withstand, transfer or reduce risks, with risk reduction preferred over withstanding or transferring risk. Apart from managing the down-side risk, there is also in some cases potential for up-side risk, where a positive impact results. For example, changing to flood-resistant crops might not only lower the down-side risk of losing a harvest during a flood, but might also increase the up-side risk by a higher yield. Maladaptation results if adaptation measures create additional risks instead of reducing them. O'Brien et al. (2012) give an example where irrigation might be beneficial in the short-term, reducing a farmer's vulnerability, but in the long-term increases vulnerability when the non-renewable source used for the irrigation is depleted. "Hard" engineering solutions can be expensive and may not cover costs and risks equally for all stakeholders across time. As an example, the Nanbéto dam in Togo reduced total days with flood conditions for downstream communities, but also increased their flood vulnerability every time an overspill and subsequent poorly managed and communicated release of water took place (Climate Centre 2017). In the United States, past building in floodplain areas downstream from dams that have exceeded their design life has become a major concern (O'Brien et al. 2012). In this case, losses and damages are being exacerbated for the more vulnerable communities. "Softer" solutions such as ecosystem restoration or stress tolerant crop varieties may provide a range of benefits now and in the future (IPCC 2014; van der Geest and Warner 2015) and can be very cost-effective sustainable solutions.

In the case of L&D risks that are "beyond adaptation" (see Box. 22.2 and introduction by Mechler et al. 2018), risks can only be absorbed, and we distinguish hard and soft adaptation limits. A soft adaptation limit means that adaptation options are currently not available to those affected, but might become available with cultural, social and economic change or technology and innovation (Dow et al. 2013). In other words, the limit is mutable. As an example, Alaskan native villages threatened by coastal erosion and inundation have, from their perspective, no available options to maintain their way of life (which is for them an intolerable risk), since protecting their infrastructure is economically not feasible (Klein et al. 2014). Hard adaptation limits occur if no adaptive actions are available now or in the future to avoid intolerable risks (Verheyen 2012; Klein et al. 2014). For example, protection against sea-level rise is in some cases considered impossible, no matter what welfare growth, institutional changes or technological innovations emerge (Dow et al. 2013). But, even hard adaptation limits can be dynamic over time. The inability to breed rice varieties that pollinate above 32–35 °C is currently considered as a hard limit (Klein et al. 2014). However, heavy investments in research might someday result in shifting pollination temperature limits upward (Dow et al. 2013).

Box 22.2 Risk management and limits approach to L&D

The risk management perspective classifies risks as either acceptable (no additional action required), tolerable (action required considering costs and other constraints) or intolerable (action required irrespective of constraints). It makes clear that, once standard adaptation in the form of DRR, CCA or development is no longer feasible in the intolerable space, transformative or curative action is required (Mechler and Schinko 2016). The limits to adaptation perspective focuses on soft and hard limits to adaptation (Klein et al. 2014; Dow et al. 2013). A cross-cutting distinction is between whether the option represents incremental, fundamental or transformative adjustment (Schinko and Mechler 2017). Kates et al. (2012) distinguish between incremental and transformational adaptation. The former aims to improve efficiency within existing technological, governance and value systems, whereas transformative adjustments may involve changes in some of the fundamental attributes of those systems. Kates et al. (2012) consider three groups of transformative actions, i.e. those adopted at a much larger scale or intensity, those that are truly new to a particular region or resource system, and those that transform places and shift locations. Schinko and Mechler (2017) use the connotation "transformative" to denote a profound change in risk management going beyond traditional adaptation measures, whereas Kates et al. (2012), with "transformational adaptation", refer to an innovative approach of adaptation and include shifting locations, which is strictly speaking no longer adaptation.

Considerable groups of vulnerable people who live in highly exposed and risk-prone places and who lack the capacity to adapt have already reached either soft or hard adaptation limits (van der Geest and Warner 2015). Apart from accepting the limit and corresponding escalating losses, one can undertake curative or transformative measures, as we explain also in Box 22.2 on risk management. In the example of Alaskan villages, a transformative measure would be to relocate residents and economic activity away from high risk and increasingly unproductive areas—even though this is deemed politically impossible, given the estimated costs of up to US$1 million per person (Huntington et al. 2012; Klein et al. 2014). If no transformative action is taken, only curative measures remain as a last resort. This involves redress and rehabilitation mechanisms, when climate change can be established as the key driver, for example, displacement and involuntary migration.

Clusters of technologies can be distinguished that are beneficial for multiple actions. Disaster risk management, such as EWS, and structural/physical technologies, such as ecosystem management, serve only adaptation purposes. Geographical information management and applications are instrumental both in the adaptation and "beyond adaptation" phase, for example for spatial or land-use planning. Technologies for poverty alleviation and livelihood security are clearly distinct. As an example, for livelihood security in the adaptation phase, one can diversify livelihoods by changing agricultural practices to ones that can cope with climate change, whereas for "beyond adaptation" one must find alternative livelihoods and shift from agriculture to, for example services. In this case, there is no longer a strong relationship between the livelihood and natural hazards.

Table 22.2 gives an overview of actions that public or private actors can take to reduce, retain, transfer or absorb climate risk (Subsidiary Body for Implementation 2012) by giving examples that are drawn from the case study on EWS. For each action, we explain the objective in terms of addressing loss and damage. We also indicate for both the private and public action if the technology required is basic, intermediate or advanced. The first column of Table 22.2 situates the action within the spectrum of policy options. Boyd et al. (2017) and the chapter by James et al. (2018) explain how different actor perspectives on L&D result in different ideas about what policy options are available for addressing L&D, both *ex ante* to address the risk of losses and damages and *ex post* to address impacts that have materialised. They distinguish the adaptation and mitigation, the risk management, the limits to adaptation and the existential perspective; we focus on the risk management and the limits to adaptation perspectives to construct the overview.

22.4 Reporting Frameworks for Global, Regional, National and Local Policies

We now turn to analysing key global agreements with their corresponding regional, national and local counterparts regarding their transparency mechanisms in relation to losses and damages and technology as a means of implementation. As tracking of the post-2015 agreements has started only to a limited extent, we include reporting under the pre-2015 agreements in our analysis.

Global Agreements and Risk Management
Figure 22.3 shows how the risk of losses and damages is associated with climate change and climate variability. These risks can be reduced, retained, transferred or addressed through climate action. There are three major global agreements which guide climate actions and priorities in addressing climate risks to different extents: the Paris Agreement on Climate Action (UNFCCC 2015), the Sendai Framework for Disaster Risk Reduction (UNISDR 2015) and the Sustainable Development Goals (SDG) (UN 2015), all agreed in 2015. The Paris Agreement distinguishes three pillars of climate action: mitigation, adaptation and L&D. Mitigation will reduce losses and damages by slowing down climate change. Adaptation will reduce risks, but without changing the level of climate change, and result in avoided losses and damage. The L&D pillar addresses losses and damages as they occur, losses and damages that mitigation failed to reduce and that were beyond the scope of adaptation (van der Geest and Warner 2015; see introduction by Mechler et al. 2018). Climate risk management (CRM) is an integration of traditional approaches of climate change adaptation (CCA) and disaster risk reduction (DRR) as well as transformational actions, and aims to provide stakeholders with relevant decision-support information and tools to face climate risks (IISD 2011; see also chapters by Handmer and Nalau 2018; Heslin et al. 2018; Heslin 2018; Haque et al. 2018; Landauer and Juhola 2018). Comprehensive risk management is used as a broader term that includes all actions aimed at reducing risk regardless of cause.

Table 22.2 Overview of public and private flood risk actions and their intended effect on losses and damages

Adjustment	Spectrum and *Timing*	Private action; *Tech level*: Examples	Public action; *Tech level*: Examples	Objective
Incremental	DRR-preparedness. *Short-term, ex ante*	*Basic*: Fishermen putting fish net around fishing pond after receiving early warning	*Basic*: NGO locating relief items closer to the predicted to-be-affected area. Increase response capacity of communities	Risk reduction; Limited increase of avoidable losses and damages
	DRR-risk reduction; CCA. *Medium-term; for next year's floods; ex ante*	*Basic*: A household raises its plinths/floors and diversifies crops	*Intermediate to Advanced*: An NMHS improves its hydro-meteorological modelling so that forecasts with better lead times and spatial resolution become available. Government-led irrigation system, building of dykes	Risk reduction; Moderate increase of avoidable losses and damages
	Humanitarian aid. *Directly after floods; ex post*	*Basic/none*: Support from within the community	*Intermediate*: Post-disaster public and donor assistance, such as relief items or cash transfers to households and money to governments for reconstruction of, e.g., roads and embankments	Risk retention; Compensation for unavoided losses and damages non-attributable to climate change
Fundamental	DRR and CCA (larger scale or intensity). *Long-term; over several years; ex ante*	*Intermediate*: Access interactive voice response service to get meteorological and agricultural advice	*Intermediate*: Improving access to information through digital inclusion, e.g. providing early warning services in first language of beneficiaries, voice SMS early warning service, nationwide coverage of mobile networks, lower taxation on mobile users	Risk reduction; considerable increase of avoidable losses and damages
	DRR and CCA (new to a particular region or resource system). *Medium to long-term; ex ante*	*Advanced*: Crowdsourcing data on water levels from citizens	*Advanced*: Dam operator changes its way of releasing water by using advanced forecasting models. Forecast based financing. A rice research institute develops flood-tolerant rice	Risk reduction; Soft adaptation limit is stretched; what was considered unavoidable before becomes avoidable

(continued)

Table 22.2 (continued)

Adjustment	Spectrum and *Timing*	Private action; *Tech level*: Examples	Public action; *Tech level*: Examples	Objective
		Intermediate: purchase micro-insurance	*Intermediate*: Micro-insurance, can be supported by mobile technology and/or public-private partnerships to ensure commercial viability	Risk transfer; Adaptation limit not changed. Insurance for unavoidable or unavoided losses and damages
	DRR and CCA (transform places). *Long term; ex ante*	*Intermediate*: Citizens contribute to constructing bio-dykes or ecological corridors	*Intermediate*: build several smaller dams instead of large dam. Green infrastructure such as bio-dykes; ecological corridors. Use of floodplains instead of building dykes	Risk reduction; Soft adaptation limit is stretched; what was considered unavoidable before becomes avoidable
	L&D curative: redress and rehabilitation. *Short term; ex post*	*None*: Involuntary migration or staying put	*Intermediate*: Financial compensation for loss and damage that can be attributed to climate change. Active remembrance (e.g. through museum exhibitions, school curricula). Counselling	Risk absorption; Adaptation limit does not change. Compensation for unavoidable losses and damages
Transformative	L&D transformative measures (shift places). *Long term; ex ante, ex post*	*None*: Voluntary permanent migration	*None*: Voluntary migration of a complete village	Risk absorption; Adaptation limit not changed. Unavoidable losses and damages are avoided by moving away
	L&D transformative measures (livelihoods). *Long term; ex ante, ex post.*	*Intermediate (not hazard related)*: Seeking training and schooling for alternative livelihoods	*Intermediate, not hazard related technology*: Alternative livelihoods. Providing training and schooling (e.g. agriculture to services industry) and access to new technologies such as e-learning	Risk absorption: Adaptation limit does not change. Unavoidable losses and damages are avoided by moving away

Examples are taken from the EWS case study discussed in this chapter, except for the one on dams building on ongoing forecast-based financing projects in Africa. *Source* Climate Centre (2017), Coughlan et al. (2016)

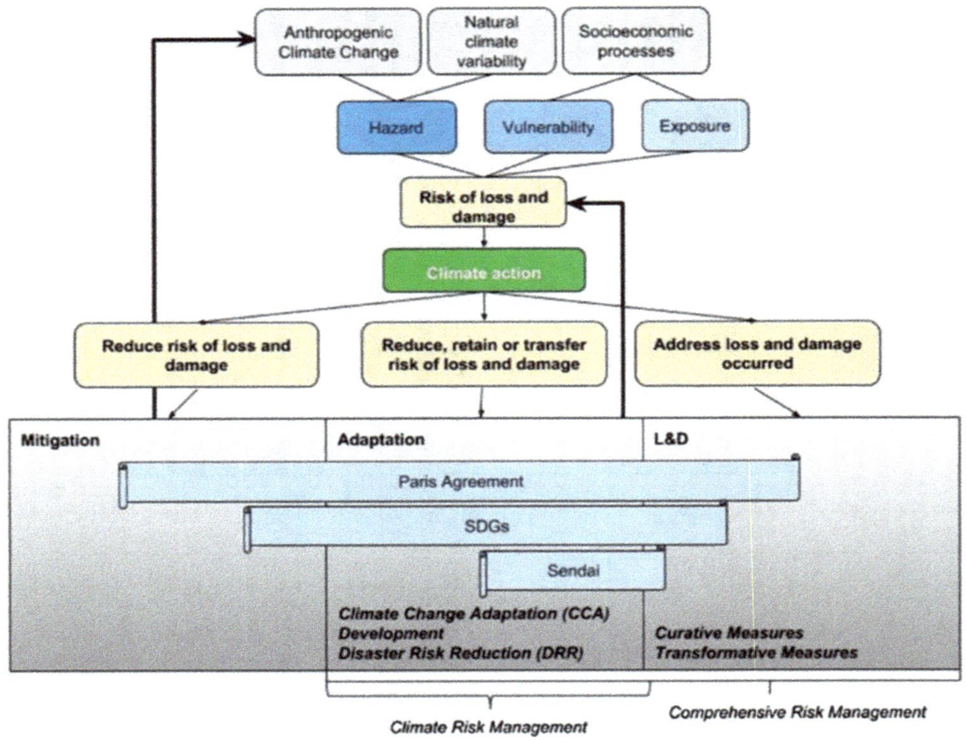

Fig. 22.3 Overview of the relationship of the risk of losses and damages to the three pillars of climate action and key global agreements (Sendai and SDG)

The Warsaw International Mechanism for Loss and Damage associated with Climate Change Impacts (WIM) is the United Nations Framework Convention on Climate Change (UNFCCC) body that has been tasked to develop this pillar (UNFCCC 2013). Sendai, as a framework tailored towards DRR, is part of adaptation. Sendai has indicators on losses and damages and includes paragraphs on relocation of human settlements,[2] but Sendai does not go into attribution of losses and damages data to climate change and leaves the implications of relocation to the climate regime. The SDG compact encompasses development in many dimensions and has synergies with all three pillars.

Notions of climate justice are relevant for all three global agreements; however, there is now a crucial global opportunity to make climate justice a more coherent part of these three agreements and to ensure that climate actions that follow from these agreements are governed accordingly. Inequities play out more in those countries where existing measures are insufficient to cope with the global warming that will continue even if the ambitious target of the Paris Agreement in terms of limiting warming is met. Therefore, we focus on adaptation, as it can reduce losses and damages for the poorest and most vulnerable in developing countries on a shorter time scale than is possible for mitigation alone. In these countries, investments into transformative adjustments for adaptation and L&D as a step change to an alternative socio-economic reality may be necessary.

Global Agreements and Transparency: Indicators and Reporting
As the different agreements evolve, methodologies and terminologies used for providing transparency do so as well. The UNFCCC uses the stringent measurement, reporting and verification (MRV) mechanism (UNFCCC 2014), which is legally binding contrary to the actual mitigation targets in the nationally determined contributions (NDC) that are not dictated by the agreement (Bridgeman 2017). The UN has review or progress reports for the SDGs, and the UNISDR speaks of monitoring and reporting for Sendai, both of which are non legally binding (UNISDR 2015; UN 2015).

The transparency mechanism for the current climate agreements for non-annex I countries starts with the climate pledge, that is (intended) NDCs, where 85% also have an adaptation component (Pauw et al. 2016). Least developed countries such as Bangladesh and Nepal express their adaptation plans through the short-term national adaptation programme of action (NAPA). Countries are also developing medium- and long-term national adaptation plans. Reporting formats on implementing the convention are currently still different for the non-annex I countries due to "common but differentiated responsibilities and respective capacities" (CBDR-RC). The reporting mechanism consists of National Communications (NC) and biennial update reports (BURs), with sections on both mitigation and adaptation. As one example, the section on adaptation in the NCs for Bangladesh, India and Nepal is much less quantitative than for mitigation (see Box 22.3). These reports present no data on the

[2]Paragraph 27(k) of the adopted Sendai resolution reads "Formulate public policies, where applicable, aimed at addressing the issues of prevention or relocation, where possible, of human settlements in disaster risk zones, subject to national law and legal systems."

consequence of adaptation measures on impacts and risks. As another example, the second NC for Bangladesh identifies as a gap that there is hardly any research related to Loss and Damage. Scattered throughout the reports is some losses and damages data, but often at a highly aggregate level or very specific.

Box 22.3 Case study findings on reporting frameworks
We assessed national- and local-level policies in relation to the three global agreements for Bangladesh, India and Nepal. In general, ministries responsible for the environment and forestry develop the national-level climate change policy and investment plans, including the adaptation part. Both Nepal and Pakistan developed local adaptation plans of action (LAPAs) in response to perceived shortcomings of the UNFCCC's NAPAs (Klinsky et al. 2014). Despite successfully integrating vulnerability assessments and prioritising adaptation projects accordingly, the national plan is still seen as an overly broad, top-down estimation that has not adequately captured local needs. Since the impacts of climate change dramatically changed from one village to the next, a top-down process such as a NAPA is considered ill-equipped to cater for meeting local needs (Chaudhury et al. 2014). In Nepal, the LAPA process started mid-2010 and covered, by 2016, 90 village development committees and seven municipalities—the lowest administrative units in the country (Government of Nepal 2016). Nepal's LAPA has succeeded in mobilising local institutions and community groups in adaptation planning and recognising their role in adaptation. However, the LAPA approach and implementation have been constrained by socio-structural and governance barriers that have prevented the integration of local adaptation needs into local plans and thus failed to increase the adaptive capacity of vulnerable households (Regmi et al. 2016). For DRR, each state and district develops its own state and district disaster management plan by adapting the national plan to its local context. The Global Network of Civil Society Organisations for Disaster Reduction has the Frontline programme in which it collects community perceptions of disasters and risk to measure threats, local capacities and underlying development factors, bringing local knowledge to national, regional and global actors. It was one of the few agencies separate from the UN and the agencies that were being assessed that also produced a review of HFA. Frontline continues its programme for the post-2015 agreements, whereby it tries to capture data from local experience and reality on all three key global agreements instead of only on Sendai, by using grounded resilience indicators. Frontline has established baselines during 2015–2016 as a basis for ongoing monitoring during the currency of these frameworks. The Nepalese government, supported by The United Nations Development Programme (UNDP) and in dialogue with development partners, implemented the MDG goals in national-level policies and measures. In some cases, local-level implementation plans, and reporting was completed. Similarly, also for the SDGs, Nepal states in its SDG 2016–2030 National (Preliminary) Report its ambition to combine the localisation of SDGs with political setups at local levels that are willing and capable of handling the development agenda (National Planning Commission 2015).

Article 13 of the Paris Agreement describes the principles for a transparency framework. The new framework will build on the existing mechanisms, but will also introduce the adaptation communication, containing adaptation priorities, implementation and support needs, plans and actions. Standardised indicators for adaptation may be useful to make comparisons across countries possible, but are considered more complex than mitigation indicators, as the impact of climate change varies greatly from one country to another. It is important to make adaptation goals more specific and to build on monitoring approaches from different sectors (Transparency Partnership 2017). The transparency framework also aims at aggregating reporting on support offered and received, and gradually converging the review arrangements for developed and developing countries (ECBI 2017). The facilitative dialogue in 2018 supports the development of the transparency framework and also makes clear how it links to the global stocktake, the collective stocktaking of progress towards achieving the paris agreement, which will start for the first time in 2023 and will consider NDCs submitted in 2020 for the period 2026–2030.

Transparency regarding the WIM mechanism in its first phase from 2013 to 2017 can be said to consist of annual work plans, which report mostly on the first two functions of the WIM, i.e. enhancing knowledge and understanding of comprehensive risk management approaches and strengthening dialogue, coordination, coherence and synergies among relevant stakeholders. It is expected that the WIM in its second phase (2017–2022) will be able to work more on its third function, i.e. enhancing action and support. In that case, the transparency mechanism will very likely become more indicator-based.

The Hyogo Framework for Action (2005–2015) (HFA) was monitored through regional, national and, for a limited number of countries, local progress reports, usually at a 3—year interval. In 2015, the UN General Assembly endorsed its successor: the Sendai Framework for DRR 2015–2030, aims to improve on some of the issues encountered under Hyogo, such as the focus in the indicators on input rather than output or outcome, and the lack of clear links to millennium development goals (MDGs) and UNFCCC (Maskrey 2016). Four of sendai's seven global targets are outcome-focused instead of input- or output-focused and have clear links to the SDGs and the climate agreements. Mysiak et al. (2015) state that the wording used in the pre-conference version of the Sendai Framework seems to have been aimed at fortifying the claims advanced under the WIM, claims in terms of accepting liability for the residual risks. Sendai focuses not only on reducing existing risks, but also on preventing new risks and strengthening resilience. Outcome targets are objective and measurable, allowing international benchmarking of progress relative to a quantitative baseline of 2005–2015. A data readiness review for 87 countries has been done (UNISDR 2017). The first progress reports are expected in 2018. Every 2 years, UNISDR publishes the Global Assessment Report for DRR (GAR) as a supportive tool for HFA and Sendai, which monitors risk patterns and trends and progress in DRR while providing strategic policy guidance to countries and the international community.

MDGs (2000–2015) worked with country progress reports usually every 3 years, covering mostly MDG 1 through 7. MDG 8 was captured through annual MDG Gap Task Force reports. After the UN defined its SDGs, both government spending and donor funding will be tailored—although to a varying degree depending on the specific country and context—to the current scores on these indicators as well as the targets that are to be reached in 2030 (Martin and Walker 2017). In 2016 some countries had already submitted a voluntary national review. Table 22.3 shows the losses and damages indicators for SDGs (the MDGs only had indicators in terms of reducing loss of environmental resources and biodiversity).

Transparency: National and Local
Governments are expected to take ownership of the key global agreements in terms of integration with national planning processes. For example, the National Disaster Management Plan of India states that the country has incorporated substantively the approach enunciated in Sendai. Focal points in each country are responsible for the collection of high-quality, accessible and timely data on the indicators. But also collecting and analysing data at scales greater than national boundaries is required, as disasters do not stop at national borders. Key global agreements and several regional, national and local policies are interrelated, and has each its specific means of implementation. Therefore, regional follow-ups and reviews are held regularly based on the national-level analyses and contribute to follow-up and review at the global level.

Means of Implementation: Technology
CBDR–RC is a principle within the UNFCCC that acknowledges the different capabilities and differing responsibilities of individual countries in addressing climate change. UNFCCC mandated the technology mechanism (TM) in 2010, and it became fully operational at the end of 2013. The TM supports parties in promoting and facilitating enhanced action on mitigation and adaptation (Paris Agreement, article 10.4). The Paris Agreement further specifies that the TM, together with the Financial Mechanism, will support collaborative approaches to research and development, and facilitate access to technology, in particular for early stages of the technology cycle, for developing country parties (Paris Agreement, article 10.5). The Climate Technology Centre and Network (CTCN) implements the mechanism through technology needs assessments (TNA), corresponding technology action plans (TAP), and TT:CLEAR, the web platform for all information related to climate technology. A TNA and TAP has been performed for Bangladesh. A TNA was started but remains unfinished in Nepal. In general, TNAs have been performed for several developing countries, but there are still many that have not received and/or requested technical assistance, and the CTCN seems understaffed (Shimada and Kennedy 2017). The WIM executive committee has established at the end of 2016 a technical expert group on comprehensive risk management and transformational approaches and engages regularly with the Technology Executive Committee.

The Technology Facilitation Mechanism (TFM) that supports the implementation of SDGs has similar characteristics as the UNFCCC's TM, but is still in its early stages, as it started about 5 years later.[3] It aims to ensure equitable access to key

[3]It has three components: (1) a United Nations interagency task team on science, technology and innovation for the SDGs (IATT) with representatives from civil society, the private sector and the scientific community; (2) a collaborative multi-stakeholder forum on science, technology and innovation for the SDGs (STI Forum), which organises calls for innovations; and (3) an online platform as a gateway for information on existing STI initiatives, mechanisms and programmes (Antic and Liu 2015).

Table 22.3 Transparency in the three key global agreements: reporting mechanisms, indicators related to impacts and risks, and means of implementation for technology, with some detail on Bangladesh, India and Nepal

Key aspects	Climate agreements	HFA/Sendai	MDGs/SDGs
Reporting in general	**NDC, NC, BUR** and **NAP, NAPA, adaptation communication** (in development). Self-reporting with strong review and validation mechanism for mitigation, not for adaptation. **WIM**: annual reporting of ExCom to COP; 2-year work plan with nine action areas (2014–2016); 5-year rolling work plan with seven strategic work streams (as of 2016). Review in 2016 and 2019. Request for Loss and Damage contact point at national level in 2016	**HFA**: global, regional and national progress reports, global assessment report. **Sendai**: Sendai Framework progress report. Self-reporting at national levels	**MDG and SDG**: national review, self-reporting
Indicators related to impacts and risks	**Paris Agreement** Article 8.4 Areas of cooperation and facilitation: (a) Early warning systems; (b) Emergency preparedness; (c) Slow onset events; (d) Events that may involve irreversible and permanent loss and damage; (e) Comprehensive risk assessment and management; (f) Risk insurance facilities, climate risk pooling and other insurance solutions; (g) Non-economic losses; and (h) Resilience of communities, livelihoods and ecosystems. **WIM**: three functions: (1) Enhance knowledge and understanding of comprehensive risk management approaches; (2) Strengthen dialogue, coordination, coherence and synergies among relevant stakeholders; (3) Enhance action and support	**HFA**: 2.2: Systems in place to monitor, archive and disseminate data on key hazards and vulnerabilities. Key question: Disaster loss databases exist and are regularly updated. 5.4: Procedures in place to exchange relevant information during hazard events and disasters, and to undertake post-event reviews. **Sendai**: A1 Number of deaths and missing persons attributed to disasters per 100,000 population; C1 Direct economic loss attributed to disasters as global gross domestic product; D1 Damage to critical infrastructure attributed to disasters; D5 Number of disruptions to basic services attributed to disasters	**MDG**: 7A reverse the loss of environmental resources. 7B Reduce biodiversity loss, achieving, by 2010, a significant reduction in the rate of loss. **SDG**: 1.5.2 Direct economic loss attributed to disasters in relation to global gross domestic product (GDP); 11.5.2 Direct economic loss in relation to global GDP, damage to critical infrastructure and number of disruptions to basic services, attributed to disasters

(continued)

Table 22.3 (continued)

Key aspects	Climate agreements	HFA/Sendai	MDGs/SDGs
Previous reporting on impacts and risks	Scattered reporting with some aggregate numbers. **Nepal NC**: over 10-year period up to 2014 more than 4,000 persons died; \$5.34 billion lost in property, land, crops and livestock. **India BUR** \$5 to 6 billion losses and damages 2013–2014. **Bangladesh NC**: rice yield losses as a function of inundation; data on infrastructure damage during last 25 years due to floods. **Bangladesh INDC**: Asian Development Bank estimated 2% GDP annual loss by 2050 due to climate change. Estimated damage of floods in 2007 more than \$1 billion	**HFA**: only reporting on level of progress achieved. No data on losses and damages. **Sendai**: data readiness review shows that only 37–55% of countries report having data on economic losses to productive assets, losses in critical infrastructure and cultural heritage, and disruptions to health, education and other basic services, with between 29 and 33% able to develop baselines	**MDGs**: reporting on increase of land area covered by forest. **SDG**: only voluntary national reviews; none yet for Bangladesh, India and Nepal available. **Nepal Preliminary report on SDG**: large earthquakes in 2015 killed nearly 9,000 people, more than 700 billion Nepalese rupees of damage (destroyed more than half a million houses and damaged more than 200,000 houses and public offices)
Means of implementation: technology	Technology mechanism such as TNA and TAP	**Sendai**: Framework with science and technology roadmap	**MDG**: stimulation ICT as enabling technology. **SDG**: TFM, e.g. science, technology and innovation for SDGs forum, global innovation exchange

Note COP Conference of the Parties, *HFA* Hyogo framework for action, *NC* national communication, *BUR* biennial update reports BUR, *NDC* nationally determined contribution, *NAP* national adaptation plan, *NAPA* national adaptation programme of action, *WIM* Warsaw International Mechanism for Loss and Damage, *MDG* Millennium Development Goal, *SDG* Sustainable Development Goal, *TNA* technology needs assessments, *TAP* technology action plan

technologies and knowledge for developing countries. It is highly likely that it will aim at avoiding overlap with what is being covered by the UNFCCC Technology Mechanism, but some degree of synergy can be expected. So far, no reporting on TFM has been done. Technology transfer was stimulated under the MDG framework as well, whereby especially ICT was put forward as an important enabling technology. The HFA framework emphasises the importance of technical assistance, technology transfer, knowledge and innovation, but means of implementation are not very well articulated. The United Nations Trust Fund for Disaster Reduction bilateral and multilateral cooperation are put forward as possible financing mechanisms. Sendai has a section on means of implementation, where it is reaffirmed that developing countries need technology transfer on concessional and preferential terms and that thematic platforms of cooperation can be used to enhance access to technology (for example global technology pools and systems to share know-how, innovation and research) (UNISDR 2015). Also, a science and technology roadmap was developed to support the framework with a set of expected outcomes, actions and deliverables, mostly aimed at the scientific community (UNISDR 2016). However, these intentions have not yet led to the establishment of tangible mechanisms such as UNFCCC's CTCN.

22.5 Reporting Framework for Technology to Address Loss and Damage and Contribute to Climate Justice

The three key global agreements and their corresponding policy frameworks at regional, national and local level—as also discussed for Bangladesh, India and Nepal—have different ways of planning, reporting and reviewing and require the involvement of many stakeholders. The SDGs and Sendai have Loss and Damage related indicators. The Paris Agreement has no specific indicators, but the NCs do contain some usually highly aggregate losses and damages data. The reporting on adaptation is usually self-reporting without a review mechanism and standardisation that allows for comparability, done at a highly aggregate level and not specific on impact achieved. All three agreements have or are working on some form of technology facilitation for adaptation, but these mechanisms are still in their infancy, except for the TNAs. Overall, it is complex if not impossible to distil from the current transparency mechanisms a comprehensive overview of the status of progress on adaptation and its role in tackling losses and damages retrospectively or prospectively.

Developing the Framework

We thus proceed to lay out an analytical framework to analyse technology needs to reduce losses and damages for decision-makers that brings together the findings of the previous three sections, see Fig. 22.4. The framework puts centre stage two repositories that each relate impacts and risks to technology and its three components, hardware, software and orgware. One repository is an inventory of technologies used to address impacts and risks; the other repository is a target list of those technologies planned to address risk. Several repositories of technology are available that aim at connecting and matching users to technologies.[4] These kinds of repositories can be used by practitioners, to select socially and environmentally sound technologies that match the needs of the poor and vulnerable/marginalised groups.

Global, regional, national and local policies have different means of implementation, i.e. technology, capacity-building and finance, as depicted on the right side

[4]For example, the ClimateTechWiki offers detailed information on several of the mitigation and adaptation technologies. It is a platform for a wide range of stakeholders in developed and developing countries who are involved in technology transfer and the wider context of low emission and low vulnerability development. The Technology Needs Assessment Database is complementary, with factsheets on several technologies. IEEE Engineering for Change created an online, decision-aid platform where users can search and compare technology-based solutions. The Flood Resilience Portal (www.floodresilience.net) is an online knowledge-sharing space that offers practical solutions to address the risks of flooding; the UN just started the Global Innovation Exchange.

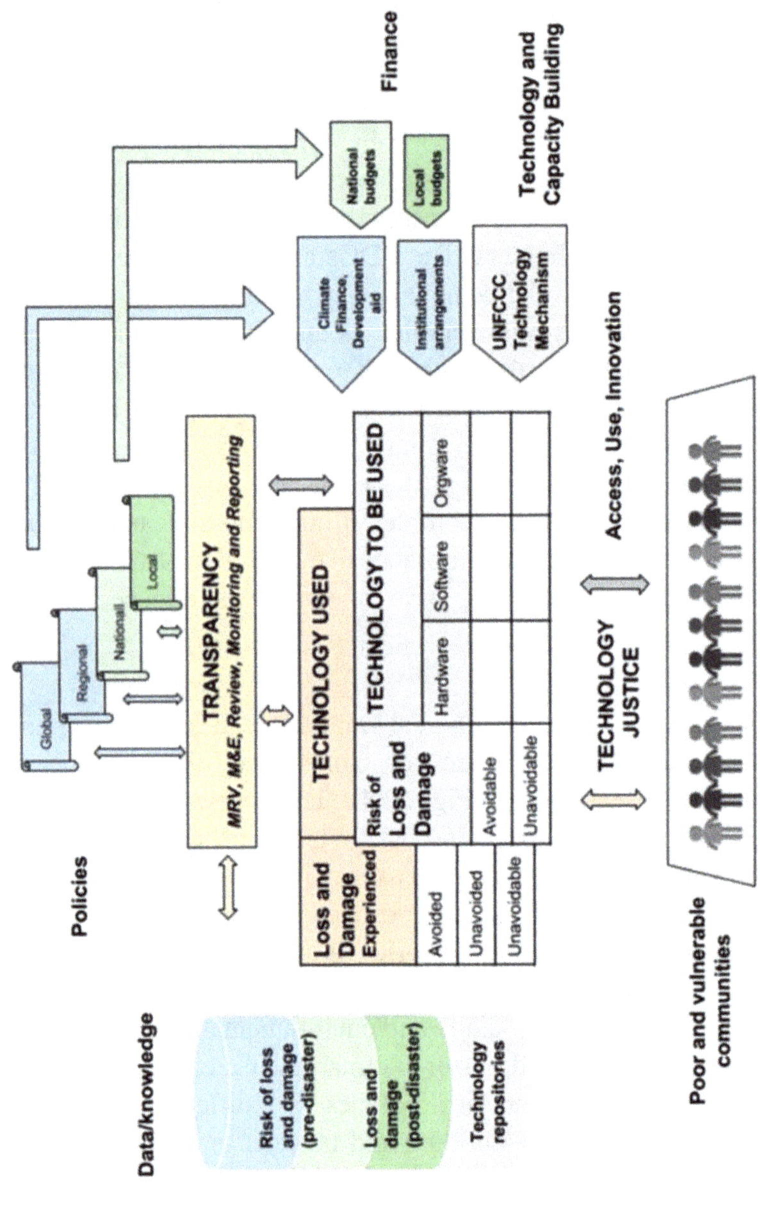

Fig. 22.4 Reporting framework for technology to address Loss and Damage and contribute to climate justice

of Fig. 22.4. The key global agreements and interrelated regional, national and local counterparts each have their own specific transparency mechanism, a way of measuring, reporting and in some cases validating progress, with each their particular focus. This plethora of reporting and reviewing mechanisms covers impacts and risks only to a limited extent and does not adequately help to unveil injustices, as the reporting is often based on self-reporting at a highly aggregate level with insufficient ground-truthed data.

Therefore, credible, timely and high-quality data is an essential input for the transparency mechanism, and as shown on the left side would be kept and updated in another repository element. Reporting frameworks need to have data on access to technology that reflects actual need and on the role that technology can play in reducing losses and damage, both backward- and-forward looking. There are several approaches, methodologies and tools available to collect pre-disaster data on the risk components, i.e. vulnerability, hazards and coping capacity, and data on the actual losses and damages (Surminski et al. 2012). To maximise utility, these databases must be inclusive, capture the poor and vulnerable, be interoperable, preferably open-access, timely (regularly updated) and represent different granularity levels from global to local. It is essential to narrow the gaps in representing the poor and vulnerable of developing countries in climate data, with the ultimate objective to provide an evidence base that can be used in the policy and funding debate around climate change, as well as for DRR and development. Apart from data, knowledge is essential to assess existing and foresee new technologies for adaptation and transformation, i.e. the repositories we referred to earlier.

Applying the Technology for Climate Justice Reporting Framework
We applied the technology justice components as explained in Table 22.1 to trans-boundary early warning systems for the Brahmaputra River (Bangladesh–India) and the Karnali River (India–Nepal).[5] Seven key experts in Nepal, India and Bangladesh provided information both in writing and through follow-up interviews.

Whereas the MDGs had no reference at all to EWS, the SDG framework has two EWS targets. Target 3d is "Strengthen the capacity of all countries, in particular developing countries, for early warning, risk reduction and management of national and global health risks." Target 13.3 is to "Improve education, awareness-raising and human and institutional capacity on climate change mitigation, adaptation, impact reduction and early warning" (SDG 2016). Article 7 and Article 8 of the Paris Climate Agreement[6] place a greater emphasis on understanding, action and support for EWS, but no reporting is as of yet available. Pre-2015 reports such as the national communications or the NAPAs do not have relevant data on early warning, except for more general statements. HFA and Sendai do have relevant reporting. Table 22.4 summarises the injustices for each of the components.

[5]The component on sustainable use does not directly apply to EWS, as EWS cause negligible intrusions such as through gauges that are put into rivers or radar installations.

[6]Article 7 is on "Enhancing adaptive capacity, strengthening resilience and reducing vulnerability to climate change" and Article 8 is loss and damage and "the importance of averting, minimizing and addressing loss and damage associated with the adverse effects of climate change".

Table 22.4 Injustices identified in current flood early warning systems in South Asia

Proposed technology for climate justice component	Injustices derived from case study (expert interviews, focus group discussions, desk research)	climate justice principle required to tackle the injustice	Adjustments required to bridge the gap
Access to services	Both national and community-based EWS do not effectively reach poor and vulnerable communities	Distributive, normative	Incremental and fundamental
Access to technology and knowledge	NMHS are limited in their possibility to improve the spatial and temporal resolution of the forecasts, as they lack the funding and capacity necessary to use the state-of-the-art technology and collect more granular data. The poor and the vulnerable can often not benefit from early warning early action information due to the digital divide	Distributive, normative	Incremental and fundamental
Use	In assessments for hard-engineering solutions for flood CRM, the impact on the poor and vulnerable is often not considered	Procedural	Incremental and fundamental
Technological innovation and implementation	There is not much room for innovation, as the available budgets usually barely cover the rolling out and scaling up of existing copycat-type technology. In addition, capacity building to roll out flood CRM at local level is often not sufficient, due to many ad hoc, short-lived project interventions	Procedural, distributive and normative	Transformative
Governance	Insufficient governance at national to local, and national to regional/neighbouring countries, interfaces. Plethora of reporting frameworks, lack of standardisation and quantitative data at sufficiently granular level. Capacity for reporting is not sufficient	Procedural and transitional	Fundamental and transformative
Finance	Limited funding for public adaptation is going to the least-developed countries, and the poor and vulnerable have very limited funding for private adaptation actions	Compensatory, distributive	Transformative

Note National Meteorological and Hydrological Services (NMHS), *CRM* climate risk management

Equitable Access to Early Warning
The focus of National Meteorological and Hydrological Services (NMHS) is on calculating accurate forecasts nationwide. However, ensuring equitable access to these forecasts also for poor and vulnerable communities is not core to their mandate. Community-based early warning systems (CBEWS) try to bridge this gap, but they do not cover all flood-prone communities, provide only very short lead times and are not well integrated with national systems, hampering their sustainability. Communities that do not receive an early warning inevitably face higher losses and damages, but even those that do receive an early warning often do not have sufficient information to take well-targeted (early) actions that could limit or avoid losses and damages. It is key to characterise the early warning-early action gap to a sufficiently quantitative extent and not—as is currently the case for HFA—in a multi-hazard, country-wide and mostly qualitative way. The self-reporting on access in the HFA, and soon Sendai, has to be interpreted carefully, as the reporting is, to our current understanding, not based on representative surveys conducted by governments among communities that depend on early warning. In general, local self-reporting seems to give a more realistic picture than national self-reporting.

Equitable Access to Technology and Knowledge
Access to services and technology is far from equitable both at the public and private level. Access to more advanced flood risk modelling and observational data, including the required advanced computational power, enables NMHS to improve the spatial and temporal precision of the EWS. This in turn allows for better targeting of adaptation actions for reducing or avoiding losses and damages. Poor and vulnerable communities face digital disparities, impeding equitable access to early warning and early action information.

Technological Innovation and Implementation
Communities are better able to manage and utilise CBEWS when they are involved in the technology development process from the onset. The dissemination, communication and response component of EWS can benefit from relatively low-tech innovations, whereas the risk modelling and monitoring and warning components require both low and high-tech innovations. Current policies and plans have identified several of these innovation needs, but available budgets usually barely cover the rolling out and scaling up of existing copycat-type technology. In addition, capacity building to roll out flood CRM at local level is often not sufficient, due to many ad hoc, short-lived, mainly project-based interventions (Khan et al. 2016).

Governance
Many organisations are involved in implementing EWS at local, national, regional and global level. Most CBEWS initiatives start at the project or pilot level and face difficulties in scaling up and becoming sustainable. It is at the national to local and national to regional/neighbouring countries' interfaces that current governance is insufficient. Governance has to occur across these different dimensions, to promote synergy and coherence and to create political and financial support for using new

technologies to reach the communities that need the information. In addition, there are a plethora of reporting frameworks and a lack of standardisation and quantitative data at sufficiently granular level. High-resolution spatial data on whether/how adaptation technologies meet the needs of the poor and vulnerable is required for the focal scale of flood impacts and interventions, but is lacking. It is complex if not impossible to distil from the current transparency mechanisms a comprehensive overview of the status of progress on adaptation and its role in reducing losses and damages. Clearly capacity for reporting is not sufficient and self-reporting of countries to the global policy agreements tends to lead to too-optimistic scoring, as is seen for example in terms of the reach of early warning into poor and vulnerable communities.

Finance
We find in the transboundary EWS case study area that costs for bridging the gap towards communities are currently not covered through structural and comprehensive funding streams. There is evidence from Bangladesh that shows that these costs form a significant percentage of the overall EWS costs. Innovations in the area of local data collection are urgently needed to reduce the current costs for data collection of water levels. Targeted crowdsourcing might be cost-effective to collect local data for flood maps as compared with costly gauges and gauge readers; at the same time, it will bring along uncertainties in relation to the continuity and validity of the collection. To convince policy makers and practitioners, it is essential that a more mature, longitudinal and standardised assessment of losses and damages at community level takes place against investments that are being made in EWS.

Overall, we suggest the framework proves to be an adequate mechanism to assess the injustices present in a flood CRM measure, such as a transboundary EWS, along the technology dimension. This assessment forms a starting point for change. In Table 22.4 we indicate in the third column which climate justice principle is applicable to tackle these injustices. For example, procedural justice means making sure the poor and vulnerable are included in evaluating a flood CRM measure. The fourth column in Table 22.4 estimates what kind of adjustment is necessary to bridge the gap between an unjust and just situation. Improving access to services can be a quick win with mostly incremental adjustments. However, funding and governance might require transformative adjustment.

22.6 Discussion and Conclusions

This chapter assessed the role of technology for the L&D debate and developed a reporting framework that links climate justice principles to access, use, innovation, finance and governance of technology to address loss and damage at the crossover from adaptation to "beyond adaptation" from the perspective of the poor and vulnerable. Application of the framework to a case study on a flood EWS showed that developing countries (as well as poor and vulnerable communities in these countries) can only use a small part of the technology spectrum available to address loss and damage as they have limited capacities and funding for innovating, accessing and using technology. They are therefore forced to implement the bare minimum largely copycat type of technology. As climate change progresses, the level of adaptation required increases, whereas if no action is taken, the technology available for adaptation remains the same. This means the adaptation deficit (Burton 2004) will increase.

We argued that attention to climate justice principles can help to motivate support for widening the technology spectrum available to developing countries and for addressing the injustices we inventoried by distributing means of implementation (technology, finance and capacity building) through underlying principles such as distributive, compensatory, transitional or procedural justice. We hold that global communities have a responsibility to ensure sustainable use of, equitable access to and inclusive innovation of technology to shape the soft adaptation limit and, once this limit is reached, to support transformative and curative measures necessary to tackle additional risks due to climate change.

In this concluding section, we build on the framework in order to develop recommendations for the Paris Agreement and WIM as to how technology can be mobilised to contribute to climate justice. As the required actions are partly in the adaptation and partly in the L&D pillar, recommendations will cover both. We organise our suggestions around the three main functions of the WIM (understanding, dialogue and support plus action).

Understanding L&D

Understanding the switch from adaptation to L&D enables improved investment in technologies for adaptation while clarifying the unavoidable risks requiring curative or transformative action. We emphasise that this will be possible up to the hard limit, after which only L&D measures are possible. The executive committee of the WIM may include in the work stream and expert group on comprehensive risk management an inventory of how technologies shape the soft limits in both developing and developed countries. It will also be important to reach a solid basis and agreement on what the hard limits from a technological point are for climate change risks, such as for sea-level rise, to avoid contentious political discussions on operationalising the L&D mechanism.

Dialogue, Coordination and Coherence on Loss and Damage

Parties may want to link dialogue, coordination and coherence to the transparency mechanism under Article 7, as the WIM does not have a transparency mechanism. Article 7 of the Paris Agreement states that each party should periodically submit an adaptation communication, which may include its priorities, implementation and support needs, plans and actions. In this context, Article 13 states that, under the transparency framework, countries are encouraged—without it being mandatory—to report information on their adaptation actions to highlight what they have done and what more needs to be done (Desgain and Sharma 2016). The transparency framework offers flexibility in the scope, frequency and level of detail of reporting, and in the scope of review (Kato and Ellis 2016). There is a window of opportunity as part of the facilitative dialogue to start a discussion on including technology in the adaptation communication and to make sure reported data captures the actual impact of adaptation on impacts and risks and represents the poor and vulnerable. However, reporting on adaptation has the risk of shifting the burden to developing countries if efforts to reduce risks are seen as their responsibility (ECBI 2017). It therefore has to go hand in hand with a further development of reporting on the WIM mechanism. It is also important to treat technology in coherence with the SDG and Sendai framework, and join forces in reporting on losses and damages in the broader sense (including L&D). A kind of devolution hub[7] that makes access to policies at global, regional, national and local level easily available and interpretable might be beneficial to stimulate coherency. In addition, standardisation of how to measure and report on losses and damages will be essential.

Action in Relation to Technology to Contribute to Climate Justice
In many instances, communities and countries still seem to have room for adaptation between the soft and hard limit, as indicated by the reported avoidable impacts and risks. Countries are expected to implement adaptation measures to the best of their capabilities (meaning up to their soft limit) to protect their populations from climate variability and/or to empower their citizens, especially those with the lowest capacity to adapt (Winkler and Rajamani 2014) ,to implement corresponding risk avoidance measures, given the common responsibility for adaptation. Governments should provide essential services for DRR, such as a basin-scale EWS making use of automated data collection, high-resolution satellite imagery and impact-based forecasting. But insufficient funding for adaptation is going to the least-developed countries, and the poor and vulnerable have limited access to technologies required for individual adaptation, let alone for keeping up with future risk trends.

Technology can play a role in creating additional adaptation options and/or shifting the soft adaptation limit. Soft adaptation limits should be levelled between developing and developed countries. This means that the objectives that shape the adaptation limit should not be different. Technologies should be shared among those countries having access and those not having access, recognising the commitment to leave no one behind. Why would an NMHS in a developing country settle for less EWS lead time than in a developed country? The technologies that do play a role in transformative actions are in general different from climate-related technologies, for example ICT technologies for distance learning or for outsourcing IT work. Technological development and proliferation has to involve all stakeholders in a fair and equal manner (procedural justice). It is essential to create funding possibilities for developing appropriate technology within existing technology mechanisms such as from the CTCN. The voices of the poor and vulnerable have to be heard. It does not all need to be high-tech; many local technologies can be adapted with investment in research, such as biodykes for flood mitigation, with the added benefit that they can be maintained by local people with existing skill sets.

The transparency framework we propose overall exposes injustices in technology innovation, access and use, with the objective of widening the technology spectrum

---

[7]Such as from the OpenInstitute, see http://www.openinstitute.com/devhubv2.

available to developing countries by distributing means of implementation (technology, finance and capacity building) through underlying climate justice principles.

Acknowledgements The Zurich Flood Resilience Alliance supported this work. The authors gratefully acknowledge input by the following experts from Practical Action: Jonathan Casey, Christine Comerford (UK), Gopal Ghimire, Dinanath Bhandari, Gehendra Gurung and Sumit Dugar (Nepal), Rigan Ali Khan (Bangladesh) and K. R. Viswanathan (India).

References

Antic A, Liu W (2015) Options of an online platform of a technology facilitation mechanism. IATT Background Paper No. 2015/2. https://sustainabledevelopment.un.org/content/documents/2153OnlineTechnology%20Facilitation%20Knowledge%20Platform%20Oct%2028%202015_clean_final.pdf. Accessed 28 Oct 2015

Boldt J, Nygaard I, Hansen UE, Trærup S (2012) Overcoming barriers to the transfer and diffusion of climate technologies. Roskilde, Unep Risø Centre on Energy, Climate and Sustainable Development

Boyd E, James RA, Jones RG, Young HR, Otto FE (2017) A typology of loss and damage perspectives. Nat Clim Change 7(10):7223

Bridgeman T (2017) Paris is a binding agreement: here's why that matters. https://www.justsecurity.org/41705/paris-binding-agreement-matters/. Accessed 4 Jun 2017

Burton I (2004) Climate change and the adaptation deficit. In: Fenech A, MacIver D, Auld H, Bing Rong R, Yin Y (eds) Climate change: building the adaptive capacity. Environment Canada, Meteorological Service of Canada, Gatineau, QC, Canada, pp 25–33

Chaudhury A, Sova C, Rasheed T, Thorton TF, Baral P, Zeb A (2014) Deconstructing local adaptation plans for action (LAPAs): analysis of Nepal and Pakistan LAPA Initiatives. Working Paper 67. CGIAR Research Program on Climate Change, Agriculture and Food Security (CCAFS), Copenhagen, Denmark. http://papers.ssrn.com/sol3/papers.cfm?abstract_id=2496968. Accessed 28 Oct 2015

Christiansen L, Olhoff A, Trærup S (eds) (2011) Technologies for adaptation: perspectives and practical experiences. UNEP Risø Centre, Roskilde

Clark D (2011) Which nations are most responsible for climate change. The Guardian April 21, 2011

Climate Centre (2017) Hydropower and humanitarian sectors joining forces to combat flood risk. http://www.climatecentre.org/news/849/hydropower-and-humanitarian-sectors-joining-forces-to-combat-flood-risk. Accessed Apr 21 2018

Coughlan de Perez E, van den Hurk B, van Aalst MK, Amuron I, Bamanya D, Hauser T, Jongman B, Lopez A, Mason S, Mendler de Suarez J, Pappenberger F, Rueth A, Stephens E, Suarez P, Wagemaker J, Zsoter E (2016) Action-based flood forecasting for triggering humanitarian action. Hydrol Earth Syst Sci 20:3549–3560. https://doi.org/10.5194/hess-20-3549-2016

Cumiskey L, Altamirano M, Hakvoort H (2014) Mobile services for flood early warning, Bangladesh: Final Report. In: Deltares, Cordaid, RIMES, Flood Forecasting and Warning Center, The Netherlands

Desgain DDR, Sharma (2016) Understanding the paris agreement: analysing the reporting requirements under the enhanced transparency framework

Dow K, Berkhout F, Preston BL (2013) Limits to adaptation to climate change: a risk approach. Current Opinion Environ Sustain 5(3):384–391

ECBI (European Capacity Building Initiative) (2017) Pocket Guide to Transparency. http://www.eurocapacity.org/downloads/Pocket_Guide_Transparency_under_UNFCCC/mobile/index.html#p=1. Accessed 24 Jun 2017

ETC Group (20110) Gene Giants Stockpile Patents on 'ClimateReady' Crops in Bid to Become Biomasters. Communiqué no. 106. http://www.etcgroup.org/en/node/5221. Accessed 28 October 2011

Etkin D (1999) Risk transference and related trends: driving forces towards more mega-disasters. Global Environ Change B: Environ Hazards 1(2):69–75

Freudenburg WR, Gramling R, Laska S, Erikson KT (2008) Organizing hazards, engineering disasters? Improving the recognition of political-economic factors in the creation of disasters. Soc Forces 87(2):1015–1038

Government of Nepal (2016) Nationally determined contributions. http://www4.unfccc.int/ndcregistry/PublishedDocuments/Nepal%20First/Nepal%20First%20NDC.pdf. Accessed Apr 2018

Hallegatte S, Vogt-Schilb A, Bangalore M, Rozenberg J (2016) Unbreakable: building the resilience of the poor in the face of natural disasters. World Bank Publications

Handmer J, Nalau J (2018) Understanding loss and damage in Pacific Small Island developing states. In: Mechler R, Bouwer L, Schinko T, Surminski S, Linnerooth-Bayer J (eds) Loss and damage from climate change. Concepts, methods and policy options. Springer, Cham, pp 365–381

Haque M, Pervin M, Sultana S, Huq S (2018) Towards establishing a national mechanism to address loss and damage: a case study from Bangladesh. In: Mechler R, Bouwer L, Schinko T, Surminski S, Linnerooth-Bayer J (eds) Loss and damage from climate change. Concepts, methods and policy options. Springer, Cham, pp 451–473

Heslin A (2018) Climate migration and cultural preservation: the case of the marshallese diaspora. In: Mechler R, Bouwer L, Schinko T, Surminski S, Linnerooth-Bayer J (eds) Loss and damage from climate change. Concepts, methods and policy options. Springer, Cham, pp 383–391

Heslin A, Deckard D, Oakes R, Montero-Colbert A (2018) Displacement and resettlement: understanding the role of climate change in contemporary migration. In: Mechler R, Bouwer L, Schinko T, Surminski S, Linnerooth-Bayer J (eds) Loss and damage from climate change. Concepts, methods and policy options. Springer, Cham, pp 237–258

Huntington HP, Goodstein E, Euskirchen E (2012) Towards a tipping point in responding to change: rising costs, fewer options for Arctic and global societies. Ambio 41(1):66–74

IISD (2011) Climate risk management technical assistance support project. Dominican country study: climate risk management in the water sector. http://unfccc.int/files/adaptation/knowledge_resources/databases/partners_action_pledges/application/pdf/iisd_furtherinfo_water_190411.pdf. Accessed 28 Oct 2015

IPCC (2012) Summary for policymakers. In: Field CB, Barros V, Stocker TF, Qin D, Dokken D, Ebi KL, Mastrandrea MD, Mach KJ, Plattner G-K, Allen S, Tignor M, Midgley PM (eds) Adaptation. 2012 intergovernmental panel on climate change special report on managing the risks of extreme events and disasters to advance climate change. Cambridge University Press, Cambridge, United Kingdom and New York, NY, USA

IPCC (2014) Climate change 2014: synthesis report. In: Core Writing Team, Pachauri RK, Meyer LA (eds) Contribution of working groups I, II and III to the fifth assessment report of the intergovernmental panel on climate change. IPCC, Geneva, Switzerland, 151 pp

James RA, Jones RG, Boyd E, Young HR, Otto FEL, Huggel C, Fuglestvedt JS (2018) Attribution: how is it relevant for loss and damage policy and practice? In: Mechler R, Bouwer L, Schinko T, Surminski S, Linnerooth-Bayer J (eds) Loss and damage from climate change. Concepts, methods and policy options. Springer, Cham, pp 113–154

Kates RW, Travis WR, Wilbanks TJ (2012) Transformational adaptation when incremental adaptations to climate change are insufficient. Proc Natl Acad Sci 109(19):7156–7161

Kato T, Ellis J (2016) Communicating progress in national and global adaptation to climate change. http://www.oecd-ilibrary.org/environment/communicating-progress-in-national-and-global-adaptation-to-climate-change_5jlww009v1hj-en. Accessed 28 Oct 2016

Khan M, Sagar A, Huq S, Thiam PK (2016) Capacity building under the Paris Agreement. http://www.eurocapacity.org/downloads/Capacity_Building_under_Paris_Agreement_2016.pdf. Accessed 28 Oct 2016

Klein RJT, Midgley GF, Preston BL, Alam M, Berkhout FGH, Dow K, Shaw MR (2014) Adaptation opportunities, constraints, and limits. In: Field CB, Barros VR, Dokken DJ, Mach KJ, Mastrandrea MD, Bilir TE, Chatterjee M, Ebi KL, Estrada YO, Genova RC, Girma B, Kissel ES, Levy AN, MacCracken S, Mastrandrea PR, White LL (eds) Climate change 2014: impacts, adaptation, and vulnerability. Part A: global and sectoral aspects. Contribution of working group II to the fifth assessment report of the intergovernmental panel on climate change. Cambridge University Press, Cambridge, United Kingdom and New York, NY, USA, pp 899–943

Klinsky S, Brankovic J (2018) The global climate regime and transitional justice. Routledge Advances in Climate Change Research, *forthcoming*

Klinsky S, Waskow D, Bevins W, Northrop E, Kutter R, Weatherer L, Joffe P (2014) Building climate equity. Creating a new approach from the ground up, World Resource Institute (WRI), Summary Report

Landauer M, Juhola S (2018) Loss and damage in the rapidly changing arctic. In: Mechler R, Bouwer L, Schinko T, Surminski S, Linnerooth-Bayer J (eds) Loss and damage from climate change. Concepts, methods and policy options. Springer, Cham, pp 425–447

Link LE (2010) The anatomy of a disaster, an overview of Hurricane Katrina and New Orleans. Ocean Eng 37:4–12

Martin, M, Walker J (2017) Financing the sustainable development goals. Lessons from government spending on the MDGs. https://policy-practice.oxfam.org.uk/publications/financing-the-sustainable-development-goals-lessons-from-government-spending-on-556597. Accessed Apr 2018

Maskrey A (2016) Monitoring progress in disaster risk reduction in the Sendai framework for Action 2015–2030 and the 2030 sustainable development agenda. http://eird.org/ran-sendai-2016/presentaciones/D2S2P1-ANDREW-MASKREY.pdf. Accessed 9 Jun 2016

Mechler R et al (2018) Science for loss and damage. Findings and propositions. In: Mechler R, Bouwer L, Schinko T, Surminski S, Linnerooth-Bayer J (eds) Loss and damage from climate change. Concepts, methods and policy options. Springer, Cham, pp 3–37

Mechler R, Schinko T (2016) Identifying the policy space for climate loss and damage. Science 354(6310):290–292

Moser SC (2010) Now more than ever: the need for more societally relevant research on vulnerability and adaptation to climate change. Appl Geogr 30(4):464–474

Munich Re NatCatService (2017) Natural catastrophe losses at their highest for four years. https://www.munichre.com/en/media-relations/publications/press-releases/2017/2017-01-04-press-release/index.html. Accessed 23 Oct 2017

Mysiak J, Surminski S, Thieken A, Mechler R, Aerts JC (2016) Brief communication: Sendai framework for disaster risk reduction–success or warning sign for Paris? Nat Hazards Earth Sys Sci 16(10):2189–2193

National Planning Commission (2015) Sustainable development goals, 2016–2030. National (Preliminary) Report. http://www.np.undp.org/content/dam/nepal/docs/reports/SDG%20final%20report-nepal.pdf. Accessed 12 Apr 2018

O'Brien K, Pelling M, Patwardhan A, Hallegatte S, Maskrey A, Oki T, Oswald-Spring U, Wilbanks T, Yanda PZ (2012) Toward a sustainable and resilient future. In: Field CB, Barros V, Stocker TF, Qin D, Dokken DJ, Ebi KL, Mastrandrea MD, Mach KJ, Plattner G-K, Allen, Tignor M, Midgley PM (eds) (2012) Managing the risks of extreme events and disasters to advance climate change adaptation. A special report of working groups I and II of the intergovernmental panel on climate change (IPCC). Cambridge University Press, Cambridge, UK, and New York, NY, USA, pp 437–486

Pauw WP, Cassanmagnano D, Mbeva K, Hein J, Guarin A, Brandi C, Dzebo A, Canales N, Adams KM, Atteridge A, Bock T, Helms J, Zalewski A, Frommé E, Lindener A, Muhammad D (2016) NDC explorer. German Development Institute/Deutsches Institut für Entwicklungspolitik (DIE), African Centre for Technology Studies (ACTS), Stockholm Environment Institute (SEI). https://doi.org/10.23661/ndc_explorer_2017_2.0

Raworth J (2012) A safe and just space for humanity: can we live within the doughnut? Oxfam Policy Practice: Clim Change Resil 8(1):1–26

Regmi BR, Cassandra S, Walter LF (2016) Effectiveness of the local adaptation plan of action to support climate change adaptation in Nepal. Mitig Adap Strateg Global Change 21.3(2016):461–478

Schinko T, Mechler R (2017) Applying recent insights from climate risk management to operationalize the loss and damage mechanism. Ecol Econ 136:296–298

Schinko T, Mechler R, Hochrainer-Stigler S (2018) The risk and policy space for loss and damage: integrating notions of distributive and compensatory justice with comprehensive climate risk management. In: Mechler R, Bouwer L, Schinko T, Surminski S, Linnerooth-Bayer J (eds) Loss and damage from climate change. Concepts, methods and policy options. Springer, Cham, pp 83–110

Shimada K, Kennedy M (2017) Potential role of the technology mechanism in implementing the Paris Agreement. http://unfccc.int/ttclear/misc_/StaticFiles/gnwoerk_static/events_SE-TEC-CTCN-COP21/d093a44fa4b34caabe125562e66b80b9/0595db8c40d34226be9b58999e59ba78.pdf. Accessed 26 Oct 2017

Simpson AL, Balog S, Moller DK, Strauss BH, Saito K (2015) An urgent case for higher resolution digital elevation models in the world's poorest and most vulnerable countries. Front Earth Sci 3:50. https://doi.org/10.3389/feart.2015.00050

Subsidiary Body for Implementation (2012) A literature review on the topics in the context of thematic area 2 of the work programme on loss and damage: a range of approaches to address loss and damage associated with the adverse effects of climate change. http://unfccc.int/resource/docs/2012/sbi/eng/inf14.pdf. Accessed 12 April 2018

Surminski S, Lopez A, Birkmann J, Welle T (2012) Current knowledge on relevant methodologies and data requirements as well as lessons learned and gaps identified at different levels, in assessing the risk of loss and damage associated with the adverse effects of climate change

Tomlinson L (2015) Procedural justice in the United Nations Framework convention on climate change. Springer International Publishing

Trace S (2016) Rethink, retool, reboot, technology as if people and planet mattered. Rugby, United Kingdom, Practical Action Publishing

Transparency Partnership (2017) Preparing for the new transparency framework—lessons learned, challenges, next steps. https://www.transparency-partnership.net/preparing-new-transparency-framework-%E2%80%93-lessons-learned-challenges-next-steps. Accessed 27 May 2017

Turner RE, Baustian JJ, Swenson EM, Spicer JS (2006) Wetland sedimentation from hurricanes Katrina and Rita. Science 314(5798):449–452

UN (2015) Transforming our world: the 2030 Agenda for Sustainable Development, A/RES/70/1. http://www.refworld.org/docid/57b6e3e44.html

UNESCAP (2015) Overview of natural disasters and their impacts in Asia and the Pacific, 1970–2014. http://www.unescap.org/sites/default/files/Technical%20paper-Overview%20of%20natural%20hazards%20and%20their%20impacts_final.pdf. Accessed 11 May 2016

UNFCCC (2006) Application of environmentally sound technologies for adaptation to climate change (FCCC/TP/2006/2). https://unfccc.int/sites/default/files/resource/docs/2006/tp/tp02.pdf. Accessed 10 Apr 2018

UNFCCC (2013) Decision 2/CP.19: Warsaw international mechanism for loss and damage associated with climate change impacts. http://unfccc.int/resource/docs/2013/cop19/eng/10a01.pdf#page=6. Cited 13 Nov 2015

UNFCCC (2014) Handbook on Measurement, Reporting and Verification for developing country parties. http://unfccc.int/files/national_reports/annex_i_natcom_/application/pdf/non-annex_i_mrv_handbook.pdf. Accessed 28 May 2017

UNFCCC (2015) Adoption of the Paris Agreement. Decision FCCC/CP/2015/L.9 https://unfccc.int/resource/docs/2015/cop21/eng/l09r01.pdf. Cited 13 Feb 2016

UNISDR (2015) Sendai framework for disaster risk reduction 2015–2030. http://www.unisdr.org/files/43291_sendaiframeworkfordrren.pdf. Accessed 31 Mar 2015

UNISDR (2016) The science and technology roadmap to support the implementation of the Sendai Framework for disaster risk reduction, 2015–2030. http://www.preventionweb.net/files/45270_unisdrscienceandtechnologyroadmap.pdf. Accessed 25 Feb 2016

UNISDR (2017) Global summary report Sendai framework data readiness review 2017. http://www.unisdr.org/files/53080_entrybgpaperglobalsummaryreportdisa.pdf. Accessed 28 Oct 2017

van der Geest K, Warner K (2015) Editorial. Loss and damage from climate change: emerging perspectives. Int J Global Warming 8(2):133–140

Verheyen R (2012) Tackling loss & damage—a new role for the climate regime. Bonn, Germany, pp 1–12

Walker G (2009) Beyond distribution and proximity: exploring the multiple spatialities of environmental justice. Antipode 41(4):614–636

Wallimann-Helmer I, Meyer L, Mintz-Woo K, Schinko T, Serdeczny O (2018) The ethical challenges in the context of climate loss and damage. In: Mechler R, Bouwer L, Schinko T, Surminski S, Linnerooth-Bayer J (eds) Loss and damage from climate change. Concepts, methods and policy options. Springer, Cham, pp 39–62

Winkler H, Rajamani L (2014) CBDR&RC in a regime applicable to all. Clim Policy 14(1):102–121

Winsemius HC, Aerts JCJH, van Beek LP, Bierkens MF, Bouwman A, Jongman B, Kwadijk JCJ, Ligtvoet W, Lucas PL, van Vuuren DP, Ward PJ (2015) Global drivers of future river flood risk. Nat Clim Change 6(4):381

World Bank (2010) Bangladesh—Economic of adaptation to climate change Main report. Washington, DC: World Bank. http://documents.worldbank.org/curated/en/841911468331803769/Main-report. Accessed 28 May 2016

Index

A

Accountability, 4, 29, 333, 334, 484, 486, 500–503, 505–507

Adaptation, 4, 5, 9–12, 14, 18, 19, 21–25, 27–31, 39–43, 50–52, 58, 63, 64, 66, 67, 74, 76–78, 83, 84, 86–90, 92, 96, 99, 105, 115, 118, 119, 122, 138, 139, 141–143, 155–157, 160–164, 167, 169, 171–174, 181, 185, 194–197, 206–208, 215, 222–227, 230–233, 247, 261–263, 270–273, 275–278, 289–299, 301–303, 305–312, 317–324, 326–328, 330, 332, 336, 343–348, 352, 353–357, 359, 360, 366, 368–373, 376, 377, 394, 395, 399, 401, 404, 406, 426–431, 433–442, 444, 452, 453, 457, 461, 462, 466, 467, 483, 484, 485, 497, 498, 503, 504, 513–518, 520–525, 527–533, 535–540

- constraints, 41, 50, 88, 225, 318, 369, 370, 517
- frontiers, 18, 24, 28, 29, 317, 318, 320–324, 330, 332, 336
- gap, 344, 355, 356
- limits, 12, 18, 22, 27, 29, 41, 42, 88, 92, 223, 225, 226, 317–320, 322, 324, 332, 336, 368–370, 373, 376, 377, 484, 514, 515, 521, 522, 526, 539, 540
- opportunities, 11, 232, 320
- capacity, 366, 369, 402, 429, 435, 438, 514

Adaptive management learning, 420

Africa, 92, 103, 161, 227, 229, 231, 323, 355, 356, 488, 490, 497, 505, 525

Agriculture, 92, 226, 227, 246, 355, 359, 374, 377, 452, 519, 522, 526

Alliance of Small Island States (AOSIS), 4, 7, 9, 41, 42, 51, 52, 55, 84, 121, 157, 158, 161, 163, 165–172, 367, 484, 486

Anthropogenic climate change, 3, 14, 15, 18, 24, 26, 46, 47, 49, 50, 57, 58, 63–67, 71, 74–78, 83, 85, 87, 95, 96, 99, 114, 116–122, 124–126, 129, 130, 134, 137, 138, 140, 142, 264, 268, 274, 287–291, 306, 366, 371, 475, 477, 484, 514

Arctic, 20, 21, 28, 30, 31, 91, 133–135, 357, 358, 425–444

Asia, 68, 91, 158, 242, 349, 350, 488, 517

Assets, 14, 16, 20, 42, 50, 51, 56, 63, 64, 69, 71, 77, 91, 162, 171, 264, 289, 299, 319, 322, 325, 333, 368, 373, 375, 395, 400, 401, 410, 443, 453, 466, 468, 469, 487–489, 491, 495, 504, 520, 532

Attribution, 4, 15, 25, 26, 29, 45, 48, 53, 63, 67–70, 85, 90–93, 95, 99, 113–145, 156, 171, 182, 198, 268, 269, 274–276, 366, 371, 373, 376, 395, 426, 477, 478, 500, 503, 505, 527

Australia, 68, 73

Avoided losses and damages, 11, 13, 19, 222, 223, 344, 523–525

B

Bangladesh, 17, 18, 21, 28, 29, 77, 84, 92, 99, 100, 102, 103, 105, 161, 237, 249, 306, 309, 312, 451–471, 502, 515, 517, 519, 527, 528, 530–533, 535, 538, 541

Barriers, 11, 28, 88, 184, 229, 232, 245, 249, 302, 320, 435, 437, 438, 440, 517, 528

R. Mechler et al. (eds.), *Loss and Damage from Climate Change*, Climate Risk Management, Policy and Governance, https://doi.org/10.1007/978-3-319-72026-5

Behaviour, 28, 54, 100, 167, 169, 199, 212, 250, 262, 305, 306, 325, 328, 330, 332, 357, 401, 485, 491, 495, 520
Behavioural change, 495
Beneficiary Pays Principle, 45, 55
Benefits of adaptation, 291, 346
Benefits of DRM, 402
Blame, 15, 25, 111–114, 114, 115, 117, 120, 124, 138, 144, 251
Borrowing, 289, 489
Boundary object, 401
Budget, 326, 332, 463, 489
Building codes, 252, 301–303, 312, 368, 369
Burden-sharing, 22, 106, 261, 263, 268, 273, 274
Burkina Faso, 229
Business, 23, 103, 185, 203, 251, 252, 293, 296, 327, 331, 335, 395, 399, 419, 443, 485, 488, 491–493
Business interruption, 327

C
Caribbean, 74, 103, 158, 248, 350, 490, 493, 496, 497
Caribbean Catastrophe Risk Insurance Facility (CCRIF), 327, 496–498, 502, 503
Catastrophe loss model, 69
Catastrophe Simulation Model (CATSIM), 103
Catastrophic loss, 324, 332, 335, 484, 493
Chad, 227, 229, 230, 251
China, 72, 73, 161, 168, 171, 172, 242, 293, 349–355
Cities, 18, 21, 99, 166, 183, 229, 240, 248–250, 273, 278, 292–298, 302, 305, 310–312, 389, 443, 476, 477
Civil law, 180–182, 475, 476
Claim, 44, 46, 48, 49, 54, 55, 58, 168, 170, 171, 182, 183, 185, 191, 194, 196, 198, 210, 216, 231, 245, 322, 324, 325, 331, 476, 477, 480, 492, 494, 497, 499, 502, 506, 519, 529
Climate change, 3–5, 7–11, 14–29, 39–41, 44, 46–51, 53, 55–58, 63–67, 70, 71, 74–78, 83–85, 87, 88, 90–93, 95, 96, 99, 100, 105, 114–140, 142–145, 156, 157, 160–164, 168–171, 179–185, 187–199, 205–208, 212–215, 217, 221–227, 230–232, 237–239, 242, 245–248, 250–253, 261–264, 266–271, 273–278, 287–292, 297–303, 305, 306, 308, 309, 311, 312, 317–319, 321, 322, 324, 325, 327, 328, 330, 331, 336, 343, 344, 345, 347, 355–359, 365–373, 376, 383, 384, 388, 393, 395, 397, 399, 400, 402, 404, 406, 416, 421, 425–434, 436, 438, 439, 441–444, 451–453, 456, 457, 461–467, 470, 471, 475–477, 479–481, 484–487, 494, 497, 501, 503, 506, 507, 513–517, 520, 522, 523, 524, 525, 527–530, 532, 535, 539
  justice, 4, 22, 23, 31, 40, 83, 86, 90, 162, 170, 428, 430, 434, 513–517, 520, 527, 533–536, 538–541
  model, 91, 128, 130, 135, 142, 143, 265–271, 292, 293, 357, 360
  modelling, 271, 274
  policy, 10, 39–41, 48, 90, 116, 216, 287, 288, 357, 376, 426, 442, 443
  regime, 172, 192, 198, 527
  risks, 4, 7, 12–15, 18, 20, 22–24, 28, 43, 52, 63, 78, 83, 85, 87, 88, 95, 96, 98, 100, 102, 105, 142, 143, 156, 160, 162–164, 252, 263, 264, 267, 272, 277, 288, 292, 317–319, 321–325, 330–333, 335, 336, 366, 377, 394, 430, 441, 442, 484, 486, 488, 498, 505, 513, 514, 518, 519, 523, 531, 536
  scenarios, 19, 278, 300, 343, 359, 418
  science, 15, 17, 91, 114, 115, 117, 118, 124, 125, 182, 261, 263, 275, 357
  sensitivity, 343, 344, 356, 357, 360
  variability, 14, 17, 26, 28, 44, 46, 47, 49, 50, 53, 54, 63–65, 71, 88, 91, 114, 117, 121, 128, 162, 277, 230, 242, 261, 266, 274, 318, 321, 366, 395, 436, 453, 514, 523, 540
Climate Change Adaptation (CCA), 5, 10, 11, 13, 18, 67, 83–85, 94, 98, 100, 181, 194, 261–264, 268, 270–272, 275, 299, 301, 366, 395, 404, 421, 452, 460, 466, 516, 522, 523, 525
Climate Risk Management (CRM), 7, 12–15, 18, 24, 28, 63, 78, 83, 85, 95, 96, 98, 142, 143, 156, 162–164, 277, 288, 292, 318, 330, 336, 377, 484, 486, 488, 519, 523, 536
Co-benefits, 215, 272, 273, 394
Common But Differentiated Responsibility (CBDR), 84, 170, 171, 213, 527, 530
Community, 29, 45, 50, 51, 58, 64, 66, 70, 91, 96, 98, 103, 119, 125, 140, 156, 168, 169, 185, 209, 213, 214, 216, 217, 223, 224, 226, 243, 248, 264, 272, 290, 303, 304, 311, 322, 367–369, 376, 377, 384, 387, 388, 394, 395, 397–404, 406–410, 413–417, 420, 421, 431, 435, 440–442,

451, 452, 460, 470, 471, 489, 495, 499, 503, 504, 507, 515, 520, 524, 528–530, 533, 536–538
Community Pays Principle (CoPP), 45, 46
Compensation, 4, 7, 9, 10, 23, 24, 29, 43–48, 52–54, 58, 83–85, 90, 95, 99, 100, 103–105, 113, 120, 122, 124, 125, 139–141, 145, 161–163, 170–174, 181, 189–191, 194, 196, 209, 212, 215–217, 261, 263, 268, 270, 273–276, 289–291, 303, 305, 312, 322, 328, 347, 426, 442, 483–486, 498–500, 505, 524, 525
Compensatory justice, 14, 24, 39, 40, 44–47, 54, 58, 83, 85, 90, 91, 94, 95, 104, 336, 516
Communication, 5, 211, 334, 373, 398, 418, 528, 531, 532, 537, 539, 540
Constructivism, 165, 166, 170
Consumption, 31, 136, 193, 386, 388, 489, 491
Context-dependence, 16, 24, 205, 208–211
Contingent credit, 488
Coping, 18, 22, 46, 58, 86, 92, 224, 309, 327, 373, 491, 497, 535
Coral reefs, 11, 26, 88, 133–135, 384
Cost, 25, 76, 103, 169, 206, 211, 212, 215, 216, 262, 277, 287, 291, 295–298, 300–303, 306, 307, 310–312, 321, 322, 325, 328, 330, 331, 333, 334, 344, 346, 347, 349, 352, 356, 357, 370, 388, 411–413, 427, 433, 437, 438, 440, 443, 484, 488, 491–493, 497, 502, 507, 520, 521, 538
Cost-Benefit Analysis (CBA), 277, 291, 295–300, 307, 311, 312, 411, 413, 520
Cost-effectiveness analysis, 277, 298, 412, 413
Credit, 326, 334, 488, 489, 493, 495, 503
  facility, 489, 503
  risk, 489
Crop, 205, 222, 223, 227, 229–232, 240, 246, 294, 325, 331, 334, 366, 369, 373–375, 377, 384, 386, 453, 488, 490, 495, 501, 519–521, 524, 532
Cultural heritage, 15, 20, 50, 51, 84, 106, 209, 210, 217, 300, 383, 384, 532
Culture, 183, 191, 209, 210, 216, 227, 229, 243, 246–248, 264, 326, 331, 384, 387, 426, 427, 433, 435, 439, 440, 442, 443, 497
Curative measures, 24, 25, 52, 55, 99, 499, 522, 539
Cyclones, 11, 67, 69, 71–73, 75, 77, 86, 88, 100, 125, 143, 224, 248, 249, 252, 369, 375, 453, 456, 457, 466

D
Damage functions, 343–345, 347, 356, 357, 358, 360
Damages, 4, 5, 7, 9–11, 13, 15–17, 19, 21, 23–29, 42, 49, 51, 63, 64, 66, 67, 76–78, 84, 86, 87, 90, 91, 95, 96, 99, 100, 102, 104, 105, 114, 115, 117, 119–122, 124–128, 130, 134, 137–145, 161, 180–183, 186–191, 194, 195, 197, 198, 206, 207, 213, 215, 216, 221–227, 228, 231–233, 237, 244–253, 261, 263, 264, 268, 273–276, 288, 289, 291, 292, 294, 295, 297, 299, 300, 305, 318, 320, 322, 323, 325, 327, 328, 331, 343–352, 355, 356, 358–360, 366, 371, 375, 383, 417, 425–428, 430, 431, 434, 436, 441, 443, 451–453, 457, 460–462, 465–470, 475, 480, 481, 483–485, 487, 495, 500–502, 504, 515, 516, 520–528, 530, 532, 533, 535, 537, 538, 540
Dams, 521, 526
Dangerous climate change, 426, 427, 430, 443
Decision-making, 10, 17, 42, 43, 56, 58, 100, 101, 156, 157, 212, 214, 217, 232, 261, 263, 270–274, 277, 278, 289, 295, 299, 319, 376, 377, 402, 411–415, 429, 435, 440, 442, 463, 494
Desertification, 11, 17, 28, 125, 237, 246, 250, 252, 330, 433
Destruction, 11, 22, 209, 456, 476
Detection and attribution, 70, 92, 129, 132, 477, 478
Development, 5, 10, 18, 20, 28–30, 64, 66, 75, 97, 98, 119, 122, 123, 126, 131, 145, 157, 158, 162–164, 167, 168, 171, 180, 182, 184, 185, 187, 194, 196, 198, 207, 213, 214, 217, 227, 232, 245, 246, 248, 251, 264, 266, 268, 270, 272, 273, 276, 277, 289, 291, 298, 301, 302, 303, 306, 308, 309, 312, 317, 319, 321, 322, 324, 325, 326, 327, 330, 334, 335, 336, 338, 367, 371, 377, 384, 393, 394, 395, 396, 397, 399, 400, 401, 402, 404, 407, 410, 414–418, 426, 430, 431, 435, 441, 444, 451, 452, 457, 459–462, 464, 467–469, 471, 486, 489, 491, 493, 499, 501–504, 506, 507, 518, 520, 522, 523, 527–533, 535, 537, 540
Development goals, 5, 30, 248, 309, 394, 523, 529
Diaspora, 20, 383, 384, 388
Disaster Risk Management (DRM) interventions, 84, 400, 401, 413

Disaster Risk Management (DRM) (*cont.*)
investment, 297, 309, 312, 376
policy, 18, 23
Disaster Risk Reduction (DRR), 5, 24, 63, 66, 76–78, 85, 119, 162, 163, 262, 276, 288, 291, 297, 301, 306, 318, 334, 366, 370, 394, 407, 410, 414, 416, 438, 439, 451, 452, 457–460, 468, 471, 485, 494, 497, 498, 504, 513, 516, 523
Displacement, 10, 17, 19–21, 25, 28, 30, 52, 83, 99, 105, 158, 171, 185, 196, 198, 227, 237, 238, 242–244, 246, 247, 249–252, 373, 383–385, 440, 442, 462, 522
Disruption, 206, 293, 531, 532
Distributive justice, 14, 24, 39, 40, 44–49, 52, 53, 55, 58, 85, 90, 91, 94, 95, 500, 516
Diversification, 157, 230, 232
Drought, 13, 17, 25, 27, 29, 64, 67–69, 71, 73, 75, 86, 91, 115, 118, 125, 126, 128, 130, 137, 143, 222, 224, 227–230, 232, 242, 245, 264, 265, 333, 369, 374, 375, 453, 456, 457, 484, 487, 495–497, 502, 519
Drylands, 17, 28, 224, 227–229

E
Early Warning Systems (EWS), 22, 49, 126, 143, 160, 196, 249, 303, 304, 369, 400, 401, 513–516, 518, 522, 523, 526, 531, 535–538, 540
East Africa, 143, 227
Economic
benefits, 413
damage, 300, 358
damages and losses, 300
development, 30, 64, 309, 312, 400, 416, 418, 426
growth, 184, 189, 289, 293, 295, 309, 326, 344, 457, 465
loss, 16, 384, 531
resilience, 10, 20, 24, 158
risk, 276
shock, 325, 327
stability, 51
Economy, 11, 165, 166, 169, 226, 243–245, 250, 252, 324, 375, 415, 427, 428, 442
Ecosystem-based
adaptation, 233, 369, 376
approaches, 376
Ecosystem services, 17, 28, 33, 50, 51, 90, 162, 209, 210, 223–225, 226, 227, 232, 233, 428, 429, 433, 440, 457
Education, 209, 226, 247, 249, 370, 371, 388, 457, 469, 520, 532, 535
Egalitarianism, 47
El Niño, 20, 126, 143, 207, 368, 375, 394, 397, 401, 416–418
Emergency plans, 20, 401
Emissions, 7, 15, 22, 24–26, 41, 45, 46, 48, 54, 55, 58, 63, 64, 67–70, 77, 78, 85, 91, 115, 118, 120, 124, 126–129, 131, 133, 135, 136, 157, 163, 167, 179, 181–186, 188–193, 195–197, 199, 265, 266, 268, 288, 293, 310, 344, 347, 348, 352, 428, 475–477, 479, 480, 499–501, 503, 514
Emitter Pays Principle, 47
Emitters, 44, 46, 48, 120, 121, 135, 140, 141, 182, 274, 475, 476, 479, 480
Employment, 20, 24, 185, 243, 245, 370, 377, 388, 459, 490, 492
Environmental benefits, 299
Environmental co-benefits, 215, 272
Environmental degradation, 92, 237, 240, 242, 244, 247, 251, 368, 370
Equity, 5, 29, 84, 170, 289, 333, 334, 411, 430, 438, 439, 441, 484, 499, 500–502, 506, 507, 520
Ethics, 15, 16, 23, 39, 40, 100
Ethiopia, 191, 231, 277, 495, 496, 501, 502
Europe, 68, 72, 73, 91, 127, 133, 158, 183, 184, 244, 245, 350, 351, 479, 488, 489
Evacuation, 20, 75, 249, 250, 400, 401
Evacuation plan, 20, 400, 401
Ex-ante DRM, 413
Expected losses, 102, 264, 332, 492
Ex-post relief, 494
Exposure, 12–15, 18, 25, 27, 29, 31, 63–67, 69–71, 74–78, 88, 91, 92, 102, 105, 113–115, 120, 126, 137, 142, 143, 248, 264, 268–270, 276, 288, 289, 292, 293, 306, 311, 317, 319, 321–323, 336, 366, 376, 407, 417, 439, 459, 497, 520
Externalities, 347
Extreme events, 9, 11, 12, 23, 52, 55, 56, 66, 67, 70, 84, 86, 99, 100, 125, 126, 129–131, 133, 206, 213, 232, 262, 271, 319, 327, 328, 331, 373, 400, 428, 430, 433, 453, 459, 485, 503, 519
Extreme risk, 290
Extreme weather, 14, 25, 29, 52, 63–67, 69–71, 75–77, 91, 114, 117, 118, 120, 123, 124, 127–131, 136, 137, 139, 143, 160, 195, 213, 222, 242, 252, 262, 275, 287, 288, 291, 311, 319, 322, 324, 330, 331, 333, 366, 485, 497, 503
Extreme weather events, 14, 25, 52, 63–67, 69–71, 77, 91, 114, 117, 118, 120, 123, 124, 127–131, 137, 139, 143, 160, 195,

213, 222, 242, 262, 275, 322, 324, 330, 331, 333, 366, 485
Extremes, 22, 28, 49, 50, 53, 57, 64, 65, 67–69, 71, 74, 75, 77, 91, 124, 136, 168, 230, 232, 267, 293, 302, 321, 375, 376, 483, 484, 504, 507

F
Fairness, 24, 90, 170
Farmers, 29, 51, 98, 226, 229, 230, 299, 324, 325, 331, 333, 334, 495, 496, 501, 519
Fiji, 31, 192, 367, 368
Finance, 10, 11, 15, 18, 19, 23, 25, 31, 55, 56, 58, 100, 101, 105, 199, 158, 160, 164, 173, 195, 213, 318, 327, 328, 343, 344, 352, 355, 356, 358, 359, 441, 452, 463, 467, 499, 501, 507, 513, 518, 520, 533, 536, 538, 539
Fiscal
 policy, 84, 100, 335
 risk, 100, 103
Fishing, 50, 229, 371, 372, 386, 433, 524
Flood, 17, 20, 22, 28, 31, 70, 72–75, 77, 84, 85, 98, 102, 103, 105, 126, 137, 206, 224, 226, 230, 231, 253, 246, 252, 261, 265, 267–269, 272, 273, 278, 289, 292–295, 297–306, 308–312, 325, 369, 393, 395–397, 399–404, 406–408, 410, 411, 414–420, 453, 454, 476, 479, 480, 490, 494, 505, 515–521, 526, 533, 536–538, 540
 barriers, 302
 protection, 85, 298, 299, 300, 301, 310, 311, 406, 414, 454, 519
 Resilience Alliance, 20, 393, 396, 397, 399, 401, 418, 420
 risk, 20, 70, 77, 84, 85, 98, 102, 103, 105, 206, 269, 272, 273, 278, 292, 293, 295, 297–299, 303–306, 308, 309, 311, 369, 393, 395–397, 399–401, 404, 406–408, 411, 414, 415, 417–420, 516–518, 524, 525, 537
Flooding, 11, 17, 25, 26, 29, 64, 69, 71–74, 77, 86, 88, 92, 123, 125, 127, 130, 135, 143, 169, 183, 208, 224, 230, 231, 246, 264, 268, 289, 292, 293, 299, 300, 302, 304–306, 312, 331, 393, 396, 397, 400, 401, 420, 429, 453, 455, 475, 476, 480, 487, 517, 519, 533
Food security, 51, 168, 205, 309, 327, 372, 375, 377, 426, 452, 457–459, 462, 465, 466

G
General Circulation Model (GCM), 266, 267
Germany, 14, 18, 21, 22, 26, 72, 73, 189, 300–303, 305, 306, 311, 312, 475, 476, 490
GHG emissions, 25, 26, 41, 91, 115, 182
Glacial lake outburst, 26, 476
Glacial retreat, 11, 15, 26, 31, 125, 133, 475, 477, 479, 487
Global Facility for Disaster Risk Reduction (GFDRR), 329, 497
Global warming, 22, 91, 92, 96, 125, 128, 136, 277, 357, 404, 406, 527
Governance, 5, 9, 11, 17, 21, 28, 31, 64, 158, 222, 227, 229, 232, 252, 262, 276, 309, 369, 370, 377, 394, 425, 435, 436, 438, 439, 441, 442, 518–520, 522, 528, 536–538
Government, 5, 9, 20, 28, 29, 41, 64, 98, 115, 118, 162, 163, 166, 169, 180–183, 187, 197, 208, 244, 251, 252, 264, 292, 308, 322, 324–326, 328, 333, 335, 372, 373, 375, 384, 389, 394, 401, 404, 407, 429, 431, 438–441, 443, 452, 453, 457, 459–464, 467, 469, 471, 485, 488–491, 493–497, 499, 502, 504, 517, 524, 528–530, 537, 540
Green Climate Fund, 141, 213–215, 344
Gross Domestic Product (GDP), 19, 74, 136, 157, 166, 299, 343, 345, 352, 358, 456, 457, 493, 531, 532

H
Hazard, 3, 12–15, 17, 25–27, 63, 64, 66, 67, 69–77, 85, 88, 102, 105, 113–115, 120, 123, 126, 137, 142, 143, 246–248, 261, 263–270, 274, 276, 288–294, 301–303, 305, 306, 311, 312, 323, 324, 331, 335, 365, 368–370, 372, 395, 399, 402, 406, 407, 416–420, 430, 436–439, 452–454, 457, 459, 466, 476, 484, 488–491, 494, 495, 497, 503–505, 514, 517, 520, 522, 526, 531, 535, 537
Health, 16, 20, 24, 28, 50, 51, 64, 95, 120, 161, 164, 191, 198, 205, 206, 208–210, 212, 217, 232, 233, 243, 247, 249, 268, 269, 298, 309, 320, 344, 359, 370, 371, 375, 388, 430, 433, 438, 441–443, 452, 462, 465, 490, 492, 532, 535
Heat, 11, 13, 25, 30, 67, 68, 73, 75, 77, 84, 91, 115, 118, 125, 127, 128, 135, 205, 222, 232, 233, 270, 348, 452, 457, 519

Herders, 229, 230, 335, 495, 502
Honduras, 172
Household, 18, 27, 29, 87, 92, 98, 103, 168, 230, 246, 247, 277, 287, 291, 301–306, 311, 324, 325, 327, 331, 386, 387, 399, 402, 406, 410, 421, 462, 483, 485, 488–491, 493, 494, 497, 498, 502, 504, 524, 528
Huaraz, 21, 22, 183, 475–477, 480, 481
Human capital, 491
Human health, 16, 24, 50, 51, 205, 206, 208, 217, 344, 430
Humanitarian assistance, 120, 459, 501, 507
Human life, 210, 217
Hurricane, 71, 73, 74, 245, 248–250, 305, 497, 503, 519

I

Incentives, 52, 290, 291, 303, 305, 306, 312, 325, 326, 328, 334, 347, 485, 491, 494, 498, 504–506
Income, 19, 53, 206, 215, 309, 325, 327, 371, 373–375, 457, 462, 488, 493, 499, 501
Incommensurability, 16, 24, 205, 208, 211, 212, 216
Index-based insurance, 230
Indian Ocean, 103, 143, 248
Indigenous people, 132, 426, 435
Indirect impacts, 66, 417, 442
Indonesia, 77, 292, 401, 406, 410, 421
Infrastructure, 28, 103, 120, 125, 126, 128, 205, 223, 232, 247, 249, 252, 268, 269, 272, 278, 294, 299–301, 336, 374, 376, 408, 410, 414, 417, 419, 427, 428, 430, 431, 433, 434, 441 443, 453, 454, 462, 487, 489, 491, 503, 521, 526, 531, 532
Innovation, 22, 23, 31, 133, 185, 230, 326, 372, 404, 414, 504, 513, 514, 516, 518–521, 530, 532, 533, 536–540
Institutions, 7, 20, 21, 29, 31, 42, 52, 98, 119, 122, 123, 162, 168, 180, 183, 184, 199, 251, 291, 320, 322, 344, 393, 394, 443, 451, 453, 457, 458, 460, 466, 468, 470, 485, 488–490, 498, 499, 501, 502, 506, 528
Insurance, 4, 7, 9, 10, 18, 21–24, 28, 29, 49, 52, 53, 56, 57, 65, 66, 69, 70, 83, 84, 101, 104, 105, 126, 137, 139, 140, 143, 158, 160, 162–165, 230, 287–291, 302, 303, 305, 306, 311, 312, 317–319, 321–328, 330–336, 372, 399, 400, 420, 441, 462, 483–502, 504–507, 520, 526, 531
Integrated Assessment Model (IAM), 343–345, 355, 356, 359
Integrated climate risk management, 288
Intergovernmental Panel on Climate Change (IPCC), 5, 7, 8, 12, 15, 23, 26, 31, 41, 46, 58, 64, 65, 67, 68, 70, 71, 74–76, 85, 87, 88, 90–92, 94, 96, 115, 127, 129, 132–135, 137, 141, 143, 206, 222–224, 228, 231, 242, 245, 246, 248, 249, 264–268, 270, 271, 275, 276, 288, 289, 318–320, 330, 347, 352, 357, 366, 383, 418, 426, 428, 431, 456, 477, 478, 494, 514, 516, 517, 520, 521
Internal displacement, 242, 243
International law, 16, 26, 46, 53, 156, 180–182, 185–193, 196–199, 245
International relations, 15, 58, 95, 155, 156
Investment, 19, 28, 30, 103, 141, 232, 277, 278, 290, 291, 297–300, 305, 306, 308, 309, 312, 323, 325, 326, 328, 345, 346, 369, 376, 395, 411, 415, 418, 462, 480, 481, 485, 491, 494, 498, 504, 513, 518, 519, 521, 527, 528, 538–540
Irreversibility, 11, 87, 344, 428
Irrigation, 229, 377, 464, 495, 496, 520, 521, 524

J

Jamaica, 158
Japan, 350
Justice, 4, 5, 7, 14, 15, 22–24, 31, 39, 40, 44–49, 52–55, 58, 83–86, 90, 91, 94, 95, 104, 106, 156, 162, 170, 171, 174, 185–190, 207, 216, 274, 336, 376, 428, 430, 434, 442, 444, 500, 513–520, 527, 533–536, 538–541
Justice principles, 23, 24, 513, 517, 538, 539, 541

K

Kaolack, 231
Karnali, 20, 393, 397, 401, 407, 408, 515, 535
Kenya, 130, 231
Kiribati, 192, 214, 215, 246, 247, 367
Knowledge, 9, 14, 16, 31, 41, 50, 55, 63, 70, 86, 87, 116, 137, 144, 157, 167, 171, 195, 205, 207–210, 212, 214, 216, 221, 224–226, 266, 275, 277, 278, 304, 359, 369, 371, 376, 377, 394, 397, 398, 402, 406, 408, 413–415, 420, 426, 430, 435, 438, 441, 442, 444, 452, 462, 467, 468, 497, 500, 518, 519, 528, 529, 531–533, 535–537

Knowledge transfer, 9, 50, 55, 139, 196, 462, 518, 520, 532
Koshi, 20

L
Lake Chad, 229, 230
Landslides, 13, 73, 86, 433
Land-use planning, 64, 522
Latin America, 72, 158, 386
Law, 16, 26, 30, 46, 53, 118, 140, 155, 156, 163, 173, 179–183, 185–193, 196–199, 206, 299, 303, 332, 475, 476, 477, 527
Legal frameworks, 180, 185, 335, 428
Liability, 26, 43–45, 48, 54, 57, 58, 83–85, 90, 91, 94, 95, 105, 113–115, 117, 124, 125, 138, 139, 140, 144, 145, 162, 170, 182, 199, 269, 366, 426, 429, 442, 475, 480, 484, 500–502, 506, 516, 529
Liberalism, 165, 169
Limit, 58, 68, 96, 189, 191, 222, 223, 226, 231–233, 271, 289, 301, 305, 306, 311, 312, 320, 325, 352, 368, 369, 371, 373, 376, 389, 395, 429, 523, 526, 537, 539, 540
Litigation, 16, 21, 26, 140, 179–183, 197, 198, 476, 481
Livelihood, 19, 20, 24, 28, 49, 57, 99, 132, 133, 135, 162, 168, 171, 206, 209, 212, 215, 216, 222, 224, 227, 229, 230, 232, 245, 247–249, 251–253, 268, 269, 293, 319, 322, 327, 365, 368–372, 375, 377, 393, 396, 397, 401, 404, 410, 414, 415, 417, 426–429, 433, 435, 439, 442, 443, 456, 457, 462, 466, 468, 493, 496, 522, 525, 531
Livestock, 28, 223, 226, 227, 229, 230, 232, 331, 335, 456, 488, 497, 532
Loans, 329, 502
Longer-term impacts, 91, 95, 224, 321, 325–327
Loss, 3–6, 9, 11, 12, 14–17, 19–23, 25, 26, 31, 32, 39, 40, 42–44, 49–52, 63–78, 83–87, 90, 91, 94–97, 99–106, 113–115, 117, 119–128, 130–132, 134, 135, 137–145, 155, 156, 158, 160–162, 168, 169, 171, 173, 174, 179–181, 184, 191, 193–197, 205–216, 221–227, 229–232, 237, 244–250, 252, 261–264, 268, 273–276, 278, 288–290, 294–296, 298, 300, 311, 317, 318, 321–328, 330–332, 335, 336, 343–347, 352, 355, 356, 358–360, 365, 366, 368, 369, 371–376, 383–387, 389, 393, 394, 396, 397, 402, 404, 410, 413, 417–419, 421, 425–431, 433–444, 451–453, 456, 457, 460–462, 465–471, 475, 480, 481, 483–486, 488, 490, 491–495, 497–502, 504–507, 513–528, 530–535, 537–540
Loss and Damage, 3–7, 9–19, 21–32, 39–58, 63–67, 75–78, 83–87, 90, 91, 94–97, 99, 100, 102, 104, 105, 113–115, 117–122, 124–127, 130, 134, 137–145, 155–174, 179–185, 193–197, 199, 205–207, 213–215, 221, 222, 224–227, 229, 231–233, 237, 244–250, 252, 261–264, 268, 270, 271, 273–276, 287, 288, 290–292, 295, 301, 311, 312, 318, 322, 323, 325, 327, 328, 331, 336, 343–347, 349, 352, 355, 356, 358–360, 365, 366, 368, 371, 372, 374–376, 393, 394, 396, 397, 404, 413, 418, 421, 425–431, 434, 436, 437, 439, 441–444, 451–453, 457, 460–462, 465–471, 475, 476, 480, 481, 483–487, 490, 494, 495, 498–501, 505, 506, 513–516, 518, 520–528, 530–535, 537–540
Loss and Damage Network, 4, 7, 31, 32
Loss modelling, 19, 66, 78, 86, 88, 100, 103, 105, 271, 274, 294, 352, 417, 418, 420, 497, 498, 519, 537
Loss of life, 20, 22, 25, 26, 50, 64, 74, 77, 126, 132, 135, 143, 209, 210, 212, 223, 300, 311, 413
Loss of lives, 216, 369, 453

M
Macroeconomy, 264, 453
Maladaptation, 326, 330, 521
Mali, 227, 229
Mangrove, 232, 233
Marshall Islands, 20, 28, 163, 171, 383–389
Mauritania, 227
Mexico, 18, 172, 188, 301, 303, 304, 311, 401, 406, 408, 421
Migration, 10, 15, 17, 19, 21, 24, 25, 28, 30, 84, 96, 97, 99, 106, 155, 158, 185, 206, 208, 214, 215, 230–232, 237–247, 249, 251–253, 365, 366, 370, 373, 384, 385, 388, 389, 416, 417, 425, 426, 430, 434–439, 442, 443, 462, 522, 526
Mitigation, 5, 7, 10, 11, 14, 19, 23, 39–41, 43, 51, 58, 83, 84, 87, 90, 115, 119, 139, 156, 163, 169, 171, 172, 180, 194, 195, 197, 206, 222, 223, 225, 232, 261–263, 273, 275, 277, 288–290, 292, 297, 301, 302, 305, 306, 311, 325, 328, 343–345,

347, 352, 356, 357, 359, 395, 406, 428, 436–438, 462, 464, 494, 514–516, 518, 523, 527, 529–531, 533, 535, 540
Moral hazard, 290, 305, 312, 491, 494, 495, 504, 505
Multi-criteria analysis, 277, 296, 298, 311, 412, 413

N
Natural hazard, 64, 67, 69, 70, 137, 246, 289, 291, 292, 301–303, 306, 311, 365, 368, 370, 372, 399, 402, 406, 488, 514, 520, 522
NELD, 16, 20, 24, 50, 51, 126, 205–210, 212–217, 223, 457
Neorealism, 165, 166
Nepal, 20, 28, 393, 397, 401, 406–408, 411, 412, 421, 515, 527, 528, 530–533, 535, 541
Netherlands, 18, 181, 277, 296, 298–300, 309, 311, 312
NGOs, 20, 162, 164, 167, 168, 368, 393, 394, 396, 399, 402, 404, 406–408, 410, 414, 415, 435, 452, 453, 459, 460, 462–464, 467, 475, 480, 488, 494, 499, 501, 506, 517, 518, 524, 525, 528
Niger, 227, 229
Nigeria, 227, 229, 250, 251
No-harm rule, 179, 187–190, 192, 197, 198
Non-economic, 5, 10, 11, 16, 23, 49–52, 56, 57, 105, 126, 128, 158, 160, 171, 205–209, 211, 212, 214–217, 232, 233, 262, 264, 297, 331, 356, 384, 443, 456, 457, 465, 466, 531
Non-economic losses (NEL/NELD), 5, 10, 16, 20, 23, 24, 50, 51, 126, 128, 158, 161, 205–208, 210–217, 223, 232, 233, 262, 264, 331, 356, 383, 384, 443, 457, 465, 466, 531
Non-monetary damages, 344
No-regrets, 215
Normalisation, 69–72, 74, 75

O
Observations, 66, 77, 120, 129, 143, 144, 168, 217, 228, 265, 332, 357, 426, 537
OECD, 277
Opportunity, 9–11, 20, 66, 96, 97, 103, 113, 116, 121, 125, 138, 158, 163, 167, 168, 171, 217, 225, 232, 240, 288, 297, 312, 320, 325, 326, 333, 371, 373, 377, 383, 384, 388, 389, 393, 397, 400, 402, 443, 468, 490, 493, 505, 516, 527, 539
Opportunity cost, 297, 493
Outmigration, 21, 28, 425, 426, 430, 434, 435, 437, 439, 442, 443

P
Pacific, 17, 19, 27, 28, 103, 158, 191, 237, 246–248, 252, 365–373, 375–377, 383, 384, 386, 490, 497, 517
Paraguay, 251
Paris agreement, 4, 5, 7, 9, 22, 24, 43, 44, 53, 57, 58, 84, 92, 99, 105, 121, 140, 157, 160–162, 168, 170–172, 183, 192, 193, 196, 197, 275, 288, 318, 395, 452, 471, 484, 485, 500, 501, 504, 516, 523, 527–531, 533, 539
Participatory approach, 207, 334, 393, 397, 401, 402, 407–409
Partnership, 4, 7, 20, 30, 290, 318, 334, 335, 393, 394, 396, 397, 399, 420, 421, 460, 486, 493, 504, 507, 525, 529
Pastoralism, 229
Pathways, 18, 97, 207, 252, 264, 266, 273, 277, 287, 291–293, 295, 306–310, 312, 321, 348, 358, 359, 415, 417, 419, 520
Peru, 20, 28, 393, 399, 401, 406, 408, 415–419, 421, 476
Philippines, 163–165, 170–172, 184
Piura, 20
Policy, 4, 5, 7, 10, 13–19, 21–26, 30–32, 39–41, 43, 48, 50, 51, 83–86, 90, 94–98, 100, 104, 105, 113–121, 123, 124, 126, 130, 136, 138, 139, 144, 145, 156, 158, 164, 180, 184, 194, 206, 208, 214, 216, 217, 223, 224, 229, 232, 237, 240, 245, 247, 263, 271–275, 277, 288, 289, 298–303, 306, 307, 310, 311, 318, 322–324, 326, 331, 335, 336, 357, 368–371, 373, 374, 376, 386, 394, 396, 398, 399, 402, 404, 406, 413, 414, 416, 417, 419, 421, 426, 442, 443, 451–453, 457–461, 465–469, 487, 489, 496–499, 513, 519, 523, 527–530, 533, 535, 537, 538, 540
Policy-advisor, 26, 32
Policy-maker, 13, 15, 114, 116, 117, 126, 136, 139, 144, 237, 263, 306, 398, 402, 413, 417, 466, 469, 538
Population, 10, 14, 17, 20, 29, 63, 64, 70, 71, 74, 77, 126, 136, 157, 158, 162, 165, 166, 184, 185, 206, 208, 222, 237, 238, 240–242, 244, 246, 249–252, 289, 293, 295, 299, 324, 345, 371, 373, 374, 377, 383–385, 388, 389, 400, 429, 436–439, 442, 443, 452, 456, 462, 466, 491, 517, 519, 531, 540

Poverty, 28, 87, 119, 227, 231, 249, 309, 325, 326, 328, 333, 370, 452, 457, 459, 461, 491, 501, 504, 506, 522
Preparedness, 20, 105, 196, 227, 301–304, 306, 395, 396, 401, 410, 414, 417, 426, 433, 441, 466, 524, 531
Private sector, 20, 163, 164, 375, 393, 394, 397, 399, 486, 530
Probability, 12, 13, 17, 20, 25, 52, 67, 101–103, 115, 129, 130, 136, 143, 192, 263, 267, 270, 272, 276, 280, 294, 295, 299, 301–303, 321, 326, 332–334, 359, 441
Probability density function (pdf), 292, 293
Profit, 22, 325, 492, 519
Projections, 19, 67, 76, 77, 130, 142, 143, 145, 207, 230, 242, 249, 264, 266–268, 271–272, 278, 293, 331, 343, 360, 384, 419, 456, 457, 465, 466
Property damage, 206
Public
  finance, 15
  good, 244
  investment, 519
  private partnerships, 290, 335, 504, 525

R

Rainfall, 17, 25, 65, 69, 71, 77, 91, 128, 222, 227–230, 233, 246, 247, 249, 261, 265, 267, 292, 324, 375, 384, 452, 453, 495
Rainfall intensity, 228
Reconstruction, 22, 184, 265, 357, 417, 460, 491, 493, 494, 497–499, 504, 524
Recovery, 10, 114, 117, 119, 139, 158, 229, 230, 232, 247, 327, 375, 395, 437, 438, 459, 460, 487, 489, 491, 494
Redistribution, 14, 30, 45, 47–49, 53, 58, 85
Refugee, 30, 174, 185, 198, 237–241, 243–245, 370, 441, 443
Regulation, 101, 181, 182, 226, 252, 301, 303, 306, 311, 312, 325, 435, 499, 505
Reinsurance, 66, 69, 137, 487, 489, 490, 492, 499, 504, 507
Relief, 22, 29, 168, 227, 326, 452, 458, 459–461, 466, 468, 470, 489, 490, 491, 493, 494, 496, 497, 499, 504, 505, 524
Relocation, 19–21, 27, 28, 49, 57, 99, 206, 214, 216, 223, 248, 365–373, 383–385, 387–389, 419, 425, 429, 430, 434–437, 439–443, 527
Remedial obligation, 179
Reserve fund, 99, 467, 488–490, 498
Resettlement, 17, 27, 237, 243, 245, 246, 252, 368, 369, 385, 441
Residual damage, 19, 263, 291, 320, 343–352, 356, 359, 360
Residual risk, 18, 76, 90, 98, 101, 263, 287, 288, 295, 301, 311, 312, 325, 327, 328, 434, 493, 529
Resilience, 10, 20, 24, 27, 52, 122, 158, 164, 229, 232, 263, 270, 273, 275, 320, 322, 324–326, 330, 331, 333, 393–397, 399–408, 410–421, 430, 436, 452, 454, 459, 462, 466, 467, 485, 486, 494–497, 506, 528, 529, 531, 533, 535
Rimac, 20, 393, 397, 401, 416, 417
Risk
  aversion, 92, 305, 493
  coping, 92
  finance, 58, 318, 467
  layer, 102–105, 486, 502
  layering, 84–86, 94, 95, 100–105, 290, 328, 329, 335
  management, 4, 9, 10, 12–16, 18, 21, 23–26, 28, 30, 31, 51, 52, 56, 58, 63, 67, 78, 83–85, 95, 96, 98, 101, 103–105, 119, 123, 138, 139, 142, 143, 156, 158, 160, 162–164, 174, 205, 207, 213, 214, 233, 262, 263, 270–273, 275–278, 287–294, 296, 297, 301, 302, 304, 306, 308, 309, 311, 312, 317–319, 321–324, 326–328, 330, 333–336, 366, 372, 376, 377, 396, 400, 401, 408, 413, 416, 418, 462, 475, 479, 484, 486–488, 491, 495–498, 514–516, 519, 520, 522, 523, 529–531, 536, 539
  modelling, 323, 399, 406, 418, 420, 519, 537
  perception, 13, 246, 250
  preference, 11, 87, 92, 96, 100, 320
  premium, 492
  reduction, 5, 9, 10, 14, 18, 24, 28–30, 49, 57, 63, 64, 66, 74, 76–78, 85, 92, 96, 97, 101, 119, 139, 162, 163, 222, 262, 263, 270, 275, 276, 287, 288, 290–292, 294, 297, 301, 303, 305, 306, 312, 317–322, 324–326, 328, 330, 333–336, 365, 370, 371, 394, 406, 407, 410, 411, 414, 416–418, 438, 439, 451, 452, 457–461, 468, 471, 483–485, 487, 491, 494–498, 504, 507, 513, 516, 521, 523–525, 535
  tolerance, 41–43, 50, 84, 92, 94, 98, 100, 103, 104, 320, 404
  taking, 30, 321, 322, 325, 326, 333, 400, 495, 496
  transfer mechanisms, 9, 288

Robustness, 265, 271, 272, 278, 344, 377, 411, 413
Rural livelihoods, 206

S
Safe operating space, 317, 319, 317, 319, 320
Safety nets, 29, 327, 333, 335, 459, 461, 484, 496, 502, 506
Sahel, 17, 28, 222, 224, 227–230, 232, 250
Saint Lucia, 13, 170
Savings, 301, 311, 325, 326, 333, 334, 488, 489, 493, 495, 496, 502
Scenarios, 19, 23, 41, 66, 77, 78, 88, 138, 265, 266, 268–273, 278, 292–298, 300, 308, 310, 311, 325, 330, 343, 344, 347, 348, 352, 358–360, 366, 368, 383, 398, 416–420, 434, 438, 462, 466
Science-policy, 7, 123, 124, 138, 399
Science-policy interface, 5
Sea level rise, 5, 9, 11, 15, 17, 21, 27, 28, 41, 42, 52, 65, 67, 86–88, 91, 92, 97, 99, 115, 125, 126, 128, 136, 139, 158, 168, 171, 193, 205, 207, 208, 223, 224, 232, 233, 237, 246–248, 251, 252, 264, 272, 292, 293, 295, 296, 299, 300, 307, 330, 366, 369, 385, 386, 425, 426, 431, 433, 437, 442, 452, 453, 456, 466, 486, 487, 521, 539
Sendai Framework for Disaster Risk Reduction, 318, 451, 471, 523
Senegal, 230, 231, 495, 496
Services, 16, 17, 27, 28, 30, 50, 51, 90, 99, 162, 164, 209, 210, 212, 221, 223–227, 231–233, 245, 247, 250, 262, 268, 269, 334, 370, 376, 388, 428, 429, 433, 440, 457, 463, 518, 519, 522, 524, 525, 531, 532, 536–540
Shock, 86, 230, 325, 327, 402, 459, 493, 503, 519
Slow-onset events, 11, 24, 66, 67, 174, 433
Small business, 23, 103, 185, 293, 296, 327, 335, 395, 396, 399, 492
Small Island Developing States (SIDS), 9, 19, 52, 88, 158, 193, 194, 246–248, 252, 365, 366, 368, 376, 442
Social
cultural impacts, 436, 466
environmental, 156, 166, 231, 238, 271, 272, 306, 366, 402, 425, 435, 436, 441, 464, 466, 514, 518, 519, 533
impact, 21, 310, 425, 426, 441
protection scheme, 232, 326, 334, 462, 506
Society, 15–17, 20, 27, 30, 32, 113, 129, 166, 169, 209, 210, 221, 222, 224–227, 231, 252, 268, 287, 296, 297, 300, 394, 396, 397, 400, 413, 415, 420, 429, 442, 443, 452, 468, 496, 518, 528, 530
Socio-ecological system, 24, 318, 320, 403
Solidarity, 4, 29, 170, 334, 372, 483, 484, 486, 488, 489, 493, 499–503, 505–507
South America, 17, 28, 133, 237, 251, 477, 478
Southern Cone, 17, 28, 237, 251, 252
South Sudan, 227
Spending, 529
Storms, 13, 17, 25, 28, 72–74, 86, 91, 128, 237, 246, 248, 249, 250, 264, 369, 433, 456, 457
Stressors, 16, 17, 207, 221, 222, 225, 232, 242, 252, 272, 317–320, 327, 331, 376, 452, 466, 516
Sudan, 227
Sudden-onset events, 10, 13, 86
Supply chain, 30, 155, 169, 174
Sustainable Development Goals (SDGs), 5, 10, 30, 248, 394, 395, 523, 527, 528–533
Sustainable economic development, 30, 266, 289, 309, 430
Systems, 10, 15, 16, 21, 22, 25, 26, 28, 49, 65, 74, 88, 92, 120, 126, 132, 133, 143, 145, 161, 169, 182, 191, 196, 197, 208, 209, 211, 217, 221, 223–227, 231, 249, 263, 265, 267, 270, 275, 288, 303, 304, 306, 317–321, 324, 334, 369, 376, 377, 395, 397–401, 403, 410, 413–417, 427, 433, 441, 444, 462, 464, 466, 494, 495, 503–506, 513, 515, 520, 522, 527, 531, 532, 535–537

T
Tax, 489–491, 498
Technology, 10, 12, 20, 22, 23, 27, 28, 30, 31, 34, 49, 55–57, 135, 160, 166, 195, 213, 232, 335, 344, 371, 373, 406, 441, 442, 462, 513–523, 526, 530–541
Technology justice, 518–520, 535
Temperature, 25, 52, 65, 67, 71, 73, 77, 91, 92, 115, 125–130, 133–136, 207, 222, 226–229, 231, 248, 265, 267, 268, 270, 345, 347–349, 252, 355, 357, 358, 369, 383, 384, 434, 453, 479, 521
Tipping point, 307, 308, 310, 356–359, 427
Trade-off, 11, 12, 19, 27, 206, 208, 278, 320, 345, 357, 513
Traditional knowledge, 208, 210, 216, 369, 377, 406, 426, 430, 435
Transformation, 4, 20, 24, 30, 31, 56, 114, 117, 368, 394, 397, 429, 435, 436, 443, 494, 535

Trends, 7, 12, 14, 15, 23, 66, 69–75, 91, 92, 128, 134, 137, 162, 228, 246, 250, 262, 264, 270, 272, 331, 416, 419, 431, 503, 529, 540
Tuvalu, 158, 171, 172, 185, 247, 248, 367

U

Uganda, 227
Unavoidable losses and damage, 11, 15, 76, 87, 90, 222, 223, 526
Uncertainty, 17–19, 26, 58, 67, 85, 113, 114, 117, 120, 121, 123, 125, 126, 130–132, 140, 142, 145, 187, 189, 230, 242, 261–272, 275–278, 292, 293, 299, 300, 306, 308, 312, 320, 326, 331, 343, 344, 347, 356–360, 402, 403, 413, 418, 419, 538
Unemployment, 370, 490
United Nations Framework Convention on Climate Change (UNFCCC), 4–11, 15, 16, 18, 22–24, 30, 31, 41, 43, 44, 46, 48, 53, 55, 58, 83, 84, 90, 92, 96, 105, 115, 116, 118–121, 125, 137, 140, 141, 144, 155–168, 171–173, 179, 192–197, 205–209, 211–214, 217, 223, 224, 237, 238, 262–264, 271, 275, 276, 287, 288, 291, 318, 336, 366, 367, 394, 426, 427, 429, 430, 435, 442, 443, 467, 469, 484, 486, 494, 501, 520, 523, 527–530, 532, 533
Urban, 77, 233, 252, 272, 278, 301, 302, 371, 400, 433
USA, 26, 72, 73, 77, 158, 164, 249, 250, 350, 351

V

Values, 12, 16, 41, 42, 50, 51, 56, 69, 136, 156, 162, 181, 190, 191, 205–212, 214–217, 223, 242, 262, 264, 267, 273, 274, 277, 278, 292, 293, 297–300, 307, 309, 319, 320, 331, 333, 334, 336, 345, 346, 347, 356–358, 368, 374, 402, 408, 413, 436, 443, 492, 493, 507, 517, 522
Vanuatu, 19, 27, 193, 365, 366, 368, 371, 373–377
Variability, 13, 14, 17, 19, 26, 28, 44, 46, 47, 49, 50, 53, 54, 63–66, 69, 71, 74, 88, 91, 114, 117, 120, 121, 125–129, 137, 143, 162, 227–230, 232, 242, 261, 264–266, 268, 269, 273–275, 318, 321, 359, 365, 366, 395, 436, 453, 514, 523, 540
Vulnerability, 12–15, 25–27, 63–67, 69, 70, 74–78, 88, 91, 92, 98, 102, 105, 113–115, 119, 120, 126, 137, 141–143, 157, 162, 169, 207, 227, 230–232, 248, 263, 264, 268–271, 275, 276, 288, 289, 291–294, 301, 303, 306, 309, 311, 312, 320, 321, 323, 324, 327, 330, 331, 376, 400, 402, 406, 407, 410, 414, 416, 417, 419, 421, 426, 428, 430, 431, 433–435, 439, 441, 443, 452, 459, 466, 467, 471, 490, 497, 519, 521, 528, 531, 533, 535

W

Warsaw International Mechanism for Loss and Damage (WIM), 4, 5, 9, 10, 16, 18, 22, 25, 28, 31, 53, 84–86, 99, 105, 106, 121, 156–158, 160, 161, 164, 165, 168, 171, 173, 180, 195, 196, 198, 199, 205, 207, 208, 212, 213, 394, 430, 451, 462, 467, 468, 471, 483–486, 494, 498, 499, 501, 504, 506, 507, 527, 529–532, 539, 540
Water deficit, 229, 277
Welfare, 19, 90, 245, 311, 320, 343, 345, 348, 491, 521
West-Africa, 17, 222
World Bank, 166, 222, 231, 249, 356, 371, 400, 456, 457, 460, 462, 489, 497, 506, 517

www.ingramcontent.com/pod-product-compliance
Lightning Source LLC
LaVergne TN
LVHW082016200926
848481LV00010B/2871
9781013271984